FIFTH EDITION

ELEMENTARY CLASSROOM MANAGEMENT

Lessons from Research and Practice

CAROL SIMON WEINSTEIN

Rutgers, the State University of New Jersey

MOLLY E. ROMANO

University of Arizona

ANDREW J. MIGNANO, JR.

Mc Graw Hill

Connect
Learn
Succeed™

ELEMENTARY CLASSROOM MANAGEMENT: LESSONS FROM RESEARCH AND PRACTICE
Published by McGraw-Hill, a business unit of The McGraw-Hill Companies, Inc., 1221 Avenue
of the Americas, New York, NY, 10020. Copyright © 2011, 2007, 2003, 1997, 1993 by The McGraw-
Hill Companies, Inc. All rights reserved. No part of this publication may be reproduced or
distributed in any form or by any means, or stored in a database or retrieval system, without the
prior written consent of The McGraw-Hill Companies, Inc., including, but not limited to, in any
network or other electronic storage or transmission, or broadcast for distance learning.
Some ancillaries, including electronic and print components, may not be available to customers
outside the United States.

This book is printed on acid-free paper.

2 3 4 5 6 7 8 9 10 DOC/DOC 1 5 4 3 2 1

ISBN-13: 978-0-07-337862-6
ISBN-10: 0-07-337862-3

Vice President, Editorial: *Michael Ryan*
Publisher: *David Patterson*
Senior Sponsoring Editor: *Allison McNamara*
Managing Editor: *Meghan Campbell*
Developmental Editor: *Beth Kaufman*
Marketing Manager: *James Headley*
Production Editor: *Jasmin Tokatlian*
Designer: *Laurie Entringer*
Production Supervisor: *Laura Fuller*
Composition: *Laserwords Private Limited*
Printing: *45# New Era Matte, R. R. Donnelley & Sons/Crawfordsville, IN*

Cover image: © *PunchStock*

Library of Congress Cataloging-in-Publication Data

Weinstein, Carol Simon.
    Elementary classroom management : lessons from research and practice / Carol Simon
    Weinstein, Molly Romano, Andrew J. Mignano, Jr.—5th ed.
        p. cm.
    ISBN 978-0-07-337862-6
    1. Classroom management—United States—Case studies. 2. Education, Elementary—
United States—Case studies. 3. Home and school—United States. 4. Children with disabilities—
Education—United States. I. Mignano, Andrew J. II. Romano, Molly. III. Mignano, Andrew J.
IV. Title.
LB3013.W45 2011
372.1102′4—dc22

                                                                                2009031678

The Internet addresses listed in the text were accurate at the time of publication. The inclusion of
a Web site does not indicate an endorsement by the authors or McGraw-Hill, and McGraw-Hill does
not guarantee the accuracy of the information presented at these sites.

ABOUT THE AUTHORS

Carol Simon Weinstein is professor emerita in the Department of Learning and Teaching at Rutgers Graduate School of Education. She received her bachelor's degree in psychology from Clark University in Worcester, Massachusetts, and her master's and doctoral degrees from Harvard Graduate School of Education. Dr. Weinstein began her research career by studying the impact of classroom design on students' behavior and attitudes. She pursued this topic for many years, writing about the ways that classroom environments can be designed to facilitate teachers' goals and to foster children's learning and development. Eventually, her interest in organizing classroom space expanded to include classroom organization and management in general. She is the author (with Ingrid Novodvorsky) of *Secondary Classroom Management: Lessons from Research and Practice* (McGraw-Hill, 2011), as well as numerous chapters and articles on classroom management and teacher education students' beliefs about caring and control. Most recently, she has focused on the need for "culturally responsive classroom management," or classroom management in the service of social justice. In 2006, Dr. Weinstein co-edited (with Carolyn Evertson) the first *Handbook of Classroom Management: Research, Practice, and Contemporary Issues* (Lawrence Erlbaum Associates, Inc.), a compendium of 47 chapters written by scholars from around the world.

Molly Romano is an assistant professor in the department of Teaching and Teacher Education at the University of Arizona. Dr. Romano received a bachelor's degree in Elementary Education, and a master's and doctoral degree in Teaching and Teacher Education, all from the University of Arizona. Before becoming an assistant professor, Dr. Romano was an elementary classroom teacher for ten years. During that time she worked as a cooperating teacher for several student teachers and also as a beginning teacher mentor. Dr. Romano has conducted research on "bumpy moments" (a term she coined to describe episodes during the practice of teaching that require additional reflection before acting) with both practicing and preservice teachers. This led to an interest in the successes and struggles of teachers, particularly during the first year of practice. Dr. Romano found that many of the "bumpy moments" and struggles of teaching identified, for both preservice and practicing teachers, were concerns about classroom management. Currently, Dr. Romano is in the process of creating a school-based master's degree program with an emphasis on mentoring and teacher leadership.

Andrew J. Mignano, Jr., is assistant superintendent of curriculum and instruction for the Freehold Township Public Schools in Freehold Township, New Jersey, where he also served as principal of the Laura Donovan Elementary School for five years. Prior to that, he was a principal and a teacher in Highland Park, New Jersey. Mr. Mignano received his bachelor's degree in elementary and special education from Rutgers College in 1974 and his master's degree in educational psychology from Kean College in 1981. During his 15 years as a teacher, he taught all levels from kindergarten to grade five, including one year teaching a special education class. Throughout his career in education, Mr. Mignano has been active as an instructional leader and a professional developer. He has been instrumental in the implementation of innovative programs in the areas of early literacy, early childhood education, writing workshop, strategic reading, inclusion, and parent involvement. Mr. Mignano has worked closely with the Office of Teacher Education at the Rutgers Graduate School of Education. He has welcomed student teachers to his schools and has also served as an adjunct professor for the seminar that accompanies student teaching.

DEDICATION

Once again—to Barbara, Courtney, Ken, Viviana, and Garnetta:

You continue to teach and inspire all who read this book.

CONTENTS

PART III   ORGANIZING AND MANAGING INSTRUCTION   199

PART IV   PROTECTING AND RESTORING ORDER 333

PREFACE

In the years since the first edition of *Elementary Classroom Management* was published, the challenges of classroom management have grown dramatically. Classes are more heterogeneous than ever, with students from a wide range of cultural and linguistic backgrounds. Children with disabilities are educated in classes alongside their peers without disabilities, and teachers may be working in co-teaching arrangements that require collaboration and coordination. Increasing numbers of children come to school with emotional and psychological problems. The recent economic crisis has increased the incidence of poverty and homelessness and created a climate of uncertainty, anxiety, and fear. Now more than ever, teachers need to know how to establish classrooms that are supportive, inclusive, caring, and orderly.

Unfortunately, beginning teachers frequently report that their teacher education programs did not prepare them for the challenges of classroom management. They call for more preparation in areas such as communicating with parents, responding to inappropriate behavior, working in diverse, multicultural settings, and helping students with special needs. They complain about courses that are too removed from the realities of schools and crave examples of real teachers dealing with the challenges of real students in real classrooms.

PROFILES OF REAL TEACHERS

Elementary Classroom Management: Lessons from Research and Practice is designed to address these concerns. As the subtitle of this book indicates, we have integrated what research has to say about effective classroom management with knowledge gleaned from practice. This is done by highlighting the thinking and the actual management practices of five real teachers: Courtney Bell (kindergarten), Viviana Love (first grade bilingual), Garnetta Chain (third grade), Barbara Broggi (fourth grade), and Ken Kowalski (fifth grade). Courtney is a first-year teacher, whereas the others are all quite experienced. Readers will come to know these five teachers—to hear their thinking on various aspects of classroom management and to see the ways they establish relationships with students and parents. Their stories provide real-life examples of the concepts and principles derived from research.

These teachers not only teach different grade levels, they also work in school districts that differ substantially in terms of race, ethnicity, and socioeconomic status. For example, Courtney's suburban district is predominantly European American (85 percent), and only 4 percent of the students are eligible for the federal free or reduced-price lunch program. In contrast, Viviana and Garnetta teach in an urban district that is 54 percent Latino and 41 percent African American, and 80 percent of the students are eligible for the federal lunch program. Because of differences such as these, their ways of managing their classrooms often look very different. But all of the teachers are able to create productive, respectful classrooms, and they all apply the same basic principles of classroom management.

THE FIFTH EDITION: WHAT'S THE SAME? WHAT'S NEW?

Just like earlier editions, the fifth edition of *Elementary Classroom Management* provides clear, practical guidance for organizing and managing classrooms. Our goal has been to write a book that is based on actual research findings yet is accessible—even enjoyable—to read. We have tried to balance the goal of providing breadth and depth of coverage with the need for a book that is easy to use and reasonable in length. We hope we have succeeded in producing writing that is clear, lively, conversational, and engaging. (Note that, for the sake of readability, we consistently use "we" and "us" even when describing incidents that involved only one of the authors.)

This edition continues to address the ongoing management tasks that teachers face—from organizing physical space, creating community, and teaching norms to responding to problem behavior and preventing violence. We also include topics that are often omitted in classroom management texts but that seem crucial, such as working with families and using time effectively. In addition, we discuss strategies for motivating students and managing the instructional formats commonly used in elementary classrooms (such as independent work, small-group work, recitations, and discussions), topics more commonly found in general methods books. Throughout the text, we emphasize the importance of positive teacher–student relationships to effective classroom management.

This edition retains several pedagogical features that instructors and students have found useful. In almost every chapter, readers can find

- *Pause and Reflect* boxes to promote engagement and comprehension.
- *Activities for Skill Building and Reflection* that are divided into three sections: "In Class, "On Your Own," and "For Your Portfolio."
- An annotated list of books and articles headed *For Further Reading.*

- A list of *Organizational Resources* describing agencies that can provide additional information.
- *Practical Tips* boxes that contain useful classroom management strategies.
- Marginal icons that alert readers to content that focuses on cultural diversity.

In addition, this edition contains two new features. First, an introduction to each of Parts I through IV provides an organizing framework for the chapters to come and summarizes their contents. Second, *Meet the Educator* boxes highlight the work of well-known speakers and writers whom beginning teachers are likely to encounter during inservice workshops or lectures. All of these educators have produced widely disseminated classroom management programs or have done work that is relevant to classroom management (examples include Alfie Kohn, Harry Wong, Jane Nelson and Lynn Lott, and Spencer Kagan).

In response to feedback from the users of the fourth edition, a few chapters have been reordered to better mesh with the way classroom management courses are organized. We have also improved coherence by moving some material from one chapter to another, eliminating redundancy, and streamlining discussions. All chapters have been updated to reflect recent scholarship and current concerns; there are more than 70 new references. New or expanded material addresses topics such as

- The importance of being both warm *and* assertive
- Presenting yourself professionally
- The norms and values of middle-class White culture
- Learning about students' lives
- Working with other adults in the classroom
- Being an active participant in the IEP and 504 planning process
- Increased use of technology for communication with parents
- Using multiple intelligences to enhance student success
- The developing elementary child
- Working with children who are poor or homeless
- Positive behavioral supports

CourseSmart
Learn Smart. Choose Smart.

This text is available as an eTextbook at www.CourseSmart.com. At CourseSmart you can save up to 50% off the cost of a print textbook, reduce your impact on the environment, and gain access to powerful web tools for learning. CourseSmart has the largest selection of eTextbooks available anywhere, offering thousands of the most commonly adopted textbooks from a wide variety of higher education publishers. CourseSmart eTextbooks are available in one standard online reader with full text search, notes and highlighting, and email tools for sharing notes between classmates. For further details contact your sales representative or go to www.coursesmart.com.

MIDDLE AND SECONDARY CLASSROOM MANAGEMENT: A COMPANION TEXT

This edition of *Elementary Classroom Management* parallels the fourth edition of *Middle and Secondary Classroom Management: Lessons from Research and Practice* (Weinstein & Novodvorsky, 2011) so that instructors who are teaching courses that include both elementary and secondary teacher education students can use the two books as a package. The principles and concepts discussed are the same, but the teachers on whom the companion book is based all work at the middle or secondary level, and the "lessons from research" are based largely on studies conducted in middle schools, junior high, and high school.

ACKNOWLEDGMENTS

As always, we express our gratitude to the teachers featured in this book. They allowed us to observe in their classrooms and shared their wisdom, frustrations, and celebrations during countless hours of interviews. In the interest of full disclosure, one point about the structure of the book needs to be made explicit. The portraits of Barbara, Ken, Viviana, and Garnetta are composites derived from material collected over a number of years, starting in 1991. In other words, we have created a portrait of each teacher by describing incidents that occurred in different years with different students at different grade levels as though they had all occurred in the same academic year with the same class. Ken and Courtney are still working in their schools (although Courtney is obviously not a first-year teacher anymore!), and Barbara has just retired, so all three were able to contribute to this new edition; however, Viviana and Garnetta both retired several years ago.

We are also grateful to the district administrators who agreed to this project and to the school counselors who took the time to speak with us and shared their perspectives. To our students, many thanks for allowing us to use your journal entries and for providing us with feedback on everything from confusing content to printing errors. It should be noted that in some cases, details from the journals have been changed to avoid embarrassment to anyone, and at times, composite entries have been created.

We express our deep appreciation to the individuals who reviewed the previous edition: Lynne Ensworth, University of Northern Iowa; Carol L. Higy, University of North Carolina at Pembroke; Sharon S. McKool, Rider University; Linda V. Neiman, Cardinal Stritch University; Catherine Reischl, University of Michigan; and Shirley E. Thompson, Valdosta State University. If there are any errors or misstatements, the fault is entirely our own.

Finally, a special thank you to Neil, Jeff, Mariel, and Daniel for their support.

Carol Simon Weinstein

Molly E. Romano

Andrew J. Mignano, Jr.

PART I

INTRODUCTION

When you hear the words "a really good teacher," what comes to mind?

We have asked our teacher education students this question, and invariably they talk about *caring*. A good teacher is a caring teacher, they say, someone who respects and supports students, who doesn't put them down, and who shows genuine interest in them as individuals. Our teacher education students also believe they have the capacity to be that kind of teacher. They envision themselves nurturing children's self-esteem, rejoicing in their successes, and creating strong bonds of affection and mutual respect.

And then these prospective teachers begin student teaching. Over the weeks, the talk about caring begins to fade away, replaced by talk of control and discipline, penalties and consequences. Students lament the fact that they were "too nice" at the beginning and conclude that they should have been "meaner." Some even seem to believe that caring and order are mutually exclusive.

The tension between wanting to care and needing to achieve order is not uncommon among novice teachers. But showing that you care and achieving order are *not* irreconcilable goals. The two actually go hand in hand. Indeed, *one of the main ways in which teachers create an orderly environment is by treating students with warmth and respect.* Common sense tells us that students are more likely to cooperate with teachers who are seen as responsive, trustworthy, and respectful, and research consistently shows this to be true.

At the same time, *one of the ways to show students you care is by taking responsibility for keeping order.* Far from just being "warm and fuzzy," caring teachers are willing to assume the leadership role that is part of being a teacher. For such teachers, caring is not just about being affectionate and respectful; it is also about monitoring behavior, teaching and enforcing norms, and providing needed organization and structure. These teachers understand that children actually crave limits—even though they may protest loudly.

In Chapter 1, you will meet five good elementary school teachers whose experiences and wisdom form the basis for this book. As you will see, they are able to combine warmth and respect with an insistence that students work hard, comply with classroom norms, and treat one another with consideration. This combination constitutes *authoritative classroom management.* To borrow terminology from the literature on parenting, authoritative classroom managers are neither dictatorial and unresponsive ("authoritarian") nor affectionate but undemanding ("permissive"). Instead, they are "warm demanders," a concept we will meet in many of the chapters that follow.

CHAPTER 1

CLASSROOM MANAGEMENT IN A CROWDED, COMPLEX ENVIRONMENT

For many prospective and beginning teachers, entering an elementary classroom is like returning home after a long absence. So much is familiar: Bulletin boards still display "Good Work" studded with As, stars, and smiling faces; alphabet charts still illustrate the proper formation of letters; bells and buzzers still interrupt lessons to announce fire drills. The familiarity of these sights and sounds makes us feel comfortable and at ease; in fact, it may lead us to think that the transition from student to teacher will be relatively easy. Yet ironically, this very familiarity can be a trap; it can make it hard to appreciate what a curious and demanding place the elementary classroom really is. Looking at the classroom as though we have never seen one before can help us recognize some of its strange characteristics and contradictions.

Viewed from a fresh perspective, the elementary classroom turns out to be an extremely crowded place. It is more like a subway or bus than a place designed for learning. In fact, it is difficult to think of another setting, except prison, where such large groups of individuals are packed so closely together for so many hours. Nonetheless, amid this crowdedness, students are often not allowed to interact. As Philip Jackson (1990) has noted, "students must try to behave as if they were in solitude, when in point of fact they are not. . . . These young people, if they are to become successful students, must learn how to be alone in a crowd" (p. 16).

There are other contradictions in this curious place. Children are expected to work together in harmony, yet they may be strangers—even rivals—and may come from very different cultural backgrounds. Students are urged to cooperate, to share, and to help one another, but they are also told to keep their eyes on their own papers, and they often compete for grades and special privileges. They are lectured about being independent and responsible, yet they are also expected to show complete, unquestioning obedience to the teacher's dictates. (This peculiar situation is captured in the cartoon that appears in Figure 1.1.)

In addition to these contradictions, Walter Doyle (2006) has pointed out six features of the classroom setting that make it even more complex. First, classrooms are characterized by *multidimensionality*. Unlike a post office, a restaurant, or other places devoted to a single activity, the classroom is the setting for a broad range of events. Within its boundaries, students read, write, and discuss. They form friendships, argue, celebrate birthdays, and play games. Teachers not only instruct but also collect milk money, take attendance, and settle disputes. They counsel students with problems and meet with parents to discuss students' progress. Somehow, the classroom environment must be able to accommodate all these activities.

Second, many of these activities take place at the same time. This *simultaneity* makes the elementary classroom a bit like a three-ring circus. It is not uncommon to see a cluster of students discussing a story with the teacher, individuals writing at their desks or on computers, pairs of students playing a mathematics game,

"I expect you all to be independent, innovative, critical thinkers who will do exactly as I say."

Figure 1.1   *Source:* Reprinted by permission of Warren.

and a small group working on a social studies mural. Still other students may be passing notes about yesterday's soccer game. It is this simultaneity—this three-ring circus quality—that makes having "eyes in the back of your head" so valuable to teachers.

A third characteristic of classrooms is the rapid pace at which things happen. Classroom events occur with an *immediacy* that makes it impossible to think through every action ahead of time. A squabble erupts over the ownership of an action figure; a student complains that a neighbor is copying; a normally silent child makes a serious but irrelevant comment during a group discussion. Each of these incidents requires a quick response, an on-the-spot decision about how to proceed. Furthermore, classroom events such as these cannot always be anticipated, despite the most careful planning. This *unpredictability* is a fourth characteristic of classrooms. It ensures that being a teacher is rarely boring, but unpredictability can also be exhausting.

A fifth characteristic of classrooms is the *lack of privacy.* Classrooms are remarkably public places. Within their four walls, each person's behavior can be observed by many others. Teachers talk of feeling as though they are always "on stage" or living in a "fishbowl" (Lortie, 1975). Their feelings are understandable. With 20 or 30 pairs of eyes watching, it is difficult to find a moment for a private chuckle or an unobserved groan. But the scrutiny goes two ways: Teachers constantly monitor students' behavior as well. And in response to this sometimes unwelcome surveillance, students develop an "active underlife" (Hatch, 1986) in which to pursue their own personal agendas. With skills that increase as they progress from grade to grade, students learn to pass notes, comb their hair, read magazines, and doodle—all, they hope, without the teacher's ever noticing. Yet even if they avoid the teacher's eyes, there are always peers watching. It is difficult for students to have a private interaction with the teacher, to conceal a grade on a test, or to make a mistake without someone's noticing.

Finally, over the course of the academic year, classes construct a joint *history.* This sixth characteristic means that classes, like families, remember past events—both positive and negative. They remember who got yelled at, who was chosen to be the paper monitor, and what the teacher said about homework assignments. They remember who was going to have only "one more chance" before getting detention—and if the teacher didn't follow through, they remember that too. The class memory means that what happens today affects what happens tomorrow. It also means that teachers must work to shape a history that will support, rather than frustrate, future activities.

Contradictory, multidimensional, simultaneous, immediate, unpredictable, public, and remembered—this portrait of the classroom highlights characteristics that we often overlook. We have begun the book with this portrait because we believe that *effective organization and management require an understanding of the unique features of the classroom.* Many of the management problems experienced by beginning teachers can be traced to their lack of understanding of the complex setting in which they work.

Past experiences with children may also mislead beginning teachers. For example, you may have tutored an individual student who was having academic difficulties, or perhaps you have been a camp counselor. Although these are valuable experiences, they are very different from teaching in classrooms. Teachers do not work one-on-one with students in a private room; they seldom lead recreational activities that children have themselves selected. Teachers do not even work with youngsters who have chosen to be present. Instead, *teachers work with captive groups of students, on academic agendas that students have not always helped to set, in a crowded, public setting.*

Within this peculiar setting, teachers must carry out the fundamental tasks of classroom management.

> ## PAUSE AND REFLECT
>
> Before going any further, jot down the words that come to mind when you hear the phrase *classroom management.* Then write the answer to this question: "What is the goal of classroom management?" After reading the next section, compare your goal statement with the statement in the book. Are they similar? In what ways (if any) are they different?

GUIDING PRINCIPLES

Sometimes, we become so preoccupied with basic management issues (such as getting everyone to sit down) that we forget that classroom management is not about achieving order for order's sake. Indeed, classroom management has two distinct purposes: *It not only seeks to establish and sustain a caring, orderly environment in which students can engage in meaningful learning, it also aims to enhance students' social and emotional growth.* From this perspective, *how* a teacher achieves order is as important as *whether* a teacher achieves order (Evertson & Weinstein, 2006). Keeping this in mind, let us consider five principles that guide the content and organization of this book. (These are summarized in Table 1.1.)

The first principle is that *successful classroom management fosters self-discipline and personal responsibility.* Let's be honest: Every teacher's worst fear

---

TABLE 1.1 Five Guiding Principles about Classroom Management

1. Successful classroom management fosters self-discipline and personal responsibility.
2. Most problems of disorder in classrooms can be avoided if teachers foster positive student–teacher relationships, implement engaging instruction, and use good preventive management strategies.
3. The need for order must not supersede the need for meaningful instruction.
4. Managing today's diverse classrooms requires the knowledge, skills, and predispositions to work with students from diverse racial, ethnic, language, and social class backgrounds. In other words, teachers must become "culturally responsive classroom managers."
5. Becoming an effective classroom manager requires reflection, hard work, and time.

is the prospect of losing control—of being helpless and ineffectual in the face of unruly, anarchic classes. Given this nightmare, it's tempting to create a coercive, top-down management system that relies heavily on the use of rewards and penalties to gain obedience. Yet such an approach does little to teach students to make good choices about how to act. Furthermore, as Mary McCaslin and Tom Good (1998) point out, "the success of a compliance model depends upon constant monitoring (if the teacher turns her or his back, students misbehave)" (p. 170). An emphasis on external control is also inconsistent with current thinking about curriculum and instruction (McCaslin & Good, 1998). It doesn't make sense to design learning activities that encourage independence, problem solving, and critical thinking and then to use managerial strategies that encourage dependence on points, popcorn parties, and punishment. This is not to discount the importance of teachers' authority; clearly, in order to be effective, you must be willing to set limits and guide students' behavior. Nonetheless, what you are aiming toward is an environment in which students behave appropriately not out of fear of punishment or desire for reward, but out of a sense of personal responsibility.

The second principle is that *most problems of disorder in classrooms can be avoided if teachers foster positive student–teacher relationships, implement engaging instruction, and use good preventive management strategies.* Let's look at these components in order. Extensive research demonstrates that when students perceive their teachers to be supportive and caring, they are more likely to engage in cooperative, responsible behavior and to adhere to classroom rules and norms (Woolfolk Hoy & Weinstein, 2006). Similarly, when students find academic activities meaningful, engrossing, and stimulating, they are less inclined to daydream or disrupt. Finally, a pivotal study by Jacob Kounin (1970) documented the fact that orderly classes are more the result of a teacher's ability *to manage the activities of the group* than of particular ways of handling student misconduct. As a result of Kounin's work, we now distinguish between *discipline*—responding to inappropriate behavior—and *classroom management*—ways of creating a caring, respectful environment that supports learning.

Third, *the need for order must not supersede the need for meaningful instruction.* Although learning and teaching cannot take place in an environment that is chaotic, excessive concerns about quiet and uniformity can hinder instruction (Doyle, 2006). For example, a teacher may wish to divide the class into small groups for a hands-on science experiment, believing that her students will learn better by *doing* than by simply *watching.* Yet her anxiety about the noise level and her fear that students will not cooperate could make her abandon the small-group project and substitute a teacher demonstration and an individual workbook assignment. In one respect this teacher is correct: A collaborative science experiment will not only be more intellectually and socially challenging, it will also be more challenging from a managerial perspective. Nonetheless, it is crucial that teachers not sacrifice opportunities to learn in order to achieve a quiet classroom. As Doyle (1985) comments, "A well-run lesson that teaches nothing is just as useless as a chaotic lesson in which no academic work is possible" (p. 33).

Our fourth principle is that *managing today's diverse classrooms requires the knowledge, skills, and predispositions to work with students from diverse racial, ethnic, language, and social class backgrounds. In other words, teachers must become "culturally responsive classroom managers"* (Weinstein, Curran, & Tomlinson-Clarke, 2003; Weinstein, Tomlinson-Clarke, & Curran, 2004). Sometimes, a desire to treat students fairly leads teachers to strive for "color-blindness" (Nieto & Bode, 2008), and educators are often reluctant to talk about cultural characteristics for fear of stereotyping. But definitions and expectations of appropriate behavior are culturally influenced, and conflicts are likely to occur if we ignore our students' cultural backgrounds. Geneva Gay (2006) provides a telling example of what can happen when there is a "cultural gap" between teachers and students. She notes that African Americans frequently use "evocative vocabulary" and "inject high energy, exuberance, and passion" into their verbal communication (p. 355). European American teachers may interpret such speech as rude or vulgar and feel compelled to chastise the students or even impose a punishment. Because the students see nothing wrong with what they said, they may resent and resist the teacher's response. As Gay notes, "The result is a cultural conflict that can quickly escalate into disciplinary sanctions in the classroom or referrals for administrative action" (p. 355).

To avoid situations like this, we need to become aware of our own culturally based principles, biases, and values and to reflect on how these influence our expectations for behavior and our interactions with students. When we bring our cultural biases to a conscious level, we are less likely to misinterpret the behaviors of our culturally different students and treat them inequitably. In addition, we must acquire cultural content knowledge. We must learn, for example, about our students' family backgrounds and their cultures' norms for interpersonal relationships. Obviously, this knowledge must not be used to categorize or stereotype, and it is critical that we recognize the significant individual differences that exist among members of the same cultural group. Nonetheless, cultural content knowledge can be useful in developing *hypotheses* about students' behavior (Weiner, 1999).

Our final principle is that *becoming an effective classroom manager requires knowledge, reflection, hard work, and time.* Classroom management cannot be reduced to a set of recipes or a list of "how to's." As we have seen, the classroom environment is crowded, multidimensional, fast-paced, unpredictable, and public. In this complex setting, pat answers just won't work. Similarly, well-managed classrooms are not achieved by following "gut instinct" or doing "what feels right." Classroom management is a *learned craft.* That means that you must become familiar with the knowledge base that undergirds effective management. You must also be ready and willing to anticipate problems, analyze situations, generate solutions, make thoughtful decisions—and learn from your mistakes.

PLAN OF THE BOOK

Elementary Classroom Management focuses first, in Part II, on ways of creating a classroom environment that supports learning and self-regulation, such as designing an appropriate physical setting, building an atmosphere of caring and respect, and developing standards for behavior. It then moves, in Part III, to the managerial tasks directly related to instruction—for example, using time wisely, motivating students to learn, organizing group work, and managing student-centered discussions. Finally, in Part IV, the book examines the inevitable challenges associated with classroom management, such as responding to inappropriate behavior and preventing and coping with violence.

Throughout the book, concepts and principles derived from research are woven together with the wisdom and experiences of five real elementary teachers. You learn about the classes they teach and about the physical constraints of their rooms; you hear them reflect on their rules and routines and watch as they teach these to students. You listen as they talk about motivating students and fostering cooperation and as they discuss appropriate ways to deal with misbehavior. In sum, *this book focuses on real decisions made by real teachers as they manage the complex environment of the elementary classroom.* By sharing these stories, we do not mean to suggest that their ways of managing classrooms are the only effective ways. Rather, our goal is to illustrate how five reflective, caring, and very different individuals approach the tasks involved in classroom management. And now, let's meet the teachers in order of the grade level taught. (Table 1.2 provides an overview of the teachers and the contexts in which they teach.)

TABLE 1.2 Featured Teachers and Their School Districts

Teacher's Name	Grade Level	District Size (students)	Students Qualified for Free or Reduced-Price Lunch	District Ethnic/ Racial Diversity
Courtney Bell	K	4,605	4%	85% European American 7% Asian American 5% Latino 3% African American
Viviana Love	1 bilingual	6,500	80%	54% Latino 41% African American 5% European American
Garnetta Chain	3	6,500	80%	54% Latino 41% African American 5% European American
Barbara Broggi	4	1,650	26%	53% European American 17% African American 16% Asian American 14% Latino
Ken Kowalski	5	7,500	12%	64% European American 20% Asian American 10% African American 6% Latino

MEETING THE TEACHERS

Courtney Bell: Kindergarten

Courtney is a 24-year-old, first-year kindergarten teacher. She was a theater arts major in college before she decided to go on for a master's degree and certification in elementary education. Reflecting on her choice of teaching as a career, she comments:

 I did not come to the decision lightly. Since everyone told me I should be a teacher, I resisted the urge. I seriously looked into a career in Drama Therapy, but after an internship in the field, I decided it wasn't for me. After a lot of soul searching, I decided I should go to graduate school in education. . . . When I decided, my parents weren't surprised. They had known this is what I should do all along. . . . When you look at my résumé, every part-time job I have ever held involved education and working with children. I think they were really relieved that I finally figured it out!

Courtney did her student teaching in a kindergarten that used *The Responsive Classroom,* an approach to teaching that integrates children's social-emotional learning with their academic learning. (See Charney, 2002; see also "Organizational Resources" listed at the end of the chapter.) She found this experience extremely rewarding, so she looked for a job in a district that would allow her to implement elements of this approach. She found one in a middle- to upper-middle-class suburban district comprising five elementary schools and two middle schools. The population of the town is relatively homogeneous in terms of race and socioeconomic

Courtney Bell

status: Of the district's 4,605 pre-K to eighth-grade students, 3 percent are African American, 5 percent are Latino, 7 percent are Asian American, and 85 percent are European American. Only 4 percent of the students qualify for the free or reduced-price lunch program. The district is known to be progressive and high-achieving. Full-day kindergarten was started in 2004.

Courtney's school, a one-story brick building constructed in the 1960s, has just added a separate wing for five new kindergarten classrooms. The five kindergarten teachers work together as a team to plan and implement the program. This makes Courtney's first year of teaching far less daunting and provides her with much-appreciated mentoring and support.

Courtney has 21 students in her class; two are Indian and the rest are European American. They vary tremendously in size: A girl who turned five right before the beginning of school is tiny, and a boy about to turn six looks like a third-grader. One child has been retained in order to give him another year in which to mature, and another child was diagnosed with Asperger syndrome during the school year. Courtney also has a student with diabetes who must leave the classroom several times a day to visit the nurse's office.

A few days before the first day of school, Courtney spoke about her desire to create a safe, joyful classroom environment for her 21 students:

 My main goal is to instill a love of learning. This is my students' first public school experience, and I want to make learning exciting and fun for them. At the same time, I want to create a warm environment where they feel they can express themselves both academically and socially. Children should feel free to take academic risks and should know they will not be ridiculed if they do not succeed. I also want all students to feel successful in my classroom. I want them to know there are things they can do, and I accept approximations and celebrate accomplishments. I believe that even something as small as a smile and the excitement in my voice as I praise a child for a job well done can make them feel good about the hard work they put into accomplishing something.

As part of her commitment to building a warm, welcoming environment, Courtney starts each day with a group gathering on the floor of the meeting area. In addition to the kindergarten traditions of calendar and weather, Courtney's morning meeting usually includes a greeting (during which every member of the circle is greeted by name) and a song or community-building activity. She also leads discussions about attendance ("How many people are in our class?" "How many people are here today?" "How many are absent?" "Who are we missing?") and about the question of the day. Finally, the class reads a morning message printed on an easel pad. On the first day of school, for example, the message read: "Good morning, class. Today is Tuesday, September 7th. We will learn names today." The morning message not only alerts students about what will be happening that day but also serves as a vehicle for discussions of letters, sounds, and punctuation.

On a typical day, Courtney moves from morning meeting to a "read-aloud," clearly a favorite activity. Often the book is part of the theme for the month—for example, apples and pumpkins, buses, penguins, families. After a snack and some sort of gross motor activity (outside on the playground or in the multipurpose room), Courtney conducts writing workshop and leads a "Word Work" lesson. Then there is lunch, followed by a rest and quiet literacy activities, during which children can curl up on the carpet with pillows and books. Math and "related arts" (such as music, art, library, and gym) are scheduled in the afternoon, and the day ends with half an hour of "choice time" in the various learning centers located around the room.

As a novice teacher, Courtney is excited and optimistic about the coming year. Nonetheless, she recognizes that this will be a year of learning:

 The stressful part of never having done this before is that I have no idea of what will work. I know that you can be a teacher for 20 years and things work beautifully every year, and then you get a class and it just doesn't work this time, but for me everything is an experiment. Everything is new. It's hard to have confidence. I mean, I'm confident that I had good training and that a lot of what I'm going to do is going to work out, but I can't be confident about everything. I guess we'll just have to see.

Viviana Love: First Grade

Viviana Love is a first-grade bilingual teacher in an urban district with 10 schools. Of the 6,500 students in this district, 54 percent are Latino and 41 percent are African American. Many of the children come from poor or low-income families, evidenced by the fact that 80 percent of the students qualify for the federal free or reduced-price lunch program. The socioeconomic conditions breed other

Viviana Love

conditions typical of urban areas—drug abuse, transiency, homelessness, teenage pregnancy, physical abuse. Viviana's school is in the heart of the small city, surrounded by single- and multifamily dwellings. It is an old but well-cared for building with a capacity for 700 students.

Viviana was born in a small town in Puerto Rico. Although her parents had only a third-grade education, they instilled in Viviana a desire to learn and a strong ambition to succeed. Her mother taught her to read and write, and with these skills Viviana began her teaching career at the age of seven. She tutored neighborhood children, and much to her delight, she sometimes received a quarter for her services! From the very beginning, Viviana knew teaching felt right.

An image of her first-grade teacher, Mrs. Hernandez, is as strong today as it was 50 years ago:

 She wore a lot of bracelets and when she went to the board . . . oh, those bracelets! I loved the chiming of the bracelets. I used to just look at them and say to myself that the first thing I'll do when I am a teacher is buy a lot of shiny bracelets—and I did. The bracelets, for me, were a glamorous symbol of high social status. I couldn't wait to write on the board with my shining bracelets.

Viviana began her professional teaching career in Puerto Rico and then moved to the United States mainland, where she has taught in the same district for 30 years. With no children of her own, Viviana "adopts" her students. "They are my children," she says. "I will do anything for them, just like mothers do for their own children. I want them to be the best." Sometimes she feels like taking them home with her, so she can give them the love and stability some of them lack. Above all, she seeks to stimulate her students' desire to learn.

Viviana's commitment to her students is evident in her first-grade bilingual classroom. With an energy level that is rare, she motivates, prods, instructs, models, praises, and captivates her students. Most instruction is delivered to the whole class, as required by the district. The pace is brisk, and Viviana clearly has a flair for the dramatic; she uses music, props, gestures, facial expressions, and shifts in voice tone to communicate the material.

Viviana's 25 students have all emigrated from the Dominican Republic, Mexico, Puerto Rico, and Honduras. Eighteen attended kindergarten here; seven are "port-of-entry" (POE) children who have just arrived in this country. Early in the school year, Viviana instructs primarily in Spanish. She moves to English as soon as possible, however, using Spanish whenever she perceives problems in comprehension. Viviana is vehement about not wanting her children segregated or labeled as disadvantaged because they are not fluent in English. She uses every available minute for instruction, even turning interruptions or unexpected events into teachable moments. Her efforts pay off: Even though her children begin the year speaking little or no English, they leave in June generally having achieved the normal first-grade objectives for the district.

Knowing that her children come from poor families, Viviana provides all the materials they need to complete class assignments. "My children cannot say they couldn't complete a project because they didn't have a magazine or scissors. I give them what they need so that there is no excuse for failure." Some people say that Viviana is strict and demands too much of first-grade students, but her students don't seem daunted by her high expectations. They look enthusiastic and speak proudly about their accomplishments.

Viviana is also valued and appreciated by the parents of the children she teaches. On the first day of school, she talks openly with the parents who have accompanied their children to school: "At home, *you're* the parents … but at school, *I'm* the mother. We're all family, one big family, all Hispanic, and we all help each other." She communicates frequently with parents, not simply to discuss children's progress in school but also to counsel parents on discipline, guide them in their search for employment, and suggest ways they can help their children learn.

Despite having lived here for 31 years, Viviana maintains strong ties with her parents, who are still in Puerto Rico. She is grateful for the love of learning and the drive to succeed that they instilled in her. She hopes to share these same gifts with her students and their families.

Garnetta Chain: Third Grade

On the outskirts of the city, in the same school district in which Viviana teaches, a low brick elementary school sits amid low-income housing projects and worn-looking factories. In a brand new addition to the building, we meet third-grade

Garnetta Chain

teacher Garnetta Chain. Garnetta's classroom belies the stereotype of the urban school. The blue-gray carpeting that covers two-thirds of the classroom creates a feeling of warmth and homeyness, while the linoleum on the other third provides a suitable flooring for messy activities. From the back wall, next to the sink, juts a peninsula of shelving and cabinets. Two aquariums with long-haired guinea pigs sit on the formica countertop, and math manipulatives of all sizes and colors fill the shelves. Brightly colored posters suggest the topics the class will be studying—the solar system, "exploring emotions," the cursive alphabet. In one corner is a library center; on the opposite wall is a collection of board games.

Garnetta, a mother of three children, has been teaching for 25 years. Although she began college intending to become a biochemist, she soon realized that she'd much rather work with children and changed her major to education. Garnetta eventually received a master's degree in elementary education; she has taught third grade for the last 13 years. This year her class is small, only 15 students; 3 are Latino and 12 are African American. It's quite a change from last year, when she had a class of 39 children and had to teach in the library because no classroom was large enough!

Garnetta is a veritable whirlwind in class. She is everywhere, all at once, making sure that her students are actively involved. When they learn about liquid measurement, she gives them water and containers for pouring and measuring. Sometimes she has them work in pairs, interviewing each other and then describing their partners in oral reports to the class. When they begin the fearsome topic of long division, they work with Unifix cubes, and it's suddenly not so scary. When they read about bread baking in their reading books, they make bread in class. Although Garnetta is required to present new concepts and skills to the whole class, she frequently uses small groups for reinforcement and enrichment. She strongly believes in the value of students teaching each other and stresses the importance of their learning to work together.

Garnetta speaks candidly of the difficulties her students face. Many of them have been victims of physical and sexual abuse. Drugs, teenage pregnancy, and violence plague the community in which they live. It is no wonder that Garnetta feels that she is there not only to provide her students with a firm academic foundation and to foster a love of learning, but also to impart moral values, give plenty of love and attention, and teach her students to feel good about themselves.

She also aims to offer a secure and safe environment. Class rules are clearly posted in her room. Garnetta feels that her children live with so much uncertainty in their lives that they need to know there is one place where they can count on consistency. She tells us, "They need to know that a no or yes answer will remain that way, whether it's Monday or Friday. They have to have limits; there need to be consequences for their behaviors so that they'll develop responsibility for their actions."

Along with limits, Garnetta provides praise and affection. We watch her calm an angry child with a soft word and prevent a disruption with a hand on a shoulder, and it's easy to see why her students come to respect and trust her. It's not unusual for students to return to her classroom years after they've moved on, just to chat or discuss a problem.

When we asked Garnetta how she maintains her optimism and enthusiasm for teaching, she replied:

> I always hope that there's somebody out there that I will reach and that I'll make a difference. I know society has a strong hold on my students and I may fail, but if someone makes something of themselves, and I've had a role in making a difference, then it's all worthwhile. I have to believe this.

Barbara Broggi: Fourth Grade

Barbara teaches in a small community that is extremely diverse in race, ethnicity, and socioeconomic status. The district's three schools serve children who live in expensive homes as well as those from low-income apartment complexes. The student population of 1,650 is 53 percent European American, 17 percent African American, 14 percent Latino, and 16 percent Asian American. About 26 percent of the children qualify for the federal free or reduced-price lunch program.

Barbara Broggi, a mother of three children, is a product of the school system in which she now teaches fourth grade. Her school houses 450 students in grades 3–6. This year, Barbara has 25 students. Like the town itself, her class is diverse

Barbara Broggi

in terms of racial/ethnic composition: 16 of her students are European American, 4 are African American, 3 are Latino, and 2 are Asian American. The class is also heterogeneous in terms of academic ability and achievement: Six students qualify for enrichment; three students have been classified as having learning disabilities; and three children receive extra "basic skills instruction." In addition, one boy has autism, and another is classified as emotionally disturbed; both of them have "child-specific aides" who stay with them all day.

Barbara never thought of becoming anything but a teacher. Her mother taught high school in the same district, and Barbara grew up with an insider's view of the profession. She was present when students dropped by to talk with her mother or to ask for extra help, and it was this close personal connection with people that first attracted Barbara to teaching. Even now, after 23 years in the classroom, it's the relationship with students that means the most to her:

 Everyday contact with my students is what makes teaching so special for me. I want to get to know them as people—not just names on a seating chart. I want them to know me, to see that I'm a person with strengths and needs just like them. If I cry when I'm reading them a sad passage from a novel, they see that I have feelings and that I'm not afraid to express them. And they learn that it's okay to express their feelings as well. I tell my students, "We're in this together. We're going to learn, work, and play together. And our common goal is to get the most out of every single day."

Barbara's classroom reflects her belief in the importance of creative expression and active participation. Students' work covers the walls and hangs from the ceiling. Science experiments are always in progress, and illustrations of novels enliven a bulletin board. Three computers remain on all day so students can write and edit and do research.

Barbara is given quite a bit of latitude in the materials and teaching strategies she uses. For example, she is an avid supporter of literature-based reading instruction, and she selects novels that touch her and that she thinks will be meaningful to her students: "During literature discussions, I can tap into a whole range of student feelings on a wide variety of subjects. And as we share ideas, we grow closer together." Barbara also uses children's literature as a springboard for teaching vocabulary, grammar, writing, and spelling.

Barbara enjoys living in the town where she teaches. She likes being able to run into parents at the local food store, at a soccer game, or in the sports collectibles card shop that she and her husband own. Parents appreciate this accessibility, and the informality of their encounters helps Barbara to establish a partnership with them. She is on a first-name basis with the parents of her students—an indication of their open, easy relationship.

Each afternoon when the dismissal bell has sounded, students of all ages cluster around the door to Barbara's classroom. They come to share some news, to complain about a perceived injustice, or simply to see what's going on in her room. It was the promise of close personal relationships with children that lured

Barbara into teaching. Now, as we watch Barbara surrounded by her present and former students, it's clear that the promise has been realized.

Ken Kowalski: Fifth Grade

The district in which Ken Kowalski teaches has a reputation for innovation. This well-regarded suburban school district currently has about 7,500 students and is gaining more than 400 a year. The student population is becoming increasingly diverse; it is now 64 percent European American, 20 percent Asian American, 10 percent African American, and 6 percent Latino. More than 50 different first languages are spoken—in particular, Spanish, Gujarati, Hindi, Cantonese, and Arabic—and the socioeconomic range is striking. Although many people think of the community as middle- to upper-middle class, a sizable number of its children live in low-cost mobile home parks. About 12 percent are eligible for the federal free or reduced-price lunch program.

At first glance, Ken's school looks as though it's situated in the middle of a park. It is surrounded by woods and grassy fields; a wooden footbridge spans a creek flowing nearby. Built in 1975, the school serves 502 students from kindergarten through fifth grade. An "open space" building, the main instructional area is a huge space that can accommodate at least 10 "classrooms." There are few permanent interior walls; instead, classroom boundaries are delineated by folding walls, file cabinets, bulletin boards, shelves, and cubbies.

Ken, a father of one child, is a fifth-grade teacher. He came to teaching in a roundabout way. After graduating from college with a degree in sociology, he became a writer and began working in an after-school program to supplement

Ken Kowalski

his income. As he came to know the children in his charge, he realized that they
needed more than arts and crafts, but he wasn't sure how to help them:

> I had gone to a parochial school as a kid, and there were 50 to 60 stu-
> dents in a class. The nuns were just overwhelmed by that many students;
> they had little time for individuals. I couldn't draw on my own personal
> experiences to help "my kids," and I didn't know intuitively what to do.
> If teaching is an art, then I came into it with no colors on my palette.

Ken decided to enroll in a teacher certification program so he could "do
something" for his at-risk students. He soon had children playing word games
and dropping by his house to talk or listen to stories. His career in teaching had
begun.

Despite the serendipitous way he entered teaching, Ken has a strong commitment to the profession and a deep attachment to his colleagues. He received two
master's degrees, one in reading and one in computer education, and regularly
takes in-service courses. Over the years, he has achieved a reputation as a master
teacher. He constantly questions what he does in the classroom, searching for the
best ways to help his students grow.

This year, Ken has 23 students in his class; there are 3 Asian Americans, 1
African American, and 19 European Americans. One student has a bilateral moderate hearing loss, and another has a learning disability and is pulled out of class
to receive special services. A number of Ken's students were in his fourth-grade
class the year before, so the relationship between them was easy and familiar from
the very beginning. Because he knows many of his students, Ken can "pick up"
from the previous year and develop plans that he knows will be intellectually
challenging. In addition, Ken is very concerned about his students' social and emotional development. This past summer, he attended an institute on the *Responsive
Classroom*, and he is eager to put some of the ideas he learned into practice. As
Ken puts it:

> Geometry is an exciting, necessary lesson, but to say that geometry is
> more important than sitting with kids and dealing with issues like teas-
> ing and humiliation is a mistake. If the kids sit there feeling miserable,
> then school is a sham—a place to come and feel terrible while you're try-
> ing to learn. Instead, school should be a place where you come to deal with the
> most important problems—which are how do you deal with people—and then you're
> ready to learn some geometry. Geometry can be fun when kids don't have to worry
> about other things.

Ken works hard to create an atmosphere of understanding, responsibility, and
mutual respect. During class, he appears relaxed and patient. When students speak
to him, he listens intently. His students know that they can confide in him; they
often use their daily journals as an opportunity to tell him about concerns. Ken
knows that writing offers a privacy that's difficult to achieve in the classroom, and
he always writes back.

Ken may have begun teaching with no colors on his palette, but he has certainly become a master of even the most subtle hues.

WHAT DO THE STUDENTS SAY?

While working on this chapter, we became curious about the perceptions of students in the classrooms of our five teachers. In particular, we were interested in their reasons for cooperating with their teachers. In each class, we met with students in small groups, either in a corner of the room or out in the hallway. We asked them to explain "why the kids in this class behave." They answered with disarming honesty, and within each class, students demonstrated extraordinary consistency.

Courtney's kindergartners first responded by saying that the children behaved well because "the kids in here are good listeners." When we probed, and asked *why* they were good listeners, they told us that they listened to Courtney "because she's a teacher and you're supposed to listen." (One child added that "we listen 'cause she's bigger than us.") We commented that "kids don't always listen to teachers, even if they're supposed to," and they agreed that this was so. After thinking for a few more minutes, several children talked about the fact that Ms. Bell was a "nice teacher" and they "all really like her." One child explained that "she lets us have lots of play time," and another reported that "she gives us choices." They also talked about how "she teaches us to be good," although they were unable to explain exactly what she did. One unusually articulate child concluded the discussion by telling us, "Since she is nice to us, we have to respect her."

Viviana's first-graders seemed to have difficulty even understanding the concept of misbehavior. For them, behaving well was the only possible course of action. Much like Courtney's students, they told us, "We gotta behave, because she's grown up and she's a teacher." Over and over, they insisted that "kids hafta listen to the teacher," that "we have to behave because she tells us to be good." When we described situations in which students *didn't* behave well, they looked at us blankly, as though they could not conceive of that possibility. One boy in Viviana's class even told us, "My mother has educated me to behave well, so I never misbehave. *I'm not allowed to misbehave.*" A few children talked about wanting Mrs. Love to be happy: "Mrs. Love is good, and she's happy when we're good. She feels good when we listen." And one boy said he behaved well so that he would learn: "If you don't listen to the teacher you might not learn, and when you grow up someone might ask you a question and you won't know the answer, and you won't be able to have a good job, and then you won't make money."

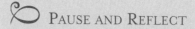

PAUSE AND REFLECT

Now that you've met the teachers, take a minute to think about their personalities and approaches to classroom management. Do you feel a special kinship with any of the five teachers? If your answer is yes, why do you feel this way? Next, reflect on your own elementary school experiences. Were there any teachers that you would characterize as especially effective classroom managers? What did they do that made them especially effective? Are there any similarities between these teachers and the teachers you've just read about

In contrast, Garnetta's third-graders had no difficulty understanding our question. They talked enthusiastically about the stickers they receive for good behavior. They proudly showed us their sticker folders, making certain we saw their favorites. They also told us about the candy they sometimes get when they've been "especially good," and about the pizza parties that they've earned. In addition, they emphasized that "Ms. Chain is real nice." We heard several variations on this theme: "Ms. Chain doesn't yell." "Ms. Chain cares about us." "Ms. Chain treats us real good. If we ask her to go somewhere, like the bathroom, she let's us go. Other teachers say wait until the other kids go." "Ms. Chain bought the guinea pigs for us—only the eighth-grade kids got guinea pigs." Students also described some of the projects they do, claiming that "in this room, we get interesting stuff to do." One girl reported that "in this class, we get to bake bread (the story in our reading book was about making bread, so she let us do that). And she's going to let us make cupcakes, and she let us go with her to get fish for the bazaar." Finally, students described some of the "consequences" that they received if they broke the rules.

In Barbara's class, the students also stressed how "nice" their teacher was, how "she doesn't yell," and how "she makes things fun, even things we don't like." They talked about their science experiments, the arts and crafts activities they had done, the books they read, and the journals they kept. They were appreciative of the fact that they were allowed to work with other students and that they were given choices. They talked about the way Barbara gives them free time and how she plays board games with them ("not like *mothers,* who never play games with kids"). One child commented, "She gives us what *we* want, so we give her what *she* wants." Finally, students made it clear that they knew their teacher's limits: "She's strict—she doesn't let us run all over her, like some teachers—but she's not mean."

We heard the same themes in Ken's class. These fifth-grade students talked about how "he makes work fun" and how "nice" he is—how he jokes, how he cares about kids, and how he really listens. One girl liked the way "we can tell him about our problems. We have journals and if we have a problem, we can write it down and tell him and he'll write back (like if you don't want to sit next to somebody or if you want to be in another reading group)." Students also mentioned the occasional use of rewards ("we get to play an extra game outside if we do a lot of good stuff") and penalties ("we have to stay in for recess and discuss what we did wrong"). The main theme, however, was the fact that "in Mr. K's class kids get to make decisions." Repeatedly, students talked about the options they were given (e.g., "we get to decide what order to do the work in"). They proudly pointed out the Students' Bill of Rights and the Student-of-the Week program. One boy earnestly described the difference between Mr. K and "other teachers": "In here, kids make up the class rules. Some teachers don't care what kids think about what the rules should be. They come in the first day, hand out a paper with rules on it, and say, 'These are the rules.' But in here, we can say what we think the rules should be."

Examining the similarities and the differences among these responses is intriguing. To some extent, the differences across classes seem to reflect developmental changes that occur in children's understanding of authority and obedience. William

Damon (1977), for example, has pointed out that very young children view authority figures as having an inherent right to be obeyed. Thus, most of Courtney's and Viviana's children insist that "we gotta behave because she's grown up and she's a teacher." Later, Damon observes, authority comes to be understood as a reciprocal relationship: One person obeys another in return for the other's assistance and favors. We hear this type of reasoning when Garnetta's students tell us "she gives us stickers and candy" and when Barbara's students cite the way "she plays games with us" (although some of Courtney's students also used this type of reasoning). At a still later age, children begin to see authority as an earned commodity; those who have acquired specific abilities and experiences are entitled to obedience. According to Damon, the authority figure's respect for the welfare and rights of the subordinate is seen as particularly important. Although this theme emerged in discussions with both Garnetta's and Barbara's students, it was most striking in our talks with Ken's fifth-graders, who repeatedly emphasized that "in Mr. K's class, kids get to have a say in what we do."

Beyond these developmental differences, we can see that students' responses largely reflect three themes—*relating to students with caring and respect; teaching in a way that is motivating and interesting; and setting limits and enforcing them.* Moreover, students' descriptions closely matched the behavior that we saw during our observations. We were repeatedly struck by the caring and sensitivity teachers showed to students, by their efforts to stimulate students' interest and engagement in lessons, and by their authoritative, "no-nonsense" attitudes. We will address these themes in the three sections of the book that follow.

PAUSE AND REFLECT

After listening to these students discuss the characteristics of effective classroom managers—caring and respect, teaching in a way that is motivating and engaging, and firmness (the ability to set and enforce limits)—take a moment to reflect on your own strengths and weaknesses in these three areas. What do you think will be your greatest challenge?

CONCLUDING COMMENTS

Courtney, Viviana, Garnetta, Barbara, and Ken teach in very different settings. Grade levels range from Courtney's kindergarten to Ken's fifth grade. The five classes differ dramatically in racial composition: Barbara's class is extremely heterogeneous, Viviana's children are all Latino, Courtney and Ken's classes are predominantly European American, and Garnetta's class is predominantly African American. Viviana and Garnetta work in a district where 80 percent of the children are eligible for free or reduced-price lunch, compared with the 26 percent figure in Barbara's district, the 12 percent figure in Ken's district, and the 4 percent figure in Courtney's. All five teachers follow district curricula that reflect state standards, but Barbara, Ken, and Courtney have more flexibility than Garnetta and Viviana in terms of implementation and choice of materials. In order to be effective, our five teachers must be sensitive and responsive to these differences in age, race, culture, socioeconomic conditions, and district policy.

Despite these differences, Courtney, Viviana, Garnetta, Barbara, and Ken are alike in many ways. Obvious similarities emerge when they talk about the tasks of classroom management. Interestingly, these five teachers rarely use the words *discipline* or *punishment, confrontation* or *penalty.* Instead, they stress the need to develop a "caring community" in which all children are contributing, valued members (Schaps, 2003; Watson & Battistich, 2006); they speak about involving students and helping them to achieve; they talk about the importance of being organized and well prepared.

It's important to remember that Courtney, Viviana, Garnetta, Barbara, and Ken are real human beings working in the complex, uncertain environment of the elementary classroom. Courtney is a first-year teacher, and as she herself admits, she is uncertain about "what will work." Viviana, Garnetta, Barbara, and Ken are experienced, skillful teachers who are extremely effective at preventing misbehavior, but even their classrooms are not free of problems. (Chapter 12 focuses specifically on the ways in which they deal with misbehavior.) Like all of us, they make mistakes; they become frustrated and impatient; they sometimes fail to live up to their image of the "ideal" teacher. By their own testimony, they are all still learning how to run more effective classrooms.

It is also important to remember that these five teachers do not follow recipes or prescriptions for classroom management, so their ways of interacting with children often look very different. Nonetheless, *underlying the differences in behavior, we often detected the same guiding principles.* In the chapters that follow, we will try to convey the ways these five teachers tailor the principles to fit their own particular contexts.

Finally, it is necessary to point out that these teachers do not work in schools where conditions are so bad that classes have to be held in stairwells or storage closets, where windows remain broken for years, and where 40 students in a class have to share a handful of books. Nor do they teach in schools that have installed metal detectors or where students regularly carry weapons. In recent years, their districts have all experienced an increase in serious problems, but violence is certainly not a common occurrence. Whether the strategies discussed here are generalizable to severely troubled schools is not clear. Nevertheless, we hope that *Elementary Classroom Management* will prove to be a useful starting point for teachers everywhere.

SUMMARY

This chapter examined some of the contradictions and special characteristics of classrooms. It argued that effective management requires an understanding of the unique features of the classroom environment and stressed the fact that teachers work with captive groups of students on academic agendas that students have not always helped to set. Within this peculiar setting, teachers must work to accomplish the two major goals of classroom management—creating a caring, orderly environment for learning and enhancing students' social and emotional growth.

Contradictions of the Classroom Environment

- Classrooms are crowded, yet students are often not allowed to interact.
- Children are expected to work together harmoniously, yet they may not know or like each other.
- Students are urged to cooperate, yet they often work in individual or competitive situations.
- Students are encouraged to be independent, yet they are also expected to conform to the teacher's dictates.

Characteristics of the Classroom Environment

- Multidimensionality
- Simultaneity
- Immediacy
- Unpredictability
- Lack of privacy
- History

Guiding Principles of the Book

- Successful classroom management promotes self-regulation.
- Most problems of disorder can be avoided if teachers foster positive teacher-student relationships, implement engaging instruction, and use good preventive management strategies.
- The need for order must not supersede the need for meaningful instruction.
- Teachers must be "culturally responsive classroom managers."
- Becoming an effective classroom manager requires knowledge, reflection, hard work, and time.

Meeting the Teachers

This chapter introduced the five teachers whose thinking and experiences will be described throughout the rest of the book. (See Table 1.2 for a summary.)

- Courtney Bell (kindergarten)
- Viviana Love (first grade, bilingual)
- Garnetta Chain (third grade)
- Barbara Broggi (fourth grade)
- Ken Kowalski (fifth grade)

Although these five teachers teach different grade levels in very different settings, they are alike in many ways. In particular, they speak about classroom management in very similar terms: They emphasize the prevention of behavior problems, mutual respect, involving students in learning activities, and the importance of being organized and well prepared.

What Do the Students Say?

When asked why they behave well in certain classes and not in others, students consistently voiced three themes: relating to students with caring and respect, teaching in a way that is motivating and interesting, and setting limits and enforcing them. We will return to these three themes in subsequent chapters.

ACTIVITIES FOR SKILL BUILDING AND REFLECTION

In Class

1. In a group, discuss the six characteristics of classroom environments and share your ideas about how these characteristics will affect you as a classroom teacher.

2. Reflect on your past experiences with children (e.g., tutoring, being a camp counselor). What did you learn from those experiences that might help you in the classroom?

3. Review the biographies of all the teachers. Identify three to four major ways in which the teachers are similar.

On Your Own

If you are a novice or preservice teacher, are you feeling the same sense of uncertainty that Courtney is expressing? Think about what some of your concerns might be. Talk to a teacher who has been teaching for two or three years and share your thoughts. Find out how that person dealt with his or her concerns.

For Your Portfolio

Pretend you are a teacher being featured in this book. What is *your* story? Think about what motivated you to choose a career in teaching and what your goals are. Write down some of the key points you would want included in your own introduction. (This can be a useful document to review before interviewing and can serve as inspiration during the often difficult first year of teaching.)

FOR FURTHER READING

Charney, R. S. (2002). *Teaching children to care: Classroom management for ethical and academic growth, K–8.* Greenfield, MA: Northeast Foundation for Children.

This book provides a lively, practical guide to creating a respectful, friendly, academically rigorous classroom. Based on Charney's experiences as a teacher and informed by work on the Responsive Classroom approach (Northeast Foundation for Children), the book illustrates ways of managing classrooms to nurture students' social and intellectual growth.

Walker, J. M. T. (Ed.) (2009). A person-centered approach to classroom management. *Theory into Practice, 48*(2), 95–159.

The articles in this theme issue of *TIP* are built around the assertion that viewing classroom management as a person-centered endeavor both is humane and leads to better teaching practice. Although the articles address classroom management at varying levels, from the individual classroom to the school to teaching about management in college classrooms, they all develop the idea that relationships are the heart of schools.

Weinstein, C. S. (Ed.) (2003). Classroom management in a diverse society. *Theory into Practice, 42(4),* 267–359.

The articles in this special theme issue of *TIP* address different aspects of classroom management in a diverse society, but they all reflect the idea that the fundamental task of classroom management is to create an inclusive, supportive, and caring environment. All the authors view classroom management in terms of human relationships—relationships between teachers and students and among students themselves.

ORGANIZATIONAL RESOURCES

REACH Center, 307 North Olympic Avenue, Suite 211, Arlington, WA 98223; 1-800-205-4932; www.reachctr.org. The REACH center has developed school curricula to promote multicultural and global awareness for elementary, middle, and high school classrooms. The center provides training in the use of these curricula, along with books and teacher guides.

The Responsive Classroom, Northeast Foundation for Children (NEFC), 85 Avenue A, P.O. Box 718, Turner Falls, MA 01376-0718; 1-800-360-6332; www.responsiveclassroom.org. The responsive classroom is a practical approach to creating safe, challenging, and joyful elementary classrooms and schools. See the website or contact NEFC for more information.

ESTABLISHING AN ENVIRONMENT FOR LEARNING

"Don't smile until Christmas."

When the three of us went through our respective teacher education programs, that bit of folk advice was all we learned about preventing inappropriate behavior. The idea was to refrain from smiling during the first few months of school so that students would perceive you as stern and serious. Then they wouldn't dare act up.

Actually, our programs didn't talk much about student behavior at all; the overwhelming focus was on what to teach and how to teach it. On those rare occasions when we did discuss students' behavior, it was always in terms of *discipline*—what to do to individuals *after* misbehavior had occurred. When we graduated from our programs and entered teaching, our ability to create respectful, productive learning environments was more a matter of good instincts and luck than of any real knowledge.

Fortunately, the situation has changed a great deal over the last 30 years. Teacher education students can now learn research-based principles, concepts, and practices for creating orderly classrooms—and smiling is definitely encouraged. The emphasis has shifted from what to do *after misbehavior occurs* (discipline) to how to *prevent it in the first place.* Discipline is still important because prevention sometimes fails, but educators now talk about the much broader concept of *classroom management* (of which discipline is only one part). As we discussed in Chapter 1, we define classroom management as *the tasks teachers must carry out to establish a learning environment that is caring, inclusive, and productive.*

Part II of this book addresses "beginning-of-the-year" tasks. Because most teachers are immediately faced with arranging classroom furniture, Chapter 2 focuses on the physical environment. It is intended to help you design a classroom setting that supports your academic and social goals. In Chapter 3, we examine ways to create a classroom community in which individuals feel connected, respected, and cared for. Chapter 4 focuses on the task of establishing and teaching expectations for behavior. We stress the fact that shared behavioral expectations (or norms) are essential if classrooms are to be safe, comfortable, and productive environments. Chapter 5 emphasizes the importance of getting to know your students—understanding and appreciating the characteristics they all share, as well as their unique, individual needs. Finally, Chapter 6 explores the benefits that accrue when teachers and families work together and suggests strategies for reaching out to families. Throughout these chapters, we learn about the beliefs and practices of our five teachers, as well as what research has to say on the topics discussed.

DESIGNING THE PHYSICAL ENVIRONMENT

Discussions of organization and management often neglect the physical character-istics of the classroom. Unless it becomes too hot, too cold, too crowded, or too noisy, we tend to think of the classroom setting as merely a backdrop for inter-action. Yet this setting can *influence the way teachers and students feel, think, and behave.* Careful planning of the physical environment is an integral part of good classroom management. Moreover, *creating a comfortable, functional classroom is one way of showing your students that you care about them.*

Environmental psychologists point out that the effects of the classroom environment can be both *direct* and *indirect* (Proshansky & Wolfe, 1974). For example, if students seated in straight rows are unable to carry on a class discussion because they can't hear one another, the environment is *directly hin-dering their participation.* Students may also be affected *indirectly* if they infer from the seating arrangement that the teacher does not really want them to interact. In this case, the arrangement of the desks is sending a message to the

PAUSE AND REFLECT

You have probably spent more than 13,000 hours as a student in elementary and secondary classrooms. Undoubtedly, some of these rooms were much more attractive and comfortable than others. Think about what made them that way. For example, was it the bulletin boards? the presence of plants? the arrangement of furniture? the lighting? Jot down the specific characteristics that made these rooms pleasant environments in which to learn, and then reflect on which ones are under the teacher's control. Keep these characteristics in mind as you read this chapter.

students about how they are supposed to behave. Their reading of this message would be accurate if the teacher had deliberately arranged the seats to inhibit discussion. More likely, however, the teacher genuinely desires class participation but simply has not thought about the link between classroom environment and student behavior.

This chapter is intended to help you develop *environmental competence* (Martin, 2002; Steele, 1973)—awareness of the physical environment and its impact and the ability to use that environment to meet your goals. Teachers who are environmentally competent can plan spatial arrangements that support their instructional plans. They are sensitive to the messages communicated by the physical setting. They know how to evaluate the effectiveness of a classroom environment. They are alert to instances when physical factors might be contributing to behavioral problems, and they can modify the classroom environment when the need arises.

As you read this chapter, remember that classroom management is not simply a matter of dealing with misbehavior. As we stressed in the first chapter, successful managers *promote students' involvement in educational activities, foster self-regulation, prevent disruption, and relate to students with care and respect.* Our discussion of the classroom environment reflects this perspective: We are concerned not only with reducing distraction or minimizing congestion through good environmental design but also with ways in which the environment can foster children's security, increase their comfort, and stimulate their interest in learning tasks. Throughout this chapter, we will illustrate our major points with examples from the classrooms of the teachers you have just met.

Six Functions of the Classroom Setting

Chapter 1 emphasized the wide variety of activities that occur in classrooms. Although we normally think of the classroom as a place for instruction, it is also a place for making friends, collecting book club money, and passing notes. It is a setting for social interaction, for trying out new roles, and for developing trust, confidence, and a sense of personal identity. Fred Steele (1973) has suggested that physical settings serve *six basic functions:* security and shelter, social contact, symbolic identification, task instrumentality, pleasure, and growth. These six functions provide a useful framework for thinking about the physical environment of the elementary classroom.

Security and Shelter

This is the most fundamental function of all built environments. Like homes, office buildings, and stores, classrooms should provide protection from bad weather, noise, extreme heat or cold, and noxious odors. Sadly, even this most basic function is sometimes not fulfilled, and teachers and students must battle highway noise, broken windows, and leaky roofs. In situations like this, it is difficult for any of the other functions to be met. Physical security is a *precondition* that must be satisfied, at least to some extent, before the environment can serve students' and teachers' other, higher-level needs.

Physical security is a particularly important issue in classes such as science and art, where students may come into contact with potentially dangerous supplies and equipment. It is essential that teachers of these subjects know about their state's safety guidelines for proper handling, storage, and labeling. The art teacher in Viviana's school, for example, is careful to store supplies according to state specifications. She also keeps herself informed about regulations regarding the kinds of materials she can order; pointed scissors and rubber cement are definitely out!

Physical security is also a matter of special concern if you have students who use wheelchairs, leg braces, or crutches or students who have unsteady gaits. Navigating through crowded classrooms can be a formidable and dangerous task. Be sensitive to the need for wide aisles and space to store walkers and crutches when they are not in use. The physical or occupational therapists working in your school can provide consultation and advice.

Often, schools provide *physical* security but fail to offer *psychological* security—the feeling that this is a safe, comfortable place to be. Psychological security is especially crucial for children who live in impoverished, unstable, or unsafe home environments. Psychological security is also particularly important in open-space settings, such as Ken's, where background noise and large interior spaces can be unsettling.

One way of enhancing psychological security is to make sure your classroom contains some "softness." With their linoleum floors, concrete block walls, and formica desks, classrooms tend to be "hard" places. But children (and adults) feel more secure and comfortable in environments that contain items that are soft or responsive to their touch. In Garnetta's classroom, we find plants, fish tanks, and beanbag chairs in which to relax; Viviana's room contains a couch and two arm chairs; and in Courtney's classroom, pillows are available for times when students want to curl up and read on the floor.

One concern about upholstered furniture and fabric-covered pillows is the possibility of spreading lice (Clayton & Forton, 2001)—and in fact, the parent of one of Courtney's students did call to express her concern:

 She said (very nicely) that she wasn't sure it was a good idea to have pillows in the classroom because she thought that it might spread disease as well as lice, since the children were putting their heads on the pillows. I explained why I had the pillows—to create a warm environment and to make it comfortable and cozy when kids are looking at books on the floor. I told her I was going to continue using the pillows, but that she could certainly tell her child that she didn't want him using the pillows and I would follow up on that. I talked to my mentor about it, and she mentioned that she has beanbag chairs that are vinyl. I'm thinking that next year, I'll do that too, or I'll get pillows with removable covers that can be washed regularly.

Other soft elements that teachers can use are stuffed, feathered, or furry animals—but make sure that none of your students are allergic to them. Warm colors, bright accents, and varying textures (such as burlap, wood, and felt) can also help to create an atmosphere of security and comfort.

Another way of increasing psychological security is to arrange classroom space so that students have as much freedom from interference as possible. In the crowded environment of the classroom, it is easy to become distracted. You need to make sure that students' desks are not too near areas of heavy traffic (e.g., the pencil sharpener, the sink, a learning center) and that noisy activities are separated from quiet ones (e.g., block play from the literacy center).

It's also helpful to create spaces where students can retreat when things get too hectic. Low partitions allow children to feel separated and private, but they still enable you to see what's going on. In addition, you might set up a few study carrels or "private offices" where children who want more enclosure can work alone, or you might provide folding cardboard dividers (three pieces of heavy cardboard bound together) that they can place on their desks. All of us need to "get away from it all" at times, but research suggests that opportunities for privacy are particularly important for children who are distractible and for those who have difficulty relating to their peers (Weinstein, 1982). Barbara recognizes this need for privacy:

 I always arrange the desks in clusters because I use a lot of small-group activities, but I've had kids who ask to sit all alone, and I allow them that opportunity. What I've found is that they usually want to be back in the group after a while. I've never permanently put a child by himself or herself, because then that child can't be part of the group activities I plan. I want the kid to be part of the cluster, but to have the right to buy out when he or she can't handle it. If I see a kid having trouble at a table, I might

Barbara uses pillows and stuffed animals to create a "soft" reading area.

say, "Look if you would like to go work by yourself, go ahead, but you can't ruin this for everyone." Or the kid might ask me for permission to go work alone. He or she can move a desk to a corner or find a little enclosed place on the floor.

Freedom from distraction is especially crucial for children with attention-deficit/hyperactivity disorder (ADHD), a neurobiological disability that interferes with an individual's ability to sustain attention. Children with ADHD have difficulty focusing attention, concentrating, listening, following instructions, and organizing tasks; they may also exhibit behaviors associated with hyperactivity—difficulty staying seated, fidgeting, impulsivity, lack of self-control. (See Chapter 5 for more information on ADHD.) You can help children with ADHD by seating them away from noisy areas, near well-focused students, and as close to you as possible so that it's easy to make eye contact (Carbone, 2001). For these children, study carrels, folding dividers, and retreat spaces are especially important.

Social Contact

Interactions among Students

As you plan the arrangement of students' desks, you need to think very carefully about how much interaction among students you want, because different arrangements facilitate different amounts of contact. Clusters of desks promote social contact since children are close together and can have direct eye contact with those across from them. In clusters, children can work together on activities, share materials, have small-group discussions, and help each other with assignments. The proximity is particularly helpful for facilitating interaction among children from different linguistic and cultural backgrounds and among children with disabilities and their peers who are not disabled.

On the other hand, rows of desks make it easier for children to concentrate on individual assignments (Bonus & Riordan, 1998; Wheldall & Lam, 1987). This seems to be particularly true for children with ADHD (Carbone, 2001) and for students who have behavior and learning problems. In one particular study, when a primary class was moved from groups to rows there was a marked increase in students' average time-on-task (Hastings & Schwieso, 1995). The improvement was even more dramatic for three particularly distractible, disruptive students, whose average time-on-task went from 16 percent to 91 percent—an increase of 75 percentage points!

It is clear that clusters of desks are most appropriate if you plan to emphasize small-group work and cooperative learning—and, in fact, research indicates that the use of clusters is now widespread in grades K–5 (Patton, Snell, Knight, & Gerken, 2001). *But it is unwise and inconsistent—even inhumane—to seat children in clusters and then give them individual tasks and tell them not to talk.* If you do that, students receive two contradictory messages: The seating arrangement is communicating that it's all right to interact, while your verbal message is just the opposite!

You might also consider putting desks in horizontal rows. (See Figure 2.1.) This arrangement orients students toward the teacher but still provides them with close neighbors on each side. Still another option, advocated by Fredric Jones and others (2007), is shown in Figure 2.2. Here, an "interior loop" allows you to "work the crowd with the fewest steps" (p. 34).

Courtney, Barbara, Garnetta, and Ken all arrange their students' desk in clusters, reflecting the value they place on collaboration. (See Figures 2.3 and 2.4 for maps of Courtney's and Barbara's classrooms.) Courtney also had to consider the amount of

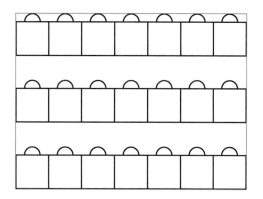

Figure 2.1   A Horizontal Arrangement

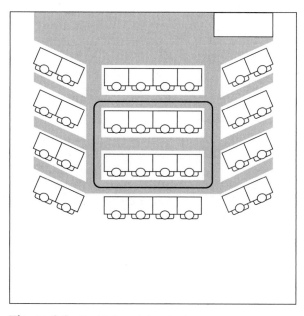

Figure 2.2   Fredric Jones's Interior Loop Arrangement
Source: Jones, F. H. (2007). *Tools for teaching.*
Santa Cruz, CA: Fredric H. Jones & Associates.
Reprinted with permission.

interaction she wanted when children were seated on the floor for morning meetings, read-alouds, and other activities. She eventually put tape on the floor to indicate two different configurations. A bright yellow oval is for morning meetings (when she encourages interaction) and during math instruction (when she wants everyone to see the manipulatives she uses for demonstrations). Four parallel rows of white tape indicate where students are to sit for read-alouds, calendar time, and literacy instruction.

In contrast to the other teachers, Viviana uses a horseshoe arrangement. (See Figure 2.5.) This layout is consistent with the teacher-directed nature of her instructional program, but it also allows students to work easily with the individuals sitting on either side. Viviana explains this choice:

 I like the desks in a horseshoe because this way everyone can see what's going on in the front of the room. They can see the work on the board or demonstrations at the small round table. But it's also a good arrangement for working with a partner. The horseshoe also lets me see everybody and get close to them.

Although our five teachers have all selected arrangements that support their normal instruction, it is important to note that they are willing to rearrange their

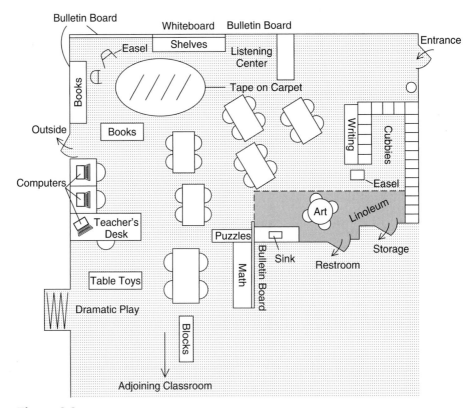

Figure 2.3   Courtney's Room Arrangement

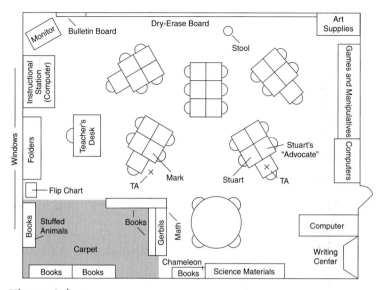

Figure 2.4   Barbara's Room Arrangement

rooms when a lesson requires a different layout. This is not typical. Research indicates that teachers are often reluctant to move the furniture in their classrooms to match the type of work they intend students to do—in other words, they prefer to change the instructional format to fit the furniture that is already

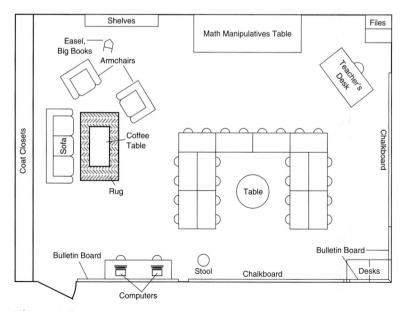

Figure 2.5   Viviana's Room Arrangement

in place (Kutnick et al., 2005). Thus teachers who have student desks in rows might opt for paired discussion rather than cooperative learning groups, because this will not require moving the furniture. We can understand this reluctance: Moving furniture can result in loss of instructional time, chaos, and confusion. But it doesn't have to be this way. Watching our teachers' students move their desks into new configurations makes it clear that students can learn to do this quietly and quickly, but they will need to be taught the procedures to follow. (See Chapter 4.)

Interaction between the Teacher and the Students

The way students are arranged can also affect interaction between the teacher and the students. A number of studies have found that in classrooms where desks are arranged in rows, the teacher interacts mostly with students seated in the front and center of the classroom. Students in this "action zone" (Adams & Biddle, 1970; Kashti, Arieli, & Harel, 1984) participate more in class discussions and initiate more questions and comments.

Educational researchers have tried to tease out the reasons for this phenomenon. Do students who are more interested and more eager to participate select seats in the front, or does a front seating position somehow produce these attitudes and behaviors? This issue has not been fully resolved, but the weight of the evidence indicates that a front-center seat does encourage participation, whereas a seat in the back makes it more difficult to participate and easier to "tune out."

Although research on the action zone has examined only row arrangements, it is easy to imagine that the same phenomenon would occur whenever teachers direct most of their comments and questions to the students who are closest to them. Keep this in mind, and take steps to ensure that the action zone encompasses your whole class. Some suggestions: (1) move around the room whenever possible; (2) establish eye contact with students seated farther away from you; (3) direct comments to students seated in the rear and on the sides; and (4) periodically change students' seats so that all students have an opportunity to be up front.

Symbolic Identification

Steele's third function involves the information that a setting provides about the people who spend time there. The key questions are these: What does this classroom tell us about the students—their interests, activities, backgrounds, accomplishments, and preferences? And what does the classroom tell us about the teacher's goals, values, and beliefs about education? Too often classrooms resemble motel rooms. They are pleasant but impersonal, revealing nothing about the people who use the space. (See Figure 2.6 for an example of a classroom that definitely reflects the interests and needs of its inhabitants.)

ASTRONAUT SCHOOL

Figure 2.6 *Source:* www.CartoonStock.com. Reprinted with Permission.

There are innumerable ways to personalize classroom space: You can post children's art work; the stories they dictate or write; charts listing heights, weights, or birthdays; and photographs. As an introductory activity, Barbara has her students write about what makes them unique (for example, one student might be a ballerina and another might like computers). The students then turn that essay into a banner made out of felt, and Barbara also makes one for herself. The essays are hung on the writing bulletin board, and the banners are displayed around the edge of the classroom all year long.

Similarly, Courtney uses student "picture cards" throughout the school year:

> **At kindergarten orientation, a few days before school began, every parent brought in a photograph of their child. I collected them and made a "picture card" for each child with the photo and his or her name. It really helped me to learn their names—even before they got to school—and the kids use the picture cards to answer the question of the day and to indicate their activity choice during free play.**

You can also personalize space by displaying materials that reflect the cultural backgrounds of the children in your class (Weinstein, Curran, & Tomlinson-Clarke, 2003). At the beginning of the year, you can create a welcome sign written in the different languages spoken by your students or their families. You might exhibit photographs of children from around the world, list accomplishments of notable people from your children's native countries, or hang posters showing art from different cultures. In Viviana's room, colorful fabric parrots from Puerto Rico hang from the ceiling; bulletin board displays are labeled in both English and Spanish; and paper flags of the Dominican Republic, Nicaragua, Mexico, Ecuador, Puerto Rico, Cuba, Peru, Honduras, and Colombia decorate one wall. Displays like these communicate respect for your students' diverse cultural backgrounds.

PRACTICAL TIPS FOR

PERSONALIZING CLASSROOM SPACE

Think about displaying the following in your classroom:

- *Student Birthdays.* You can honor the individual students in your classroom by creating a birthday cake made out of laminated paper for each month, and adding paper candles with each student's name and date of birth on the appropriate month. Not only does this provide a visual representation for the students and allow them to see which of them have birthdays around the same time, but it also provides a record for the teacher of whose birthdays to remember as each new month arrives.

- *Map of the World.* Students can learn about geography and develop cultural awareness by having a map of the world on permanent display in the room. Periodically during the school year, you can bring the class together to discuss questions such as "Where have you been?" and "Where were you born?" For younger students, a note can be sent home for a parental response to these questions. You can mark student responses on the map with colored pins or draw lines from student names to the corresponding place on the map.

- *Word Wall.* Have a designated wall space for words that are used often to be posted as students learn or need them throughout the school year. At the beginning of the year, each student's name can be posted under the appropriate letter of the alphabet.

- *Student of the Week Bulletin Board.* A specific board or wall space can be decorated to highlight a student of the week. When it is their turn, students can bring in pictures, certificates, artwork, and other artifacts representing their interests. Teachers can use this board to introduce themselves on the first day of school.

- *Best Work from Each Student.* Allow each student in your class to select his or her best piece of work to display on a classroom wall. This practice encourages students to be self-evaluative and take pride in their work, while also avoiding the danger of having the work of only a few students posted. To this end, you might want to have a designated spot labeled for each child.

In addition, consider ways in which you can communicate something about your own cultural background and experiences. You might want to hang your favorite art prints, display pictures of your family, or exhibit your collections of "precious objects." Other suggestions for how you might personalize your classroom space can be found in the nearby Practical Tips box.

Finally, look critically at commercial materials before posting them on your classroom walls and ask yourself whether they really contribute to students' learning. Patricia Tarr (2004) believes that commercial material can "silence" children when they overpower student work, or when what is displayed does not reflect who the learners are in terms of gender, ethnicity, and culture. The following questions, adapted from Tarr, are useful when planning what to display in the room:

- Why am I displaying these materials and for whom?
- What image of a learner is conveyed by the materials displayed?
- How can the walls invite active participation and learning?

- Does the display honor children's voices and work?
- How can the walls reflect the lives, families, cultures, and interests of the learners?
- What is the atmosphere of the classroom, and how do the materials on display contribute to this atmosphere?
- What are the assumptions about how children learn, and how are these reflected by the classroom walls?

Task Instrumentality

This function concerns the many ways in which the environment helps us to carry out the tasks we need to accomplish. Think about the tasks and activities that will be carried out in your classroom. Will students work alone at their desks on independent assignments? Will they work cooperatively on activities and projects? Will you instruct the whole class from the chalkboard, easel, whiteboard, overhead projector, or video projector connected to a computer? Will you work with small reading groups? Will students do research using the Internet? Will they rotate among learning centers? Will they engage in dramatic play, block play, arts and crafts, or science experiments?

For each of these tasks, you need to consider the physical design requirements. For example, if you plan to meet with small guided reading groups, you have to think carefully about where to locate the small-group area. Do you want it near a chalkboard or a bulletin board? In any case, its location should not be distracting to students working independently. You also want to be able to monitor the rest of the students while you are working with the small group.

This year, Ken is lucky enough to have four computers in his room, Barbara and Garnetta each have three, and Viviana and Courtney have two (plus one on Courtney's desk for her own work). This is substantially better than having only one computer per classroom (or none), a situation that exists in many schools. A single computer can be used for noninstructional activities, such as record keeping, or used as a whole-group presentation tool (Bolick & Cooper, 2006). Multiple computers can be used as information or learning centers for students. Unless the placement of the computer center is dictated by the location of electrical outlets and wiring for Internet access, you need to think carefully about where to create those centers. If students are going to work in pairs or in small groups, place the stations in an area where clusters of students can gather round without creating traffic congestion and distraction. Also be sure to keep the computers away from water and from chalkboards (dust can cause a problem).

Whatever tasks will occur in your classroom, there are a few general guidelines you need to keep in mind. These are listed in the accompanying Practical Tips box.

Pleasure

The important question here is whether students and teachers find the classroom attractive and pleasing. To the already overworked teacher preoccupied with covering the curriculum, raising test scores, and maintaining order, aesthetic concerns

PRACTICAL TIPS FOR

**ARRANGING YOUR CLASSROOM TO MAXIMIZE TASK
INSTRUMENTALITY**

- *Make sure that frequently used classroom materials are accessible to students.*
  Materials such as crayons, pencils, paper, dictionaries, rulers, and staplers should be
  easy to reach. This will minimize the time spent preparing for activities and cleaning
  up. Decide which materials will be kept in students' desks and which will be kept on
  shelves.

- *Organize shelves and storage areas so that it is clear where materials and
  equipment belong.* It is useful to label shelves so that everyone knows where things
  go. (For very young children, you can use picture labels as well as print.) This will
  make it easier to obtain materials and to return them. You should also have some sort
  of a system for the distribution and collection of students' work (such as in–out boxes
  or individual student mailboxes).

- *Plan pathways through the room to avoid congestion and distraction.* Paths to the
  water fountain, pencil sharpener, trash can, and coat closet should be clearly visible
  and unobstructed. These high-traffic areas should be as far from students' desks as
  possible. Make sure that your pathways don't go through work areas. For example,
  you don't want children to have to walk through a literacy corner in order to get
  something from the coat closet. Children shouldn't have to walk behind the small-
  group reading area in order to get a needed dictionary. Are pathways wide enough for
  students who use walkers or wheelchairs?

- *Plan enough space for the children to line up at the door* (Clayton & Forton, 2001).
  Allowing about nine inches between each child and the next, you can estimate the space
  you will need for students to line up without bumping into furniture or each other.

- *Design a seating arrangement that allows students to have a clear view of
  instructional presentations.* If possible, students should be able to see instructional
  presentations without turning their desks or chairs around.

- *Provide students with a place to keep their belongings (lunch boxes, backpacks,
  skateboards, etc.).* This is especially important if your classroom doesn't have desks
  with storage space.

- *Decide where to put your desk (or get rid of it!).* The location depends on where you
  will be spending your time. If you will be constantly moving about the room, your desk
  can be out of the way, in a corner perhaps. If you will use your desk as a conference
  area or as a work station, then it needs to be more centrally located. But be careful:
  With a central location, you may be tempted to remain at your desk for long periods of
  time, and this cuts down on your ability to monitor students' work and behavior. All
  five of our teachers have their desks off in a corner or in the back of the room.

- *Separate incompatible activities.* If you plan to set aside spaces for particular
  activities, think carefully about their relative locations. Make sure to separate activities
  that don't go well together: noisy/quiet, messy/neat, and wet/dry (for example, the
  computers should be far away from the sink!).

may seem irrelevant and insignificant (at least until parent conferences draw near).
Yet given the amount of time that you and your students spend in your classroom,
it is worth thinking about ways to create a pleasing environment. In Garnetta's
room, plants line the windowsill; Barbara uses large pieces of boldly patterned

wrapping paper to cover bulletin boards; and Viviana's colorful cloth parrots create a festive air.

The classic study on environmental attractiveness was conducted by Abraham Maslow and Norbett Mintz (1956). These experimenters compared interviews that took place in an "ugly" room with those that took place in a "beautiful" room. Neither the interviewer nor the subject knew that the real purpose of the study was to assess the impact of the environment on their behavior. Maslow and Mintz found that interviewers assigned to the ugly room complained of headaches, fatigue, and discomfort. Furthermore, the interviews *finished more quickly* in the ugly rooms. Apparently, people in the ugly room tried to finish their task as quickly as possible in order to escape from the unpleasant setting.

Identifying specific characteristics that everyone considers pleasing has been difficult. Nonetheless, there are some principles to keep in mind when thinking about ways to create an attractive classroom. In general, people seem to respond positively to the presence of *variation.* In other words, they seem to enjoy being in environments that contain both warm colors and cool colors; open, spacious areas and small, cozy corners; hard surfaces and soft surfaces; textures that are smooth and those that are rough (Olds, 1987). However, it is important that this variation be moderate and orderly. A lack of stimulus variation can lead to monotony, but too much variation can produce feelings of anxiety and chaos, especially if that variation lacks patterning or predictability.

Growth

Steele's (1973) last function is particularly relevant to classrooms, because they are settings specifically intended to promote children's development. This function is also the most difficult to pin down, however. Although it's easy to see that environments should be functional and attractive, it's less obvious that they can be designed to foster growth. Furthermore, growth can refer to any number of areas— learning to tie one's shoes, increasing one's self-confidence, learning to cooperate. For simplicity, we will restrict our discussion to ways in which the environment can promote children's *cognitive development and academic achievement.*

Psychologists have found that the opportunity to explore rich, stimulating environments is related to cognitive growth. Your classroom should be more than a place where children listen to instruction, complete workbook pages, and demonstrate mastery of skills. It should be a setting that *invites children into the learning experience* (Strong-Wilson & Ellis, 2007)—*to explore, observe, investigate, test, and discover.* This means that in addition to the standard readers, dictionaries, and workbooks, your classroom should contain a wide variety of materials such as puzzles, brainteasers, math manipulatives, science equipment, and art supplies.

When you are stocking your classroom, it is useful to think about materials that are "open"—water, paint, clay—and those that are "closed"—puzzles, workbooks, tracing patterns (Jones & Prescott, 1978). Its location on an open-closed continuum describes the extent to which a material or object dictates *one right answer.* For example, children have many options when creating with clay, but there is only one right way to complete a wooden puzzle. Materials such as blocks, Legos, and Tinker Toys lie somewhere in the middle of the continuum: Although these materials impose some restrictions on what can be done with them, they still invite experimentation and improvisation. Analyzing materials in terms of openness can help you to structure a setting that promotes creativity and divergent thinking.

The environment can also foster children's growth by stimulating their interest in reading and writing. Unfortunately, despite a wealth of research that demonstrates the link between "print-rich classroom environments" and increased reading achievement, many classes have only the most basic libraries (Morrow, Reutzel, & Casey, 2006). Lesley Morrow (2005) encourages teachers to provide children with the opportunity to have pleasurable experiences with literature: to read daily to children, to discuss the stories, to schedule recreational reading periods, and to integrate literature with other areas of the curriculum. These literacy activities can be supported by the presence of well-organized literacy centers. In addition to a well-stocked library corner, there can be a writing center, with paper of all kinds, index cards, markers, pens, pencils, and story-starters, and a "working with words" center, with magnetic letters, individual dry-erase boards, letter trays with letters for making words, and word and letter games (e.g., Lotto). Stocking imaginative play centers (such as building and dramatic play areas) with situation-specific literacy-related objects (telephone books, cookbooks, coupons, store ads, maps, calendars, etc.) can also promote children's literacy activity (Morrow, Reutzel, & Casey, 2006).

Viviana has created a "mini-living room" in her classroom, complete with a sofa and arm chairs salvaged from a school storage closet. A coffee table overflows with

Viviana reads a story to her class in the "living room."

newspapers, books, and magazines, and a small rug and pillows enable children to sit comfortably on the floor. Viviana tells us why she has provided this center:

For many of my children, the only thing they do in the living room is watch television and play video games. I want them to realize that you can sit in the living room and read a good book. Every day I sit on the sofa and have them sit around me on chairs and pillows. I read a story or an article from the day's newspaper (which I bring in). Then I let someone take the newspaper home. The kids love our "living room," and I feel so good when I see them curled up on the sofa with a book.

See Figure 2.7 (adapted from Morrow, 2005) for a checklist you can use to create, evaluate, and improve the literacy environment of your classroom. A note of caution if you do choose to create a literacy center as suggested in the checklist: Plan set times for students to use the center. Too many teachers design and equip literacy centers and then don't provide opportunities for children to use them. Some teachers allow children to go to the center only if they are finished with their "real work." This means that children who work slowly may never get to use the center. It also conveys the message that the activities done in the literacy center are not considered as important or valuable as those done at desks under the teacher's direct supervision. By creating set times for students to visit the literacy center, you are providing opportunities for all students to become equally engaged in this rich literacy environment.

> ### ✎ PAUSE AND REFLECT
>
> We have heard teachers in the intermediate and middle school grades comment that the six functions of the classroom setting are interesting but that they are more applicable to primary classrooms. We disagree. Think about how an intermediate or middle school teacher can use the six functions of the classroom in planning and setting up a classroom environment that is developmentally appropriate to their students.

THE TEACHER AS ENVIRONMENTAL DESIGNER

Steele's six functions give us a way of thinking about the environment, but they don't provide an architectural blueprint. If you think about the various roles that settings play, you will realize that the functions not only overlap but may actually conflict. Seating that is good for social contact may be bad for testing. Room arrangements that provide children with privacy may be poor for monitoring and maintaining order. As you think about your room and your own priorities, you will have to determine which functions will take precedence over others. In this section of the chapter, we describe a process for you to follow as you design your classroom.

Think about the Activities the Room Will Accommodate

The first step in designing a classroom is to decide what activities your room is to accommodate. For example, if you are teaching a kindergarten or primary classroom, you may wish to create areas for sharing time, reading aloud, small-group

THE LITERACY CENTER

____ Center located in a quiet area of the room

____ Area surrounded by low partitions to provide protection from distraction and intrusion, but still visually accessible

____ Children involved in designing the center (e.g. develop rules, select a name for center, develop materials)

____ Soft elements present (e.g. pillows, beanbag chairs, plants, stuffed animals)

____ Bulletin board nearby to post children's book reviews and jackets of featured books

____ Center uses about 10% of the classroom space and fits five to six children at a time

THE LIBRARY CORNER (LOCATED WITHIN THE LITERACY CENTER)

____ Featured books displayed so that front covers are clearly visible

____ All other books stored on bookshelves with spines facing outward

____ Organizational system for shelving books

____ Five to eight books per child in classroom

____ Twenty new books circulated every two weeks

____ Books represent three to four grade levels

____ Variety of books available, including: (a) picture books, (b) picture storybooks, (c) traditional literature, (d) poetry, (e) realistic literature, (f) informational books, (g) biographies, (h) chapter books, (i) easy-to-read books, (j) riddle and joke books, (k) participation books, (l) series books, (m) textless books, (n) television-related books, (o) brochures, (p) magazines, and (q) newspapers

____ Head sets and audiotapes of books

____ Literature props to accompany select books (e.g., felt boards with story characters, puppets)

____ Check-out/check-in system for children to take out books daily

____ System for recording books read (e.g., 3 × 5 cards hooked onto a bulletin board)

____ Sign-up chart for students who want to read aloud to classmates or to children in younger grades

THE WRITING CENTER (LOCATED WITHIN THE LITERACY CENTER)

____ Tables and chairs

____ Writing posters and a bulletin board for children to display their writing

____ Writing utensils (e.g., pens, pencils, crayons, felt-tipped markers, colored pencils)

____ Writing materials (e.g., a variety of paper in all sizes, booklets, pads)

____ Computer

____ Materials for making books (e.g., cardboard, staplers)

____ Message board for children to post messages for the teacher and other students

____ A place to store individual students' word lists or dictionaries

____ Folders for children to place samples of their writing

CONTENT-AREA LEARNING CENTERS (LOCATED IN OTHER PARTS OF THE ROOM)

____ Environmental print (e.g., signs related to themes, directions, rules)

____ Calendar

____ Current events board

____ Appropriate books, magazines, and newspapers

____ Writing utensils in all centers

____ Varied types of paper in all centers

____ A place for children to display their literacy work

Figure 2.7   Checklist for Creating and Improving the Literacy Environment
Source: Adapted from Morrow, 2005 and Morrow & Weinstein, 1982, 1986.

reading instruction, whole-group math instruction, blocks, dramatic play, computers, and arts and crafts. An intermediate grade teacher might want to accommodate whole-group literature discussions, small-group work, media presentations, "hands-on" projects, and testing. List these activities in a column and, next to each activity, note whether it poses any special physical requirements. For example, art and science areas should be near a sink, and the literacy center should be in a quiet area of the room. Also consider which activities involve objects that cannot be moved, such as the projection screen and equipment that needs an electrical outlet or wiring for Internet access.

Don't get discouraged if you find your room is not well suited for certain activities you would like to do. Instead, try to think of ways to compensate. Barbara, for example, has no running water in her room. So, to the dismay of the custodians, she gets two buckets of water each day (one for washing and one for water colors or science projects) and keeps them in a convenient place. As she puts it, "It's nice not to have to run down the hall every time someone spills juice."

Think about Whether the Children in Your Classroom Have Special Needs That Require Environmental Modifications

As we've already mentioned, you may have to make sure that aisles are wide enough to accommodate students who use wheelchairs, leg braces, walkers, or crutches. In addition, a special type of desk might be needed for a student in a wheelchair, and a cushion with a back might enable that student to join the other children on the floor.

If you have students with hearing impairments, as Ken does this year, it's desirable to minimize background noise by placing felt or rubber caps on chair and table legs. (Tennis balls work well!) Covering table surfaces with fabric and lining study carrels with acoustical tile or corkboard can also help cut down on noise (Mamlin & Dodd-Murphy, 2002).

Also think about special needs when assigning seats to students. We've already discussed seating for students with ADHD. But other students may also require special seating assignments. For example, make sure that visually impaired students can easily see what you are writing on the board. Similarly, if you have students with a hearing impairment who need to lip-read, locate their seats so they can see your face at all times.

Barbara has to think carefully about where to seat Stuart, a student with autism. Stuart's individualized education program (IEP) says that he can leave the classroom and take a walk in the hallway whenever he gets overstimulated or out of control, so Barbara has placed him near the doorway. (See the map of Barbara's classroom.) In addition, Stuart needs to be seated in the same cluster with one of two students who serve as his "advocates"; they have gone to school with him since he entered the general education classroom and understand his body language and vocalizations.

Think about the Needs of Other Adults in the Classroom

As more and more students with special needs are educated in general education classrooms, it becomes increasingly likely that you will be working with other adults (e.g., special education teachers providing in-class support, paraprofessionals, instructional aides). In fact, a recent study of 18 elementary schools found that teachers were more likely to have at least one additional adult in their classrooms than to be alone with their students (Valli, Croninger, & Walters, 2007).

Resource teachers or instructional aides require, at a minimum, a place to store materials and equipment and a place to sit, so you will need to decide where these will be. When designing her classroom, Barbara needed to consider where to seat the full-time aides (called "teaching associates" or TAs) who work with Stuart and Mark, a child with an emotional disorder. (See the floor plan for the location of their seats.) Each aide has a chair next to the student he's assisting, but they also share a student desk (next to Stuart) for storage of any materials they might need. (We will address these issues in greater depth in Chapter 5, when we discuss co-teaching between general and special education teachers.)

Draw a Floor Plan

Before actually moving any furniture, draw a number of different floor plans and select the one that seems most workable. The classroom diagrams shown earlier contain some useful symbols, or you may create your own. As you decide where to place furniture and equipment, consider the special requirements noted on your list of activities, as well as the room's "givens"—the location of outlets, chalk-boards or whiteboards, windows, built-in shelves, computer wiring, permanently installed TV monitors, and phones. Also keep in mind our discussion of psychological security, social contact, and task instrumentality.

It may be helpful to begin by deciding where you will conduct whole-group instruction (if at all) and the way students will be seated during this time. Think about where the teacher's desk should be; whether frequently used materials are stored on shelves or in cabinets that are accessible to you and your students; and whether pathways are clear. Remember, there is no one right way to design your classroom. The important thing is to make sure that your spatial arrangement supports the teaching strategies that you will use and the kinds of behaviors you want from your students (Bonus & Riordan, 1998; Wengel, 1992).

Involve Students in Environmental Planning

Although a great deal can be done before the start of school, it is a good idea to leave some things *undone* so that your students can be involved in the design process. You might solicit children's ideas for room design and then select those that seem most feasible. You might also rotate responsibility for some aspect of the environment among small groups of students (for instance, each group could have an opportunity to design a bulletin board display). Inviting children to participate in environmental planning not only helps to create more responsive physical arrangements but also allows them to voice their opinions and to share in meaningful decision making. And children can be perceptive and imaginative in describing the classroom they'd like to have (Pointon & Kershner, 2000). For example, Barbara designs the initial classroom arrangement and then begins a process of negotiation once the students weigh in with their opinions:

 I try to give the kids a say in how things are arranged. We have a deal: Sometimes I make the final decision, and sometimes they do. Whichever, we agree to live with the arrangement for a designated period of time. Then if we don't like it, we can change it. Last year my class decided they wanted the round table in the center of the room with the desks in a horseshoe around it. I hated this, but I lived with it for a month. Then I told them exactly why I didn't like it: I had no privacy, and all the noise faced the front of the room. So together we changed the arrangement.

Try the New Arrangement, Evaluate, and Redesign

Use Steele's (1973) six functions of the environment as a framework for evaluating your classroom design. For example, does the classroom provide opportunities for retreat and privacy? Does the desk arrangement facilitate or hinder social contact among students? Do displays communicate information about the students and their work? Are frequently used materials accessible to students? Does the room provide pleasure? Does it contain materials that invite children to explore and to extend their interests and abilities?

As you evaluate the effectiveness of the classroom setting, stay alert for behavioral problems that might be caused by the physical arrangement. For example, if a small cluster of students suddenly becomes inattentive when their desks are moved next to the hamster cage, it is likely that an environmental change is in order, rather than detention. If students rarely demonstrate interest in reading during free-choice time, it may be due to the way the books are displayed. If the classroom floor is constantly littered despite your appeals for neatness, the underlying problem may be an inadequate number of trash cans.

Improving your room does not have to be tedious and time-consuming. Small modifications can bring about gratifying changes in behavior. In one case, kindergarten students were found to be inattentive and disruptive when crowded around a teacher reading a story (Krantz & Risley, 1972). Just spreading the children out in a semicircle markedly improved their attentiveness. In fact, this simple environmental modification was as successful as a complicated system of rewards and privileges that the experimenters had devised!

CONCLUDING COMMENTS

Our five teachers design their rooms differently, but they are all environmentally competent teachers who attend to Steele's six functions. They strive to make their classrooms more comfortable places by including elements of softness (security and shelter). They arrange students' desks to match the instructional practices they implement (social interaction). They personalize the room by posting students' work and displaying artifacts related to the curriculum (symbolic identification). They think hard about where activities will take place, where materials should be stored, where their own desks should be, and how to overcome constraints (task instrumentality). They have well-stocked literacy centers (growth). And even with all their planning, they realize that they will have to see how the arrangement actually works and that they might have to change things around.

Like Courtney, Viviana, Garnetta, Barbara, and Ken, you need to think about the various functions of the physical setting when you arrange your own classroom space. Environmental competence is an integral part of effective classroom management. Remember—designing the physical environment entails far more than just decorating a few bulletin boards.

SUMMARY

In this chapter we discussed how the physical environment of the classroom influences the way teachers and students feel, think, and behave. We stressed the need for teachers to be aware of the direct and indirect effects of the physical environment. This awareness is the first step to developing "environmental competence." We suggested ways to design a classroom that will support your instructional goals, using Steele's six functions of the environment as a framework for discussion.

Security and Shelter

- Add elements of softness.
- Arrange space for freedom from interference.
- Create a "retreat" area.

Social Contact

- Consider how much interaction among students you want.
- Think about whether you are making contact with *all* of your students.

Symbolic Identification

- Personalize your classroom space so that it communicates information about you and your students.

Task Instrumentality

- Make sure that frequently used materials are accessible to students.
- Make it clear where things belong.
- Plan pathways to avoid congestion and distraction.
- Plan adequate space for students to line up by the exit door.
- Arrange seats for a clear view of presentations.
- Offer students a personal space in which to keep belongings.
- Locate your desk in an appropriate place or get rid of it.
- Separate incompatible activities.

Pleasure

- Use a variety of colors and textures to create an aesthetically pleasing environment.

Growth

- Stock your room with a variety of activities, both "open" and "closed."
- Create a rich literacy environment.

Careful planning of the physical environment is an integral part of good classroom management. When you begin to design your room, think about the activities it will accommodate, any special needs your students may have, and the needs of other adults in the classroom.

Invite your students to participate in the planning process. Try your arrangement, evaluate it, and redesign as necessary.

ACTIVITIES FOR SKILL BUILDING AND REFLECTION

In Class

1.   Consider the following seating arrangements. For each one, think about the types of instructional strategies for which it is appropriate or inappropriate. The first one has been done as an example.

Arrangement	Instructional Strategies for Which This Arrangement Is Appropriate	Instructional Strategies for Which This Arrangement Is Inappropriate
Rows	*Teacher or student presentations; audio-visual presentations; testing*	*Student-centered discussions; small-group work*
Horizontal Rows		
Horseshoe		
Small Clusters		
Circle		

2.   Examine Figure 2.8, which shows the floor plan of a first-grade room where the teacher is experiencing difficulty with classroom management. According to the teacher, there are five primary problems: (1) Children at the small-group table are frequently distracted. (2) Clean-ups and transitions between activities take too long. (3) There is conflict between children in the library corner and those playing with puzzles and games. (4) When the teacher is working with a small group, the children who are not in the group have difficulty staying on task. (5) A student with ADHD (seated next to the teacher's desk) feels isolated and ostracized. He still has difficulty staying on task even though he is seated by himself, but when he sits in a cluster, he disrupts the other students.

   Think about the ways in which the environment might be contributing to the first four problems. How would you rearrange the room? Also consider where you might seat the child with ADHD.

On Your Own

1.   Visit an elementary classroom, draw a classroom map, and evaluate the physical layout in terms of Steele's six functions of the environment. Use the bullets under each of Steele's functions, as presented in the chapter summary, as a checklist. For

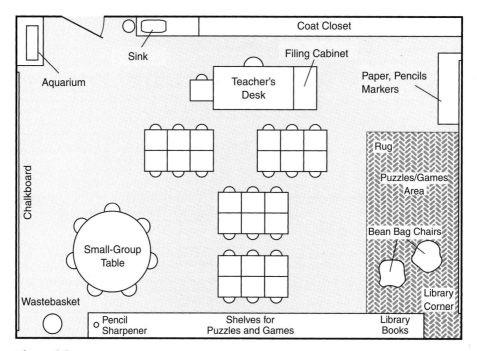

Figure 2.8   Floor Plan of First-Grade Room

example, to evaluate security and shelter, ask yourself: Does the classroom contain elements of softness? Do children have freedom from interference? Is there a place for a student to retreat? After examining all six functions, decide what you might change, if anything.

2. Have students in your classroom, or in a classroom that you are observing, compose a "wish poem" (Sanoff, 1979) by completing the phrase "I wish my classroom . . . ." Here is an excerpt from the responses written by the kindergartners of a student teacher who tried this activity (with the original spellings and translations):

I wish my classroom had a gold fish.
I wish my classroom wasn't hot and I wish my classroom was quiet.
I wus my classroom wus nis (was nice).
I wish my classroom it cmptr (had a computer).

For Your Portfolio

Design your ideal classroom. Draw a map of the room and write a brief commentary explaining your design decisions.

FOR FURTHER READING

Clayton, M. K., with Forton, M. B. (2001). *Classroom spaces that work*. Greenfield, MA: Northeast Foundation for Children.

This practical guide for designing K–6 classrooms draws on Clayton's 30 years of teaching experience. It offers concrete suggestions for arranging furniture, selecting and organizing materials, eliminating clutter, storing supplies, setting up a meeting area, creating meaningful displays, and accommodating special needs.

Nations, S., & Boyett, S. (2002). *So much stuff, so little space: Creating and managing the learner-centered classroom.* Gainesville, FL: Maupin House Publishing.

Susan Nations is a literacy resource teacher for grades K–5, and Suzi Boyett is a second-grade teacher. This little book shares the lessons that they have learned about organizing space, creating a homelike environment, attacking clutter, "sprucing up," and making sure everything has a place in a crowded classroom.

ORGANIZATIONAL RESOURCES

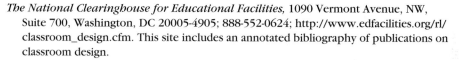

The National Clearinghouse for Educational Facilities, 1090 Vermont Avenue, NW, Suite 700, Washington, DC 20005-4905; 888-552-0624; http://www.edfacilities.org/rl/classroom_design.cfm. This site includes an annotated bibliography of publications on classroom design.

Learn NC K–12 Teaching and Learning, 140 Friday Center Drive CB #7216, The University of North Carolina at Chapel Hill, Chapel Hill, NC 27599-7216; 919-962-8888; http://www.learnnc.org/lp/pages/BasicEnv1. The University of North Carolina at Chapel Hill School of Education finds the most innovative and successful practices in K–12 education and makes them available to teachers and students. The site includes articles on the physical climate of the classroom, arranging for independence, working with available space, and sample classroom floor plans.

BUILDING RESPECTFUL, CARING RELATIONSHIPS

Some years ago, we supervised a student teacher named Annie, who had been placed in a fourth-grade classroom. One of us had taught Annie in a course on campus and had some concerns about her organizational ability. Nevertheless, we weren't prepared for what occurred during our first visit to her classroom. Annie was teaching a lesson on quotation marks. Although it wasn't exactly captivating, it wasn't awful. But her students' behavior *was*. They chatted, rummaged through their desks, and completely ignored the lesson. Furthermore, throughout the period, a steady stream of students walked up to Annie, asked to go to the restroom, and left the room. We watched in disbelief as a student left about every three minutes; at one point, five or six students were out at the same time. Yet Annie never asked students to wait until she had finished teaching or until the previous person had returned.

When the period was over and we met with Annie to discuss the lesson, we asked her to talk about the students' behavior. We wondered how she interpreted the students' lack of interest in her lesson and their obvious desire to leave the room. We also wanted to know why she had never said "no" when a student asked to leave the room. We remember her answer clearly: "I want to show the children that I care about them. I don't want to rule this classroom like a dictator. If I said no when someone asks to go to the bathroom, that would be showing them that I don't respect them."

Annie never did create the atmosphere of mutual respect she desired; in fact, she never completed student teaching. Her commitment "to care"—which she defined as "never say no"—led to a situation so chaotic and so confused that no learning, teaching, *or* caring was possible.

WHY IS SHOWING CARE IMPORTANT?

Over the years, we have thought a lot about Annie and her efforts to establish a respectful, caring environment. Although Annie was ultimately unsuccessful, we understand and applaud the high priority she placed on positive teacher–student relationships. Both common sense and research tell us that students are more likely to cooperate with *teachers whom they see as caring, trustworthy, and respectful* (Cornelius-White, 2007; Gregory & Ripski, 2008; Osterman, 2000; Woolfolk Hoy & Weinstein, 2006). This appears to be especially true for Black and Hispanic students, who frequently perceive that their teachers (generally European American) fail to understand their perspectives, accept them as individuals, honor their cultural backgrounds, or demonstrate respect (S. R. Katz, 1999; Nieto & Bode, 2008; Sheets, 1996). Indeed, Angela Valenzuela (1999) argues that the immigrant Mexican and Mexican American high school students she studied in Houston need to feel *cared for* before they can *care about* school.

But gaining cooperation is certainly not the only reason for developing respectful, supportive relationships with students. If we want children to be seriously engaged in learning, to share their thoughts and feelings, to take risks, and to develop a sense of social responsibility, then we need to organize classrooms in such a way that students feel safe and cared for—emotionally, intellectually, and physically. If we want students to feel a sense of connectedness and trust, then we must work to create classroom communities where students know that they are needed, valued members of the group. If we want students to accept and appreciate diversity—ethnic, racial, gender, class, ability/disability—we must model that behavior.

In retrospsect, Annie's problem was not the high priority she placed on being caring and on creating positive relationships with her students. *Her problem was the way she thought about caring.* Clearly, never saying "no" doesn't work. So what does? How can you show students that you care about them?

This chapter begins by considering ways of showing caring and respect for students. We then turn to relationships among students themselves and discuss strategies for creating a caring community in which students feel respected, trusted, and supported by one another. As you read, keep in mind the characteristics of classroom groups that we discussed in Chapter 1. Recall that, unlike most other social groups, students do not come together voluntarily. They are a captive audience, and they are often required to work on tasks they have not selected and in which they may have little interest. Remember, too, that

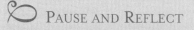

PAUSE AND REFLECT

Before going any further, think about a teacher you had in elementary school who showed caring and respect for students. In specific behavioral terms, what did this teacher *do* to communicate that he or she cared about you?

classroom groups are formed somewhat arbitrarily; students do not usually choose their peers *or* their teachers, yet they are expected to cooperate with both. Recalling these special characteristics makes it easier to see why teachers must work deliberately to create cohesion, cooperation, and a sense of community.

WAYS OF SHOWING CARE AND RESPECT FOR STUDENTS

Be Welcoming

Beginning teachers are often told not to smile until Christmas so that students will perceive them as serious and tough. We don't agree. A smile is a simple, effective way to be welcoming. You can also welcome students by standing at the classroom door and greeting them at the beginning of the day. This not only ensures that students enter the room in an orderly fashion but also gives you an opportunity to say hello, comment on a new book bag, and ask how things are going. If you have students who are not native English speakers, learn a few phrases in their native language so you can welcome them to your class each day with a few words from their homeland. Ken tells about a girl in his class who had recently come from Mexico and was feeling unhappy and uneasy in her new setting:

 One day she came in, and I said, "Buenas dias," and she got this huge grin on her face. When I saw her reaction, I tried to learn some common Spanish phrases. Whenever I'd use them—in my awful accent—she'd smile and correct me. It was really something; it changed the whole nature of our relationship.

 Most important, learn students' names (and any preferred nicknames) as quickly as possible. You also need to learn the correct pronunciation, especially for names that are unfamiliar. In our teachers' classes, for example, there are children whose names can be a challenge: Isatu ("eye-sa-too"); Iaesi ("ee-si"); Wei Hou ("wee-how"); Hiji ("Hai-jai"); Daniel ("Donny-el"); Ayesha and Aisha (pronounced identically).

Learn about Students' Lives

In addition to welcoming your students, another way of showing care and respect is to learn about their lives and interests. For example, you can ask your students to complete an information sheet asking about their favorite subjects, about what they want to learn about in school, about what they like to do at home, and about their families. Scheduling a one-on-one lunch with each of your students is another way of getting to know your students. You can also assign weekly writing assignments (or drawings for younger children) that ask students to tell something special, such as "My favorite thing in class this week was . . ." or "The best part of my weekend was . . ." (Cartledge & Lo, 2006).

Another idea comes from JoBeth Allen (2008), who was part of a teacher study group in Georgia that used photography to learn about students' families. With a small grant, the study group teachers bought three cameras for each classroom and invited students to photograph what was important to them in their homes and neighborhoods. Students took the cameras home on a rotating basis, and students and family members wrote personal stories, memories, poetry, and letters about the photos.

Be Sensitive to Children's Concerns

In essence, being sensitive to children's concerns means thinking about classroom events and activities from a student's point of view. Sitting next to someone you dislike, for example, can make life in school very unpleasant. For this reason, Barbara allows students to have input whenever she changes the seating:

 I ask students to write down a list of three students they'd like to sit next to. I tell them that I'll do my best to see that they sit next to one of their choices, but I explain that I'm counting on them to make wise choices— to choose someone who can act as a partner, someone they can sit next to without causing a commotion or interfering with others. . . . When I decide on the seating, I try to honor their requests, but I can also separate overly social kids or kids who just don't get along. In this way, I can prevent problems from occurring. The kids really like this system. They realize I'm trying to be considerate of their feelings, but I'm also protecting their opportunity to learn.

Another way of showing sensitivity to students' concerns is by remembering the very public nature of classrooms and keeping grades as private as possible. Most students don't want their peers to know when they've gotten a poor grade, and public announcements are less likely to increase motivation than to generate resentment. Even if you announce only the As, you can embarrass students. A fifth-grader we know was mortified when her teacher held her test up in front of the whole class and announced that "Laura was obviously the only one who studied!" And what does an announcement like that convey to the student who normally receives Ds, but studied really hard and earned a C?

Sensitivity also means discussing inappropriate behavior quietly and privately. In the following vignette, Garnetta deals with an overly exuberant child in a sensitive manner:

Garnetta's class is learning to count money. Garnetta tells each table group to work together to draw as many combinations of $0.35 as possible, using dimes, quarters, nickels, and pennies. The students were very excited. Leon seems about to burst. Standing up, he waves his arms and yells, "We got six [combinations]!" Then "We got seven!" Garnetta walks over to him, bends down low, and speaks softly. Leon sits down and continues working with his group; he is still engaged and excited, but he no longer yells. It appears that other students have paid scant attention to the interaction.

Like Garnetta, all of our teachers avoid public reprimands whenever possible. Public reprimands are humiliating—and humiliation will surely poison your relationship with students. Moreover, verbal abuse can have long-term negative effects. A recent Canadian study (Brendgen, Wanner, Vitaro, Bukowski, & Tremblay, 2007) found that elementary students, from kindergarten through fourth grade, who were "picked on" by the teacher (defined as behaviors such as scolding, criticizing, or shouting) were more likely to display behavior problems in young adulthood.

Establish and Enforce Clear Expectations for Behavior

Establishing and enforcing clear norms for behavior makes the classroom a safer, more predictable environment and communicates that you care about your students' well-being. With clear rules and routines, there is less likelihood of confusion, misunderstanding, and inconsistency—and more likelihood that teachers and students can engage in warm, relaxed interactions. Clear expectations also establish you as the classroom leader; this is especially important if you are working with African American students, who generally expect teachers to be authoritative— to speak in a firm voice, establish a no-nonsense atmosphere, demand respect, and convey high expectations (Brown, 2004; Gordon, 1998; Irvine, 2002; Milner, 2006; Obidah & Teel, 2001).

Research has demonstrated the long-term benefits to students of organized classrooms with clear norms. In one study (Catalano, Haggerty, Oesterle, Fleming, & Hawkins, 2004), elementary teachers from schools in high-risk neighborhoods were trained in the use of proactive classroom management techniques (e.g., establish consistent classroom expectations and routines at the beginning of the year; give clear, explicit instructions for behavior; recognize desirable student behavior). Not surprisingly, the students of those teachers demonstrated a higher level of school bonding and fewer problem behaviors than students in a control group. What is even more noteworthy is the fact that when those students were followed into high school, their levels of school attachment, commitment, and academic achievement were higher than those in the control group, and school problems, violence, alcohol abuse, and risky sexual activity were reduced. (Establishing norms for behavior is addressed more fully in Chapter 4.)

Be Fair

It seems obvious that caring teachers must strive for fairness. But it's not always so simple. Being fair generally involves "making judgments of students' conduct and academic performances without prejudice or partiality" (M. S. Katz, 1999, p. 61). In terms of classroom management, this translates into ensuring that rules apply to everyone, no matter what. On the other hand, being fair can also imply recognition that people may need different, personalized treatment, and being caring certainly seems to demand that we acknowledge students' individuality. From this perspective, treating everyone the same is *unfair*. So what is a teacher to do?

This dilemma is especially salient for Barbara: Her class includes Stuart, a child with autism, and Mark, a child who has been classified as emotionally disturbed.

Barbara is well aware that she needs to make special accommodations for both Stuart and Mark, but she wanted to make sure that their peers understood the reasons for the differential treatment. To provide an opportunity for the children who were not disabled to discuss what it was like to be in class with Stuart and Mark, Barbara led "share circles" on a day when the two boys were not present. Discussion revealed that students were very understanding and tolerant of Stuart. When he walked around the room at will, or made noises during silent reading time, students attributed his behavior to his autism. In contrast, they considered Mark to be "sort of normal" and believed that he should be able to control his behavior. This made his occasional refusals to work or his aggressive outbursts confusing, and students expressed resentment about the special privileges Mark sometimes received (e.g., getting to use the computer while they were doing class work). Having learned this, Barbara has worked hard to explain how "different students have different needs, so always treating everybody the same is not fair." She has also explained about "visible" and "invisible" disabilities and has emphasized the fact that invisible disabilities require students to be more sensitive and understanding. Her efforts appear to have paid off: Subsequent discussions with students indicated increased acceptance of Mark's outbursts and his special treatment.

Research suggests that students generally understand the need for accommodations. One particular study explored the perceptions of 98 students in grades 1 through 6 regarding the acceptability of teachers' differentiating academic work, as well as rules and rewards, to meet the diverse needs of students with learning and behavior problems (Fulk & Smith, 1995). Students were individually interviewed and asked two "yes" or "no" questions regarding management: "Pretend there is a student in your room who gets in trouble a lot for not following school rules. Would it be OK with you if this student got special rewards for behaving better that other students did not get?" "Would it be OK with you if the teacher gave this student extra chances or different rules while he or she learned to behave better?" Overall, most students favored special rewards (72 percent) and extra chances or different rules (67 percent); only first-graders, with a 53 percent "no" response, were split on the acceptability of differential treatment. Interestingly, students explained their responses not only in terms of the effect on students with problem behavior ("Because he needs more help with his behavior than other kids. He may someday get to be like us if he works hard and gets special things.") but also in terms of the effect of inappropriate behavior on the class as a whole ("His bad behavior affects others, so special rewards for everyone would be better."). The researchers conclude, "Teachers may be more concerned about equal treatment of students than students are" (Fulk & Smith, 1995, p. 416). (We return to this topic in Chapter 12, when we discuss the issue of consistency.)

Be a Real Person (as Well as a Teacher)

Beginning teachers often puzzle over the extent to which they should share information about their personal lives. We remember having teachers who refused to reveal their first names—as though that would somehow blur the boundary between teacher and student and diminish their authority. On the other hand, there are teachers who are extremely open. In an article on "Building Community from Chaos" (1994), Linda Christensen, a high school English teacher in Portland, Oregon, writes:

> Students have told me that my willingness to share stories about my life—my father's alcoholism, my family's lack of education, my poor test scores, and many others, opened the way for them to tell their stories. . . . And through their sharing, they make openings to each other. Sometimes a small break. A crack. A passage from one world to the other. And these openings allow the class to become a community. (p. 55)

As a new teacher, it's probably wise to find a happy medium between these two extremes and share limited information (about families, vacations, cultural and athletic activities, hobbies, or pets, for instance). Before you start your first teaching job, be sure to review any online profiles you may have on sites such as MySpace or Facebook. Make sure your profiles don't reveal more than you would want your students (and their parents) to know about you.

After some deliberation, Courtney decided to share the fact that she had a fiancé named David:

I keep a picture of the two of us on my desk, which the girls especially loved. David also came to read to the class at Thanksgiving and for the end-of-the-year program. You would have thought a rock star came to school, the kids were so excited. I told them I was getting married in the summer, and it became a really big thing. At the end of the year, two parents worked with the class to produce a book called "David is a lucky man because . . .," and every child filled out a page. What an incredible surprise!

As you gain experience and confidence, you can decide whether you want to share more information about your personal life. But Garnetta suggests that you think about the *reason* for disclosing personal stories:

Why do you want to share information? Is it to get students' attention? to enhance a lesson? to model how to share during sharing time? to build a relationship with the children? There needs to be a purpose. Don't tell about your life just to tell.

Another way of showing your humanity is to admit when you don't know something. Teachers sometimes feel that they have to be the "sage on the stage," but it can be beneficial for students to see that even "experts" don't know all the answers all the time. The best way to encourage students to take risks in the process of learning is to take risks yourself.

It's also important to apologize if you make a mistake. The following excerpt comes from a student teacher in middle school:

> *The class was working [on their creative writing assignments and posters] when I heard one student, Gary, [who was] sitting on the floor by David's*

desk, say to David, "Please stop kicking me." I heard David reply, "I'm not kicking you." I watched the two of them for the next few minutes. . . Gary continued drawing on the poster on the floor, while David sat at his desk writing. Then I saw it, David swung his leg repetitively forward, kicking Gary several times in the back. . . . I rose to tell David that I needed to speak to him privately, took him into the farthest corner of the room, and said softly to him, "You need to stop doing that immediately." He said, "I really didn't know I was doing that!" Then I said, "I think you do and I'd like you to stop." [Later] I had the chance to speak with another teacher about what happened. She had had David in previous years, "It's possible he's telling you the truth," she said. "He has Tourette syndrome and occasionally he can have involuntary body movements."

I had been aware of David's Tourette syndrome . . ., having looked at his file. But I had noticed only that he had trouble with occasional tics and sudden spoken outbursts. I went to find him in his next class. He came out of the class and I explained to him that I had thought it had been intentional, and that I might have been wrong in thinking that way. Then I said that I would like for us to speak more often and keep open communication so that we can understand each other better. He agreed to do this.

Keep in mind that presenting yourself as a real person to your students doesn't mean that you should dress like them. Students, and also parents, tend to respect teachers who dress professionally. If you are coming straight from college, your clothes may be too casual for the classroom. Use other teachers as a model, or ask the principal about expectations for professional dress. You should also learn about school policy on piercings and tattoos.

Promote Autonomy by Sharing Responsibility

Providing opportunities for students to participate actively in classroom decision making, planning, and goal setting contributes to their feelings of being connected and supported (Osterman, 2000). There are many ways of allowing students to have a say in what happens in the classroom. For example, Ken sometimes allows students to select the novels they will read in small groups:

 I brought in about a dozen sets of novels and had the kids examine them when they had some free time. They know there have to be three or four groups. They talked with one another about the books. I'd hear them say, "This looks good. Would you want to read this with me?" You know, it's funny. Teachers say, "You can't do this. Kids will just pick the books their friends read." I say, "That's right. And that's OK. In fact, that's exactly what adults do." When a friend says a book is good, that's when you want to read it. Kids are no different. Anyway, after everyone had a chance to peruse the books, we took about 30 or 40 minutes one day to set up the groups. Generally, the kids were really cooperative. For example, one boy said, "I really wanted to read *Treasure Island*, but no one else picked it, so I'll take *Dies Drear* instead."

Ken also allows his class to have input into the daily schedule. He'll tell them, "It's 1:45 and we have three things to do. What order should we do them in?" Sometimes, students are allowed to select the two assignments they will do in class and the one they will bring home for homework.

Like Ken, Barbara tries to build choice into the curriculum. During one visit late in the school year, we watched Barbara introduce a new project—writing a newspaper based on the novel they had just finished reading. In the following vignette, Barbara allows individuals not only to select the topic on which to write but also to decide whether they will work alone or in groups.

BARBARA: Should we work in groups or not? [Students raise their hands in response to her question.] Edward?

EDWARD: I personally don't want to work in groups. I have an idea about what I want to do and how I want to do it, and it would be better if I could work alone.

BARBARA: Are there people who feel differently? How do you feel, James?

JAMES: I'd like to work in pairs.

BARBARA: Why?

JAMES: Because it's easier. You get more work done quickly.

EDWARD: I don't mind pairs either, just not a large group.

ISATU: I go to enrichment, and it would help if I had a partner so I'd know what to do when I come back.

BARBARA: That's a good point. Jill?

JILL: Sometimes I prefer to work alone because I have serious thinking to do.

BARBARA: OK, here's what we're going to do. You changed how I was thinking. I was thinking of having you work in threes, but you convinced me that pairs and singles would be good. . . . You get yourselves organized, and then come over to the round table and tell me what you want to write about and if you're single or pairs.

Although it is easier to share decision making with students in higher grades, Courtney, Viviana, and Garnetta also try to create opportunities for students to exercise independent judgment. For example, instead of assigning classroom jobs, Garnetta puts the list on the board and allows children to choose the two jobs they would like to do. She makes an effort to give students their first choice. When Viviana's first-graders work on spelling words, they have the option of using the spelling word in a sentence, drawing and labeling a picture showing the word, or incorporating the word in a sentence that describes a magazine picture. Whenever Courtney introduces a new math activity, she conducts a lesson with the whole group so that everyone can become familiar with it. Then the activity becomes an option during "math choice time," along with four or five activities she's already introduced. Students examine the options, which are listed on a pocket chart along with the number of students who can select each activity, and then place their picture cards next to their selections.

Sharing decision making can be difficult for teachers. When you're feeling pressured to cover the curriculum and to maximize learning time, it's easier to make the decisions by yourself. Involving students can be "messy" and time-consuming, and allowing students to make decisions about their own behavior means that they'll sometimes make the wrong decisions. Nonetheless, a "short-term investment of time" can lead to "a long-term gain in decision-making ability and self-esteem" (Dowd, 1997).

Reduce the Use of Extrinsic Control

Another way of increasing students' experience of autonomy is to decrease the use of extrinsic rewards and punishments. None of us likes to feel controlled or manipulated, and we generally experience external regulation as alienating (Reeve, 2006b; Ryan & Deci, 2000). Indeed, research has revealed that there is a *negative* relationship between the use of external control and student engagement (Kim, Solomon, & Roberts, 1995); this is critical, because student engagement is, in turn, significantly related to sense of community. What seems clear is that the more students feel externally regulated, the less they show interest and effort, and the more they tend to disown responsibility for negative outcomes (Ryan & Connell, 1989). This hardly makes for a caring community.

Instead of imposing lots of rewards and penalties, our five teachers try to help students think about and understand the importance of making the classroom a good place to be. When problems occur, they typically take a "teaching" or problem-solving approach, rather than an approach based on punishment. When Viviana's children become distracted by the rubbery spider rings that are popular at Halloween time, Viviana doesn't direct students to put them away. Instead she says, "If you can pay attention and wear the ring, fine. If you think you'll have trouble, then take it off and put it in the desk."

Similarly, Ken calls class meetings to discuss persistent behavioral problems instead of simply handing out punishments:

> Every day, the class would come back from playing outside and complain about kids being too aggressive—pushing, grabbing the ball, fighting. Finally, we had a class meeting. I said to them, "According to the Bill of Rights, everyone in this class has the right to go outside almost every day. [See Chapter 4.] But everyone also has the right to be treated nicely and not to be disturbed. So what are we going to do?"
>
> It would have been a lot easier to just impose the consequences by myself, without deliberation. Meeting with students to discuss what to do is really time-consuming. But I'm convinced that this is the way kids develop responsibility for their own behavior. And when I do bench someone, it's not because I'm mean or nasty; it's because that's what the class decided.
>
> You really have to do this a lot in September and October. Later on everyone's too hysterical about standardized tests. But no one objects if you take a lot of time at the beginning of the school year; that's when you're supposed to be setting the tone. And in the long run, student decisions save time. There is less misbehavior when students help to decide.

Be Inclusive

In recent years, the term *inclusive education* has been used to refer to the practice of placing students with disabilities in general education classrooms, rather than segregating them in special classrooms or schools. But the term can also be used more broadly, to describe classes in which differences related not only to disability but also to race, class, ethnicity, gender, cultural and linguistic background, religion, and sexual orientation are acknowledged, understood, and respected.

This, of course, is easier said than done. Before we can acknowledge and respect differences, we need to recognize that we are often afraid and suspicious of those differences. As we mentioned in Chapter 1, sometimes we deny even *seeing* differences. It is not uncommon, for example, for our European American teacher education students to pride themselves on being color-blind, assuming that being color-blind is "fair and impartial when it comes to judging people on their race" (Nieto & Bode, 2008, p. 75). Yet to deny cultural or racial differences is to deny an essential aspect of people's identity—and recognizing those differences does not make us racist.

In addition to *acknowledging* differences, creating inclusive classrooms means learning about disabilities, cultures, races, or religions that we've never before encountered. For example, you can't acknowledge and respect behaviors that have cultural origins if you have no idea that the behaviors are rooted in culture. Teachers may be shocked when Southeast Asian students smile while being scolded if they are unaware that the smiles are meant not as disrespect, but as an admission of culpability and an effort to show that there is no grudge (Trueba, Cheng, & Ima, 1993). Similarly, teachers who do not realize that Pacific Islanders value interpersonal harmony and the well-being of the group may conclude that these students are lazy when they are reluctant to participate in competitive activities (Sileo & Prater, 1998). Teachers who are unaware that the culture of most American Indians tends to emphasize deliberate thought may become impatient when those students take longer to respond to questions (Nieto & Bode, 2008).

A particularly heated debate about students' use of Ebonics, or Black English, illustrates the problems that occur when teachers are unaware of the cultural origins of language. Ernie Smith (2002), an African American linguist, notes that teachers often equate the use of Ebonics with deficiency:

> Teachers and other school officials often used such terms as "talking flat," "sloven speech," "corrupt speech," "broken English," "verbal cripple," "verbally destitute," "linguistically handicapped," and "linguistically deprived" to describe the language behavior of my Black classmates and me. They suggested that our language differences were deficiencies that were related to physical and/or mental abnormalities. Often during Parent-Teacher Conferences or at Open House Conferences, my teachers were not hesitant to suggest to my parents, and to parents of other children, that we should be assigned to the school speech clinic for speech therapy or to the school psychologist for a diagnostic examination, and treatment for possible congenital mental disorders. (pp. 17–18)

Not surprisingly, this negative reaction to children's home language frequently leads to alienation from school. As Lisa Delpit argues in *The Skin That We Speak* (2002), "language is one of the most intimate expressions of identity" so "to reject a person's language can only feel as if we are rejecting him" (p. 47). Rejection like this has no place in an inclusive classroom; instead, inclusive teachers honor students' home language while teaching them the importance of learning to speak Standard English—what Delpit (1995) calls the "language of the culture of power." In other words, our goal is to enable students to "code switch" according to the norms of the setting.

It's unrealistic to expect beginning teachers (or even experienced ones!) to be familiar with all of the cultures that might be represented in their extremely diverse classrooms. Certainly, developing this kind of "cultural literacy" takes time and effort. Some specific suggestions are listed in the accompanying Practical Tips box.

Creating inclusive classrooms also means challenging practices of *exclusion* (Sapon-Shevin, 2003). When students make such comments as "You can't be in our group!" or "Go away! We don't want to work with you," it's important to convey that excluding others is unacceptable ("What you said is hurtful, and in this classroom we treat everyone with kindness"). In addition, it is useful to explicitly address issues of exclusion during class discussions: "Let's talk about what happened today when Mark wanted to join the girls in the dramatic play area." "What shall we do about the fact that some of you think you should be able to choose whom to work with, but then other students feel left out and sad?" "What can you do when you see someone is left out?" Mara Sapon-Shevin notes that teachers are sometimes hesitant to initiate discussions of exclusion, fearing that they will make matters worse. But, she observes, if we wait until everyone feels ready to address issues like these, "we may wait a very long time. Failing to address what all the students have already observed communicates that exclusion is inevitable" (pp. 26–27).

> ## ⤧ PAUSE AND REFLECT
>
> In her book *You Can't Say You Can't Play,* Vivian Gussin Paley (1992) describes how she introduced that rule to her kindergarten class. In other words, excluding children from joining a group was not allowed. What do you think about such a rule? Is it fair? Can it work? Would you ever contemplate having such a rule in *your* classroom?

Search for Students' Strengths

In *The Culturally Responsive Teacher* (2007), Ana Maria Villegas and Tamara Lucas tell the story of Belki Alvarez, an eight-year-old girl from the Dominican Republic. As the oldest child in the family, Belki was responsible for getting her brother and sister ready for school and caring for them until her parents came home from work. On weekends, she joined her mother at a community street fair, selling products prepared at home, negotiating prices with customers, and handling financial transactions. She also served as an English language translator for her parents. But Belki's teachers didn't see this competent, responsible child. They saw only a youngster lacking in language and math skills and made no effort to tap into her life experiences. In other words, they focused on her deficits, rather than her strengths.

Searching for deficits makes a certain amount of sense. After all, if we can identify what students don't know or can't do, we can try to fix the problems. But responsible teaching also involves searching for strengths. In *Teaching to Change*

PRACTICAL TIPS FOR

DEVELOPING CULTURAL LITERACY

- **Examine your own taken-for-granted beliefs, values, and assumptions and reflect on how they are influenced by your cultural, racial, and socioeconomic identity.** As we noted in Chapter 1, many European Americans consider their beliefs and values to be correct and universal, not realizing that these beliefs and values are products of their particular cultural background. Developing cultural literacy begins by examining one's own cultural norms. For example, a White middle-class worldview emphasizes individual achievement, independence, and competition. This is in stark contrast to the worldview of more collectivist cultures (e.g., Asian, Latino, and Native American), which avoid displays of individual accomplishment and, instead, stress cooperation, harmony, and working for the good of the group. One worldview is not necessarily better than the other—but they are certainly different. Failing to appreciate and respect these differences can lead to misunderstanding and miscommunication.

- **Explore students' family backgrounds.** Where did the student come from? Was it a rural or an urban setting? Why did the family move? How long has the student been in this country? How many people are in the family? What are the lines of authority? What responsibilities does the student have at home? What are his or her parents' beliefs with respect to involvement in the school and in their child's education? Do they consider teachers to be experts and therefore refrain from expressing differences of opinion? Is learning English given high priority?

- **Explore students' educational background.** If students are new to this country, how much previous schooling have they had? What kinds of instructional strategies are they used to? In their former schools, was there an emphasis on large-group instruction, memorization, and recitation? In students' former schools, what were the expectations for appropriate behavior? Were students expected to be active or passive? independent or dependent? peer-oriented or teacher-oriented? cooperative or competitive?

- **Be sensitive to cultural differences and how they may lead to miscommunication.** How do students think about time? Is punctuality expected or is time considered to be flexible? Do students nod their heads to be polite or to indicate understanding? Do students question or obey authority figures? Do students put their needs and desires before those of the group, or vice versa? Are expressions of emotion and feelings emphasized or hidden?

- **Use photographs to communicate without words.** Take pictures of the children engaged in various activities to take home to parents; display photographs around the room; invite students to bring in pictures of themselves and their families; use photographs for get-acquainted activities.

- **Develop a portfolio for each child.** Make a list of everything the child can do without using language (build, sort, match, categorize, sequence, copy, draw, mimic, make faces, pantomime). Note interactions with other people. Determine which instructional activities the student enjoys the most and which he or she tries to avoid. Think about whether these preferences might reflect cultural values. Find out what activities the child pursues after school. Include photographs of the child and samples of work.

Sources: Kottler, 1994; Sileo & Prater, 1998.

the World (1999), Jeannie Oakes and Martin Lipton argue that when teachers and students have a caring relationship, they work together to find competence: "The student's search is his own discovery of what he knows and how he knows it. The teacher's search—an act of care and respect—is also discovering what the student knows and how he knows it" (p. 252).

Ken feels strongly about the importance of searching for students' strengths:

 It's really important to build a schedule and design activities that will lead to success, not just reaffirm that the kid fails a lot. Teachers have got to work with children's strengths and interests, not just their weaknesses. A lot of the time, teachers say, "These are the areas where the child has problems, so I've got to spend all the time on remediating these." But skills are all interdependent; they can be taught in the context of activities that kids find interesting and appealing, activities that they can succeed on. Children need to learn hope and success as much as they need to learn academic skills.

Develop Communication Skills

Another way of showing students that you care is by being a good listener. This means being attentive, demonstrating empathy, asking appropriate questions, and helping students solve their own problems. In the following sections, we will examine each of these. As you read, keep in mind that as a teacher, you are required by law to report child abuse or neglect, so there may be times when you will need to go beyond merely listening. It's important to let your students know that if you do learn about any abuse, you will need to report the information to the appropriate child welfare agency.

Attending and Acknowledging

Giving a student your complete, undivided attention is the first and most basic task in being helpful (Kottler & Kottler, 1993). It is rare for individuals to be fully attentive to one another. Have you ever tried to talk with someone who was simultaneously organizing papers, posting articles on the bulletin board, or straightening rows of desks? Divided attention like this communicates that the person doesn't really have time for you and is not fully paying attention.

Attending and acknowledging involve both verbal and nonverbal behaviors. Even without saying a word, you can convey that you are totally tuned in by orienting your body toward the student, establishing eye contact, nodding, leaning forward, smiling, or frowning. In addition, you can use verbal cues. Thomas Gordon (2003) recommends "acknowledgement responses" or "empathic grunting"—the little "uh-huhs" and phrases ("Oh," "I see," "Mmmmm") that communicate, "I'm really listening." Sometimes, when a student needs additional encouragement to talk more, you can use an explicit invitation, what Gordon calls a "door opener," such as "Tell me more," "Would you like to say more about that?" "Do you want to talk about it?" "Want to go on?"

Active Listening

Attending and acknowledging communicate that you are totally engaged, but they do not convey whether you really *understand.* Active listening takes the interaction one step further by having you reflect what you think you heard. This feedback allows you to check out whether you are right or wrong. If you're right, the student knows that you have truly understood. If you're off target, the student can correct you, and the communication can continue. Examples of active listening appear in Table 3.1.

TABLE 3.1 Examples of Active Listening

STUDENT:	Wait 'til my mom sees this test grade. She's gonna flip out.
TEACHER:	You think she'll be really mad at you?
STUDENT:	Yeah, she expects me to come home with all As.
TEACHER:	Sounds like you're feeling really pressured.
STUDENT:	Well, I am. You'd think that getting a B was like failing. My mom just doesn't understand how hard this is for me.
TEACHER:	So you think a B is an OK grade in a tough course like this, but she thinks that you can do better.
STUDENT:	Yeah, she has this thing that if I come home with a B, I'm just not working.
TEACHER:	That's rough. I can see how that would make you feel like she doesn't appreciate the efforts you're making.
STUDENT:	I can't believe I have to be home at 10:00! It's crazy! All my friends have a later curfew—or they don't have any curfew at all!
TEACHER:	So you think your parents are a lot stricter than the other kids' parents.
STUDENT:	Well, they are! I mean, I know it's 'cause they care about me, but it's really a pain to have to be home earlier than everyone else. I feel like a dork. And besides, I think I'm responsible enough to have a later curfew.
TEACHER:	So you're not just embarrassed, you're mad because they don't realize how responsible you are.
STUDENT:	All along she's been telling me how we'll be best friends forever, and then she goes and gets a best friend charm with Mira.
TEACHER:	When something like that happens, you feel really abandoned.
STUDENT:	I don't want to go to School-Base [for mental health counseling]. Only crazy kids go to School-Base!
TEACHER:	Going to School-Base is kind of embarrassing . . .
STUDENT:	Yeah. My friends are going to give me a really hard time.
TEACHER:	You think they're going to say you're crazy.
STUDENT:	Yeah, I wanna go, but I don't want people to make fun of me.
TEACHER:	I can understand that. It's really rough when people make fun of you.
STUDENT:	I had the worst nightmare last night! I mean, I know it was just a dream, but I just can't get it out of my head. This bloody guy with a knife was chasing me down this alley, and I couldn't get away.
TEACHER:	Nightmares can be scary.
STUDENT:	Yeah, and I know it's babyish, but I just can't shake the feeling.
TEACHER:	Sometimes a bad feeling from a nightmare stays with you a long time . . .

If you're new to active listening, you may find it useful to use the phrase "You feel . . ." when you reflect what you heard. Sometimes, novices feel stupid when they use this technique, as though they're simply parroting what the person just said. As they gain more skill, however, they become better able to *paraphrase* what they hear, and the interaction becomes far more subtle.

You can also use active listening to respond to the nonverbal messages contained in students' facial expressions and body language. For example, if you see that a student entering the room looks really angry, you might be able to ward off problems by recognizing that something is wrong. Here is a recent journal entry from a student teacher who did this without even knowing about active listening:

> *I was writing the "Do Now" on the marker board when all of a sudden I heard a loud crash behind me—the sound of a backpack crammed full of books hitting the floor. I turned around, and there was John sulking in the seat directly behind me. Obviously, I could not let this slide, so I quickly finished writing the "Do Now" for the rest of the class to begin while I attended to John. I came up to him, squatted down to his level, and asked, "What's wrong? You seem really upset"—not knowing at the time that this was a communication strategy called Active Listening. His immediate response was "Nothing." I paused, trying to come up with something "teacher-y" to say and in that pause of 10 seconds, John spoke! The problem was that he was mad at his parents. He had broken his book bag the day before, and because he had to use the same broken bag the next day, he was extremely embarrassed. We talked about his anger, and he started to work once he had vented. The next day he came into class with a different book bag—an old but functional one. I took notice, and even though he was mad that his bag was an old one, he was glad I paid attention to him and his problem.*

Active listening is not always this easy. Student teachers with whom we work often want to reject it out of hand; many find it unnatural and awkward, and they would much prefer to give advice, not simply communicate that they understand. But knowing that someone really understands can be profoundly important, especially to children who often feel misunderstood. In addition, active listening provides an opportunity for students to express their feelings and to clarify their problems. It can also help a teacher defuse strong feelings without taking the responsibility away from the student for solving the problem.

Questioning

When people tell us their problems, we often want to ask them questions in order to get more information. As a teacher, you need to be careful about this practice:

> The problem with questions, as natural as they may come to mind, is that they often put the child in a "one down" position in which you are the interrogator and expert problem solver. "Tell me what the situation is and I will fix it." For that reason, questions are used only when you can't get the student to reveal information in other ways. (Kottler & Kottler, 1993, p. 42)

If you must ask questions, they should be open ended—requiring more than a one-word response. Like active listening, open-ended questions invite further exploration and communication, whereas closed-ended questions cut off communication. Compare these questions:

"What are you feeling right now?" versus "Are you feeling angry?"

"What do you want to do?" versus "Do you want to tell your father?"

There is one notable exception to the rule of avoiding questions whenever possible: This rule does not apply when it is important to get very specific information in a potentially dangerous situation, such as when a student is discussing suicide (Kottler & Kottler, 1993). Then it is both appropriate and advisable to ask specific questions: "Have you actually tried this?" "Will you promise not to do anything until we can get you some help?"

Problem Solving

Instead of trying to solve students' problems, you can guide them through a process that helps them to solve their *own* problems. In problem solving, students define their problem, specify their goals, develop alternative solutions that might be constructive, narrow the choices to those that seem most realistic, and put the plan into action (Kottler & Kottler, 1993).

In the following example, we see how Barbara used this approach to solve a problem her students were experiencing at the end of recess each day. Note that she makes certain everyone agrees on what the problem is, that she doesn't allow students to evaluate suggestions during the brainstorming phase of the activity, that she herself speaks against suggestions she doesn't like, and that she doesn't have students vote on the solution but, instead, works for consensus.

BARBARA: A few weeks ago, you were very upset about what was happening when you came in from the playground at the end of recess. We let it go for a while to see if the problem would go away by itself, but lately people have been telling me that things are still pretty bad out there. [Students begin to murmur in agreement and to comment on what is happening.] Can you tell me exactly what happens?

STUDENT: When the aide blows the whistle to come in, everyone gets in a big clump in the little alleyway by the door and then everybody pushes and shoves, and people start to fight, and then the aides get mad, and people get sent to the office. . . .

BARBARA: Wait. [She draws a map of the playground and the school on the board.] Now let's see if I understand. Everyone clumps up right here? OK, so this is the problem. We're all agreed on what it is? [There are signs of agreement.] Now, let's brainstorm some solutions. Remember, when we brainstorm, we let everyone have their say without evaluating. We'll evaluate all the suggestions at the end.

STUDENT: The doors are always kept closed until after we're lined up, and everyone gets smushed in. If they were left open all the time, we could get in easier. [Barbara writes on board: "#1. Leave doors open all the time."]

BARBARA: Another idea? [She continues to solicit ideas and to write down each suggestion in a numbered list on the board. Ideas include opening the door right before the whistle is blown, having classes go in different doors, lining up classes in different places, and having more aides. During this process, when a child verbally agrees with a suggestion, Barbara reminds the children not to evaluate, that they are still generating solutions.]

BARBARA: Are there any more ideas? [Suggestions seem to be at an end.] OK, our next job is to quietly read these suggestions and think about them. Take two or three minutes to discuss the suggestions with your table group. . . . [Students discuss the suggestions in their small groups.] OK, what we'll do now is discuss each one and decide what we think about each suggestion. [As students state positive or negative reactions, Barbara puts a plus or a minus sign by each suggestion that is mentioned.]

STUDENT: I like the idea of using more doors because that way kids would be separated and there wouldn't be so much pushing and shoving.

STUDENT: I like the one about more aides. If there were more aides, then they could stop kids from pushing.

STUDENT: I don't think that's a good idea because it would cost money and the school doesn't have the money.

BARBARA: I'm going to write a dollar sign next to this one so you can think about the issue of money.

STUDENT: I like the idea of the teachers picking up the classes, but I don't think the teachers would like it.

BARBARA: Let me give you my perspective on that. Even though I adore you, my lunch time is very precious to me, and I would not appreciate giving up part of that time every day to come pick you up.

STUDENT: Our table likes the idea of having two classes by the wall and two by the fence.

STUDENT: Why don't we vote?

BARBARA: I don't want to vote because then there are winners and losers. But let's see if there are some we can eliminate. Let's sift out the ones that we think won't work. For example, I'm telling you that the one about having the teachers pick up the classes won't work because the teachers won't want to give up lunch. Let's look at the suggestions that have no marks next to them and the ones that have minus signs next to them. [She points to each one and asks, "Do you think this would work?" For each, the class says "no," and she erases.] OK, there are three left. Does anyone have any objection to these three? [One girl has reservations about one and explains why.] Do you think you could live with it? [The girl indicates that she is willing to go along with the class.] Well, I think these three make a good package that we can present to [the principal]. Let's talk tomorrow about how we want to present these ideas.

Be Careful about Touching

In recent years, the fear of being accused of sexual harassment and physical abuse has made teachers wary of showing students any physical affection. This is a particularly salient issue for males (King, 1998). Indeed, one of our male student teachers recently wrote this entry in his journal:

> *I had occasion to talk to a student who had a death in the family. She was pretty upset. After explaining that she needn't worry about her class work for that day, I tried my best to comfort her. It's funny, under any other circumstances I would have put an arm around a person in that state, but in this case, I wasn't sure if that would be right.*

Our student is not alone in his concern. A study of male teacher education students who were about to begin their careers revealed a tension between their natural inclinations to be warm, caring, and affectionate to children and the fear that their behavior would be misconstrued as sexual (Hansen & Mulholland, 2005). Fortunately, the anxiety about showing physical affection to children decreased somewhat as the teachers became more experienced. One teacher reported, for example, "I don't have any hassles if a child come[s] up to hold hands. It isn't an issue . . . that's what children do." The young male teachers also found other ways of expressing their affection—for example, by talking and listening with empathy.

Although our five teachers have all been told to avoid touching children, they do not want to forgo all physical contact. Ken still pats students on the back when he's praising them for particularly fine work. When children reach out to hug Barbara and Viviana, they still hug back. And Garnetta tells us:

There was a time when I actually stopped hugging or touching in any way because of the bad publicity, but I just couldn't continue doing that. I felt like I just didn't bond as well with that class. My children are young, and they need love. But you do have to be careful.

It's important to remember that Ken, Barbara, Viviana, and Garnetta have been in their districts for many years and have solid reputations. Courtney, on the other hand, is a new teacher, so she has made sure to speak with her mentor teacher about the situation. Like Courtney, you should speak with your colleagues about the policy in effect in your school; some schools actually direct teachers to "teach but don't touch." Even if there is no explicit prohibition against touching children, you need to be cautious so that your actions are not misinterpreted. For example, when children stay after school, keep the door open or make sure that other students or teachers are around. Give your hugs in front of others. Give "high fives" instead of hugs (Jones & Jones, 2010).

Ask the Students How They Feel about the Classroom Environment

In *Beyond Discipline: From Compliance to Community* (1996), Alfie Kohn suggests that teachers begin the school year by asking students about ways of building feelings of safety:

> A teacher might say, "Look, it's really important to me that you feel free to say things, to come up with ideas that may sound weird, to make mistakes—and not to be afraid that other people are going to laugh at you. In fact, I want everyone in here to feel that way. What do you think we can do to make sure that happens?" (pp. 110–111)

It's also a good idea to ask students to provide you with feedback about their perceptions of the classroom environment. "What Is Happening in This Class?" (Fraser, McRobbie, & Fisher, 1996) is a questionnaire designed to assess a variety of classroom dimensions, including student cohesiveness, teacher support, involvement, cooperation, and equity. Some of the items from the questionnaire appear in Table 3.2. If you periodically administer some of these items, you can get a sense of how students are feeling about your classroom environment.

BUILDING CARING RELATIONSHIPS AMONG STUDENTS

A great deal has recently been written on ways of fostering supportive, trusting relationships among students. As Mara Sapon-Shevin (1995) reminds us:

> Communities don't just happen. No teacher, no matter how skilled or well intentioned, can enter a new classroom and announce, "We are a community." Communities are built over time, through shared experience, and by providing multiple opportunities for students to know themselves, know one another, and interact in positive and supportive ways. (p. 111)

It is clear that our five teachers work hard to provide opportunities for students to know one another and to interact. Following are some of their suggestions, along with some from educational writers interested in students' social and emotional learning.

Model and Recognize Prosocial Behavior

Teachers frequently exhort students to treat one another with respect. Yet exhortation is unlikely to be effective unless teachers themselves are respectful. As Mary Williams (1993) tells us, "'Do as I say, not as I do' clearly does not work" (p. 22). Williams was interested in learning how respect was taught and learned by students in middle school classrooms (grades 6–8). She found that respect was best taught through modeling. According to students, teachers "have to follow the values themselves" (p. 22). Students resented teachers who told them to be kind and to respect others and yet exhibited favoritism, treated students "like babies," didn't listen, and gave "busywork."

In addition to modeling, it's important to promote and recognize the prosocial behavior of your students. For example, teachers can encourage kindness by

TABLE 3.2 Items from the "What Is Happening in This Class?" Questionnaire

Student Cohesiveness
I know other students in this class.
Members of the class are my friends.
I work well with other class members.
In this class, I get help from other students.

Teacher Support
The teacher takes a personal interest in me.
The teacher considers my feelings.
The teacher helps me when I have trouble with the work.
The teacher talks with me.
The teacher is interested in my problems.

Involvement
My ideas and suggestions are used during classroom discussions.
I ask the teacher questions.
I explain my ideas to other students.
I am asked to explain how I solve problems.

Cooperation
I cooperate with other students when doing assignment work.
When I work in groups in this class, there is teamwork.
I learn from other students in this class.
Students work with me to achieve class goals.

Equity
The teacher gives as much attention to my questions as to other students' questions.
I have the same amount of say in this class as other students.
I am treated the same as other students in this class.
I receive the same encouragement from the teacher as other students do.

Items are scored 1, 2, 3, 4, and 5, respectively, for the responses *almost never, seldom, sometimes, often,* and *almost always.*

Source: Adapted from Fraser, McRobbie, & Fisher, 1996.

having a "kindness box" into which students drop brief notes about acts of kindness they do or witness (Beane, 1999). Periodically, the teacher pulls out a note and reads it aloud. Other strategies include assigning students "kindness pals," for whom they do random acts of kindness; having a "kindness reporter," who watches for acts of kindness, briefly describes them in a notebook, and reports at the end of the week; and collaboratively writing "Our Big Book of Kindness."

Provide Opportunities for Students to Get to Know One Another

To build community, our five teachers create opportunities for students to learn about one another and to discover the ways in which they are similar and different. For example, on the first day of school, Ken has his students create personalized CD covers with a title, an illustration, and 12 song titles that tell something important about themselves. By the end of the period, he has learned a good deal about the self-perceptions of his students, and they have learned more about each other.

Similarly, Garnetta begins the school year by having students pair up and interview each other with a set of questions that she and the class have formulated. After the children have interviewed their partners, they introduce each other to the class. Then they write up their interviews, affix them to photographs that Garnetta takes of each child, and post them on a bulletin board.

Viviana reads her class *The Important Book* (1949) by Margaret Wise Brown. Each child then makes a banner proclaiming what is important about himself or herself—and what is *most* important ("The important thing about Juanita is that she is smart, she can speak Spanish, she likes to skate, she loves pizza, etc. But *the most important thing* is that she is smart."). "Find Someone Who" is an introductory activity that Barbara likes to use. Students must find one person in the class who fits each of the descriptions (e.g., someone who "has the same favorite television show as you do," "someone who went to Disney World this summer"). When Barbara writes the descriptions, she tries to incorporate multiple intelligences: "someone who likes to draw cartoons," "someone who likes to hike," "someone who read more than six books this summer." Later in the year, when students have developed a sense of trust, you can include items related to race, cultural and linguistic background, and disability, and have students solicit information from their peers, along with a signature (Sapon-Shevin, 1995)—for example, "Find someone who has a family member with a disability. What's something that this person has learned by interacting with the person who has a disability?" or "Find someone whose parents come from another country. What's one tradition or custom that this person has learned from his or her parents?" (Sapon-Shevin, 1995). Some additional getting-acquainted activities are listed in the accompanying Practical Tips box. (Figure 3.1 shows one student's opinion of these activities.)

Figure 3.1   *Source:* FOXTROT © 2006, Bill Amend. Reprinted with permission of UNIVERSAL UCLICK.

HELPING YOUR STUDENTS TO GET ACQUAINTED

- **Guess Who?** Have students write a brief autobiographical statement (family background, hobbies, extracurricular activities, etc.), which they do not sign. Collect the statements, read each description, and ask students to write the name of the individual they believe wrote the description. (You can participate too.) After all the descriptions have been read, reread them and ask the authors to identify themselves. Ask students how many classmates they correctly identified (Jones & Jones, 2010).

- **Two Truths and a Lie (or Two Facts and a Fiction)** Have students write down and then share three statements about themselves, two of which are true and one of which is a lie. For example, Molly might write, "I sang a solo in my Junior High musical," "I played waterpolo in high school," and "I have two dogs." Students guess which one is the lie, and then she tells the truth (she doesn't have any dogs). The activity can be done as a whole class or in small groups. In either case, because the activity allows students to select what to disclose about themselves, there is little chance of embarrassment. It also provides opportunities for students to discover common interests and experiences and to test assumptions and stereotypes (Sapon-Shevin, 1999).

- **Little-Known Facts about Me** This is a variation of the previous activity. Students write a statement about themselves that they think others won't know. The papers are folded, collected, put in a box, and shaken. Students take turns drawing a paper and reading the statement aloud. Everyone guesses who wrote the little-known fact (Sapon-Shevin, 1999).

- **Lifelines** Each student draws a line on a piece of paper and then marks 6 to 10 points representing important events in their lives that they are willing to share (e.g., the birth of a sibling, the death of a close family member, the time they starred in the school play, when they moved to this school). Students then get into pairs and share their life stories. Members of each pair could also introduce each other to the rest of the class, referring to points on the lifeline (Sapon-Shevin, 1999).

- **Your Inspiration** Have students bring in pictures of people or things that inspire them, along with an accompanying quotation. Post these items on a bulletin board (Schmollinger et al., 2002).

- **What Are You Most Proud of Yourself For?** Have students write their individual responses to this question on paper in the shape of a footprint. Post these on a bulletin board in the shape of a path labeled "success" (Schmollinger et al., 2002).

Hold Class Meetings

This year, as a result of having attended the Responsive Classroom institute, Ken decided to begin each day with a "morning meeting" (Kriete, 2002, 2003). He and his students sit in a circle on the floor and *greet each other* by name; they may pass a handshake around the circle, give a high-five, or toss a ball to the student they are greeting. *Sharing* comes next; during this phase of the morning meeting, a few students present news they wish to share, and others ask questions and comment. Ken's goal is to make sure that everyone gets to share once during the week, although he admits that this does not always happen. After sharing, the class engages in a *group activity*—a game, song, chant, or poem—designed to build

Ken's class begins each day with a "morning meeting."

community and create group identity. Finally, during *news and announcements,* Ken and his students discuss what they will be doing during the day. According to Ken, morning meeting has been a tremendous help in creating a sense of caring and belonging.

Courtney also begins her day with a morning meeting in which academics and social-emotional activities are closely linked. Late in September, for example, we watched as Courtney's kindergartners came in, put their backpacks in their cubbies, and took their seats on the floor in a circle. Courtney gave each student a Unifix cube and explained that they were going to be making an attendance stick with all the cubes. As each child added his or her cube to the tower, the class chanted the number of the students who were present. Then Courtney led a brief discussion on how many children were in the class, how many were present, and how many were absent. The meeting continued with a group greeting. Today it was a silly chant, using each child's name in a rhyme:

"Rillibee Rollabee Rope, An elephant sat on Hope."

"Rillibee Rollabee Rawn, An elephant sat on Shawn."

"Rillibee Rollabee Ralex, An elephant sat on Alex."

After the greeting came a song ("This school is your school, this school is my school . . ."), and then Courtney chose the "star of the day" by randomly pulling a name card from a box. Calendar activities and the "morning message" followed: "Good morning, class! Today is Monday, _____. _____ is the star of the day." Courtney asked students to help her fill in the blanks.

Jane Nelsen, Lynn Lott, and Stephen Glenn (2000) recommend a somewhat different type of class meeting, one that follows the agenda shown in Figure 3.2.

1. Express compliments and appreciation.
2. Follow up on earlier solutions applied to problems.
3. Go through agenda items that students and teachers have written in a special notebook.
     Discuss ways of solving the problems that are brought up.
     a. Share feelings while others listen.
     b. Discuss without fixing.
     c. Ask for problem-solving help.
4. Make future plans for class activities (e.g., field trips, parties, projects).

Figure 3.2 Class Meeting Format
     Source: Nelson, Lott, & Glenn, 2000.

The goal is to provide a safe time and place for everyone to develop an attitude of caring and concern for others and to learn the skills necessary for cooperation and problem solving. For more information on the ideas of Nelson and Lott, see Box. 3.1.

Use Cooperative Learning Groups

Research suggests that there are few opportunities for interaction among students during the school day (Osterman, 2000). These findings are disturbing in light of innumerable studies attesting to the power of cooperative learning to promote the development of positive peer relations. More specifically, cooperative learning facilitates interaction and friendship among students who differ in terms of achievement, gender, cultural and linguistic background, and race; it also fosters the acceptance of students with disabilities and increases positive attitudes toward being in class (Good & Brophy, 2008).

David and Roger Johnson (1999), two prominent researchers in the field of cooperative learning, distinguish among three types of cooperative learning. In *formal cooperative learning,* teachers assign students to small, heterogeneous groups that work together on carefully structured tasks; groups may stay together for anywhere from one class period up to several weeks. In *informal cooperative learning,* students work together in "temporary groups" that might last from a few minutes to a whole period. For example, during a whole-class presentation, Garnetta frequently tells her students to "turn to your neighbor and talk about how you'd tackle this problem." Finally, *cooperative base groups* are long-term, heterogeneous groups in which students support one another's academic progress and emotional well-being. Members of the base group can collect assignments for absent students and provide assistance when they return, tutor students who are having problems with the course material, check homework assignments, and provide study groups for tests. It's helpful to have base groups meet several times a week for 5 to 15 minutes. (See Chapter 10, "Managing Small-Group Work," for a more detailed discussion of cooperative learning.)

MEET THE EDUCATORS   BOX 3.1

MEET JANE NELSEN AND LYNN LOTT

Jane Nelsen and Lynn Lott are therapists and educators who write, lecture, and conduct workshops for parents and teachers on "Positive Discipline." Their work is grounded in the ideas of Alfred Adler (1870–1937) and Rudolf Dreikurs (1897–1972), two Viennese psychiatrists who advocated treating children respectfully and kindly, but firmly. Nelsen and Lott's collaboration began in 1988, with the book that is now entitled *Positive Discipline for Teenagers.* Since then, the Positive Discipline series has grown to include titles that address different age groups, settings (e.g., home, school, and child care), and types of families (e.g., single parents, blended families).

Some Major Ideas about Classroom Management

1. Methods of classroom management must be based on *caring and mutual respect,* with the goal of creating a climate that is nurturing to self-esteem and academic performance.
2. In order to convey caring, teachers need to be aware of five pairs of behaviors that affect their relationships with students. In each pair, the first behavior is a *barrier* to good relationships and the second is a *builder* of good relationships: (1) Assuming, rather than Checking; (2) Rescuing/Explaining, rather than Exploring; (3) Directing, rather than Inviting/Encouraging; (4) Expecting, rather than Celebrating; and (5) Using "Adultisms" (when you forget

that children are not mature adults) rather than Respecting.
3. *Class meetings* not only help to minimize discipline problems but also help students develop social, academic, and life skills.
4. To ensure that class meetings are effective, teachers need to take time to teach students the *Eight Building Blocks:* (1) Form a circle; (2) Practice compliments and appreciations; (3) Create an agenda; (4) Develop communication skills; (5) Learn about separate realities; (6) Recognize the four reasons why people do what they do; (7) Practice role-playing and brainstorming; and (8) Focus on nonpunitive solutions.

Selected Books and Articles

Positive Discipline in the Classroom, Revised 3rd Edition: *Developing Mutual Respect, Cooperation, and Responsibility in Your Classroom* (Nelsen, Lott, and H. Stephen Glenn, Prima, 2000)

Positive Discipline for Teenagers, Revised 2nd Edition (Nelsen & Lott, Prima, 2000)

Positive Discipline: A Teacher's A-Z Guide, Revised 2nd Edition: *Hundreds of Solutions for Every Possible Classroom Behavior Problem* (Nelsen et al., Prima, 1996)

Website: www.positivediscipline.com

Teach Social-Emotional Skills

During one visit, we watched Viviana teach her first graders a lesson on feelings and anger management:

VIVIANA: [After showing her class pictures of people with different kinds of feelings, such as happiness, excitement, anger, and love, she shows the class a picture of a boy by a fence with a ball and bat.] What do you think this boy is feeling?

STUDENT: Sad.

STUDENT: Lonely.

VIVIANA: Why do you think he is sad and lonely?

STUDENT: Because the other children won't let him play ball with them.

VIVIANA: What could you do to fix things?

STUDENT: Invite him to play.

VIVIANA: [Viviana then holds up a picture of a girl taking a doll from another girl.] What do you think this little girl is feeling? [She points to the girl who is having the doll taken away.]

STUDENT: She's mad.

STUDENT: She doesn't want her to do that.

VIVIANA: What could the little girl do about it?

STUDENT: She can count to 10.

VIVIANA: Right, we have talked about how we should all deal with our feelings. Sometimes I get angry too, but I count to 10 or do something until I cool off. You can hop, jump, ride a bike . . .

STUDENT: And then you can talk to her and tell her that you don't want her to do that.

VIVIANA: Yes, then you can talk with the person about what made you angry and you are less likely to say words you might regret later on.

Viviana's lesson is designed to enhance her students' "emotional competence"—the ability to understand and manage social-emotional situations (Woolfolk Hoy, 2007). Individuals with emotional competence can identify and regulate their feelings, solve problems by generating alternative solutions and selecting the best action, show respect and empathy for others, and communicate effectively. There are now a raft of programs designed to foster skills such as these; in fact, all of our teachers work in districts that have implemented a formal curriculum focused on social-emotional learning (SEL). Even if your school has not adopted such a program, it's important to teach and reinforce SEL in your own classroom.

There is great diversity in approaches, but generally the programs fall into two categories: those that train the entire student body in social-emotional skills and conflict resolution strategies and those that train a particular cadre of students to mediate disputes among their peers (Johnson & Johnson, 1995). An example of a program that targets the entire student body is *Second Step—A Violence Prevention Curriculum* for preschool through ninth grade created by the Committee for Children (www.cfchildren.org) and used in Garnetta and Viviana's district. Once or twice a week, teachers teach explicit lessons on empathy, anger management, impulse control, and problem solving; they then try to reinforce the lessons during the day, using naturally occurring classroom incidents. Research on the curriculum has indicated that *Second Step* leads to moderate decreases in aggression and increases in neutral and prosocial behavior in school (Grossman et al., 1997).

Children in Barbara's school also participate in a broad-based program. Designed by psychologists Maurice Elias and John Clabby, the program focuses on social decision making and social problem solving (SDM/SPS; Elias & Clabby, 1988, 1989). It is based on two premises: first, that a hierarchy of skills underlies

1. Look for signs of different feelings.
   Recognize your feelings of stress, anxiety, or uncertainty as a signal to begin problem solving, rather than a feeling to be eliminated or ignored; also recognize signs of others' feelings.
2. Tell yourself what the problem is.
   "I feel nervous because I have a test tomorrow."
   "I'm worried because those kids look really tough."
3. Decide on your goal.
   "I want to do well on that test."
   "I want to keep away from those tough kids."
4. Stop and think of as many solutions to the problem as you can.
   "I'll study in the library tonight instead of staying home. That way I won't be able to talk on the phone."
5. For each solution, think of all the things that might happen next.
   "Of course, if I meet friends in the library, I might waste time talking to them."
6. Choose your best solution.
7. Plan it and make a final check.
8. Try it and rethink it.

Figure 3.3   Skills Children Are Taught to Use in SDM/SPS
Source: Elias & Clabby, 1988.

competent interpersonal behavior, in particular, social–cognitive problem-solving skills; and second, that children can be taught these skills so that they can analyze, understand, and prepare to respond to everyday problems, decisions, and conflict. Whereas traditional approaches to social decision making have often been organized around a particular issue (drug and alcohol use, violence, nutrition), SDM/SPS reflects the belief that children need to learn social–cognitive skills that can be applied to a variety of decision-making situations. Figure 3.3 lists the sequence of skills that children are taught to use.

The health teacher in Barbara's school has incorporated SDM/SPS into the health curriculum for all third- and fourth-graders. There, children are taught to deal with conflicts by being their **BEST:** monitoring **B**ody posture, making **E**ye contact, **S**aying nice words, and using a respectful **T**one of voice. In the classroom, teachers reinforce the SDM/SPS curriculum by having children complete "Hassle Logs" when they are having a problem. (Figure 3.4 shows a Hassle Log completed by a third-grade girl when her classmate started to "bug" her. Figure 3.5 shows a Hassle Log that uses a different format.)

In contrast to these broad-based programs, peer mediation programs select a few students to guide disputants through the problem-solving process. The advantage of using peers as mediators rather than adults is that students can frame disputes in a way that is age-appropriate. Generally working in pairs, mediators explain the ground rules for mediation, provide an opportunity for disputants to identify the problem from their differing perspectives, explain how they feel, brainstorm solutions, evaluate the advantages and disadvantages of each proposed solution, and select a course of action. These steps can be seen in the example of a peer mediation that appears in Figure 3.6.

Figure 3.4   Hassle Log Completed by Third-Grade Girl

Peer mediation programs are becoming increasingly popular in schools across the country, and thus far, anecdotal evidence suggests that they can substantially reduce violent incidents. Some researchers contend that peer mediation actually has more impact on the mediators than on the disputants, because the former acquire valuable conflict resolution skills and earn the respect of their peers (Bodine & Crawford, 1998; Miller, 1994). If this is so, it means that high-risk students—not just the "good kids"—must be trained and used as mediators.

Obviously, peer mediation is not an option when the conflict involves drugs, alcohol, theft, violence, or other criminal actions. But mediation can help to resolve disputes involving behavior such as gossiping, name-calling, racial putdowns, and bullying, as well as conflicts over property (e.g., borrowing a book and losing it). Even then, mediation must be voluntary and confidential. In cases where school rules have been violated, mediation should not substitute for disciplinary action; rather, it can be offered as an opportunity to solve problems and "clear the air."

PAUSE AND REFLECT

Think about how you might introduce SEL to your students. What skills would you emphasize? Would you devote a specific time during the week to giving an explicit lesson on social-emotional skills or would you just try to take advantage of "teachable moments"?

Curb Peer Harassment and Bullying

Efforts to promote prosocial behavior have to be accompanied by intolerance for antisocial behaviors that might threaten the safe and caring community. Every day, students suffer name-calling, teasing, ridicule, humiliation, social exclusion, ostracism, and even physical injury at the hands of their peers. When this peer harassment is repeated over time (rather than being infrequent or incidental), is

Hassle Log

Name _____ Homeroom Teacher _____

Date _____ Grade _____

Time of day: (Circle one)   morning   afternoon   evening

Where were you? _____

Who was involved? _____

What is the **problem?** _____

_____

What did you do? _____

_____

How did you **feel** before you did this? _____

_____

What was your **goal** (what were you trying to do)? _____

_____

How satisfed are you with the way(s) you have tried to solve the problem?

(Circle one)   not at all   only a little   okay   pretty satisfied   very satisifed

How easy or hard was it for you to keep calm and stay in control of yourself?

(Circle one)   very easy   pretty easy   okay   pretty hard   very hard

****************What else could you have done to be your **BEST?**************************

Think of as many possible **solutions** as you can.

Solutions (what I could do)   **Consequences** (what could happen)

Figure 3.5   Another Type of Hassle Log

intended to cause harm, discomfort, or fear, and involves an imbalance in strength or power, it becomes *bullying* (Hyman et al., 2006; Olweus, 2003). Boys bully other students more often than girls do, and their bullying tends to be physical. Girls typically use more subtle, "relational" bullying, such as excluding someone from the group and spreading rumors.

Peer harassment and bullying are not limited to the upper elementary grades. In a study of 25 kindergarten through third-grade classrooms (Froschl & Gropper, 1999), teasing and bullying were found to be common reactions to perceived differences among peers. The study also documented the distressing fact that teachers rarely intervened; indeed, teachers and other adults were uninvolved in or ignored *71 percent* of the observed incidents of teasing and bullying.

One probable reason for the lack of intervention is that bullying has traditionally been considered "socially acceptable" (Crothers & Kolbert, 2008). Bullies can be popular, and their behavior is often dismissed as normal. When the bullies are males, for example, it is not uncommon for adults to comment that "boys will be boys." In fact, almost one-third of teachers in the United States perceive bullying as "normative behavior" that victims must learn to resolve (Hyman et al., 2006). Another reason for not intervening may be the fact that a lot of peer harassment and bullying takes place in hallways and in the lunchroom, places where teachers may feel they don't have jurisdiction.

Conflict: Billy and Juan sit next to each other during math class. While working independently on completing problems, Billy has the habit of humming as he figures out the equations. This makes it very difficult for Juan to concentrate and get his work done.

JUAN: Would you shut up with that humming?
BILLY: (Humming louder) What, did someone say something?
JUAN: Seriously, I'm going to come over there and make you be quiet.
BILLY: I'd like to see you try.

Teacher overhears and asks the boys if they would like to go to mediation. They agree.

Mediation Step 1: Introductions and Explanation of Rules

MEDIATOR 1:   [Introduces self and other Mediator] We will serve as your peer mediators. What are your names? (Boys respond and Mediator writes them on form.)

MEDIATOR 2:   We are not here to judge or punish you, but to simply help you work through your conflict. Everything we say here will be held in confidence, unless something discussed is illegal, harmful, or a sign of abuse.

MEDIATOR 1:   We need you both to agree to some rules before we begin. They are:
               1) Allow others to speak without interruption.
               2) Treat others with respect and avoid put-downs.
               3) Take responsibility and be willing to solve the problem.

MEDIATOR 2:   Do both of you agree to the rules? (If both agree, move on to Step 2.)

Mediation Step 2: Listening and Understanding the Problem

MEDIATOR 1:   Juan, please tell us your side of the story.
      JUAN: I was trying to work and this loser is humming so loud I can't think!
MEDIATOR 1:   Please be respectful and refrain from putting him down or calling names.
      JUAN: Sorry. I was trying to work and he was humming VERY loud.
MEDIATOR 1:   His humming was disrupting your work. How does that make you feel?
      JUAN: I'm really mad because it happens every day.
MEDIATOR 1:   You are angry because you feel that he is intentionally humming loudly.
MEDIATOR 2:   Billy, what is your side of the story?
     BILLY: I was working and minding my own business, and yes, I was humming.
MEDIATOR 2:   How do you feel about this situation?
     BILLY: I'm frustrated because Juan is so sensitive!
MEDIATOR 2:   You would like to keep humming and you think Juan is overreacting.
               Is this correct? (Billy agrees.) Is there anything else either one of you would like to say? (If yes, continue taking turns. If no, go to Step 3).

Mediation Step 3: Brainstorming Solutions

MEDIATOR 1:   You've both heard the other's side of the story. Think about what you could do to solve this problem now or in the future. We're going to write down all your ideas and we can decide what to do later. (Juan suggests he can ask Billy to stop humming in a nicer manner; Billy suggests he can change seats; Juan suggests he could wear earplugs; Billy says he can hum in his head.)

MEDIATOR 1:   Any other ideas? (If none, go to Step 4)

Mediation Step 4: Reaching an Agreement

MEDIATOR 2:   Let's look at all the solutions you both suggested. Which ones might help solve this conflict? (The boys decide that moving seats is impractical, and it is unfair that Juan would have to wear earplugs. Juan suggests, and Billy agrees, that Billy should hum in his head, and Juan will remind him if he gets loud enough to be a distraction.)

MEDIATOR 2:   Is this conflict solved? (If both boys agree yes, they sign an agreement on the Peer Mediation form. If they disagree, they go back to Step 3 for more solutions.) Thank you for being willing to work out your conflict. We will check back with you in a few days to see how your new solution is working.

Figure 3.6 Peer Mediation Script

Taking peer harassment seriously and intervening to stop it—wherever it occurs—is crucial if teachers are to build safer, more caring classrooms. You need to be alert to hurtful comments about race and ethnicity, body size, disabilities, sexual orientation, unfashionable or eccentric dress, use of languages other than English, and socioeconomic status. You need to make it clear that disrespectful speech and slurs—even when used in a joking manner—are absolutely unacceptable. Stephen Wessler (2008), director of the Center for the Prevention of Hate Violence at the University of Southern Maine, urges teachers to respond immediately to instances of peer harassment:

> Whether in the hallway or the classroom, teachers must speak up when students use degrading language or stereotypes. In a busy hallway, these interventions can be short. Making eye contact with a student and saying, "I heard that," "We don't talk like that here," or "That word is hurtful" sends the message that bias-motivated slurs and jokes are not acceptable. These low-key interventions break the pattern of escalation and stop some students from continuing to use degrading words. They also model for students what they can do to interrupt hurtful language themselves. And finally, when teachers speak up, they send a message of hope to those students who constantly hear slurs but feel that no one cares. (p. 47)

Because much peer harassment and bullying occurs out of teachers' sight and hearing, it is important to teach students how to "stand up and speak up" when they witness unacceptable behavior (Wessler, 2008). Robert Marzano and colleagues (2005) suggest three simple rules for students to adopt to prevent bullying among students: (1) We will not bully other students. (2) We will help others who are being bullied by speaking out and getting adult help. (3) We will use extra effort to include all students in activities at our school. Some schools actually have students sign an anti-bullying pledge. (See Figure 3.7.)

It's also important to help students understand what behaviors constitute peer harassment and bullying. For example, teasing is the most frequent bullying behavior at all ages, but it can be difficult for students to draw the line between playful exchanges and hurtful harassment. Whether an exchange represents teasing or friendly banter may have to do with the social level or popularity of the individuals involved (Hoover & Oliver, 2008). If a higher-status student mocks a lower-status student, the exchange is likely to be seen as an attack. Teasing someone of the same status is more likely to be interpreted as playful. Here are some other guidelines about teasing (adapted from Hoover & Oliver, 2008) to help your students understand what is and what isn't appropriate:

Ask whether teasing about a certain topic is hurtful, and if it is, don't tease about that topic.

Watch for body language that conveys that teasing bothers someone.

Stand up for a student who is being teased.

Speak up if teasing about a certain topic bothers you.

Be careful about using humor, especially sarcasm.

Avoid teasing someone you don't know well.

We, the students of the _____ school district, agree to join together to stop bullying.

BY SIGNING THIS PLEDGE I AGREE TO:

- Treat others respectfully.
- Try to include those who are left out.
- Refuse to bully others.
- Refuse to watch, laugh or join in when someone is being bullied.
- Tell an adult.
- Help those who are being bullied.

Signed by

_____

Date

_____

Figure 3.7   Anti-Bullying Pledge
Source: Harrison, 2005.

Never tease people about sex, being a boy or girl, their bodies, or their family members.

Refrain from teasing someone who seems to be having a bad day.

Accept teasing that is meant in a friendly way.

To raise awareness of bullying, it's also useful to incorporate reflective activities into the curriculum whenever possible. In language arts, students can read fiction related to the topic of harassment and bullying; in math, they can conduct surveys and analyze the results; in art classes, they can depict their feelings about name-calling and put-downs or draw pictures of peaceful, prosocial behaviors (Bickley-Green, 2007). Very young children can explore the concept of human difference by creating a chart about how they are the same and different. First-graders can tell stories and draw pictures about when they had the courage to stand up for a friend who was being teased. Children can build a wall of blocks that represents the kinds of things that keep people from being friends and discuss ways to remove the barriers.

Be Alert for Instances of Cyber-Bullying

In the last few years, peer harassment and bullying have expanded from school grounds to cyberspace, as "cyber-bullies" use e-mail, cell phone and pager text messages, instant messaging, Web logs, and online "slam books" to pursue their victims. A student in Fairfax County, Virginia, for example, decided to do a survey on the top five "hated kids" in the sixth grade and set up a website where students could vote (Lisante, 2005). Fortunately, the parents of one "winner" reported the survey to the principal, which prompted an in-school program on the damage that cyber-bullying can cause.

Online harassment is less visible to adults than "offline" harassment, and adults who are unfamiliar and uncomfortable with the new technologies may have no sense of the nature or magnitude of the problem. At the same time, cyber-bullying can be vastly more humiliating to victims. Rumors, ridicule, embarrassing pictures, and hateful comments can be circulated among a huge number of peers with just a few clicks, and home no longer provides a safe haven from the taunting. Furthermore, youngsters may say things online that they would never say in person, mainly because of the feeling of anonymity and the distance from the victim. As one student comments, "Over the Internet you don't really see their face or they don't see yours, and you don't have to look in their eyes and see they're hurt" (Leishman, 2002, cited in Shariff, 2004). Cyber-bullying also seems to have a particular appeal for girls, who prefer "relational aggression" rather than physical harassment and often try to avoid direct confrontation (Harmon, 2004).

Some strategies for dealing with cyber-bullying appear in the accompanying Practical Tips box.

Be Alert for Student-to-Student Sexual Harassment

On May 24, 1999, in a case called *Aurelia Davis v. Monroe County Board of Education,* the Supreme Court ruled five to four that any school district receiving federal money can face a sex-discrimination suit if they are "deliberately indifferent" to information about "severe, pervasive, and objectively offensive" harassment among students (Walsh, 1999).

The *Davis* case started as a lawsuit brought by the mother of a Georgia schoolgirl who was *in fifth grade* when she began to experience what her family describes as five months of sexual harassment by the 11-year-old boy who sat next to her. According to the plaintiff's brief to the Court, the boy "repeatedly attempted to touch [the girl's] breasts and vaginal area, . . . told her in vulgar terms that he want[ed], . . . to get in bed with her, . . . placed a doorstop in his pants and behaved in a sexually harassing manner" (Gorney, 1999). Meanwhile, the girl and her family made repeated requests for help from school officials, who are accused of ignoring their pleas. The *Davis* case illustrates the fact that worry about student-to-student sexual harassment is not confined to high schools.

Sexual harassment is generally defined as *unwanted and unwelcome sexual attention.* This includes a wide range of behaviors:

> leering, pinching, grabbing, suggestive verbal comments, pressure for sexual activity, spreading sexual rumors, making sexual or sexist jokes, pulling at another student's clothing, cornering or brushing up against a student in a sexual way, insulting comments referring to students' sexual orientation, date rape, sexual graffiti about a student, or engaging in other actions of a sexual manner that might create a hostile learning environment. (Hyman, 1997, p. 318)

It can sometimes be difficult for you—and your students—to distinguish between harmless teasing and sexual harassment. When you are faced with this situation, it's helpful to keep in mind the fact that whether harassment has occurred is truly "in the eye of the beholder." In other words, the determining factor is "how the person on the receiving end is affected by the behavior, not what the other person means by the behavior" (Strauss with Espeland, 1992, p. 15). Kissing,

PRACTICAL TIPS FOR

DEALING WITH CYBER-BULLYING

- Develop an explicit policy for acceptable in-school use of the Internet, and include it in the school handbook (or your class rules). The policy should spell out what constitutes cyber-bullying and should list consequences. It should also include information about whom to contact if a student feels victimized.
- Educate yourself about the technology tools used by your students. Don't give students the opportunity to exploit your ignorance.
- Make sure that children and young people are aware that bullying will be dealt with seriously.
- Ensure that parents/guardians who express concerns about cyber-bullying are taken seriously.
- Explain to students that they:
  - Should never share or give out personal information such as their address, school, or phone number.
  - Should not post identity-revealing photos of themselves online or post photos of friends without their permission.
  - Should limit access to their online profiles (in Facebook or MySpace) to their friends and should be cautious about accepting friend requests, especially from people they don't know.
  - Should not delete messages; they do not have to read them, but they should show them to an adult they trust. Messages can be used to take action against cyber-bullies.
  - Should not open a message from someone they don't know.
  - Should *never* reply to a bullying message.
  - Can block the sender's message if they are being bullied through e-mail or instant messaging.
  - Can forward the messages to their Internet Service Provider
  - Should tell an adult.
  - Should show the message to the police if it contains physical threats.
  - Should speak out against cyber-bullying.
  - Should never send messages when they are angry.
  - Should never send messages they wouldn't want others to see.
- Make parents aware of the fact that all of the major Internet Service Providers offer some form of parental controls. For example, AOL has developed "AOL Guardian," which reports whom youngsters exchange messages with and what websites they visit and monitors chat rooms for children 13 and under.
- Encourage parents to keep computers in a public room in the house.
- Invite members of the local police department to come to school to speak with parents and students about proper Internet use.
- Make sure ethics is included in any computer instruction given at your school.
- Consult with the following resources: *Surfswell Island: Adventures in Internet Safety* (www.disney.go.com/surfswell), *NetSmartz* (www.netsmartz.org), *CyberSmart! Education Company* (www.cybersmart.org), and *i-SAFE* (www.isafe.org).

Sources: Adapted from Franek, 2005/6; Keith & Martin, 2005; Lisante, 2005; and the National Crime Prevention Council, 2003, at www.mcgruff.org.

touching, and flirting that the recipient likes or wants is *not* sexual harassment (although it is certainly inappropriate and may be an indicator that either child is the victim of sexual abuse; see Chapter 5).

In recent years, an increasing number of districts have written and distributed sexual harassment policies for both students and school personnel. These generally define sexual harassment, outline the procedures to follow when you learn about an incident of sexual harassment, and spell out the consequences. It's important that you obtain a copy of this policy and follow the specified procedures. Remember, the Supreme Court's ruling in the *Davis* case means that you must take complaints seriously and intervene. If you don't, you may be accused of "deliberate indifference" (Gorney, 1999).

CONCLUDING COMMENTS

Alfie Kohn (1996) suggests that it would be helpful if we all reflected on "what makes school awful sometimes" (p. 114). We recently followed his advice. With our students, we reminisced about the awful times we had experienced. Here are some of our students' memories:

> *In fourth grade, we were told we would have current events on Fridays— one article summarized and brought in to read aloud to the class. On the first Friday, I forgot, along with eight others, to do the assignment. The teacher made all those who forgot stand up while she harshly rebuked us in front of the class. Then she went around and we each had to say why we forgot it. Then she made us write a letter to our parents explaining why we would never forget current events again . . .*

> *In first grade, I had to go to speech therapy because I had a difficult time pronouncing my THs. So when it was time to go my teacher would say, "Okay, all the kids who don't know how to talk right, line up at the door."*

> *Looking back, first grade to about sixth grade was not too good for me. . . . I was always the forgotten kid. Teachers would rarely call on me because I was so quiet and because I never raised my hand for fear of saying the wrong thing, fear of being in the spotlight, fear of being embarrassed. That was also the case among my peers. My views or ideas were always ignored. . . .*

> *In second grade, my teacher took off two gold stars which I had accumulated by my name. (To give some background: There was a huge poster on one bulletin board with everyone's name on it. Your goal was to collect stars of different colors for different achievements. Gold stars were the highest prize.) She did this in front of the class, and it humiliated me. What had I done to receive such harsh punishment? Well, I picked my nose . . .*

PAUSE AND REFLECT

Think about your most memorable memory of school. Was it an instance in which you felt humiliated, threatened, or powerless? If so, what could you do to ensure that kind of experience never happens to your students? If you are fortunate enough not to be able to recall a negative experience from school, think about what made school a safe environment for you and how you can work to create that for your students as well.

For too many children, school is a place where they feel humiliated, threatened, ridiculed, tormented, teased, powerless, and betrayed. But teachers who can "remember when school was awful" are more inclined to build a safer, more caring classroom community. Of course, in this era of high-stakes testing and pressure for academic excellence, you might be reluctant to take the time needed to build community—and it *will* take time. But keep this in mind: Building community will eventually lead not only to a more harmonious classroom but also to greater motivation, academic engagement, and achievement (Watson & Battistich, 2006).

SUMMARY

This chapter began by discussing the key role that positive teacher–student relationships play in classroom management. The chapter then considered ways of showing students that you care about them and ways of building caring relationships among students.

Ways of Showing Care and Respect for Students

- Be welcoming.
- Learn about students' lives.
- Be sensitive to students' concerns.
- Establish and enforce expectations for behavior.
- Be fair.
- Be a real person as well as a teacher.
- Promote autonomy by sharing responsibility.
- Reduce the use of extrinsic control.
- Be inclusive.
- Search for students' strengths.
- Develop communication skills:
    Attending and acknowledging.
    Active listening.
    Open-ended questioning.
    Problem solving.
- Be careful about touching.
- Ask the students how they feel about the classroom environment.

Building Caring Relationships among Students

- Model and recognize prosocial behavior.
- Provide opportunities for students to get to know one another.

- Hold class meetings.
- Use cooperative learning groups.
- Teach social-emotional skills.
- Curb peer harassment and bullying.
- Be alert for instances of cyber-bullying.
- Be alert for student-to-student sexual harassment.

For too many students, school is a place where they feel humiliated, threatened, ridiculed, tormented, teased, powerless, and betrayed. Teachers who are mindful that school can be awful are better able to create a safe, caring community for their students.

ACTIVITIES FOR SKILL BUILDING AND REFLECTION

In Class

1. Think about the teachers you had in elementary school. Select one teacher who showed caring to students and one teacher who did not. Write a paragraph on each teacher, providing details and examples to illustrate what each teacher actually did. Share these in small groups.

2. In the following bits of conversation, students have confided in teachers about problems they are experiencing, and the teachers have responded in ways *not* suggested in this chapter. Provide a new response for each case, using the communication skills discussed in this chapter: acknowledging, active listening, asking open-ended questions, and problem solving.

    STUDENT: My parents won't allow me to go out on weekends like the other kids. They say they trust me, but then they don't show it!

    TEACHER: Well, I'm sure they have your best interests at heart. You know, you really shouldn't gripe. You're pretty young, and after all, a lot of kids don't have parents who care about them. I see a lot of kids whose parents let them do anything they want. Maybe you think you'd like that, but I'm sure you wouldn't.

    STUDENT: I can't stand my stepmother. She's always criticizing me and making me come home right after school to watch my sister, and making me feel really stupid.

    TEACHER: Oh, come on now, Cinderella. I'm sure it's not that bad.

    STUDENT: My sister told me she thinks she's pregnant. She made me promise not to tell our folks, but I'm really scared. I think they should know. I'm scared she's going to try to get rid of it by herself. What do you think I should do?

    TEACHER: I think you should tell your parents.

On Your Own

1. Interview a few elementary students about their definitions of caring teachers. Ask them to identify the ways in which teachers show caring to students.

2. Do some planning for the first week of school. First, think about how you will introduce yourself to your students. What will you tell them about yourself? Second, plan a way of learning about your students' lives. (Will you have students write a letter to you? Will you have them answer specific questions?) Third, plan an introductory activity designed to help students become acquainted.

3. Visit an elementary school classroom that you have never been in before. Record your immediate thoughts when you walked into the room about how it feels to be a student in that room. Observe the class for a little while and jot down any ways in which the teacher is promoting a safe and caring community, as well as your ongoing impressions about the tone of the classroom.

For Your Portfolio

Document the ways in which you work (or will work) to create a caring, safe classroom community. Include artifacts such as welcoming letters to students, lesson plans on social-emotional skills, and getting-to-know-you activities.

FOR FURTHER READING

Bondy, E., & Ross, D. D. (2008). The teacher as warm demander. *Educational Leadership, 66*(1), 54–58.

> Teachers who are "warm demanders" demonstrate their caring for students by deliberately building relationships, learning about students' cultures, and communicating an expectation of success. Then they "relentlessly insist on two things": that students treat the teacher and one another respectfully, and that they complete the academic tasks necessary for successful futures.

Kriete, R. (2002). *The morning meeting book.* Greenfield, MA: Northeast Foundation for Children.

> This volume, part of the "Strategies for Teachers" series, provides step-by-step guidelines for implementing Morning Meeting, a key component of the Responsive Classroom approach to teaching and learning. It is clear, concise, and reader-friendly.

Espelage, D. L., & Swearer, S. M. (Eds.) (2004). *Bullying in American schools: A social-ecological perspective on prevention and intervention.* Mahwah, NJ: Lawrence Erlbaum Associates.

> Espelage and Swearer argue that bullying is not just a matter of a "few bad kids" who make life miserable for other people. Rather, bullying has to be understood across family, peer, school, and community contexts, and interventions have to target the multiple environments that youngsters inhabit. Part III of this book examines "classroom characteristics associated with bullying." Chapters address teachers' attitudes toward bullying, the influence of peers and teachers on bullying among young children, and classroom ecologies that support or discourage bullying.

Correa-Connolly, M. (2004). *Ninety-nine activities and greetings: Great for morning meeting . . . and other meetings too.*

This book features a collection of activities and greetings that are appropriate for use with students in grades K–8. This book is meant to complement Kreite's *The Morning Meeting Book* (described above).

Watson, M., in collaboration with Ecken, L. (2003). *Learning to trust: Transforming difficult elementary classrooms through Developmental Discipline.* San Francisco: Jossey-Bass.

This book describes Laura Ecken's efforts to develop positive, nurturing relationships with the children in her inner-city, full-inclusion, ungraded class of seven- and eight-year-olds. Watson shows how attachment theory can provide teachers with a basis for meeting children's needs for autonomy, belonging, and competence; creating a caring community of serious learners; and maintaining a safe and productive classroom.

ORGANIZATIONAL RESOURCES

The Anti-Defamation League (ADL), 823 United Nations Plaza, New York, NY 10017; 1-800-343-5540; www.adl.org. Dedicated to combating anti-Semitism, hate crime, and bigotry through programs, services, and materials. (The *ADL Material Resource Catalog* offers a wealth of resources, including lesson plans, curriculum guides, and lists of children's books.)

The Southern Poverty Law Center, 400 Washington Avenue, Montgomery, AL 36104; 334-956-8200; www.teachingtolerance.org. The Teaching Tolerance project provides teachers at all levels with ideas and free resources for building community, fighting bias, and celebrating diversity.

The Northeast Foundation for Children, 85 Avenue A Suite 204, P.O. Box 718, Turner Falls, MA 01376; 1-800-360-6332; www.responsiveclassroom.org. Offers professional development programs, workshops, and resources on the Responsive Classroom; designed to help educators integrate the teaching of social and academic skills.

The Child Development Project, Developmental Studies Center, 2000 Embarcadero, Suite 305, Oakland, CA 94606; 1-800-666-7270; www.devstu.org. An elementary school program with the explicit goal of integrating into the school day a focus on children's social and moral development; sees community as the foundation of classroom management and caring relationships as the foundation of community.

Collaborative for Academic, Social, and Emotional Learning (CASEL), Department of Psychology (M/C 285), University of Illinois at Chicago, 1007 West Harrison St., Chicago, IL 60607; 312-413-1008; www.casel.org. Dedicated to the development of children's social and emotional competencies and the capacity of schools, parents, and communities to support that development. CASEL's mission is to establish integrated, evidence-based social and emotional learning (SEL) from preschool through high school.

ESTABLISHING NORMS
FOR BEHAVIOR

The first day of a new academic year can be scary, even for students who have been in school several years. There are so many unknowns: What will the teacher be like? Who will be in my class? Will I be able to find my room? And, of course, there are all those "what if" questions: What if I have to go to the bathroom? What if my pencil point breaks? What if the teacher asks me a question and I don't know the answer?

To understand what students are feeling, try to recall a time when your unfamiliarity with cultural norms and customs made you uncomfortable and insecure. Perhaps you visited a shop in a foreign country and weren't certain whether it was appropriate to bargain with a vendor. Or perhaps you had dinner in an unusually elegant restaurant and felt unsure about proper table etiquette.

In each of these situations, *not knowing what was expected* caused insecurity, discomfort, and self-consciousness. All of us feel more competent when we understand the norms for appropriate behavior, and elementary students are no exception. Indeed, a study on motivation in the classroom (Skinner & Belmont, 1993) showed that third-, fourth-, and fifth-graders were more likely to work harder and to be more persistent when they perceived their teachers as providing clear expectations. The message is apparent: *Well-defined norms for behavior can help to dispel the "what ifs" and enhance feelings of safety, security, and competence.*

Clear expectations for behavior have another major benefit. As we have emphasized in earlier chapters, classes are crowded, complex settings in which individuals engage in a wide variety of activities. *Well-defined norms decrease the complexity of the classroom.* They minimize confusion and prevent the loss of instructional time. They enable you and your students to carry out "housekeeping" tasks (e.g., taking attendance, distributing materials, collecting homework) smoothly and efficiently so that time for learning and teaching is maximized.

In this chapter we describe research that demonstrates the importance of classroom norms. We then discuss some principles to guide you in establishing norms for your own classrooms. We'll also learn how Courtney, Barbara, Garnetta, Ken, and Viviana introduce norms to their students and what they think about this central task of classroom management.

RESEARCH ON EFFECTIVE CLASSROOM MANAGEMENT

Prior to 1970, teacher preparation programs could offer beginning teachers only limited advice about classroom management. Teacher educators shared useful "tricks of the trade" (e.g., flick the lights for quiet), stressed the importance of firmness and consistency, and warned prospective teachers not to smile until Christmas. But research identifying the behaviors of effective managers was unavailable, and it was simply not clear why some classrooms functioned smoothly while others were chaotic.

That situation changed in 1970, with the publication of Jacob Kounin's study of orderly and disorderly classrooms. Kounin set out to compare teachers' methods of responding to misbehavior. To his surprise, he found that the reactions of good classroom managers were not substantially different from the reactions of poor classroom managers. What *did* differ were the strategies that teachers used to *prevent* misbehavior. Effective classroom managers constantly monitored students' behavior. They displayed what Kounin called *withitness:* They were aware of what was happening in all parts of the room, and they communicated this awareness to students. They also exhibited an ability to *overlap*—to do more than one thing at a time—certainly a desirable skill in a setting where so many events occur simultaneously! Furthermore, effective managers kept lessons moving at a brisk pace, so that there was little opportunity for students to become inattentive and disruptive.

Kounin's work led researchers to wonder how effective managers began the school year, and a series of studies was launched to investigate this topic. One project (Emmer, Evertson, & Anderson, 1980) involved observations of 27 self-contained third-grade classrooms in an urban district. During the first three weeks of school, researchers observed extensively in each classroom and kept detailed records of what occurred. Observations were then stopped, but they resumed in November and continued until the end of the school year. On the basis of the November through May data, the researchers identified more effective and less effective managers. They then went back to the information collected at the beginning of the year and compared what the teachers had done during the first three weeks of school. Striking differences were apparent—even on the very first day of school!

Among the major differences documented was the way teachers handled rules and routines. *Effective managers had clear rules for general conduct* (e.g., "Be prepared for class"), *as well as procedures or routines for carrying out specific tasks* (e.g., going to the restroom). Furthermore, effective managers spent much of the first few days teaching these rules and procedures to students—as carefully as they taught academic content—and they continued to review during the first three weeks of school.

In contrast, the ineffective teachers did not have well-defined rules or procedures. One new teacher, for example, had no routines for going to the restrooms, using the pencil sharpener, or getting a drink of water. As a result, children wandered about, coming and going as they pleased. Although ineffective managers did have rules, the rules were often vague ("Be in the right place at the right time") and were not clearly explained. Ineffective managers frequently introduced rules casually, neglecting to teach them to students in a careful, deliberate way.

A more recent study revisited the question of how effective managers begin the school year (Bohn, Roehrig, & Pressley, 2004). The researchers observed the first few days of school in the classrooms of two "more effective" and four "less effective" primary grade teachers. Despite the 25 years separating this study from the earlier one, the results were strikingly similar. For example, although all six primary grade teachers introduced procedures, only the two more effective teachers made sure that the students practiced the procedures until they were able to perform them well. This later work also reported some new findings that reflect our changing ideas about classroom management. In particular, the researchers found that the more effective teachers did a great deal to foster self-regulation during the first few days of school, stressed the importance of community, and conveyed the expectation that students would be "good community members" (p. 285).

In sum, the research on classroom management at the beginning of the school year has helped to clarify what effective managers do to create order in their classrooms. This work underscores the importance of (1) *deciding how you want your students to behave* and (2) *making these expectations absolutely clear to students.* Let's look at each of these steps separately.

DEFINING YOUR EXPECTATIONS FOR BEHAVIOR

Before the first child enters your classroom, you need to think about how you expect your students to behave. Not only do you need to decide on *norms for students' general conduct* (commonly referred to as classroom rules), you also need to identify the *behavioral routines or procedures* that you and your students will follow in specific situations. For example, when students arrive in the morning, are they to hang up their coats, go immediately to their desks, and take out a book? Or may they chat quietly with neighbors, sharpen pencils, and play games? When students need paper for an assignment, will they get it themselves, will you have a paper monitor, or will you distribute it yourself? When students have to use the restroom, are they to ask permission or simply get a pass and leave? When students are working at their seats, may they help one another or must they work individually?

Because these seem like such trivial, mundane issues, it is easy to underestimate their contribution to classroom order. But lessons can fall apart while you try to decide how to distribute paper, and students feel anxious if they're unsure whether answering a classmate's question during seatwork is considered helping or cheating. As we will see, behavioral norms may vary from class to class, but no class can function smoothly without them.

> ## PAUSE AND REFLECT
>
> We have distinguished between norms for general conduct (*rules*) and the procedures that students will follow in specific situations (*routines*). In order to make sure that you grasp the distinction, consider the following expectations. For each one, decide whether it is a rule or a routine. (1) At the end of the day, students are to put their chairs upside down on top of their desks. (2) Students are to be courteous. (3) We listen respectfully when people are talking. (4) When we're doing writing workshop, put your name at the top of the page on the right side. (5) During small-group work, students may talk quietly to their group members. We will review this list later in the chapter.

Planning Norms for General Conduct

Effective managers typically have four or five general rules of conduct (Akin-Little, Little, & Laniti, 2007). These rules describe the behaviors that are necessary if your classroom is to be a good place in which to live and work—for example, "Respect other people's property," "Keep your hands to yourself," and "Follow directions." In Garnetta's classroom, she and the children decided on the following rules:

Be respectful.

Raise your hand to talk.

Settle disagreements peacefully and without fighting.

Listen when someone is talking.

Think before you do something.

As you reflect on rules for your own classroom, there are four guidelines to keep in mind. These are summarized in Table 4.1. First, *rules should be reasonable and necessary.* Think about the age and characteristics of the children you are teaching, and ask yourself: What rules are appropriate for them? For example, it is unreasonable to require kindergartners to "sit quietly at your desks at all times." Given young children's irresistible need to move, establishing such a rule will only result in squirming, fidgeting, and frustration.

Also ask yourself whether each rule is necessary. Is there a compelling reason for it? Will it make the classroom a more pleasant place to be? Will it increase children's opportunity to learn? A second-grade teacher whom we know established a strict "no talking" rule during snack time (while children sat at four-person clusters of desks). It was difficult for students (and for us!) to understand why they should be forbidden to talk quietly while eating. Although the teacher was able to enforce the rule, her class perceived it as arbitrary and unfair.

Second, *rules need to be clear and understandable.* Because rules are often stated in very general terms ("Be polite"), they may be too abstract for children to

TABLE 4.1 Four Guidelines for Planning Classroom Rules

Guidelines	Questions to Think About
1. Rules should be reasonable and necessary.	What rules are appropriate for this grade level? Is there a good reason for this rule?
2. Rules need to be clear and understandable.	Is the rule too abstract for students to comprehend? To what extent do I want my students to participate in the decision-making process?
3. Rules should be consistent with instructional goals and with what we know about how people learn.	Will this rule facilitate or hinder students' learning?
4. Classroom rules need to be consistent with school rules.	What are the school rules? Are particular behaviors required in the halls, in the cafeteria, during assemblies, etc.?

comprehend. When planning your rules, you need to think of specific examples to discuss with students. For instance, Barbara's most basic rule for general conduct is "Be courteous." She makes sure that "courtesy" is spelled out in terms of real behaviors: "When you play with someone who's being left out." "When you listen politely when someone's speaking." "When you don't tease." "When you don't call people names." "When you say please and thank you."

Many teachers (including Courtney, Garnetta, and Ken) believe that rules are more understandable when they are generated by students and teachers working together. They hope that this will increase students' willingness to "buy into" the rules and make it clear that they are active participants in classroom decision making. At the present time, there is no clear evidence that generating rules with students is better than simply presenting and discussing them. What does seem essential is making sure that everyone understands what the class norms are and how they apply (Carter & Doyle, 2006).

A third guideline to keep in mind is that *rules should be consistent with instructional goals and with what we know about how people learn.* The first chapter discussed the principles guiding this book. One principle was that the need for order should not supersede the need for meaningful instruction. As you develop rules for your classroom, think about whether they will *facilitate or hinder the learning process.* For example, a second-grade teacher we know had a "no erasures" rule for written work done in class. Her reason was clear: Children tended to create holes in their papers when they erased, and the results were messy and difficult to read. Unfortunately, not being allowed to erase created a lot of anxiety; some students actually became more focused on not making mistakes than on what they were writing. Although the rule was well-intended, it interfered with children's learning.

In the pursuit of order, teachers sometimes prohibit talking during independent seatwork assignments. Or they may refrain from using cooperative learning activities for fear that students will be too rowdy. Obviously, such restrictions are necessary at times, but it is sad when they become the status quo. Educational psychologists who study the ways children learn stress the importance of children's interaction. Much of this thinking is based on the work of the Soviet psychologist Lev Vygotsky, who believed that children's intellectual growth is fostered through collaboration with adults who serve as coaches and tutors and with more capable peers (Wertsch, 1985). Interestingly, research on the use of small groups indicates that these interactions benefit the *tutor* as well as the person being tutored. Researchers found, for example, that children who provide explanations for their peers also show increased achievement themselves (Webb, 1985). Given the important role that interaction plays in children's learning and cognitive development, it seems sensible not to eliminate interaction, but to spend considerable time teaching children how to behave in these situations. (We will address this topic more fully in Chapter 10.)

Finally, *classroom rules need to be consistent with school rules.* For example, some schools require students to possess a pass when they leave the classroom; if this is the case, you need to establish the same rule. Your school may hold an orientation meeting for new teachers where school rules and procedures are explained. If not, see whether there is a school handbook and consult with office staff and other teachers. In particular, find out about behaviors that are expected during assemblies, in the cafeteria and library, and on the playground. You also need to know about any administrative procedures for which you are responsible (e.g., taking attendance, collecting lunch money, supervising fire drills, communicating with parents).

Planning Routines for Specific Situations

So many different activities occur in classrooms that trying to decide on procedures or routines for specific situations can be daunting. Gaea Leinhardt and her colleagues observed the behavior of effective classroom managers and categorized the routines they used (Leinhardt, Weidman, & Hammond, 1987). We have adapted their three-category system to provide you with a way of thinking about routines for your own classroom.

Class-Running Routines

These are *nonacademic routines* that enable you to keep the classroom running smoothly. This category of routines includes *administrative duties* (taking attendance, recording the number of students who are buying lunch each day, distributing school notices), *procedures for student movement* (entering the room at the beginning of the day; leaving the room at the end of the day; leaving the room to go to the bathroom, the nurse, the library, or lockers; lining up to go to "specials" such as art, music, and physical education; fire drills; moving around the room to sharpen pencils, use learning centers, or get materials), and *housekeeping routines* (cleaning chalkboards, watering plants, storing personal items such as book bags and coats, cleaning out desks, maintaining storage for materials used by everyone).

Without clear, specific class-running routines, these activities can consume a significant part of the school day. Research on the way time is used in second-grade classrooms has indicated that, on average, noninstructional activities (transitions, waiting, housekeeping) consume almost 20 percent of the time spent in the classroom—more than the amount of time spent in mathematics instruction (Rosenshine, 1980). This figure is undoubtedly higher in classrooms that are not well managed.

By defining how children are to behave in these specific situations, you can save precious minutes for instruction. You also enable children to carry out many of these routines without your direct supervision, freeing you to concentrate on instruction. For example, Barbara allows her students to take a laminated cardboard pass and go to the bathroom without asking permission—as long as the class is not in the middle of a lesson. Having a single pass means that only one child can be out of the room at a time, and of course Barbara makes sure that no one leaves the room an unreasonable number of times. With these safeguards in place, the routine runs smoothly and saves Barbara from innumerable interruptions.

Another important class-running routine should outline what students are expected to do with any electronic devices they may bring to school, including cell phones and MP3 players. Although these devices are much more prevalent in the older grades, students at younger ages are also starting to carry and use them. If your school does not have a policy for such devices, you will have to establish appropriate policies for your classroom. For example, Barbara's school allows cell phones to come to school, but they must stay in student lockers or backpacks. If electronic devices are brought into the classroom, those devices are confiscated and students' parents must come and pick them up at the office. Even if it seems impossible that your young students would have cell phones or MP3 players, it is a good preventive measure to have an appropriate routine in place in case the situation occurs.

Lesson-Running Routines

These routines *directly support instruction by specifying the behaviors that are necessary for teaching and learning to take place.* They allow lessons to proceed briskly and eliminate the need for students to ask questions such as "Do I have to use pen?" "Should we number from 1 to 20?" and "What do I do if I'm finished?"

Lesson-running routines describe what items students are to have on hand when a lesson begins, how materials are to be distributed and collected, what kind of paper or writing instrument is to be used, and what should be done with the paper (folded into eight boxes; numbered from 1 to 10 along the left margin; headed with name, date, and subject). In addition, lesson-running routines specify the behaviors that students are to engage in at the beginning of the lesson (e.g., have books open to the relevant page, silently sit and wait for instructions from the teacher) and what they are to do if they finish early or if they are unable to finish the assignment by the end of the time allotted.

Homework procedures can also be considered lesson-running routines, because the pace and content of a lesson often depend on whether students have done their homework assignments. You need to establish routines for determining quickly which students have their homework and which do not, as well as routines for checking and collecting assignments.

Also think about what routines will be followed when students are absent. How will you keep track of work for absent students? How will students learn what the day's assignments are? How will work get home to students who are absent? How many days will students have to complete work they missed?

Interaction Routines

These routines refer to the *rules for talk*—talk between teachers and students and talk among students themselves. Interaction routines specify *when talk is permitted and how it is to occur.* For example, during a whole-class discussion, students need to know what to do if they want to respond to a question or contribute a comment. All five of our teachers, like many others, usually require students to raise their hands and wait to be called on, rather than simply calling out. In this way, the teachers can distribute opportunities to participate throughout the class and can ensure that the conversation is not dominated by a few overly eager individuals. The teachers can also check on how well the class understands the lesson by calling on students who do not raise their hands.

It's often hard to keep track of which students have had an opportunity to speak. To avoid this problem, Ken sometimes uses "the cup system"—a coffee mug containing popsicle sticks with students' names. He shakes the cup, pulls out a name, and then places the popsicle stick on the side after that student has participated.

During some lessons (e.g., counting by fives), you may want students to respond chorally rather than individually. A simple signal can be used to indicate that the rules for talk have changed. Viviana, for example, uses hand gestures. When she wants students to raise their hands, she shoots her arm into the air as she asks the question. When she wants a choral response, she reaches out both hands, palms up, in a clear invitation for all to respond.

Barbara also suspends the normal rules for talk at times. For example, during a "great books discussion," she encourages her students to respond directly to one another. It's amazing how difficult they find this to be, at least at first; students repeatedly seek her permission to talk, despite her frequent reminders that they can comment without first being called on.

Interaction routines also include *procedures that students and teachers use to gain each other's attention.* For example, if students are busy working and you need to give additional instructions, how will you signal that you want their attention? Will you say, "Excuse me," as Garnetta does, or will you clap your hands, flick the lights, or ring a bell? Conversely, if you are busy working with a small group or an individual, and students need your assistance, how will they communicate that to you? Will they be allowed to call your name or leave their seats and approach you? Will they turn over a "help" sign at their desks, or perhaps raise a red flag?

Finally, you need to think about the rules that will govern *talk among students*. When 20 to 30 students sit so close to one another, it's only natural for them to talk. You must decide when it's all right for students to talk about the television show they saw last night (e.g., during recess and free time) and when their talk must be about academic work (e.g., during cooperative learning activities or peer conferencing). You also need to think about times when students may talk quietly (e.g., during independent work or writing workshop), and when you need to have absolute silence (e.g., when you are giving instruction or during a test). Table 4.2 summarizes the three types of routines we have just discussed.

As we wrap up our discussion of planning for norms and routines, let's go back to the first Pause and Reflect box, which asked you to indicate whether each

---

TABLE 4.2 Summary of Classroom Routines

Class-Running Routines: Nonacademic routines that enable the classroom to run smoothly

Administrative routines
   Taking attendance
   Recording lunch orders
   Distributing school notices
Routines for student movement
   Entering the room at the beginning of the day
   Leaving the room at the end of the day
   Going to the restroom
   Going to the nurse
   Going to the library
   Going to "specials" (art, music, PE)
   Fire drills
   Sharpening pencils
   Using learning centers
   Getting materials
Housekeeping routines
   Cleaning chalkboards
   Cleaning desks
   Watering plants
   Storing personal items (backpacks, coats)
   Cleaning desks
   Maintaining common storage area

Lesson-Running Routines: Routines that directly support instruction by specifying the behaviors that are necessary for teaching and learning to take place
   What to bring to the lesson
   Collecting homework

Recording who has done homework
Returning homework
Moving in and out of centers
Writing workshop responsibilities
Distributing materials
Preparing paper for assignment (heading, margins, type of writing instrument)
Collecting in-class assignments
What to do when assignments have been completed

Interaction Routines: Routines that specify when talk is permitted and how it is to occur

Talk between teacher and students
   During whole-class lessons
   When the teacher is working with a small group
   When the teacher needs the group's attention
   When the students need the teacher's help
Talk among students
   During independent work
   During center time
   During peer conferencing
   During cooperative activities
   During small-group work
   During free time
   During transitions
   During loudspeaker announcements
   When a visitor comes to speak with the teacher

expectation was a rule or a routine. The first example, students putting chairs on desks at the end of the day, is a class-running routine. It helps with housekeeping, in this case quite literally, because it makes it easier to clean the floor if the chairs are out of the way. The second example, "Students are to be courteous," is a rule. As discussed earlier, Barbara uses this rule and explains to her students specific ways in which they can show that they are following this rule in the classroom. The third example, "We listen respectfully when people are talking," is a rule that enables the students and teacher to hear each other more clearly. Asking students to write their name on the page at the writing center, our fourth example, is a lesson-running routine that allows students to take responsiblity and be account-able for their work. Finally, the fifth example, talking quietly during small-group work, is an interaction routine. It specifies one of the times when student–student talk is acceptable.

THE FIRST FEW DAYS OF SCHOOL: TEACHING STUDENTS HOW TO BEHAVE

Learning how to behave in school is not always easy. Too often, students have to guess the rules for appropriate behavior from teachers' indirect statements such as "I see someone whose hands are not folded" [translation: Students' hands should be folded now] (Shuy, 1988) or "I don't see any hands" [translation: Students should raise their hands if they wish to speak] (Gumperz, 1981). Students must also be sensitive to cues provided by nonverbal behavior, such as voice tone and pitch, posture, tempo and rhythm of speech, and facial expression. Sometimes students "misbehave" simply because they have misinterpreted these subtle cues! As shown in Figure 4.1, you will need to teach rules and routines explicitly so that your students have the same understandings as you do about what is expected from them.

Moreover, misinterpretation is especially likely when teachers and students come from different cultural backgrounds. As we noted in Chapter 1, definitions and expectations of appropriate behavior are culturally influenced. Most schools

Figure 4.1   *Source:* CALVIN AND HOBBES © 1995, Watterson. Distributed by UNIVERSAL UCLICK. Reprinted with permission. All rights reserved.

enact the values and norms of middle-class, European American cultures; in other words, these values and norms are not culturally neutral (Levin & Nolan, 2003) and may, in fact, conflict with those of other cultural groups.

To minimize the possibility of confusion, you need to teach students rules and routines as deliberately and thoroughly as you would teach academic content. In fact, during days 1–4, teachers and students may spend *more time on management issues than on academic content* (Leinhardt, Weidman, & Hammond, 1987). This may seem like an unreasonable amount of time to invest in rules and routines, but your investment should pay off later when your class runs smoothly (Cameron, Connor, & Morrison, 2005).

See Box 4.1 for information on Harry and Rosemary Wong, two educators who have written about the importance of teaching rules and routines during the first days of school.

MEET THE EDUCATORS   BOX 4.1

MEET HARRY AND ROSEMARY WONG

Harry Wong, a popular educational speaker and consultant, taught middle school and high school science, garnering numerous teaching awards. Rosemary taught kindergarten through grade 8. The couple now have their own publishing company (Harry K. Wong Publications), of which Rosemary is CEO. Together they wrote *The First Days of School*, which has sold over 3 million copies, making it the best-selling book ever in education. The Wongs have also produced the DVD series *The Effective Teacher*, which won the Telly Award for best educational video of the past 20 years and was awarded the first-place Gold Award in the International Film and Video Festival.

Some Major Ideas about Classroom Management

- What you do on the first days of school will determine your success or failure for the rest of the school year.
- Effective teachers introduce rules (i.e., expectations of appropriate student behavior), procedures, and routines on the very first day of school and continue to teach them throughout the first week of school.
- The number one problem in the classroom is not discipline; it is the lack of procedures and routines.

- A procedure is a method or process for how things are to be done in a classroom. When the procedure becomes automatic, it is a routine.
- Effective teachers have procedures for taking roll, exchanging papers, sharpening pencils, entering the classroom, starting class, leaving the classroom, and so on.
- The three steps to teaching procedures are (1) explain clearly; (2) rehearse (until class procedures become class routines); and (3) reteach when necessary and reinforce (give specific praise).

Selected Books and Articles

The First Days of School: How to Be an Effective Teacher by Harry and Rosemary Wong (Mountain View, CA: Harry K. Wong Publications, 2004)

Monthly columns by the Wongs can be found at http://teachers.net/wong. Some examples are

- "An Amazing Kindergarten Teacher" (May 2008)
- "Schools That Beat the Academic Odds" (April 2008)
- "Wrapping the Year with Rap!" (December 2007/January 2008)

Website: www.effectiveteaching.com

Teaching Norms for General Conduct

It's not enough to state norms for general conduct and expect students to understand or remember them. You need to *define terms* as clearly as possible, *discuss rationales,* and *provide examples.* Let's see what this looks like in action. We begin with Barbara.

On the morning of the first day of school, Barbara taught students her most basic norm: "Be courteous." Note how she solicits examples, explains why certain behaviors are necessary, comments on students' attentiveness, and checks to see that students understand.

BARBARA: I guess it's time now to talk about fourth grade. This is a big step for you. People have a lot of expectations of fourth-graders. Let's discuss some of those expectations. I expect you to be courteous. What does that mean? What are some examples of being courteous?

STUDENT: Not being rude.

BARBARA: That's right, but give me an example of not being rude.

STUDENT: Not slamming the door on somebody.

BARBARA: Good. What's another example?

STUDENT: Listen to people when they're talking.

BARBARA: Yes. I can see that you people don't have any problem with that, because you're listening now as we're talking. Another example of being courteous? [Students can't think of any.] Let's say we're having a lesson and someone walks in to talk to me. What could you do to be courteous?

STUDENT: Sit quietly.

STUDENT: Whisper quietly.

BARBARA: Good. It's important for you to know that it's all right with me if you whisper quietly. But I need to know that you know what whispering quietly means. So go ahead and do that. [Students whisper.] All right, I can live with that. That was fine. OK, so you can sit silently, or you can whisper quietly What else?

STUDENT: You can read a book.

BARBARA: Yes, that's a good idea. Do you think you could get up and walk around? [Students murmur no and shake their heads.] Right, because as soon as the person leaves we'll resume the lesson, and we'll lose time if you're all around the room. Is there anything else you could do when I'm speaking with someone?

STUDENT: Continue working on our work.

BARBARA: Absolutely. You know, we're going to be living here together all day long, and we're going to be friends. We're going to be like a family. So we have to treat each other courteously and learn to care about one another.

As this example illustrates, teaching students norms for general conduct doesn't have to be unpleasant or oppressive. Interestingly, Barbara doesn't even use the word *rule* as she discusses her expectations for students' behavior. Nor does she post rules on a bulletin board, although many effective managers do. When we asked her about this, she explained her reasoning:

> Even if a rule is stated positively, the word rule itself has a negative connotation. From a child's perspective, rules are made up by adults to tell kids, "These are the things you can't do, and these are the things you have to do, and if you don't follow the rules you get punished." I also think that children think the rules are only for them, not for the teacher. I much prefer to talk about the way we all need to treat each other. When I talk about the need for courtesy, I try to make it clear that *I* need to be courteous too, not just the children. I also want to communicate that there is no question in my mind that we will all be courteous, so I don't talk about penalties or punishments, or what will happen if people *aren't* courteous.

Garnetta takes a very different approach. In the following scenario, we see how she tries to make the need for norms vivid for her third-grade students. Note how her students readily suggest classroom rules, consequences, and rewards. In fact, Garnetta needs to do little prompting during the discussion. Her students' responses reflect their experiences at school, where teachers have been taught *Assertive Discipline,* a program developed by Lee and Marlene Canter (Canter & Canter, 2001). In classrooms using Assertive Discipline, it is common to see a set of posted rules, rewards, and consequences.

GARNETTA: We're going to go on an imaginary trip, on a boat. [She describes what the boat is like.] But a storm comes up and the boat capsizes, and we all go overboard. Luckily, we find a lifeboat. We all get on the little lifeboat, and we get to an island. Things are real nice for a few days, but after a while they get kind of disorganized. [She elaborates on how kids begin to take other kids' clothes and other kids' food, how people do whatever they want to do.] So we have a problem. We're missing something we need to make life on the island better for us all. What are we missing?

STUDENT: Rules.

GARNETTA: Right. We need to make some rules. What would be some good rules for our island?

STUDENT: Don't mug somebody.

STUDENT: Don't snatch somebody's food.

STUDENT: Don't take anybody's clothes.

STUDENT: Don't beat nobody up.

GARNETTA: These are really fine rules for our island. . . . But what if somebody didn't follow them, what if someone did something wrong?

STUDENT: Make them do 15 pushups.

GARNETTA: What do we call that?

STUDENT: Consequences.

GARNETTA: Right. What are consequences?

STUDENT: If you break the rules, you gotta pay the price.

GARNETTA: Let's say that everyone did everything just right. What could we do then?

STUDENT: We could get rewards. [Students begin to murmur: Yeah, we could get some treats, some candy, some popcorn parties.]

GARNETTA: Yes, we could have some wonderful treats. Life on the island would be a lot better then. But, you know, we have to leave the island and come home, because school is starting. We build a new boat and we come back to school. Now let's think about what we need in our class. How can we make it good in here?

STUDENT: We gotta have rules and consequences and rewards here too.

GARNETTA: Okay, you want to suggest a rule?

STUDENT: Stay in your seat. [Garnetta writes what students say on the board.]

STUDENT: Raise your hand to be recognized.

GARNETTA: Excellent rule.

STUDENT: Think before you do something.

GARNETTA: Oh, I like that one. Yes I do.

Students continue to suggest rules. Then Garnetta solicits ideas for consequences (call parents; stay after school; no treats or special games) and rewards (send a good note home to parents; stickers or other treats; movies). When students have no more ideas, Garnetta brings the activity to a close.

GARNETTA: Let's go over these lists and review, and then I'll write them up on posters. We'll be talking some more about these in the days to come. [The class reads the lists out loud with her. A boy wants to add "Don't name call" to the list of rules. Garnetta agrees to add it.]

Later in the day, Garnetta talked with us about her approach to teaching about rules:

 I talk with them a lot about why we need rules. I think they need a very clear structure to follow, especially since some of them come from homes where there's very little structure. The rules need to be clear, and they need to understand what happens if you follow the rules and what happens if you don't follow them. You can see that they're very used to talking about rules, consequences, and rewards, because everyone in the school uses the same kind of system. They know what kind of behavior is expected here, and they know what happens if you misbehave.

We turn now to Courtney. As a new teacher, Courtney thought long and hard before school began about how she wanted to approach rule-setting in her kindergarten classroom. She decided to follow the model that she had witnessed during student teaching, based on *The Responsive Classroom* (Denton & Kriete, 2000):

 On the third day of school, we're going to talk about our hopes and dreams for kindergarten. I'll start by talking about my own hopes and dreams— I want us all to learn, to make friends, to become a community—and

I'll draw a picture of me living out these hopes and dreams. And then the kids are going to do the same. They're going to think about something they want to get out of kindergarten (learning to read, learning to write, riding the bus) and then they'll draw a picture. Then, the next day, we'll share our hopes and dreams for kindergarten.

The next week of school, we're going to revisit the hopes and dreams and talk about what we as a class need in order to accomplish them. And that's how we'll develop our rules. For example, if someone wants to learn to read, we need to be good listeners. They'll probably come up with a lot of things like "Don't hit" and "Don't punch." That night, I'll look at the things they came up with and think about how we can group those rules. The next day, I'll approach the kids and say something like "We have 'Don't hit,' and 'Don't punch,' and 'Don't call each other names,' so how can we group these together?" I'm hoping to come up with a list of about five general rules. Each table will be assigned one rule to illustrate.

I really hope that this will work; it worked out beautifully last year, but my cooperating teacher has been doing this for several years. We'll just have to see.

Courtney followed her plan, and the first day's activity went well. Students generated a list of their hopes and dreams for school (to play, learn math, make new friends, etc.), and Courtney posted the words on an easel pad. When it came time to think about what rules would be needed to achieve these hopes and dreams, however, students seemed to become fixated on the physical activities they knew were inappropriate. Suggestions came steadily: "No running," "No climbing up the slide," "No rocking on our chairs," "No hitting somebody," "No jumping," "No biting," "No running in the hallway," "No doing cartwheels," "No walking on hands," "No karate." Courtney tried to steer them toward considering what they *should* do and away from the gymnastic, but when she asked for additional items, they continued in the same vein: "No throwing," "No throwing baseballs."

The next day, Courtney led the class in a discussion about how these suggestions could be grouped in about five positively stated rules, and they finally had their list: "Listen," "Keep our hands to ourselves," "Do our best," "Be respectful," and "Walk in school." But she found she had to provide more direction than she had anticipated:

 They kept focusing on no hitting, no biting, no kicking, and no cartwheels (that was a favorite), and no matter how much I tried to get them to focus on the positive—what we *should* do—I couldn't get them beyond the "no's." I finally said, "Well, if we're not going to do any of these things, we're going to keep our hands to ourselves." And I made that a rule. I also suggested "Do our best" and "Be respectful," and I defined that for them. Being respectful is about being a good friend and about using our words to work out a conflict and not calling other children names, and sharing materials and toys, and from their illustrations, I could see they understood.

The next day, I wanted to reinforce the rules, so I asked, "What is one of the important rules we decided on?" and I got "No hitting," "No cartwheels," "No sitting back on your chair." That's what really seemed to stick in their minds. This didn't work out exactly the way I had hoped. They just didn't make the leap from hopes and dreams to the rules. I still love the general approach, and I want to do it again next year, but I'm going to have to think about how to frame it differently so they're not so focused on the playground!

Finally, let's consider Ken's approach to teaching norms. Instead of rules, Ken prefers to speak in terms of students' rights, as well as the classroom "laws" that are necessary to protect those rights. In the following scenario, Ken talks to his students about what those rights might be. Note how Ken allows all suggestions (as long as they were seriously contributed) but indicates that further refinement will be needed.

 KEN: I want to spend some time thinking about what your rights in school are. I want to do a brainstorming session and write down things that you consider a right in school. OK, what rights do you think you should have? (Ken moves to blackboard and calls on children. As children state rights, Ken writes down what they say; sometimes he rewords a bit if student gives him permission.)

STUDENT: The right to whisper when the teacher isn't talking.

STUDENT: The right to be treated nicely, politely.

STUDENT: The right to not have people take your things.

STUDENT: The right to a two-minute break between every working period.

STUDENT: The right to work and learn without being bothered.

STUDENT: The right to a snack every day.

STUDENT: The right to sit next to whoever you want. (Ken writes: "The right to choose a table.")

STUDENT: The right for the table to stay together unless it wants to break up.

KEN: That's really an elaboration of the previous right, so I won't write it down, OK?

STUDENT: The right to privacy—so no one else takes what you have. So no one touches your stuff without permission.

STUDENT: The right to use chairs on the floor to lean.

KEN: Can I write down, "The right to be comfortable?" (Boy agrees.)

STUDENT: The right to chew gum, without blowing bubbles. (Everyone begins to murmur, "yeah . . .")

KEN: We'll put it up, but we'll have to think about it. I like the way you qualified it about the bubbles.

STUDENT: The right to make choices about the day's schedule.

STUDENT: The right to free work time.

Suggestions appear to be at an end. A few kids mutter things like "There must be more things to put up that we haven't thought about." Ken stands silently and waits. Kids are unable to come up with much more.

KEN: I don't think this is complete yet. But I'm going to copy this down and post it. We're going to have to work on this, and define things more carefully, especially the chewing gum.

In the next few days, Ken and his students continue to revise and refine the Students' Bill of Rights. When they are all satisfied with the list, he writes the Bill of Rights in final form and posts it in the classroom. Ken then turns to the discussion of "laws" needed to protect those rights. As Ken tells it, "That's when the kids start saying, 'You have to do what the teacher says.' They expect me to protect their rights, and I do accept that responsibility. But I also tell them that we have to work together on this." After Ken and his students decide on laws that will safeguard their rights, Ken types the list, preserving students' actual language. (See Figure 4.2.)

Later, Ken shared with us his thoughts about the whole process:

I think every teacher should do this every year. The Students' Bill of Rights teaches you so much about the kids in your class; the list always reflects their concerns and their views of what classrooms are all about.

You can see where they're from, what's happened to them in the past, what their expectations are. Making a bill of rights forces them to open up . . . to think about what they'd really like the classroom to be. It almost becomes a wish list—we wish we had these things. And then, of course, it forces me to ask myself, why not? Why can't they have these things? After all, if they're willing to take on the responsibilities, well, then, why shouldn't they enjoy the rights?

Some of the things on the list seem a lot more special than they really are. Take the two-minute break between classes, for example. In reality, every time you switch classes, it takes about that long anyway. So you define it as the break. You're acknowledging that it takes that long and saying that it's all right to talk during that time. In other words, it legitimizes something that's going to happen anyway.

Another thing—you read the literature on how we want kids to be fluent idea-producers, to be able to make choices, to engage in problem solving, to critique ideas. Well, here's a real-life problem: What rights should you have in this

---

LAWS TO PROTECT OUR RIGHTS

1. Follow directions the first time.
2. Speak nicely, be courteous, and respect other people, their feelings and their things. Follow the Bill of Rights.
3. Laugh at the right time for the right amount of time.
4. Respect others' right to learn. Do not distract others. Don't be nosy. Don't yell. Remember to get quiet at countdown.
5. Talk at the right times with the right tone of voice and volume.
6. Transitions and movements are calm, quiet, careful, and elegant.
7. Follow all classroom and school procedures, like: bathroom, pencil, lunch and recess, dismissal.

Figure 4.2 Laws to Protect Our Rights

classroom and what laws do we need to protect them? The kids have to live with the list they come up with; it stares them in the face every day. And it makes the classroom more real and changes the way kids think about classroom behavior. I hear kids say to other kids, "This place is different; we have rights here."

It's important to note that when Courtney, Garnetta, and Ken invite their students to generate a list of rules or rights, the teachers have already thought long and hard about the norms that need to be in place for their classrooms to run smoothly. They make it clear that they are beginning a process of *negotiation,* not simply accepting anything that students might suggest. For example, Ken was wary about the suggestion that students have the right to chew gum in class. He knew from experience that this could lead to management prob-

> ### ✎ Pause and Reflect
>
> Some teachers would be leery about trying Ken's approach with their students, and others would recommend that novice teachers stay away from this approach altogether. If you were to use this approach, what would you have to keep in mind and what pitfalls might you need to plan for?

lems (e.g., loud popping sounds during instruction and sticky gum on the underside of desks) and worked with his students to create a solution they could all live with.

Teaching Routines for Specific Situations

Teaching students how to carry out behavioral routines is much like teaching them how to add or subtract. Research shows that effective classroom managers *explain and demonstrate procedures,* allow students to *practice* them, *provide feedback* to students about their performance, and then *reteach* the procedures if necessary (Emmer, Evertson, & Anderson, 1980). Such thoroughness is particularly important at lower grade levels, when children have had little experience with the routines of school and when new instructional strategies are introduced (e.g., writing workshop, literature circles, centers).

Viviana teaches her first-graders how to behave in specific situations when the need arises. On the first day of school, for example, she taught them to turn their chairs around to face her when she gives instruction to the whole group. Even though the whole process lasted less than a minute, Viviana managed to demonstrate the behavior, had students practice, provided feedback, and explained the rationale for the routine:

 All right children, I want you to turn your chairs around to face me. Let me show you how to do that. [She selects a child, stands her up and turns her chair around to demonstrate.] Did you all see that? José, can you do that? [The child turns his chair around properly.] Good for you. Now let me see everyone's chair like that. [She makes a big thing of looking up and down each row checking the chairs.] Very, very good. You did that very well. By turning your chairs around like this, you won't have to strain your necks trying to see what I'm doing [she twists her neck around to illustrate], and I'll be able to see everybody's beautiful face.

Throughout the day, Viviana reinforces this procedure repeatedly: "Turn your chairs around and face me. Very good, you remember how."

Courtney also believes in teaching routines in context. The following excerpt is from our observations on the first day.

Courtney stands by the door; students are outside in the hallway. Before they enter the room, she tells them to find their seats, take off their backpacks, and sit down. When everyone is seated, she explains how to put things away in their cubbies.

COURTNEY: Do you remember where your cubbies are (from kindergarten orientation)? How will you know which is your cubby?

STUDENT: Our names are on the cubbies.

COURTNEY: Right. Steven, will you show everyone how to hang up your jacket? [He does so.] OK, now everyone who has a jacket, get up and go hang it up. [They do.] Good job. Now open your backpacks and take out your lunch or snack bags. Michael, will you help us? Put your lunch box in the bin by the door so that we can take them to the multipurpose room when it's time for lunch. [Michael puts his lunch box in the bin.] Okay, now everyone get up and put your lunch boxes away. . . . Now Mary, let's use your backpack to show everyone how to put backpacks away. First, you zip it up so things don't fall out [Mary does so], and then put it in your cubby by the handle. [She does.] How did she put her backpack in the cubby? I want you to raise your hand if you know.

STUDENT: She hung it up.

COURTNEY: How?

STUDENT: By the handle.

COURTNEY: Right. Now everyone put your backpack away.

As the day progresses, Courtney teaches many other routines: how to "freeze" when she blows a train whistle for attention (a signal coordinated with their first thematic unit on trains); how to get up, push in their chairs, and come to morning meeting; where and how to sit during morning meeting (in a circle, with "pretzel feet"); how to participate in discussions (by raising their hands); how and when to go to the restroom; where to put their papers when they are finished with an activity; how to line up by the door at lunchtime. Although everything went smoothly, Courtney still felt overwhelmed by it all. Several days later she commented:

I just wasn't prepared for the fact that they didn't know how to do anything. The simplest act—come over and sit on the carpet—required a mini-lesson. And I was just very flustered. . . . There are so many things to teach them! But the next day, we went over things all over again, and I could see that at least some of them were beginning to get it. At this age, they're not going to get all of these routines immediately. In the morning, I say the same thing over and over: "Sit down, open your backpack, take out your folder with work and messages, put your lunch bag in the bin, then put the folder and backpack in your cubby. Your folder goes under the crayons." And I just try to say it the same way every time. I realize now how hard those multistep things are for them.

Although Courtney felt that she was spending an inordinate amount of time teaching these kinds of routines, in November she felt the time had been well spent:

 Overall, things have been going well. The class has really settled into the routines, and I'm actually surprised that by five years old, they are able to learn the routines so well. And they don't like it when you change the routines either, like on half-days. I'm really amazed at how much they are creatures of routine at this age. You'd think they'd like some changes, but the consistency is very important and seems to be necessary. They like to know what's coming next.

CONCLUDING COMMENTS

Courtney, Barbara, Garnetta, Ken, and Viviana all have well-defined expectations for student behavior, and they make these expectations absolutely clear. Nonetheless, the five teachers have somewhat different expectations, and they introduce rules and routines in different ways. These differences reflect their beliefs about what works best for their own particular students in their own particular contexts. Courtney wants the rules to emerge from students' "hopes and dreams," although, as she put it, the class wasn't completely successful in making the "leap." Viviana prefers to teach her expectations for behavior in context; Garnetta uses a framework of rules, rewards, and consequences; Barbara's norms flow from the basic principle of courtesy; and Ken and his students formulate a bill of rights and a set of laws to protect those rights.

As a beginning teacher, you would be wise to adopt a deliberate, thorough approach to teaching and reviewing rules and routines. Once you've gained experience—and a reputation—you might try a less formal approach. Also keep in mind that rules and routines are not invented in a single year, polished and fully developed. Instead, they will evolve over time, products of your experience and creative efforts.

One final note: We once heard a professor of education recount the story of her daughter's first week of kindergarten (Delpit, 1995). After each of the first four days of school, the mother asked her daughter what she had learned. The child's answers were succinct: On the first day she learned "to sit still"; on the second day she learned "to walk in a straight line"; on the third day she learned "to raise her hand"; and on the fourth day she learned "to be quiet." On the fifth day,

PAUSE AND REFLECT

You have listened in on each of our five teachers as they set up rules and procedures in their classrooms. Which teacher has an outlook most like yours? Is there a particular style that resonates with you, or will you borrow an idea from Barbara and add one from Garnetta? As you develop your own management style, keep in mind the ways in which these teachers approach their classrooms, and use their thoughts to develop your own ideas.

the mother decided not to ask any more questions!

Obviously, the teacher in this story did a thorough job of teaching her students how to behave, and it's likely that she had few behavior problems in succeeding weeks. Nonetheless, we find this story somewhat sad and disturbing. Although we have emphasized the importance of establishing behavioral expectations early in the year, rules and routines should not be the *most salient* aspect of schooling for children. As you plan the first few weeks, make sure that you balance the teaching of rules and routines with a variety of learning activities that students will find meaningful, enjoyable, and memorable. We want our students to understand that they will learn more in our classes than simply how to behave.

SUMMARY

This chapter discussed two important functions of classroom norms: (1) to provide a structure and predictability that help children to feel safe and secure, and (2) to reduce the complexity of classroom life, allowing you and your students to concentrate on teaching and learning. We outlined two broad categories of behavioral expectations—*rules for general conduct* and *routines for specific situations*—and emphasized the need to teach these explicitly.

Decide on Rules for General Conduct That Are

- Reasonable and necessary.
- Clear and understandable.
- Consistent with instructional goals and with what we know about how people learn.
- Consistent with school rules.

Plan Routines for Specific Situations

- Class-running routines.
    Administrative duties.
    Procedures for student movement.
    Housekeeping responsibilities.
- Lesson-running routines.
    Use and distribution of materials.
    Paper headings, homework procedures, what to do if you finish early.
- Interaction routines.
    When and how talk is permitted.
    How students and teachers get each other's attention.

Teach Norms Explicitly

- Define terms.
- Discuss rationales.
- Provide examples.

Teach Routines Carefully

- Explain.
- Demonstrate.
- Practice.
- Give feedback.
- Reteach.

Remember, developing good rules and routines is only the first step. For rules and routines to be effective, you must actively teach them and then review them on a regular basis. Time spent on rules and routines in the first weeks of school will pay off in increased instructional time throughout the year. Make sure, however, to balance the teaching of rules and routines with learning activities that are meaningful and memorable.

ACTIVITIES FOR SKILL BUILDING AND REFLECTION

In Class

1. Working together in small groups, develop a set of rules for general conduct. About five rules should be sufficient. For each rule, think of ways to make the rules more meaning-ful (e.g., modeling expected behaviors, providing examples, discussing hypothetical scenarios). Think about which rules are most important to you and why.

2. Use Table 4.2 to help you think through the ways you expect your students to behave in specific situations. In a small group, consider different routines you might use for at least one item in each category (class running, lesson running, interaction). Then, think about which routines should be taught the first day. In other words, decide on priorities so you can teach routines when it is most appropriate (and when they are most likely to be remembered).

3. You may decide, as Ken has, that developing a Students' Bill of Rights is the strategy that best suits you and your students. During the brainstorming session, you may be confronted with some unexpected suggestions from your students. This can be prob-lematic: On the one hand, you don't want to squelch student initiative by vetoing too many of their ideas; on the other hand, you are the adult in charge, and know what you and the school can tolerate.

    A little practice on what to say to "unusual" ideas might help. Listed below are some student suggestions. What would be your response? Is there a way to incorporate or modify a suggestion to make it workable for you? Is there a way to say no in a manner that makes sense to the student? Give it a try!

    a. We should be able to walk around the classroom without our shoes on.

    b. We deserve stickers for bringing in our homework every day.

    c. We should be able to bring toys to school.

    d. We should have a joke-telling time every day before lunch.

    e. We should be able to select one day a week when we don't have to do homework.

    f. We should be able to write notes to each other.

    g. We should be able to call you by your first name.

    h. We should be able to lie down on the floor to do our work.

On Your Own

If you are teaching, student teaching, or observing another teacher's classroom, keep a reflective journal on developing and teaching rules and routines. Using the routines listed in Table 4.2, note which routines cause the most problems, the nature of the problems, and how you might respond to those problems. Also note which routines work particularly well.

For Your Portfolio

Write a brief statement on the rules that will guide behavior in your classroom. Will you develop and distribute them yourself? If so, what rules will you select? Will you generate rules with students? If so, how will you do this? Describe the specific approach you will take.

FOR FURTHER READING

Bohn, C. M., Roehrig, A. D., & Pressley, M. (2004). The first days of school in the classrooms of two more effective and four less effective primary-grades teachers. *The Elementary School Journal, 104*(4), 269–287.

    This journal article describes the ways that two exemplary teachers began the school year. Consistent with previous research published more than two decades ago, these two teachers emphasized rules and procedures during the first few days of school, closely monitored students and responded to their needs, rewarded appropriate behavior, and carefully organized instruction. However, some differences from the earlier research were also noted. Specifically, the two exemplary teachers did much to foster self-regulation in students during the first few days of school and conveyed the expectation that students would be good community members.

Brady, K., Forton, M. B., Porter, D., & Wood, C. (2003). *Rules in school.* Greenfield, MA: Northeast Foundation for Children.

    One of the Strategies for Teachers series, this book provides practical suggestions for involving K–8 students in generating classroom rules that grow out of their hopes and dreams.

Denton, P., & Kriete, R. (2000). *The first six weeks of school.* Greenfield, MA: Northeast Foundation for Children.

    This is another book in the Strategies for Teachers series, showing K–6 teachers how to structure the first six weeks of school. Detailed guidelines are presented for building community, creating rules and routines, introducing curriculum, establishing high expectations, and integrating social-emotional and academic learning.

Marzano, R.J., with Marzano, J. S., & Pickering, D. J. (2003). *Classroom management that works: Research-based strategies for every teacher.* Alexandria, VA: Association for Supervision and Curriculum Development.

Chapter 2 in this book focuses on rules and procedures. The authors first discuss research confirming the importance of classroom norms. They then outline a series of "Action Steps" that teachers can take to identify appropriate rules and procedures and to involve students in their design.

KNOWING YOUR STUDENTS AND THEIR SPECIAL NEEDS

Getting your class list at the beginning of the school year always brings a sense of anticipation, excitement, and curiosity: What are these children like? What do they know? How do they think? What strengths do they bring? What struggles do they face? Where do they come from? Over the first few weeks and months of school, you begin to formulate answers to these questions. Gradually, you gain an understanding of *who these children are.* (See Figure 5.1 for an example of how one teacher understands her young students.) This understanding enables you to tailor your teaching to their specific needs and to find ways of building connections. And *knowing your students is essential if you are to build an inclusive, caring environment for learning.*

Knowing your students means recognizing and appreciating the ways in which each student is a unique individual, as well as understanding the common characteristics of early and middle childhood. Undoubtedly, your class will comprise students with a wide range of abilities, social skills, and emotional maturity. In addition, your class will probably include children with "special needs." Although this term is generally used to refer to children with disabilities, children who are learning English as a second language also have special needs. Likewise, children who are growing up in unstable or abusive circumstances may have physical, emotional, or psychological problems that must be addressed.

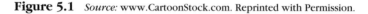

"I'll have the decaf. Twenty-one second graders will
provide me with enough stimulation."

Figure 5.1   *Source:* www.CartoonStock.com. Reprinted with Permission.

This chapter begins by looking at some of the common developmental characteristics of elementary-age children and considering the implications for classroom management. Then we consider strategies for supporting children who are English-language learners. Next, we examine ways of helping children with disabilities and attention-deficit/hyperactivity disorder (ADHD), the most commonly diagnosed behavior disorder among children in the United States (Coles, 2000). We then discuss the needs of children who are troubled—specifically, those who suffer from the problems associated with substance abuse and child abuse and neglect. Finally, we discuss approaches to working with children who are poor or homeless.

THE DEVELOPING ELEMENTARY CHILD

With entrance into school, children move from a family setting into sustained contact with the larger world. This transition provides opportunities for children to compare themselves with their peers in terms of appearance, abilities, and behaviors. Thus the elementary years are a critical period for the development of self-concept. Social comparison leads children to conclude that they are very good at some things, just OK at others, and not very good at still others (Berk, 2009). Consider this 11-year-old's description of herself:

> I'm a truthful person. I'm not pretty. I do so-so in my studies. I'm a very good cellist. I'm a very good pianist. I'm a little bit tall for my age . . . I am a very good swimmer. I try to be helpful. . . . Mostly I'm good, but I lose my temper. . . . I don't know if I'm liked by boys or not. (Montemayor & Eisen, 1977, p. 318)

The elementary years are also marked by rapid gains in the capacity to regulate emotions. Between ages six and eight, children are increasingly able to reflect on their feelings and to distinguish between *experiencing* an emotion and *expressing* it. They learn their culture's *emotional display rules,* specifying when, where, and how to express emotions appropriately (Berk, 2009). This is particularly useful for communicating negative emotions in ways that are acceptable to others.

School-aged children also begin to understand a wider range of emotions and are no longer restricted to describing their feelings in terms of "happy," "sad," and "mad." In addition, they learn to use multiple cues to discern the way others are feeling, an ability that leads to increases in empathy. Strides in language and cognitive abilities also enable children to understand the perspective of others and to imagine themselves in "the other person's shoes."

The transition from home to school is also marked by a growing independence from parents and caregivers and a greater emphasis on peer relationships. Friendships become more important, and children have a growing desire to be accepted and liked. As children become more social, play becomes more cooperative, but this also brings more opportunities for conflict (Carter & Doyle, 2006). Fortunately, during the early school years, children are increasingly able to engage in social problem solving—ways of resolving disagreements that are acceptable to both sides—and they learn to substitute persuasion and compromise for grabbing, hitting, and biting (Berk, 2009).

The elementary years also bring about transformations in children's moral reasoning. They develop a stronger sense of right and wrong, and their concept of distributive justice—the allocation of goods and resources—changes (Berk, 2009; Nucci, 2006). In kindergarten and first grade, for example, cries of "That's not fair! He got more than I did!" are not uncommon. At this age, children think of justice in terms of strict equality: Each person should get exactly the same amount, whether it's snacks, turns in a game, or chances to share something during "show and tell." From age six to age seven, children begin to take merit into account; thus, they may now suggest that someone who has worked especially hard should get something extra. From eight to nine, children are able to recognize differences in circumstances, and they can understand that children who are disadvantaged in some way should be given special consideration.

Development within the moral domain also leads to changing ideas about the fairness of classroom practices. Prior to third grade, for example, children tend to think that it is fair to allow peers to work together on a test and that a fair test yields equal test scores; in contrast, older children believe that group testing is unfair, because it would conceal individual differences (Nucci, 2006).

Children's understanding of *morality* (right and wrong) must be distinguished from their understanding of *social convention* (norms, fashion, rules of etiquette, and so on). If being in your seat when the bell rings is a class rule, students who are chatting by the water fountain are violating a rule (a social convention), but they are not immoral. In the conventional domain, children begin by believing that norms are "real and right" (Woolfolk Hoy, 2007) and not to be violated. Later, they recognize that conventions are arbitrary and thus can vary: Some teachers require students to be in their seats when the bell rings, and some don't. Still later, they understand that rules have social value; they may be arbitrary, but they are helpful in maintaining order. This understanding leads to a greater willingness to comply (at least until adolescence!).

Classroom management practices must not only be matched to students' developmental levels, they should also contribute to students' social, emotional, and moral growth (Nucci, 2006). It is critical that classrooms have clear expectations for behavior that reflect basic moral norms. As Larry Nucci (2006) writes, children "expect schools to have rules governing actions such as hitting and hurting and stealing personal property, and state that it is wrong for schools or teachers to permit such behaviors because of the harm that they cause" (p. 717). Moreover, teachers must be trustworthy, dependable, and in control of their own emotions:

> Young children are particularly susceptible to the positive effects of adult displays of emotional warmth, and the negative impact of adult displays of anger. . . . Thus, constructing an emotionally caring environment for young children means that teachers should be even-tempered, and refrain from emotional outbursts. (Nucci, 2006, p. 716)

Erikson's Theory of Psychosocial Development

According to Erikson (1963), individuals move through eight stages of psychosocial development, each with its own goals and concerns. At each stage, the individual faces a developmental "crisis" or conflict. Successful resolution of the crisis leads to a positive outcome; unsuccessful resolution has a negative effect on passage through subsequent stages, as well as on the individual's emerging sense of self and relationship with others.

In Stage 1 (birth to 6–18 months), the basic developmental conflict is between *trust and mistrust.* If the infant's need for food and care are met with sensitivity, consistency, and responsiveness from caregivers, the child will develop trust that the world is a safe place. In contrast, a child who is neglected or abused may develop a sense of mistrust. In Stage 2 (18 months to 3 years), the conflict is between *autonomy and shame/doubt.* During this stage, children strive to master basic motor skills and begin to assume some responsibility for self-care (e.g., feeding, dressing). With increasing competence, they develop feelings of autonomy and confidence; if their efforts are not supported and reinforced, however, they may experience feelings of shame and doubt their abilities to negotiate the world. Erikson's third stage (3–6 years) focuses on *initiative versus guilt.* Now children are "on the move"—actively engaged in new activities, many undertaken independently and with peers. If adults support these new activities, children's sense of purpose and ambition flourish; if adults are interfering or overly protective, children may conclude that everything they want to do is "wrong" and begin to develop a sense of guilt.

When children move from the family into school, they must reestablish the first three stages in an institutional setting (Woolfolk Hoy, 2007): They must learn to trust unfamiliar caregivers (teachers), act autonomously in a more complex environment, and show initiative on school tasks while conforming to a new set of rules. In addition, elementary children face the psychosocial challenge of Erikson's fourth stage (6–12 years)—*industry versus inferiority.* In this stage, children must deal with demands to learn new skills and achieve new goals. They are required to demonstrate the capacity to focus on the task at hand, persist at challenging tasks, and cooperate with others. Success in meeting these new demands results in an increasing sense of competence and self-assurance; failure or difficulty (and negative comparisons with others) can lead to feelings of inferiority.

Attachment Theory

Like Erikson's theory of psychosocial development, attachment theory posits that children's early relationships with their primary caregivers (usually the mother) can affect the nature of relationships throughout life (Ainsworth, 1964, 1967; Bowlby, 1969, 1973). When caregivers respond with sensitivity and consistency, children develop trust in themselves, their caregivers, and the world. They are likely to become resilient, self-confident, cooperative, independent individuals, able to form close friendships. On the other hand, when caregivers are unresponsive, inconsistent, or rejecting, children develop an insecure, anxious attachment relationship. They may come to believe that the world is an unsafe place and that others cannot be trusted to provide care. When they get older, they are likely to be less resilient, to have negative self-concepts, and to distrust others, with a limited ability to form positive relationships. They may be angry and defiant or passive and withdrawn.

For children entering school with an insecure or anxious attachment to their primary caregiver, a connection with a trustworthy, consistent, nurturing adult is absolutely critical (Watson, 2003). Unfortunately, these are precisely the children it is hard to like. They may have few social skills, low self-confidence, little trust that adults will care for them, and "the belief that survival depends on their ability to manipulate and coerce others" (Watson, 2003, p. 281). They may be angry and defiant and have little or no empathy for others. Teachers must make even greater efforts to help them control their harmful behavior and teach them the social and emotional skills they did not learn during their early years.

In *Learning to Trust: Transforming Difficult Elementary Classrooms through Developmental Discipline* (2003), Marilyn Watson argues that knowledge of attachment theory can help teachers believe in the "ultimate goodwill" of "chronically misbehaving" children (p. 8). Instead of perceiving them as selfish individuals who need to be controlled by rewards and punishments, attachment theory encourages us to see them as anxious, insecure children who need (and crave) a responsive, nurturing relationship with a caregiver. Watson acknowledges that while teachers are building these relationships, they also have to find nonpunitive ways to prevent children from disrupting the classroom and hurting others. The primary goal is to build a community in which everyone feels cared for and safe.

ENGLISH-LANGUAGE LEARNERS

The past two decades have seen a significant increase in the number of school-aged children who speak a language other than English at home. According to community surveys conducted from 2005 through 2007, 54 million people, or nearly 20 percent of the general population aged five and over, speak a language other than English at home (U.S. Census Bureau, 2008). This is up from 14 percent in

1990 and 11 percent in 1980. California has the largest percentage of non-English-language speakers (42 percent), followed by New Mexico (36 percent), Texas (34 percent), New York (29 percent), Arizona and New Jersey (each about 28 percent), Nevada (27 percent), and Hawaii (24 percent). The 2000 U.S. census indicated that Spanish is the non-English language spoken most frequently at home, followed by Chinese, French, German, Tagalog, Vietnamese, Italian, Korean, Russian, Polish, and Arabic (Shin with Bruno, 2003).

The growth in the language minority population is reflected in public school enrollments. It has been estimated that in the 2005–2006 school year, over 5 million English-language learners (ELLs) were enrolled in public schools (pre-K to 12th grade). This represents more than 10 percent of the total school enrollment, and a 57 percent increase from 1995–1996 (NCELA, 2007).

Federal legislation provides funding and encouragement for programs to assist these children; however, there are no federally mandated programs like those provided for children who have disabilities. Instead, laws vary substantially from state to state. The state in which you teach may mandate such services or merely permit them; it may even prohibit them! Despite this variability, state laws generally call for the identification and assessment of second-language learners and describe options for special services. One option is a *bilingual education program,* such as Viviana's, which teaches children in their native language as well as in English, thus allowing them to learn academic subjects while they're learning English. In some states, if there are a given number of second-language learners in a district, speaking a common native language at approximately the same grade level, the district is required to provide bilingual programs.

PAUSE AND REFLECT

Bilingual education programs are extremely controversial, and in some states, laws have been passed restricting bilingual education and substituting programs that stress the use of English. Even the parents of some English-language learners oppose bilingual education, contending that it hinders children's learning of English. At the same time, scholars in bilingual education stress the importance to children of receiving instruction in their first language to build on their existing literacy skills. What do *you* think about this issue?

When English-language learners come from many different language backgrounds, bilingual education programs are not practical. In this case, schools typically place children in regular English-only classrooms and pull them out for instruction from a teacher specially trained in teaching *English as a Second Language* (ESL). Because the focus is on learning English, children with different native languages can be in the same room. A few years ago, for example, Ken had six students—from Mexico, Korea, India, Sri Lanka, and Turkey—who regularly left his room for ESL instruction; there they joined students who spoke Russian, Hebrew, and Chinese.

In general education, English-only classrooms, English-language learners will undoubtedly have problems if they are expected to "sink or swim" and if teachers are unwilling to make any modifications. ELLs may be able to function admirably, however, if you implement some of the environmental supports used in "sheltered instruction" or "Specially Designed Academic Instruction in English" (SDAIE). A comprehensive model of SDAIE includes five components

(Diaz-Rico & Weed, 2009). First—and crucial—is the *teacher's attitude;* unless the teacher is open and willing to learn from students, SDAIE cannot be successful. The second component is *content;* lessons must have both subject matter and language objectives, and lessons must be planned and implemented with language in mind. Third is an emphasis on *comprehensibility;* lessons must include explicit strategies that enhance children's understanding (e.g., modeling, frequent comprehension checks, adjustment in use of language). Fourth are *connections,* reflecting the importance of connecting curriculum to students' background and experiences. The final component is *interaction;* students in a sheltered English classroom need frequent opportunities to work together, to clarify concepts in their native language, and to represent learning in a variety of ways. (See Diaz-Rico & Weed, 2009, for additional information on these five components.)

Having a number of English-language learners in your class will add to the cultural richness and global understanding of your students. It may also be a source of stress, especially for new teachers. Questions are likely to arise about how to meet the needs of your second-language learners without shortchanging the rest of the class; however, incorporating some sheltered English strategies into your teaching and following the suggestions listed in the accompanying Practical Tips box should benefit *everyone.*

CHILDREN WITH DISABILITIES AND ADHD

Stuart is an autistic child in Barbara's classroom. His vocal speech is very limited and difficult to understand, but he is able to type independently to communicate. For brief exchanges, Stuart uses an electronic organizer; for more elaborate interactions, academic writing, and note taking, he uses a laptop. In mathematics, he uses a calculator. Stuart's individualized education program (IEP) specifies that in addition to these accommodations, he is to have a full-time, male aide (a "teacher associate," or TA) to assist him during the day. The TA helps to refocus Stuart when his attention wanders and to calm him when he becomes frustrated, distressed, or agitated. Stuart appears to be flourishing in the general education classroom. In February, when asked how things were going, Stuart typed this message: "SCHOOL IS REALLY THE GREATEST."

Malika is in Garnetta's third-grade classroom. Her skills in reading and math are far below those of her classmates. In addition, Malika is extremely immature: She cries a lot, gets frustrated easily, and frequently falls out of her chair. Sometimes Garnetta finds Malika sitting under her desk. She is often defensive and denies her involvement in any misbehavior ("I didn't do it!"). Classified as "learning disabled," Malika has an individualized education program that specifies the goals and objectives for the academic year and how instruction is to be modified to meet her needs. In addition, it specifies that Malika is to go to a resource room every day, where a special education teacher provides instruction in reading and math.

PRACTICAL TIPS FOR

HELPING ENGLISH-LANGUAGE LEARNERS

- Provide a safe, welcoming environment for language risk taking. Be aware of your own biases toward cultures that differ from your own.

- Take time to learn about the discourse patterns of cultures other than your own so that you don't misinterpret students' words, gestures, or actions.

- Communicate the expectation that all students can succeed, and show students that you are eager to help them do so.

- Increase time and opportunities for meaningful talk.

- Find ways for all students to participate in group activities, giving them roles that are less dependent on language use (e.g., have them draw pictures or serve as timekeepers).

- Encourage English speaking while honoring students' first language and culture. Allow students to use their native language at appropriate times (e.g., when they need to process new material with another person who shares their language, or when they need to construct meaning from a reading selection).

- Encourage children to tell about their culture. Listen carefully and ask questions. View ethnic and linguistic diversity within a classroom not as a problem but as an asset from which both teachers and students can profit.

- Build on and utilize students' background knowledge and personal interests.

- Encourage students to write about topics of their choice and for real-world purposes.

- Encourage parents to develop and maintain their primary language at home.

- Learn and use some second language yourself with students.

- Emphasize collaborative over individual work.

- Emphasize doing rather than telling.

- Speak a bit more slowly, and enunciate clearly, with your mouth in direct view of the students.

- Make the language of the text comprehensible by interpreting it in simple, everyday language.

- Offer periodic summaries.

- Paraphrase questions and statements to allow for different levels of proficiency. Use synonyms to clarify the meaning of unknown words.

- Control vocabulary and sentence structure (for instance, if you use idioms such as "It's raining cats and dogs," explain what they mean).

- Ask questions that require different degrees of English proficiency in responding (e.g., nonverbal signals to communicate agreement or disagreement, "yes or no" questions, questions that call for single-word or short answers).

- When students respond to your questions, focus on the content of the response, rather than on its form.

- Use objects, video, pictures, and/or movement to increase comprehensibility and provide a context for learning.

- Apply Specially Designed Academic Instruction in English (SDAIE) strategies across the curriculum. Often known as "sheltered instruction," SDAIE focuses on core curriculum content and uses a rich variety of techniques and materials, such as artifacts, visuals, video, storyboarding, movement, role plays, and collaborative learning.

(continued on next page)

- Think aloud and model a variety of reading comprehension strategies (e.g., making connections, predicting, inferring).

- Use a variety of reading supports, such as text tours and picture walks (to preview material), graphic organizers (story maps, character analyses), and text signposts (chapter headings, bold print).

- Use a variety of writing supports, such as group composing, graphic organizers, and drawing-based texts.

Sources: Cary, 2007; Henning, 2008; Romero, Mercado, & Vazquez-Faria, 1987.

Stuart and Malika's presence in general education classrooms, the supplemental services they receive, and their individualized education programs are a direct result of the Individuals with Disabilities Education Act (reauthorized as IDEA 2004 and also referred to as the Individuals with Disabilities Education Improvement Act or IDEIA), federal legislation mandating a "free appropriate public education" for all children with disabilities. According to IDEA, *disability* is defined as mental retardation; a hearing impairment, including deafness; a speech or language impairment; a visual impairment including blindness; serious emotional disturbance; an orthopedic impairment; autism; traumatic brain injury; other health impairment (e.g., limited strength or vitality due to chronic or acute health problems such as asthma or diabetes); a specific learning disability; deaf-blindness; or multiple disabilities.

Sometimes called the "mainstreaming law," IDEA requires *students with disabilities to be educated with their peers without disabilities to the maximum extent appropriate, with the supplementary aids and services needed to help them achieve.* The general education, mainstream class needs to be considered the "least restrictive environment." However, the law also requires schools to have available a *continuum of alternative placements* (e.g., a special classroom or school, hospital, residential institution) if the nature or severity of a child's disability precludes the possibility of a satisfactory education in a general education setting.

How schools implement the guidelines set forth by IDEA varies greatly. For example, in Barbara's school there are no-self contained special education classrooms. Rather, students with special needs are given assistance within the regular classroom and are pulled out for only part of the day to receive additional resource help. On the other hand, Courtney's school has one "full inclusion classroom" at each primary grade level, co-taught by one general education teacher and one special education teacher.

✂ PAUSE AND REFLECT

What do you think about the inclusion of children with disabilities in the general education classroom? Do your views depend on the kind of disability (e.g., physical, emotional, cognitive)? What are your specific concerns, if any, about teaching in inclusive classrooms?

In the following sections, we summarize the characteristics of students with learning disabilities, emotional and behavioral disorders, autism and Asperger syndrome, and ADHD, and we suggest some strategies for working effectively with these students. We then discuss a variety of general strategies that may be useful as you work to achieve a classroom that is truly inclusive.

Learning Disabilities

More students are identified as having "specific learning disabilities" than any other type of disability. Of the 10 percent of school-age children identified as having disabilities, just over 50 percent of this group (or 5 percent of the total school-age population) are diagnosed as LD, and the number has been increasing dramatically (Vaughn, Bos, & Schumm, 2003). It is estimated that every public school classroom contains at least one student with a learning disability, and probably several more (Henley, Ramsey, & Algozzine, 2002).

It is difficult to get a satisfactory definition of LD because there are many types of learning disabilities, and children diagnosed with LD are a heterogeneous group. The IDEA defines *learning disabilities* as a "disorder in one or more of the basic psychological processes involved in understanding or in using language, spoken or written," which results in learning problems that are not explained by some other disability (such as mental retardation). Many schools make a diagnosis of LD when there is a "severe discrepancy" between intellectual ability and academic performance. However, the discrepancy criterion is a source of concern to many parents and educators, since children have to struggle for several years before the disparity between achievement and ability is severe enough to allow diagnosis. This means that most students with LD do not qualify for services until late second or third grade—a practice that seems to set these children up for failure (Vaughn, Bos, & Schumm, 2003).

The reauthorization of IDEA in 2004 allows schools to use a child's *response to intervention* (RTI) as part of the procedures to identify students with learning disabilities. RTI involves two components: (1) implementation of an intensive intervention and (2) ongoing assessment to monitor student progress or response (Richards, Pavri, Golez, & Murphy, 2007). If early intervention fails to benefit the child, then he or she many qualify as having a specific learning disability. (See Pietrangelo & Giuliani, 2008 in the further reading section for more information on this practice.)

Although it is difficult to list a set of characteristics that adequately describe all children with LD, Table 5.1 presents some signs that may indicate a learning disability. If a child displays a number of these problems, then teachers should consider the possibility of a learning disability and seek advice from special services personnel.

Ken learned that one of his students had a learning disability when he met with each of his students and their families before the school year began. This early discovery allowed Ken the time to talk with the student's parents about their expectations, review the child's individualized education program (IEP) carefully,

TABLE 5.1 Possible Indicators of a Learning Disability

When a child has a learning disability, he or she

- May have trouble learning the alphabet, rhyming words, or connecting letters to their sounds.
- May have trouble blending sounds into words.
- May make many mistakes when reading aloud, and repeat and pause often.
- May not understand what he or she reads.
- May confuse similar letters and words, such as *b* and *d, was* and *saw.*
- May have real trouble with spelling.
- May have very messy handwriting.
- May have difficulty with fine motor activities.
- May have trouble remembering the sounds that letters make or hearing slight differences between words.
- May have trouble understanding and following directions.
- May have trouble organizing what he or she wants to say or not be able to think of the word he or she needs for writing or conversation.
- May confuse math symbols and misread numbers.
- May not be able to retell a story in order.
- May not know where to begin a task or how to go on from there.

Source: Adapted from Fact Sheet 7 of the National Dissemination Center for Children with Disabilities (2004).

and do some reading on this student's particular areas of need. Ken talked to us about this process:

 I formulated the idea that this student could grow and learn as much as anyone else in my classroom. This would be a task that the student and I would share. For my part, I typed up a list of ways that I could help the student, and the student agreed to help by being accountable and responsible. When work is missing there are no excuses, just a plan to get it done. We made an agreement to try our best to work together.

Reviews of research indicate that three teaching strategies are particularly powerful in promoting the academic success of students with LD (Vaughn, Gersten, & Chard, 2000). First, teachers need to match tasks to the student's abilities and skills, sequencing examples and problems to allow high levels of student success. Second, small-group instruction with no more than six students appears to be especially beneficial. Finally, students with LD need to learn self-questioning strategies (i.e., to ask themselves questions while reading or working on a mathematics problem). Teachers can model this by thinking aloud about text being read or mathematics problems to be solved. These instructional practices are hardly revolutionary, but unfortunately, they are too rarely implemented in classrooms (Vaughn, Gersten, & Chard, 2000).

Emotional Disturbance and Behavioral Disorders

The terms *emotional disturbance* and *behavioral disorder* are often used interchangeably. Although IDEA uses the term *emotional disturbance,* many professionals prefer the term *behavioral disorder,* which they feel is less stigmatizing (Vaugh, Bos, & Schumm, 2003).

IDEA defines an emotional disturbance as a condition characterized by one or more of the following: an inability to learn that cannot be explained by intellectual, sensory, or health factors; an inability to build or maintain satisfactory interpersonal relationships with peers and teachers; inappropriate types of behavior or feeling under normal circumstances; a general, pervasive mood of unhappiness or depression; or a tendency to develop physical symptoms or fears associated with personal or school problems. As you can see, like the term *learning disabilities,* the term *emotional disturbance* actually encompasses a variety of conditions, from conduct disorders to depression.

When teachers are asked to talk about "problem children," they tend to speak about those who are disruptive, aggressive, and defiant and whose behaviors interfere with others—children whose behavioral disorders are *externalizing* (Vaughn, Bos, & Schumm, 2003). Listen to what Barbara has to say about Mark, the boy in her class who has a diagnosis of emotional disturbance:

> Mark is often sullen and always thinks that he's being treated unfairly. He has a "short fuse," and little things (like another child telling him what to do) will trigger an outburst of screaming, throwing things, and shoving. He has difficulty concentrating, so reading is hard for him, and his fine motor skills are poor. This leads to frustration, and frustration leads to outbursts. He can't process what I'm saying when his emotions take over and he's in the middle of one of his storms. His body gets rigid and he absolutely can't be touched when he's in that mode. But he will respond to a single, sharp comment, like "stop" or "don't." Then he needs time to calm down. He goes to a "cool-off space" that he chose. For Mark, it's sitting quietly by the gerbils, but I've had other kids who curled up on the rug with a pillow, or sat at their desk with their head down. Whatever, it's a calming down routine that we agreed on ahead of time for "getting past the moment." More than anything, it's important for Mark to know that I like him and I care about him. He needs to trust me, to know that I won't do anything that would hurt him.

Students like Mark have a "conduct disorder" (CD), characterized by a "repetitive and persistent pattern of behavior in which the basic rights of others or major age-appropriate societal norms or rules are violated" (American Psychiatric Association, 2000). It's easy to identify students who display this kind of behavior, but what do you do about it? First, it's essential to be proactive. Too often, teachers react only to the student's negative behaviors, but students with CD must learn how to behave more appropriately. This means monitoring students' behavior closely, so that you can prompt, recognize, and reward acceptable behaviors (i.e., "catch 'em being good") and anticipate and head off unacceptable behavior.

Second, students with CD can benefit from direct teaching of appropriate social behavior, with rewards provided for the display of these behaviors, as well as a response-cost procedure in which points (or tokens) are lost for inappropriate behavior (Ostrander, 2004). Third, exploring the intent or purpose of the unacceptable behavior may reveal what a student needs in order to behave more appropriately and to learn, such as getting help with a difficult or frustrating assignment. (This is discussed more fully in the section on functional behavioral assessment in Chapter 12.) Some additional suggestions are listed in the Practical Tips box. Also refer to the section on defiance in Chapter 12 and to the section on de-escalating potentially explosive situations in Chapter 13.

Children with emotional disturbance may also show a pattern of *internalizing* behaviors, such as shyness, withdrawal, anxiety, and depression (Vaughn, Bos, & Schumm, 2003). Consider the following journal entry written by a student teacher we know:

> *I'm really worried about one of my kids. She's unbelievably shy and withdrawn. It took me a long time to even notice her. She never participates in class discussions, never raises her hand, and never volunteers for anything. When I call on her, she looks down and doesn't answer, or her answer is so soft that I can't hear her. I've watched her during lunch time in the cafeteria, and she doesn't seem to have any friends. The other kids aren't mean to her—they act like she doesn't even exist—and that's sort of the way I feel too!*

PRACTICAL TIPS FOR

HELPING CHILDREN WITH CONDUCT DISORDER

- Make sure your classroom environment is organized, predictable, and structured.
- Plan and implement activities to promote a sense of community (see Chapter 3).
- Actively work on establishing positive relationships; provide consistent, positive attention and decrease negative comments.
- Closely monitor behavior, and acknowledge and reward positive behavior.
- Directly teach social skills (e.g., anger management skills).
- Provide structured choices ("Would you prefer to do your math or your writing first?" "Do you want to do this alone or work in a group?").
- Have a plan for removing the child if he or she has a tantrum.
- Learn to anticipate and de-escalate problem situations (see Chapter 13).
- Use self-management approaches (see Chapter 12) such as self-monitoring, self-evaluation, and self-instruction.
- Develop and implement contingency contracts (see Chapter 12).
- Make sure that instruction is appropriate for the student's level of ability, because frustration and academic failure can exacerbate students' emotional/behavioral problems.

TABLE 5.2 Indicators of Early-Onset Depression

Indecision, lack of concentration, or forgetfulness

Change in personality, such as increased anger, irritability, moodiness, agitation, or whining

Change in sleep patterns and appetite

Loss of energy

Lack of enthusiasm or motivation

Loss of interest in personal appearance and hygiene

Hopelessness, helplessness, and sadness

Frequent physical complaints, such as headaches and stomachaches

Thoughts of suicide or death

Low self-esteem, frequently expressed through self-blame and self-criticism

Withdrawal from friends and activities once enjoyed

Poor school performance

Students like this, who act sad, reserved, withdrawn, or irritable, may actually be suffering from childhood depression. Table 5.2 lists the signs that suggest depression in children.

It is important to consult with a guidance counselor or school psychologist if you are concerned that a child is depressed (Schlozman, 2001). Certainly, journals, drawings, or essays that suggest suicidal or homicidal thoughts warrant a formal referral. In addition, teachers need to understand that depressed students often feel as though they have little to contribute. To counter these feelings, you need to communicate respect and confidence in the student's abilities, minimize the possibility of embarrassment (e.g., by calling on depressed students to answer questions that have no clearly correct answer), and encourage them to assist younger or less able students. Most important, you need to forge a connection with the depressed student. Adults who suffered from depression when they were younger frequently remember the efforts of a specific teacher as key to their recovery (Schlozman, 2001).

Pervasive Developmental Disorders: Autism and Asperger Syndrome

Autism and Asperger syndrome are two "pervasive developmental disorders" (PDDs) or "autism spectrum disorders" (ASDs), a cluster of disorders characterized by marked impairments in the development of social interaction and communication skills. Biological and neurological in origin, autism and Asperger syndrome (AS) are generally evident by three to five years of age (Hagin, 2004). Just how frequently PDDs occur is not entirely clear. However, the Centers for Disease Control and Prevention (2007) reported that autism spectrum disorders affect approximately 1 child in every 150. Furthermore, the prevalence of PDDs appears to be increasing dramatically. For example, between 1998 and 2003, there was an increase of 244 percent in identified cases of autism (Vaughn, Bos, & Schumm, 2003). Why this is happening is unclear. Some educators hypothesize that the increase is due to better assessment measures, changes in diagnostic criteria, and growing awareness of PDDs among parents and professionals, rather than to an actual rise in incidence (Hagin, 2004).

Children with autism display a lack of responsiveness and unawareness of social situations; for example, they may make little or no eye contact, show little awareness of social situations, and exhibit a lack of interest in sharing enjoyable activities with other people. In addition, they may have little or no spoken language, and those who do develop language may use it idiosyncratically (e.g., repeating sentences said to them, a condition known as echolalia). Finally, individuals with autism often exhibit restricted, repetitive patterns of behavior (e.g., body rocking or hand flapping; inflexible adherence to routines or rituals) and have a consuming preoccupation with specific topics (e.g., train schedules). Hypersensitivity to sensory input such as noise, lights, and touch is also common. Autism is four times more common in boys than in girls (National Dissemination Center for Children with Disabilities, 2003).

There is ongoing debate about whether Asperger syndrome (AS) is an independent diagnostic category or a mild form of autism (Myles, Gagnon, Moyer, & Trautman, 2004). In fact, the Individuals with Disabilities Education Act (IDEA) does not recognize AS as a specific disability category, so children with Asperger syndrome are often served under the diagnostic labels of autism, behavior disorders, or learning disabilities. Like autism, AS is characterized by marked impairment in social interaction. However, children with AS often desire interaction—they just lack the skills and knowledge needed to initiate and respond appropriately in social situations. For example, they often demonstrate an inability to understand the perspectives of others and have difficulty understanding nonverbal social cues. Although individuals with AS have no clinically significant delay in cognition and do not have delayed language development, they have difficulty understanding the subtleties of language, such as irony and humor (National Dissemination Center, 2003) and their voice quality may be flat, stilted, and "robotic." They also have a restricted range of interests or obsessions, developing an exhaustive knowledge of one topic (e.g., monsters, numbers, or movies) on which they give long-winded lectures. In addition, children with AS tend to have poor motor skills and to be clumsy and uncoordinated. Like those with autism, children with AS show an "apparently inflexible adherence to specific, nonfunctional routines or rituals" (American Psychiatric Association, 2000, p. 84).

Listen to Courtney describe a student in her class who was eventually diagnosed with Asperger syndrome:

 Brittany is very bright, but she doesn't like to work and won't write. She gets very upset at any change in the routine. If I have to terminate an activity, she will scream and run to the door, yelling, "That's it, I quit. I'm out of here." We made a quiet spot for her by the dramatic play area, so that she can go there when she is upset. She'll scream and cry whenever she is upset, which of course is disruptive to the rest of the class. She'll say, "I have my crazy brain today" or "I drank evil juice at lunch." If a student walks by her that she doesn't like, she will scream. Although she has some inappropriate interactions with other children and plays a lot by herself, she is also incredibly sweet. The students will play a tag game with her, and when she catches them, she will hug them. It doesn't seem to upset them, and rather they seem to like it.

It is important to note that manifestations of autism and AS can range from mild to severe. Thus, two children with the same diagnosis may function very differently and require different kinds and amounts of support. Although there are no cures for PDDs, educational interventions can be effective in bringing about improvements. Students with autism can benefit from augmentative and alternative communication systems. For example, they can learn to point to a picture on a communication board to indicate preferences during lunch, free play, or academic work (Vaughn, Bos, & Schumm, 2003). Because students with autism and AS adhere rigidly to routines, it is essential that you create and follow a consistent classroom schedule. It's helpful to use a Velcro board displaying pictures of the daily activities next to clocks showing the times at which the activities occur. If a change in the schedule is necessary, you can communicate this by rearranging the pictures. See the Practical Tips box for additional suggestions on helping children with AS; also refer to Kline and Silver (2004) for a comprehensive discussion.

PRACTICAL TIPS FOR

HELPING CHILDREN WITH ASPERGER SYNDROME

- *Establish a "home base,"* a safe area in which a student can calm down, away from the overstimulation of the classroom (such as a counselor's office, a resource room, or the nurse's office). Home base should *not* be used for time-out or punishment.

- *Use "priming" to familiarize students with academic material prior to its use in school.* Priming can reduce the stress associated with new tasks and increase success. A typical priming session lasts 10–15 minutes and is held in a quiet space the evening or morning before the materials are to be used.

- *Modify the environment:*
  Seat the child in an area free of distraction.
  Keep the child's space free of unnecessary materials.
  Use checklists to help the student be organized.
  Provide opportunities for the student to move around.

- *Modify instruction:*
  Because fine motor skills can make handwriting difficult, let the student type
      or record responses.
  Because verbal information can be difficult to process, use visual supports
      whenever possible.
  Color-code assignments.
  Provide the student with a skeletal outline of the main ideas.
  Schedule short, frequent conferences with the student to check for
      comprehension.
  Break assignments into shorter tasks.
  Allow the student to use a computer or calculator.

Source: Myles, Gagnon, Moyer, & Trautman, 2004.

Attention-Deficit/Hyperactivity Disorder

Although teachers often find it particularly challenging to work with children who have attention-deficit/hyperactivity disorder (ADHD), this condition is *not* included in IDEA's definition of children with disabilities. For this reason, students with ADHD are not eligible for services under IDEA unless they also fall into other disability categories (e.g., learning disabilities, serious emotional disturbance, other health impairment). They may, however, be able to receive special services under Section 504 of the Rehabilitation Act of 1973. Section 504 prohibits discrimination on the basis of disability by recipients of federal funds and requires that public schools that receive federal funding address the needs of children with disabilities. As defined in Section 504, a person with a disability is any person who has a physical or mental impairment substantially limiting a major life activity such as learning. Thus children with ADHD may fit within that definition.

No diagnostic test for ADHD is currently available, but Table 5.3 lists the symptoms that suggest an individual has ADHD. Five conditions must be met for a positive diagnosis: (1) Six or more symptoms listed in the table must be present; (2) the symptoms have to have persisted for at least six months; (3) the symptoms have to have appeared before seven years of age; (4) the symptoms must result in impaired functioning in at least two settings; and (5) the symptoms must not occur exclusively during the course of another pervasive developmental or psychotic disorder, and must not be accounted for by another mental disorder. Keep in mind that any one of the behaviors can be normal, especially in young children. It is when a child frequently displays a large number of these behaviors at a developmentally inappropriate age that the possibility of ADHD should be considered.

It is estimated that 3 to 5 percent of school-age children in the United States have ADHD, with far more boys than girls affected (Wodrich, 2000). The reason for the disparity is not clear. Some researchers believe the explanation lies in brain biochemistry or structure; others point to the way boys are socialized, which may make it harder to sit quietly and attend. Still others suggest subtle discrimination on the part of elementary teachers, who are predominantly women (Wodrich, 2000).

Children with ADHD often have difficulties in school. They may be underproductive or disorganized, failing to complete their work or even losing it. They may also have problems with memory, language, visual perception, and fine motor control, which interfere with academic achievement. Indeed, as many as 35 percent of children with ADHD may have learning disabilities, compared with 3 percent of all children (Wodrich, 2000). Finally—and not surprisingly—children with ADHD may have problems meeting behavioral expectations and getting along with other children.

⌘ PAUSE AND REFLECT

In recent years, dramatic increases in the number of children who have been diagnosed and treated for ADHD have stirred debate not only about the possibility of overdiagnosis but even about whether the disorder really exists. Skeptics criticize teachers for wanting to suppress children's natural enthusiasm and energy, parents for failing to provide appropriate guidance and discipline, and physicians for overmedicating. What do you think about this?

TABLE 5.3 Symptoms of Attention-Deficit/Hyperactivity Disorder

Either (1) or (2):

(1) Six (or more) of the following symptoms of inattention have persisted for at least 6 months to a degree that is maladaptive and inconsistent with developmental level:

Inattention

    (a) Often fails to give close attention to details or makes careless mistakes in schoolwork, work, or other activities.

    (b) Often has difficulty sustaining attention in tasks or play activities.

    (c) Often does not seem to listen when spoken to directly.

    (d) Often does not follow through on instructions and fails to finish schoolwork, chores, or duties in the workplace (not due to oppositional behavior or failure to understand directions).

    (e) Often has difficulty organizing tasks and activities.

    (f) Often avoids, dislikes, or is reluctant to engage in tasks that require sustained mental effort (such as schoolwork or homework).

    (g) Often loses things necessary for tasks or activities (e.g. toys, school assignments, pencils, books, tools).

    (h) Is often easily distracted by extraneous stimuli.

    (i) Is often forgetful in daily activities.

(2) Six (or more) of the following symptoms of hyperactivity-impulsivity have persisted for at least 6 months to a degree that is maladaptive and inconsistent with developmental level:

Hyperactivity

    (a) Often fidgets with hands or feet or squirms in seat.

    (b) Often leaves seat in classroom or in other situations in which remaining seated is expected.

    (c) Often runs about or climbs excessively in situations in which it is inappropriate (in adolescents or adults, may be limited to subjective feelings of restlessness).

    (d) Often has difficulty playing or engaging in leisure activities quietly.

    (e) Is often "on the go" or often acts as if "driven by a motor."

    (f) Often talks excessively.

Impulsivity

    (g) Often blurts out answers before questions have been completed.

    (h) Often has difficulty awaiting turn.

    (i) Often interrupts or intrudes on others (e.g., butts into conversations or games).

Source: Reprinted with permission from the *Diagnostic and statistical manual of mental disorders*, Text Revision, Fourth Edition. (Copyright 2000), American Psychiatric Association.

In order to help children with ADHD, your classroom needs to be predictable, secure, and structured. Behavioral expectations must be clear, and consequences must be fair and consistent. The Practical Tips box offers some more specific suggestions.

PRACTICAL TIPS FOR

HELPING CHILDREN WITH ADHD

- Provide structure, routine, predictability, and consistency.
- Make sure that behavioral expectations are clear.
- Tape a copy of the schedule on their desks.
- Seat them close to you, among attentive, well-focused students (the second row is better than the first).
- Make frequent eye contact.
- Make sure their desks are free of distractions (provide cardboard dividers to block out distractions).
- Provide a quiet work area or a "private office" to which children can move for better concentration.
- Provide headphones to block out noise during seatwork or other times that require concentration.
- Provide opportunities to move around in legitimate ways (e.g., exercise breaks, doing errands).
- Use physical contact to focus attention (e.g., a hand on a shoulder).
- Develop private signals to help focus attention.
- Ease transitions by providing cues and warnings.
- Use positive reinforcement and behavior modification techniques.
- Modify assignments:
  Cut the written workload.
  Break the assignment into manageable parts.
- Limit the amount of homework.
- Allow more time on assignments or tests.
- Assist with organization (e.g., assignment pads; checklists; color-coded notebooks for different subjects; accordion folders for loose papers).
- Try to give students at least one task each day that they can do successfully.
- Try to call students when they are paying attention; use their first names before calling on them.
- Provide extra sets of books to keep at home so that children are not overwhelmed after an absence and to prevent problems caused by forgetting books.
- Provide access to a computer, along with keyboard and word processing instruction; do not remove access to the computer as a penalty.
- DO NOT PUNISH; DO NOT ASSUME CHILDREN ARE LAZY; DO NOT GIVE UP.

Sources: Adapted from Rief, 1993 and CHADD Facts, 1993.

General Strategies for Helping Children with Disabilities and ADHD

Obtain Access to Support and Services

To obtain appropriate assistance for students who may have special needs, you must become familiar with the procedures and resources in your own school.

The best way to do this is to speak with people who can provide guidance and direction—experienced teachers, the principal, the school nurse, special educators, school psychologists, and guidance counselors. Ken emphasizes that

> **what's important is that you talk with people. The more you talk with people, the less the problem is just yours, and that makes it easier to deal with. You also need to keep in mind that if you go to one special services person and you're in the wrong place, they'll bounce you to the** right place. And be sure to build rapport with people involved in special services. If you build rapport, you're going to get help.

Exactly what kind of help will you receive when you make contact with your school's special services personnel? Generally, the first step is to provide you with additional suggestions for addressing the child's needs. These suggestions may include adjusting the curriculum, tutoring by a peer or an aide, implementing a behavior modification plan—even something as simple as changing the child's seat. If these interventions are not successful, and special services personnel believe the child should be considered for placement in special education, the classroom teacher initiates a formal request for evaluation.

Specific referral procedures vary from district to district, but the teacher usually completes a form describing the child's academic performance and classroom behavior and the interventions that have already been tried. The form used in the district in which Garnetta and Viviana teach asks for the following information:

- Family information (parents' birthplace, education, occupation, residence, and marital status; siblings).
- Contact with parents with regard to problem.
- Steps that the teacher has taken to deal with the problem.
- Description of the child's social and emotional adjustment (e.g., relationship with other children, attitude toward authority, effort, special interests and aptitudes).
- Previous schools attended.
- Attendance record for last two years.
- Standardized test data.
- Achievement level in reading and mathematics.
- Remedial services received.
- Health record (to be completed by the school nurse).

IDEA requires that parental consent be obtained before a child can be evaluated. When parents give their permission, the referral process can proceed: The child is given a variety of tests, a conference is held with parents, and the results of the evaluation are discussed. If it is determined that the student's problems result from a disability, a classification is agreed upon, and an individualized education

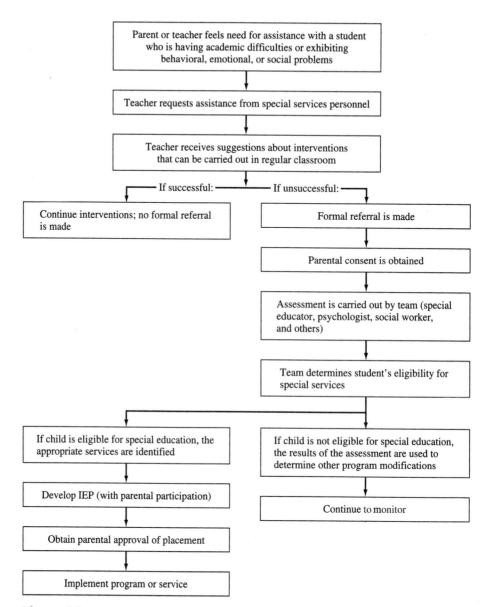

Figure 5.2   A Typical Referral Process

program is developed (as will be discussed in the following section). A flow chart outlining this generic referral process appears in Figure 5.2.

It's important to approach special services armed with specific information about the child and about the interventions you've already tried. Complaints such as "He's driving me crazy," "She constantly demands attention," or "He just can't hack it in fourth grade" are not helpful. The more detailed your information can be, the more likely you are to receive assistance. Here are some of our teachers' suggestions about the kinds of information to bring:

- An overall description of the child (both strengths and weaknesses).
- A detailed description of the child's inappropriate behavior:

  When does the child exhibit the behavior?
  How frequently does the child exhibit the behavior?
  What antecedent events set off the behavior?
  What is the duration of the behavior?
  What is the reaction of other students in the class?

- A detailed description of the child's academic difficulties (with work samples to support your description).
- Information about the family (if possible).
- Efforts on your part to correct or deal with the problem.
- How you'd like to be helped or what type of help you believe the child needs.

Once you've reported a problem, it's human nature to expect everybody to drop whatever they're doing and provide you with immediate help. But special services tend to be overworked and understaffed, and help is not always prompt. Barbara reminds us:

 You're dealing with the problem every day, and you're frustrated. You want an immediate resolution, but you have to be realistic. Special services is a slow process. I'm not the only person they deal with. They work with all the teachers in the building and with the kids who are already classified. It can take a long time for a child to be evaluated. But special services people will come in and consult with me. They'll give me ideas for working with a child, strategies I've forgotten to use. Or they'll fill me in on family histories. You've got to remember that they're not miracle workers. They're not wonders. But they will validate my problem, provide me with advice and support, and give time and understanding to a student.

Be an Active Participant in the IEP and 504 Planning Process

Once a student has been formally evaluated and it is determined that the student qualifies for special services, a meeting will be called to decide the extent to which accommodations will be provided for the particular student. IDEA requires that an individual education program (IEP) be developed for each student with a disability. IEPs are developed by a team made up of a representative of the local education agency (e.g., an administrator who can commit school district resources), the student's general education teacher, the special education teacher who will have primary responsibility for implementing the IEP, parents or guardians, a person who can interpret the instructional implications of the evaluation results, the student (when appropriate), and other individuals at the discretion of the parent or school.

Similarly, a student who is eligible for special services under Section 504 of the Rehabilitation Act will have a "504 plan" outlining the accommodations and services needed to ensure that the student receives an appropriate education. Like the IEP, a 504 plan is developed by a team, although the team's composition is not specified by law.

Some students in elementary classrooms already have an IEP or 504 plan developed during their previous year(s) of school. It is your responsibility as their current teacher to follow the accommodations and guidelines set forth in that plan, and to make sure that you properly document all progress toward meeting their goals. In extreme cases, the compliance of individual teachers and the schools and/or districts in which they work has been questioned; that is, it has been alleged that they did not follow the student's IEP or 504 plan. This year, for example, the parents of a student in Ken's school district filed a lawsuit claiming that their child's teacher failed to follow their child's IEP. Thus it is critical that you diligently attend to each child's IEP and keep track of the accommodations made to ensure that you have implemented the IEP or 504 plan as it was intended.

Each student's IEP or 504 plan is reviewed each year, and teachers have an important role in suggesting new goals and accommodations for the student. You can be an active participant in the process by providing data and work samples from the student and by suggesting approaches that you believe might be effective in meeting the child's specific needs. The ideal situation involves teachers, parents, school administrators, special education teachers, and (when appropriate) the students themselves working as a team to provide the most effective educational experience for all students with special needs.

Create an Accepting Climate

The success of inclusion largely depends on a teacher's ability and willingness to create a positive atmosphere that is accepting of individual differences. You can promote a positive climate by making it clear that all students are accepted, valued members of the class, establishing norms that emphasize belonging and respect, and implementing group activities that foster interaction between students with disabilities and their nondisabled peers (Soodak & McCarthy, 2006). Students with special needs may display significant social deficiencies and have difficulty establishing friendships (Meadan & Monda-Amaya, 2008); in this case, you can help students find common interests, regardless of their abilities or special needs (Grandin, 2007). When social interaction is fostered through commonalities, students are more likely to accept each other as equal members of the classroom community. See Chapter 3 for additional ideas.

Coordinate and Collaborate with Special Education Teachers and Paraprofessionals

As inclusion has become more widespread, so too has the practice of having general educators co-teach with special educators. *Co-teaching* is defined as two or more people sharing responsibility for planning, teaching, and evaluating some or all of the students assigned to a classroom (Villa, Thousand, & Nevin, 2008).

Co-teaching, also known as collaborative teaching or cooperative teaching, can take a variety of forms (Cook & Friend, 1995). For example, in the "one teaching, one assisting" model, one teacher takes responsibility for instruction while the other offers assistance and support to individuals or small groups. In "parallel teaching," teachers jointly plan instruction, but each delivers it to a heterogeneous group consisting of half the class, and in "team teaching," both teachers share the planning and instruction of students.

Although co-teaching can be very effective, it also poses challenges for both parties. Some of these difficulties stem from inadequate school supports (e.g., lack of common preparation time), personality conflicts, and a lack of clarity about roles and responsibilities in co-taught classrooms. In order to avoid these problems, it is essential to discuss the roles that each teacher will play in the general education classroom. The Practical Tips box lists strategies for enhancing the likelihood that co-teaching will be successful.

The use of paraprofessionals or teaching assistants has become another popular method of supporting students with disabilities in general education classrooms. (This is the model used in Barbara's classroom, where both Stuart and Mark have paraprofessionals known as teacher associates.) In fact, in many schools, having a paraprofessional accompany a student with disabilities to class is the "primary or exclusive" way in which inclusion is accomplished (Giangreco & Doyle, 2002, p. 2). Paraprofessionals can play a vital role in inclusive classrooms, but all too often, they become the student's actual instructor, while the teacher becomes

Practical Tips for

ENHANCING THE SUCCESS OF CO-TEACHING

- **Take baby steps.** Discuss your respective understandings of co-teaching. Begin by having a special educator provide in-class support so that you become comfortable working together. Examine various models of co-teaching.

- **Assess the school environment.** Discuss the kind of administrative support that is needed (especially with respect to common planning time). Find out whether such support will be forthcoming.

- **Get to know your partner.** Discuss your expectations with respect to roles and responsibilities regarding
    Planning whole-class instruction
    Planning modifications for individual students
    Conducting instruction
    Grading
    Parental contact
    Discipline

- **Use good communication.** Recognize the other person's frame of reference, and use good listening skills to ensure that miscommunication does not occur. Respect each teacher's expertise. Talk about how to ensure that both teachers are actively involved and that neither feels over- or underutilized.

Source: Adapted from Murawski, 2005.

the delegator (Giangreco & Doyle, 2002). When this happens, we have a situation in which those who are least qualified to teach are responsible for instructing the students who present the most complex challenges.

If you have paraprofessionals in your classes, it is critical that you remain engaged with the students who have disabilities and not turn their education over to someone who may be uncomfortable with the subject matter and know little about it. As Barbara says,

> **As the classroom teacher, you have to know what you want to have happen. You are in charge. It's your class. A teacher associate can edit instruction, but it is your job to lead the instruction.**

You also need to discuss explicitly what your respective roles and responsibilities will be with respect to instruction and behavior management. Paraprofessionals can provide support by carrying out a variety of noninstructional activities (e.g., preparing materials, taking attendance) as well as instructional tasks (e.g., assisting students during independent work, providing additional practice opportunities to reinforce previously taught material), but they should not have primary responsibility for a student's learning.

Examine your Classroom Environment for Possible Mismatch

It's important to remember that problems do not always reside exclusively within a child. Sometimes problems are the result of a discrepancy between a child's needs and the classroom environment. Barbara shares this example of an obvious mismatch:

> **I have a boy in my class who's 5 feet 6 inches and weighs about 200 pounds. He's constantly picking up his desk with his knees and dropping it on the floor. It's disturbing and disruptive, but I can't blame him. I've had a request in for months for a bigger desk, but so far nothing has happened. Meanwhile, he's always fumbling and bumping into things and knocking things over. It's easy to get frustrated with him—he's got lots of other problems too—but it's clear that one contributing factor is that the physical setting is just too small for him!**

As Barbara's story points out, we sometimes think of a child as disabled, when actually the problem is the result of a *disabling situation* (Gearheart, Weishahn, & Gearheart, 1992). Before concluding that "the entire problem is the kid," examine your classroom situation and reflect on ways the environment may be contributing to the child's difficulties. Here are some questions that our teachers ask themselves when they reflect on ways in which their classroom settings might be exacerbating students' problems:

- Where is the child sitting? Is the seat near a source of distraction? Is it too far from the teacher?
- Is sitting in clusters too difficult for the child to handle? Should I move the child to a pair or to individual seating?

- What type of academic work am I providing? Are assignments too mechanical? too dry? too long? Do they require too much independence? Do I ever allow choice?

- How do I speak with the child? How do I praise the child? *Do* I praise the child?

- What rules and routines have I set up and are they contrary to the student's ability to comply? Am I expecting quiet behavior too long? Am I setting the child up for failure?

- Am I allowing an appropriate amount of time for completing assignments? for transitions?

Reflect on the Appropriateness of Your Expectations

Sometimes, in our efforts to be understanding and sympathetic, we lower our expectations so much that we teach students to accept less from themselves as well. We water down curriculum; we forgive inappropriate behavior; we place children in safe environments where they will never be asked to do things we are sure they can't do. And when, in fact, they cannot do them, when they behave inappropriately, and when they do not learn, our beliefs seem justified.

On the other hand, it's important not to set unreasonably high expectations that children cannot meet. Your expectations have to be achievable, appropriate, and flexible. Viviana shares this incident:

 Last year I had a child who had just moved here as a first-grader. This boy would learn something one day and forget it the next. I couldn't understand what was going on. I began to get so frustrated; I'd say, "But you knew this yesterday!" The child was frustrated too, of course. Finally, I talked with the parents about the problem. The mother told me that she had been taking him to a clinic for lead poisoning. When he was a baby, he had eaten the paint chips in his apartment. I said, "Why didn't you tell me? I wouldn't have gotten so frustrated with him!" Once I understood the problem, my entire attitude changed. That didn't mean I left him in the corner not doing anything, but I understood what was causing his memory problems.

Use Group Work and Cooperative Learning to Foster Real Inclusion

Teachers sometimes think that all support and assistance must come from them. But students can serve as *tutors* on academic tasks, *buddies* who assist with difficult activities, or *advocates* who "watch out" for the welfare of children who have special needs (Gearheart, Weishahn, & Gearheart, 1992). Ken tells us about a two-person team he created that has been beneficial to both students:

 I have one kid, Jeannie, who goes to a resource room, and another kid, Suzanne, who's considered "gifted and talented." When the class works on Voyage of the Mimi activities on the computer, they function as a team. Let's say their task is to find a whale that's caught in a trap. You're someplace in the ocean, you've got different nautical instruments, and you're supposed to get to the whale. I know that Jeannie isn't going to be able to follow the complicated instructions on her own, and she doesn't have the patience to go through the necessary six or seven steps to come close to the whale. She's just not accurate enough. Also, you never get it on the first shot, so you have to deal with that frustration, and she's easily frustrated. But she can be a valuable part of the team. She can work the rulers to plot the points on the map, for example. And Suzanne can do the planning and the strategizing. She's not held back at all. Together, they do fine.

Research has demonstrated that cooperative learning can promote positive social relationships between children with disabilities and their peers. The use of cooperative learning can help to minimize the problem of children with special needs being isolated and rejected *socially,* even though they are included *physically* in the regular classroom. This year, for example, Barbara has teamed up for science with a special education teacher who teaches a self-contained class. Each day during science, the special education teacher and her class come to Barbara's room where children work in cooperative learning groups:

All the children are integrated into cooperative learning teams. Each member of the group always has a special job, like materials gatherer, timekeeper, reader, recorder. Since the special ed kids have a communication disability, they have problems with reading and writing, but they don't get out of the reading and writing responsibilities. Instead, they all have a "buddy" from my class who helps them do their jobs. There's been no embarrassment or nervousness about this at all. They know they have trouble with reading and writing, and my kids know they have trouble, and everyone approaches the matter very matter-of-factly. It's been really wonderful. The special ed teacher and I have a great time working together, and the kids really enjoy it.

Unfortunately, research indicates that cooperative learning is not always this successful. In a study of cooperative learning in grades 3 through 6 (O'Connor & Jenkins, 1996), researchers observed 22 children with mild disabilities and 12 average-performing children. They classified only 40 percent of the disabled students as successfully participating in cooperative groups. Successful participation depended on the selection of suitable partners, careful monitoring, the teaching of cooperative behaviors, and the establishment of a cooperative ethic.

CHILDREN WHO ARE TROUBLED

During one meeting, our four experienced teachers spoke sadly about the increasing problems their students face. They talked about six children sleeping in one bed; about absent fathers and drug-addicted mothers; about parents who are in and out of jail; about a youngster finding the body of his older brother who had committed suicide; about a child sleeping, eating, and doing homework in the car while his mother delivered newspapers; about a first-grader who had to bring her mother home from a bar every afternoon after school. As they talked, their anger and compassion were obvious. Also obvious was their recognition that in today's society, teachers have to deal with issues that were unimaginable in an earlier era—issues that require knowledge and skills far beyond those needed to be an effective instructor.

To help the troubled children in your class, *you need to be alert to the indicators of potential problems.* As an adult immersed in the culture of youth, you will probably develop a good idea of what the behavior of a typical elementary student is like. This enables you to detect deviations or changes in a student's behavior that might signal the presence of a problem. Learn to ask yourself a series of questions when you notice atypical behavior (Kottler & Kottler, 1993):

- What is unusual about this student's behavior?
- Is there a pattern to what I have observed?
- What additional information do I need to make an informed judgment?
- Whom might I contact to collect this background information?
- What are the risks of waiting longer to figure out what is going on?
- Does this student seem to be in any imminent danger?
- Whom can I consult about this case?

Viviana tells us how she tries to be alert to problems her students might be experiencing:

Even when I'm giving a lesson, I'm always scanning the room from one end to the other. You have to have your eyes all over. When the children are supposed to be paying attention, it's easy to notice behavior that might mean there's a problem—sleeping, putting a head down on the desk, masturbating, fidgeting. I also watch for bruises. The other day, for example, Carlita came in with a bruise under her eye. I said, "How did you get that bruise?" She said that she had fallen. I was not too concerned because I have known the family for a long time—I had two of Carlita's siblings—and there's never been any indication of abuse. But I decided to consult with the school nurse anyway. She examined the bruise, got the same story from Carlita, and talked with her grandmother, who happens to work in the cafeteria. She said, "You know, Carlita has a bruise under her eye." The grandmother said that she knew, that Carlita had fallen. Since the story checked out, we decided to leave it at that. But I still watch. If a child seems to be "falling" too much, then I report it to DYFS [Division of Youth and Family Services].

Substance Abuse

Substance abuse affects elementary classrooms in two ways: when children from chemically dependent families enter school and when children themselves are substance abusers. Let's turn first to the problems of children from chemically dependent families.

Amanda's father is an alcoholic who becomes aggressive and abusive when he drinks. At age 13, Amanda is her mother's primary source of support and works hard to make her family appear normal. She has assumed many adult responsibilities that would normally be carried out by the father of a household. At school, she is a very successful student; her teachers describe her as superdependable and motivated. They don't realize that she is filled with feelings of inadequacy and confusion and that her behavior is prompted by a compulsive need to be perfect. Nor do they notice that in between classes and at lunch time, Amanda spends most of her time alone. Amanda avoids forming friendships because she is afraid of revealing the family secret.

Ricky, Amanda's 10-year-old brother, is a fourth-grader whose teacher describes him as sullen, disrespectful, and obstructive. He frequently fights with other children and is often in the principal's office being reprimanded for some antisocial behavior. His mother claims not to understand his behavior; she reports that Ricky never acts this way at home and implies that the teacher is the cause of his perpetual negative attitude. Yet he often runs around the house, screaming and tearing things apart. At the core of Ricky's behavior is anger: He is enraged by the rejection he feels from his alcoholic father and resentful that his mother spends so much time wallowing in self-pity. He soothes his pain by planning ways to run away. He is on the verge of jumping into his own life of addiction. (Powell, Zehm, & Kottler, 1995)

It is estimated that *one in every four children* sitting in a classroom comes from a family in which one or both parents are addicted to drugs or alcohol (Powell, Zehm, & Kottler, 1995). When these children of alcoholics/addicts (COAs) are angry and disruptive like Ricky, it is relatively easy to recognize that a problem exists; it is far more difficult when children are compliant perfectionists like Amanda. Leslie Lillian, the student assistance counselor (SAC) at Ken's school, stresses that COAs can exhibit a wide variety of behaviors (see Table 5.4):

Some children become perfectionists. It's as if they think to themselves, "I'm not going to disturb anything, I'm not going to do anything wrong, so no one can be angry with me." Some children become class clowns; maybe they've found that making people laugh breaks the tension, or maybe they're seeking attention. Others become very angry; they may begin to lie, or steal, or cheat. Some become sad and melancholy; everything about them says, "Nurture me." We see a whole spectrum of reactions—and it's the same spectrum of behaviors that we see in kids from violent homes.

It's important to understand that for COAs, family life revolves around the addiction. Rules are arbitrary and irrational, boundaries between parents and children are blurred, and life is marked by unpredictability and inconsistency. Leslie comments: "These kids never know what they're going home to. One day, they may bring a paper home from school that's gotten a low grade, and the parent might say, 'That's OK, just do it over.' Another day, they might get beaten up for bringing home a paper like that." One of the most frustrating aspects of working with COAs is the realization that you do not have the power to change the child's home life. Instead, you must concentrate on what you *are* able to do during the

TABLE 5.4 Characteristics of Children of Alcoholics/Addicts

Difficulty in creating and maintaining trusting relationships, often leading to isolation

Low self-esteem

Self-doubt

Difficulty in being spontaneous and open, caused by a need to be in control and to minimize the risk of being surprised

Denial and repression because of the need to collaborate with other family members in keeping "the secret"

General feelings of guilt about areas for which the child had no responsibility

Uncertainty about his or her own feelings and desires caused by shifting parental roles

Seeing things in an "all or nothing" context, which sometimes manifests itself in a perfectionist fear of failure

Poor impulse control, which may result in acting-out behavior, probably caused by lack of parental guidance, love, and discipline

Potential for depression, phobias, panic reactions, and hyperactivity

Preoccupation with the family

Abuse of alcohol and/or drugs

Source: Adapted from Towers, 1989.

six hours each day that the child is in school. Many of the strategies are not different from those we have espoused for all children. (See the Practical Tips box.) For example, it is essential that you establish clear, consistent rules and work to create a climate of trust and caring.

In addition, you should find out whether your school has student assistance counselors or other special services personnel who can provide help. Find out whether support groups for COAs are available. For example, Tonia Moore, the student assistance counselor in Barbara's district, runs groups alone or with the school's guidance counselor. She speaks about the benefits that joining such a group can bring:

> *There's such a sense of relief. The comments are always the same: "I thought I was the only one." "I didn't know anyone else was going through this stuff." The shame is so great, even at a very young age, and the need to keep it all a secret is so hard. There's instant camaraderie. We do activities that help to build self-esteem. We do role playing to get at feelings—being disappointed, being unsafe, being embarrassed, and being angry.*

A second way that substance abuse can affect elementary classrooms is when *children themselves abuse drugs and alcohol.* At the elementary level, the problems of COAs are far more prevalent, but it would be naive to think that there is no substance abuse among youngsters at the intermediate grade levels. Indeed, studies indicate that drinking frequently starts at very young ages. Data from recent surveys show that approximately 10 percent of 9- to 10-year-olds have already started drinking, and nearly one-third of young people begin drinking before age

PRACTICAL TIPS FOR

HELPING CHILDREN OF ALCOHOLICS/ADDICTS

- *Be observant.* Watch your students not just for academic or behavior problems, but also for the more subtle signs of addiction and emotional distress. Remember that COAs can be overachieving, cooperative, and quiet, as well as disruptive and angry.

- *Set boundaries that are enforced consistently.* When chaos exists at home, some sense of order is crucial at school.

- *Be flexible.* Although it is necessary to set boundaries, classroom rules that are too rigid and unyielding may invite students to act out.

- *Make addiction a focus of discussion.* Find a way to deal with this subject. Incorporate addiction into literacy instruction (e.g., through children's literature, writing), science, social studies, etc.

- *Make it clear that you are available.* Communicate that you are eager to talk to children. Reach out to the troubled child in a gentle, caring way. "I notice you are having some difficulty. I just want you to know that I care about you. Call me any time you are ready to talk. And if you would rather speak to someone else, let me find you someone you can trust."

- *Develop a referral network.* Find out what services are available to help, and refer the child for appropriate professional care.

- *Accept what you can do little about.* You can't make people stop drinking or taking drugs.

Source: Adapted from Powell, Zehm, & Kottler, 1995.

13 (National Institute on Alcohol Abuse and Alcoholism, 2004/2005). Moreover, 12- to 18-year-olds who drink report that they began doing so between two and three years earlier, when they were about 9 to 15, respectively (Substance Abuse and Mental Health Services Administration, 2003).

To a large extent, student assistance counselors rely on teachers to refer students who might be having problems with alcohol and other drugs or who might be at risk for such problems. But teachers may be particularly reluctant to make referrals about suspected drug use because they are unsure about the indicators. Tonia Moore is very sensitive to this problem:

> *Teachers tell me, "I have no idea what substance abuse looks like. It wasn't a part of my training. I wouldn't know when to refer a student." I tell them, that's OK. You can't tell substance abuse just by looking. There has to be a chemical screening. But you can see changes in behavior. You know enough about kids to know when somebody's behavior has changed, or if their behavior is different from all the other kids. You don't need to know the student is using; you just need to suspect that there may be drug use or a problem related to drug use.*

What are the behaviors that might lead you to suspect drug use and to make a referral? Figure 5.3 shows the behavior checklist used in Ken's district. Many

Academic Performance
_____Drop in grades
_____Decrease in participation
_____Inconsistent work
_____Works below potential
_____Compulsive overachievement

School Attendance
_____Change in attendance
_____Absenteeism
_____Tardiness
_____Class cutting
_____Frequent visits to nurse or counselor
_____Frequent restroom visits
_____Frequent requests for hall passes

Social Problems
_____Family problems
_____Job problems
_____Peer problems
_____Relationship problems
_____Runaway
_____Constantly borrowing money

Physical Symptoms
_____Staggering/stumbling, poor coordination
_____Incoherent or slurred speech
_____Glossy, bloodshot, or dark eyes
_____Smelling of alcohol/marijuana
_____Vomiting, nausea
_____Deteriorating physical appearance
_____Sleeping in class
_____Physical injuries
_____Frequent physical complaints
_____Dramatic changes in musculature

Extracurricular Activities
_____Lack of participation
_____Possession of drugs/alcohol
_____Involvement in thefts and assault

_____Vandalism
_____Talking about involvement in illegal activities
_____Possession of paraphernalia
_____Increasing noninvolvement
_____Decrease in motivation
_____Dropping out/missing practice(s)
_____Not fulfilling responsibilities
_____Performance changes

Disruptive Behavior
_____Defiance of rules
_____Irresponsibility, blaming, lying, fighting, cheating
_____Problem with authority figures
_____Sudden outbursts, verbal abuse
_____Obscene language or gestures
_____Attention-getting behavior
_____Frequently in wrong areas
_____Hyperactivity, nervousness
_____Lack of motivation, apathy
_____Extreme negativism

Atypical Behavior
_____Difficulty in accepting mistakes
_____Overly sensitive or defensive
_____Erratic behavior
_____Boasts about alcohol or drug use
_____Change of friends
_____Depression
_____Disoriented
_____Inappropriate responses
_____Withdrawn/difficulty relating
_____Sexual behavior in public
_____Unrealistic goals
_____Seeking adult advice without a specific problem
_____Rigid obedience
_____Constantly seeks approval

Figure 5.3   The Behavioral Checklist Used in Ken's District

schools use forms that are very similar to this one. Keeping your school's behavior checklist handy can help you stay alert to the possibility that students are using drugs or living with addiction in their families.

It's important to distinguish between situations in which a pattern of behavior problems suggests possible drug use *outside of school* and situations in which a student appears to be *under the influence of drugs during school, at school functions, or on school property.* When you see students who might be "under the influence," you cannot wait to fill out a behavior checklist; you need to alert the appropriate personnel as soon as you possibly can. Tonia Moore explains one of the reasons:

> *It used to be that teachers would come to me at the end of the day and say, "I was really worried about X today. I think he was really on something." That's no good. I need to know at the time. After all, that student could fall down the stairs, or the student could leave the building . . . and get killed crossing the street. We have to deal with the problem immediately. It can really be a matter of life and death.*

Because you cannot be sure that a student is using drugs just by looking, it's important not to be accusatory when you talk with the student. Ken would ask, "Are you feeling OK? You don't look like yourself. Would you like to go to the nurse?" He would then alert the nurse that he was sending her a student whose behavior suggested possible drug or alcohol use. Making a referral like this is not easy, but you need to remember that turning away and remaining silent can send the message that you condone the behavior—or that you don't care enough to do anything.

One final note: If you suspect that a student is in possession of drugs or alcohol in school (e.g., in a purse or backpack), it's important to bring that person to the appropriate school official rather than undertaking a search by yourself. In a landmark case (*New Jersey v. T.L.O.*, 1985), the United States Supreme Court ruled that a school official may properly conduct a search of a student "when there are reasonable grounds for suspecting that the search will turn up evidence that the student has violated or is violating either the law or the rules of the school" (Fischer, Schimmel, & Kelly, 1999). In other words, students in school have fewer protections than are normally afforded to citizens under the stricter "probable cause" standard (Stefkovich & Miller, 1998). Nonetheless, searching a student's belongings is best left to an administrator who is aware of the subtleties of the law. (We will discuss this further in Chapter 12.)

Abuse and Neglect

During one meeting with our teachers, they related sad, frightening stories that illustrate the important role teachers serve in identifying victims of abuse. Listen to Garnetta:

> Libby had moved from another country with her mother and sisters, and they were living in her grandmother's house. Her father stayed back home, but within three or four years, he rejoined his family. Shortly after, I noticed physical bruises on Libby's arms and legs. I also noticed that her older brother had bruises too. We reported the case to DYFS (Division of Youth and Family Services), and they sent a caseworker to the home to investigate. DYFS reported back to us that the father admitted he had hit the children because

they hadn't gone to bed when he told them to. Apparently this wasn't the first time. According to the mother, when the children were very young, the father had been jailed for "hurting" the children.

Libby and her brother are not alone. The National Child Abuse and Neglect Data System reported that approximately 900,000 children were victims of maltreatment in 2006 (U.S. Department of Health and Human Services, 2008). To protect these young people, most states have laws requiring educators to report suspected abuse to the state's "child protective service" or "child welfare agency." Although definitions of abuse vary, states generally include nonaccidental injury, neglect, sexual abuse, and emotional maltreatment. It is essential that you become familiar with the physical and behavioral indicators of these problems. (See Table 5.5.)

Unfortunately, the signs of abuse can be difficult to detect. As Table 5.5 indicates, teachers not only need to watch for physical evidence, they must also be alert to behavioral indicators such as apprehension when other children are upset, reluctance to go home at the end of the school day, and wariness of adult contact. Children who give improbable explanations for their injuries, refuse to talk about them, or pretend they don't hurt may also be victims of physical abuse.

Teachers are often reluctant to file a report unless they have absolute proof of abuse or neglect. They worry about invading the family's privacy and causing unnecessary embarrassment to everyone involved. Nonetheless, it's important to keep in mind that *no state requires the reporter to have absolute proof before reporting.* What most states do require is reasonable "cause to suspect" or "believe" that abuse has occurred (Fisher, Schimmel, & Kelly, 1999). If you are uncertain whether abuse is occurring, but have reasonable cause to suspect it, you should risk erring on the side of excessive care in safeguarding the youngster and file a report. Waiting for proof can be dangerous; it may also be illegal. If a child is later harmed, and it becomes clear that you failed to report suspected abuse, both you and your school district may be subject to civil and criminal liability. Also keep in mind that every state provides immunity from any civil suit or criminal prosecution that might result from the reporting of suspected child abuse or neglect—as long as you have acted "in good faith" (Fischer, Schimmel, & Kelly, 1999).

It's essential that you learn about the reporting procedures in your state *before* you are faced with a situation of suspected child abuse. Some states explicitly name the school personnel who are required to file the report. Other states have more general provisions that require reporting by "any person" who works with children; this would clearly include teachers, nurses, therapists, and counselors (Fischer, Schimmel, & Kelly, 1999). States also vary with respect to the form and content of reports required. Most states require an oral report, followed by a more detailed written report, and some states also have a 24-hour, toll-free "hot line." Generally, you should be prepared to provide the student's name and address; the nature and extent of the injury or condition observed; and your own name and address (Fischer, Schimmel, & Kelly, 1999).

The variation among states underscores the importance of becoming familiar with the procedures and resources in your own school. The best way to do this is to speak with people who can provide guidance and direction: experienced

TABLE 5.5 Physical and Behavioral Indicators of Child Abuse and Neglect

Type of Abuse or Neglect	Physical Indicators	Behavioral Indicators
Physical Abuse	Unexplained • bruises or welts • burns • fractures • lacerations or abrasions	Wary of adult contact Apprehensive when other children cry Behavioral extremes; aggressiveness or withdrawal Frightened of parents; afraid to go home; reports injury by parents
Physical Neglect	Consistent hunger, poor hygiene, inappropriate dress Consistent lack of supervision, especially in dangerous activities or for long periods Constant fatigue or listlessness Unattended physical problems or medical neglect Abandonment	Begging, stealing food Extended stays at school (early arrival and late departure) Constantly falling asleep in class Alcohol or drug abuse Delinquency States there is no caretaker
Sexual Abuse	Difficulty in walking or sitting Torn, stained, or bloody underclothing Pain or itching in genital area Bruises or bleeding in external genitalia, vaginal, or anal areas Venereal disease, especially in preteens Pregnancy	Unwilling to change for and participate in PE Withdrawal, fantasy, or infantile behavior Bizarre, sophisticated, or unusual sexual behavior or knowledge Poor peer relationships Delinquent or runaway Reports sexual assault by caretaker
Emotional Maltreatment	Habit disorders (sucking, biting, rocking) Conduct disorders (antisocial, destructive) Neurotic traits (sleep disorders, speech disorders, inhibition of play) Psychoneurotic reactions (hysteria, obsession, compulsion, phobias)	Behavioral extremes; aggressiveness or withdrawal Inappropriately adult or infantile behaviors Developmental lags Attempted suicide

Source: Adapted from Governor's Task Force on Child Abuse and Neglect, 1988.

teachers, the principal, the school nurse, the school psychologist, and the student assistance counselor.

CHILDREN LIVING IN POVERTY

More than one in six (13.3 million) children in the United States are considered poor, meaning they live below the federal poverty line for a family of four, which in 2008 was $21,200 (Children's Defense Fund, 2008). How many are homeless is not clear, because there are no regular surveys of homeless children in the United States; however, a frequently cited statistic is 1.3 million homeless children in any given year (National Law Center on Homelessness and Poverty, 2008). The economic crisis that began in 2008 has dramatically increased these numbers. Even as we write this, a growing number of newspaper articles and television newscasts are reporting on the surge of "tent cities" as people lose their jobs and homes (e.g., McKinley, 2009).

Children and adolescents living in poverty obviously face enormous challenges. They are far less likely than children from middle-class backgrounds to have access to adequate physical, dental, and mental health care. They may suffer from physical, emotional, and psychological problems, experience developmental delays, exhibit academic and behavioral difficulties, and be at risk for school failure. For homeless children, living arrangements are varied and far from adequate: Some double up with other family members or friends; others live in shelters, emergency foster care, abandoned buildings, vehicles, or motels; still others are on the street (National Coalition of Homeless Children and Youth, 2008).

School can be a haven for children living in poverty. But what can you possibly do? First, *effective teachers are wary of claims about a "culture of poverty" whose members have shared (often negative) traits.* From this perspective, those who are poor are a homogeneous group with characteristics that differ starkly from those who are middle-class. These characteristics include *language patterns* (casual rather than formal), *values* (money is to be spent rather than saved), *worldviews* (a focus on the present rather than on the future), *ways of interacting with others* (physically rather than verbally), and *daily life* (noisy and chaotic rather than quiet and orderly). The idea of a culture of poverty has become popular among administrators and teachers, and numerous professional development workshops on this topic are offered throughout the country (e.g., Payne, 2005). Although these programs are intended to help teachers better educate poor children, some critics dispute the existence of a culture of poverty and contend that there is no research evidence to support this notion (e.g., Bomer, Dworin, May, & Semingson, 2008). They argue that traits like those listed above are undoubtedly to be found in *some* poor individuals (and in some who are not poor!) but that they do not define all poor people. Moreover, these critics warn that this characterization of poor people can lead teachers to engage in *deficit thinking*—a tendency to attribute school failure to internal deficiencies such as lack of motivation, rather than to external factors such as inadequate funding to schools that serve poor students. Teachers who engage in deficit thinking are likely to overlook or dismiss the strengths of poor students, to "blame the victim," and to adopt negative stereotypes.

Second, effective teachers of poor or homeless students are "bearers of hope" (Landsman, 2006). They believe in the ability of all their students to learn, even if they're wearing dirty clothes or come to school hungry. Such teachers examine and monitor their assumptions. On the one hand, they are careful not to assume that poor students will be unable to meet class expectations; on the other hand, they don't assume that students will be able to complete homework assignments in a comfortable, quiet room at a desk stocked with all needed materials. They do not lower their expectations in terms of class participation and work, but they show flexibility and compassion (e.g., by extending a due date). They try to give their students as much choice and control over assignments as possible, so that the students can feel they have a say in their education.

Third, teachers of poor or homeless adolescents work especially hard to build a supportive, trusting relationship. They listen respectfully and respond empathically, using active listening skills to keep the lines of communication open (see Chapter 3). They are alert to opportunities to provide assistance. Viviana, for example, routinely sends home the addresses and phone numbers of the Salvation Army, Catholic Charities, family planning organizations, dental clinics, and food distribution centers. At times, she also provides direct help:

> **Rents are very high around here, so two and three families rent an apartment together. Three families might rent a three-bedroom apartment, with a whole family sleeping in one bedroom. This means that some of the kids have to sleep on the floor. This year I have a girl in my class who used to fall asleep every day. I asked her, "Why are you so sleepy?" She told me that she has to sleep on the floor; there are eight in her family and they all sleep in one room with two beds. I had a folding bed that I had bought to use when my nephew came to visit. I went to her house and asked the mother if she could accept it. I said, "Do you mind if I give you the folding bed?" She was very pleased, and the girl doesn't fall asleep anymore.**

As a postscript to this anecdote, it's important to recognize that Viviana is viewed as her students' "second mother." There is even an expression for this in Spanish: "*La maestra es la segunda mama,*" and this is the way Viviana introduces herself to her students' parents (see Chapter 6). She also shares a first language and a Latina identity. These factors undoubtedly increase the likelihood that her offers of assistance are perceived as helpful and respectful rather than as intrusive or critical. Seek advice from a parent advocate or liaison if you are considering offering direct help but are uncertain how families will respond.

Some strategies for helping children who are poor or homeless are listed in the Practical Tips box.

CONCLUDING COMMENTS

We strongly believe that teachers are responsible for all the children in their classes, including those with special needs. This may mean communicating and collaborating with special support personnel to provide children with appropriate educational experiences. It also means actively teaching and including children with special needs when they are in your room—not putting them in the back and ignoring them, like the teacher in this journal entry written by one of our students:

> *There's a boy in my classroom who goes to a resource room every day for reading and math. When he's in the classroom, he sits in a back corner, basically doing nothing. My cooperating teacher gives him some*

PRACTICAL TIPS FOR

HELPING STUDENTS WHO ARE LIVING IN POVERTY

Provide basic "survival" assistance:

- Keep granola bars and other healthful snacks on hand.
- If students live where things get stolen, allow them to leave school materials in school.
- Keep basic toiletries in your room for students who don't have access to personal hygiene items.
- Have extra school supplies on hand.

Be sensitive when disciplining:

- Think about whether students are purposefully misbehaving or whether they are behaving in ways that are acceptable in their home culture. Explain that their behavior may be all right at home but not at school, and explain why.
- Don't penalize students who are asleep without talking to them first; maybe they have no bed or quiet place to sleep.
- If students laugh when disciplined, recognize that this may be a way to save face. Teach other behaviors that are more appropriate.
- If students make inappropriate or vulgar comments, have them generate (or teach them) other phrases that are more acceptable for school and can be used to say the same thing.
- If students are physically aggressive, tell students that aggression is not an option in school. Have them generate (or teach them) other, more appropriate options.

Encourage academic achievement:

- Examine what and how you're teaching. Do you assume that students living in poverty will not be going to college anyway, so it's OK if they're getting a watered-down curriculum?
- Give students as much choice in and control over their assignments as possible so that they feel that they have a say in their education.
- Include topics that are familiar and relevant.
- Teach ways of keeping materials organized.
- Help students to set goals and to keep track of progress.
- Use rubrics that show levels of performance so students can begin to critique their own assignments.
- Maintain realistically high expectations.

Provide special help for students who are frequently changing schools:

- Assign a buddy who can show them the ropes.
- Explicitly welcome them to class.
- Have a special lunch with them.
- If you know they will be leaving, create a "memory book" for them to take.
- Coordinate with the homeless education liaison in your school.

Sources: Grossman, 2004; Landsman, 2006; Payne, 2005.

worksheets to do but doesn't even really monitor to see if he does them. He never includes him in any of the class's activities. Sometimes the boy wanders around the room, looking at what the other kids are doing, and I get the feeling he'd like to do the lesson too, but my teacher doesn't make any attempt to involve him. When I asked about the boy, my teacher told me he can't do anything for the child, that his learning disabilities are just too great. He said he doesn't have the necessary expertise to help him—that he's not a special educator. So he just lets him sit. It makes me want to cry.

When students have special needs, it's more important than ever to create a classroom that is safe, orderly, and humane. You may not be able to eliminate a child's disability, but you can make sure that your classroom is not disabling. You may not be able to change youngsters' relationships with their families, but you can work to establish positive teacher–student relationships. You may not be able to provide students with control over impoverishted, unstable, chaotic home lives, but you can give them opportunities to make decisions and to have some control over their time in school. You may not be able to change students' lives, but you can try to make their time in school as productive and meaningful as possible.

SUMMARY

Building a caring, inclusive classroom begins with knowing who your students are. Today's classrooms contain children from a wide range of cultural and linguistic backgrounds, and many are learning English as a second language. Children with disabilities are frequently educated alongside their nondisabled peers. A greater number of children are growing up in circumstances that put them at risk for physical, emotional, and psychological problems. This chapter reflects our belief that teachers are responsible for all the children in the class—not just for those who are easy to teach.

The Developing Elementary Child

- The elementary years are a critical period for the development of
    Self-concept
    The capacity to regulate emotions
    The ability to understand the perspectives of others
    Social problem solving
    Understanding of morality and social convention
- From age 6 to 12, children are in Erikson's Stage 4—industry versus inferiority—during which they must cope with demands to learn new skills or risk developing a sense of inferiority and failure.
- According to Bowlby and Ainsworth, the nature of our early attachment relationships can affect the relationships we form throughout life. When caregivers are inconsistent, unresponsive, or rejecting, children develop an insecure, anxious attachment

relationship. They come to believe that others cannot be trusted to provide care and are likely to become anxious and mistrustful, with a limited ability to form relationships.

English-Language Learners

- Provide a safe environment for language risk taking.
- Avoid idioms and complex sentences.
- Ask questions that allow for different levels of proficiency in responding.
- Encourage English speaking while honoring students' first language.
- Offer periodic summaries and paraphrases.
- Emphasize collaborative over individual work.
- Emphasize process over product.
- Apply SDAIE strategies across the curriculum.
- Encourage children to write about topics of their choice and for real-world purposes.

Children with Disabilities and ADHD

- A diagnosis of LD is made when there is a "severe discrepancy" between intellectual ability and academic performance or when students fail to respond to an early, intensive intervention.
- Emotional disturbance and behavioral disorders can be externalizing (e.g., conduct disorder) or internalizing (e.g., depression).
- Autism and Asperger syndrome are two pervasive developmental disorders, a cluster of disorders characterized by marked impairments in the development of social interaction and communication skills.
- ADHD is not included as a disability in IDEA; however, children may receive services under Section 504 of the Rehabilitation Act of 1973. ADHD is characterized by inattention, hyperactivity, and impulsivity.

General Strategies for Helping Children with Disabilities and ADHD

- Obtain access to support and services.
- Be an active participant in the IEP and 504 planning process.
- Create an accepting climate.
- Coordinate and collaborate with special education teachers and paraprofessionals.
- Examine your classroom environment for possible mismatch.
- Reflect on the appropriateness of your expectations.
- Use group work and cooperative learning to foster real inclusion.

Children Who Are Troubled

- Substance abuse:
  - Students may be children of alcoholics/addicts (COAs) and/or may be abusing drugs and alcohol themselves.
  - COAs can benefit from support groups.
  - Teachers must be watchful for students who may be abusing drugs and alcohol and refer such students to the student assistance counselor or other appropriate persons.
  - Distinguish between situations in which drugs are being used outside of school and situations in which students are under the influence during school.
- Abuse and neglect:
  - Educators are required to report suspected abuse and neglect to the state's child protective service.

No state requires the reporter to have absolute proof before reporting.

Most states require "reason to believe" or "reasonable cause to believe or suspect."

Children Living in Poverty

- Be wary of claims about a "culture of poverty" whose members have shared (often negative) traits.
- Strive to be a "bearer of hope."
- Work hard to build a supportive, trusting relationship.
- Look for opportunities to provide assistance.

Sometimes the problems that students bring to school can be overwhelming, especially for beginning teachers who are still learning the basics. And in fact, there may be students whose problems are so great that you just cannot help. Nonetheless, you can still try to create a classroom environment that is safe, orderly, and humane. You can show students you care by working to make their time in school as meaningful and productive as possible.

ACTIVITIES FOR SKILL BUILDING AND REFLECTION

In Class

1. In small groups, consider the following scenario.

At XYZ School, a meeting of the special services team was called to discuss two children who were having academic and emotional difficulties. The teacher of each child was invited to describe the situation. Mr. Ryan, a fifth-grade teacher, made the following presentation:

Mr. Ryan began by saying that he thought Olivia was having some difficulties at home that were affecting her ability to do her work in school. "Olivia's academic problems have been evident since the beginning of the school year. She's reading at a third-grade level, and she's doing fourth-grade math." He distributed reading and math worksheets for the committee to see. "However, recently her work and her work habits have gotten worse. I've talked to Olivia and her mom. Since her mother started working nights, Olivia has shown little interest in school. In a typical week, she'll have her homework done only one or two days, and she rarely finishes assignments in class. She has difficulty following oral directions and is slow at getting her ideas down on paper. Here are two typical writing papers; in each case, she only managed to get down two sentences in 25 minutes, and you can see that her handwriting is somewhat immature." He showed the committee two papers. "I have tried to limit the number of directions I give her, and when oral directions are given, I also write them on the board. I've offered after-school help, but she needs to get home to watch her little sister. She's also having problems socially; in the last two weeks, she's gotten into five fights with the children in the class." He referred to a note pad he had brought. "On November fifth, for example, she accused another child of stealing a pencil and an eraser from her desk. It resulted in a lot of name-calling and loud insults. We finally found the pencil and eraser in the back of her desk, behind all her papers and books. I was worried about her before the problems at home surfaced, and now I'm really at a loss for how to help her. Do you have any ideas for me?" He took out a pen and opened the note pad to a clean sheet.

After Mr. Ryan's presentation, the team discussed ways of helping Olivia. Mr. Ryan left the meeting feeling that his concerns had been taken seriously and that he had received useful advice. Next Mrs. Teller, a third-grade teacher, presented her concerns about Daniel:

Mrs. Teller began by stating that it was about time that someone did something for Daniel. "He has been disturbing my class since September. Look at his work." She handed out papers with many red circles and negative comments. "His work is sloppy, and he never finishes anything. I keep him after school and call his mother and still he doesn't try to get any better. He's one year below level in reading and still can't figure out long vowel sounds. I've had it with him. He doesn't seem to listen to me anymore. In all my years of teaching third grade, this boy is the worst one yet! He always interrupts the lesson by fooling around. I always end up yelling at him or sending him to the principal. What can you do to help me? I think he belongs in a special class."

The team members told Mrs. Teller that they needed more information before they could provide meaningful assistance and asked her to attend the next meeting when Daniel's case would again be discussed. Based on the guidelines presented in this chapter and the model provided by Mr. Ryan, rewrite Mrs. Teller's presentation to make it more effective.

2. Working together in a small group, imagine that you are a general education teacher working in a co-teaching arrangement with a special education teacher. Generate a list of issues that you would want to discuss before beginning to teach together. In particular, consider what expectations you have with respect to planning and delivering instruction and with respect to classroom management. Then assume the role of the special education teacher and repeat the process.

3. In a small group, read the following scenario and then discuss the questions that are listed below.

Joanne Wilson's fifth-grade class has 23 students. One has been identified with learning disabilities, and he struggles with the novels the class is reading, as well as the writing assignments. In addition, two students are recent immigrants with very limited English, and one student has ADHD. Although he is supposed to be on medication, he sometimes skips a dose; on days like that, he "bounces off the walls" and accomplishes very little academic work. Ms. Wilson is very concerned about these students' academic progress, and she doesn't know where to turn. An in-class support (ICS) teacher provides some assistance two days a week, but they have no planning time and so she functions more like an aide than a real teacher. Ms. Wilson is also painfully aware that the class is not a cohesive community; although there is no blatant disrespect, the other students generally ignore the students with special needs and are reluctant to work with them in cooperative groups.

Questions

a. What strategies could Ms. Wilson use to help create a more inclusive, more accepting climate?

    b. For each student with special needs (i.e., the student with LD, the two ELLs, and the student with ADHD), think of one strategy that Ms. Wilson could use to enhance his or her academic progress.

    c. What kinds of help could Ms. Wilson ask from the ICS teacher?

On Your Own

1. In the school where you are observing or teaching, interview the principal or the director of special services to learn about the district's policies and procedures for supporting children with disabilities. Are any children with severe disabilities being educated in the general education classroom? If so, what kinds of special supports are being provided for those children? Interview a teacher about his or her attitudes toward including a child with special needs who would previously have been educated in a special education classroom or sent to a special school.

2. In the school where you are observing or teaching, interview the principal or an ESL teacher about the district's policies and programs for supporting children who are English-language learners. How many languages are represented in the school? Interview a teacher in an English-only classroom who has English-language learners in his or her classroom. How does the teacher provide supports for English-language learners?

3. In the school where you are observing or teaching, interview the student assistance counselor, a guidance counselor, or the director of special services to determine what services are available for children who come from substance-abusing families.

For Your Portfolio

Policies governing the reporting of suspected abuse and neglect vary from state to state. Find out what policies apply in your state. Also find out whether your school has particular policies and procedures that you are to follow. In particular, get answers to the following questions:

Who is required to report abuse and neglect?
When should you report child abuse? (When you have reasonable cause to suspect? reasonable cause to believe?)
To what state agency do you report?
What information must be included in the report?
Do you have to give your name when reporting?

Compile your findings into a set of guidelines that you keep in your portfolio.

FOR FURTHER READING

Cary, S. (2007). *Working with second language learners: Answers to teachers' top ten questions.* Portsmouth, NH: Heinemann.

    Ten questions from teachers were chosen with the following criteria in mind: veracity (meaning that they were asked by real teachers teaching real kids), frequency, relevancy, and difficulty (they needed to be challenging). Questions include: How do I assess a student's English? How do I find useful information on a student's cultural background? How do I make my spoken language more understandable? How do I get my reluctant speakers to speak English?

Gorski, P. (2008). The myth of the "culture of poverty." *Educational Leadership, 65*(7), 32–36.

In this reader-friendly, provocative article, Paul Gorski refutes "common and dangerous myths about poverty." Chief among them, he argues, is the "culture of poverty"—the idea that "poor people share more or less monolithic and predictable beliefs, values, and behaviors." Gorski looks at some of the stereotypes held about poor people and concludes that teachers must consider how their class biases affect their interactions with students.

Kline, F. M., & Silver, L. B. (Eds.) (2004). *The educator's guide to mental health issues in the classroom.* Baltimore, MD: Paul H. Brookes.

This book is dedicated to "general education classroom teachers who are charged with serving ALL students!" It is designed to serve as a reference for educators who work with students who have mental health issues and who need to collaborate with mental health workers. Chapters address biologically based disorders (e.g., ADHD), biologically based and/or psychologically based disorders (e.g., substance abuse), and behavioral disorders (e.g., oppositional defiant disorder).

Pietrangelo, R., & Giuliani, G. (2008). *Frequently asked questions about Response to Intervention: A step-by-step guide for educators.* Thousand Oaks, CA: Corwin Press.

This book answers the most commonly asked questions about Response to Intervention (RTI). The text is designed to help both general and special education teachers better understand this approach and learn the purposes and benefits of this service delivery model.

Snell, M. E., & Janney, R. (2000). *Social relationships and peer support.* Baltimore, MD: Paul H. Brookes.

This book is part of a series of reader-friendly teachers' guides to inclusive practices. This guide focuses on ways of facilitating positive peer relationships in an inclusive classroom. Topics include creating a positive atmosphere, establishing peer support programs, teaching social skills, and building friendship groups.

Soodak, L. C., & McCarthy, M. R. (2006). Classroom management in inclusive settings. In C. M. Evertson & C. S. Weinstein (Eds.), *Handbook of classroom management: Research, practice, and contemporary issues.* Mahwah, NJ: Lawrence Erlbaum Associates.

This chapter reviews research-based practices that promote positive academic, social, and behavioral outcomes for students in inclusive classrooms. Practices include teacher-directed strategies (such as building classroom community and establishing programs that foster acceptance and friendship), peer-mediated strategies (such as cooperative learning and peer tutoring), and self-directed strategies (such as self-monitoring). The authors stress the role of teachers in creating classrooms in which all students have greater access to the general education curriculum.

Villa, R. A., Thousand, J. S., & Nevin, A. I. (2008) *A guide to co-teaching: Practical tips for facilitating student learning,* 2nd ed. Thousand Oaks, CA: Corwin Press.

This book highlights the benefits and challenges of co-teaching and addresses both the NCLB requirement that all students have access to highly qualified teachers and the IDEA requirement that students with disabilities have access to the general education curriculum. The following four types of co-teaching models are described in detail: supportive, parallel, complementary, and team teaching.

ORGANIZATIONAL RESOURCES

Autism Society of America, 7910 Woodmont Ave. Suite 300, Bethesda, MD 20814-3067; 800-3AUTISM (800-328-8476); www.autism-society.org. This society seeks to improve the lives of those affected by autism by increasing public awareness, advocating for appropriate services, and providing the latest information on treatment, research, and advocacy. Its website includes links to resources and local referrals.

Center on Addiction and the Family (COAF), 164 West 74th Street, New York, NY 10023; 646-505-2060; www.coaf.org. COAF works to promote the healing of families affected by substance abuse. Its website includes information on the impact of substance abuse and how to work with children and families.

Children and Adults with Attention-Deficit/Hyperactivity Disorder (CHADD), 8181 Professional Place, Suite 150, Landover, MD 20785; 800-233-4050; www.chadd.org. CHADD is a nonprofit organization serving children and adults with ADHD. It runs the National Resource Center on ADHD, a national clearinghouse for evidence-based information about ADHD.

The Council for Exceptional Children, 1110 North Glebe Rd., Suite 300, Arlington, VA 22201; 888-232-7733; www.cec.sped.org. CEC is the largest international professional organization dedicated to improving educational outcomes for students with disabilities and those who are gifted.

Center for Research on Education, Diversity, and Excellence (CREDE), 1640 Tolman Hall, University of California, Berkeley, CA 94720-1670; 510-643-9024; www.crede.org. CREDE is a federally funded research and development center focused on improving the education of students whose ability to reach their potential is challenged by language or cultural barriers, race, geographic location, or poverty. It offers a wide range of multimedia products.

Learning Disabilities Association of America (LDA), 4156 Library Road, Pittsburgh, PA 15234-1349; 412-341-1515; www.ldanatl.org. LDA is the largest nonprofit volunteer organization advocating for individuals with learning disabilities. This website includes links to information for teachers and parents.

National Center for Homeless Education, 1100 West Market St., Suite 300, Greensboro, NC 27403; 1-800-308-2145; www.serve.org/nche. This site serves as a clearinghouse for information and resources on the educational rights of homeless children and youth.

WORKING WITH FAMILIES

"I had no idea his mother lost her job and his father hasn't been around for a month. No wonder he's been so belligerent!"

"Her grandmother has been so good about checking her assignment pad every night and making sure she's doing her homework. She really's working with me on this."

"His father comes in to read to the class whenever he has a day off. He provides such a fabulous role model!"

Comments like these can be heard in teachers' rooms all across the country. They reflect some of the benefits that accrue when teachers and families establish positive, productive relationships. A growing body of evidence shows that family involvement in schooling is linked to students' academic achievement (Anderson & Minke, 2007). But family–school relationships also have definite payoffs in terms of classroom management.

First, *knowing about children's home situations provides insight into their classroom behavior.* It's easier to understand why John seems so listless if you're aware that his mother is undergoing chemotherapy, and Jana's anxiety about getting all As is understandable if you appreciate how much her parents pressure her to succeed. Furthermore, these insights can help you decide what course of action to take when dealing with a child's problems. You don't want to suggest that a parent read to a child if the parent can't read, or send a note home if it will lead to a beating.

Second, *when families understand what you are trying to achieve, they can provide valuable support and assistance.* Most parents want their children to succeed in school and will do what they can to help. But they can't work in a vacuum. They need to know what you are trying to achieve and how you expect children to behave in your classroom. Familiarizing parents with your curriculum, routines, and policies minimizes confusion, misinterpretations, and conflict.

Third, *families can help to develop and implement strategies for changing behavior.* Working together, parents and teachers can bring about improvements in students' behavior that it would be impossible for either to achieve working alone. Garnetta shares this example:

> I had this boy in my class who was extremely disruptive. He wouldn't work, kept "forgetting" his homework, distracted other children, wandered around the room. You name it; he did it. The three of us— the mother, the boy, and I—talked about what we could do, and we decided to try a system of home rewards. We agreed that I would send a note home each day, reporting on the boy's behavior. For every week with at least three good notes, his mother let him rent a video game. In this way, the child's access to video games was directly dependent on his behavior. This system really made a difference!

Finally, *parent volunteers can make classroom management easier by assisting in the classroom.* Parents can staff learning centers, read to children, help during writing conferences, and perform some of the clerical and housekeeping duties that eat up a teacher's time. In the crowded, fast-paced, unpredictable world of the elementary classroom, an extra pair of hands (and eyes) can be a lifesaver.

Despite the many benefits of close communication and collaboration, parents and teachers are often at odds with one another. What causes this adversarial relationship and what can teachers do to avoid it? In this chapter, we examine three challenges to close working relationships—teacher reluctance to involve parents, parent reluctance to become involved, and changes in the family and American society. We then turn to our teachers and to the literature on parent involvement to suggest ways in which families and schools can work together to *overcome* those challenges.

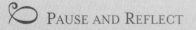

PAUSE AND REFLECT

What are some of the challenges to close working relationships between parents and teachers? Before reading on, think about three possible answers to each of the following questions:

- Why would teachers sometimes be reluctant to involve parents in their child's schooling?
- Why would parents sometimes be reluctant to become involved?
- How does the changing nature of the family affect parent–teacher collaboration?

CHALLENGES TO FAMILY–TEACHER COOPERATION

Teacher Reluctance to Involve Families in Schooling

A primary reason for teachers' reluctance to work with families is the *extra time and energy that is required.* Teaching is physically and emotionally exhausting, and reaching out to parents is sometimes viewed as one more burdensome task. For example, telephoning 30 parents and talking for 10 minutes to each means five hours of work (Epstein & Becker, 1982). This is obviously in addition to planning lessons and activities, grading papers, organizing cooperative learning groups, and creating bulletin board displays, so it's understandable when teachers wonder whether the extra time required is worth the trouble.

Teachers' perceptions of families undoubtedly also contribute to their reluctance to seek greater parental involvement. Many teachers recognize that time is often a scarce commodity for parents, limited by responsibilities at work, household chores, and caring for other family members. The teachers question whether it is fair to ask already burdened parents to spend time working with children on academic activities or assisting in school. As Ken told us:

Some parents are really stressed out. One family I'm thinking about owns their business. They work unbelievable hours. Meanwhile, I'm telling them to read to their kid. C'mon, are they going to do the accounts, or are they going to read to their kid? They're going to do the accounts. It's understandable.

Other teachers have been burned by encounters with angry, irresponsible, or apathetic parents. They would tend to agree with the statement that "far too many parents—and not just disadvantaged ones—simply don't give a damn. For them, school is a free babysitting service" (Walde & Baker, 1990, p. 322).

Another reason for teachers' reluctance to involve parents is *the worry that parents may not understand their role in the classroom.* Some parent volunteers intervene when they shouldn't (e.g., imposing their own punishments for inappropriate behavior instead of consulting the teacher); they may instruct students in ways that contradict what the teacher has demonstrated; or they may violate confidentiality by sharing student records and relaying sensitive information. When situations like these occur, teachers may wonder if parent volunteers are more of a hindrance than a help.

Finally, teachers may be reluctant to involve parents because of the *authority and autonomy they enjoy within their classrooms.* Teachers are often exposed to criticism. Parents may blame them for children's problems or question their professional competence. It's not surprising that teachers sometimes become guarded and protective of their "turf," especially if they lack confidence in their skills and expertise. Indeed, teachers who report higher levels of *teacher efficacy* (teachers' beliefs that they can teach and that their students can learn) are more likely to reach out to parents (Hoover-Dempsey, Bassler, & Brissie, 1987).

Parent Reluctance to Become Involved in Schooling

Although most parents strongly value involvement in their children's learning, actual involvement often falls short of school expectations (Drummond & Stipek, 2004). Among the most obvious reasons are the *competing demands of work*. This is especially so in low-income households, which are more likely to be single-parent families or to have two parents who work full time. Low-income parents may also have two or more jobs, work evenings and nights, or have jobs with inflexible or unpredictable hours.

In addition to the difficulties imposed by work, there are more subtle reasons for parental reluctance to become involved. Some adults have unhappy—even traumatic—memories of their own experiences as students. According to Sara Lawrence-Lightfoot (2003), parents' encounters with schools are shaped by their own autobiographical stories—"their own childhood histories, their own insecurities, and their own primal fears" (p. xxii). These "ghosts" from the past may make parents hostile to schools and teachers and less than eager to return for conferences or open houses (see Figure 6.1 for a humorous example). Listen to this father describe his reasons for not participating more fully in his son's schooling:

> They expect me to go to school so they can tell me my kid is stupid or crazy. They've been telling me that for three years, so why should I go and hear it again? They don't do anything. They just tell me my kid is bad. . . . See, I've been there. I know. And it scares me. They called me a boy in trouble but I was a troubled boy. Nobody helped me because they liked it when I didn't show up. If I was gone for the semester, fine with them. I dropped out nine times. They wanted me gone. (Finders & Lewis, 1994, p. 51)

Other families may *feel guilty* when their children have difficulties in school. They may become defensive and uncooperative when teachers try to discuss their child's problem or may be too embarrassed to disclose troubles they are having at home. Rather than deal with the child's problem, these families may try to deny what is occurring and to avoid communication with the teacher.

Still other families may be *intimidated or unnerved by schools*. This is particularly so when parents are poor, are uneducated, or have limited proficiency in

Figure 6.1   *Source:* Rose is Rose © Pat Brady & Don Wimmer. Reprinted with permission of United Features Syndicate. All rights reserved.

English. Some may find teachers and administrators unresponsive to their requests (Gutman & McLoyd, 2000); others may even fear teachers, viewing them as authority figures who must not be questioned (Lindeman, 2001). Immigrant parents in particular may be confused by educational practices that are different from their own; they may not know the words (e.g., *standards, student-centered, cum file, grade equivalence*) that would enable them to have a meaningful exchange.

One study interviewed 11 Latino families about family involvement in schooling (Chrispeels & Rivero, 2000). Nine of the 11 families felt they had little influence on what happened at school and left decisions in the hands of the teacher. Mrs. Andres was typical:

> My daughter's report card from fourth grade arrived with all Bs. In third grade she came out with excellence and an A. We waited for the next report card and again she got all Bs. . . . She told me, "My teacher says that she will not give any As because that will make the children who get an F feel bad." My daughter said that in that case she would not try hard because she was not going to get an A. (p. 22)

Although Mrs. Andres felt this was unfair, she did not ask the teacher for an explanation: "In a way I felt that the teacher could say, 'Well, who tells you that your daughter deserves an A?' My fear of that comment kept me from going to ask" (p. 22).

Finally, it is important to recognize that some families *do not view participation at school as part of their parental roles* (Hoover-Dempsey & Sandler, 1997). They may believe that schooling should be left to the professionals or that they are showing their support for teachers by not interfering. Immigrant families may not even realize that parental involvement is expected and valued: "In most countries outside the United States, the unspoken norm is that it's the teacher's job to educate a student and that participation from parents shows disrespect for the teacher's expertise" (Sobel & Kugler, 2007). Asian American families, for example, generally hold high expectations for their children's academic success; nonetheless, they tend to view educational matters as the province of the school (Fuller & Olsen, 1998). Similarly, Latinos typically perceive their role as ensuring their children's attendance; instilling respect for the teacher; encouraging good behavior in school; meeting their obligations to provide clothing, food, and shelter; and socializing children to their family responsibilities (Chrispeels & Rivero, 2000; Trumbull, Rothstein-Fisch, Greenfield, & Quiroz, 2001). Parental presence at school (attending conferences and back-to-school night; volunteering in class; fundraising) is *not* a key component of this role.

A good example of how both the demands of work and parents' definition of involvement can affect involvement comes from Gerardo Lopez (2001), who studied the Padillas, an immigrant, migrant family whose children were all very successful in school. Their parental involvement, however, took the form of exposing their children to their hard work in the fields and teaching them that without an education, they might end up in the same situation. Here is an excerpt from one interview:

INTERVIEWER: Now I want to know if you or your wife are involved in the schools in one way or another? For example, like volunteers or in the Parent's Committee.

MR. PADILLA: No sir . . .

> INTERVIEWER: Hmmm. Haven't you gone to a parents' meeting or something like that?
>
> MR. PADILLA: No. Not really. It's just that we're always busy with work. We rarely go to the school.
>
> INTERIVEWER: Not even to a conference with the teachers?
>
> MR. PADILLA: Well, maybe once in a while. But it's really difficult. There's a lot of work.
>
> INTERVIEWER: So how are you involved in your children's education?
>
> MR. PADILLA: Well, I have shown them what work is and how hard it is. So they know that if they don't focus in their studies, that is the type of work they'll end up doing. I've opened their eyes to that reality.
> (p. 427)

As Lopez points out, if the Padillas' "involvement" were defined by their presence at bake sales or back-to-school nights, they would appear to be uninvolved in their children's education. Yet they were *highly* involved in fostering their children's positive attitudes toward school. Clearly, we need to be cautious about assuming that parents who do not attend school events are unconcerned and uncaring. Teachers who equate parent involvement with presence at school are likely to overlook or underestimate the involvement that occurs at home (Anderson & Minke, 2007; Lee & Bowen, 2006).

Changes in the Family and American Society

In 1955, 60 percent of American households consisted of a working father, a homemaker mother, and two or more school-age children (Hodgkinson, 1985). Teachers sent letters home addressed to "Dear Parents," reasonably confident that two parents would read them, and schools scheduled "parent conferences" with the expectation that parents were the primary caregivers of their children.

Times have changed. The typical family of the 1950s is still called "normal" in everyday conversation, but less than one-quarter of all households conform to this model (Heilman, 2008). Today, about half of all marriages end in divorce (Heuveline, 2005), and about half of today's children will spend some portion of childhood in a single-parent family (Heilman, 2008), without the human or economic resources available to those growing up in two-parent families. In some cases, the significant adults in children's lives are not their parents at all, but grandparents, aunts, uncles, brothers, sisters, or neighbors. The "stay-at-home" mother is vanishing; indeed, 65 percent of all preschoolers have mothers in the work force (Coontz, 2007). Between 8 and 10 million children are being raised in gay and lesbian families (Child Welfare Information Gateway, 2008). With a surge in immigration from Central and Latin America, the Middle East, Southeast Asia and the Pacific, and Russia and Eastern Europe, many students come from homes where a language other than English is spoken, and their families are unfamiliar with schools in the United States.

These changes in American society have made communication and collaboration more difficult than ever. Nonetheless, research has found that *teachers' attitudes and practices—not parents' educational level, marital status, or workplace— determine whether families become productively involved in their children's schooling* (Epstein, 2001; Griffith, 1998). In other words, it's the teacher that makes the difference. For this reason, you must not only understand the challenges to parent involvement but also be aware of the ways in which families and schools can work together. (Note that in this chapter, when we refer to "parents," we are referring to all the various types of caregivers that your students may have in their lives, not just birth parents.)

OVERCOMING THE CHALLENGES: FOSTERING COLLABORATION BETWEEN FAMILIES AND SCHOOLS

Joyce Epstein and her colleagues at Johns Hopkins University have studied comprehensive parent involvement programs and have identified six different types of family–school collaboration. These are listed in Box 6.1. The first four of Epstein's six categories provide a framework for our discussion. (For more information and to learn about the last two types, see Epstein and colleagues, 2002, listed in Box 6.1).

Helping Families to Fulfill Their Basic Obligations

This category refers to the family's responsibility to provide for children's health and safety, to prepare children for school, to supervise and guide children at each age level, and to build positive home conditions that support school learning and behavior. Schools can assist families in carrying out these basic obligations by providing workshops on child development and parenting skills; establishing parent-support groups; creating parent resource centers and toy-lending libraries; providing child care for parents to attend meetings; and referring families to community and state agencies when necessary (Brown & Beckett, 2007).

Asking teachers to assume responsibilities for the education of *families,* in addition to the education of *children,* may seem onerous and unfair. Not surprisingly, some teachers hesitate to become "social workers," a role for which they are not trained. Others feel resentful and angry at parents who do not provide adequate home environments. Although these attitudes are understandable, you need to remember that your students' home environment shapes their chances for school success. As the number of distressed families grows, helping families to carry out their basic obligations becomes increasingly critical.

What can you, as a teacher, realistically do to assist families in carrying out their basic obligations? Although you will probably not be directly involved in planning parent education workshops or leading support groups, you can play an important *indirect role.* You can photocopy and share relevant articles from journals and magazines. You can let families know about available materials, motivate and encourage them to attend programs, bring transportation and child care problems to the attention of appropriate school personnel, and help families to arrange car pools (Greenwood & Hickman, 1991).

MEET THE EDUCATORS   BOX 6.1

MEET JOYCE EPSTEIN

Joyce Epstein is professor of sociology at Johns Hopkins University and director of the Center on School, Family, and Community Partnerships. She began research on parent involvement in elementary schools in 1981 and then extended her inquiries to middle schools and high schools. In 1996, Epstein and her colleagues established the National Network of Partnership Schools, which assists schools, districts, and states in using research-based approaches to develop programs of family involvement and community connections and to meet the requirements of No Child Left Behind for parent involvement. The Network now includes over 1,200 schools located in 21 states.

Some Major Ideas about Family, School, and Community Partnerships

1. Well-designed programs of school, family, and community partnerships benefit students, families, and schools.
2. There are six types of involvement for comprehensive partnership programs.
   - Type 1: Parenting—Help all families establish home environments to support children as students.
   - Type 2: Communicating—Design effective forms of school-to-home and home-to-school communications about school programs and children's progress.
   - Type 3: Volunteering—Recruit and organize parent help and support.
   - Type 4: Learning at Home—Provide information and ideas to families about how to help students at home with homework and other curriculum-related activities, decisions, and planning.
   - Type 5: Decision Making—Include parents in school decisions, developing parent leaders and representatives.
   - Type 6: Collaborating with the Community—Identify and integrate resources and services from the community to strengthen school programs, family practices, and student learning and development.
3. In order to create a lasting, comprehensive partnership program, each school needs an Action Team for Partnerships (ATP) to assess present practices and needs, develop options for action, implement selected activities, evaluate next steps, and coordinate practices.

Selected Books and Articles

Epstein, J. L. (2001). *School, Family, and Community Partnerships: Preparing Educators and Improving Schools.* Boulder, CO: Westview Press.

Epstein, J. L., Sanders, M. G., Simon, B. S., Salinas, K. C., Jansorn, N. R., & Van Voorhis, F. L. (2002). *School, Family, and Community Partnerships: Your Handbook for Action* (2nd ed.). Thousand Oaks, CA: Corwin Press.

Hutchins, D. J. Greenfeld, M. D., & Epstein, J. L. (2008). *Family Reading Night.* Larchmont, NY: Eye on Education.

Website: www.partnershipschools.org

You can also educate families about relevant school-based resources (e.g., guidance counselors, psychologists, social workers, and school nurses), as well as community and state agencies. Listen to Viviana's story of Santiago, a child who had come from Nicaragua:

 Right away I noticed that Santiago had a lot of difficulty sitting still and paying attention. Sometimes he seemed like he was in another world. One day, shortly after school began, I talked with his grandmother when she came to school to pick him up. She told me that Santiago's father was still in Nicaragua and that Santiago lived with her, his mother, an older sister,

and two little ones. She told me that Santiago had terrible problems sleeping, that he would wake up crying and fanning himself—as if he were trying to get flies away from him. She told me that Santiago had seen lots of people killed in Nicaragua, that he had seen bodies lying in the street, decomposing and covered with flies. I told the grandmother that we needed to get professional help for him and that I would see what I could do.

The next day, I found out that there was a Spanish-speaking person at a local mental health clinic, and I gave the grandmother the phone number. I told her to give the number to the mother, and I urged her to call. The clinic gave them an appointment right away and told the mother to bring all members of the family. It was such a good thing that they did! They found out that Santiago's older sister was contemplating suicide! As for Santiago, after working with him a number of times, they decided he needed medication to calm him down.

The change in Santiago was unbelievable. He was able to sit still, to pay attention, to do his work. He did fine after that. The mother came to see me and said, "Mrs. Love, you saved my family. My daughter was going to kill herself, and I didn't even know it." But she was worried about Santiago's medication; I assured her that they knew how much to give Santiago. We talked about her family and her jobs—she was working three jobs! Later, I found out the mother was laid off from two of the three jobs, and she didn't know what to do. I helped her go to welfare.

In addition to providing this sort of indirect assistance, there are times when it may be appropriate to work *directly* with families. You might be able to help them communicate more effectively with their children. If kindergartners are worried about separation, for example, you could share information with parents or caretakers about active or empathic listening (see Chapter 3). If sixth-graders are arguing about curfews, you might be able to encourage parents to provide necessary limits. Barbara remembers a child with many behavior problems, both at home and in school:

 The mother really wanted him in my class, and I agreed to take him—with the stipulation that she listen to my suggestions about how to handle him at home. She was at her wit's end with the boy, so she agreed. I helped her learn how to say no to her son and how to reward his good behavior. The mother, the child's therapist, and I worked together as a team, and eventually we saw a lot of improvement in his attitude toward school and his relationship with his mother. It was a lot of work, and it was discouraging at times. But we were able to reach a very difficult child, and we got to the point where he was controllable in class. This not only made him feel good, it also caused less of a distraction to the rest of the class. It was worth the trouble.

As you reflect on how to help families with parenting responsibilities, keep in mind that there are cultural differences in beliefs about child rearing, and these differences may lead to cultural clashes between home and school. Parents from collectivistic cultures, for example, may emphasize respect, obedience, helpfulness, and responsibility to the family, whereas teachers from individualistic cultures stress individual achievement, independence, and self-expression (Trumbull, Rothstein-Fisch, Greenfield, & Quiroz, 2001). If these differences are not acknowledged and respected, teachers' and schools' efforts to help families with parenting are likely to cause resentment and suspicion.

Communicating with Families

 It's the first day of school in New Brunswick. In Viviana's classroom, 19 parents are standing around the sides and the back of the room. The children are seated boy–girl and according to height. Viviana speaks in Spanish to the parents. She introduces herself and explains how she seated the children. She explains that they're the parents at home, but she's the mother in school. She says that they are all family, one big family, all Hispanic, and that they should come in if they need help; they are not alone.

She discusses the importance of homework and attendance. She explains that she is very firm about both. She will give a zero if children do not bring in their homework. She tells the parents that she gives homework every day but not on weekends, so the children can relax. She says that parents should not let their children fool them about being sick and not able to come to school. She says the school has a nurse and can check their children and send them home if they're really sick.

Viviana moves to a round table in the front of the room where workbooks are displayed. She picks up each workbook and explains that there is much work ("mucho trabajo") this year: spelling, social studies, English, math, science, health. Again, she emphasizes that the children must attend school in order to master the skills they need for first grade.

Viviana asks whether the parents have any questions or comments. A woman in pink thanks her for her comments about being one big family. Then Viviana invites the parents to introduce themselves. They go around the room, saying who they are and pointing to their children. After the introductions are complete, the parents leave, kissing their children goodbye on the way out.

Epstein's second category of family–school involvement refers to the school's obligation *to communicate about school programs and children's progress.* Communications include the kind of face-to-face interaction that Viviana has on the first day of school and at open houses and parent–teacher conferences, as well as report cards, progress reports, memos, e-mail messages, newsletters, and phone calls. This is certainly the most commonly accepted way to work with parents, and there is no doubt that these communications are essential. The crucial question, however, is not only whether these communications occur but *when they occur, whether they are being understood, and whether they lead to feelings of trust and respect or of alienation and resentment.*

Viviana welcomes parents on the first day of school.

All of the teachers stress the importance of communicating with families early in the school year—*before* stressful situations occur. As Ken reminds us:

It takes effort for teachers to contact a parent, and so they often wait until some problem arises. Because of this, "communication" begins to have a negative connotation. We've got to communicate with parents even when there is no problem—when we've got good things to tell— and the more communication the better. If you develop a personal connection with parents early, you have an easier time approaching them when you do have a concern.

Given Ken's attitude, it is not surprising that he was part of a program this year in which teachers in his district held parent conferences *before school began.* The focus of the conferences was to hear "parents' hopes and dreams for the coming year for their child," to learn "one important thing they want their child to learn this year," and to find out about "special needs and future problems that might arise." Ken hopes that "these early conferences will make it clear that parents and teachers are *partners* in the education of the children."

It is clear that the five teachers with whom we are working are able to establish productive partnerships with families, and the next few sections of this chapter describe some of the ways they do this. In addition, the accompanying Practical Tips box lists some suggestions for communicating with parents who are particularly hard to reach.

PRACTICAL TIPS FOR

REACHING "HARD TO REACH" PARENTS

Step 1: Try to figure out why parents are hard to reach. Ask yourself (or someone in the school or community who would know) the following questions.

- Do parents speak English?
- Do parents come from cultures that do not identify parent involvement as a priority? Do they come from cultures that believe schooling should be left to the educators?
- Do parents have work schedules that conflict with conferences?
- Do parents live far from the school? Do they have transportation?
- Do parents have other children who would require babysitting during parent–teacher meetings?
- Do parents know where the school is?
- Are the parents homeless (and therefore have no good address for receiving written communications from school)?

Step 2: Develop outreach strategies to address the underlying issue. For example:

- Make sure that parents receive messages in their native language.
- Make sure that written communications are easy to read, warm, and friendly.
- Figure out how to get messages to parents who are homeless.
- Schedule conferences at flexible times to accommodate parents with conflicting work schedules.
- Provide child care for meetings, conferences, and events.
- See whether neighbors or friends can be used as liaisons.
- Offer use of a language translator to aid communication.
- Determine whether meetings can be held in a more convenient, more familiar, more neutral location.
- Arrange for home visits (with appropriate security).
- Make it clear that you value the language, culture, knowledge, and expertise of parents and family members.

Source: Adapted from Swap, 1993.

E-mails, Websites, Newsletters, and Notes

So often, parents have no idea what is happening to their children for the six hours of each school day. Hungry for information, they appreciate a note—electronic or paper—about current projects, future activities, and children's progress. One or two weeks before school begins, Barbara sends home a letter addressed to her students and their families (see Figure 6.2). In it she talks about schedules, snacks, the curriculum, and homework policies. But the letter conveys more than this basic information: It communicates her desire for an open, ongoing relationship and sets the stage for the year ahead.

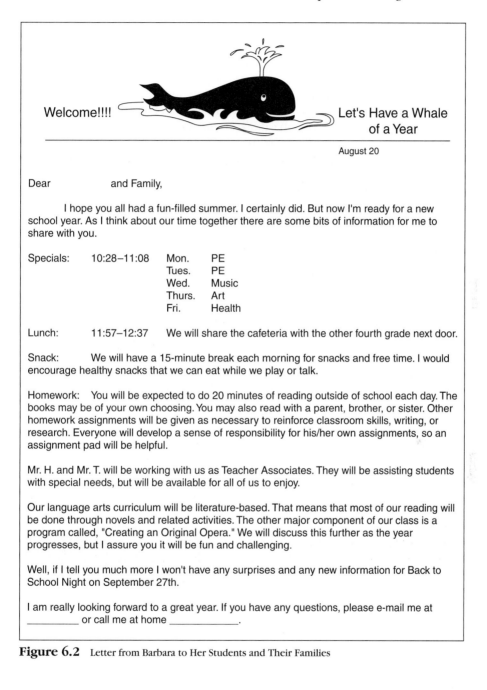

Welcome!!!!   Let's Have a Whale
of a Year

August 20

Dear _____ and Family,

I hope you all had a fun-filled summer. I certainly did. But now I'm ready for a new school year. As I think about our time together there are some bits of information for me to share with you.

Specials: 10:28–11:08   Mon.   PE
                                 Tues.   PE
                                 Wed.   Music
                                 Thurs.   Art
                                 Fri.   Health

Lunch: 11:57–12:37   We will share the cafeteria with the other fourth grade next door.

Snack: We will have a 15-minute break each morning for snacks and free time. I would encourage healthy snacks that we can eat while we play or talk.

Homework: You will be expected to do 20 minutes of reading outside of school each day. The books may be of your own choosing. You may also read with a parent, brother, or sister. Other homework assignments will be given as necessary to reinforce classroom skills, writing, or research. Everyone will develop a sense of responsibility for his/her own assignments, so an assignment pad will be helpful.

Mr. H. and Mr. T. will be working with us as Teacher Associates. They will be assisting students with special needs, but will be available for all of us to enjoy.

Our language arts curriculum will be literature-based. That means that most of our reading will be done through novels and related activities. The other major component of our class is a program called, "Creating an Original Opera." We will discuss this further as the year progresses, but I assure you it will be fun and challenging.

Well, if I tell you much more I won't have any surprises and any new information for Back to School Night on September 27th.

I am really looking forward to a great year. If you have any questions, please e-mail me at _____ or call me at home _____.

Figure 6.2   Letter from Barbara to Her Students and Their Families

To facilitate the process of writing positive notes and memos, it's helpful to write each student's name on an envelope and place the envelopes in a convenient, obvious place. Once or twice a week, you can pull out an envelope and jot a brief, positive note to the family of that student. When all the envelopes are gone, you'll know that you've communicated once with each family (Gruber, 1985). It's also a good idea to make a "communication card" for each student on which to jot down any extra contact you have with a family member by phone, via e-mail, or in person.

Weekly newsletters also help to keep parents informed about what is happening in school. In the lower grades, you can have a class meeting right before dismissal to review and record the day's events. On Fridays, you can fill in the newsletter just before lunch (see the form in Figure 6.3) and then duplicate and send it home at the end of the day (Gruber, 1983). In the higher grades, students can fill out the form themselves at the end of each day or write a letter to parents on Fridays describing five events that occurred during the week. Some teachers also send out monthly newsletters, giving highlights of the past month and previewing the upcoming weeks (see Figure 6.4).

In recent years, Ken and Barbara have used electronic mail and the Internet to facilitate communication with parents. Barbara has created a website for her class that lists class assignments and due dates, links that might help in doing assignments, links to the Internet Public Library (IPL), the weekly schedule, news about current and upcoming events, requests for supplies or assistance, and photographs

OUR WEEKLY NEWSLETTER WEEK OF_____	
LITERACY	
MATHEMATICS	
SOCIAL STUDIES	
SCIENCE	
HEALTH	
ADDITIONAL NOTES	

Figure 6.3 A Sample Newsletter Format

CLASSROOM TIMES

Teacher: _____   Date: _____

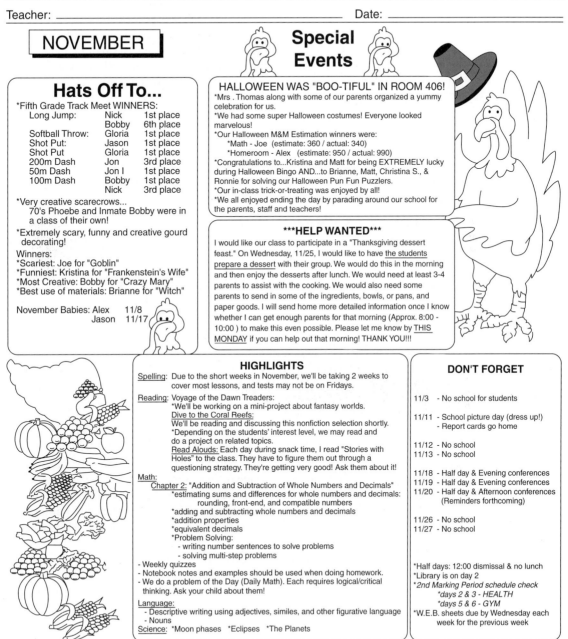

NOVEMBER

Hats Off To...

*Fifth Grade Track Meet WINNERS:

Long Jump:	Nick	1st place
	Bobby	6th place
Softball Throw:	Gloria	1st place
Shot Put:	Jason	1st place
Shot Put	Gloria	1st place
200m Dash	Jon	3rd place
50m Dash	Jon I	1st place
100m Dash	Bobby	1st place
	Nick	3rd place

*Very creative scarecrows...
   70's Phoebe and Inmate Bobby were in
   a class of their own!

*Extremely scary, funny and creative gourd
   decorating!

Winners:
*Scariest: Joe for "Goblin"
*Funniest: Kristina for "Frankenstein's Wife"
*Most Creative: Bobby for "Crazy Mary"
*Best use of materials: Brianne for "Witch"

November Babies:	Alex	11/8
	Jason	11/17

Special Events

HALLOWEEN WAS "BOO-TIFUL" IN ROOM 406!
*Mrs . Thomas along with some of our parents organized a yummy
celebration for us.
*We had some super Halloween costumes! Everyone looked
marvelous!
*Our Halloween M&M Estimation winners were:
   *Math - Joe (estimate: 360 / actual: 340)
   *Homeroom - Alex (estimate: 950 / actual: 990)
*Congratulations to...Kristina and Matt for being EXTREMELY lucky
during Halloween Bingo AND...to Brianne, Matt, Christina S., &
Ronnie for solving our Halloween Pun Fun Puzzlers.
*Our in-class trick-or-treating was enjoyed by all!
*We all enjoyed ending the day by parading around our school for
the parents, staff and teachers!

HELP WANTED

I would like our class to participate in a "Thanksgiving dessert
feast." On Wednesday, 11/25, I would like to have the students
prepare a dessert with their group. We would do this in the morning
and then enjoy the desserts after lunch. We would need at least 3-4
parents to assist with the cooking. We would also need some
parents to send in some of the ingredients, bowls, or pans, and
paper goods. I will send home more detailed information once I know
whether I can get enough parents for that morning (Approx. 8:00 -
10:00) to make this even possible. Please let me know by THIS
MONDAY if you can help out that morning! THANK YOU!!!

HIGHLIGHTS

Spelling: Due to the short weeks in November, we'll be taking 2 weeks to
   cover most lessons, and tests may not be on Fridays.

Reading: Voyage of the Dawn Treaders:
   *We'll be working on a mini-project about fantasy worlds.
   Dive to the Coral Reefs:
   We'll be reading and discussing this nonfiction selection shortly.
   *Depending on the students' interest level, we may read and
   do a project on related topics.
   Read Alouds: Each day during snack time, I read "Stories with
   Holes" to the class. They have to figure them out through a
   questioning strategy. They're getting very good! Ask them about it!

Math:
   Chapter 2: "Addition and Subtraction of Whole Numbers and Decimals"
      *estimating sums and differences for whole numbers and decimals:
         rounding, front-end, and compatible numbers
      *adding and subtracting whole numbers and decimals
      *addition properties
      *equivalent decimals
      *Problem Solving:
         - writing number sentences to solve problems
         - solving multi-step problems
- Weekly quizzes
- Notebook notes and examples should be used when doing homework.
- We do a problem of the Day (Daily Math). Each requires logical/critical
   thinking. Ask your child about them!

Language:
   - Descriptive writing using adjectives, similes, and other figurative language
   - Nouns
Science: *Moon phases *Eclipses *The Planets

DON'T FORGET

11/3 - No school for students

11/11 - School picture day (dress up!)
   - Report cards go home

11/12 - No school
11/13 - No school

11/18 - Half day & Evening conferences
11/19 - Half day & Evening conferences
11/20 - Half day & Afternoon conferences
   (Reminders forthcoming)

11/26 - No school
11/27 - No school

*Half days: 12:00 dismissal & no lunch
*Library is on day 2
*2nd Marking Period schedule check
   *days 2 & 3 - HEALTH
   *days 5 & 6 - GYM
*W.E.B. sheets due by Wednesday each
   week for the previous week

Figure 6.4   Example of a Monthly Newsletter

of class activities. (Note that children's pictures can appear on the website only if parents give permission.)

Although Ken has not established a class website, he takes five minutes at the end of each school day to send an e-mail message to all parents with Internet access. In the message, he lists homework assignments, shares highlights of the day, and suggests topics to discuss over dinner. Ken makes a point of sending the e-mail to parents' work addresses: "I want parents to get it *before* they leave for home. My goal is to make it unnecessary to ask, 'Do you have any homework?' and 'What did you do in school today?'" Ken also uses e-mail to communicate with parents when special situations arise:

I'm too social to make a short phone call. But I can send a short e-mail message letting them know their son had a great day, their daughter cried today, their child didn't have homework. It's easy and effective.

Teachers like Ken see the value in utilizing e-mail as a quick and efficient tool to communicate with parents. E-mail enables you to maintain a paper trail of conversations and to send a message to large groups of parents without having to contact each one individually. With e-mail (as well as snail mail), you can choose your words carefully and deliberately, an advantage you may not have when you're interacting with parents in "real time."

On the other hand, we do have a few words of caution regarding e-mail. First, a clear "digital divide" exists between those parents who have access to e-mail and those who don't (Thompson, 2008). Even when parents do have e-mail, they may not check it as frequently as teachers would like, so you can't assume that parents will read your messages in a timely fashion. Second, e-mail seems to encourage sloppiness and inaccuracy, so be sure to edit your e-mails for misspellings or grammatical errors. Third, be careful about using e-mail to discuss sensitive issues or problems. E-mail doesn't allow you to convey your concerns in a calm, quiet tone of voice or to "soften" your message with smiles, gestures, or body language; nor can you see or hear parents' reactions. For this reason, e-mail may be more likely to lead to misinterpretations than face-to-face interactions or even phone calls. Further, e-mail can also be made public with the simple touch of a few computer keys (intentional or not). You will want to keep this in mind as you compose e-mail messages to parents and save sensitive or personal issues for phone calls or face-to-face interactions.

We asked Courtney, Barbara, Ken, Garnetta, and Viviana to share the guidelines they keep in mind when they draft memos, e-mails, and newsletters to families. Their responses appear in the accompanying Practical Tips box.

The last guideline in this Practical Tips box deserves some additional comment. Be prepared for the fact that parents will not always follow this advice and will write notes to you when they are angry or upset about something. Try not to let the tone of the letter discourage you from dealing with the issue. If the incident is explained and the teacher uses active listening, most conflicts can be defused and resolved.

PRACTICAL TIPS FOR

DRAFTING MEMOS, E-MAILS, AND NEWSLETTERS

- Memos, e-mails, and newsletters should be written in clear, concise language and should be edited for any misspellings or grammatical errors.

- Check e-mail at the beginning, middle, and end of every day—and don't let it pile up.

- Don't use educational jargon; it's a turn-off to parents. Remember that you won't be there to clarify what you meant.

- When writing a note to a family, make sure you know the last name of the parent or guardian to whom you are writing. Often, the parent and the child do not have the same last name.

- Tell children what is in the note. Not going behind their back is a sign of respect.

- If families don't read English, memos and notes should be written in their native language. (In Barbara's school, volunteer parents work as "parent advocates" to help teachers communicate with families who are Chinese, Filipino, Hispanic, Indian, Israeli, Japanese, Portuguese, and Russian.)

- Send home lots of positive notes, such as "happygrams," award certificates, and success stories. Parents love to hear when their children are doing well.

- End letters with an invitation to call or meet with you if there is any question about the contents.

- Don't write notes and letters in anger. If you're communicating about a problem, wait until you've calmed down, and think carefully about what you want to say.

Phone Calls

At the beginning of the school year, all five of our teachers find out when and how to contact the families of their students by telephone. (They're also careful about checking school records to see which parent, in cases of divorce, should be contacted.) Some businesses have strict policies about employees' receiving phone messages, and a call during work hours may result in a reprimand. In cases like this, it's better to call in the evening or to send a note home. Garnetta says that she sometimes has to call at 10:30 in the evening to reach working parents. In all cases, you will want to start a phone call by asking the parent if this is a good time to talk. This can help you avoid catching the parent at a bad time, and it lets them know they have the option to talk at another, more convenient time.

All of the teachers also let parents know when they can receive telephone calls during the school day. (Barbara and Ken even give parents their home phone numbers; they say that no parent has ever abused this access.) If parents call the school and leave a message, our teachers are prompt to return the call the same day so that parents know they care. One of Courtney's initial concerns was that parents were going to call with a question to which she didn't know the answer, but she has since learned that parents prefer an honest response: "I finally realized it's okay to say that I'm not 100 percent sure and that I'll have to get back to them or that we'll have to figure it out together."

Like memos and notes, phone calls should not be reserved for problems. Parents like to hear about their children's successes and improvement. And, of course, if you've made contacts like these, it's easier to call when a problem *does* arise. Ken recalls a sensitive situation that occurred not too long ago:

The class was having a discussion about drug abuse. I was talking about peer pressure to use drugs. I noticed this boy wasn't paying attention and doing a lot of talking, so I said something like "Kids will try to convince you to use drugs, just like they try to convince you to talk when we're having a class discussion." The boy stopped talking, looked at me, and said, "Are you saying I'm going to use drugs?" We talked about what I had meant, and things were OK, but I realized I needed to call home in order to head off trouble. I didn't want the boy to go home and say, "Mr. K. said I'm gonna use drugs." I called home right after school. I was really glad that I had already spoken to these parents a lot, so that we had a good relationship going. I began by telling the parent that I was generally concerned about the boy's behavior in class lately (which I was) and that I felt something was going on. We talked about that for a while, and then I said, "By the way, this happened in school today. . . ." It was really important for me to talk about this with the parents, so that the situation didn't get misinterpreted.

Home Visits

Visiting students' homes is not very common, but it can be a valuable way of learning about students' lives and reaching parents who are reluctant to come to school. Visits to the homes of immigrant students can be particularly helpful in learning about family background, experiences, values, strengths, and challenges. During the visit, you can discuss how the child benefits when the home and school work together, invite parents to visit your classroom, and encourage them to call you if they have questions or concerns.

In some school districts, teachers are encouraged to visit the homes of all students before school begins in order to listen and to learn about each family. Other districts have created the position of home visitation coordinator or parent educator; this person is responsible for regularly visiting students' homes to discuss important events in the family's life, the child's progress in school, and ways in which parents can support and extend their child's learning (Olmsted, 1991).

Garnetta and Viviana stress the need to know about the community before you venture out. Both of them used to make regular home visits, but they are now far more cautious. Garnetta tells us:

A while back, I visited a child's home to talk about her progress in school and just to connect with the family. We had a nice visit. But two or three days later, I learned that her mom and dad and the older children were found guilty of possessing and selling drugs. I could have been in their home when the drug bust was made! Experiences like this have made me leery. I want to know the setting I'm walking into before I visit a parent's home these days.

Viviana has had similar experiences. As a result, she now asks another person (such as the school security guard) to go with her when she makes a home visit. She also asks for assistance from the district's Bilingual Community Liaison Coordinator, who is responsible for visiting children's homes.

If you are thinking about making home visits, consider the recommendations listed in the Practical Tips box.

PRACTICAL TIPS FOR

MAKING HOME VISITS

- Make appointments in advance and follow up with reminders. Try to schedule visits when key family members will be home.
- Plan on brief visits, but follow the family's lead on how long to stay.
- Expect the unexpected (e.g., cancellations, unfamiliar situations and surroundings, sharing of emotional and troubling information).
- If a translator or interpreter is present, look at the family member to whom you are speaking, rather than at the interpreter.
- Remember—parents and family members are experts on their children, so observe, listen, and learn.
- Good questions to guide discussions, especially during the first visit, include
    What are your child's interests and favorite activities?
    What are your child's strengths?
    What do you think your child needs to work on most?
    What does your child want to learn about most?
    What have you discovered about how your child learns best?
    What does your child already know a lot about?
    What are your goals for your child this year?
    Would you like to visit or volunteer in your child's classroom?
    What activities do you do with your child after school and on weekends?
    How do you spend time together?
    What are the favorite topics of conversation?
    What kind of reading or writing do you do together?
    Are there any home/family circumstances that I need to be aware of in order to
        help your child?
    What does your child talk about when he or she mentions school?
    What things about schools in the United States seem different from the learning
        opportunities you had as a child?
    How did your life in other communities differ from your life here?
    What do you particularly enjoy about this community?
    What things at school make your child feel included?
    What are you most proud of about your son or daughter?
    Are there any ways you would like to participate at school that you may not have
        had the opportunity to try?

Sources: Adapted from Ginsberg, 2007; Kyle & McIntyre, 2000.

Report Cards

Report cards have been the traditional way of communicating with families about a child's progress in school. Unfortunately, they are often not very informative. What exactly does it mean when children receive a C in reading? Are they on grade level or not? Are they having problems with vocabulary? with comprehension? with decoding? To clarify or elaborate on students' grades, it's a good idea to write narrative comments. Avoid bland, general statements such as "Maia did a lovely report." You can take a few brief notes during the marking period about accomplishments or behaviors and then use sentence stems such as "Jessica's best work of the quarter was . . .," "Jonathan has shown improvement in . . .," "This term I was glad to see Connor . . .," "Ask Sarah to talk about . . .," "This term Melissa challenged herself . . ." (Power & Chandler, 1998, p. 80). It is always a good policy to make sure that you say at least one positive thing about the student's performance on each report card.

Another common problem with report cards is timeliness. During discussions with our five teachers, they repeatedly emphasized that parents need to know how their children are doing throughout the marking period. In other words, the report card should never come as a shock.

Some schools formalize the process of keeping parents informed. Garnetta and Viviana, for example, are required by their district to write progress reports for all of their children every four weeks. These summarize children's strengths, as well as areas that need improvement.

In addition to sending home letters and progress reports, you may want to develop a comment sheet to accompany the report card so that parents can easily write back to you. A comment sheet like this can tell you a lot about the clarity of the report card and the concerns that parents may have. Most parents will appreciate this opportunity to communicate and feel that you value their participation.

Back-to-School Night

For many parents, open house or back-to-school night is the first opportunity to meet you and to see the classroom. It's also the first opportunity you have to show parents all the great things you've been doing and to tell them about the plans you have for the future. Barbara says, "I put a lot of time, effort, and energy into my teaching, and I'm proud of it. I'm enthusiastic about what I do, and I want to share this with my parents. Plus, I like to show off!" Despite Barbara's enthusiasm, back-to-school night can be anxiety-producing, especially for beginning teachers. Listen to Courtney, reflecting on her first experience:

 I first met the parents at kindergarten orientation, but my focus was really on the children. I met the parents so briefly that by the time we got to back-to-school night, I didn't even really remember which parent belonged to which child. I was definitely nervous; it wasn't a lack of confidence, exactly, but the realization that I didn't have a reputation to stand on. I wanted to make a good impression; after all, you want them to think you're capable and that you're doing right by their children. I'm 24 years old and straight out of school. I was talking to them as an authority figure, and I was the youngest one in the room! I kept telling myself that I knew more about the curriculum than they did, but I was also afraid that they'd ask me questions I didn't know the answers to!

Although Courtney was anxious about back-to-school night, the evening actually went very well—partly because she thought carefully about how to orchestrate the event. In retrospect, however, she wishes she had allowed more time for the parents to share some of their thoughts:

> It never occurred to me to ask the parents what their most important goal was for their child. Next year I think I'll ask about this, and I want to ask the children as well. Then I'll compile the information and discuss it at parent conferences. I think it would help me to learn where the parents are coming from and to discuss whether their goals are realistic. Something like this would help us to all be on the same wavelength. It would also be good to check on progress toward the goal at the parent–teacher conference in the spring.

Given the hectic schedules of many parents, it may take some ingenuity to get a good turnout for back-to-school night. In Viviana's school, a sit-down dinner was held on back-to-school night this year in order to entice parents to come and to make them feel welcome. You might also consider holding a supplemental "back-to-school Saturday morning" for parents who work nights and may not be able to attend school functions scheduled on weekday evenings. (Providing coffee and doughnuts could also increase attendance!) Another idea was devised by a student teacher we know: She made a videotape of her class in action, recording two or three minutes of each major activity and making sure that every child in the class was included. She and her cooperating teacher publicized the fact that the video would be shown at back-to-school night, and they were rewarded by a substantially larger group than in previous years. Another benefit was that parents who were unable to attend could borrow the videotape to watch at home or at school. (Note that videotaping of children requires parental permission, so check with a school administrator about protocol.)

In addition to the regular back-to-school night, Ken has started having his own series of "parent evenings," each devoted to a different content area. On "science night," "social studies night," and "writing night," clusters of students make presentations about what they are doing in school in each subject. He reports that parents are extremely enthusiastic, but—take note—some of the other teachers in the building are unhappy with him.

Some guidelines suggested by our teachers for back-to-school night are listed in the next Practical Tips box.

Parent–Teacher Conferences

Schools generally schedule one or two formal parent–teacher conferences during the school year. Interestingly, these meetings are often a source of frustration to both teachers and parents. Parents resent the formality of the situation and find the limited conference period frustrating. As one mother puts it, "Ten minutes is ridiculous, especially when other parents are waiting right outside the door. I need time to tell the teacher about how my child is at home, too" (Lindle, 1989, p. 14).

PRACTICAL TIPS FOR

BACK-TO-SCHOOL NIGHT

- To increase attendance, don't just rely on the notices sent to parents by the school. Send a special invitation to families, indicating how much you are looking forward to meeting them. You might send an e-mail invitation or post a prominent announcement about the night on your class website. You can also have your students create invitations for their own families.

- Make sure the classroom looks especially attractive and neat. Bulletin boards should display the work of all children, not just a few.

- If you want parents to sit in their children's seats, make sure there are name tags on the desks. Have your students write notes to their parents and leave them on their desks.

- Greet parents at the door, introduce yourself, find out who they are, and show them where their child sits.

- Make sure your presentation is succinct and well organized. Parents want to hear about your goals, plans, and philosophy, as well as the curriculum, schedules, and policies governing homework and absences. Create a PowerPoint presentation; incorporate photographs of the children.

- Have a packet of materials or a hand-out (with statement of goals, class schedules, homework policies, etc.) for parents to take home.

- Send the packet of materials or the hand-out home for parents who were unable to attend back-to-school night. Include a note indicating how sorry you were that they had to miss the evening and how much you are looking forward to meeting them.

- Inform parents about support staff (teachers' aides, basic skills instructors, special education teachers) who work in the classroom, and introduce them if they are present.

- If parents raise issues that are unique to their child, let them know in a sensitive way that the purpose of open house is to describe the general program. Indicate that you will be more than happy to discuss their concerns during a private conference. You may want to have a sign-up sheet available for this purpose.

- Listen carefully to questions that parents have. Provide an opportunity for parents to talk about their goals and expectations for their children in the coming school year. This can begin the two-way communication that is so crucial for family–school collaboration.

- Provide a sign-up sheet for parents who are able to participate in classroom activities (e.g., as a teacher's aide, guest speaker, or chaperon on field trips).

- If refreshments are being served after the class meetings, join in conversations with parents. Clustering with the other teachers separates you from parents and conveys the idea that there is a professional barrier.

Teachers, too, are sometimes unhappy with these formal conferences. Many find the scheduling to be grueling. Ken observes, "It's hard to be pleasant, alert, sensitive, and productive when you're seeing families every 15 minutes for five or six hours in a row!" Moreover, teachers agree with parents that the brief time allotted often precludes meaningful exchange. Finally, teachers complain about the lack of attendance: "The parents you *don't* need to see show up, while the ones you desperately want to talk with don't come."

Despite the problems, parent–teacher conferences are sometimes your only opportunity to have face-to-face interaction with members of a child's family, so it's important to encourage families to participate. Amazingly, all four experienced teachers report that they generally have 100 percent attendance at parent–teacher conferences. This is obviously not an accident. By conference time, Viviana, Garnetta, Barbara, and Ken have already established a close relationship with families through notes, calls, and home visits. They schedule conferences when parents can come, even if this requires making appointments before school begins or in the evening. If necessary, they use "incentives" to encourage attendance. Viviana, for example, enlists her children's aid by promising a surprise to each child whose family attends. She also distributes report cards at conferences, rather than sending them home with children.

All of our teachers stress the need to prepare carefully for conferences. Barbara tells us:

> **The first thing I do is collect samples of students' work and place them in individual folders. Using the report card as a model, I also prepare a profile of each student's academic progress and behavior. This helps to focus the conference and ensures that all important areas are discussed. I try really hard to make the classroom particularly inviting. The students' work is displayed, and the room is neater than usual. I usually set up a table with adult-sized chairs so that we're both sitting on the same level. On the table I put a vase of flowers and a bowl of fruit or candies. Conference time is physically taxing. I need the refreshments, and I offer them to parents as a sign of hospitality.**

Conferences can be tense—especially if you're meeting with family members for the first time—so all five teachers begin by trying to put parents at ease. They engage in small talk or share a funny incident that happened in school. They suggest leading with something positive: "Your son is a delight to have in class" or "Your daughter appears to be really interested in the topics we've been studying." One note of caution in this regard: Immigrant Latino parents (and others from collectivistic cultures) may be uncomfortable hearing extended praise of their children, since praise singles a child out from the group (Trumbull, Rothstein-Fisch, Greenfield, & Quiroz, 2001). If this is a concern, teachers can share pictures of the student involved in various activities during the school day; this is especially helpful if family members have limited proficiency in English.

Next, the teachers inform parents about the child's progress, pointing out both strengths and weaknesses. Discussing weaknesses was the part that worried Courtney the most:

> **I was most nervous about presenting information that they wouldn't like, whether academic or social. But what I found out was that in most cases, the parents knew their children very well. When I said something like "Your child tattles a lot" or "Your child struggles in this area," they already knew! I was feeling like, "This is my first class, who am I to tell them, but**

it worked out fine. And, of course, if they didn't know what I was telling them, they really needed to hear it!

When delivering information about the areas that need improvement, it's important to be specific and calm, conveying confidence that the problems can be solved. In addition, it's helpful to document your reports to parents by showing samples of students' work that you have collected for this purpose. Our five teachers also explain any strategies they are using to bring about improvements in academic work or behavior and try to enlist parents' support or assistance.

Although they try to provide parents with substantive information, our teachers emphasize *the need to listen.* They always allow time for parents to ask questions, and they solicit parents' suggestions. Remember, a conference should be a two-way conversation, not a monologue. *It's also critical not to assume that poor parents, uneducated parents, or parents with limited English proficiency have nothing of value to offer.* A mother in one study expressed her frustration this way: "Whenever I go to school, they want to tell me what to do at home. They want to tell me how to raise my kid. They never ask what I think. They never ask me anything" (Finders & Lewis, 1994, p. 53).

Ellen Kottler (1994) stresses the importance of encouraging families from non-English-speaking backgrounds to help you understand their children's educational and cultural background. For example, you might ask them about past educational experiences, whether the child is experiencing any cultural conflicts, what their educational goals for the child are, whether English is used at home, and whether there are any special needs or customs you need to take into consideration. If you are meeting with parents who are using an interpreter, keep in mind that your conversation is with the parents, not the interpreter. You should speak to and make eye contact with the parents. Speak no more than two or three sentences at a time, and then pause for the interpreter to speak.

You also need to be sensitive to cultural differences in communication styles. Cultures shape the nature of verbal interaction, providing norms for who can initiate conversation, whether it's all right to interrupt, and how long to pause between a question and its answer (Swap, 1993). If these norms are not shared, partners may feel uncomfortable. The following example of conversation between Athabaskan Indians and Whites in Alaska illustrates how misunderstanding can arise because of different communication styles:

> [A] white speaker often will ask a question, then pause, waiting for the Indian speaker to reply; then, when it appears the listener has nothing to say, the white speaker will speak again. The Indian, who wishes to reply, but is accustomed to longer pauses between speakers, is not given an adequate opportunity to speak.
>
> On the other hand, when Indian speakers do have the floor, they are interrupted frequently because they take what are perceived by whites to be "lengthy" pauses between thoughts. As an Athabaskan woman said to one of us, "While you're thinking about what you're going to say, they're already talking." Hence, Indian speakers often say very little and white speakers seem to do all the talking. (Nelson-Barber & Meier, 1990, p. 3, as cited in Swap, 1993, p. 91)

In addition, you need to recognize that different cultures hold different views about appropriate classroom behavior. For example, a European American teacher may encourage students to participate actively in classroom discussions, to voice their opinions, and to ask questions. In contrast, some Latino and Asian American parents may expect their children to be quiet and obedient and not to contradict the teacher or ask questions (Scarcella, 1990). It's also important to understand that Latino immigrant parents may be primarily interested in the child's social and moral development. For example:

> [A] dominant (although not always welcome) theme these parents introduce into parent–teacher conferences is children's behavior.... [They ask], "Como se porta mi hijo/a?" ("How is my son/daughter behaving?") The teacher may try to direct the conversation toward the child's academic achievement, only to be asked again about the child's behavior. Teachers may encounter similar questions from Vietnamese-American or Japanese-American parents. (Trumbull, Rothstein-Fisch, Greenfield, & Quiroz, 2001, pp. 17–18)

Regardless of the family's cultural background, Ken stresses the need to be as responsive as possible:

> Sometimes parents have a particular request—for example, maybe they want to know immediately if a kid misses an assignment. Teachers sometimes resist requests like this and say, "That's not the way I do it. This is the policy in my class. The first time a child misses an assignment, I only give a warning, the second time...." I tell parents, "If you want it that way, we'll do it that way." I try to understand what the situation is at home and to be accommodating. And, you know, it's the greatest feeling when a parent walks away from a conference and says thank you—thank you for understanding and for being responsive, thank you for not telling me I'm a bad parent.

If a parent is angry or upset with a particular approach or incident, our teachers also try hard not to respond with anger and defensiveness. Instead, they use the communication skills outlined in Chapter 3, such as acknowledging and active listening. As Viviana points out:

> It's important to let the parents get it out of their system. Don't fight it. Let it go. Most times the parents are reacting to what was told to them by their child and that is not always accurate. Once the emotions are spent, find out what prompted the tirade. Gather information. Then you can tell parents how you see the situation.

Our teachers emphasize the importance of not closing doors to further communication. When a problem needs to be resolved, they try to reach consensus on possible solutions, determine who will be responsible for doing what, and schedule a follow-up meeting. If a conference is not going well, they might suggest another meeting, perhaps with the principal or guidance counselor on hand to mediate the discussion.

Name _____ Grade _____ Date _____

1   Select 3 pieces of work to share and tell why those were selected.

   a   _____

       _____

       _____

   b   _____

       _____

       _____

   c   _____

       _____

       _____   _____

2   This year I'm most proud of:

3   I consider these to be my strengths:

4   A target area for improvement is:

5   Things I will do to try to improve are:

6   Overall, my fourth-grade experience has been:

7   Additional comments, if needed:

                           _____

                                          Signature

Figure 6.5   Student Conference Organizer

At the end of each conference, our teachers take a minute to summarize any decisions that have been made and to thank parents for coming. Sometimes they follow up by sending a note home, expressing their appreciation for parents' attendance and reporting on children's subsequent progress.

Some schools offer three-way conferences that include the teacher, the parent or caretaker, and the child (Bailey & Guskey, 2001). Barbara, for example, provides parents with the option of having a regular two-way conference or a three-way conference, during which children can show pieces of work that they feel represent their best efforts and share the goals they have for the rest of the year. Barbara restricts three-way conferences to the spring, because students are more experienced by this time at setting goals and assessing their own work. If families opt to have a three-way conference, students must prepare for the conference by completing the organizer shown in Figure 6.5.

Research indicates that the three-way conference has distinct advantages over the traditional parent–teacher conference. One study (Minke & Anderson, 2003), for example, compared traditional parent–teacher conferences with conferences that included students as participants ("family–school conferences"). Families chosen to participate in the project had children with mild learning or behavior problems. Two primary findings emerged with respect to traditional conferences. First, both teachers and parents agreed that conferences are important opportunities for an exchange of information; second, both groups approached conferences with trepidation. Parents used words such as *worried, nervous, overwhelmed, angry,* and *apprehensive* to describe their emotions, and teachers described their feelings of *exhaustion* and *relief* when conference days were over. In contrast, both parents and teachers felt that the family–school conference model increased trust and communication and provided greater opportunities to learn about each other and the child. Adults were particularly impressed by students' "unexpectedly mature behavior" and their "honest, insightful comments about their own learning" (p. 60). Indeed, "Teachers often noted that the child was the first one to bring up 'bad news,' which teachers saw as relieving them of a worrisome burden and greatly reducing parental defensiveness" (p. 60). Evidence also suggested that family–school conferences could be conducted in the same 15–20 minutes usually allotted to routine, two-party conferences. It should be noted, however, that three-way conferences like this require training and careful preparation. (See Bailey & Guskey, 2001, for practical strategies and suggestions.)

> ⌘ PAUSE AND REFLECT
>
> Teachers often complain about the fact that the parents you don't need to see are the ones who come to parent-teacher conferences, whereas the parents you really do need to see are the ones who don't show up. Review the possible reasons for parents' absences from these events. Then think of three specific actions you might take to encourage participation in parent-teacher conferences. Also consider how you could follow up with parents who don't attend.

In addition to formally scheduled parent–teacher conferences, our teachers look for chances to have more casual face-to-face meetings. As we saw earlier, Viviana capitalizes on the fact that many of her children's parents bring their children to school on the first day. Other opportunities occur in the morning, when her parents walk their children to school, or at the end of the day, when they come to pick them up.

Interestingly, all of our teachers agree that if parents show up unexpectedly during the teaching day, they will meet with them on the spot if they are not directly involved with students (i.e., if the visit occurs during a prep period, at lunch time, or before or after school). As Garnetta tells us:

If a parent felt it necessary and important to show up, you take care of it! They're not just coming in to chitchat. You cannot turn the parent away. If you do, there will be hurt feelings and anger. Parents need to feel you are accessible.

Sending Home Student Work

Many teachers send students' work home so that families can see how their children are doing in school, but the work doesn't always arrive in very good condition. Sometimes it doesn't arrive at all! To avoid this problem, some teachers collect work over a week and then send it home in special envelopes that parents sign and return ("Friday folders"). If you're concerned that poor papers will be "lost" on the way, you can indicate on the envelope how many items should be inside. A parent response sheet might also accompany the work, to make it easier for parents to write back

When you're sending home student work and tests, it's important to keep in mind that your written comments may be carefully scrutinized. Does children's work contain suggestions for improvement and specific praise for work well done, or is it marked up with red slashes, zeros, and minus signs? Remember, whatever you write on a paper is a communication to both child and parent.

You also need to think carefully about the kind of work you're sending home. Fill-in-the-blank worksheets are generally not products that children are proud to share, and they're unlikely to stimulate dinner conversation about what's happening in school. Social studies projects, science laboratory reports, and writing samples are not only more interesting, they're also more informative about what students have learned.

Ken believes strongly in the need to send home this kind of meaningful work. When students finish reading a novel, for example, he has them assemble a packet of the writing they've done about the story. He sits with each child, and together they evaluate the work as a whole. He might use items from the report card as a guide and ask students, "What grade would you give yourself for comprehension, for vocabulary, for making inferences?" Both the packet and the evaluation sheet are then sent home. Parents review the work and the evaluation, make their own comments on the sheet, and send it back so that Ken can see whether everyone is in agreement.

Family Involvement in School

Epstein's third type of family–school involvement refers to family members who come to school to attend student performances, athletic events, or other programs. It also refers to parents and other volunteers who assist in classrooms or in other areas of the school.

If you're teaching in a district where there has never been much parent involvement in school, special efforts may be needed to convince parents that you really want them to participate in the life of the school. When Bruce Davis (1995) became principal of an urban elementary school with no history of parent involvement, he immediately instituted a weekly awards assembly on Friday morning at 8:30 to which parents were invited. At the assembly, 44 students—two from each classroom—were honored as "students of the week" and "super readers of the week." Davis used the assemblies as an opportunity to welcome parents to the school, to remind them about upcoming events, to make announcements of interest, and to encourage parents to become involved. He reports that about

50 parents attended each week, many with cameras and video recorders; some came *every week,* just to keep up with school news.

Classroom volunteer programs usually involve relatively few people, but even a few parents can provide considerable support. Ken has at least one parent come in every day for an hour to assist children during reading time. In Garnetta's classroom, a mother comes in once a week to *assist with learning activities.* Depending on the day, she may work with small groups or individuals, read aloud, type stories into a computer, staff a learning center, or supervise the production of a puppet show. She also helps to carry out *clerical and housekeeping chores,* such as preparing bulletin boards, organizing games and toys, filing work samples, and collecting book club money. (Note that she does *not* tutor low-achieving children, who are most in need of the expertise of certified teachers.)

Parents can also enrich the curriculum by sharing information about their jobs, hobbies, and cultural backgrounds. When Barbara's class reads *In the Year of the Boar and Jackie Robinson* (Lord, 1984), a novel about a little girl who comes to the United States from China, Barbara has parents who have come from other countries discuss their immigration experiences.

If you decide to invite parents to participate in your classroom, you need to think carefully about how to recruit them. Sometimes parents don't volunteer simply because they're not sure what would be expected or how they could contribute. As we mentioned earlier, back-to-school night offers a good opportunity to make a direct, in-person appeal and to explain the various ways parents can assist. You might also send an invitation and a survey to families, soliciting their involvement. One kindergarten teacher we know periodically sends home "classified ads," listing specific jobs that need to be done and requesting parents' help.

Using family members as volunteers in the classroom requires you to assess parents' strengths, interests, and availability and determine appropriate roles for them to play. You need to plan and coordinate activities, assign meaningful tasks, and provide direction and possibly even training. Despite these added responsibilities, the benefits can be substantial. Not only do you receive much-needed assistance in the classroom; parents obtain a better understanding of the classroom and become more comfortable in the school environment.

Parents of Youngsters with Special Needs

According to the Individuals with Disabilities Education Act (IDEA), parents of children with disabilities have a legal mandate to participate in the planning of their children's individualized education program (IEP). Because inclusion is now widespread, you are likely to have contact with parents of children with disabilities and, ideally, to be involved in the annual IEP meetings (at which a teacher must be present). For example, Barbara participated in the meetings for Stuart (the child in her class who has autism) and for Mark (the child with an emotional disorder). In Stuart's case, Barbara met with Stuart's mother, his caseworker (the school psychologist), his teacher-associate, his math teacher, the speech therapist, and Stuart himself to review his current IEP, discuss his academic and social goals, and consider strategies to facilitate his progress. One reason why the meeting was productive was that all members of the team had already interacted informally on numerous occasions. In fact, Barbara had invited Stuart and his parents to come over for dinner in August—*before school even began:*

 When I have a child with a disability in my room, I don't wait for formal, mandated meetings or even for parent–teacher conferences. I know that Stuart's mother is anxious every time he gets a new teacher, so I wanted to give them the opportunity to get to know me in a less formal setting. I also wanted to get to know them a little. It's clear that Stuart and his mother have a very special bond. . . . I truly believe that the dialogue I'll have with her is a really important piece. She has a very clear view of Stuart and she can be my biggest help.

In contrast, Mark's mother was not an active participant in his education because of her work schedule (she worked nights and slept days) and language (she spoke very little English, so she couldn't help him with reading). This didn't mean she didn't care; she just couldn't be as fully involved.

Family Involvement in Learning Activities at Home

Epstein's fourth type of involvement refers to the ways in which families can assist their own children at home in learning activities that are coordinated with ongoing classwork. Interestingly, many parents say this is the kind of involvement they want most (Brandt, 1989). On the other hand, parental participation in learning activities at home may conflict with some families' beliefs about the importance of independence and self-sufficiency. For example, a mother in one study explains why she stays out of her daughter's schooling:

> It's her education, not mine. I've had to teach her to take care of herself. I work nights, so she's had to get up and get herself ready for school. I'm not going to be there all the time. She's gotta do it. She's a tough cookie. . . . She's almost an adult, and I get the impression that they want me to walk her through her work. And it's not that I don't care either. I really do. I think it's important, but I don't think it's my place. (Finders & Lewis, 1994, p. 52)

Clearly, this mother is concerned for her child's well-being, but she sees independence as critical if her daughter is to survive and succeed.

It is important to think carefully about realistic ways in which families can participate in learning activities at home, especially if children come from one-parent families or families in which both parents work outside the home. During one meeting, we asked our teachers to describe the ways they try to involve families in learning activities. Their responses can be grouped into three categories.

Activities Involving Reading and Books

Families can create a supportive literacy environment at home in many ways. Our teachers provide a variety of suggestions to parents, such as getting their children a library card; setting aside a special place to keep books; subscribing to a children's magazine; reading road and street signs while walking, driving, or riding some-where; writing notes to children; helping children make birthday cards for friends and relatives; and limiting television and video games.

Our teachers also encourage parents to read aloud to their children, but this can be a problem if parents aren't able to read in English (or at all). Viviana turns the tables: She gives her students books to read to their parents. She recalls how excited Eduardo's mother was the first time he read to her. She actually came to school the next day to tell Viviana how beautifully Eduardo had read, how he had translated each page, and how he had discussed the story with her in Spanish. Viviana tells us, "The parents are learning from the kids."

Activities Involving Joint Homework Assignments

In conjunction with *In the Year of the Boar and Jackie Robinson,* Barbara has students interview family members about their ethnic background. Students make a family scrapbook with photographs, drawings, maps, and reports of interviews they've conducted. According to Barbara, "The really neat thing is that parents find out things they didn't know either. They have to call their parents and aunts and uncles and cousins to find out information."

A program called "Teachers Involve Parents in Schoolwork" (TIPS), developed by Joyce Epstein, colleagues, and teachers (1995), provides teachers with interactive homework assignments that require students to involve family members. For exam-ple, in math, middle-school students might have to ask family members for their shoe sizes or height and then compute the averages; in science, students might conduct a simple experiment using liquids of different thickness and then discuss the results with a family partner. (See the website for the National Network of Partnership Schools in the list of organizational resources at the end of this chapter.)

Supervising Homework

In a study of 69 parents of first- through fifth-grade students, parents generally belie-ved that involvement in homework was a "given" of parenthood (Hoover-Dempsey, Bassler, & Burow, 1995). Many parents, however, expressed ambivalence about how much help they should provide and how independent their children should be. In addition, parents worried that they couldn't provide adequate help because they were unfamiliar with the topic being studied ("You would think I could do fourth-grade work, but sometimes I can't"); because they didn't understand the new way subjects were taught ("My [math] language was different, because that was 30-years-ago language"); or because competing demands on their time made it difficult to help as much as they felt they should (pp. 444–445). Despite their wor-ries, parents did not want less involvement in their children's learning at home; they simply wanted "to know better how to be involved" (p. 447).

Helping children with their homework can be especially problematic for par-ents who are not fluent in English and have had little formal schooling themselves. Research indicates that parents have special difficulty with the "reams of work-book pages and ditto sheets" that children bring home (Delgado-Gaitan, 1992,

p. 510). Because these tasks depended on subject matter knowledge covered in the classroom, they often caused a great deal of confusion and frustration.

You can support parents' desire to be involved by providing explicit information about your homework expectations and specific suggestions for working with children at home. Even simple suggestions such as "Read for 15 minutes most nights"; "Say 'Let's go over this together"; or "Do about five math problems each night" are appreciated (Hoover-Dempsey, Bassler, & Burow, 1995).

Our teachers try to reassure parents by emphasizing the importance of simply monitoring their children's schoolwork and setting limits ("Doing math in front of the TV is not working" or "You have to do your homework before you go out to play"). In fact, a recent review of research on parent involvement in homework (Patall, Cooper, & Robinson, 2008) concluded that of all the various types of parent involvement in homework, *setting rules about when and where homework should be done may have the most beneficial effect on students' achievement.* And this kind of involvement doesn't require years of higher education. A survey of middle-school students' homework practices (Xu & Corno, 2003) found that family members were especially helpful in arranging the environment (e.g., finding a quiet area, creating space for the child to work, turning off the television) and in helping children control their emotions (e.g., calming a frustrated child, providing encouragement when a child is upset). The homework helper's educational level was unrelated to effective homework assistance.

Parents can also help simply by asking to see their children's papers; this prevents papers from going directly into the trash can from the bookbag. In Garnetta's class, for example, each student has a homework pad provided by the school. At the end of each school day, children copy the assignments listed on the chalkboard. Parents are required to review the homework pad each night and to sign it. When children come to school each morning, they put their homework and the pads on their desks for Garnetta to check. Garnetta remembers one boy who forged his father's signature. Because she had taught his brother, she knew what his father's signature looked like and she informed the boy that "the jig was up." As she puts it, "There was no use jumping all over the kid, but I wanted to make sure he took responsibility for getting the pad signed."

PAUSE AND REFLECT

Homework is a controversial subject. For example, in *The End of Homework: How Homework Disrupts Families, Overburdens Children, and Limits Learning*, Etta Kralovec and John Buell argue that homework actually promotes discrimination. Children who are able to get support and assistance from their families (the "haves") can surge ahead, while those who come from families that are unable to help them (the "have-nots") fall further and further behind. What do you think about this issue?

CONCLUDING COMMENTS

This chapter has described different ways in which teachers can reach out to families. Our suggestions vary considerably in terms of how commonly they are used and how much time and energy they demand. As you get to know your students and their family situations, you will be able to decide which practices are most appropriate and most feasible. Of course, you need to be realistic: As a beginning teacher, you may have to delay major efforts to facilitate communication and collaboration with families. Nonetheless, remember that family involvement can be crucial to children's success and that *extending specific invitations to participate has been shown to have a powerful impact on family involvement at home and in school* (Anderson & Minke, 2007).

SUMMARY

This chapter began by discussing the benefits of working closely with families. We then examined the challenges to family–teacher cooperation and stressed that teachers' attitudes and practices—not the educational level, marital status, or workplace of parents—determine whether families become productively involved in their children's schooling. Finally, we presented strategies for overcoming the challenges and for fostering collaboration between families and schools.

Benefits of Working Closely with Families

- Knowing about a student's home situation provides insight into the student's classroom behavior.
- When families understand what you are trying to achieve, they can provide valuable support and assistance.
- Families can help to develop and implement strategies for changing behavior.
- Parent volunteers can make classroom management easier by assisting in the classroom.

Challenges to Family–Teacher Cooperation

- Teachers are sometimes reluctant to involve families in schooling because of

    The extra time and energy that are required.
    Their perceptions that families are too overburdened, apathetic, and irresponsible, or that they lack the skills needed.
    The level of authority and autonomy teachers enjoy within their classrooms.

- Parents are sometimes reluctant to become involved in schooling because

    They have competing demands from work.
    They have unhappy memories of school.
    They believe schooling should be left to the experts.
    They feel guilty if their children are having problems.
    They find schools intimidating and threatening places.
    They do not see involvement in schooling as a part of their role.

- Changes in the family and in America society mean that

    The number of single–parent families has increased.
    The "stay-at-home" mother is vanishing.
    The significant adults in children's lives may not be parents, but grandparents, neighbors, aunts, uncles, or others.
    Many children come from non-English-speaking homes.

Fostering Collaboration between Families and Schools

- Schools can assist families in carrying out their basic obligations by providing parent education, establishing parent–support groups, and referring families to community and state agencies.
- Teachers need to communicate about school programs and students' progress through memos, e-mails, notes, phone calls, report cards, progress reports, and face-to-face interactions (e.g., back-to-school night, parent conferences).
- Family members can serve as volunteers in classrooms.
- Families can assist their children at home on learning activities:
   Activities involving reading and writing.
   Activities involving joint homework assignments.
   Supervising homework.
   Providing encouragement and support.
   Setting limits.

As a beginning teacher, you have to decide what you can realistically accomplish with respect to communication and collaboration with parents. Nonetheless, you need to remember that family involvement is critical to children's success. In this age of single parents, mothers who work outside the home, and children who come from diverse cultural backgrounds, meaningful family–school collaboration has never been more challenging, but it has never been more vital.

ACTIVITIES FOR SKILL BUILDING AND REFLECTION

In Class

1. Working in small groups, students read the vignettes below (one per group) and do the following:
   - Discuss the information provided in the vignette.
   - Make a list of other information you might like to get and how you might get it.
   - Make a list of possible ways you might address the issue aside from talking to the parent/guardian/family. What might some underlying issues be?
   - Think about what you will you do to prepare for the conference.
   - Decide how you will structure the meeting so that you can state your information in a productive way without being defensive.
   - Role-play the conversation that you might have with the family member about this issue.

Vignette 1

You have your third-grade students sitting in clusters that are heterogeneous in terms of race, ethnicity, gender, and achievement level. You often have students work on cooperative learning activities in their clusters, and you encourage students to help one another on their academic tasks. At parent conferences, the father of a Pakistani girl in your class requests that you move his child to an all-girl group. As he explains, his culture frowns on girls and boys sitting together, and he was extremely unhappy when he learned about the seating arrangement in your classroom.

Vignette 2

You are teaching fourth grade and everything seems to be going well. It is November, and you feel prepared for your first parent–teacher conferences. Ronald is a good student who completes all of his work. He is reading way above grade level and writes wonderful, imaginative stories. You are looking forward to sharing his work with his mother. She looks at his work and listens to you, but then she expresses her serious concern about Ronald's handwriting. She believes that his penmanship is very poor and can't understand why you are not addressing this problem. She is quite upset about this and feels that you are neglecting an important part of her son's education.

Vignette 3

It is parent–teacher conference night for your second-grade class. You are eager to talk to Deirdre's parents, because the other children have been complaining about her. Almost every day, two or three students tell you that Deirdre has pinched them, hit them, or said a bad word. When you ask her about it, she is silent. She is compliant, but she will not answer your questions. She speaks at other times during the day, but she shuts down when you ask her about these incidents. You have never seen or heard her do any of the things that the other students accuse her of, but the overwhelming number of complaints leads you to believe that they are true. When her father comes in for the conference, you explain the situation. He seems to be most concerned about what the other children are doing to Deirdre to provoke her. He does not really address her silence. He also mentions that he has taught her to defend herself if someone bothers her.

Vignette 4

You have a student in your fourth-grade class who is failing to complete her homework. She is an academically competent student in class; she does most of her class work and is friendly and easygoing. You have asked the student repeatedly to do her homework, yet she comes in almost daily with little or none of it complete. When you ask her why she has not done the work, she answers by saying, "I don't know." You have sent two letters home and have left one phone message for her family. Her mother shows up unexpectedly at the end of a school day, demands to speak with you, and tells you that her daughter is complaining that you are picking on her and do not like her.

2. In an effort to involve parents in their children's education, you planned a project that required students and their families to work together. The activity involved collecting 15 different leaves, identifying them, and creating a booklet or chart to display the collection in an interesting way. As you survey students about their progress, you realize that two of your students are not receiving any help from home. In a small group, discuss four ways in which you can help these children, either by trying to get the families involved or by providing alternative assistance.

On Your Own

1. In getting ready for the school year, you have decided to send a letter to the family of each student in your class. The point of the letter is to introduce yourself, describe the curriculum, highlight a few upcoming projects, and provide information about what to expect the first day. Select a grade level and write such a letter. As you write, think

about the need to create a warm tone, to be clear and organized, to avoid educational jargon, and to stimulate interest and excitement about school.

2. Anita is extremely "forgetful" about doing homework assignments. She has received innumerable zeros and regularly has to stay for detention to make up the work. You have called her mother to report on this behavior and to ask for assistance, but her mother does not want to get involved. As she puts it, "I've got all I can do to handle her at home. What she does with schoolwork is your responsibility!" Interview two experienced teachers about what they would do in a case like this, and then formulate your own course of action based on what you learn.

For Your Portfolio

Demonstrate your capacity to communicate with families by including two or three artifacts (such as newsletters, interactive homework, requests for parental help with homework, invitations to class events, student award certificates, or checksheets to be used at parent conferences).

FOR FURTHER READING

Allen, J. B. (2007). *Creating welcoming schools: A practical guide to home–school partnerships with diverse families.* New York: Teachers College Press.

   This book contains many practical strategies for engaging families in schools, learning about diverse cultures, and building partnerships between school and home.

Bailey, J. M., & Guskey, T. R. (2001). *Implementing student-led conferences.* Thousand Oaks, CA: Corwin Press.

   In a student-led conference, students take the responsibility of communicating their progress, while teachers serve as facilitators. This very helpful book provides suggestions for preparing, conducting, and evaluating student-led conferences. It includes sample conference announcements and formats, portfolio planners, reproducible letters, and parent and student response forms.

Davis, C., & Yang, A. (2005). *Parents and teachers working together.* Turners Falls, MA: Northeast Foundation for Children.

   This is another book in the "Strategies for Teachers" series, reflecting the Responsive Classroom approach to teaching and learning. Carol Davis is an experienced teacher and a Responsive Classroom consultant. Together with Alice Yang, she provides elementary teachers with practical ideas for collaborating with parents all year long. Easy-to-adapt letters and forms offer further guidance. Topics include working with diverse family cultures, setting the stage for a positive relationship early in the school year, talking with parents about child development, inviting parents into the classroom, involving parents who can't make it to school, and helping parents understand classroom practices.

Delgado Gaitan, C. (2004). *Involving Latino families in schools: Raising student achievement through home–school partnerships.* Thousand Oaks, CA: Corwin Press.

   Concha Delgado Gaitan provides strategies for including Latino parents with the goal of increasing student achievement. She stresses three conditions of increased parental participation: connecting to families, sharing information with parents, and supporting continued parental involvement. Among the topics examined are Latino families' aspirations for their children, the communication systems needed between schools and Latino families, and techniques to foster Latino parent involvement.

Henderson, A. T., Mapp, K. L., Johnson, V. R., & Davies, D. (2007). *Beyond the bake sale: The essential guide to family-school partnerships.* New York: The New Press.

This book compiles tips from principals, teachers, and parents on how to build strong collaborative relationships and improve interactions between the home and school. Each chapter includes a checklist designed to help assess the current state of your school, family, and community partnerships; identify areas in need of improvement; and develop strategies to strengthen and enhance your partnership programs.

Lawrence-Lightfoot, S. (2003). *The essential conversation: What parents and teachers can learn from each other.* New York: Ballantine Books.

According to Lawrence-Lightfoot, "beneath the polite surface of parent-teacher conferences . . . burns a cauldron of fiery feelings." For parents, there is no more dreaded moment; for teachers, these meetings engender feelings of uncertainty, defensiveness, and exposure. This book focuses on the experiences of 10 exemplary teachers in an effort to understand how parents and teachers "negotiate the treacherous and tender terrain" between them.

ORGANIZATIONAL RESOURCES

The Family Involvement Network of Educators (FINE), Harvard Family Research Project, 3 Garden Street, Cambridge, MA 02138; 617-495-9108; www.hfrp.org. FINE brings together thousands of stakeholders committed to promoting strong partnerships among schools, families, and communities. FINE provides information about family involvement, including teaching tools, training materials, and research reports. Members can receive a free subscription to the FINE e-mail newsletter, which regularly highlights new resources for strengthening family, school, and community partnerships.

The National Network of Partnership Schools, Johns Hopkins University, Center on School, Family, and Community Partnerships, 3003 North Charles Street, Baltimore, MD 21218; 410-516-8800; www.partnershipschools.org. NNPS provides information on implementing comprehensive, goal-oriented programs of school, family, and community partnerships. Check out the interactive homework assignments (TIPS) and the collections of "Promising Partnership Practices" on its website.

The National Parent Teacher Association (PTA), National Headquarters, 541 N. Fairbanks Court, Suite 1300, Chicago, IL 60611-3396; 312-670-6782; www.pta.org. The National Parent Teacher Association (PTA) and its state affiliates have produced a set of standards for family–community–school partnership. Teachers, schools, and parents can use these standards to assess their own efforts. Additionally, the website provides materials for parents on how to help their children learn and how they can join their local PTA.

PART III

ORGANIZING AND MANAGING INSTRUCTION

Educators sometimes talk about classroom management and instruction as though the two were completely distinct and separate aspects of teaching. From this perspective, management and instruction occur in chronological sequence. First you establish rules, routines, and consequences; build positive relationships with students; and promote community. Then you begin to teach.

In contrast, we see these two tasks as closely entwined—even inseparable. As we pointed out in Chapter 1, in order to avoid problems of disorder, teachers not only must foster positive student–teacher relationships and use good preventive management strategies, they also must implement well-paced, organized, and engaging instruction. When students find academic activities purposeful and interesting, they are less likely to become inattentive and disruptive.

In this section, we consider ways of managing instruction and instructional time to promote students' involvement and learning. Chapter 7 looks at the amount of time available for instruction and discusses ways to make sure you aren't wasting this precious resource. Chapter 8 argues that teachers are responsible for stimulating students' motivation and offers a variety of motivational strategies drawn from research, theory, and the practice of our five teachers. Chapters 9 through 11 examine four instructional situations that regularly arise in elementary classrooms: independent work (also known as seatwork), small-group work (including cooperative learning), recitations (question-and-answer sequences), and discussions. For each of these, we describe the unique managerial challenges, or "pitfalls," that teachers need to be aware of and then suggest ways to structure the instructional situation to increase the probability of success. We draw on the experiences and wisdom of our five teachers to illustrate how to use these instructional modes effectively.

Our discussion in Chapters 9 through 11 is based on the premise that what constitutes appropriate and orderly behavior varies across these types of instruction. For example, calling out may be perfectly acceptable in a student-centered discussion but be inappropriate during a teacher-directed recitation. Similarly, students may be encouraged to work together during a cooperative learning activity but be prohibited from helping one another during an independent writing assignment. Students have the right to know how you expect them to behave when they're participating in independent work, small-group work, recitations, and discussions. Thus, in addition to the rules for general behavior presented at the beginning of the year, you must think about the behaviors that are appropriate and desirable in each of these instructional situations and make your behavioral expectations absolutely clear.

MAKING THE MOST OF CLASSROOM TIME

On the first day of school, the academic year seems to stretch out endlessly. If you're a beginning teacher, you may wonder how you'll ever fill all the hours of school that lie ahead—especially if you're not even certain what you're going to do *tomorrow.* And yet, as the days go by, you may begin to feel that there's never enough time to accomplish everything you need to do. With assemblies, fire drills, announcements over the intercom, recess, clerical tasks, and holidays, the hours available for instruction seem far fewer than they did at first. Indeed, by the end of the year, you may view time as a precious resource—not something that has to be filled (or killed), but something that must be conserved and used wisely. (Of course, your students may not share this view, as Figure 7.1 illustrates!)

This chapter focuses on the issues of time and time management. Guiding the chapter is the premise that the wise use of time will maximize opportunities for learning and minimize opportunities for disruption. First, we look at the amount of school time that is actually available for teaching and learning. Then we consider strategies for using classroom time efficiently. We discuss four complementary approaches—maintaining activity flow, minimizing transition time, holding students accountable, and

PAUSE AND REFLECT

Keeping in mind that the average student spends 1,080 hours per year in school, estimate either the number of hours or the percent of time that students are actually involved in productive learning (that is, engaged in meaningful, appropriate academic tasks). Then read on to see what researchers have calculated and find out whether you are on target.

Figure 7.1   *Source:* CALVIN AND HOBBES © 1993, Watterson. Distributed by UNIVERSAL
UCLICK. Reprinted with permission. All rights reserved.

limiting the disruption caused by students leaving the room for special instruction
("pullouts").

HOW MUCH TIME IS THERE, ANYWAY?

Although this seems like a straightforward question, the answer is not so simple.
In fact, the answer depends on the kind of time you're talking about (Karweit,
1989). Most states mandate a school year of approximately 180 days, with a school
day of six hours. This amounts to more than 1,000 hours of *total time* each year.
But flu epidemics break out, and boilers break down; snowstorms cause delayed
openings, and teacher workshops require early closings. Factors such as these
immediately reduce the time you have available for teaching; the remaining hours
are called *attended time.*

Even when school is in session and students are present, only about five hours
of the day are available for teaching and learning, with the remaining time going
for lunch, recess, and other breaks. Moreover, the way these five hours of *available
time* are actually used varies tremendously from teacher to teacher. Ideally,
most of the available time would be *instructional time.* But in some classes, noninstructional activities such as taking attendance, collecting lunch money, distributing materials, and reprimanding misbehaving students consume more time than
they should. This was vividly illustrated in a study examining how much instruction was delivered to students in grades 2, 5, and 8 in a large urban district (Smith,
2000). Out of a 330-minute day, 300 minutes were available for instruction. About
half of the observed teachers were very effective managers, and in their classrooms, noninstructional time was only about 14 percent. In the other half of the
classrooms, noninstructional activities consumed as much as 30 percent of the
available time. Thus students in those classes received only 200 minutes of instruction each day—two-thirds of the district's official mandate. An excerpt from one
observer's log conveys some of the problems:

> 9:00 A.M. Students are straggling in from the rain. As they enter, the teacher
> directs them to get out of their coats and to their desks. The kids chatter with one
> another as their classmates enter. At 9:15 A.M., after they stand to say the pledge

of allegiance, the teacher begins to take attendance and to collect money from a candy sale. There is confusion about what has and has not been turned in yet. She then hands out some worksheets and asks students to get out their language arts books, but several students do not have their books. There is a short lecture about this and an emotional explanation from one upset student. Students move around to buddy up so everyone has a book. The attendance officer comes to collect paper work. At 9:30 A.M., they settle in and begin work on a vocabulary assignment. (Smith, 1998, p. 9)

Even when teachers are actually teaching, students are not necessarily paying attention. We must consider still another kind of time—*engaged time,* or time-on-task. Let's suppose that while you are teaching, some of your students choose to pass notes about Halloween costumes, play with the latest action figures, or stare out the window. In this case, the amount of time you are devoting to instruction is greater than the amount of time students are directly engaged in learning. This is not atypical. Research documents the fact that students tend to be "on task" about 70 percent of the time (Rosenshine, 1980). Again, there are sizable variations from class to class. One study of time use in elementary schools found that some classes had an engagement rate of only 50 percent (i.e., the average student was attentive about one-half of the time), while in other classes the engagement rate approached 90 percent (Fisher et al., 1980).

Finally, we need to think about the amount of time students spend on work that is meaningful and appropriate—what Herbert Walberg (1988) calls *productive time.* Teachers sometimes get so caught up in ensuring that students are on task that they fail to select tasks that are educationally beneficial. We once saw second-graders spend 20 minutes of a 60-minute language arts lesson coloring the animal pictures on a vocabulary worksheet. The students seemed totally engaged. But how did the activity enhance students' reading skills? Unfortunately, this example is not unusual; in fact, one educational observer has concluded that the reason so many students reach the upper grades without reading skills is that they spend their time on the "crayola curriculum" (Schmoker, Oct. 24, 2001).

This chapter began by asking, "How much time is there, anyway?" Figure 7.2 depicts the answer to this question. The bar at the far left shows the number of hours of *total time* in the typical mandated school year—1,080. For the sake of argument, we will assume that student absences and school closings reduce this figure by 10 days, or 60 hours. Thus the second bar indicates that *attended time* is 1,020. One hour of each day is generally spent in lunch and recess, so only 850 hours are *available for instruction* (bar 3). Given the need to carry out clerical and administrative tasks, we have only 680 hours of actual *instructional time* (bar 4). If students pay attention 80 percent of that time, *engaged time* is 544 hours (bar 5). And assuming that students work on meaningful, appropriate tasks for 80 percent

PAUSE AND REFLECT

Most teachers are surprised when they see how little time is actually spent in productive learning. What are some practices that erode the time available? What are some practices that you could use to maximize the opportunity for productive learning? Keep these considerations in mind as you read the next section of the chapter.

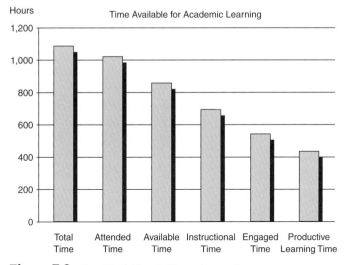

Figure 7.2   How Much Time Is There, Anyway?

of the time they are engaged, we see that *productive learning time* is just 435 hours—only 40 percent of "mandated" total time.

Obviously, these figures are estimates. But the graph summarizes our fundamental point: *The hours available for learning are far more limited than they initially appear.*

INCREASING OPPORTUNITY TO LEARN

Over the years, time has been a popular topic for reform-minded educators. In 1983, for example, the National Commission on Excellence in Education declared that we were "a nation at risk" because of "a rising tide of mediocrity" in our educational system. The report advocated a variety of reforms, including recommendations to extend the school day to seven hours and to lengthen the school year to 200 or 220 days. A decade later, the National Education Commission on Time and Learning (1994) also stressed the need for more time. It characterized teachers and students as "prisoners of time" and paraphrased Oliver Hazard Perry's dispatch from the War of 1812: "We have met the enemy and they are [h]ours" (p. 1).

More recently, an education task force established by the Center for American Progress and the Institute for America's Future reached the same conclusions about the need for more time. In a report titled "Getting Smarter, Becoming Fairer" (Renewing Our Schools, 2005), the task force observes that "the allocation and use of time today is still tied to an agrarian economy . . ., where children were needed to help in the fields during the after-school hours and summer months" (p. 15) and asserts that "abruptly thrusting American children out of the clasroom door in the middle of the afternoon is a wasted opportunity" (p. 18). The first recommendation of the task force is to increase the amount of time that children spend in school by lengthening the school day and, in the case of low-performing schools, the school year.

Despite the cogency of these reports, the six-hour, 180-day school year is still the norm in the United States. For this reason, it is essential to consider ways of increasing students' productive learning time within the constraints of the traditional school day. We will discuss four strategies for achieving this goal: *maintaining activity flow, minimizing transition time, holding students accountable,* and *managing "pullouts."* (See Table 7.1 for a summary.) Of course, these strategies not only maximize time for learning but also help to establish and maintain classroom order.

Maintaining Activity Flow

Tom Good and Jere Brophy (2008) observe that "four things can happen" when students must wait with nothing to do, and "three of them are bad: (1) students may remain interested and attentive; (2) they may become bored or fatigued, losing interest and ability to concentrate; (3) they may become distracted or start daydreaming; or (4) they may actively misbehave" (p. 79). Given the three-to-one odds that waiting will result in undesirable behavior and a loss of valuable learning opportunities, it's essential for teachers to learn how to maintain the flow of classroom activities.

TABLE 7.1 Increasing Students' Learning Time

- *Maintain activity flow*
  Avoid flip-flopping.
  Avoid "stimulus-bound events" (being pulled away from the ongoing activity by
    an event or object that doesn't really need attention).
  Avoid overdwelling and fragmentation.

- *Minimize transition time*
  Prepare students for upcoming transitions.
  Establish clear routines.
  Have clear beginnings and endings: Bring first activity to a halt, announce the
    transition, monitor the transition, make sure everyone is attentive, begin
    second activity.

- *Hold students accountable*
  Communicate assignments clearly.
  Monitor students' progress.

- *Manage pullouts*
  Coordinate with special services to schedule pullouts so they are not too
    disruptive.
  Create a schedule showing when various students are present and when the
    whole class is together. Establish a policy and procedures for having students
    who are pulled out complete work they missed.

Once again, we turn for guidance to the classic work of Jacob Kounin (1970). Kounin investigated differences in teachers' ability to initiate and maintain activity flow in classrooms. He then looked for relationships between activity flow and students' engagement and misbehavior.

Kounin's research identified many differences in the ways teachers orchestrated classroom activities. In some classrooms, activities flowed smoothly and briskly, whereas in others, activities were "jerky" and slow. Kounin even developed a special vocabulary to describe the problems he observed. For instance, he found that some ineffective managers would terminate an activity, start another, and then return to the first activity. Kounin called this *flip-flopping*. It is illustrated by the following situation: A teacher finishes reviewing math problems with the class and tells students to take out their reading books. She then stops and says, "Let's see now. How many got all the [math] problems right? . . . That's very good. . . . All right, now let's get at our readers" (p. 94).

Kounin also observed *stimulus-bound events,* situations in which teachers are "pulled away" from the ongoing activity by a stimulus (an event or an object) that really doesn't need attention. Kounin describes the case of a teacher who is explaining a math problem at the board when she notices that a student is leaning on his left elbow as he works the problem. She leaves the board, instructs him to sit up straight, comments on his improved posture, and then returns to the board.

Sometimes teachers slow down the pace of activity by *overdwelling*—continuing to explain when students already understand or preaching at length about appropriate behavior. Another type of slowdown is produced when a teacher breaks an activity into components even though the activity could be performed as a single unit—what Kounin called *fragmentation:*

> The teacher was making a transition from spelling to arithmetic as follows: "All right everybody, I want you to close your spelling books. Put away your red pencils. Now close your spelling books. Put your spelling books in your desks. Keep them out of the way." [There's a pause.] "All right now. Take out your arithmetic books and put them on your desks in front of you. That's right, let's keep everything off your desks except your arithmetic books. And let's sit up straight. We don't want any lazy-bones do we? That's fine. Now get your black pencils and open your books to page sixteen." (p. 106)

Flip-flops, stimulus-boundedness, overdwelling, and fragmentation—these are all threats to the flow of classroom activities. Not only do they result in lost learning time, they can have a significant effect on children's behavior. When activities proceed smoothly and briskly, children are *more involved in work and less apt to misbehave.* Indeed, as Kounin concluded three decades ago, *activity flow plays a greater role in classroom order than the specific techniques that teachers use to handle misbehavior.*

During one visit to Garnetta's classroom, we watched the skillful way she maintained the flow of activity in her math class. Students were working in groups, using colorful cubes to solve division problems. For no apparent reason, there were innumerable interruptions that day. A messenger from the office wanted to know the number of children who had signed up for a special Saturday program; a child came to borrow an overhead projector for another teacher; and there was an announcement over the loudspeaker about after-school activities. All these interruptions occurred within a 15-minute period. Garnetta worked valiantly to keep the momentum going. She told the messenger from the office, "I'm in the middle of a lesson. I'll find out later and let the office know." When she turned to get the overhead projector, she first gave her class a task to do: "I'm going to give you a really tough problem while I take care of this business—88 divided by 2! Let's see if you can do that one!" The big number (88) bought Garnetta some additional time and created a special challenge for students. We heard murmurs like "That's not tough," and "Oh, that's easy," as they immediately began to manipulate the blocks to solve the problem.

Later, we talked with Garnetta about the way she had managed to keep activities moving. With a good deal of fervor, she told us:

 This can be a difficult group. If there's any "down time" at all, things can get out of hand. If students have to sit and wait while paper is being passed out, that provides an opportunity for trouble. If they have to wait until I've written problems on the board, they get fidgety. It's important to keep them actively involved and participating. That's also why I tend to have them work in groups, rather than call on one student at a time.

Minimizing Transition Time

Kounin identified "flip-flopping" as one problem that can occur during transitions between activities. But transitions are vulnerable in other ways. An analysis by Paul Gump (1982, 1987) helps us to understand why transitions can be so problematic. First, Gump observes, there may be difficulty "closing out" the first activity—especially if students are deeply engaged. (Ironically, the very involvement that teachers strive to achieve makes it more difficult to get students to switch activities!) Second, transitions are more loosely structured than activities themselves (Ross, 1985). Because there's usually more leeway in terms of socializing and moving around the room, there is also more opportunity for disruption. In fact, a study of 50 classes taught by student teachers (Arlin, 1979) found that there was almost twice as much disruption (such as hitting, yelling, and obscene gestures) during transitions as during nontransition time.

Third, students sometimes "save up" problems or tensions and deal with them during the transition time. They may seek out the teacher to complain about a neighbor, ask for permission to retrieve a book from a locker, or dump out the contents of their bookbags in search of a lost homework assignment. Although these behaviors are legitimate—and help to protect the adjacent activities from disturbance—they also make transitions more difficult to manage. Finally, there may be delays in getting students started on the second activity. Teachers may be held up because they are dealing with individual children's concerns or are busy assembling needed materials. Students may have difficulty settling down, especially if they are returning from physical education or recess.

Gump's analysis suggests that teachers can reduce the potential for chaos by *preparing students for upcoming transitions, by establishing efficient transition routines, and by clearly defining the boundaries of lessons* (Ross, 1985). These guidelines are especially important for children with attention-deficit/hyperactivity disorder and those with autism, who may have particular difficulty with transitions and changes in routine (McIntosh et al., 2004).

Advance Preparation

Marshall Arlin's (1979) research revealed that transitions were far more chaotic when student teachers failed to warn students about the imminent change of activity. This often occurred because student teachers didn't even realize the period was about to end:

> The lesson was still continuing when the bell would ring. Not having reached any closure, the teacher, with some degree of desperation, would say something like "OK, you can go," and pupils would charge out of the room, often knocking each other over. (Sometimes, pupils did not even wait for the signal from the teacher.) The teacher might then remember an announcement and interject to the dispersing mob, "Don't forget to bring back money for the trip!" (p. 50)

In contrast, other student teachers in Arlin's study were able to prepare students for the upcoming transition. If they were about to dismiss the class to go to lunch, they made sure that desks were in order and that students were quiet and ready to leave. They made announcements while students were still seated and then lined children up in an orderly fashion.

Our five teachers are very skillful "clock watchers." They take care to monitor time and to inform students when an activity is drawing to a close. In the following scene, we see Garnetta warn her students that they will be changing activities in two minutes. We also see her spur them along by counting aloud, although she times her counting to match students' progress. Finally, she praises students for their cooperation:

 10:15 **Ladies and gents, you have approximately two minutes to finish up whatever sentence you're working on. Then put your papers in your creative writing book and sit up straight to show me you're ready to go to Basic Skills.**

10:17 **OK, I'm starting to count. One. We've got one person ready, now two people, four people. Table 2 looks excellent; Table 1 is excellent. I'm on two. (She circulates, walking closer to those who are not yet ready and watching as more and more students sit up straight.) I'm up to three. Table 1 is good; Table 2, beautiful. [At table 3, Robert is still putting things in his desk.] Almost everyone is ready to go. Robert, are you ready? [He sits up straight.] Table 3, lovely.**

10:18 **[She speaks in a very quiet voice] OK, everyone knows our hallway rules. . . . Are we going to talk in the hallway? [Kids murmur, "No . . ."] Table 2 line up, Table 3, Table 1 [Children all push in their chairs and line up quietly.] Table 1, I really like the way you lined up.**

10:19 **The class leaves the room in an orderly, quiet line.**

Not only do our teachers warn their students about upcoming transitions, they also prepare them for the activities that will occur after lunch, recess, or special classes. Here, we see Ken call his class together five minutes before they are to go to lunch. He reviews what the afternoon's activities will be and makes sure all students have their materials out and ready:

KEN: Folks, I'd like everyone at their tables. [He pauses while students return to their seats from the various parts of the room where they have been working.] Now, before we go to lunch, I want to take five minutes so that you're all set for this afternoon. What are you going to need for this afternoon?

STUDENT: Page 39, page 40 [worksheets the students have been working on], and our newspapers.

KEN: Good. Take a minute to get those together and put them on your desks. What else?

STUDENT: We need our private journals with the answers to the questions.

KEN: Right. Get your private journals ready and on your desks.

STUDENT: We need our book reports.

KEN: Good. Is your book report on your desk?

STUDENT: We need our peer tutoring logs.

KEN: Yes. Get them out. I'm going to try to look at them this afternoon. We'll also watch the health video if we have time. Any problems? [Several students inform him about places they have to go that afternoon—to a second-grade class for peer tutoring, to band practice, to a yearbook meeting.] OK, folks, see you later. [Students get up, get their coats, and leave for recess.]

Because transitions and unpredictability are problematic for children with ADHD and those with autism, a timer or hourglass can help them to see how much time they have left. It can also be helpful to tape a detailed schedule on their desks so they can keep track of what's going to happen when. In *Time to Teach, Time to Learn* (1999), Wood advises teachers to show the times *graphically* so that there is consistency between the schedule and the classroom clock. Wood also suggests that children have a watch that matches the clock (sweep hand or digital readout), so they are reading the time in the same way on their wrist and on the wall.

The Use of Transition Routines

In Chapter 4 we talked about the need to have clear, specific routines in order to keep the classroom running smoothly. At no time is the use of routines more important than during transitions. Well-established routines provide a structure to transitions that helps to prevent confusion and lost time. Once again, this is particularly important for children who struggle with transitions. They can benefit from having a job to do, such as signaling the beginning and end of the transition, collecting papers, or timing the transition with a stopwatch (Wood, 1999).

Barbara has instituted a routine for entering the room in the morning and settling in. This routine helps to ease the transition from home to school. When students come in, they immediately check the chalkboard to find out what they are to begin doing. Sometimes the board says "SQUIRT," and students know to begin Sustained, Quiet, UnInterrupted Reading Time. Sometimes the board says "JOURNALS":

It's 8:30. Students enter the room, glance at the board, go to their seats, and take out their journals. They quickly begin writing, as Barbara circulates. She gets the attendance form and silently notes attendance while students are working. Without a word, she hands the form to a boy who takes it to the office. He comes back in one minute. Barbara says, "Thank you, David." She continues to circulate, occasionally commenting to a child.

Viviana has a routine that she uses whenever she erases boardwork in preparation for a new activity. The routine not only provides a structure that helps keep children engaged during the transition but also reinforces her first-graders' reading skills.

Children are creating sentences by unscrambling words written on the chalkboard. They come to the last set of words:

can play us with you

One child volunteers: "Can you play with us?" Viviana acknowledges that the sentence is correct and asks whether children can think of any other. No one can. Viviana praises the children for their good work and tells them that they will do more scrambled words another day. Then she says, "Now let's erase the board." As she goes to erase each word, she pauses, and the children read it aloud. When all the words have been erased, Viviana begins the next part of her lesson. "OK children, now we're going to work a little bit with two vowel sounds."

Courtney uses cueing and signaling to alert her students when writing workshop is about to end. At the beginning of the year she was extremely explicit. Five minutes before the end of writing workshop, Courtney would call for attention: "Writers, hands up (a signal to put their pencils or markers down and listen). We have five more minutes of writing time." At the end of writing workshop, Courtney would say, "One, two, three, hands up. Writers, writing workshop time is over. Put your caps on your markers. Close the stamp pad. Put your papers in your folders. Monitors, put the buckets and bins away." Later in the year, when Courtney judged that her students no longer needed such explicit instructions, she changed her routine. As she told us:

Now I just put on a CD and play a song that lasts about one minute and 20 seconds and has two verses. This way students know that when the first verse is done, their transition time is about half over. As soon as the children hear the music, they know to get ready for writing workshop. And the same thing at the end: When the music starts, they begin cleaning up, and table monitors return the materials to the shelf.

In many classrooms, the transition routines are implicit, and students are expected to figure out what to do by picking up on subtle cues. This may be fine for the majority of students, but those with ADHD, autism, or other disorders may have trouble and end up getting reprimanded. If you have students like this in your class, it is essential (and only fair) to spend time teaching students how to make efficient, orderly transitions. Suggestions are listed in the accompanying Practical Tips box.

Clear Beginnings and Endings

Transitions proceed more smoothly if teachers bring the first activity to a halt, announce the transition, allow time to make sure that everyone is attentive, and then begin the second activity (Arlin, 1979). In other words, smooth transitions are characterized by well-defined boundaries.

Sometimes, in an effort to maintain activity flow, teachers rush into the second activity without checking to be sure that students are "with them." One classroom observer writes: "Several times I noticed over 15 children continuing the previous activity while the teacher was giving directions for the new activity" (Arlin, 1979, p. 50). Needless to say, those teachers then became exasperated when students asked questions about what to do.

PRACTICAL TIPS FOR

TEACHING TRANSITIONS

- Think about the transitions that occur during the period, such as
  Entering and leaving the classroom.
  Putting materials away and preparing for the next task.
  Cleaning up a work area.
  Moving from group work to independent work.
  Turning in homework.
  Choosing partners for small-group activities.

- Explicitly teach the expected transition behavior.
  Model the behavior using both correct and incorrect examples.
  Provide opportunities for students to practice.
  Provide feedback.
  Reteach if needed.

- Provide precorrections (reminders of the expected behavior *before* the transition begins).

- Provide positive reinforcement for efficient, orderly transitions.
  Give specific praise or special privileges and activities.
  Use tangible rewards if necessary.

- Actively supervise the transition.
  Scan the room, looking for both appropriate and inappropriate behavior.
  Walk around the room, using proximity to encourage students to engage in the appropriate behavior.
  Interact with students during the transition, providing reminders and specific praise.

Source: McIntosh et al., 2004.

Our five teachers also make certain that students are listening before they begin an activity. Often, they'll preface lessons with remarks designed to "grab" students' attention. Garnetta, for example, uses verbal cues like these:

"Let's get everything put away now. I want everybody with me 100 percent for this. It's important."

"Put everything else away. Now we're going to have some fun."

"We're doing this for the first time, so you all have to be quiet and listen very carefully."

Courtney finds that chants work especially well in kindergarten. She'll call out "One, two, three, eyes on me" or "Tootsie roll, lollipop, we were talking, now we stop," and children chant a response. Rhythmic clap patterns that students have to emulate are also effective.

Although it's important to make sure that students are attentive before proceeding with a new lesson, Gump (1982) warns that waiting *too long* can cause a loss of momentum. He reminds us that a new activity will often "pull in" nonattending children. Gump writes, "Waiting for absolute and universal attention can sometimes lead to unnecessarily extended transition times" (p. 112). Clearly, teachers need to find the happy medium between rushing ahead when students are inattentive and waiting so long that momentum is lost. It's a delicate balancing act.

Holding Students Accountable

During a visit to Ken's class, we watched as Janice tried to get Monica to stop working on an assignment and do something with her. It wasn't clear exactly what Janice wanted to do, but Monica's reaction was unambiguous. "No," she responded firmly, "I want to do this *now*. I don't want to do it at recess, I don't want to do it at lunch time, and I don't want to do it for homework. I want to do it now."

Observing this interaction, we thought of Walter Doyle's (1983) comment that students tend to take assignments seriously only when they are held accountable for them. Your own school experiences probably testify to the truth of this statement. Even as adults, it takes a good deal of self-discipline, maturity, and intrinsic motivation to put your best effort into work that will never be seen by anyone. And elementary students are *children*. Unless they know that they will have to account for their performance, it is unlikely that they'll make the best use of class time.

Furthermore, students are *unable* to make good use of their time if they are confused about what they're supposed to be doing. Teachers sometimes tell students merely to "get to work" and are immediately bombarded by questions: "Can I use pen?" "Do I have to write down the problems or can I just put the answers?" "Do we have to reduce to lowest terms?" "Can I work on the rug?" When this happens, precious class time has to be spent clarifying the original instructions.

In order to help children use their time wisely, teachers must *communicate assignments and requirements clearly* and *monitor students' progress* (Evertson & Emmer, 2009). Before students begin work, for example, you should explain what the students will be doing and why, how to get help, what to do with completed work, what to do when they're finished, and how long they'll be spending on the task. You also need to make sure that students are familiar with your work standards—for example, what kind of paper to use, whether they should use pencil or pen, how to number the page, and whether or not erasures are allowed. After giving instructions, it's a good idea to have students explain what they will be doing in their own words. Simply asking "Does everyone understand?" seldom yields useful information.

During one visit to Garnetta's classroom, we watched her explain to her class that they were going to read about the life of Martin Luther King Jr., and then write summaries. She emphasized that the summaries should be brief, containing only the most important ideas. Moreover, she stressed that they needed to be written in the students' own words:

I don't want you to just copy the information from the story. You've got to use your . . . [points to head; children call out "BRAINS"]. That's right, your brains. You and your partner will read the story, decide what the important facts are, and then write them down in your own words. Let's make sure that everyone understands this. I'm going to read the beginning of one of the stories in our reader. [Garnetta opens the reader and reads a few paragraphs. The children are clearly familiar with this story. Then she closes the book.] In your own words, what is happening in this story? What did I just read? [Children raise their hands. Garnetta calls on individuals to tell the story.] Good. You are summarizing the story. You're not telling the whole thing—only the most important things. And you're not just copying the words from the book. You're picking out the most important information, discussing it with your partner, and then you're writing it down *in your own words.*

Writing instructions and work assignments on the board or providing other visual cues can often be helpful. Some students with learning problems cannot remember a laundry list of materials, so a chart with stick-on pictures of paper, pens, pencils, rulers, and books can be used to nonverbally communicate what children will need. The same is true for very young children. Courtney learned that students had a lot of trouble with multistep tasks (e.g., those that require writing, cutting, coloring, and pasting), especially if the steps had to be done in a particular order. To make things easier for students, she not only goes through the directions orally but also places on the whiteboard magnetic cards that list the steps. (See Figure 7.3.)

In Ken's class, the day's assignments are already on the chalkboard when students enter the classroom in the morning. A small chalkboard at the side of the room indicates how the morning will be structured. Each reading group is listed (by the title of the novel being read), along with its assignments and the time it will be meeting with Ken. After the morning meeting, Ken reviews the assignments with the class and checks that everyone knows what to do that morning. On the

Figure 7.3   Courtney's Magnetic Cards

larger, front chalkboard is the schedule for the afternoon, along with due dates for the week's special assignments.

Communicating assignments clearly is especially important if you are working with low-achieving students or students who have a history of "forgetting" work. Barbara has devised a homework procedure that she uses with her low math class. At the beginning of the month, she provides each student with a folder in which all the assignments for the month are stapled. On the cover of the folder is a calendar, showing exactly what homework students are to do each night. In this way, students can't claim they "didn't know what to do," and if they're absent (a common occurrence among low-achieving children), they still know what the assignment is. One of Barbara's calendars appears in Figure 7.4.

Once you've given directions for an assignment and your class gets to work, it's important to monitor how students are doing by circulating around the room (Fisher et al., 1980). This practice enables you to keep track of students' progress, to identify and help with problems, and to verify that assignments are matched to students' ability. Circulating also helps to ensure that students are using their time well. Observations of our five teachers revealed that they rarely sit down, unless they're working with a small group. In all five rooms, the teacher's desk is out of the way and is used for storage rather than as a place to sit.

MARCH

SUN	MON	TUE	WED	THU	FRI	SAT
			1	2	3	4
5	6	7	8	9 Multiplication, Division Page 44	10 Word Problems Page 45	11
12	13 Fractions Pages 48–49	14 Symmetry Page 55	15 Subtraction Page 57	16 Multiplication, Division Page 59	17 Money Page 60	18
19	20 Word Problems Page 61	21 Check-up Page 64	22 Multiplication 2 Digit by 1 Digit Page 67	23 Multiplication Page 68	24	25
26	27 Subtraction Page 69	28 Bar Graph Page 74	29 Addition, Subtraction Page 78	30 Multiplication Page 87	31 Check-up Page 84	

Figure 7.4   Barbara's Assignment Calendar

Viviana's children are working with Pattern Blocks, wooden blocks that come in several different shapes and colors. The task is to use four blocks of the same color and shape to cover outlined figures drawn on a worksheet. While they work, Viviana circulates, checking each child's paper: "You're supposed to use only one color. You're using two." "These are not the same shape, are they?" "Good for you. You are right!"

In classrooms where learning centers are prevalent, other forms of monitoring student performance and ensuring student accountability may be needed. A sign-in form by each learning center, for example, enables students to indicate that they have worked in a particular center; even kindergarten children can learn to check off or sign their names. The teacher can then pass by each center and readily determine which children have completed the centers. In addition, many teachers use response sheets that require students to perform some sort of written

Garnetta monitors students' progress on written work.

work associated with the center. This can consist of a simple fill-in-the-blank form, a small project, a review sheet, or a self-generated narrative. Requiring students to sign in and put something down in writing sends a clear message: The work done in centers is important, and students are accountable.

To monitor whether students are regularly completing assignments, it's important to *establish routines for collecting and checking classwork and homework.* Some teachers keep file folders for each child. These contain all of the worksheets and assignments for the day. Children complete their work and put it back in the file folders, which are then returned to the teacher's desk to await checking. Other teachers appoint student monitors to collect each assignment. If the monitors alphabetize the papers, it simplifies the task of noting whose work is missing. In some classes, students are assigned numbers, which they put at the top of every assignment. This enables the monitors to put the work in numerical order, another way of making it easy to scan assignments.

Checking or grading all the work done each day is an arduous task. One student teacher recently wrote about "the looming mountain of paperwork that a teacher must perpetually climb":

> *Sometimes I'm not sure if I'm a teacher or certified [public] accountant! However, my experience . . . has enabled me to find ways to reckon with the ponderous load. Simple things like color-coordinated folders . . . or writing the names of absent students on quiz sheets to keep track of make-up work, are "tricks" that I am extremely grateful to have been shown along the way.*

Like this student teacher, you need to find ways to "make a molehill out of a mountain" (Shalaway, 1989). We asked our teachers how they handle the paperwork. Their ideas are listed in the Practical Tips box.

PRACTICAL TIPS FOR

HANDLING PAPERWORK

- Model your record keeping after the report card you use. In this way, you'll be sure to have sufficient documentation for each category of the report card. For example, if the report card reads, "Is able to grasp main idea," make sure that you have attended to this skill, that you have examples of each child's achievement in this area, and that you have recorded their progress.

- Give the students some of the responsibility for keeping records. Teach them to keep track of their own progress. For example, they can construct a bar graph to record the number of spelling words they get right each week. Even kindergartners can date-stamp their assignments.

- Whenever possible, correct in-class work while students are doing it or as a group immediately afterward.

- Collect in-class worksheets and then redistribute them randomly for grading as a group. If students are assigned numbers, which they put at the top of their papers instead of their names, no one knows whose paper they're checking.

- Monitor that students complete in-class worksheets (e.g., a set of math problems) and homework, but don't grade these. Grade only quizzes and tests.

- Instead of correcting and grading every homework assignment, give periodic quizzes to check what students are learning.

- Give quizzes with 5 questions instead of 25.

- If you're drowning in paperwork, you're giving too much. Pare it down!

Managing Pullouts as Efficiently as Possible

With the movement toward inclusive education, children with special needs are increasingly served by special services personnel who are "pulled in" to the general education classroom. Nonetheless, "pullouts" are still common. For example, students with learning disabilities may go to a resource room to work on reading and study skills; those who are "gifted and talented" may leave for an enrichment program; those with limited proficiency in English may receive instruction in English as a Second Language. In addition, the whole class may go to "specials" such as art, music, and physical education. Given all these comings and goings, you may sometimes feel more like an air traffic controller than a teacher; furthermore, it may seem as though there is no time for whole-class instruction. One student teacher recently wrote about this problem in her journal:

> *I am so frustrated as of this journal entry!! Where is there any time in the day?!! My kids get pulled out for so many different things that I rarely have a solid hour with them all together! How can anyone teach the subjects that all students are supposed to get? Three kids go out on three days at different times for compensatory education. One girl goes out four days a week at different times for a one-hour block of resource room. Three more students go out three days at different times for a*

HOTS (higher-order thinking skills) program. . . . Three-quarters of the class goes out once a week for chorus, band, and art club (and these are not even the specials, like music, gym, art, and library). Fourteen of my 24 kids go out of the room at scattered times throughout the entire week for music lessons. There is NO time in the day, and there is absolutely no consistency for the kids!!!

There is also no simple solution for this problem. All of our teachers face it to some extent, and all of them find it frustrating. The best approach is to try to have input into scheduling. If you can work closely with special services personnel, you can develop a schedule that will minimize the fragmentation and ensure that there are some time periods when you will be able to instruct the whole class or a small group without excluding somebody. For example, it can be helpful to schedule "G & T" (gifted and talented), basic skills, and ESL (English as a Second Language) all at the same time. In this way, a large number of children can be out of the room simultaneously, rather than at different times throughout the whole day. (At Barbara's school, these special services are now scheduled right before first period—8:00 to 8:40—so that children do not have to be pulled out during the regular school day.) If you have students who require the maximum instruction possible in reading and math, make sure that you don't schedule your own instruction in these content areas while they are out of the room. On the other hand, if children go to a resource room *instead* of receiving regular class instruction in these areas, then it's a good idea to schedule your own literacy and math instruction at that time.

Regardless of the scheduling, you need to be familiar with your school's policy about requiring students who are pulled out to complete missed work. Consider another student teacher's journal entry:

It seems to me that my special ed students are confused about what is expected of them, where they are supposed to be, whose class they belong to, etc. I certainly know that I feel very confused in regard to teaching them. Basically, they are out of class almost half of the school day. When they return to the classroom from being in the Resource Room, I often don't know what to do with them. . . . For example, is it fair to hold these children responsible for work that they weren't in class for? How fair is it to let them slide? Should I try to take them aside and explain what the class is doing? Amazingly, I have never been given a straight answer about whether or not these children are responsible for the work they missed. The "policy" seems to vary from week to week. This "laissez-faire" attitude is likely to doom students to always needing special services. It appears that there is little orchestration of objectives and material between the regular classroom teacher and special services personnel.

Usually, if children come into the class after being in the Resource Room, I have them simply join in with the class (or with their cooperative groups) wherever the class may be. But then it dawns on me that these are the children who are least likely to be able to pick up concepts in the middle of things and that a more effective routine needs to be established. Special needs children can get lost so easily!

PAUSE AND REFLECT

This student teacher argues that the children who are least able to handle transitions and the most likely to "get lost" are the very children who face the most transitions as part of their daily schedule. What are your thoughts about this situation? Think about ways in which you could ease a child's transition into a class already in progress. What systems or structures could you put in place so that students would know what to do when they re-enter your classroom?

If your school also has a "laissez-faire" approach to this issue, you will have to establish your own policy. You will also need to think carefully about the procedures you want to implement to make children's leaving and reentry as smooth as possible. You might appoint a special "buddy" for each student who is pulled out; buddies are responsible for orienting the students upon their return to the regular classroom. It can also help to have a special folder or box for each child who is pulled out so that you don't forget to put aside assignments or materials for children who are out of the room.

CONCLUDING COMMENTS

Tracy Kidder's book *Among Schoolchildren* (1989) describes one year in the life of Chris Zajac, an elementary teacher who's feisty, demanding, blunt, fair, funny, and hard-working. At the very end of the book, Kidder describes Chris's thoughts on the last day of school. Although she is convinced that she belongs "among schoolchildren," Chris laments the fact that she hadn't been able to help all her students—at least not enough:

> Again this year, some had needed more help than she could provide. There were many problems that she hadn't solved. But it wasn't for lack of trying. She hadn't given up. She had run out of time.

Like Chris, we all run out of time. The end of the year comes much too quickly, and some children's needs are much too great. We hope the concepts and guidelines presented in this chapter will help you to make good use of the limited time you have.

SUMMARY

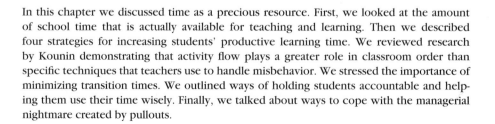

In this chapter we discussed time as a precious resource. First, we looked at the amount of school time that is actually available for teaching and learning. Then we described four strategies for increasing students' productive learning time. We reviewed research by Kounin demonstrating that activity flow plays a greater role in classroom order than specific techniques that teachers use to handle misbehavior. We stressed the importance of minimizing transition times. We outlined ways of holding students accountable and helping them use their time wisely. Finally, we talked about ways to cope with the managerial nightmare created by pullouts.

Types of Time

- Total time: the time the state mandates that school be in session.
- Attended time: the time students are actually in school.
- Available time: the time remaining after activities such as lunch, recess, and assemblies are removed.
- Instructional time: the time that is actually used for instruction.
- Engaged time: the time a student spends working attentively on academic tasks.
- Productive time: the amount of engaged time during which students are doing work that is meaningful and appropriate.

How to Increase Hours for Learning

- Maintain activity flow by avoiding
    - Flip-flopping.
    - Stimulus-bound events.
    - Overdwelling.
    - Fragmentation.
- Minimize transition time by
    - Defining boundaries to lessons.
    - Preparing students for transitions.
    - Establishing routines.
- Hold students accountable by
    - Communicating assignments and requirements clearly.
    - Monitoring students' progress.
    - Establishing routines for collecting and checking classwork and homework.
- Manage pullouts as efficiently as possible:
    - Try to have input into scheduling.
    - Create a schedule showing periods of time when various students are present and when the whole class is together.
    - Establish (or find out about) a policy regarding the responsibility of pulled-out students to complete work they missed.
    - Establish procedures for smooth transitions when students return to the classroom.

By using time wisely, you can maximize opportunities for learning and minimize disruption in your classroom. Think about how much time is being spent on meaningful and appropriate work in your room, and how much is being eaten up by business and clerical tasks. Be aware that the hours available for instruction are much fewer than they first appear!

ACTIVITIES FOR SKILL BUILDING AND REFLECTION

In Class

1. Read the following vignette and identify the factors that threaten the activity flow of the lesson. Once you have identified the problems, explain how you would avoid them if you were the teacher.

Mrs. P. waits while her second-grade students take out their fraction circles to begin the math lesson. When most of the children have placed the circles on their desks, she begins to remind the class of the work they did on fractions the previous day. As she explains the tasks they are about to do, she notices that Jack doesn't have his circles.

"Jack, where are your circles?"

"I don't know."

"This is the third time you don't have your circles. You didn't have them last week, and you had to stay in at recess one day and you also lost free time. What did I tell you would happen if you lost your circles one more time?"

"You were going to call my mother."

"That's right. Now go and write your name on the board while I see if I have an extra pack for you to use."

Mrs. P. goes to the supply closet and pulls out a pack of fraction circles for Jack. She then instructs the class to place the bag of shapes on the top left side of their desks.

"Take out the blue circle and place it directly in front of you." She checks to see that all students have complied.

"Now take out one of the four red pieces and place it on the blue circle. Be careful not to drop it, and do this without talking to your neighbor."

Mrs. P. circulates to see whether the children are following directions. "Now take out another red piece and place it on the blue circle."

The children do so. Mrs. P. then directs them to take out two remaining red pieces and place them on the blue circle "one at a time."

"How many red pieces did you use to cover the blue circle?"

The class responds, "Four."

"And what is one piece called?"

"One-fourth."

"I'd like everyone to say it together, please."

"One-fourth!"

"Did I hear the back table? I want everyone to repeat it with strong voices!"

"ONE-FOURTH!"

"Excellent. Now what are two pieces called?"

"Two-fourths."

"I still didn't hear everyone. Let's hear Rhonda's table. (Rhonda's table responds.) OK, how about Shakia's table? (They respond.) And now Reggie's table. Good."

As she passes Rob's desk, she notices a pink slip of paper. "Class, I almost forgot. Those children who have permission forms for the zoo trip need to give them to me now, so I can get them to the office."

Children proceed to hunt through their desks. Several ask permission to go get their book bags. Once all the slips are collected, Mrs. P. returns to the lesson and goes on to talk about thirds. She directs the children to put away the red pieces, to take out the three green pieces, and to cover the blue circle with the green pieces. Mrs. P. checks that students know each green piece is "one-third." At the completion of this activity, Mrs. P. directs the students to put away the fraction circles and to take out their spelling books.

"OK, children, turn to page 37 in your spellers and let's review the words for this week. Tanya, please read the first word and use it in a sentence."

As Tanya begins, Mrs. P. interrupts: "I'm sorry, Tanya, but I just realized that I forgot to tell you all what the math homework is. Everyone, take out your assignment pads and write down the assignment as I write it on the board." She takes a piece of chalk and writes, "Math—page 25, even problems only." The children copy the assignment. Mrs. P. scans the room to make sure everyone has written the assignment. When all the children are done, she directs them to return to their spellers. "All right, now where were we? Tanya, you were doing number one." When Tanya finishes, Mrs. P. has the class spell the word out loud and then moves on to the next word. The class is on the fourth word when the bell rings for lunch.

"Oh my, I don't know where the time went. OK, boys and girls, get ready for lunch. We'll continue with spelling when you get back."

2. You want your fourth-grade students to do a research report on a famous inventor. They will also be creating their own inventions. As you plan this project, you will need to consider how to hold your students accountable. In a small group, share your ideas about how you will (a) convey requirements clearly and thoroughly, and (b) monitor student progress.

On Your Own

1. Observe an elementary class for one complete class period, carefully noting how much of the period is actually used for *instructional* purposes. For example, let's suppose you elect to observe a 50-minute mathematics lesson. While you are observing, you note that the first five minutes of the period are spent checking to see who does and who does not have the homework (a clerical job). Then, in the middle of the period, the teacher asks students to get into groups of four, and moving into groups takes up another five minutes. Next an announcement comes on over the loudspeaker, and the class discusses the announcement for another three minutes. Finally, the teacher wraps up class five minutes before the end of the period and gives everyone free time. Conclusion: Out of 50 minutes of available time, 18 minutes were spent on noninstructional activities, leaving only 32 minutes of actual instructional time.

2. Interview two teachers about their policies and procedures with respect to pullout instruction. Do they require students who are pulled out to complete the work they missed? If so, when do students do the work? How do they reorient students when they return to class? Do they see any alternatives to pullout instruction?

For Your Portfolio

Develop a transition routine for each of the following situations. Remember, your goal is to use time wisely.

    a. Beginning of the school day
    b. Snack time
    c. Returning from gym
    d. Moving from small-group time to independent seatwork

FOR FURTHER READING

Gabrieli, C., & Goldstein, W. (2008). *Time to learn: How a new school schedule is making smarter kids, happier parents, and safer neighborhoods.* San Francisco, CA: Jossey-Bass.

Using common sense, experience, hard data, and personal observation, the authors of this book argue that the current school day is obsolete and out of step with the reality of working families without a stay-at-home parent. The additional one to two hours of the "new school day" enable students to master core academic subjects, receive individualized instruction and tutoring, and participate in the arts, music, drama, and sports.

Gettinger, M., & Seibert, J. K. (1995). Best practices for increasing academic learning time. In A. Thomas & J. Grimes (Eds.), *Best practice in school psychology—III,* pp. 943-954. Washington, DC: National Association of School Psychologists.

This chapter reviews the findings on the relationship between academic learning time and student achievement. Gettinger and Seibert suggest ways to assess time use and identify areas for improvement in order to maximize learning time. Although the chapter is intended for school psychologists, it should be helpful to teachers themselves.

Smith, B. (2000). Quantity matters: Annual instructional time in an urban school system. *Educational Administration Quarterly, 36*(5), 652-682.

The official time policy of the Chicago public elementary schools is to provide students with 300 minutes of instruction per day for 180 school days per year. This adds up to 900 hours of instruction annually. But on the basis of classroom observation records, field notes, teacher interviews, school calendars, and other documents, this report concludes that nearly half of Chicago students may be receiving only 40 to 50 percent of the recommended hours. The reasons for this erosion of instructional time are discussed, and recommendations are outlined.

ENHANCING STUDENTS' MOTIVATION

Midway through student teaching, a young woman in a fifth-grade placement came to seminar at her wits' end. "I give up with these kids," she told the group.

> *My cooperating teacher and I can threaten with zeroes, call their parents, keep them in at recess—nothing works. They just don't care, and I'm just about ready to quit! I want a placement in kindergarten, where kids still want to learn things!*

As we talked further, it seemed as though she believed that motivation is entirely the student's responsibility; to be successful in school, students must arrive motivated, just as they must arrive with notebooks and pencils. She also seemed to think that motivation is a stable characteristic, like eye color. From this perspective, some individuals come to school wanting to learn, and some don't. This can be a comforting point of view: If motivation is an innate or unchangeable characteristic, then we don't have to spend time and energy figuring out ways to motivate students.

A contrasting view holds that motivation is an acquired disposition amenable to change. It can also be situation specific, varying with the nature of the particular activity. Thus students can be enthusiastic about reading one of J. K. Rowling's

Harry Potter books but can appear bored and uninterested when it's time to do spelling sentences.

According to this latter perspective, teachers are responsible for trying to stimulate students' engagement in learning activities. It may be gratifying (and a lot easier) when students come to school already excited about learning; however, when this is not the case, teachers must redouble their efforts to create a classroom context that fosters students' involvement and interest. Unfortunately, research indicates that this does not always happen. In fact, teachers' actions may actually "magnify" students' initial levels of motivation (Skinner & Belmont, 1993). When children enter the classroom already motivated, teachers tend to respond positively and to provide additional support, affection, and encouragement. When children enter the classroom exhibiting a *lack* of motivation, however, teachers may respond negatively and become coercive and neglectful—thus exacerbating students' initial lack of interest.

This chapter focuses on ways to enhance students' motivation. We begin by reflecting on what is realistic and appropriate with respect to motivating students. We then examine the factors that give rise to motivation. Finally, we consider a variety of motivational strategies drawn from research, theory, and the practice of our five teachers.

> ### ∞ PAUSE AND REFLECT
>
> Think of a time when you were extremely motivated to learn. It might have been when you were preparing to take the test to get your driver's license or the winter you learned to ski. Why were you motivated to learn? What supported you in your learning? What made it a successful experience? Try to relate your experiences to what you will be doing every day in your classroom.

WHAT IS REALISTIC? WHAT IS APPROPRIATE?

Many of the teacher education students with whom we've worked believe that teachers motivate students *by making learning fun.* In fact, they frequently mention the ability to design activities that are enjoyable and entertaining as one of the defining characteristics of the "good teacher." Yet, as Jere Brophy (2004) reminds us, "schools are not day camps or recreational centers" (p. xii), and teachers are not counselors or recreational directors. Given compulsory attendance, required curricula, class sizes that inhibit individualization, and the specter of high-stakes standardized testing, trying to ensure that learning is always fun is unreasonable and unrealistic. Bill Ayers (1993), a professor of education who has taught preschool through graduate school, is even more blunt. According to Ayers, the belief that good teachers make learning fun is one of the common myths about teaching:

> Fun is distracting, amusing. Clowns are fun. Jokes can be fun. Learning can be engaging, engrossing, amazing, disorienting, involving, and often deeply pleasurable. If it's fun, fine. But it doesn't need to be fun. (p. 13)

Probably all of us can remember situations in which we were motivated to accomplish an academic task that was not fun but that nonetheless seemed worthwhile and meaningful. The example that immediately comes to our minds is learning a foreign language. Neither of us has ever been very good at languages, and we were anxious and self-conscious whenever we had to speak in language class. We found conversation and oral exercises painful; role-plays were excruciating. Yet we each took at least four years of a foreign language in high school and college because we were determined to communicate as fluently as possible when we were finally able to go abroad.

Brophy (2004) refers to this kind of drive as *motivation to learn*—the "tendency to find academic activities meaningful and worthwhile and to try to get the intended learning benefits from them" (p. 15). He distinguishes motivation to learn from *intrinsic motivation,* in which individuals pursue academic activities because they find them pleasurable. At times, of course, you may be able to capitalize on students' intrinsic interests so that the learning activities will be perceived as fun. But it's unlikely that this will always be the case. For this reason, teachers need to consider ways of developing and maintaining students' motivation to learn.

An Expectancy × Value Framework

It is helpful to think about stimulating motivation to learn in terms of an expectancy-value model (Brophy, 2004; Wigfield & Eccles, 2000). This model proposes that motivation depends on *students' expectation of success* and *the value they place on the task* (or on the rewards that it may bring, such as being able to speak fluent Spanish). The two factors work together like a multiplication expression (expectancy × value): If either one is missing (i.e., zero), there will be no motivation.

The expectancy × value model suggests that you have two major responsibilities with respect to motivation. *First, you need to ensure that students can successfully perform the task at hand if they expend the effort.* This means creating assignments that are well suited to students' achievement levels. It may also mean helping students to recognize their ability to perform successfully. Consider the case of Hopeless Hannah (Stipek, 1993). During math class, Hannah frequently sits at her desk doing nothing. If the teacher urges Hannah to try one of the problems she is supposed to be doing, she claims she can't. When the teacher walks her through a problem step by step, Hannah answers most of the questions correctly, but she insists that she was only guessing. Hannah considers herself incompetent, and she interprets her teacher's frustration as proof of her incompetence. She is a classic example of a student afflicted with "failure syndrome" (Brophy, 2004).

Fortunately, extreme cases such as Hannah's are uncommon (Stipek, 1993). But we've probably all encountered situations where anticipation of failure has led to avoidance or paralysis. A lengthy term paper assignment is overwhelming, so we procrastinate until it's too late to do it really well. Calculus is daunting, so we take general mathematics instead. If failure is inevitable, there's no point in trying. And if we rarely try, we rarely succeed.

A second responsibility of teachers is to help students recognize the value of the academic work at hand. For example, Satisfied Sam (Stipek, 1993) is the class clown. He earns grades of C+ and B−, even though he's clearly capable of earning As. He's popular with his peers and often fools around with them on the school grounds after school. At home, Sam spends hours at his computer, reads every book he can find on space, loves science fiction, and has even written a short novel.

But he displays little interest in schoolwork. If assignments coincide with his personal interests, he exerts effort; otherwise, he simply sees no point in doing them.

In order to motivate Sam, you need to help him see that class activities can be valuable or enjoyable. Sam likes to interact with peers, so he might participate willingly in small-group activities. Relating class assignments to his interest in science fiction could also prove helpful. At the very least, you can point out the value of the *rewards* that successful completion or mastery will bring. For example, Sam may see little value in learning history, but he may still recognize that a passing grade is required for promotion.

In accordance with the expectancy $\times$ value model, Brophy (2004) has reviewed relevant theory and research and derived a set of strategies that teachers can use to enhance students' motivation. The following sections of this chapter are largely based on Brophy's work (see Table 8.1). We begin with strategies that focus on the first variable in the model—students' expectations of success.

As you read, keep in mind that *none of these strategies will be very effective if you have not worked to create and sustain a safe, caring classroom environment* (Chapter 3). Before students can become motivated, they must feel safe from humiliation, must understand that it's all right to take risks and make mistakes, and must know that they are accepted, respected members of the class (Urdan & Schoenfelder, 2006). In fact, a supportive environment is an "essential precondition" for the successful use of motivational strategies (Good & Brophy, 2008, p. 148).

PAUSE AND REFLECT

Now that you have read about the expectancy $\times$ value model of motivation, think back to instances in your own life when you felt unmotivated about a particular task or assignment. See whether you can apply the model to these instances to help explain your lack of motivation. Were you expecting to fail? Did you see little value in the task?

TABLE 8.1 Brophy's Strategies for Enhancing Motivation to Learn

Strategies for Increasing Expectation of Success
- Provide opportunities for success.
- Teach students to set reasonable goals and to assess their own performance.
- Help students recognize the relationship between effort and outcome.
- Provide informative feedback.
- Provide special motivational support to discouraged students.

Strategies for Increasing Perceived Value
- Relate lessons to students' own lives.
- Provide opportunities for choice.
- Model interest in learning and express enthusiasm for the material.
- Include novel/variety elements.
- Provide opportunities for students to respond actively.
- Allow students to create finished products.
- Provide opportunities for students to interact with peers.
- Provide extrinsic rewards.

Source: Brophy, 2004.

STRATEGIES FOR INCREASING EXPECTATIONS OF SUCCESS

Provide Opportunities for Success

If tasks appear too difficult, students may be afraid to tackle them. You need to make sure that instruction is on an appropriate level for each student. You may have to modify assignments for different students, make assignments open-ended so that a variety of responses can be acceptable, allow extra time, or provide additional help. For example, when Courtney's students have writing workshop, she makes sure that they have the tools they need to be successful. Although an alphabet chart is posted on the wall, Courtney gives some students personalized letter strips and personalized word walls so that they can use them during writing. She may also provide children with different worksheets based on their writing skills. For example, during one lesson, Courtney read students *Click, Clack, Moo—Cows That Type* (Cronin, 2000), in which Farmer Brown's cows find a typewriter and type out their demands. Then the children had to think about what Fuzzy (the stuffed toy mouse in their classroom) might ask for if he could write. The follow-up assignment was to write a letter explaining what Fuzzy would like. Some children drew a picture and wrote their sentences on blank lines. Other had a "template" to follow that simplified the task (see Figure 8.1). A differentiated assignment like this increases all children's chances of success.

Another example of differentiated assignments comes from Carol Tomlinson (1999):

> Today, [Ms. Cunningham's first-grade] students will work at a learning center on compound words. Students' names are listed at the center; one of four colors is beside each name. Each student works with the folder that matches the color beside his or her name. For example, Sam has the color red next to his name. Using the materials in the red folder, Sam must decide the correct order of pairs of words to make familiar compound words. He also will make a poster that illustrates each simple word and the new compound word they form. Using materials in the blue folder, Jenna will look around the classroom and in books to find examples of compound words. She will write them out and illustrate them in a booklet. Using materials in the purple folder, Tijuana will write a poem or a story that uses compound words that she generates to make the story or poem interesting. . . . In the green folder, Dillon will find a story the teacher has written. It contains correct and incorrect compound words. Dillon will be a word detective, looking for "villains" and "good guys" among the compound words. He will list [these] on a chart . . . and then write them correctly.

Another way of enhancing the probability of success is to vary instructional approaches so that students with different strengths have equal access to instruction. Numerous schools have developed programs based on Howard Gardner's (1995, 1998) theory of "multiple intelligences" (MI). According to Gardner, people have at least eight types of intellectual capacities. (These are listed in Table 8.2.) Schools have traditionally emphasized the development of linguistic and logical-mathematical intelligences (and have favored those who are relatively strong in these), while they have neglected and undervalued the other intelligences. Although Gardner does not advocate one "right way" to implement a multiple intelligences education, he

Dear Miss Bell,

Fuzzy is _tired_ [D|A|R T_____.

He would like _couch_ C A A W A C H_____.

Sincerely,

Figure 8.1   Courtney's Differentiated Assignments

does recommend that teachers approach topics in a variety of ways, so that more students will be reached and more can experience "what it is like to be an expert" (1995, p. 208). With this in mind, Barbara plans curriculum units that allow for a wide range of activities, from report writing, to puppet shows, to murals, to hands-on demonstrations and experiments. As Barbara puts it,

> I want all students to have the chance to work in ways that are comfort-able for them, but I also want to "stretch" them and have them work in ways that are less comfortable. Children who are artistic should have the chance to do murals, but they also have to do writing!

Dear Miss Bell,

Fuzzy   needs   a   friend
FESE NEDS A FREND

to   be   happy
TOOBEHAPPY

Sincerely,

Figure 8.1   *Continued*

Obviously, incorporating all the intelligences into every topic is impossible. And Gardner himself claims that trying to do this is a waste of effort and one of the ways in which MI theory is misused (Gardner, 1998). Nonetheless, the theory of MI can suggest varied ways of having students engage with academic content. By routinely integrating tasks involving two or three different intelligences into your planning, you can provide students with greater opportunities for success.

One other consideration regarding student success is important to mention here. Keep in mind that the process of learning something new often involves temporary failure and possibly some frustration (Alfi, Assor, & Katz, 2004). It's important that you allow your students to experience temporary failure in the

TABLE 8.2 Gardner's Multiple Intelligences

Type of Intelligence	Description
Linguistic	Capacity to use language to express and appreciate complex meanings; sensitivity to the sounds, rhythms, and meanings of words
Logical-mathematical	Capacity to reason and recognize logical and numerical patterns; to calculate, quantify, consider propositions and hypotheses
Spatial	Capacity to perceive the visual world accurately; to think in three-dimensional ways; to navigate oneself through space; to produce and understand graphic information
Musical	Sensitivity to pitch, melody, rhythm, and tone; capacity to produce and appreciate different forms of musical expression
Bodily-kinesthetic	Capacity to use the body and to handle objects skillfully
Interpersonal	Capacity to understand and interact effectively with others; to discern accurately the moods and emotions of others
Intrapersonal	Capacity to understand oneself; perceptiveness about one's own moods, emotions, desires, motivations
Naturalist	Capacity to understand nature and to observe patterns; sensitivity to features of the natural world

Sources: Arends, 2008; Campbell, Campbell, & Dickinson, 1999.

safety of your classroom, so that they can develop needed coping skills and a sense of mastery that will contribute to their motivation to continue learning.

Teach Students to Set Reasonable Goals and Assess Their Own Performance

Some children think anything less than 100 on a test is a failure, whereas others are content with a barely passing grade. You may have to help students set goals that are reasonable and obtainable. On the first day of school, Garnetta has her students write about their goals for third grade. These are discussed and posted on the front bulletin board, where they can serve as daily reminders: "I want to learn how to write in cursive." "I want to know times tables and divided by." "I will try to get strait [sic] A's." "I want to learn multiplication." And from a new child, "I want to make new friends." Similarly, on the first day of school, Ken gives his students their report cards from the previous year and copies of their standardized achievement test scores. He asks them "to sit and reflect and begin to set some goals." He encourages them to write these down. Then he distributes a blank report card to each student, telling them to "think about what you'd like to get in each subject." He stresses that this is "just the beginning" of the process and that they will continue to develop real objectives for the academic year.

Help Students Recognize the Relationship between Effort and Outcome

Like Hopeless Hannah, some youngsters proclaim defeat before they've even attempted a task. When they don't do well on an assignment, they attribute their failure to lack of ability, not realizing that achievement is often a function of effort. Other students may be overconfident—even cocky—and think they can do well without exerting much effort. In either situation, you have to make the relationship between effort and outcome explicit. Whenever possible, point out students' improvement and help them to see the role of effort: "See, you did all your math homework this week, and it really paid off. Look at how well you did on the quiz!"

During a visit to Courtney's classroom, we watched her teach students what to do if they "get stuck" during writing workshop. At this stage of writing workshop, students are mainly drawing, and Courtney stresses that this is a perfectly good way of representing your ideas. But sometimes children are anxious about not being able to draw well enough. With students gathered on the rug in front of the easel pad, Courtney begins by describing what she saw during the last workshop session:

Writers, last week I saw lots of wonderful things. I saw people think and then put that down on paper. But I also saw people get stuck, because they said, "This is too hard to draw." So today, I'm going to show you what to do if you get stuck.

This past weekend, my window was open and I wanted to push it down, but it was stuck. So let's say I decide to draw that. The window is easy. [On the easel paper she draws a window.] There are flowers on the sill. [She adds flower pots with flowers.] But, uh oh, I don't know how to draw me. Maybe I'll just draw more flowers. No, I'll do the best I can. That's what writers do. [She draws herself in front of the window.] Now, David came and helped me. [David is her fiancé.] I want to draw David, but that's hard. Should I just draw more flowers or should I just do my best? [The children tell her to do her best.] OK, I'll just do my best. [She draws David.] Gee, that's pretty good. [She turns back to the students.] Do you see how I tried my best? That was smart of me. Writers do that. Turn to your neighbor and tell them what you would do if you got stuck. [Children tell one another that they would just do their best.] OK, writers, eyes up here. I heard so many people say, "I would just try my best." That's wonderful.

Provide Informative Feedback

Sometimes turning in work to a teacher is like dropping it down a black hole. Assignments pile up in huge mounds on the teacher's desk, and students know that their papers will never be returned—graded or ungraded. From a student's perspective, it's infuriating to work hard on an assignment, turn it in, and then receive no feedback from the teacher. But a lack of academic feedback is not simply infuriating; it is also detrimental to students' motivation and achievement.

The Beginning Teacher Evaluation Study (Fisher et al., 1980) documented the importance of providing feedback to students:

> One particularly important teaching activity is providing academic feedback to students (letting them know whether their answers are right or wrong, or giving them the right answer). Academic feedback should be provided as often as possible to students. When more frequent feedback is offered, students pay attention more and learn more. *Academic feedback was more strongly and consistently related to achievement than any of the other teaching behaviors.* (p. 27; emphasis added)

If you circulate while students are working on assignments, you can provide them with immediate feedback about their performance. You can catch errors, assist with problems, and affirm correct, thoughtful work. As Viviana comments:

I always correct papers as my children are doing them. That's the time to explain and correct mistakes. If children don't understand the first problem, they'll get all the rest wrong. This also allows students to take their work home every day, so parents can see how they're doing. Correcting work as students do it also means that I don't have to take home a huge stack of papers every night, and I can use that time for planning.

Sometimes you're unable to monitor and correct work while it's being done. In this case, you need to check assignments once they've been submitted and return them to students as soon as possible. You might also decide to allow your students to check their own work. Ken believes this has numerous educational benefits:

If I correct assignments, I'm doing all the important work—the editing, the problem solving, the analyzing of mistakes. That's what the kids should be doing, or at the very least, I should be doing it in front of them. They learn best by correcting their own mistakes, rather than reading somebody else's comments. And the most important stuff must be talked about. I prefer to have students discuss and correct work together, either in their small reading and math groups or as a whole class. I tell them, "Today at 2:00 you need to be ready to share your newspaper articles." We discuss what they've done, and the feedback session becomes an extension of the assignment.

Some teachers also encourage peer feedback in order to reduce their workload and to reinforce the idea that students can learn from one another. Even kindergartners can be introduced to this practice. For example, when Courtney's students begin learning to "write for readers" (that is, to use conventional spacing and spelling so that readers can understand what's written), Courtney teaches students what to say if they are unable to read their partners' work (e.g., "I can't read that because your words are all squished together" or "I can't read that word because you didn't write enough sounds"). Although she admits that "only a few can really do this effectively," Courtney still believes that it's important for students to start learning how to give peer feedback from the very beginning of their schooling experience.

If you choose to use peer feedback, be aware of some inherent problems (Latham, 1997). First, without proper training, students may not be able to provide high-quality feedback. When providing feedback on written work, for example, students may respond to "lower-order concerns," such as syntactic errors, rather than to more substantive concerns, such as the development of ideas (Ching, 1991). That's why teacher modeling is so crucial. Second, although Lev Vygotsky (1978) argues that interactions with more able peers can help students work in their zone of proximal development, a classwide system of peer feedback inevitably requires some students to receive feedback from *less* able peers (DiPardo & Freedman, 1988). Finally, some students may not value feedback received from their peers. One study (Zhang, 1995) found that students whose native language was not English overwhelmingly preferred teacher feedback to student feedback.

Whether you correct work while it's being done, at home over a cup of coffee, or together with your students, the important point is that students *need to know how they are progressing*. It's also important to give feedback in terms of *absolute standards or students' own past performance rather than in terms of peers' performance* (Brophy, 2004). Thus, instead of saying, "Congratulations! You received the sixth-highest grade in the class," you could say, "Congratulations! You went from a 79 on your last quiz to an 87 on this quiz." Similarly, you can point out strengths and weaknesses and add a note of encouragement for further effort ("You've demonstrated a firm grasp of the perspectives of the slaveholders and the abolitionists, but not of the slaves themselves. Check the chapter again, and add a paragraph to round out your presentation.").

Provide Special Motivational Support to Discouraged Students

For students with limited ability or learning disabilities, school may be a constant struggle to keep up with classmates and to maintain a sense of enthusiasm and motivation. Such students not only require instructional assistance (e.g., individualized activities, extra academic help, well-structured assignments, extra time) but may also need special encouragement and motivational support. Unfortunately, teachers sometimes develop counterproductive behavior patterns that communicate low expectations and reinforce students' perceptions of themselves as failures. Table 8.3 lists some of the behaviors that have been identified.

As Brophy (2004) points out, some of these differences are due to the behavior of the students. For example, if students' contributions to discussions are irrelevant or incorrect, it is difficult for teachers to accept and use their ideas. Moreover, the boundary between *appropriate differentiated instruction* and *inappropriate differential treatment* is often fuzzy. Asking low achievers easier, nonanalytic questions may make instructional sense. Nonetheless, it's important to monitor the extent to which you engage in these behaviors and to reflect on the messages you are sending to your low-achieving students or those with learning disabilities. If you find that you are engaging in a lot of the behaviors listed in Table 8.3, you

TABLE 8.3 Ways in Which Teachers May Communicate Low Expectations

1. Waiting less time for low achievers to answer a question before giving the answer or calling on someone else.
2. Giving answers to low achievers or calling on someone else rather than helping.
3. Rewarding inappropriate behaviors or incorrect answers.
4. Criticizing low achievers more often for failure.
5. Praising low achievers less often for success.
6. Paying less attention to low achievers.
7. Seating low achievers farther away from the teacher.
8. Demanding less from low achievers than they are capable of learning.
9. Being less friendly in interactions with low achievers; showing less attention and responsiveness; making less eye contact.
10. Providing briefer and less informative answers to questions from low achievers.
11. Showing less acceptance and use of low achievers' ideas.
12. Limiting low achievers to a low-level, repetitive curriculum with an emphasis on drill and practice tasks.

Source: Brophy, 2004.

may be "merely going through the motions of instructing low achievers, without seriously working to help them achieve their potential" (Brophy, 2004, p. 129).

Research on gender bias in the classroom has revealed that teachers may also communicate low expectations to their female students (Sadker, Sadker, & Zittleman, 2009). Therefore, it is important to monitor your interactions with female and male students to make sure you aren't sending an unintended message to either group.

ENHANCING THE VALUE OF THE TASK

Recall that the students in the classes of our five teachers stressed that "good teachers" teach in a way that is motivating. As one student wrote, "Not everything can be fun . . . , but there are ways teachers can make [material] more interesting and more challenging" (see Chapter 1). This student intuitively understands that motivation to learn depends not only on success expectations but also on students' perceptions of the value of the task or of the rewards that successful completion or mastery will bring. Remember Satisfied Sam? Seeing no value in his course assignments, he invests little effort in them, even though he knows he could be successful. Because students like Sam are unlikely to respond to their teachers' exhortations to work harder, the challenge is to find ways to convince them that the work has (1) *intrinsic value* (doing it will provide enjoyment), (2) *utility value* (doing it will advance their personal goals), or (3) *attainment value* (doing it will affirm their self-concept or fulfill their needs for achievement, understanding, skill mastery, and prestige) (Brophy, 2004; Eccles & Wigfield, 1985).

Let's consider some of the strategies that teachers can use to enhance the perception of value.

Relate Lessons to Students' Own Lives

A study of the motivational strategies of first-year teachers (Newby, 1991) demonstrated that students are more engaged in classrooms where teachers provide reasons for doing tasks and relate lessons to students' personal experiences (see Figure 8.2). Unfortunately, *the study also found that first-year teachers use these "relevance strategies" only occasionally.*

Observations of our five teachers provide numerous examples of attempts to link academic tasks to children's lives. In math class, for example, Barbara often creates word problems that incorporate her students' names and interests: "Mark collects baseball cards. His collection is worth $57.85. He purchases five new cards valued at $6.35 . . . ." When Ken's class does writing, the topics come from the students' own lives. He asks them to write about what they're good at, what they can teach others, how they feel about school. Viviana and Garnetta teach map skills by having students make maps of the classroom and the neighborhood. Garnetta's students also play a game in which they write the directions to their houses. These are then read aloud and students try to guess whose house is involved.

For Courtney's kindergartners, "taking the bus to school is a big deal," so this year, Courtney designed a thematic unit around the school bus. Students kept "bus journals," in which they wrote their questions about buses and recorded the answers; they counted the number of seats in a school bus and measured tire circumference; they built buses from Legos and blocks; they used actual bus parts to create settings for their dramatic play; they did bus jigsaw puzzles and painted pictures of buses in the art center.

When students are not from the dominant culture, teachers must make a special effort to relate academic content to referents from the students' own culture—what Gloria Ladson-Billings (1994) calls *culturally relevant teaching.* This practice not only helps to bridge the gap between the two cultures, it also can usher in the study of cultural referents in their own right. The case of Carter Forshay, an African American man in his late 20s, provides a compelling example (Ladson-Billings, 2001).

Figure 8.2   *Source:* ADAM @ HOME © 2008 by UNIVERSAL UCLICK. Reprinted with permission. All rights reserved.

As a first-year teacher, Carter was committed to fostering the literacy skills of his third-grade students, all African Americans. To his dismay, he discovered that his students "absolutely hated writing" (p. 19):

> Every time Carter attempted to come up with an exciting and motivating topic on which to write, his students balked. . . . "Aww, Mr. Forshay, I don't want to do this." "Writin' is too hard." "I don't have nothin' to say; why are you makin' us write this stuff?" "Why can't you just give us some worksheets? We can do them!" (p. 19)

Knowing that his students loved music, Carter decided that "helping kids connect with music might be a way to help them connect with writing" (p. 20). He chose a CD by trumpeter Wynton Marsalis containing the song "Blue Interlude: The Bittersweet Saga of Sugar Cane and Sweetie Pie." Just as in "Peter and the Wolf," various melodies in "Blue Interlude" reflect particular characters.

> During the first lesson Carter played the CD and questioned the students about what they thought the action was and how they thought the characters were behaving and feeling. From there, Carter encouraged the students to take turns role-playing the characters and their interactions.

Although Carter's students were initially reluctant to do the role plays, they eventually became more enthusiastic and more theatrical. Carter concluded the first lesson by having students record the traits of each character in the piece.

On subsequent days, students outlined the story they had created, developed dialogue, and wrote and illustrated their own drafts. As Ladson-Billings comments, "The students who no one thought would write had become writers" (p. 21).

Provide Opportunities for Choice

One of the most obvious ways to ensure that learning activities connect to individuals' personal interests is to provide opportunities for choice. Moreover, research has shown that when students experience a sense of autonomy and self-determination, they are more likely to be intrinsically motivated (Ryan & Deci, 2000b) and to "bond" with school (Roeser, Eccles, & Sameroff, 2000).

Mandated curricula and high-stakes standardized testing thwart opportunities for choice, but there are usually alternative ways for students to accomplish assignments. Researchers asked 36 teachers about the types of instructional choices they gave their students (Flowerday & Schraw, 2000). Although types of choices varied as a function of content areas and grade levels, all teachers agreed on six main types of choice: (1) topics of study (for research papers, in-class projects, and presentations); (2) reading materials (type of genre and choice of authors); (3) methods of assessment (exam versus final project); (4) activities (book report or diorama); (5) social arrangements (whether to work in pairs or small groups and choice of group members); and (6) procedural choices (when to take tests, what order to study prescribed topics, and when assignments were due). Teachers also expressed the belief that choice has a positive effect on students' motivation by increasing their sense of ownership and self-determination, interest, and enthusiasm. Despite this belief, however, teachers tended to use choice as a *reward* for effort and good behavior, rather than as a *strategy for fostering* effort and good behavior. Thus teachers were most likely to give choices to students who were already self-regulated.

It's easy to understand why teachers would provide choice to students who have previously shown that they are responsible, motivated, and well-behaved. (It certainly seems safer!) But we strongly believe that teachers need to use choice in a more proactive way to motivate students like Satisfied Sam. In fact, research has shown that providing choice to students with emotional and behavioral disorders is an effective way of increasing engagement and appropriate behavior (Jolivette, Wehby, Canale, & Massey, 2001). Consider the hypothetical case of Isaac (Jolivette, Stichter, & McCormick, 2002), a seven-year-old first-grader with emotional and behavioral disorders. Isaac's teacher reported that he performed below grade level in mathematics and that he was noncompliant and off-task during seatwork activities. He frequently ripped up his math worksheet and threw it to the floor, verbally disrupted the student next to him, and walked around the room instead of working. In response, his teacher took away privileges such as free time and moved his desk away from those of his peers. Isaac's inappropriate behaviors only escalated.

Although some teachers may believe that Isaac doesn't "deserve" the opportunity to make choices, if we think of choice as a motivational strategy rather than as a reward, we can see that it might be useful here. There are a variety of choice possibilities (Jolivette, Stichter, & McCormick, 2002). For example, Isaac might be allowed to decide when he will begin his math worksheet—after carrying out his daily housekeeping tasks (straightening the workbook shelf and sharpening pencils) or before. He might also be allowed the option of taking 30-second "mini-breaks" while working on the math problems; this could be particularly useful if he finds the work difficult. Isaac could also make decisions about the writing utensil (pencil, pen, or colored pencil) and eraser he wants to use, and where he wants to sit. If more than one worksheet is assigned, he can decide on the order in which to complete them. Such choices are likely to provide Isaac with a reassuring predictability and a sense that he has control over his environment.

Model Interest in Learning and Express Enthusiasm for the Material

Before Barbara introduces students to the novel *Mr. Popper's Penguins* (Atwater, 1966), she first discloses that "penguins are one of my favorite animals." Her enthusiasm for penguins is apparent—on the first day of school, students' name tags prominently feature a picture of a penguin; a five-foot-high, plastic penguin stands in the library corner; stuffed animal penguins perch on Barbara's desk; and as days go by, dates on the class calendar are covered by paper penguins.

Enthusiasm like this is exhibited by all five teachers, and it appears to be a very important characteristic of teachers who foster involvement, effort, and learning (Patrick et al., 2001). It's not unusual to hear our teachers make comments like "This is really going to be interesting," "Now this is my favorite part," "Wait 'til you see what happens next," "I just love this book, and I'm excited to share it with you."

Include Novelty/Variety Elements

Garnetta's students play "Wheel of Fortune" to practice vocabulary. Barbara distributes the advertising flyers from supermarkets, assigns each child a designated amount of money, and has her students "go shopping." Viviana's students jump, hop, clap, and march when she's teaching them about verbs that depict action. When Ken's students learn about sampling procedures, they work with M&M's, extrapolating from a small bag in order to predict how many of each color would be contained in a half-pound bag. Courtney's students use shaving cream, sand, salt, finger paints, and wax sticks to practice writing upper- and lowercase letters.

Provide Opportunities for Students to Respond Actively

So often the teacher talks and moves, while students sit passively and listen. In contrast, when Ken's class studies probability, students work in small groups, gently tossing tacks and graphing how many land with the points up and how many land with the points down (and it's *not* 50–50). Barbara's students make bubble solution, go outside to blow bubbles, and discuss what they saw, how the bubbles felt, and what they looked like. Then they come back in and write poems, essays, or stories about the experience. Courtney's students learn a chant and a hand motion for each letter of the alphabet (for the letter A, for example, they mime biting an apple).

Allow Students to Create Finished Products

Too much school time is devoted to exercises, drills, and practice. Students practice writing, but rarely write. They practice reading skills, but rarely read. They practice mathematical procedures, but rarely do real mathematics. Yet creating a

Courtney's students use materials such as salt, sand, and shaving cream to practice writing the alphabet.

Garnetta's students carry out a science experiment.

finished product gives meaning and purpose to assignments and increases students' motivation to learn. After Garnetta's students finish their research on the solar system, each child constructs an eight-foot mural of the planets that she or he can take home. When Viviana's students learn about seeds, they construct displays for the district's Academic Fair. Barbara's students participate in the "Invention Convention": They define a problem (e.g., scratching your back in an out-of-the-way place) and then construct an invention to solve the problem. In addition, students write ads for their inventions, and these ads are compiled in a book that resembles a Sears catalog. When Ken's students have a writing assignment, the due date is called the "publication date." At that time, they "celebrate authorship" by reading and discussing their work (and, of course, by sharing some treats). Courtney's students create class books for the library corner modeled after those she's read to them. For example, after hearing *It Looked Like Spilt Milk* (Shaw, 1947), students used white paint on blue paper to draw clouds that looked like an object of their choice. Captions followed the format of the book (e.g., "Sometimes it looked like a baseball bat, but it wasn't a baseball bat").

Provide Opportunities for Students to Interact with Peers

All five teachers allow students to work in pairs or small groups to accomplish tasks (a topic we will explore further in Chapter 10). For example, Courtney's students have writing workshop partners who provide peer feedback, and Viviana's students work in pairs during math, manipulating Unifix cubes to demonstrate two-digit numbers. In Ken's class, students form simulation teams to experience firsthand the hardships of pioneer life. Garnetta's class divides into "food groups" when they are studying nutrition. Barbara's students have spelling partners because "spelling can be tedious."

Provide Extrinsic Rewards

Some effective managers find it useful to provide students with rewards for engaging in the behaviors that support learning (such as paying attention and participating) and for academic achievement. The use of rewards in classrooms is based on the psychological principle of *positive reinforcement:* Behavior that is rewarded is strengthened and is therefore likely to be repeated. Although rewards do not increase the perceived value of the behavior or the task, they link performance of the behavior or successful completion of the task to attractive, desirable consequences.

Rewards can be divided into three categories: social rewards, activity rewards, and tangible rewards. *Social rewards* are verbal and nonverbal indications that you recognize and appreciate students' behavior or achievements. A pat on the back, a smile, a thumbs-up signal—these are commonly used social rewards that are low in cost and readily available.

Praise can also function as a social reward. In order to be effective, however, praise must be *specific and sincere.* Instead of "Good paper," you can try something like this: "Your paper shows a firm grasp of the distinction between metaphor and similes." Instead of "You were great this morning," try "The way you came into the room, took off your baseball caps, and immediately got out your notebooks was terrific." Being specific will make your praise more informative; it will also help you to avoid using the same tired, old phrases week after week, phrases that quickly lose all impact (e.g., "Good job"). If praise is to serve as a reinforcer, it also needs to be *contingent on the behavior you are trying to strengthen.* In other words, it should be given only when that behavior occurs, so that students understand exactly what evoked the praise.

 Viviana's students sit quietly while she speaks with a visitor by the door. When she turns back to the class, she tells them: "Thank you for being so quiet just now. It was so helpful. I was able to talk to Mrs. Johnson without being interrupted. By being quiet you really helped me."

In addition to pats on the back and verbal praise, some teachers institute more formal ways of recognizing accomplishment, improvement, or cooperation. For example, they may display student work, provide award certificates, nominate students for school awards given at the end of the year, or select a "Student of the Week." Ken has developed an interesting variation on this program. Instead of deciding on the student of the week by himself, he and his students work together to develop the criteria (see Figure 8.3), and students vote each week to choose the recipient (another way of sharing responsibility and decision making with students). We asked Ken how he made sure that the weekly vote didn't degenerate into a popularity contest. Here's his response:

 Every Friday afternoon we sit in a circle and nominate people. Nominations have to be supported with references to the criteria. For example, "I nominate Paul. He helped me in math this week," or "I nominate Leah. She shared her snack with me," or "She helped a new

student." When the list of nominees is complete, each child gets a ballot and we vote. The winner receives a certificate to take home, and we all write a note to the student giving three reasons why he or she deserved it.

The class created the rule that you can win twice, but you can't win a third time until everyone in the class has won. Now maybe a kid who hasn't been picked begins to feel uncomfortable. I think that's OK. Maybe he'll think about not getting picked and begin to modify his own behavior. Maybe he'll hold a door for the other kids or stack chairs. I'll talk privately to a kid who isn't selected: Why do you think you haven't been chosen? What do you think you could do in order to be chosen as student of the week? When I see him begin to change his behavior, I make sure to point that out: "I want to thank Robert for holding the door for all of us." It's funny, I thought maybe this year I wouldn't do Student of the Week, but the class really wanted it. . . . And they do choose well.

In addition to social rewards, teachers sometimes use *special activities* as rewards for good behavior or accomplishment. (The accompanying Practical Tips box lists activities that may be reinforcing.) In fact, Fredric Jones (Jones et al., 2007) believes that the activities students enjoy are the best overall incentives. He recommends that teachers allow students to have "preferred activity time" (PAT) when they act responsibly. Students can also earn "bonus PAT" by saving time during transitions and "being in the right place at the right time with the right stuff" (p. 273). (See Jones's book *Tools for Teaching* for detailed advice about instituting a PAT incentive program.)

Finally, teachers can use *tangible, material rewards* for good behavior—cookies, stickers, award certificates, candy, baseball cards, pencils. For example, Barbara's math class has particular difficulty remembering to bring in homework.

The student of the week is a person who
 1. is neat in work.
 2. does homework.
 3. is friendly to all classmates.
 4. can be trusted and can be relied on.
 5. helps others.
 6. listens to the teacher's instructions.
 7. respects other people's property.
 8. is kind to people.
 9. is responsible.
10. shares with other people.
11. treats everyone equally.
12. cooperates with students and teachers.
13. has self-control.
14. doesn't curse or talk back.
15. doesn't give up and always tries his or her hardest.
16. doesn't hurt others' feelings.
17. uses gifts and talents well.

Figure 8.3   Criteria for Student of the Week

PRACTICAL TIPS FOR

CHOOSING ACTIVITIES AS REWARDS

- Be first in line.
- Choose a game to play with a friend.
- Choose a game for the class to play.
- Choose a story for the teacher to read to the class.
- Have 10 minutes of free time.
- Take care of the class pet.
- Take home the class pet for the weekend.
- Keep a favorite stuffed animal on your desk for a day.
- Have breakfast or lunch with the teacher.
- Read a story to a class in a lower grade.
- Read a story to the principal.
- Use the computer alone or with a friend.
- Listen to music through earphones.
- Work with special art materials.
- Lead a game.
- Be excused from a homework assignment.
- Chew gum at a specified time.
- Keep score during a class game.
- Create a bulletin board display.
- Check out a classroom game to take home.
- Have a private, three-minute talk with the teacher.

In order to encourage this behavior, Barbara gives out stickers that can then be traded for special privileges. Garnetta's students all have sticker folders they made out of cardboard, and Garnetta dispenses cats, pumpkins, stars, and hearts of every conceivable size, texture, and smell. In addition to the rewards she distributes in class, there is a schoolwide recognition program. By following established school rules, students earn points that can be used at the school store to purchase novelty items.

Problems with Rewards

The practice of providing extrinsic rewards has been the focus of considerable controversy. In particular, educators have debated the legitimacy and ultimate value of *material* or *tangible* rewards. Even among our five teachers, there is disagreement. Ken, Garnetta, and Barbara all use tangible rewards to some extent, whereas Viviana and Courtney generally do not, preferring to rely on praise and recognition.

One objection is that giving students tangible rewards in exchange for good behavior or performance is tantamount to bribery. Proponents of this position argue that students should engage in appropriate behavior and activities for their own sake: They should be quiet during independent work time because that is the socially responsible thing to do; they should do their homework so that they can practice skills taught during class; they should learn multiplication tables because they need to know them. Other educators acknowledge the desirability of such intrinsic motivation but believe that the use of rewards is inevitable in situations where people are not completely free to follow their own inclinations. Even Richard Ryan and Edward Deci, two psychologists who strongly endorse the importance of self-determination and autonomy, acknowledge that teachers "cannot always rely on intrinsic motivation to foster learning" because "many of the tasks that educators want their students to perform are not inherently interesting or enjoyable" (Ryan & Deci, 2000a, p. 55).

Another objection to the use of rewards is the fact that they are attempts to control and manipulate people. When we dispense rewards, we are essentially saying, "Do this, and you'll get that"—an approach not unlike the way we train our pets. Indeed, Alfie Kohn, author of *Punished by Rewards: The Trouble with Gold Stars, Incentive Plans, A's, Praise, and Other Bribes* (1993), contends that rewards and punishments are "two sides of the same coin" (p. 50). Although rewards are certainly more pleasurable, they are "every bit as controlling as punishments, even if they control by seduction" (p. 51). According to Kohn, if we want youngsters to become self-regulating, responsible, caring individuals, we must abandon attempts at external control and provide students with opportunities to develop competence, connection, and autonomy in caring classroom communities. For more information on Kohn's work, see Box 8.1.

Another major concern is that rewarding students for behaving in certain ways actually *undermines their intrinsic motivation to engage in those behaviors.* This question was explored in an influential study conducted by Lepper, Greene, and Nisbett (1973). First, the researchers identified preschoolers who showed interest in a particular drawing activity during free play. Then they met with the children individually. Some children were simply invited to draw with the materials (these were the "no-reward" subjects). Others were told they could receive a "good-player" award, which they received for drawing (the "expected-reward" subjects). Still others were invited to draw and were then given an unexpected reward at the end (the "unexpected-reward" subjects). Subsequent observations during free play revealed that the children who had been promised a reward ahead of time engaged in the art activity half as much as they had initially. Children in the other two groups showed no change.

This study stimulated a great deal of research on the potentially detrimental effects of external rewards. Although the results were not always consistent, this research led educators to conclude that *rewarding people for doing something that is inherently pleasurable decreases their interest in continuing that behavior.* A common explanation for this effect is the *overjustification hypothesis.* It appears to work like this: Individuals being rewarded reason that the task must not be very interesting or engaging, because they have to be

MEET THE EDUCATORS   BOX 8.1

MEET ALFIE KOHN

Alfie Kohn writes extensively on education, parenting, and human behavior. He is a frequent lecturer on topics such as "the deadly effects of 'tougher standards'"; the use of "A's, praise, stickers, and contests" to "bribe" students to learn; "the case against competition"; "teaching children to care"; and "the homework myth." *Time* magazine described Kohn as "perhaps the country's most outspoken critic of education's fixation on grades [and] test scores."

Some Major Ideas on Motivation

- "How do I get these kids motivated?" is a question that reflects a "paradigm of control," and external control "is death to motivation" (Kohn, 1993, p. 199).
- "Do rewards motivate people? Absolutely. They motivate people to get rewards." (Kohn, 1993, p. 67).
- People who are trying to earn rewards generally end up doing worse on many tasks than people who are not. Like punishment, rewards are a form of control, designed to bring about compliance.
- In contrast, the three Cs create the conditions for "authentic motivation": *collaboration* (learning together), *content* (things

worth knowing), and *choice* (autonomy in the classroom). When students have opportunities to work cooperatively on learning activities built around their interests, questions, and real-life concerns, and when they share responsibility for deciding what gets learned and how, there is no need for rewards.

Selected Books and Articles

The Homework Myth: Why Our Kids Get Too Much of a Bad Thing (De Capo Books, 2006)

The Case against Standardized Testing: Raising the Scores, Ruining the Schools (Heinemann, 2000)

The Schools Our Children Deserve: Moving beyond Traditional Classrooms and "Tougher Standards" (Houghton Mifflin, 1999)

Beyond Discipline: From Compliance to Community (Association for Supervision and Curriculum Development, 1996/2006)

Punished by Rewards: The Trouble with Gold Stars, Incentive Plans, A's, Praise, and Other Bribes (1993/1999)

Website: www.alfiekohn.org

---

rewarded (i.e., provided with extra justification) for undertaking it. In other words, what was previously considered "play" is now seen as "work" (Reeve, 2006a). Another explanation focuses on the possibility that external rewards conflict with people's need for autonomy and self-determination. This explanation argues that interest in a task decreases when individuals perceive rewards as attempts to control their behavior.

The detrimental effect of extrinsic reward on intrinsic motivation has been—and continues to be—hotly debated. In fact, reviews of the research (Cameron, 2001; Cameron, Banko, & Pierce, 2001; Cameron & Pierce, 1994; Deci, Koestner, & Ryan, 1999, 2001) have reached contradictory conclusions about the effects of expected tangible rewards. According to Judy Cameron (2001), it's all right to say, "If you complete the assignment with at least 80% accuracy, you'll get a coupon for something at the school store at the end of the period" (expected reward contingent on completion and specified level of performance), but it's *not* all right to say, "Work on the assignment and you'll get a coupon for something at the school store at the end of the period" (noncontingent reward). In contrast, others contend that expected "tangible rewards offered for engaging in, completing, or doing well at a task" are *all* deleterious to intrinsic motivation (Deci, Koestner & Ryan, 1999, p. 656). With respect to verbal rewards and unexpected tangible rewards, the reviews are more consistent: Both sets of researchers conclude that verbal praise can enhance intrinsic motivation and that unexpected tangible rewards have no detrimental effect. Further, most researchers acknowledge that external rewards can help develop intrinsic motivation when the initial interest level in the task is low (Williams & Stockdale, 2004). For example, elementary students may not initially find the value in reading books, particularly if the books are challenging or above their current reading level. You might offer incentives for reading those books initially (such as having a book chart with stickers for completed books) and then phase out this reward as the students start to enjoy those reading books and realize that they are improving their fluency and comprehension.

At the present time, caution in the use of external rewards is in order. As you contemplate whether or not to use rewards in your classroom, keep in mind the suggestions listed in the Practical Tips box.

> ### ✎ PAUSE AND REFLECT
>
> How are rewards used in classrooms you have observed? Now that you have read different views about the use of external rewards, what are your thoughts on the role that rewards might play in your classroom?

MOTIVATING UNDERACHIEVING AND DISAFFECTED STUDENTS

Finding ways to enhance students' motivation is particularly daunting when students are disaffected, apathetic, or resistant. As Brophy (2004) observes, such students find academic tasks relatively meaningless and resist engaging in them, even though they know they could be successful. Some may even be fearful that school learning "will make them into something that they do not want to become" (p. 205). This fear is apparent in some African Americans and other students of color who equate academic achievement with "acting White." A seminal paper published two decades ago (Fordham & Ogbu, 1986) describes how bright Black students may "put brakes on" their academic achievement by not studying or doing homework, cutting class, being late, and not participating in class. Not surprisingly, resistance to being perceived as "acting White" has been the subject of heated debate ever since, but a recent study (Fryer, 2006) provides empirical evidence to support this phenomenon.

Motivating resistant, underachieving, or apathetic students requires "resocialization" (Brophy, 2004, p. 307). This means using the strategies described in this chapter in more sustained, systematic, and personalized ways. Extrinsic rewards may be especially useful in this regard (Hidi & Harackiewicz, 2000). When extrinsic rewards trigger engagement in tasks that students initially view as boring or irrelevant, "there is at least a chance" that real interest will develop (p. 159). Resocialization also means combining high expectations for students with the encouragement and support needed to achieve those expectations—in short, showing students that you care about them as students and as people.

PRACTICAL TIPS FOR

USING REWARDS

- *Use verbal rewards to increase intrinsic motivation for academic tasks.* It seems clear that praise can have a positive impact on intrinsic motivation, especially if it is specific, sincere, and contingent on the behavior you are trying to strengthen. But remember that individual public praise may be embarrassing to older students and to those from cultures that value the collective over individual achievement.

- *Save tangible rewards for activities that students find unattractive.* When students already enjoy doing a task, there's no need to provide tangible rewards. Save tangible rewards for activities that students tend to find boring and aversive.

- *If you're using tangible rewards, provide them unexpectedly, after the task performance.* In this way, students are more likely to view the rewards as information about their performance and as an expression of the teacher's pleasure, rather than as an attempt to control their behavior.

- *Be extremely careful about using expected tangible rewards.* If you choose to use them, be sure to make them contingent on completion of a task or achievement of a specific level of performance. If you reward students simply for engaging in a task, regardless of their performance, they are likely to spend less time on the task once the reward is removed.

- *Make sure that you select rewards that students like.* You may think that animal stickers are really neat, but if your sixth-graders do not find them rewarding, their behavior will not be reinforced.

- *Keep your program of rewards simple.* An elaborate system of rewards is impossible to maintain in the complex world of the classroom. The fancier your system, the more likely that you will abandon it. Moreover, when rewards become too salient, they overshadow more intrinsic reasons for behaving in certain ways. Students become so preoccupied with collecting, counting, and comparing that they lose sight of why the behavior is necessary or valuable.

- *Think about ways to provide recognition without rewards.* Although rewards and recognition are often used interchangeably, in fact they are very different. Rewards are based on criteria set by teachers to control students' behavior and motivate learning. Recognition, on the other hand, involves noticing, validating, describing, or acknowledging. For example, instead of handing out stickers or points for "good work," you can provide time each day for students to reflect on, record, and share their accomplishments. (See Cameron, Tate, MacNaughton, & Politano, 1997, for ideas on how to provide recognition without rewards.)

Barbara remembers a student who "didn't want to do much of anything" but who was an avid skateboarder. She tells us what happened when she paired him up with a high school student who also loved to skateboard:

I called the high school student and asked him who his English teacher was, and she and I were able to coordinate. The tenth-grader worked with my student on a "How to Skateboard" book. I worked after school with them and helped them to put the book together. Three things made this a successful intervention. First, working with a tenth-grader was a real kick for my student. Second, they were able to use technology, and that in itself is a real motivator. Finally, he knew I had paid attention to him, that I cared enough about him to do this. He began to demonstrate more willingness to do other work.

As Barbara's anecdote illustrates, the perception that Barbara really cared was critical to the student's willingness to work hard, and studies consistently support this contention. As we mentioned in Chapter 1, a substantial body of research exists on students' perceptions of "good teachers" (Woolfolk Hoy & Weinstein, 2006). This research clearly demonstrates that students respond positively and care more about learning when teachers show how much *they* care for their students. For example, research demonstrates that when middle-school students perceive their teachers as caring and supportive, they are more likely to be academically moti- vated, to engage in classroom activities, and to behave in prosocial, responsible ways (Wentzel, 1997, 1998, 2006).

Perceiving that teachers care appears to be especially important for students who are alienated and marginalized and for those who are at risk of school failure. Ann Locke Davidson (1999), for example, interviewed 49 adolescents represent- ing diverse socioeconomic, cultural, and academic backgrounds. Data revealed not only students' appreciation and preference for teachers who communicated interest in their well-being, but also students' willingness to reciprocate by being attentive and conscientious. This was particularly evident in the responses of "stigmatized" students who faced "social borders"—differences between their aca- demic world (school) and their social world (home and community) in terms of values, beliefs, and expected ways of behaving.

Describing Wendy Ashton, a teacher who prodded students to achieve, one stu- dent commented, "She won't put you down, she'll talk to you and she'll go, 'Yeah, you know I love you. You know I want you to make something out of yourself, so stop messing around in class'" (p. 361). Davidson speculates that students who do not face social borders might be more accepting of teachers who are relatively distant and impersonal, because the students basically trust school as an institution. However, when students face the social divisions that can lead to alienation and mar- ginalization, it is essential for teachers to be attentive, supportive, and respectful.

As the comment about Wendy Ashton suggests, this kind of caring is less about being "warm and fuzzy" and more about being a "warm demander"—someone who provides a "tough-minded, no-nonsense, structured, and disciplined classroom environment for kids whom society has psychologically and physically abandoned" (Irvine & Fraser, 1998). Researchers identified a small group of teachers like this during a three-year study in two urban districts that served diverse student popula- tions (Corbett, Wilson, & Williams, 2005). Both districts were desperately trying to find ways to close the achievement gap that existed between lower- and higher- income students. The researchers interviewed parents, students, teachers, and administrators and visited the classrooms of a sample of teachers from each grade level in each school. Their observations and interviews enabled them to identify a set of teachers who *simply refused to let students fail.* One of the teachers was Mrs. Franklin, an African American sixth-grade teacher whose school served mostly students of color. Mrs. Franklin believed that too many teachers had given up on their students and didn't expect very much. As she put it, "Kids aren't the problem; adults are the ones finding the excuses." Mrs. Franklin didn't give her students an excuse not to do well. Her grading policy required any student work earning a grade lower than a C to be done over. Interestingly, interviews with students revealed that rather than resenting the strict grading policy, they appreciated it. As one student reported, "My teacher never let people settle for D or E; she don't let people get away with it. She gives us an education. Other teachers don't care what you do. They pass you to be passing. Here, I pass my own self " (p. 10).

CONCLUDING COMMENTS

A while back, a professor of educational psychology told us that learning about classroom management would be unnecessary if prospective teachers understood how to enhance students' motivation. Although we thought his argument was naive and unrealistic, we understood—and agreed with—its underlying premise, *that students who are interested and involved in the academic work at hand are less likely to daydream, disrupt, and defy.* In other words, management and motivation are inextricably linked.

As you contemplate ways to increase your students' expectations for success and the value they place on academic tasks, remember that motivating students doesn't happen accidentally. You need to make the topic of motivation an integral part of every lesson plan. Fortunately, the motivational strategies discussed in this chapter are consistent with current thinking about good instruction, which emphasizes students' active participation, collaborative group work, and the use of varying assessments (Brophy, 2004).

Finally, remember the suggestions in Chapter 3 for creating a safer, more caring classroom. As we have stressed, students are more motivated when they perceive that teachers care about them. In Brophy's (2004) words, "You can become your own most powerful motivational tool by establishing productive relationships with each of your students" (p. 380).

SUMMARY

Although teachers are responsible for enhancing motivation, this chapter began by questioning the belief that "good teachers should make learning fun." We argued that such a goal is unrealistic and inappropriate given the constraints of schooling—compulsory attendance, required curricula, class sizes that inhibit individualization, and the specter of high-stakes standardized testing. A more appropriate, realistic goal is to stimulate students' *motivation to learn,* whereby students pursue academic activities because they find them meaningful and worthwhile.

An Expectancy × Value Framework
- Motivation depends on (1) students' expectation of success and (2) the value they place on the task (or on the rewards that it may bring).
- If either factor is missing, there will be no motivation.

Strategies for Increasing Expectations of Success

- Provide opportunities for success.
- Teach students to set reasonable goals and assess their own performance.
- Help students recognize the relationship between effort and outcome.
- Provide informative feedback.
- Provide special motivational support to discouraged students.

Enhancing the Value of the Task

- Relate lessons to students' own lives.
- Provide opportunities for choice.
- Model interest in learning and express enthusiasm for the material.
- Include novelty/variety elements.
- Provide opportunities for students to respond actively.
- Allow students to create finished products.
- Provide opportunities for students to interact with peers.
- Provide extrinsic rewards:

   Keep in mind the different types of rewards: social rewards, special activities, and tangible rewards.

   Be aware that rewarding people for doing something they already like to do may decrease their interest in continuing that behavior.

   Think carefully about when and how to use rewards.

Motivating Underachieving and Disaffected Students

- Be sensitive to the possibility that students of color may fear accusations of "acting White" if they strive to achieve academically.
- Recognize that resistant, apathetic students need to know you care about them. Research on students' perceptions of "good teachers" demonstrates that they want teachers who make sure they do their work, maintain order, are willing to help, explain assignments clearly, vary instruction, and take the time to get to know them as people.
- Demonstrate care by using the strategies described in this chapter in more sustained and systematic ways.

By working to ensure that students are engaged in learning activities, you can avoid many of the managerial problems that arise when students are bored and frustrated. Management and motivation are closely intertwined.

ACTIVITIES FOR SKILL BUILDING AND REFLECTION

In Class

In the following two vignettes, the teachers have directed the activity. In a small group, discuss ways they could have involved students in the planning, directing, creating, or evaluating.

1. Mrs. Peters felt that the unit her fourth-grade class completed on folk tales would lend itself to a class play. She chose Paul Bunyan and Pecos Bill as the stories to dramatize. The students were excited as Mrs. Peters gave out parts and assigned students to paint

scenery. Mrs. Peters wrote a script and sent it home for the students to memorize. She asked parents to help make the costumes. After three weeks of practice, the play was performed for the lower-grade classes and the parents.

2. Mr. Wilkins wanted his sixth-grade class to develop an understanding about ancient civilizations. He assigned a five-part project. Students had to research four civilizations (Egyptian, Mesopotamian, Indus Valley, and Shang); write a biography of Howard Carter, a famous archaeologist; describe three pyramids (the step pyramid, the Great Pyramid, and the Pyramid of Sesostris II); outline the reigns of five kings (Hammurabi, Thutmose III, Ramses II, David, and Nebuchadnezzar); and make a model of a pyramid. He gave the class four weeks to complete the projects and then collected them, graded them, and displayed them in the school library.

On Your Own

Interview an experienced, effective teacher about the motivational strategies that he or she finds particularly effective with disaffected, resistant students.

For Your Portfolio

1. Design an assignment that will enable students of varying achievement levels to experience success. For example, the task might vary in complexity or in the amount of scaffolding you provide; it might be open ended, allowing a variety of acceptable responses; it might require the use of different reference materials; or it might allow students to choose the format in which they demonstrate their understanding (e.g., a report, poster, or role play). Refer to the example from Tomlinson (1999) presented earlier in the chapter.

2. Select a topic in a content area of your choice, and design a lesson or activity that incorporates at least one of the strategies for enhancing perceived value. For example, you might relate the material to students' lives, provide opportunities for choice, allow students to work with peers, or produce a final product.

FOR FURTHER READING

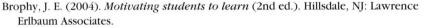

Brophy, J. E. (2004). *Motivating students to learn* (2nd ed.). Hillsdale, NJ: Lawrence Erlbaum Associates.

>   This excellent book is written explicitly for teachers and offers principles and strategies to use in motivating students to learn. It is not a "bag of tricks" but the product of the author's comprehensive, systematic review of the motivational literature.

Cameron, C., Tate, B., MacNaughton, D., & Politano, C. (1997). *Recognition without rewards: Building connections.* Winnipeg, Manitoba: Peguis Publishers.

>   This guidebook for teachers is based on the premise that reward systems interfere with learning. In lieu of rewards intended to manage behavior and motivate learning, the authors suggest that teachers provide recognition—noticing, validating, describing, or acknowledging learning that is already taking place. The book contains practical strategies, examples, and reproducible masters.

Denton, P. (2005). *Learning through Academic Choice.* Turners Falls, MA: Northeast Foundation for Children.

This book guides teachers step by step through the process of introducing Academic Choice, as a means of increasing students' motivation and academic skills and building community in the classroom. This practical and comprehensive book includes ways to build a strong foundation for Academic Choice in the classroom, the details of planning an Academic Choice lesson, and a wide range of specific lesson plans and activity lessons for grades K–6.

Dolezal, S. E., Welsh, L. M., Pressley, M., & Vincent, M. M. (2003). How nine third-grade teachers motivate student academic engagement. *The Elementary School Journal, 103*(3), 239-267.

This article reports on a study of nine third-grade classrooms in eight Catholic schools. Student academic engagement varied dramatically among the classes. In high-engagement classes, teachers used a wide array of positive motivational strategies, whereas in low-engagement classes, teachers used approaches that appeared to undermine student motivation. An appendix at the end of the article provides a comprehensive description of strategies that enhance student engagement and of those that diminish it.

Kohn, A. (1993). *Punished by rewards: The trouble with gold stars, incentive plans, A's, praise, and other bribes.* Boston: Houghton Mifflin.

Kohn argues that our basic strategy for motivating students ("Do this and you'll get that") works only in the short run and actually does lasting harm. Instead of rewards, Kohn suggests that teachers provide the "three C's"—collaboration, content (things worth knowing), and choice. The result, he maintains, will be "good kids without goodies."

Reeve, J. (2006). Extrinsic rewards and inner motivation. In C. M. Evertson & C. S. Weinstein (Eds.), *Handbook of classroom management.* Mahwah, NJ: Lawrence Erlbaum Associates.

As Reeve notes, "Extrinsic rewards are ubiquitous in educational settings." For this reason, it's important for teachers to understand how rewards can be presented to students in ways that support, rather than interfere with, students' inner motivational resources. This chapter discusses the different types of extrinsic rewards, whether they work, what their side effects are, and how rewards can be used to support autonomy.

CHAPTER 9

MANAGING INDEPENDENT WORK

Independent work is a common instructional activity in elementary school. (Some would say it's *too* common, a position we'll discuss shortly.) In this situation, the majority of children work independently on tasks while the teacher meets with individuals or small groups. We devote an entire chapter to this instructional situation because independent work can be particularly difficult for beginning teachers to manage; even for experienced teachers, independent work poses a challenging set of pitfalls that must be well understood if they are to be avoided.

To be honest, this chapter almost didn't get written. Independent work is also referred to as *seatwork,* and this term has very negative connotations, particularly among educators who promote students' active participation and collaboration. Indeed, when we asked Courtney, Viviana, Garnetta, Barbara, and Ken to talk about their views on independent work, we found heated differences of opinion. On one hand, Ken told us he uses seatwork every day: "I teach both mathematics and reading in small groups. I can't see any other way to do it, especially given the heterogeneity of my class. That means the rest of the class *has* to work on their own. If you want to individualize instruction, seatwork is inevitable." Ken thought a chapter on the topic would be "invaluable, even fascinating, for new teachers."

On the other hand, Barbara—normally so soft-spoken and gentle—was vehemently negative: "I *hate* seatwork," she told us, "and I make a point to avoid it

252

While Ken meets with a small group, the rest of the class works independently.

whenever possible. I don't know why you'd ever want to have a chapter like this in the book." Similarly, Garnetta and Viviana claimed they never used seatwork, so they couldn't really contribute to the chapter. As Garnetta asserted, "If you write a chapter like this, it won't be about us." Finally, Courtney told us, "I don't think it's developmentally appropriate in kindergarten to have kids sit and do seatwork for extended periods of time." To these four teachers, seatwork clearly meant "filling in the blanks." The term itself conjured up images of bored, passive children, sitting alone at their desks, doing repetitive, tedious worksheets.

We debated, we moralized, and we shared anecdotes about the awfulness or the usefulness of seatwork. Eventually, we came to realize that there was no fundamental difference of opinion among us. We all agreed that teachers sometimes need to assign independent work so they can meet with an individual or a small group (although the five teachers differ considerably in the amount of time they do this). We agreed that seatwork is too often busywork, that it frequently goes on for too long, and that too many teachers use it as a substitute for active teaching. And we agreed that teachers need to provide independent work that fosters meaningful learning.

This chapter examines the ways in which Ken, Barbara, Courtney, Garnetta, and Viviana work to make independent assignments worthwhile and engaging. We also discuss the unique challenges that seatwork poses—for both teachers and students—and provide suggestions for meeting these challenges. To set the stage for this discussion, we begin by

✑ PAUSE AND REFLECT

The term *seatwork* has negative connotations, and the question of whether to assign seatwork often provokes debate. What has your experience as a student been with seatwork, and what types of seatwork have you observed in classrooms? Someone once told us that seatwork is a necessary evil. What do you think?

considering three questions: (1) What does research say about the amount of time students spend doing seatwork? (2) What do they generally do during this time? and (3) What are the purposes of seatwork? Throughout this discussion the terms *independent work* and *seatwork* are used interchangeably.

SEATWORK: HOW MUCH, WHAT, AND WHY?

The amount of time that elementary students spend doing seatwork has long been a cause of concern among educators. For example, a cross-cultural study (Stigler, Lee, & Stevenson, 1987) found that first- and fifth-grade children in the United States typically spent 51 percent of their mathematics time working alone, compared with 9 percent in Taiwan and 26 percent in Japan. Furthermore, American children spent only 46 percent of their class time in activities led by the teacher; in Taiwan and Japan, the comparable figures were 90 percent and 74 percent. With some dismay, the investigators concluded that classes in the United States "were organized so that American children were frequently left to work alone at their seats on material in mathematics that they apparently did not understand well" (p. 70). Similar dismay has been voiced by researchers examining the reading instruction provided to students with learning disabilities and emotional disturbance or behavioral disorders (Vaughn, Levy, Coleman, & Bos, 2002). Synthesizing results across 16 studies conducted between 1975 and 2000, the researchers determined that

> independent seatwork dominated reading instruction. To the extent that this work is closely linked with practice to reinforce previously learned skills, it could be valuable. However, the findings from this study reveal that students with disabilities spend 40% or more of their instructional time during reading doing independent seatwork . . . . Students cannot possibily benefit from this extensive amount of time spent on independent seatwork. (p. 11)

Figures like these prompted Linda Anderson (1985) to ask, "What are students doing when they do all that seatwork?" The answer is that in many classrooms, seatwork time is spent completing workbook pages and worksheets. Indeed, it has been estimated that in the course of a school year, an elementary child might complete a thousand workbook pages and skill sheets in reading alone (Anderson, Hiebert, Scott, & Wilkinson, 1985)! The vast majority of worksheets focus on discrete skills that students are to practice and foster learning only at low cognitive levels. A typical first-grade reading worksheet, for example, might ask a child to circle all the pictures that begin with a particular consonant. In mathematics, a first-grade worksheet might have students do basic addition problems printed inside balloons and then color the balloons according to a key (e.g., color the balloon red if the sum is 6; color the balloon blue if the sum is 8). Figure 9.1 compares the time spent in three kinds of seatwork tasks in Germany, Japan, and the United States. As you can see, students in the United States spend nearly all their seatwork time practicing procedures. Clearly, if we want our students to become independent thinkers and problem solvers, we need to rethink the types of work we assign.

Why do American children engage in so much seatwork? What purpose does it serve? The answer to these questions depends on whether we look at seatwork

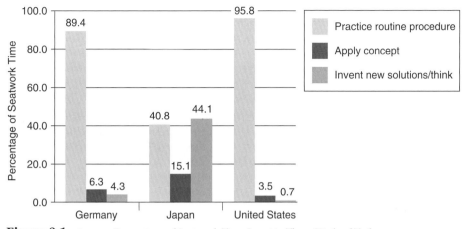

Figure 9.1   Average Percentage of Seatwork Time Spent in Three Kinds of Tasks
Source: U.S. Department of Education, National Center for Education Statistics, Third
International Mathematics and Science Study, Videotape Classroom Study, 1994–95.

from an instructional or a managerial perspective (Anderson, 1985; Anderson,
Brubaker, Alleman-Brooks, & Duffy, 1985). From an *instructional perspective,* the
purpose of seatwork is to give students an opportunity to practice skills, synthesize and apply new knowledge, and develop independent work habits (such as
learning to pace themselves and to check their work). Seatwork can also serve as
a diagnostic tool for the teacher, providing a check on students' understanding
(Chilcoat, 1990). From a *managerial perspective,* the purpose of seatwork is to
keep students involved for a predictable period of time in quiet tasks that do not
require close teacher supervision. As Ken pointed out, this way of organizing the
class enables teachers to work with individuals and small groups and—theoretically
at least—to tailor instruction to students' diverse needs. In other words, seatwork
helps teachers deal with the heterogeneity of their classrooms.

THE PITFALLS OF INDEPENDENT WORK

The Challenges for Teachers

Independent work poses unique managerial and instructional problems for
the teacher. (These are summarized in
Table 9.1.) *The first challenge is to coordinate the instructional and managerial purposes of seatwork—namely, to
select or create tasks that promote students' academic achievement yet can be
done independently.* This is easier said
than done. If tasks are simple enough
for students to complete on their own

> **PAUSE AND REFLECT**
>
> Kindergarten and first-grade teachers sometimes find it
> difficult to carve out time for small groups, especially early
> in the year, because students are not very independent, can't
> read, and need constant teacher support. We also know that
> worksheets sometimes take center stage in first grade as a
> way to keep students busy while the teacher meets with
> small groups. What types of engaging, meaningful work
> could these young students do that would enable the teacher
> to turn his or her attention to a small group?

TABLE 9.1 The Challenges of Seatwork

For the Teacher	For the Student
1. Selecting or creating seatwork that promotes academic achievement, yet can be done independently	1. Completing assigned work on their own
2. Matching seatwork to students' varying levels of achievement	2. Understanding how and when to obtain the teacher's help
3. Keeping track of what the rest of the class is doing	3. Understanding the norms for assisting peers
4. Keeping students on task	4. Learning how to be effective in obtaining help from peers
5. Dealing with the varying paces at which students work ("ragged" endings)	
6. Collecting, correcting, recording, and returning seatwork assignments	

(fulfilling the managerial purpose), they may present minimal cognitive demands. And if tasks are more academically demanding (achieving the instructional purpose), students may need considerable support from teachers.

Unfortunately, research suggests that too many of the worksheets assigned to students satisfy the managerial function of seatwork at the expense of the instructional function (Anderson, 1994). An analysis of reading workbooks, conducted by the National Academy of Education's Commission on Reading, concluded that many workbook exercises drill students on skills that have little value in learning to read. Consider the following task, cited in the commission's report *Becoming a Nation of Readers* (Anderson, Hiebert, Scott, & Wilkinson, 1985):

> Read each sentence. Decide which consonant letter is used the most. Underline it each time.
>
> 1. My most important toy is a toy train.
> 2. Nancy, who lives in the next house, has nine cats.
> 3. Will you bring your box of marbles to the party?

As the report's authors point out, if children can already read the sentences, it is unlikely that their reading ability will be improved by asking them to underline consonants. On the other hand, if they *cannot* read the sentences, it is difficult to see how underlining consonants will help.

A second challenge for teachers is to ensure that seatwork is matched to students' varying levels of achievement. Researchers observed two high achievers and two low achievers in six first-grade classrooms (Anderson, Brubaker, Alleman-Brooks & Duffy, 1985). They also talked with students about what they were doing and why. They found that children were often unable to successfully complete the tasks they were given:

> Randy could not read all of the words used in the standard board assignment, which involved copying sentences with blanks and selecting a word from a list

of options. Every time observers noted him doing this type of assignment, he became "stuck" (his word) because he could not decode the key words to make the choice and proceed.

On a ditto with nine pictures of seasonal activities, Sean was to cut out and paste on the name of the season that matched the picture. After he quickly completed the assignment, the observer questioned him about it. He had matched only two out of eight correctly, he could not read any of the seasons' names, and he was not sure in what season one sledded, flew a kite, went camping in a tent, or went swimming outdoors. (Anderson, Brubaker, Alleman-Brooks, & Duffy, 1985, p. 130)

Third, teachers need to keep track of what the rest of the class is doing when working with an individual or a small group. Careful monitoring requires the ability to *overlap* (Kounin, 1970)—to deal with simultaneous situations without becoming so immersed in one that you ignore the other. Overlapping can be a challenge for even the most experienced teachers. Ken honestly admits that's he's been concerned about this for years:

> **I've had people observe my classes to determine whether students doing seatwork are really working. They generally say that the kids are on task and that the talk I hear centers on work. But if you're working with a small group on the other side of the room, and kids are encouraged to help each other, how can you ever really be certain?**

A fourth challenge is keeping students engaged so that they do not lose interest and become uninvolved, especially if the seatwork period is long. Seatwork requires students to pace themselves through assignments. Because there are no external signals (such as teachers' questions) to push students along (Gump, 1982), children may begin to doodle, pass notes, comb their hair, and sharpen pencils—until the teacher reminds students to get back to work. In fact, research has shown that engagement in seatwork often follows a predictable cycle (deVoss, 1979): Students begin their assignments; attention wanes; the noise level increases; the teacher intervenes; the children return to the assignment. This cycle can repeat several times, until a final spurt when students rush to complete their tasks before seatwork time is over.

A fifth challenge that teachers face is to accommodate the varying pace at which students work. They may *begin* seatwork at the same time, but they never *finish* at the same time. Viviana observes that "it's common for some students to be on the second problem, while others are on number 10." Garnetta tells us that "Maria finishes everything in a minute—and if she doesn't have anything to do she'll create havoc." Ken contrasts Dana and Jessica:

> **Dana races to get everything done, and then she lords it over the others who are still working. Jessica is always ready to cry because she's the slowest; even if you gave her 10 times as much time as everybody else, she still wouldn't finish.**

Finally, *a sixth challenge is to collect, correct, record, and return all the paperwork assigned as seatwork—or to use activities that rely less on workbooks and skill sheets.* We once observed second-graders complete eight language arts work-sheets during an hour-and-a-half of seatwork time. Since there were 27 students in this class, a quick calculation told us that this teacher would have *216* worksheets to grade that evening—in this one content area alone! That much paperwork can be unbearably tedious for both teachers and students, and we had to wonder about the educational value of all those worksheets. Ken also thinks about the issue of paperwork from an *environmental* point of view: "It's easy to use reams of paper, and if the work isn't really necessary—if it's really just busywork and you end up throwing a lot of it out—then you feel terribly guilty."

The Challenges for Students

We sometimes get so caught up in the problems that seatwork poses for *teachers* that we overlook the problems for *students.* In this section of the chapter, we consider four of the special challenges that students must confront when doing independent seatwork. (Refer again to Table 9.1.)

First, because the teacher is often unavailable, students have to complete assigned work on their own. This statement may seem obvious, but it has sev-eral not-so-obvious implications. In order to complete assignments, students must maintain an internal push even if tasks are boring and personally irrelevant. They must remain free from distraction amid the crowded social environment of the classroom. They must decipher directions that are sometimes unclear. They must monitor their comprehension and recognize when they understand and when they do not.

Research reveals that children often develop elaborate strategies that enable them to finish their work even when they don't understand it. For example, they may mark answers by matching the length of the word to the length of the blank, use pictures as cues for the correct answers, or simply ask others for answers.

> Beth, unable to read enough of the *Weekly Reader* articles necessary to answer the questions, simply copied the questions and wrote answers that seemed logi-cal to her, without consulting the articles. In the one instance when she did look, she searched for a number word to answer "How many legs does a grasshopper have?" She came to the phrase "five eyes" in the article and copied the number five. (Anderson, Brubaker, Alleman-Brooks, & Duffy, 1985, pp. 131–132)

Students like Beth define success in terms of putting down an answer and finishing the assignment, even if the work makes no sense to them. As Richard, one of the target students, gleefully commented, "I don't know what it means, but I did it" (Anderson, Brubaker, Alleman-Brooks, & Duffy, 1985, p. 132).

A second challenge that independent work poses for children is understand-ing how and when to obtain the teacher's help. Because the teacher is generally interacting with an individual or with a small group, gaining the teacher's attention is a lot like trying to get the attention of a store clerk who is busy with another customer (Cazden, 1988). Students must learn the appropriate ways to obtain assistance: Do they simply raise their hands and hope the teacher notices? May they call the teacher's name? Are they allowed to get out of their seats and walk over to the teacher? Must they wait until the teacher is finished with a particular group before asking their question? Unless procedures for obtaining the teacher's help are explicit, students who encounter problems with their work may become frustrated, unengaged, and disruptive.

In addition to learning the appropriate ways to obtain the teacher's help, *students must meet a third challenge—understanding and accepting the norms for assisting peers.* In some classes, teachers encourage students to work collaboratively, whereas in other classes, giving or receiving help is tantamount to cheating. This latter situation can present a real dilemma for students. On one hand is their need to follow the teacher's directions—and to stay out of trouble. On the other hand is their need to complete the assignment successfully and to assist friends who are having difficulty (Bloome & Theodorou, 1988). (Figure 9.2 shows that students sometimes develop elaborate strategies to avoid giving peer assistance.)

Students' understanding and acceptance of the norms for helping peers can also be influenced by culture. Providing assistance may be especially valued by children with cultural roots in collectivist societies (e.g., African, Asian, Hispanic, and Native American). In collectivist cultures, people assume responsibility for one another's welfare, and the focus is on working toward the common good (Cartledge with Milburn, 1996). Thus children from these cultures may resist teachers' directives to work independently. In contrast, children from individualistic cultures (e.g., English-speaking countries) may value individual effort and self-sufficiency; they may resist teachers' efforts to encourage peer assistance.

Finally, *a fourth challenge for students is learning how to be effective in obtaining help from peers.* It is important to recognize that even in situations where helping peers is permitted or encouraged, not all students are able to gain assistance. For example, students who are low in social status may be ignored or even rejected when they seek help. A study conducted by Elizabeth Cohen (1984) illustrates this phenomenon. Cohen observed children in grades 2 through 4 working at learning centers. Students were told that they had the right to ask for help and that they also had the duty to assist anyone who asked for help. Cohen

Figure 9.2 *Source:* CALVIN AND HOBBES © 1993, Watterson. Distributed by UNIVERSAL UCLICK. Reprinted with permission. All rights reserved.

found that children's social status was positively related to the amount of peer interaction. Moreover, the more children talked and worked together, the more they learned from the curriculum. She concludes, "Those children with high social status have more access to peer interaction that, in turn, assists their learning. In other words, the rich get richer" (p. 184).

Children's ability to obtain peer assistance also depends on their ability to be "effective speakers." Research by Louise Wilkinson and her colleagues (Wilkinson & Calculator, 1982) indicates that students are more likely to get appropriate responses from their peers when their requests are *direct, made to a specific, designated listener, and perceived as sincere* (i.e., the listener believes that the speaker really wants the information and does not already know the answer). Furthermore, effective speakers are flexible and persistent: If initially unsuccessful in obtaining help, they can *revise* and *repeat* their request. Even first-grade students can be specific and persistent, as in the following example:

AMY: OK, what, what's that word?

JOE: Don't ask me.

AMY: I'll ask him. What's that word (to Dave)?

JOE: Dave, do you know what we should write, like here?

AMY: Right here. (Several seconds elapse.)

I want you to look at my paper. (Several seconds elapse.)

Listen to this.

I've got these words.

I keep gettin mixed up, Dave.

Dave, I keep gettin . . .

The words requested by Amy are provided by Dave. (Wilkinson & Calculator, 1982, p. 87)

DESIGNING AND IMPLEMENTING EFFECTIVE INDEPENDENT WORK

The research on seatwork sheds light on the special challenges or pitfalls associated with independent work. How can you avoid—or at least minimize—these pitfalls? In this section of the chapter, we propose seven guidelines derived from both the research on seatwork and the collected wisdom of our five teachers. These are presented in the accompanying Practical Tips box.

Assign Work That Is Clear and Meaningful

During one visit to Barbara's classroom we saw her assign some dictionary skill sheets to her students. Later, when we discussed the assignment, Barbara told us what she had thought about when she selected and screened the pages:

 I wanted to provide students with work they could do without me, so I could work with individuals who needed help on the ads for their inventions [a special language arts/science project they were working on].

PRACTICAL TIPS FOR

USING INDEPENDENT WORK EFFECTIVELY

- Assign work that is clear and meaningful. Ask yourself:
  - *What is the purpose of the task?*
  - *Is the task related to current instruction? Are students likely to see the connection?*
  - *Are students likely to see the task as something worth doing or something boring and unrewarding?*
  - *Are the directions unambiguous and easy to follow?*
  - *Does the task provide students with an opportunity to practice important skills or to apply what they are learning?*
  - *Does the task provide students with the opportunity to think critically or to engage in problem solving?*
  - *Does the task require reading and writing, or does it simply ask students to fill in the blank, underline, or circle?*
  - *Does the task require higher-level responses or does it emphasize low-level, factual recall and "drill and kill" practice of isolated subskills?*
  - *Is there a reason the task should be done in school (e.g., the need for coaching by the teacher) rather than at home?*
  - *Will students be able to accomplish the task without assistance? If not, how will assistance be provided?*
- Match the work to varying achievement levels.
- Make sure that oral directions are clear.
- Monitor behavior and comprehension.
- Teach children what to do if they get stuck.
- Plan for ragged endings.
- Find alternatives to workbook pages (e.g., authentic reading and writing, listening activities, working on ongoing projects, learning center tasks).

First, I looked at whether the skills on these pages meshed with the objectives of the fourth-grade curriculum. Then I made sure that the material had been previously presented by the librarian or by me, so that the pages would be practice and reinforcement—not instruction. We've worked on dictionary skills before—at the library, in spelling—so there was nothing new in these workbook pages. Then I checked the format to make sure it was familiar and understandable, and I checked that the directions were clear. If the pages had been confusing, that would have defeated the whole purpose.

Courtney also makes sure that her students work with materials and activities that are familiar and understandable. While she meets with some students in a guided-reading group, the other children can choose from a number of "file folder games"—simple, homemade activities that review various literacy skills. For example, students might have to match upper- and lowercase letters, pictures with the same beginning sounds, or pictures of rhyming words. But all these have been previously introduced to the whole group:

> **In the beginning of the year, I don't do guided reading, so that gives me a chance to introduce all the independent activities. Since the kids can't read directions, all the activities need to be explained and modeled and practiced ahead of time. For example, we might practice matching rhyming pictures. Later, I can create new games with different pictures for rhyming, but they know just what to do because the process will be the same. I tell them, "I'm going to give you another game to play today, but it's just like the other ones you've done."**

As Barbara's and Courtney's comments illustrate, they are careful to plan and evaluate the tasks they give students to complete during class. The Practical Tips box lists some of the questions that the teachers ask themselves before they assign independent work.

Match the Work to Varying Achievement Levels

When your classroom includes children who vary in ability and achievement level, it's necessary to differentiate independent work assignments. Carol Tomlinson (1999) advises teachers to think in terms of differentiating *content* (what students will learn and the materials that represent that learning), *process* (the activities that students will do), *product* (how students will demonstrate what they understand and can do), and/or *learning environment* (the conditions that set the tone and expectations of learning). For example, in order to teach classification, you might take your first-graders on a nature walk to gather objects that they will all classify as living or nonliving. Then they will classify by other attributes, such as shape, size, color, and type of object. Some children will classify the actual objects, whereas others—those who are early readers—will have both objects and cards with the objects' names. Some of the early readers will have one or two cards; others will have many. Because students are using different materials, this is an example of *differentiating by content*. (See Tomlinson, 1999, for additional examples.)

Sometimes, the only differentiation that is needed is to break large assignments into a series of smaller ones, particularly for children who have difficulty sustaining attention. Consider the case of Jay, a 10-year-old boy with mild mental retardation who had difficulty completing his math assignments (Wallace, Cox, & Skinner, 2003). Jay often worked slowly and sporadically, was frequently off task, and typically completed only 6 out of the 30 math problems on his worksheet. In an attempt to increase the number of problems Jay completed, his teacher cut his worksheet into six smaller sheets, each containing only five problems. When Jay finished one sheet, he received praise from the teacher and was given the next sheet to complete. Jay's completion rate improved substantially, and he actually appeared to enjoy doing the math problems. In fact, the researchers report that one day, when the teacher told Jay he could choose a free-time activity after completing his 30 problems, Jay asked for more math sheets instead!

Make Sure Oral Directions Are Clear

Once assignments have been selected or created, it is important to explain them clearly before sending children off to work. Unfortunately, research indicates that this does not always occur (Davidson, 2007; Emmer, Evertson, & Anderson, 1980). Less effective managers tend to state instructions vaguely and fail to check whether children understand the tasks. Not surprisingly, this results in off-task behavior, considerable talk as children tried to figure out what to do, and frequent interruptions of the teacher.

Furthermore, Linda Anderson's (1985) research on seatwork revealed that even when teachers provided introductory explanations, they rarely focused on the purpose of the seatwork or the strategies to be used. Instead, they emphasized procedural directions. Anderson recommends that teachers explain *why students are doing what they're doing, describe the strategies to be used, and do a few examples.* Indeed, studies of effective instruction (Rosenshine, 1980) demonstrate that students make fewer errors on seatwork when teachers provide "guided practice" before allowing students to work independently. As Viviana comments, "If I can catch students making a mistake on the first problem, I can prevent them from making that mistake all the way through the assignment!" Modeling and "thinking aloud" also increase the likelihood that students will be able to do their work successfully.

During one visit to Garnetta's classroom, we watched her introduce a letter-writing activity that was to be done as independent work while Garnetta met with individuals who needed additional support. She began by reminding students about a visitor who had come the previous week:

GARNETTA: Last week, we had a visitor, Miss Kinsey, who came and brought us all ice cream. I think we should thank her in some way. . . . We could send her thank-you notes, and we could send her pictures of us eating the ice cream. [The students agree and enthusiastically recall the ice cream (vanilla with chocolate-covered almonds). Then, Garnetta reviews the format for writing letters.]

GARNETTA: OK, what's the first thing that goes on our letter?

STUDENT: The heading.

GARNETTA: What goes in the heading? Edwin?

EDWIN: Dear . . .

GARNETTA: No, that's in the greeting. [Pauses. No one volunteers.] I'll give you a hint. [She writes the number 35 on the board.]

STUDENT: The address!

GARNETTA: Good. [She writes the school's address on the board.] What's next? Something really important comes next.

STUDENT: The date!

GARNETTA: Yes. [She writes the date.] OK, we've got the heading now. What comes next?

STUDENT: The greeting.

In this manner, Garnetta continued to review the format for letters. She left the model format on the chalkboard so that students could refer to it as they wrote their letters. She then instructed students that their letters had to contain at least five sentences (*not* five lines) and explained that the letter was to be written *independently*. She explained what to do if they were not sure how to spell a word. She answered students' questions and told them that after they had finished their first draft, they should have another student check it. Then they were to write the final letter and draw the picture they would send. She showed them the paper to use for their final copies and put out paper and markers for their pictures.

There is an interesting postscript to this episode. About 10 minutes into the letter writing, a student went over to Garnetta to show her his letter. She quickly scanned the page. Then she threw her hands up, gave a rueful laugh, and held a quiet but intense conference with him. He got a clean sheet of paper and returned to his desk to start again. We were curious. The directions had been so clear. What could have possibly gone wrong? During a free moment, Garnetta came over and told us what had happened. Instead of a thank-you note to Ms. Kinsey, the boy had written a letter to a substitute who had been there the week before, apologizing for his poor behavior! We learned a good lesson: Even clear and thorough directions don't ensure that everyone will carry out the assignment as you intended!

Monitor Behavior and Comprehension

When children have to work on their own, without close teacher supervision and interaction, it's not uncommon for them to become distracted and lose the momentum needed to complete their assignments. For this reason, it is particularly important for you to monitor students' behavior.

In the following examples, we see the way Courtney is able to *overlap* (Kounin, 1970)—to monitor the behavior of students doing independent work, while continuing to work with an individual or a small group. Just as if she had "eyes in the back of her head," Courtney manages to deal with simultaneous situations:

 Courtney is at the art table helping two children each count out six Pepperidge Farm goldfish crackers to take home in a small plastic bag (to go along with a book they have been reading on the first 12 days of kindergarten). The rest of the children are working with Pattern Blocks, creating designs from brightly colored hexagons, trapezoids, squares, and triangles. She scans the room and notices two children who appear to be arguing over the blocks. When the children at the art table finish their counting task, she tells them to go to their cubbies, put their baggies away, then go back to their seats, and send two more people to the art table. During the exchange, Courtney moves over to the two disputants, kneels down, quietly intervenes, and returns to the art table to meet with the next two children.

In addition to monitoring behavior, it's essential to monitor students' *understanding of their assignments*. Recall the distinction between *engaged time* and *productive time* discussed in Chapter 7. Clearly, it's not enough for students to remain busy and on task. They must also understand what they are supposed to do and carry out their tasks successfully.

Monitoring comprehension can be particularly difficult when you're also involved with a small group of students. One hint is to spend the first five minutes of independent work time circulating throughout the room. Once you've checked that students understand what to do, you can convene your first small group. It's also a good idea to circulate in the time between small-group sessions, checking on students' progress and helping with problems.

 Standing at the front of the room, Barbara gives instructions for a writing assignment and announces that she will be working with individuals at her desk. Slowly, she makes her way to her desk, stopping at various students' desks to see that they have begun to work. At Larry's desk, she crouches down: "You need to begin writing. Put these things away [the remnants from an earlier snack and a game he brought from home]. Now, what memory are you going to write about? [She discusses various ideas for the writing assignment.] Yes, those would be good memories to write about. OK, you've got a bunch of ideas. Now get started." She circulates some more and then sits down at her desk and begins to confer with two students who need help on a project. When she finishes with them, she walks over to a student who had been whispering. Barbara instructs her to turn her desk around so she is not facing other students. She checks the girl's work and quietly discusses her progress on the assignment. She does another loop through the room, glancing at students' papers, answering questions, and providing assistance. Then she returns to her desk, where another child is waiting to discuss her work.

Watching Barbara monitor seatwork, we were struck by the very quiet, discreet way she interacted with each child. This kind of discretion appears to be important for students' achievement. Researchers have found that contact with individual students during seatwork was positively related to achievement only when it was private and discreet (Helmke & Schrader, 1988). They speculate on two reasons for this finding. First, audible comments may disturb everyone's concentration and progress; second, loud, public comments may be embarrassing and may have a negative effect on students' motivation or willingness to ask questions.

Fredric Jones and colleagues (2007) offer additional advice for giving help to individual students during seatwork: "Praise, prompt, and leave" (p. 18). According to Jones, teachers should give help in 20 seconds or less for each student. Instead of questioning students ("What did we say was the first thing to do?") and providing individual tutoring, teachers should praise something the student has done correctly ("Good job up to here"), give a straightforward prompt ("Follow the model on the chalkboard"), and leave. In this way, teachers can circulate quickly and efficiently and minimize the time that students spend waiting for assistance.

Teach Children What to Do If They Get Stuck

When children encounter problems with seatwork assignments, they need to know what to do. In particular, students need to understand how and when they can obtain your help. Effective managers often establish the rule that they cannot be interrupted during their time with small groups; however, they make it clear that they will be available for help in between group meetings. They tell students to skip tasks that are causing problems and to work on something else in the meantime.

Some teachers devise special systems that students can use to indicate their need for assistance. They may give children a "help" sign or a small red flag to keep on top of their desks. A child who needs help turns the help sign up or raises the red flag. In some classrooms, students sign up for help on the chalkboard or on a clipboard.

Systems like these enable you to scan the room periodically to determine who needs assistance and to provide help at an appropriate time. This practice is far preferable to allowing children to come up to your desk or small-group meeting area whenever they need help. We've seen classrooms where long lines of children were allowed to form by the teacher's desk. Not only is this distracting to other students, it's also a waste of time for the children waiting in line.

In addition to teaching children the procedures for obtaining the teacher's help, you need to make it clear whether students may ask peers for assistance. Most of the time, our five teachers not only *allow* peer assistance but explicitly *direct* students to help one another. This ensures our teachers uninterrupted time to conduct small-group instruction or work with individual students. Garnetta tells us:

I believe that students learn from other students. Sometimes students understand the concept better when other students are teaching it. I try to have students work together as much as possible in order to avoid having students sitting there not knowing what to do or interrupting my work with small groups.

In order to promote peer assistance, Barbara and Courtney teach their students, "Ask three, then me." Explicit encouragement like this may be necessary, because students are often reluctant to ask peers for help. A study of third-, fifth-, and seventh-graders' attitudes toward seeking help (Newman & Schwager, 1993) sheds light on this reluctance: Across all grade levels, students saw the teacher as not only more likely to facilitate learning but also less likely to think they were "dumb" for asking questions.

It's also important to note that all of the teachers work hard to explain what "helping" really means. They take pains to explain to students that simply providing the answer is not helping, and they stress the futility of copying. As Viviana tells us:

In the beginning of the year we talk a lot about what is helping and what is doing it for the other person. We role-play different situations. For example, we look at a page in the math book, and I pretend I don't know how to do a problem. I ask someone for help. Then I ask the class, "Was that good help? Was that explaining or was that doing the work for me?"

Although all our teachers firmly believe in the value of peer assistance, there are also times when they do *not* allow students to help one another. In these situations, they are careful to explain that the ground rules are different:

 It is almost the end of the school year. Barbara is explaining that students will be writing an essay that will go into their writing folders. These will then be given to the fifth-grade teachers so they can see the progress that students made in fourth grade. Barbara emphasizes the fact that students must work alone: "The only thing that is different about today's assignment is that it is to be done independently. What does independently mean?" [Boy responds, "Alone."] "Yes. You may not help one another. You may not have anyone edit or proofread your essay. I don't want to hear any peer conferencing today. This is to be a silent activity."

> ### ✍ PAUSE AND REFLECT
>
> During seatwork, students are bound to need assistance at one time or another as they attempt to complete their assignments independently. Think about what systems you might employ for those students by considering the following questions: Will you allow students to come to you for help, even if you are busy working with other students? Will you allow students to request and receive help from other students? How will students indicate that they need assistance from you or their peers?

Plan for Ragged Endings

Because students finish seatwork at varying times, they need to know what to do when they're done. Activities should be provided that are educational, but enjoyable. If students learn that they'll be given additional (perhaps tedious) work that others don't have to do, they may dawdle or pretend they haven't finished. Consider the following anecdote:

> During a visit to a second-grade classroom, [an observer watched] a child who was spending most of his time staring out the window or doodling on his paper. The observer finally approached the child and asked if she could be of any assistance. Much to her surprise, the child indicated that he understood the work. When asked why he was staring out the window rather than working on his assignment, the boy pointed to a girl several rows away and said, "See her? She does all her work real fast and when she's done she just gets more work." (Jones & Jones, 1986, p. 234)

In the classrooms of our five teachers, there are numerous activities for students who finish before others. They can work on a computer; they can do free reading, extra-credit assignments, or journal writing; they can tackle brainteasers and puzzles; they can work with manipulative materials, such as Tangrams (seven plastic shapes that form a square when positioned properly) or Pattern Blocks. Finishing early also means that students can resume work on long-term, ongoing projects, such as social studies reports, science experiments, or book reviews.

Find Alternatives to Workbook Pages

Reliance on commercially prepared workbooks can lead to boredom and off-task behavior. Our five teachers provide students with innumerable alternatives to "filling in the blank." Viviana seems to speak for them all:

I rarely give my children worksheets to fill out. I really dislike them. Most of them don't make the children think. They're not challenging; they become tedious. Some of those skill sheets make children do so many problems—many more than they need. If they can do the first 5 right, why give them 95 more? That's when children get bored and tired. I try to give my children work that will challenge them to think and to express themselves.

We asked Viviana, Courtney, Ken, Barbara, and Garnetta to share some of their ideas for meaningful assignments that students can do while teachers are working with individuals or small groups. Some of their suggestions are listed in Table 9.2.

TABLE 9.2 Alternatives to Worksheets

Authentic reading activities (Individual silent reading or paired or partner reading)
- Be sure that students have access to a variety of genres (including comic books, magazines, and newspapers) and to books on a variety of topics (including sports and cars).
- Provide direct instruction on how to behave during the independent-reading time.
- Teach students how to select books that are right for their ability.
- Build in accountability (such as reading logs or conferences).

Authentic writing activities
- Provide prompts or suggested topics for students who have a hard time thinking about what to write.
- Have available samples of various kinds of writing for students to use as models (e.g., plays, newspaper editorials, letters, biographies).
- Have students keep notebooks that they use just for writing.
- Specify a designated length of time for the writing (e.g., 10 minutes) or a designated amount (e.g., "about a page").

Listening
- Provide books on tape so that even less confident readers can follow along in the text and enjoy more complex books.
- Provide multiple copies of books so that a small group of children can sit with their own book or partners can share a book.

Ongoing projects
- Use seatwork time as an opportunity for students to continue work on long-term projects.

Learning centers
- Think about how your students will know which centers to go to and how many will be allowed in each center.
- Think about how students will be held accountable for the work they do at centers.
- Design activities that can be done by students with varying abilities.

Courtney's students use a "choice board" to indicate the learning centers they want to visit.

CONCLUDING COMMENTS

In this chapter, we have tried to provide you with an understanding of the pitfalls and challenges associated with independent seatwork, as well as suggestions for avoiding, or at least minimizing, these problems. We hope you will keep these in mind as you decide on the kinds of activities students will do during seatwork time, the way you will introduce seatwork assignments, and the rules and procedures you will establish to guide behavior.

As you plan seatwork tasks, remember that even young children are capable of doing activities that are challenging and thought-provoking. For example, we recently observed Courtney's kindergarten class during literacy time. While Courtney met with a guided-reading group, the other students worked independently at a number of centers. Some children were at the listening center, where they listened to taped stories and followed along in the book; others were playing a "sight word game" that Courtney had created; still others were in the library corner looking at books they had chosen from the class library. As you can see, these "seatwork" activities don't even require students to be at their seats!

The extent to which you will use independent seatwork in your classroom will depend on a number of factors—the heterogeneity of your class, the grade level you teach, district policy, the ability of your students to work without close teacher supervision, and your beliefs about the appropriateness of whole- or small-group instruction. Indeed, Courtney, Viviana, Garnetta, Barbara, and Ken vary greatly in their use of independent seatwork. For example, Ken always teaches reading in small groups, because he has concluded that this practice best allows him to match students' interests with pieces of literature. The inevitable consequence is daily seatwork for those not meeting in the small group. In contrast, Barbara prefers to teach reading as a total class, selecting a piece of literature that children at varying levels of achievement can read together. Thus she has less need to plan independent seatwork assignments for her students.

As you decide on the extent to which you'll use seatwork, keep in mind the tradeoff that is involved. The primary advantage of seatwork is that it enables you to work with children in a small group and tailor instruction to individual needs. The primary disadvantage is that children not in the small group must work on their own, without close teacher supervision and interaction. Fortunately, this disadvantage can be alleviated by using *group work*—the topic of our next chapter.

Summary

If you plan to work with students individually or in small groups, you will need to use some form of independent work, or seatwork. In this chapter we discussed some of the challenges seatwork presents to teachers and students. We also offered some suggestions for creating meaningful, appropriate assignments that students can do instead of traditional worksheets and workbook pages.

The Pitfalls of Independent Work

Challenges for the teacher

- Assigning work that promotes students' achievement but that can be done independently.
- Matching seatwork to varying levels of achievement.
- Monitoring the class.
- Assigning work that maintains students' interest.
- Coping with "ragged" endings.
- Handling the paperwork.

Challenges for the students

- Completing work on their own.
- Understanding how and when to get the teacher's help.
- Understanding norms for assisting peers.
- Learning how to be effective in obtaining help from peers.

Designing and Implementing Effective Independent Work

- Assign work that is clear and meaningful.
- Match work to varying achievement levels.
- Present seatwork assignments clearly.
- Monitor behavior and comprehension.
- Teach children what to do if they get stuck.
- Plan for ragged endings.
- Use alternatives to traditional seatwork assignments.

Think about how much time your students spend working independently, with peers, and with you. As you decide on time allocations for various kinds of groupings, remember the tradeoff that is involved: Seatwork enables you to work with children in small groups and to tailor instruction to individual needs, but it also means that children who are *not* in the small group must work on their own. Also keep in mind the limitations of commercially prepared seatwork, and choose seatwork assignments carefully. Find alternatives to workbook pages whenever possible. Many sources of quality seatwork are available—you don't have to create it all yourself. Seatwork does not have to mean busywork!

ACTIVITIES FOR SKILL BUILDING AND REFLECTION

In Class

1. The following skills or concepts could all be reviewed with a worksheet. In a small group, select four, and for each one, think of a more active, engaging independent activity that would also provide an opportunity for review and reinforcement.

    For example, teach letter formation in first grade by tracing letters in sand or salt, using finger paints, or making letters from clay.

Grade Level	Skill/Concept	Worksheet Alternative
Kindergarten	The number "4"	
1st grade	Recognizing sight words	
2nd grade	Double-digit addition	
3rd grade	The sequence of events in a story	
4th grade	Using quotation marks	
5th grade	The parts of a flower	
6th grade	Geography terminology	
7th grade	French vocabulary	
8th grade	Character analysis in a short story	

2. Select a workbook page or obtain a worksheet and bring four copies of it to class. In a small group, examine the worksheets, using the following questions as a guide. If you identify problems, suggest ways to improve the page.
    - Are the directions clear?
    - Does the page organization facilitate students' understanding of the task?
    - Does the activity reinforce the intended skill?
    - Is the task meaningful?
    - Are the pictures a help or a distraction?

On Your Own

1. Analyze the weekly schedule of the class you are teaching or observing. Determine how much time is allocated to independent work. During that seatwork period, observe

three "target" students. (Try to select a high-, average-, and low-achieving student.) Note what activities each child is required to do during seatwork time. (Are the activities the same across achievement levels?) Every two or three minutes, record whether the children are on task or off task. If possible, ask the children to explain what they are doing and why.

2. Interview two to four elementary students to learn their perceptions of seatwork. If possible, select students who vary in terms of achievement level. Include the following questions in your interview:

    In what subject is seatwork used most? least?
    When is seatwork useful/useless? interesting/boring?
    What does your teacher generally do when the class is doing seatwork?
    Are you generally allowed to ask for help from peers or do you have to work alone?
    Are your peers willing to help you? Are they able to help you?

For Your Portfolio

Select a grade level, a content area, and an instructional objective (such as, "Students will be able to write capital and lowercase letters" or "Students will be able to distinguish between *needs* and *wants*"). Then design three independent work activities that all target that objective. Differentiate the activities so that advanced students, average students, and struggling students can have an assignment well matched to their abilities. In a brief commentary, explain what the objective is and how you are differentiating.

FOR FURTHER READING

Marriott, D. (1997). *What are the other kids doing?. . . while you teach small groups.* Cypress, CA: Creative Teaching Press.

> The purpose of this book is to provide teachers in grades 1 through 3 with ideas for self-directed literacy center activities that are meaningful and manageable and that will involve students independently while you are working with small groups. Reproducible masters are included.

Pincus, A.R.H. (2005). What's a teacher to do? Navigating the worksheet curriculum. *The Reading Teacher, 59*(1), 75–79.

> Despite the explosion of new instructional practices in reading, having students complete worksheets during seatwork is still very common. This article suggests that teachers ask themselves three questions when examining worksheets: (1) Does the worksheet aim at a research-based goal? (2) Does the worksheet employ effective and efficient means to reach that goal? (3) How can this worksheet best be used?

Tomlinson, C. A. (2003). *Differentiation in practice: A resource guide for differentiating curriculum. Grades K–5.* Alexandria, VA: Association for Supervision and Curriculum Development.

> Tomlinson begins with a "primer" on differentiation and then provides actual instructional units in language arts, social studies, science, and mathematics. Each unit contains an introduction, an overview chart, a unit description (a step-by-step explanation of what takes place in the classroom), and a commentary by the teacher who created the unit. Samples of differentiated product assignments, rubrics, and homework handouts are included.

Tomlinson, C. A. (Ed.). (2005). Differentiated instruction. Special theme issue of *Theory Into Practice, 44*(3).

This issue of *TIP* examines the concept of differentiated instruction from a variety of perspectives. Authors define the need for differentiated instruction, clarify some of the issues involved, and provide specific guidance for making classrooms more effective and efficient for all learners in today's schools.

MANAGING SMALL-GROUP WORK

Keep your eyes on your own paper.

Work without talking to your neighbor.

Pay attention to the teacher.

If you need help, raise your hand.

Do your *own* work.

These are the norms of the traditional classroom, a setting in which students have little opportunity to interact, assist one another, and collaborate on tasks (see Figure 10.1). Phrases like these are so much a part of the way we view classrooms that four-year-olds who have never even attended kindergarten use them when playing school.

This lack of interaction is unfortunate, especially in today's heterogeneous classrooms. There is substantial evidence that small-group work can yield affective, social, and academic benefits. Working with peers on tasks can enhance students' motivation, especially for those students who have negative attitudes toward school and classroom work (Pell et al., 2007). Small-group work can also have positive effects on achievement, as students debate and discuss, ask questions, explain, and evaluate the work of others (Walters, 2000). When children work in heterogeneous groups, they can develop relationships across gender, racial, and ethnic boundaries (Kutnick, Ota, & Berdondini, 2008; Oortwijn, Boekaerts, Vedder, & Fortuin, 2008). Group work can also help to integrate children with disabilities into the general education classroom (Johnson & Johnson, 1980;

"This class will stimulate your ideas and thoughts. And remember — no talking."

Figure 10.1 *Source:* Reprinted by permission of Warren.

Madden & Slavin, 1983). Finally, as Rachel Lotan (2006) observes, group work can help teachers build more caring, equitable classrooms in which "students serve as academic, linguistic, and social resources for one another and are accountable to each other individually and as members of a group" (p. 525).

Given all these benefits, why are some teachers still reluctant to use group work in elementary classrooms? Part of the answer has to do with the teacher's responsibility for keeping order and covering curriculum. In the crowded, complex world of the classroom, it's easier to keep order and cover curriculum when teachers do the talking and students do the listening. Furthermore, if the school culture equates orderly classrooms with quiet classrooms, teachers may feel uncomfortable when group work raises the noise level. Consider this student teacher's journal entry:

> *Every time I read about group work it sounds so great I'm ready to use it every day. Then I attempt it in the classroom and I start having second thoughts. I love the learning that comes out of it, but I never feel in control when it is happening. The part that really upsets me is that I really do not mind if the class gets loud. It's the other teachers and the principal I worry about. There have been a few times when I was using cooperative learning and someone has come in to ask if I need any help, or they will take it upon themselves to tell my class to be quiet. This really makes me angry. I feel like the only acceptable noise level is no noise at all.*

Effective group work in classrooms also requires a long-term commitment from teachers (Kutnick, Ota, & Berdondini, 2008). *Successful group work will not just happen.* If you want your students to work together constructively, you must plan the groups and the tasks carefully, teach students new norms, and provide opportunities for them to practice the behaviors that are required. This takes time, and you may want to heed Ken's words of caution:

 If you want to do it right, you have to allot sufficient time to teach students how to work together. In some schools, this could be viewed as taking time away from "covering the curriculum," especially in this era of high-stakes testing and accountability. It's a good idea to get administrative support before launching cooperative group work. That way, when your principal comes in to observe, he or she will understand what you're doing and why. You won't get asked, "Where is this in the curriculum guide?"

Finally, like seatwork, group work has its own set of pitfalls that can make it particularly difficult for teachers to manage. In this chapter, we examine those special pitfalls. Then we discuss ways in which they can be minimized, drawing on the experiences of our five teachers as well as the research and scholarly literature on group work.

THE PITFALLS OF GROUP WORK

Let's begin by considering the recent experience of a student teacher named Tom. During an evening seminar for student teachers, Tom told us about his first attempt to use group work with his fourth-grade class:

I couldn't wait to get my students into small groups. I didn't want to be like my cooperating teacher—she does all the talking and students are never allowed to work together. They seem so passive and so isolated from one another. Although she wasn't particularly enthusiastic about small-group work, she gave me her blessing. I was really excited. I was sure that the kids would respond well if they were given the chance to be active and to interact. I told the kids that they could choose their own groups. I figured that being allowed to work with friends would be really motivating.

Well, just getting into groups was chaotic. First we had to move the desks from rows into clusters. Then there was lots of shouting and arguing about who was going to be in which group. The whole process took about 10 minutes and was really noisy. My cooperating teacher was not pleased, and I was really upset when I saw what happened. My class is real heterogeneous—I've got Blacks, Whites, Hispanics, Asian Americans. Well, the groups turned out really segregated. They also tended to be just about all boy or all girl. Even worse—I have a boy in my class who has a learning disability and is real hyperactive, and nobody wanted to work with him at all. I ended up making a group take him, and they were pretty nasty about it. And there's another kid who's real shy and quiet; I had to get her into a group too. It was really embarrassing for both of them.

Finally, I got everyone settled down and they started to work on the assignment. We've been talking about seeds and plants, and each group was supposed to plan an experiment that they would actually carry out to demonstrate what plants needed in order to grow. I emphasized that they were supposed to work together and make sure everyone contributed to the plan.

Well, it was a real mess. A couple of the groups worked out OK, but one group argued the whole time and never got anything written. In another group—all boys—they decided to just let the kid who was smartest in science plan the experiment. He kept coming up and complaining that no one else would do any work. And it was true. The rest just sat and fooled around the whole time. Another group had three girls and one boy. The boy immediately took charge. He dominated the whole thing; the girls just sat there and let him tell them what to do.

I had pictured everyone cooperating, helping one another, contributing ideas. But it didn't work out that way at all. And the noise—it just kept getting louder and louder. I kept turning off the lights and reminding them to use their "indoor voices." For a few minutes, they'd get quieter, but then it would get loud again. Finally, my cooperating teacher stepped in and yelled at everybody. I was really humiliated. I just couldn't control them. Right now I'm pretty turned off to using cooperative groups. I think maybe she's right. Maybe these kids just can't handle working together. Maybe I should just go back to having everyone sit and listen to me explain the lesson.

PAUSE AND REFLECT

You have just read Tom's experiences and thoughts about group work. Tom began with great intentions and optimism. Where did the lesson begin to fall apart? What did he do that contributed to the problems with his lesson? What suggestions might you give to Tom?

Unfortunately, Tom's story is not unusual. It illustrates all too vividly what can happen when teachers don't understand the problems associated with group work and don't work to prevent them from occurring. Let's take a closer look at four of these problems.

First, as Tom discovered, *allowing children to form their own groups often leads to segregation among students in terms of gender and ethnicity.* Have you ever had lunch in the cafeteria of a desegregated school? One glance is enough to see that members of each ethnic and racial group tend to sit together. Similarly, at the elementary level, it is typical for boys to prefer sitting with boys, and girls with girls. It is important to recognize that strong forces operate against the formation of cross-ethnic, cross-gender friendships; left to their own devices, most children will choose to be with those they perceive as similar (Webb, Baxter, & Thompson, 1997). An even greater barrier to friendship exists between children with disabilities and their nondisabled peers. The Individuals with Disabilities Education Act (IDEA) requires the inclusion of children with disabilities in regular mainstream classrooms whenever possible, but their mere physical presence is not enough to ensure that these children will be liked, or even accepted.

A second problem of group work is the *unequal participation of group members.* Sometimes this is due to what Garnetta calls the "freeloader" phenomenon, where one or two children in the group end up doing all the work while the others sit back and relax. We saw this occur in Tom's class, when one group decided to have the best science student design the group's experiment. Although this might be an efficient approach to the task, it's not exactly a fair distribution of responsibility. And those who are freeloading are unlikely to learn anything about designing science experiments.

Unequal participation can occur for other, more poignant reasons as well. In a study of students' perceptions of doing mathematics in a cooperative learning group (King, Luberda, Barry, & Zehnder, 1998), Brett, an average achiever, reported that he often failed to understand the task; consequently, he either withdrew from participation or engaged in distracting, off-task behavior. Similarly, Peter, a low achiever, "was aware that the other students seldom asked for his ideas and if he suggested ideas they never listened to him" (p. 8). In order to save face, he engaged in "silly," "weird" behaviors.

Brett and Peter are good examples of the "discouraged" and "unrecognized" categories in Catherine Mulryan's (1992) typology of passive students (outlined in Table 10.1). It is worth keeping these categories in mind. Although a desire to freeload may be at the root of some students' passivity, it is also possible that uninvolved students are feeling discouraged, despondent, unrecognized, bored, or superior.

Just as some individuals may be passive and uninvolved in the group activity, others may take over and dominate the interaction (Cohen, 1994a, 1994b). Frequently, the dominant students are those with high academic status in the classroom—those who are recognized by their peers as successful, competent students. At other times, the dominant students are those who are popular because they are good athletes or are especially attractive. And sometimes dominance simply reflects the higher status our society accords those who are White and male. Indeed, research has shown that in heterogeneous groups, males often dominate females (Webb, 1984), and Whites dominate African Americans and Hispanics (Cohen, 1972; Rosenholtz & Cohen, 1985).

A third pitfall of group work is *lack of accomplishment.* In Tom's class, a significant amount of instructional time was wasted while children formed groups, and some groups didn't get anything done even when they had finally formed. The unproductive groups seemed to view the opportunity to interact as an opportunity to socialize. Their behavior undoubtedly distracted students who were trying to work. Furthermore, the noise and disruption was of particular concern to Tom's cooperating teacher and upsetting to Tom, who repeatedly asked students to use their "indoor" voices—without success.

Finally, a fourth problem associated with group work is children's *lack of cooperation* with one another. Tom tells us that "one group spent the whole time arguing." Although this kind of behavior is disappointing, it should not be surprising. Tom's students had apparently had little experience in cooperative groups, and they had clearly not internalized the norms for successful group work. Children who are used to keeping their eyes on their own papers may find it difficult to work with their classmates. Those who are used to asking the teacher for help may be reluctant to turn to their peers, perhaps because they don't

TABLE 10.1 Six Categories of Passive Students

Category	Description	Typical Achievement Level
Discouraged student	The student perceives the group task to be too difficult and thinks it better to leave it to others who understand.	Mostly low achievers
Unrecognized student	The student's initial efforts to participate are ignored or unrecognized by others, and he or she feels that it's best to retire.	Mostly low achievers
Despondent student	The student dislikes or feels uncomfortable with one or more students in the group and does not want to work with them.	High or low achievers
Unmotivated student	The student perceives the task as unimportant or "only a game," with no grade being assigned to reward effort expended.	High or low achievers
Bored student	The student thinks the task is uninteresting or boring, often because it is seen as too easy or unchallenging.	Mostly high achievers
Intellectual snob	The student feels that peers are less competent and doesn't want to have to do a lot of explaining. She or he often ends up working on the task individually.	High achievers

Source: C. Mulryan, 1992.

want to appear "dumb." Some may have trouble giving clear, thorough explanations to their peers. Those who are not "effective speakers" may lack the skills needed to obtain assistance (Wilkinson & Calculator, 1982; refer to Chapter 9 for the characteristics of "effective speakers"). Students whose cultural backgrounds have fostered a competitive orientation may have difficulties functioning in cooperative situations. And students who are used to being passive may be unwilling to assume a more active role. As Elizabeth Cohen (1994a) reminds us, it is a mistake to assume that individuals (children *or* adults) know how to work together in a productive, collegial manner.

Lack of cooperative behavior—and of a cooperative *ethic*—is especially problematic when teachers rely on group work as a strategy for promoting inclusion and accommodating the needs of children with disabilities. Rollanda O'Connor and Joseph Jenkins (1996) observed 22 children with mild disabilities as they worked in cooperative-learning reading lessons with their nondisabled peers. The investigators classified only 40 percent of the students with disabilities as successfully participating in cooperative groups. The following scenario illustrates an unsuccessful interaction. Here Jake, a fifth-grader with a learning disability, has been paired with a nondisabled peer for partner reading. Then they rejoin two other members of their group to work on a set of literacy tasks:

> The teacher cajoled the pair into starting, then listened to the first few exchanges before walking away. Jake read unevenly, hesitating before multisyllable words and making long pauses between phrases. His partner played with papers and rocked back in his chair when he should have been following Jake's reading and correcting his errors. When Jake stopped reading, his partner knocked softly on Jake's head, saying: "Jake, anybody in there?" . . . By the time they finished their reading and returned to the group of four, the other two group members had proceeded through the first few tasks without them. Jake noted their progress and sighed. He pounded the back of the list of questions with his ballpoint pen, making many small perforations. His partner asked the group, "What are we supposed to do, anyway? Aren't we supposed to work as a team?" The other two ignored the partner and Jake, who continued to jam his pen through the paper more vehemently. (pp. 40–41)

DESIGNING AND IMPLEMENTING EFFECTIVE GROUP WORK

This section of the chapter considers some general strategies for avoiding the pitfalls of group work, based on research and the experiences of our five teachers. (These strategies are summarized in the accompanying Practical Tips box.)

Decide on the Type of Group to Use

Students can work together in a variety of ways. Susan Stodolsky (1984) has identified five different types of group work: helping permitted, helping obligatory, peer tutoring, cooperative, and completely cooperative. The first three types of groups can be considered "collaborative seatwork" (Cohen, 1994a). All of them involve children assisting one another on individual assignments. In a *helping permitted* group, children work on their own tasks, and they are evaluated as individuals; however, they are allowed—but not required—to help one another. *Helping obligatory* situations differ only in that children are now *expected* to offer mutual assistance. In *peer tutoring,* the relationship between the students is not one of equals: Rather, an "expert" is paired with a student who needs help, so assistance flows in only one direction. In recent years, peer tutoring has been recommended as a particularly useful way of meeting the needs of students from culturally and linguistically diverse backgrounds (Webb & Palincsar, 1996).

Cooperative groups differ from these helping situations in that children now share a common goal or end, instead of working on completely individual tasks. In a simple *cooperative group,* some division of responsibilities may occur. For example, a group researching the Civil War might decide that one child will learn about the

PRACTICAL TIPS FOR

DESIGNING AND IMPLEMENTING EFFECTIVE GROUP WORK

- *Decide on the type of group to use:*
  - *Helping permitted*—children are allowed to assist one another on individual assignments.

  - *Helping obligatory*—children are expected to help one another.

  - *Peer tutoring*—a more skillful peer assists a less skillful peer.

  - *Cooperative*—children share a common goal or end; some division of responsibilities may occur.

  - *Completely cooperative*—students share a common goal and there is little or no division of labor; all members of the group work together to create the group product.

- *Decide on the size of the group:*
  - Partners are usually more appropriate for younger children.

  - Groups of four or five are generally recommended, and six is the upper limit.

- *Decide on group composition:*
  - Think carefully about achievement level, gender, cultural/linguistic background, race/ethnicity, ableness, and social skills.

- *Structure the task for positive interdependence;* have students
  - Share materials.

  - Work toward a group goal, grade, or reward.

  - Share information.

  - Share talents and multiple abilities.

  - Fulfill different roles (materials person, timekeeper, recorder, facilitator, reporter, etc.).

- *Ensure individual accountability:*
  - Make sure that all group members are held responsible for their contribution to the goal.

  - Assess individual learning.

  - Monitor individual effort and progress during group work time.

  - Differentiate responsibilities according to students' individual needs.

- *Teach students to cooperate:*
  - Help them to understand the value of cooperation.

  - Provide training in group skills.

  - Provide the chance to evaluate their group work experiences.

- *Monitor learning, involvement, and cooperative behavior.*

causes of the war, while another learns about famous battles, and a third learns about important leaders. Tasks are carried out independently, but all students' assignments have to be coordinated at the end in order to produce the final joint product.

More complex is a *completely cooperative group.* Here, not only do students share a common goal, but there is little or no division of labor. All members of the group work together to create the group product. This was the type of group work that Tom tried to implement when he directed his fourth-grade students to plan an experiment demonstrating what plants need in order to grow.

It is important to keep these distinctions in mind as you plan group work. *Different types of groups are suitable for different types of activities, and they require different kinds of skills* (see Table 10.2). In helping situations, for example, students are ultimately responsible for completing individual tasks. Although these students need to know how to ask for help, how to explain and demonstrate (rather than simply providing the right answer), and how to provide support and encouragement, they do not need the more complex skills required in truly cooperative situations where they share a common goal. For this reason, helping situations are particularly useful when working with young children or those who are new to group work. Educators of young children often recommend Think-Pair-Share, in which students work on a question or problem individually and then pair up with another student to share responses and report to the teacher. "Sidework" such as this, followed by interaction, may be more appropriate for very young children than full collaboration (Dowrick, 1993).

TABLE 10.2 Different Types of Groups

Type of Group	Skills Required	Example of an Activity
Helping permitted	How to ask for help How to explain	Students plant their seeds independently but can ask others for help when watering them
Helping obligatory	How to ask for help How to explain How to provide support and encouragement	Using newspapers to learn about geography and current events, students help one another but complete an individual worksheet
Peer tutoring	How to ask for help How to explain How to provide support and encouragement	Tutor helps tutee to complete a set of math problems
Cooperative group	Divide group task into individual tasks Coordinate individual efforts to produce final group product	M&M™ activity: students count the number of candies in individual bags and then pool their figures
Completely cooperative	Take turns Listen to one another Coordinate efforts Share materials Collaborate on a single task Resolve conflicts Achieve consensus	Building a landfill that doesn't leak toxins into the ground

As an example of a helping situation, let's consider the following activity that we observed in Ken's class:

Ken's students have been using newspapers to learn about geography and current events. Today, each student is to look through the newspaper and find five articles from cities in the state (other than their hometown), five articles from other states, and five articles from countries other than the United States. Students are expected to help one another, but each student is to complete an individual worksheet on which the geographical location, page number, and title of each article are to be listed. Then each student is to select an article to read in more depth and to write about how he or she "relates" to it. For example, what ideas does it trigger? What else do I know about the topic? Why is the article particularly interesting to me?

Students have the newspapers spread out all over their tables and on the floor. As we watch, we see lots of discussion about the assignment. Much of the talk is simple commentary on the articles students are finding. But there are also requests for assistance: "I can't find a fifth article on a New Jersey city." "Is Franklin in New Jersey?" "I don't know how to relate to this article. Relating is hard. How do you think I should relate to this?"

In contrast to helping situations, cooperative groups require skills beyond requesting and giving appropriate assistance. Students must be able to develop a plan of action; they must be able to coordinate efforts toward a common goal; they must be able to evaluate the contributions of their peers and give feedback in a constructive way; they must monitor individuals' progress toward the group goal; and they must be able to summarize and synthesize individual efforts.

During one visit to Garnetta's classroom, we observed a good example of a cooperative activity. The class was divided into groups of four or five to do a math activity involving prediction and graphing. Although students were required to carry out individual tasks, they had to coordinate their individual efforts if the groups were to be successful:

Garnetta introduces the math activity by explaining that each student is going to receive a bag of M&Ms. The first task is to predict how many of each color are in the bag. Predictions are to be recorded on a "Candy Facts" page; a bar graph is then to be constructed and colored with the appropriate M&M colors. Once predictions have been made, students are to open their bags and count the actual number of M&Ms of each color. This information is also to be recorded and then graphed.

Garnetta also explains that once all students in the group are finished with the actual count, their figures are to be pooled. In other words, students are to find out the total number of each color in the group. This information is to be entered on a large "group graph" taped to the chalkboard. Each group member is to color at least one of the bars with the appropriate color.

There is subdued excitement as group members begin to make predictions and color their graphs. Predictions vary tremendously. There are lots of comments on each other's predictions: "That's way too high. There couldn't be that many!" "You think that's all the reds? No way!" When children begin to open their bags, the excitement mounts. Again, there is lots of comparing and commenting: "You got hardly any oranges!" "I got more light browns than anyone at the table!" "You should line yours up like I did."

When it's time to pool the individual numbers of each color, students call out their totals. In some groups, one person does the addition for everyone. In other groups, every group member writes down the numbers and does the addition. There are quite a few discrepancies: "I got 65 light browns." "Uh-oh, I got 58." Garnetta offers each group a calculator so they can check their work.

In this math lesson, students were required to carry out an individual task. We can consider this a division of labor, because each student counted the M&Ms in only one bag. In order for the group to complete the entire assignment, however, each member needed to do the task correctly. This structure provided an incentive for group members to monitor everyone's progress and to help one another. Moreover, students had to coordinate their individual efforts in order to produce a joint product—the group tally of each M&M color.

Completely cooperative groups with no division of labor present even greater challenges. Not only must students be able to take turns, listen to one another carefully, and coordinate efforts, but they must also be able to share materials, collaborate on a single task, reconcile differences, compromise, and reach a consensus. Consider the following activity observed in Barbara's class, part of a science unit on the environment:

 Barbara's class has been studying the environmental problems associated with garbage. Today's lesson is about landfills. Barbara explains what each group of five is to do: "The objective for today's activity is to build a landfill that doesn't leach toxins into the ground. On your lab tray are most of the materials you will need. You have a plastic container [a two-liter bottle from soda, with the top and bottom cut off]. You also have clay, cheesecloth, raisins, leaves, and plastic. All these can be used in your landfill. You'll also have to get soil from the big bucket on the side of the room, and a beaker of water from the water bucket. The only thing you can't use are the three little pieces of sponge. When you have built your landfill and you're satisfied that it won't leak, I'll come around and put red food coloring— the "toxin"—on each sponge. Then you'll put the three sponges on the top of the landfill and make it rain by pouring water from your beaker. We'll watch to see if the toxin comes through. If it doesn't, then your group has made a state-of-the-art landfill. You'll have 15 minutes to work."

Before the groups begin to work, Barbara reviews the roles for each group member. The materials person gets the lab tray, the dirt, and the water for the group; the timekeeper keeps track of the time; the recorder writes down what the group decides to do and draws a diagram of the group's landfill; the facilitator makes sure that everyone has a chance to participate; and at the end of the lesson, the reporter will tell the class what happened.

In this activity, students had different roles to play, but they still needed to work together on the building of the landfill. They had to develop one plan, explain the reasons for their ideas, listen respectfully to one another, reject ideas without being destructive, reach consensus on which ideas to try, and take turns building the landfill. These are not easy skills to learn—even for adults.

As these three examples illustrate, the more interdependent students are, the more skills they need to cooperate successfully. In Tom's case, we can see that he began with the most complex kind of group work. He set up a situation in which students who were not even used to helping one another were expected to cooperate completely. Moreover, he assigned an intellectually demanding task that required creativity and problem solving. His students not only had to contend with an unfamiliar social situation, they also had to grapple with an unusually challenging academic task.

It's a good idea to use simpler types of groups when you are just starting out. Spencer Kagan has developed a vast array of simple group structures that can be used at a variety of grade levels and in many content areas. To learn more about Kagan, see Box 10.1.

Decide on the Size of the Group

To some extent, the size of the group you use depends on the task you assign. Pairs are appropriate when students are revising or editing written material or assessing each other's open-ended responses to a math problem using a rubric. Groups of two are also easier for beginning teachers to manage (Johnson, Johnson, Holubec, & Roy, 1984), and teachers of younger students often prefer pairs to larger groups that require more elaborate social skills (Edwards & Stout, 1989/90).

This is definitely true of Courtney, who frequently has her students work in pairs:

 It's much easier for my students to work with one other person than to work with three or four. I remember one time in particular when I tried a larger-size group, and it didn't work very well. We had been studying shapes (triangles, rectangles, ovals, squares, etc.), and each child had been assigned a shape and they had to make a page for our shape book. They had to draw a picture from the shape (like one child had a triangle, and drew a face underneath and made the triangle into a hat). So they had practice making pictures out of shapes. Then we went on to make shape murals. As a class, we brainstormed a list of settings for the shape murals, like the ocean, New York City, Disney World. Each group of four or five kids had a different setting, and they had to work together using shapes to create the picture. They had shape pieces to glue, and then they could draw with markers. What I found was that some of the groups were able to work together toward the common goal, but other groups just didn't coordinate what they were doing. For example, on the ocean mural, we had kites all over the paper—kites on the bottom and kites on the top. It was clear that they didn't all agree where the sky was going to be! In retrospect, I realize that I didn't teach them how to work together in the larger group, and I underestimated how hard it was going to be for them.

MEET THE EDUCATORS   BOX 10.1

MEET SPENCER KAGAN

Spencer Kagan is a former clinical psychologist and professor of psychology and education. In 1989 he created Kagan Publishing and Professional Development, which offers materials, workshops, and graduate courses on topics such as cooperative learning, multiple intelligences, and brain-friendly instruction. Dr. Kagan developed the concept of "structures," content-free ways of organizing social interaction among students. His structures are used in classrooms worldwide.

Some Major Ideas about Cooperative Learning

1. In a traditional classroom, teachers use structures such as "whole-class question-answer." In this structure, the teacher asks a question, students raise their hands to respond, and the teacher calls on one person. This is a *sequential structure,* in which each person participates in turn, giving little time per pupil for active participation. This also leads to competition among students for the teacher's attention.
2. Teachers can increase opportunities for student participation by following the *simultaneity principle* (for instance, if all students pair up to discuss a question, half the class is talking at any given moment).
3. From a wide array, teachers select the structures that are most appropriate for their specific objectives. Some structures are useful for team building or for developing communication skills; others are most suitable for increasing mastery of factual material or for concept development.

- "Numbered Heads Together" is appropriate for checking on students' understanding of content. Students "number off" within teams. When the teacher asks a question, team members "put their heads together" to make sure that everyone knows the answer. The teacher calls a number, and students with that number raise their hands to answer.
- In "Timed Pair Share," students pair up to share their responses to a question posed by the teacher. First Student A talks for a minute, and then Student B has a turn. This simultaneous interaction allows all students to respond in the same amount of time that it would have taken for just two students if the teacher had used the more traditional "whole-class question-answer" structure.

Publications

Kagan, S. (1994). Cooperative learning and the gifted: Separating two questions. *Cooperative Learning, 14*(4), 26–28.

Kagan, S., & High, J. (2002). Kagan structures for English Language Learners. *ESL Magazine, 5*(4), 10–12.

Kagan, S. (2006). Cooperative learning: The power to transform race relations. *Teaching Tolerance, 30,* 53.

Kagan, S., & Kagan, M. (2008). *Kagan Cooperative Learning.* San Juan Capistrano, CA: Kagan.

Website: www.kaganonline.com

Viviana also prefers to use pairs, and she provides step-by-step directions for her students' partner work. She doesn't simply put them in pairs and tell them to get to work.

 Viviana's students are working on place value. She gives each child a worksheet that is divided into a 10s column and a 1s column. She explains: "Now children, we're going to play a game. I'm going to give each pair of students a set of number cards. Put the cards between you and your partner." She distributes the cards and checks to see that everyone has a partner. "Now, one person take the two top cards and put them side by side so that you make a two-digit number. Now, form the number on your worksheet using the 10s blocks and the 1s blocks. I want you to work individually and then check with your partner to see how your partner has made the number."

As the children work, Viviana walks around and checks what they are doing. Each partner makes the number on the place value worksheet by placing blocks in the appropriate columns. Then the partners confer. Sometimes they have represented the numbers exactly the same way. Sometimes, they discover that they have represented the numbers differently; for example, one child makes 67 with 6 10s and 7 1s; her partner has made 67 with 5 tens and 17 ones. They discuss the difference. Viviana helps them to see that they have each created 67 but in different ways. When pairs have completed the first number and checked their work with their partner, Viviana instructs them to reverse the two digits. She tells them: "Now remember, you don't have the same number, even though you are using the same cards. With a six and a seven you can make 67 or you can make 76."

In situations where the academic task requires a division of labor, it makes sense to form groups larger than two. Groups of three are still relatively easy to manage, but you need to make sure that two students don't form a coalition, leaving the third isolated and excluded (Cohen, 1994a).

In general, educators recommend cooperative groups of four or five (Cohen, 1994a), and six is usually the upper limit (Johnson, Johnson, Holubec, & Roy, 1984). Keep in mind that as group size increases, the "resource pool" also increases; in other words, there are more heads to think about the task and more hands to share the work. It is also true, however, that the larger the group, the more difficult it is to develop a plan of action, allocate turns for speaking, share materials, and reach consensus.

Decide on Group Composition

In addition to deciding on the type and size of your groups, you must think carefully about group composition. As we mentioned earlier in the chapter, group work enables children to develop relationships with those who are different from themselves. Indeed, recent research (Oortwijn, Boekaerts, Vedder, & Fortuin, 2008) has found that multiethnic teams are more effective for reducing interethnic bias than ethnically homogeneous teams. For this reason, educators (e.g., Slavin, 1995) generally advise teachers to form groups that are heterogeneous with respect to ethnicity, as well as race, linguistic background, and ableness. On the other hand, it is important to be sensitive to the fact that trying to achieve heterogeneity can place a burden on students who must be separated from those with whom they feel most comfortable. In other words, it can be hard being the only student of color in a group or the only student whose native language is Spanish.

Teachers also need to consider whether small groups will be heterogeneous or homogeneous with respect to achievement level. At times, homogeneous groups can be useful; for example, you may want to form a helping group of several students who are all working on a particular mathematics skill. In general, however, educators recommend the use of groups that are heterogeneous in terms of academic performance (Cohen, 1994a; Slavin, 1995).

One reason for this recommendation is that heterogeneous groups provide more opportunities for asking questions and receiving explanations. But keep in mind that creating academically heterogeneous groups does not guarantee that students will actually engage in these behaviors. Research indicates that students' interactions in groups mirror the behavior of their teachers (Webb, Nemer, & Ing, 2006): If teachers model the role of the teacher as active problem solver, with students as passive recipients of instruction, this is the behavior that students demonstrate in small groups. Research also suggests that the productivity of the group is more a function of the interactions among the students than of their ability levels (Webb & Mastergeorge, 2003). Thus, preparing students for group work by modeling productive helping interactions appears to be more important than the academic heterogeneity of the group.

Another variable you need to consider when deciding on group composition is social skill. Some children have unusual leadership abilities; others are particularly adept at resolving conflicts; still others are especially alert to injustice and can help ensure that everyone in the group has a chance to participate. When you form groups, it makes sense to disperse children such as these so that each group has the benefit of their talents.

On the other hand, some children have extreme difficulty working with others. It makes sense to disperse *these* students too. As Garnetta points out:

Some children are really volatile—they come to school angry and disrupt whatever group they're in. Some children freeload and don't do anything; they just want to play. Some kids dominate. Some kids prefer to work individually. You have to be really careful whom you place these kinds of kids with—and you certainly don't want to put them all together in one group!

Because group composition is so important, it is risky to allow students to select their own groups. We saw what happened in Tom's class: Students segregated themselves according to gender and ethnicity; friends elected to be together—and did more socializing than work; the student with a learning disability and the social isolate were excluded. Experiences like this lead Ken to believe that students should rarely be allowed to select their own groups:

If you allow children to select their own groups without carefully structuring the situation, you're inviting problems—especially if you're a beginning teacher. Just about the only time I allow my students to choose their own groups is when they're selecting novels to read. In that case, the groups are built upon the selection of the novel; it's not just "I want to work with this person," although that certainly enters into it.

Interestingly, Garnetta and Barbara allow their students to choose their own groups more frequently than Ken does, but not until the students have had substantial experience working in various kinds of groups with almost everyone in the class. Courtney usually lets her students choose their own partners for individual activities (e.g., when they want a "reading buddy"), but when students are going to be working together for an extended period of time (e.g., in writing workshop), she assigns partners on the basis of achievement level and who will work well together. As she puts it, "I've found that it doesn't work very well when their skill levels are really far apart. I want the partners to be of varying skill levels, but it seems to work better when they're more closely matched. That way they are able to learn from one another."

Teachers develop different systems for assigning students to groups. When Barbara forms heterogeneous groups, for example, she first writes each student's name on a note card, along with information about achievement and interpersonal relationships (e.g., with whom the student doesn't get along). Then she ranks students in terms of achievement level and assigns a top-ranked student and a bottom-ranked student to each of the groups. Next she distributes the average students, keeping in mind the need to balance the groups in terms of gender, ethnicity, and social skill. Having each student's name on a note card enables her to shuffle students around as she tries to form equivalent groups that will work well together. Barbara comments, "It's impossible to form perfect groups, but at least this system gives me a fighting chance!"

Barbara pays special attention to the group assignment of children with disabilities. For example, when placing Stuart (the child with autism) in a group, she also includes one of his "student advocates," as well as a child who needs extra help and can benefit from the presence of Stuart's teacher associate. When she assigns Mark (the child who is classified as emotionally disturbed) to a group, she is extremely careful to put him with children who are unlikely to "set him off" and become involved in volatile interactions. She also allows Mark to "opt out of group work if he's having a really bad day. But it's always his choice."

Structure the Task for Positive Interdependence

If you want to ensure that students cooperate on a task, you have to create a situation in which they need one another in order to succeed. This is called positive interdependence, and it's one of the essential features that transforms a group work activity into true cooperative learning (Antil, Jenkins, Wayne, & Vadasy, 1998). One simple strategy for promoting interdependence is to require group members to *share materials* (Johnson, Johnson, Holubec, & Roy, 1984). If one member of a pair has a page of math problems, for example, and the other member has the answer sheet, they need to coordinate (at least a little) if they are both to complete the problems and check their answers. By itself, however, sharing materials is unlikely to ensure meaningful interaction.

Another way to create interdependence is to create a *group goal*. For example, you might have each group produce a single product, such as a report, a science demonstration, a puppet show, or a story. Near the end of the year, when Viviana's students learn about "school helpers" (e.g., the nurse, the principal, a counselor, the librarian), she divides her class into groups. Each group interviews a different helper, and each member of the group has to ask a different question (e.g., "What is your job?" "How do you help people in the school?"). After the interviews, the group creates a poster about their school helper, with each student writing one sentence. (Note that Viviana structured the task in such a way that every child in the group had to participate in order for the group to produce its group product. If she hadn't done this, one person in the group could have done all the work while the others remained uninvolved.)

Another way to stress the importance of collaborating is to give a *group grade* or *group reward.* For example, suppose you want to encourage students to help one another with spelling words. You can do this by rewarding groups on the basis of the total number of words spelled correctly by all the members of the group (Johnson, Johnson, Holubec, & Roy, 1984). Similarly, you can give bonus points to every math group in which all students reach a predetermined level of achievement. Some teachers give each group member a number (such as 1 to 4) at the beginning of class, and then spin a numbered spinner or toss a die to select the number of the group member whose homework or classwork paper will be graded (Webb & Farivar, 1994). Then everyone in the group receives that score. Such a practice clearly increases the pressure on group members to make sure that everyone's homework or classwork is complete and well done.

Another way of promoting collaboration is to structure the task in such a way that students are dependent on one another for *information* (Johnson, Johnson, Holubec, & Roy, 1984). In Garnetta's M&Ms math lesson, for example, group members had to pool their individual data to get a group count of the M&Ms of each color. They needed each other in order to produce the group graph. Even in kindergarten, Courtney finds that she can promote collaboration this way. She describes a math activity in which children compared "towers" they had individually constructed:

Everyone had their own bucket of cubes, all one color, and each child took a handful of cubes and made a tower. Then, working in groups of four, the children had to compare their four towers: Whose is the tallest? the shortest? And so on. Then they passed the towers around the group so that everyone could record the information on graph paper.

(This activity, done in groups of four, was much more successful than the shape mural activity Courtney described earlier, probably because the task required much less group planning and coordination.)

Jigsaw, one of the earliest cooperative learning methods (Aronson et al., 1978), is a good example of a group work situation in which students need one another if they are to complete the task successfully. Here, heterogeneous teams are responsible for learning academic material (usually a narrative, such as a social studies chapter) that has been divided into sections. Each team member reads only one section of the material. The teams then disband temporarily, and students meet in "expert groups" with other people who have been assigned the same section. Working together, they learn the material in these expert groups and then return to their home teams to teach it to their teammates. Everyone is responsible for learning all the material, so successful task completion requires students to listen carefully to their peers. One note of caution, however. A recent study (Souvignier & Kronenberger, 2007) found that students tend to learn the section they are assigned and gain less from the material their peers present. Thus students may benefit from explicit instruction in how to teach the material effectively to their peers.

You can also foster interdependence by creating rich, complex tasks that require *multiple abilities* (e.g., reading, writing, computing, role playing, building models, spatial problem solving, drawing, creating songs, public speaking). By convincing your students that *every* member of the group is good at *some* of these tasks and that *no* member of the group is good at *all* of them, you can reduce the differences in participation between high- and low-status students and enable those who are often left out to contribute (Cohen, 1994a, 1994b, 1998). Listen to Ken:

When ecosystem teams work on *A Field Trip to the Sea* [an interactive CD-ROM on marine life], everyone has to pitch in to carry out the research and create a poster presenting their information. Some have special leadership ability, and they can organize the group for the library research. Some people are really good at spelling and handwriting, but they're terrible artists. Others have terrible handwriting, but they're great artists. Some people can design the layout, while others are the speakers.

Finally, you can assign *different roles* to group members, requiring each role to be fulfilled if the group is to complete the task. In the landfill lesson that Barbara conducted, each group contained a materials person, a timekeeper, a recorder, a facilitator, and a reporter. In *Heritage,* a social studies simulation that Ken uses (Wesley, 1976), students form three-person racing teams that plot a course of travel from San Diego, California, to Bangor, Maine, stopping along the way at 15 important historical sites. Each team member plays a specific role—the driver, the navigator, or the leader. In each round of play, students change roles. The leader rolls the dice at the beginning of each round of play and selects a "fate card," which adds or subtracts miles that the team "travels." The driver computes the number of points the team earns each day and the miles gained or lost; he or she also moves the team's car symbol along the plotted course of travel on a large class map and writes a "diary entry" for the day. The navigator keeps a "daily travel log," recording the number of miles gained or lost during the round of play, the number of hours traveled, the road and weather conditions, and other important information.

Even very young children can learn to carry out roles like these. One way of reminding them about their individual responsibilities is to place a different symbol on each person's desk. For example, you can give each student a star of a different color (Edwards & Stout, 1989/90). The child with the red star reads the instructions, the blue star records what the group does, the yellow star gets the materials, and the green star monitors the noise level.

Ensure Individual Accountability

As we discussed earlier in the chapter, one of the major problems associated with group work is unequal participation. Sometimes children refuse to contribute to the group effort, preferring to freeload. Sometimes more assertive children dominate, making it difficult for others to participate. In either case, lack of participation is a genuine problem. Those who do not actively participate will not learn anything about the academic task; furthermore, the group is not learning the skills of collaboration.

One way to encourage the participation of all group members is to make sure that everyone is held responsible for his or her contribution to the goal and that each student's learning is assessed individually. *Individual accountability* is another essential feature of cooperative learning—and it is one that teachers most often neglect (Antil, Jenkins, Wayne, & Vadasy, 1998).

There are several ways to establish individual accountability. You can require students to take individual quizzes on the material and receive individual grades; you can have each student complete an identifiable part of the total group project; or you can call on one or two students from each group to answer a question, explain the group's reasoning, or provide a demonstration. When Garnetta did the M&Ms lesson, for example, all students had to complete their own set of worksheets with their individual predictions and actual counts, as well as the group tally.

Ken's *Heritage* simulation (Wesley, 1976) provides another good example of a task that fosters individual accountability as well as group cooperation. The number of miles that each team travels during a round of play is determined by the number of points the team accumulates. Team members earn points by carrying out the specific responsibilities associated with their particular roles; for example, the daily travel log is worth 10 points, and diary entries are worth 20 points. The better these are, the more miles the team is allowed to travel. In addition, each team member also has to complete three research reports on a historical site. Each research report is worth 40 points, so there is substantial incentive to do a good job. *Heritage* is structured so that the team will suffer if individuals do not participate or if they fail to do acceptable work; in other words, the success of the team depends on each person's contribution. This structure allows teachers to assign individual grades and to provide a group goal—being the first team to reach Bangor, Maine.

In addition to planning tasks so that individuals are held accountable, you need to monitor students' efforts and progress during group work time. Our five teachers continually circulate throughout the room, observing each group's activity. In this way they can note problems, provide assistance, and keep students on task. They are also careful to build in progress checkpoints. For example, Barbara occasionally stops the groups' activity and asks each group to report, either orally or in writing, on what they've accomplished. Similarly, Ken divides large assignments into components that are due every few days. This enables him to keep track of how well the groups are functioning.

If your groups include children with learning disabilities or those who have limited proficiency in English, you may have to differentiate tasks by complexity and quantity so that everyone can participate and everyone can succeed. For example, let's suppose that all members of a heterogeneous group are assigned a segment of a biography of Harriet Tubman (Schniedewind & Davidson, 2000). Students with special needs can review a relatively short portion of the book with a resource teacher before the class assignment, while those who can comprehend more complex material read more demanding sections. The critical point is that all group members receive segments that provide an appropriate challenge. After reading, students report their findings to one another and are held responsible for learning the material in all segments.

Ann Nevin (1993) describes several cooperative learning situations in which teachers have made adaptations for students with especially challenging educational needs. For example, one teacher developed a science lesson so that Bobby, who was visually impaired and nonverbal, could be included:

> In a lesson in which the objective was for all students to identify different fruits by their seeds (color, size, shape, and number), each group was to complete a poster and, as a group, present it to the rest of the class. Posters were expected to include four or five different fruits and their seeds. Bobby's objective was to tactually explore each fruit and to stay with the group. The objective was explained to the students, and they were asked what other things Bobby could do to be part of the group's activities. The students suggested that Bobby paste some materials onto the poster instead of drawing them. Once all the groups had completed and corrected their posters as necessary, each made and ate a fruit salad. (Nevin, 1993, p. 52)

PAUSE AND REFLECT

Teachers sometimes use the terms *group work* and *cooperative learning* interchangeably. But in fact, cooperative learning is a form of group work, and group work is not always cooperative learning. It is important to be able to explain to students, parents, and even administrators the type of small-group work you will be using in your class. With this in mind, identify the key elements of cooperative learning that set it apart from other types of group work.

Teach Students to Cooperate

As the classroom teacher, *it is your responsibility to teach students to work together.* This means teaching them a new set of norms (Cohen, 1994a):

Ask peers for assistance.

Help one another.

Explain material to other students.

Check that they understand.

Provide support.

Listen to your peers.

Give everyone a chance to talk.

Learning these new norms is not a simple process; students do not learn to cooperate in one 30-minute lesson. On the other hand, research indicates that a moderate amount of training can make a substantial difference. Robyn Gillies and Adrian Ashman (1998) examined the effect of two 1-hour training sessions on first- and third-graders' group work behaviors and interactions. During the first session, children were introduced to group work procedures (e.g., breaking the activity into smaller tasks with each member accepting responsibility for completing one task, encouraging equal participation, and sharing resources). The second session, held on the following day, focused on practicing interpersonal and small-group skills to promote group cooperation (e.g., listening to each other, providing constructive feedback, sharing tasks fairly, and resolving differences amicably). In subsequent group work sessions, the children who had received training exhibited more cooperative behaviors and fewer noncooperative behaviors than their peers who had not been trained. Impressively, this difference was still evident two years later, when the third-grade children (now fifth-graders) were once again observed working in groups (Gillies, 2002).

We can think about the process of training in terms of three stages: learning to value cooperation, developing group skills, and evaluation. Let's consider each of these briefly.

Valuing Cooperation

Before students can work together productively, they must understand the value of cooperation. This is especially important for high achievers who may prefer to work alone, without having to assist others whom they perceive to be less able. Similarly, when cooperative learning is used to facilitate the inclusion of students with disabilities, nondisabled peers may not be inclined to provide support for children with disabilities (O'Connor & Jenkins, 1996).

If students are going to work in the same groups over a period of time, it's often helpful to have them engage in a nonacademic activity designed to build a team identity and to foster a sense of group cohesion. For example, when Barbara forms cooperative groups that will work together for several weeks, she begins by instructing them to decide on a team name. They then create a banner displaying the team name and an appropriate logo. Sometimes Barbara gives each member of a team a marker of a different color; individuals can use only the marker they have been given, but the banner must contain all the colors. In this way, everyone has to participate in its creation.

Another activity that is useful for team building (particularly at the primary level) is making a "Things the_____ Team Likes" book (Graves & Graves, 1990). Each group gets a stack of pictures, and each student gets a turn to select a picture for the book. No picture can be included, however, unless all teammates agree that they like the picture. Once there's agreement, pictures are pasted on tagboard or construction paper, and team members provide labels or captions. This activity can be extended by having teams create "Things the_____Team Likes to Do" books or even "Things the_____Team Hates to Do" books.

Group Skills Training

Recently, a student teacher wrote in her journal:

> After my first disaster with working in groups, I decided I needed to write out a lesson plan for teaching my class how to participate in cooperative learning. I taught it just as I would a math lesson. I realized I could not expect them to know how to do something successfully if I had never taught them how. I would never expect them to be able to add two-digit numbers without training and practice; group work is the same thing.

This student teacher has learned an important lesson: Training in group skills requires systematic explanation, modeling, practice, and feedback. *It's not enough simply to state the rules and expect students to understand and remember.* And don't take anything for granted. Even basic guidelines such as "Don't distract others" and "Use indoor voices" may need to be taught.

A particularly important skill to teach and encourage is asking for help. In Chapter 9, we discussed the difficulty that some students have in obtaining assistance. (See the section on effective speakers.) But even students who are effective communicators may be reluctant to turn to their peers. For example, a study of students' attitudes toward seeking help (Newman & Schwager, 1993) found that third-, fifth-, and seventh-grade students generally preferred to seek help from the teacher rather than from classmates. Students saw the teacher not only as more likely to facilitate learning but also as less likely to think they were "dumb" for asking questions. To counteract such attitudes, you may need to give explicit instructions about when, of whom, and how to ask questions (Farivar & Webb, 1991). You can also encourage this behavior by reminding students that asking other group members can help them learn, by stressing that they're not alone in needing help, or by not responding to requests unless they're unsuccessful in obtaining help from their peers. (Remember the phrase that Barbara and Courtney use: "Ask three, then me.") Keep in mind that low achievers—those most in need of academic help—are likely to be the most passive in seeking it (Newman & Schwager, 1993).

It's helpful to begin by analyzing the group work task you have selected in order to determine what specific skills the students need to know (Cohen, 1994a). Will students have to explain material? Will they have to listen carefully to one another? Will they have to reach a consensus? Once you have analyzed the task, select one or two key behaviors to teach your students. Resist the temptation to introduce all the required group skills at once; going too far too fast is sure to lead to frustration.

Next, explain to your students that they will be learning a skill necessary for working in groups. Be sure to *define terms, discuss rationales, and provide examples.* Johnson and Johnson (1989/90) suggest that you construct a "T-chart" on which you list the skill and then—with the class—record ideas about what the skill would look like and what it would sound like. Figure 10.2 shows a T-chart for "sharing."

Finally, you need to provide opportunities for students to practice the skill and to receive feedback. You might have students role-play; you might pair the skill with a familiar academic task so that students can focus on using the social skill (Carson & Hoyle, 1989/90); or you might have students engage in exercises designed to teach particular skills.

Regardless of the type of practice you provide, you need to give students feedback about their performance. They need to know how often and how well they have engaged in the new behavior. As Ken observes:

 Social skills need to be constantly reinforced. I have to tell my kids every day that I appreciate the way they're cooperating, or that I saw some groups doing a terrific job of explaining problems. As far as I'm concerned, teaching these skills is as important as teaching them math or the language arts.

Sharing	
Looks Like	**Sounds Like**
Leave the markers in the middle of the table where all can reach.	Here's the marker.
Offer the markers to somebody else when finished using.	Thanks for handing me the marker.
Return markers to middle of the table.	I'm done with the marker; does anybody want it?
Take turns with the markers.	Anybody need the red marker?

Figure 10.2   A T-Chart for Sharing

In addition to providing feedback himself, Ken has found it effective to designate a "process person" for each group. This individual is responsible for keeping track of how well the group is functioning; for example, he or she may monitor how many times each person speaks. At the end of the group work session, the process person is able to share specific data that the group can use to evaluate its ability to work together.

Evaluation

To learn from their experiences, students need the chance to discuss what happened and to evaluate how successful they were in working together. A simple approach to evaluation is to ask students to name three things their group did well and one thing the group could do better next time (Johnson & Johnson, 1989/90). You can also have students consider more specific questions, such as

Did you use "indoor voices"?

Did you take turns?

Did everyone carry out his or her job?

Did everyone get a chance to talk?

Did you listen to one another?

What did you do if you didn't agree?

For young children, a checklist like the one in Figure 10.3 can be helpful.

After individual groups have talked about their experiences, it is often helpful to have groups report to the whole class. You can encourage groups to share and compare their experiences by asking, "Did your group have a similar problem?" "How many groups agree with the way they solved their problem?" "What do you recommend?"

Unfortunately, there are times when teaching group skills and providing opportunities for practice and evaluation are just not enough to get particular children to cooperate. Some youngsters are so troubled, volatile, or hostile that they cause conflict no matter where they're placed. When this occurs, you may have no recourse but to exclude them from the activity and devise an individual assignment

Name_____   Date_____

How was I in group today?
Did I . . .

                                  YES   NO

1. Share ideas?
2. Encourage others?
3. Let others speak?
4. Listen to others?
5. Do my job?

Figure 10.3 A Checklist for Evaluating Group Skills

for them. In cases like this, Barbara tells students, "If you absolutely can't work with the group, then you'll just have to carry the whole load by yourself."

Monitor Learning, Involvement, and Cooperative Behavior

During cooperative learning activities, Courtney, Viviana, Garnetta, Barbara, and Ken constantly circulate throughout the room, listening, assisting, encouraging, prodding, questioning, and, in general, ensuring that students are involved, productive, and working collaboratively. Research confirms that teacher monitoring helps to promote a high level of student involvement in group activities (Emmer & Gerwels, 2002). Monitoring also helps to promote the successful participation of children with disabilities. A study of cooperative learning as an inclusion strategy (O'Connor & Jenkins, 1996) found that monitoring enabled teachers to make public statements validating the contributions of students with disabilities—what Elizabeth Cohen (1998) calls "assigning competence." Consider this example from Viviana's class:

 Viviana stops to listen to Jorge's cooperative group as they work on a math assignment to create four story problems using money. The students were outlining a story in which three items were being bought, and they wanted to know how much change would be received from one dollar. Viviana overhears Jorge, a low-ability student, point out that the three items add up to more than one dollar. She remarks, "Jorge's discovery is a good one. I know he goes to the store for his mom and has experience with this." After Viviana leaves, we notice Jorge taking a more active role in the group. Viviana's comment appears to have validated Jorge's contribution and raised his status in the group. Even though his writing skills and knowledge of number facts are poor, his group now looks to him for his knowledge about spending.

In addition to circulating throughout the room, all five teachers have a signal for gaining students' attention. This allows them to provide needed instructions to the whole class or to bring the activity to a close. A study of 13 elementary teachers in six urban schools (Emmer & Gerwels, 1998) found a variety of group attention

Barbara checks in with a cooperative learning group.

PAUSE AND REFLECT

Now that you've read about managing group work, go back to your original suggestions for Tom. What additional ideas might you offer him? What are some key changes he could make to ensure that his next attempt at group work will be more successful?

signals (e.g., "Stop, look, and listen," "Clap if you can hear me," "Fold your hands," "Thumbs up if you can hear me," "Hands on head," and rhythmic clapping). Signals requiring an overt student response were more effective than those that simply asked for students' attention.

CONCLUDING COMMENTS

Even though this chapter is entitled "Managing Small-Group Work," we have seen that there are actually a number of different group work situations, each with its own set of uses, procedures, requirements, and pitfalls. As you plan and implement group work in your classroom, it's important to remember these distinctions. Too many teachers think that cooperative learning is putting students into groups and telling them to work together. They also assign tasks that are inappropriate for the size of the group; they use heterogeneous groups when homogeneous groups would be more suitable (or vice versa); they fail to build in positive interdependence and individual accountability; and they fail to appreciate the differences between helping groups and cooperative learning. The following example would be funny—if it weren't true:

> One of our colleagues recently described an example of "cooperative learning" in his son's school. The classroom teacher informed the students that [they] would be using cooperative learning. His son was paired with another student. The two

students were required to complete two separate parts of a project but were expected to complete the work outside of class. A grade was assigned to each part of the project and a group grade was given. In this instance, one child received an "F" as he failed to complete the required part of the project. The other child received an "A." The group grade was a "C," thus rewarding the student who had failed to complete the work, and punishing the child who had completed his work. In this use of "cooperative learning," there was no opportunity for the students to interact, and the attempt to use a group reward (the group grade) backfired. Although this scenario is not recognizable as cooperative learning to most proponents of cooperation, the classroom teacher described it as such to the students' parents. (O'Donnell & O'Kelly, 1994, p. 322)

This example illustrates the need for teachers to acquire an understanding of the intricacies of group work in general and cooperative learning in particular. We hope this chapter has sensitized you to some of the problems that can arise and has provided you with a set of strategies for minimizing those problems. Group work is an extremely challenging instructional approach, and successful management requires careful planning and implementation.

Despite the potential pitfalls, we believe that group work should be an integral part of elementary classrooms—particularly as you work to establish a caring, supportive community. The classroom is not just a place where students learn academic lessons. It's also a place where students learn *social lessons*—lessons about the benefits of helping one another, about relationships with students from other ethnic groups, about accepting children with disabilities, and about friendship. As a teacher, you will determine the content of these lessons. When it is planned and implemented well, group work can provide students with opportunities to learn lessons of caring, fairness, and self-worth.

SUMMARY

We began this chapter by talking about the potential benefits of group work and about some of the special challenges it presents. Then we suggested strategies for designing and implementing effective group work.

Benefits of Group Work

- Less idle time while waiting for the teacher to help.
- Enhanced motivation.
- More involvement in learning.
- Greater achievement.
- Decreased competition among students.
- Increased interaction across gender, ethnic, and racial lines.
- Improved relationships between students with disabilities and their peers.

The Pitfalls of Group Work

- Segregation in terms of gender, ethnicity, and race.
- Unequal participation.

- Lack of accomplishment.
- Lack of cooperation among group members.

Designing and Implementing Effective Group Work

- Decide on the type of group to use (helping permitted, helping obligatory, peer tutoring, cooperative, completely cooperative).
- Decide on the size of the group.
- Decide on group composition.
- Structure the task for interdependence.
- Ensure individual accountability.
- Teach students to cooperate.
- Monitor learning, involvement, and cooperative behavior.

Group work offers unique social and academic rewards, but it is important to understand the challenges it presents and not to assume that, just because a task is fun or interesting, the lesson will automatically run smoothly. Remember to plan group work carefully, prepare your students thoroughly, and allow yourself time to develop experience as a facilitator of cooperative groups.

ACTIVITIES FOR SKILL BUILDING AND REFLECTION

In Class

1. Working in a small group, consider each of the following cases and choose which type of group work you would use (helping permitted, helping obligatory, peer tutoring, cooperative group, completely cooperative group) in each situation. Briefly share your choice and your reasoning.

   a. You are teaching your heterogeneous math class how to tell time. Eight of the 17 students pick up the concept quickly, but the remaining students are having some difficulty.

   b. Your third-grade class is divided into three literature groups. Each group is reading a different novel, but each group has to define 10 vocabulary words you have drawn from its book. Your main goal is for each child in each group to have the definitions correctly written to use as a study guide for a future quiz.

   c. In your homogeneous fifth-grade math class you are reviewing the decimal equivalents of fractions. You want children to use flash cards to assist them in memorizing the equivalents.

   d. In sixth grade, your science class is studying rocks and minerals. You would like the students to work in groups of three to study the three types of rocks (igneous, metamorphic, and sedimentary). Each group is to create a large poster showing the characteristics of each type of rock and some examples.

   e. Your fourth-grade class just read tall tales in their literature anthology. To capitalize on their enthusiasm, you have them form groups to write and perform (complete with scenery and costumes) a play or puppet show based on one of the tall tales.

You would like each member of the group to enjoy the many aspects of this project, from writing to acting.

2. You want your class to work on editing and peer conferencing skills with the mystery stories they've been writing. It is important to you that students be able to give and receive constructive criticism and feedback. You have decided to have the students work in groups of three. How will you model the skills you want them to practice? What roles might you assign to facilitate achievement of the objective? What forms of accountability will you build in? How will you monitor the group work? Discuss these questions in your small group.

On Your Own

Observe a cooperative learning activity. In what ways has the teacher tried to promote positive interdependence and individual accountability?

For Your Portfolio

Design a cooperative learning lesson on a topic of your choice. Write a brief commentary describing (a) the social skills that are required in this lesson and how you will teach them; (b) the way(s) in which you built in positive interdependence and individual accountability; and (c) how students will evaluate their group interaction.

FOR FURTHER READING

Emmer, E. T., & Gerwels, M. C. (2002). Cooperative learning in elementary classrooms: Teaching practices and lesson characteristics. *The Elementary School Journal, 103(*1), 75–91.

    This article describes a study of 18 elementary teachers who were experienced users of cooperative learning. More successful and less successful lessons (based on assessments of student engagement, performance, and cooperation) are compared. Lesson success was associated with higher levels of individual or group accountability, teaching monitoring, feedback, and the use of manipulative materials.

Gillies, R. M. (2007). *Cooperative learning: Integrating theory and practice.* Los Angeles: Sage.

    This book situates cooperative learning within the context of No Child Left Behind and high-stakes testing, arguing that cooperative learning has the potential to transform schools and lead to student success on standardized tests. Chapters in the book deal with establishing successful cooperative groups, promoting student discourse, and assessing small-group learning.

O'Donnell, A. (2002). Promoting thinking through peer learning. Special theme issue of *Theory into Practice, 41*(1), 60 pp.

    The articles in this special issue of *TIP* address different aspects of cooperative or peer learning—for example, who learns in a group, what changes as a result of interaction, and how we can assess learning from peer interaction. Contributors suggest ways in which peer learning can promote thinking and point to key considerations that are important in achieving that goal.

Schniedewind, N., & Davidson, E. (2000). Differentiating cooperative learning. *Educational Leadership, 58*(1), 24–27.

This article provides "guiding tenets" and examples of how to differentiate assignments and responsibilities within heterogeneous cooperative groups.

ORGANIZATIONAL RESOURCES

Cooperative Learning Center at the University of Minnesota, 60 Peik Hall, University of Minnesota, Minneapolis, MN 55455; 612 624-7031; www.co-operation.org. Co-directed by Roger T. Johnson and David W. Johnson, the CLC is a research and training center focusing on how students should interact with each other as they learn and on the skills needed to interact effectively.

The International Association for the Study of Cooperation in Education (IASCE), P.O. Box 390, Readfield, Maine 04355; 207-685-3171; www.iasce.net. Established in 1979, IASCE is the only international, nonprofit organization for educators interested in cooperative learning to promote academic achievement and democratic, social processes. The website provides an annotated list of Web pages related to cooperative learning.

Managing Recitations and Discussions

Much of the talk that occurs between teachers and students is unlike the talk you hear in the "real world." Let's consider just one example (Cazden, 1988). In the real world, if you ask someone for the time, we can assume that you really need to know what time it is and will be grateful for a reply. The conversation would probably go like this:

"What time is it?"

"2:30."

"Thank you."

In contrast, if a teacher asks for the time during a lesson, the dialogue generally sounds like this:

"What time is it?"

"2:30."

"Very good."

Here, the question is not a request for needed information, but a way of finding out what students know. The interaction is more like a quiz show (Roby, 1988) than a true conversation: The teacher *initiates* the interaction by asking a question, a student *responds,* and the teacher *evaluates* the response or *follows up* in some way (Abd-Kadir & Hardman, 2007; Mehan, 1979). This pattern of interaction

(I-R-E or I-R-F) is called *recitation,* and several studies (e.g., Stodolsky, 1988) have documented the substantial amount of time that students spend in this instructional activity.

Recitation frequently has been denounced as a method of instruction. Critics object to the active, dominant role of the teacher and the relatively passive role of the student. They decry the lack of interaction among students. They condemn the fact that recitations often emphasize the recall of factual information and demand little higher-level thinking. The following example illustrates this kind of recitation. In this excerpt, fourth-grade students are talking about one of *Aesop's Fables,* "Androcles and the Lion." This is the story of an escaped slave named Androcles who earns a lion's gratitude for removing a large thorn stuck in one of the lion's paws:

> MR. LOWE: OK, let's start at the very beginning. What is the name of the slave?
> STUDENT: Androcles?
> MR. LOWE: Right. Now how was Androcles treated by his master?
> STUDENT: Cruelly.
> MR. LOWE: Good. So what did Androcles do?
> STUDENT: He escaped.
> MR. LOWE: Ah, yes. He escapes and he heads for the forest. He's wandering around and he meets a . . . a what, Jane?
> JANE: A lion.
> MR. LOWE: Yes, a lion. And something's wrong with the lion. What's wrong, Ari?
> ARI: He has a cut in his paw.
> MR. LOWE: Not exactly a cut. Tasheika?
> TASHEIKA: A thorn is stuck in his paw.
> MR. LOWE: Absolutely. A thorn. And this moaning, whimpering, distressed lion holds out his paw for Androcles, and Androcles does what?
> STUDENT: Takes the thorn out.
> MR. LOWE: Right—and the lion is . . . what, class?
> STUDENTS: [Silence]
> MR. LOWE: How does the lion feel toward Androcles?
> STUDENTS: [Students murmur a variety of responses.] Grateful. Happy. He likes him. Loving.

An additional criticism focuses on the public evaluation that occurs during recitation. When the teacher calls on a student, everyone can witness and pass judgment on the response. In fact, as Phil Jackson (1990) comments, classmates "frequently join in the act":

> Sometimes the class as a whole is invited to participate in the evaluation of a student's work, as when the teacher asks, "Who can correct Billy?" or "How many believe that Shirley read that poem with a lot of expression?" (p. 20)

Questions like these exacerbate the "negative interdependence" among students that recitations can generate (Kagan, 1989/90). In other words, if a student is unable to respond to the teacher's question, the other students have a greater chance to be called on and to receive praise; thus, students may actually root for their classmates' failure.

Despite the validity of these criticisms, recitation remains an extremely common feature of elementary classrooms. What is there about this instructional strategy that makes it so enduring in the face of other, more highly touted methods?

We thought hard about these questions during one visit to Barbara's classroom, and our observation of a recitation she conducted provided some clues. The students had just read the first few chapters in their new novel, *The Cay* (Taylor, 1969). Barbara asked them to take out their books and to get ready to talk about what they had read. She perched on her stool in the front of the room.

BARBARA: Let's review what you read last night. First of all, what is a cay? [One girl raises her hand.] Only one person? [She pauses and a few more hands go up. Barbara calls on a volunteer.] Maggie?

MAGGIE: An island.

BARBARA: Any particular kind of island?

STUDENT: A very small island.

BARBARA: OK. What did you find out about where the island was? [A boy raises his hand, but then lowers it.] Ben, you put your hand down, but you wanted to say something?

BEN: It's near Aruba.

BARBARA: Good. What else? [Barbara calls on a nonvolunteer.]

STUDENT: In the Caribbean.

BARBARA: OK. [Barbara directs students to look at their individual maps and locate the island. When she is satisfied that everyone has located the island, she continues.] This story takes place in what time in history?

STUDENT: 1942.

BARBARA: Good. What important thing was happening then?

STUDENT: It was the middle of World War II.

BARBARA: Right. Where did most of the fighting take place in World War II?

STUDENT: Europe.

BARBARA: OK, but are they in Europe? [She calls on a nonvolunteer.]

STUDENT: No.

BARBARA: Then why are they affected? [Barbara sounds very puzzled.]

STUDENT: It's a world war, so it affects a lot of places.

BARBARA: True, but why this place?

STUDENT: Because there are three submarines there.

BARBARA: But why?

STUDENT: Because of a supply of oil that was there.

BARBARA: So what? Why is oil important?

STUDENT: It's worth a lot of money.

BARBARA: Why?

STUDENT: Because it's rare and we need it.

BARBARA: OK, it's an important natural resource that's not plentiful everywhere.

Barbara's recitation helped us to identify five very useful functions of class-room recitations. First, the recitation enabled Barbara to review some basic facts about the story and to check on students' comprehension (Leahy, Lyon, Thompson, & Wiliam, 2005). Second, by asking intellectually demanding questions (such as why the war affected people in the Caribbean), Barbara was able to prod her students beyond low-level factual recall to higher levels of thinking. Third, the recitation permitted Barbara to involve students in the presentation of material (Roby, 1988). Instead of telling students where the island was located, for example, or why it was affected by the war, Barbara brought out the information by asking questions. Fourth, the recitation gave her a chance to interact individually with students, even in the midst of a whole-group lesson. In fact, our notes indicate that Barbara made contact with 12 different students in just the brief interaction reported here. Finally, through her questions, changes in voice tone, and gestures, Barbara was able to maintain a relatively high attention level; in other words, she was able to keep most of her students "with her."

Later, Barbara reflected aloud on her use of recitation in this lesson:

 Obviously, this was a teacher-directed lesson: One of my major goals was to get specific information to everyone without standing there and telling them. Because of this, all the talk was filtered through me. This was real different from a true discussion, when I'd encourage students to talk directly with one another and I'd pretty much stay out of things.

One of the things I like about recitations is that I can push my kids to give more complete responses than they would in writing. Fourth-graders are more comfortable talking than writing, so their oral responses tend to be more complete than their written ones. During a recitation, I can encourage them to expand on what they're saying, to substantiate their positions. I can also use their verbal responses as a model for the kinds of answers that I'd expect on a written test or in a paper.

The recitation also allows me to find out what they don't have straight and to clear up misconceptions that they have about the material. I can also find out what they bring to the lesson. For example, in this lesson, I was really impressed by how much they had learned about geography in their social studies class. Since they go to another teacher for social studies, I didn't realize they knew so much about maps and climate. And they also knew more about World War II than I had anticipated.

As we can see, Barbara's recitation session was hardly a "quiz show" in which passive students mindlessly recalled low-level, insignificant facts. On the other hand, both the pattern of talk (I-R-E) and the primary intent (to assess students' understanding of the reading) set it apart from another type of verbal interaction—the *discussion.* (Table 11.1 summarizes the differences between recitation and discussion.)

In contrast to recitation, discussion is a form of verbal interaction in which individuals work together to consider an issue or a question. The discussion is intended to stimulate a variety of responses, to encourage students to consider

TABLE 11.1 Differences between Recitations and Discussions

Dimension	Recitation	Discussion
1. Predominant speaker	Teacher (2/3 or more)	Students (half or more)
2. Typical exchange	Teacher question, student answer, teacher evaluation (I-R-E)	Mix of statements and questions by mix of teacher and students
3. Pace	Many brief, fast exchanges	Fewer, longer, slower exchanges
4. Primary purpose	To check students' comprehension	To stimulate variety of responses, encourage students to consider different points of view, foster problem solving and critical thinking, to examine implications
5. The answer	Predetermined right or wrong; same right answer for all students	No predetermined right or wrong; can have different answers for different students
6. Evaluation	Right/wrong, by teacher only	Agree/disagree, by student and teacher

Source: Adapted from Dillon, 1994.

different points of view, to foster problem solving, to examine implications, and to relate material to students' own personal experiences (Good & Brophy, 2008). In a discussion, individuals may offer their understandings, relevant facts, suggestions, opinions, perspectives, and experiences. These are examined for their usefulness in answering the question or resolving the issue (Dillon, 1994).

In order to make the distinction between recitation and discussion clear, let's consider another example, this time from Ken's class.

Eight students are sitting at the reading table with Ken, about to discuss the book they have been reading, *George Washington's Socks* **by Elvia Woodruff (1991). They roll a die to see who goes first. A "two" comes up, so the second person from the end, Eric, goes first. Eric asks the other students an analysis question that he has prepared on the reading assignment. [Analysis questions require students to go beyond simple recall or comprehension to a deeper examination of the meaning.]**

ERIC: **Should Adam Hibbs have returned the General's cape instead of Matt?**

SUZANNE: **In a way, yes . . . because he was the soldier and Matt wasn't the soldier.**

CHARLENE: **I don't think so. Adam Hibbs should not have returned it because he could get in a lot of trouble for leaving his post.**

LAUREN: I think Adam should have returned it because he was older and then he wouldn't have fallen on the bayonet.

The interaction becomes heated; several students speak at the same time. Ken looks at Eric and quietly murmurs to him.

KEN: You might want to get some control of this discussion.
ERIC: OK, hold on. Jamie, what do you think?
JAMIE: For me, it's kind of in the middle . . .
NEIL: Yeah, for me too, it's right smack in the middle. In a way I think he should have left it there, because he returns the cape and then—
SUZANNE: [interrupting Neil] The captain says, "You're in the war."
NEIL: And it's just a cape. What's the big deal? Somebody else could've given him a cape.

The discussion continues for a few more minutes. Then Ken asks Eric to read the answer he has prepared to his own question.

KEN: Comments about Eric's answer?
CHARLENE: If Adam Hibbs hadn't let Matt go, then maybe he wouldn't have gotten hurt.
LAUREN: Some of your answer goes along with the question, but then in the end, I think you were talking about something else . . .
KEN: [Listens to a few more comments made on Eric's answer.] What a great analysis question! You saw all the debate, discussion it generated. I don't even have to judge the question; you can judge for yourself from the reaction. OK, let's hear another question. Suzanne? [Ken calls on the next student, and a similar discussion ensues.]

As we can see from this excerpt, the predominant pattern in this interchange was not I-R-E (teacher initiation, student response, and teacher evaluation), but initiation (by a student in the teacher's role) followed by multiple responses (I-R-R-R). Ken essentially stays out of the interaction, except for making sure that students have an opportunity to speak when the interaction gets excited and pushing students to probe more deeply. In contrast to the recitation, students speak directly to one another. They comment on one another's contributions; they question, they disagree, and they explain.

Recitation and discussion are often confused. Teachers often say that they use discussion a great deal, when in fact they are conducting recitations. For example, in an observational study (Alvermann, O'Brien, & Dillon, 1990), 24 middle school teachers reported using discussion. Yet only 7 could actually be observed doing so; the others were using recitation or lecture interspersed with questions. These findings are consistent with observations of 1,000 elementary and secondary classrooms across the country, in which discussion was seen only *4 to 7 percent of the time* (Goodlad, 1984). It is clear that real discussion is very rarely used in classrooms.

James Dillon (1994) suggests three major reasons for the infrequency of classroom discussion. First, discussion does not come naturally; it has to be learned, and it is difficult—for both students and teachers. Second, teachers themselves have had few experiences with classroom discussions and may not have received training and guidance in leading them. Finally, school culture is generally not supportive of discussion. If teachers feel pressured to "cover the curriculum" and to have students do well on standardized tests, they may consider discussion a luxury they cannot afford. In addition, providing opportunities for discussions means that teachers have to give up their role as *leader* and assume the role of *facilitator*. This can be difficult for teachers who work in schools that emphasize control and who are used to dominating, or at least directing, the conversation.

Educational critics frequently decry the use of recitation and promote the use of discussion, but both types of interaction have a legitimate place in the elementary classroom—if done well. This chapter begins by examining the managerial problems and pitfalls associated with recitations. Next, we consider what our teachers and the research have

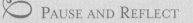

PAUSE AND REFLECT

Even if you are unfamiliar with the term *recitation*, you have probably participated in many such question-and-answer sessions during your years in school. In contrast, your experiences with student-centered discussions may be far more limited. Reflecting on the differences between these two, consider the appropriateness of both instructional strategies for the grade level you teach (or want to teach). Can you think of instances when a student-centered discussion would be appropriate? If so, when would you use such discussions?

to say about minimizing these problems and implementing effective recitations. We then turn to a consideration of discussions and offer some guidelines for managing this pattern of interaction.

THE PITFALLS OF RECITATIONS

The first pitfall of recitations is *unequal participation* among students. Imagine yourself in front of a class of 25 children. You've just asked a question. A few children are wildly waving their hands, murmuring "ooh, ooh," and clearly conveying their desire to be called on. (See Figure 11.1 for an example of a student very eager to participate.) Others are sitting quietly, staring into space, their expressions blank. Still others are slumped down as far as possible in their seats; their posture clearly says, "Don't call on me."

Figure 11.1   *Source:* FOXTROT © 2006, Bill Amend. Reprinted with permission of UNIVERSAL UCLICK. All rights reserved.

In a situation like this, it's tempting to call on a child who is eager to be chosen. After all, you're likely to get the correct response—a very gratifying situation! You also avoid embarrassing children who feel uncomfortable speaking in front of the group or who don't know the answer, and you're able to keep up the pace of the lesson. But selecting only those who volunteer or those who call out may limit the interaction to a handful of students. This can be a problem. Students tend to learn more when they are actively participating (Morine-Dershimer & Beyerbach, 1987). Furthermore, because those who volunteer are often high achievers, calling only on volunteers is likely to give you a distorted picture of how well everyone understands. Finally, restricting your questions to a small number of students can communicate negative expectations to the others (Good & Brophy, 2008): "I'm not calling on you because I'm sure you have nothing to contribute."

Unequal participation can be a particular problem if you have English-language learners (ELLs) in your classroom. Although ELLs can become proficient in conversations with their peers after about two years of exposure to English, it can take five to seven years for them to acquire grade-level proficiency in academic discourse (Cummins, 2000). Thus it may be difficult or intimidating for ELLs to take an active role in recitations.

Another drawback of recitations is *the danger of losing pace, focus, and student involvement.* A popular television program of the 1960s capitalized on the fact that *Kids Say the Darndest Things.* The title of the show aptly describes what can happen during a recitation. When you ask your question, you might receive the response you have in mind. You might also get answers that indicate confusion and misunderstanding, ill-timed remarks that have nothing to do with the lesson ("There's gum on my shoe"), or unexpected comments that momentarily throw you off balance. All of these threaten the smooth flow of a recitation and can cause it to become sluggish, jerky, or unfocused.

Threats like these require you to make instantaneous decisions about how to proceed. It's not easy. If a student's answer reveals confusion, for example, it's essential to provide feedback and assistance. On the other hand, staying with that student can cause the lesson to become so slow that everyone else begins to daydream and fidget. During recitations, you are frequently confronted with two incompatible needs: the need to stay with an individual to enhance that child's learning and the need to move on to avoid losing both the momentum and the group's attention.

At one point in Barbara's lesson on *The Cay,* we saw a good illustration of this tension. Students had been talking about the problems faced by the main character, when Jessica suddenly raised her hand and asked, "If I got stranded on an island in the Caribbean, would it be possible for me to live?" The question was clearly out of sequence, but Barbara allowed it to stand. In fact, she responded, "*I* don't know." Turning to the class, she asked, "What do *you* think? Could Jessica survive?" That initiated a long interchange on the relevant factors: presence of food, water, shelter, temperature, animals, and so on. Eventually, Barbara returned students' attention to the book, by specifically asking how this discussion was related to the characters they read about.

When we discussed this incident with Barbara after her lesson, she explained why she decided to pursue Jessica's question:

> Jessica's question really floored me, and I was tempted to go on. We had been moving at a nice clip, and I didn't want to lose the flow. I also didn't want to lose the focus of the discussion. But she seemed sincere—it didn't seem like a ploy to get us off the topic—and she hardly ever participates. This book is really a challenge for her. I decided to let the question stand because I wanted to bring her into the conversation, to "move her up" in the eyes of the other kids, and to give her some credibility. Also, I decided I could use the question to bring up some of the problems that Philip, the character in the book, has to face. But I was taking a risk. It's so easy for a lesson to get way off target. When you're standing up there, it can get really scary. Sometimes you don't have a clue what they're going to bring up when you ask a question. It's hard to tell a child we can't talk about that now, but if you follow every tangent someone brings up, you'll never get anywhere. If I decide not to talk about a question or a comment a child brings up, I try to write it on the board and remember to talk about it later, maybe during free time or lunch.

The third pitfall of recitations concerns the *difficulties teachers may have in monitoring students' comprehension.* Recitations provide an opportunity for teachers to check students' understanding, but doing so is not always easy. Recently, a fifth-grade teacher told us about a lesson taught by her student teacher, Rebecca. The class had been studying the human body, and halfway through the unit, Rebecca planned to give her students a quiz. On the day of the quiz, she conducted a brief review of the material by firing off a series of questions on the respiratory and circulatory systems. Satisfied with the high percentage of correct answers, Rebecca then asked, "Before I give out the quiz, are there any questions?" When there were none, she added, "So everybody understands?" Again, there was silence. Rebecca told the students to close their books and distributed the quiz papers. That afternoon, she corrected the quiz. The results were an unpleasant shock; a large number of students received Ds and Fs. During a conference with her cooperating teacher after the lesson, she wailed, "How could this happen? They certainly knew the answers during our review session!"

This incident underscores the difficulty of gauging the extent to which all members of a class really understand what is going on. As we mentioned earlier, teachers sometimes get fooled because they call only on volunteers—the students most likely to give the correct answers. In this case, Rebecca's cooperating teacher had kept a "map" of the verbal interaction between teacher and students and was able to share some revealing data: During a 15-minute review, Rebecca had called on only 6 of the 19 children in the class, and all of these had been volunteers. Although this allowed Rebecca to maintain the smooth flow of the interaction, it led her to overestimate the extent of students' mastery. Moreover, as Rebecca's cooperating teacher pointed out to her, asking "Does everyone understand?" is unlikely to yield an accurate assessment of comprehension.

There's no accountability built into questions like this; in other words, they don't require students to demonstrate an understanding of the material. In addition, students who do not understand are often too embarrassed to admit it. (They may not even realize they don't understand!) Clearly, you need to find other ways to assess whether your class is "with you."

The final pitfall of recitations is *incompatibility with the communication patterns that children bring to school.* Although the I-R-E format of recitations is a staple of schools, it stems from White, middle-class values and represents a way of communicating that is not well matched with the discourse styles of many students from different cultural backgrounds (Arends, 2008). For example, recitation generally follows a "passive-receptive" discourse pattern: Students are expected to listen quietly during teacher presentations and then respond individually to teacher-initiated questions. African American students, however, may be accustomed to a more active, participatory discourse pattern ("call-response"). When they demonstrate their engagement by calling out prompts, comments, and reactions, European American teachers may interpret the behavior as rude and disruptive (Gay, 2000). Native Americans may also find the format of recitations unfamiliar and uncomfortable: "In Native-American culture, there is no naturally occurring situation in which a single adult authority regulates who speaks, when they speak, at what volume they speak, and to whom they speak" (Henning, 2008, p. 138). When Native American students are reluctant to participate, European American teachers may conclude that they are uninterested.

In addition to cultural background, gender differences in discourse style may affect students' participation in recitations. As the linguist Deborah Tannen (1995) notes, boys and girls learn different ways of speaking as they are growing up:

> The research of sociologists, anthropologists, and psychologists observing American children at play has shown that, although both girls and boys find ways of creating rapport and negotiating status, girls tend to learn conversational rituals that focus on the rapport dimension of relationships whereas boys tend to learn rituals that focus on the status dimension. (p. 140)

According to Tannen, girls learn to downplay status differences and to stress the ways in which everyone is the same. They also learn that sounding too sure of themselves will make them unpopular. At the same time, boys generally recognize and expect differences in status; in fact, they learn to use language to negotiate their status in the group by displaying their abilities and knowledge. Boys in leadership positions give orders, challenge others, and "take center stage by telling stories or jokes" (p. 140). When we consider these very different styles of communication, it is easy to see that the I-R-E pattern of discourse, with its public display of knowledge and its inherent competition, is more compatible with boys' communication styles than with those of girls (Arends, 2008).

Research on gender and classroom talk has also indicated that "teachers demonstrate a clear bias in favor of male participation in their classes" (Grossman & Grossman, 1994):

> Teachers are more likely to call on a male volunteer when students are asked to recite; this is also true when they call on nonvolunteers. When students recite,

teachers are also more likely to listen to and talk to males. They also use more of [males'] ideas in classroom discussions and respond to them in more helpful ways. (p. 76)

Similarly, *How Schools Shortchange Girls* (1992), a study commissioned by the American Association of University Women (AAUW), revealed that males often demanded—and received—more attention from teachers. One study of elementary and middle school students (Sadker, Sadker, & Thomas, 1981) found that boys called out answers eight times more often than girls did. Furthermore, when the boys called out, teachers typically listened to the comment. In contrast, when girls called out, they were usually told to "Please raise your hand if you want to speak." Another study found that even when boys do not volunteer, the teacher is more likely to solicit their responses (Sadker & Sadker, 1985).

Why would teachers allow male students to dominate classroom interaction by calling out? Linda Morse and Herbert Handley (1985) suggest three possible reasons: (1) the behavior is so frequent that teachers come to accept it; (2) teachers expect males to be aggressive; and (3) the call-outs may be perceived by teachers as indicators of interest. Whatever the reasons, teachers need to be sensitive to gender differences in participation and use strategies to ensure that both males and females have opportunities to participate.

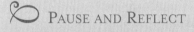

PAUSE AND REFLECT

Reflect on your own experiences with communication patterns that students bring to school. Have you noticed any gender differences in communication styles or any differences between students from different cultural backgrounds? How have these differences affected participation in class recitations or discussions?

DESIGNING AND IMPLEMENTING EFFECTIVE RECITATIONS

In this section, we suggest six strategies for minimizing the pitfalls associated with recitations. As in previous chapters, these are based on research on teaching, discussions with our five teachers, and observations of their classes. (The accompanying Practical Tips box provides a summary of our suggestions.)

Distributing Chances to Participate

During one visit to Courtney's classroom, we watched her doing a shared reading of a poem, "The Land of Many Colors," which was printed on an easel pad. Courtney read each line of the poem, and the students echoed her. Then they tried a choral reading. Afterwards, Courtney asked the children, "Who can come up here and find a new sight word?" Hands waved wildly; it was clear that everyone wanted a chance. Courtney reached into a can, pulled out a brightly colored popsicle stick, called on Daniel, and put the stick to the side. Daniel got up from his seat on the carpet, moved to the easel, took a piece of red translucent tape,

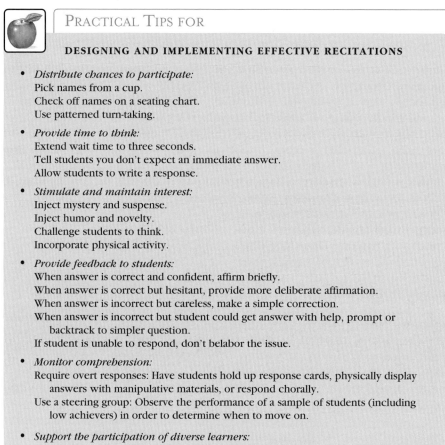

PRACTICAL TIPS FOR

DESIGNING AND IMPLEMENTING EFFECTIVE RECITATIONS

- *Distribute chances to participate:*
  Pick names from a cup.
  Check off names on a seating chart.
  Use patterned turn-taking.

- *Provide time to think:*
  Extend wait time to three seconds.
  Tell students you don't expect an immediate answer.
  Allow students to write a response.

- *Stimulate and maintain interest:*
  Inject mystery and suspense.
  Inject humor and novelty.
  Challenge students to think.
  Incorporate physical activity.

- *Provide feedback to students:*
  When answer is correct and confident, affirm briefly.
  When answer is correct but hesitant, provide more deliberate affirmation.
  When answer is incorrect but careless, make a simple correction.
  When answer is incorrect but student could get answer with help, prompt or
      backtrack to simpler question.
  If student is unable to respond, don't belabor the issue.

- *Monitor comprehension:*
  Require overt responses: Have students hold up response cards, physically display
      answers with manipulative materials, or respond chorally.
  Use a steering group: Observe the performance of a sample of students (including
      low achievers) in order to determine when to move on.

- *Support the participation of diverse learners:*
  Be conscious of your pattern of asking questions. Track whom you call on, how often
      you call on them, and how you respond to their answers.
  Become familiar with the discourse patterns characteristic of your culturally diverse
      students.
  Teach explicitly about the discourse patterns that are expected in school.
  Incorporate "alternative response formats" designed to engage all students rather than
      just one or two.

and put it over the word "like." Later, we talked to Courtney about her use of the popsicle sticks:

Using the "Pick Me" sticks helps me to make sure that I get around to everyone. Once a person's name is called, I keep that stick out of the can so everyone gets a chance. I find that unless I use a system like this, I have trouble keeping track of who's gotten a chance to participate and who hasn't. And some kids are so eager to volunteer that they'd probably monopolize the whole lesson.

Courtney doesn't use the popsicle sticks for every lesson, and we are certainly not suggesting that you do so. There are times when you won't want to call on students randomly, preferring to select particular individuals for particular questions. Nonetheless, the system helps Courtney sustain students' attention and distribute participation widely and fairly. It also enables her to keep the pace moving, because she doesn't have to deliberate each time she calls on someone.

Instead of a can (or Ken's "coffee mug system," described in Chapter 4), some teachers use a list of names or a seating chart to keep track of who has spoken, placing a tick mark by the name of each child who participates. Other teachers use "patterned turn taking," calling on students in some designated order. The research evidence on the usefulness of this practice is inconclusive. Some educators (e.g., Kounin, 1970) argue that patterned turn taking leads to inattention, because children know exactly when they will be called on. But research by Jere Brophy and Carolyn Evertson (1976) found that the use of patterned turn taking in small reading groups leads to higher achievement. One explanation for this finding is that patterned turn taking allows more reading to occur—no time is lost deciding who goes next. Another explanation is that the use of a pattern ensures that everyone has an opportunity to interact with the teacher.

Whichever system you choose, *the important point is to make sure that the interaction is not dominated by a few volunteers.* Some children are just not comfortable speaking in class and seek to avoid the risk of appearing foolish or stupid. In a study of teacher–student verbal interaction in four sixth-grade classrooms (Jones & Gerig, 1994), *32 percent of the students were classified as "silent."* During interviews, these students typically described themselves as shy (72 percent) and lacking in self-confidence (50 percent). Karen explained her silence by referring to an incident that happened *four years earlier:*

> I talk just a little in class. I'm afraid that what I say, someone won't like. When I was in the second grade, we were going to have a Thanksgiving dinner thing and students were going to be Pilgrims. I raised my hand and said I would like to be an Indian and would wear my hair in braids. Nobody said anything, and the teacher just went "Um hum," and it was embarrassing. (p. 177)

Our five teachers are well aware of the need to encourage shy students to participate. Listen to Barbara:

It's your job to keep everyone involved and to bring in the kids who are not talking. I generally ask, "What do you think?" or "Do you agree with what Peter said?" If a kid isn't comfortable talking, I may not call on them as frequently, and when I do, I try to be especially gentle. I'll ask something I know they know, or I'll call on them as soon as I see any gesture that indicates they're thinking about raising their hand. I also try to validate what the kid said, something like, "Peter just told us . . . ." But however I do it, I eventually get to everyone, and my kids know that.

"Getting to everyone" can be a daunting task, especially in a large class. One useful strategy is to use *response cards*—small chalkboards or dry-erase boards—on which students write one- or two-word responses to your questions. Response cards not only increase the rate of active student response; they also seem to improve students' academic achievement and engagement (Narayan et al., 1990).

Another strategy is to allow several students to answer a question instead of "grabbing" the first answer and moving on. In the following interaction, we see Garnetta increase participation by following this practice.

GARNETTA: **What do you do when you experiment?**
 STUDENT: **Invent things.**
GARNETTA: **OK, what else?**
 STUDENT: **Investigate!**
GARNETTA: **Good! That's a big word. What does investigate mean?**
 STUDENT: **When you be trying to find something out.**
 STUDENT: **When you be a detective and try to find something out.**
 STUDENT: **Finding out the facts—looking and finding out.**
GARNETTA: **Out of sight! (Writes on board: look at something, find out the facts, be a detective.)**

At times, distributing participation is difficult not because children are reluctant to speak and there are too *few* volunteers, but because there are too *many.* The more teachers stimulate interest in a particular lesson, the more students want to respond. This means greater competition for each turn (Doyle, 1986), and "bidding" for a chance to speak can become loud and unruly. During one visit to Garnetta's class, we watched her deal with this situation. She and the students were talking about a movie they had just seen, *A Connecticut Yankee in King Arthur's Court.* The children were incredibly excited about the movie and were eager to share their reactions.

GARNETTA: **Let's think about the ways people lived at the time of King Arthur. What did you see in the movie that was the same as the way we live now? [There are lots of "oohs," and calls of "Ms. Chain" as children compete for a chance to respond.] So many people want to talk, let's just go around, and hear one from everybody. Aleesha, you start.**
ALEESHA: **They rode horses and we ride horses. [Garnetta continues to call on students in order.]**

Garnetta was able to use a "round-robin" pattern of turn taking because her class is small (15 students). This approach might not work as well in a larger class, where too many children remain unengaged as they wait for their turn and where children seated at the "end of the line" sometimes feel cheated because they have nothing new to add. An alternative strategy is to have each child write a response and share it with one or two neighbors. This allows everyone to participate actively. You might then ask some of the groups to report on what they discussed.

One final thought: While you're thinking about ways to distribute participation widely, keep in mind the suggestions we made in Chapter 2 when we talked about the action zone phenomenon: (1) move around the room whenever possible; (2) establish eye contact with students seated farther away from you; (3) direct comments to students seated in the rear and on the sides; and (4) periodically change students' seats so that all students have an opportunity to be up front.

Providing Time to Think

Envision this scenario: You've just asked a well-formulated, carefully worded, higher-level question designed to stimulate critical thinking and problem solving. And you're met with total silence. Your face begins to feel flushed, and your heart beats a little faster. What to do now?

One reason why silence is so uncomfortable is that it's hard to interpret: Are students thinking about the question? Are they asleep? Are they so muddled they're unable to respond? Silence is also troubling to teachers because it can threaten the pace and momentum of the lesson. Even a few seconds of silence can seem like eternity. This helps to explain why many teachers wait less than *one second* before calling on a student (Rowe, 1974). Yet research demonstrates that if you extend *"wait time"* to *three or four seconds,* you can increase the quality of students' answers and promote participation. Extending wait time is also helpful to students with learning disabilities, who tend to process information more slowly than their peers.

Sometimes it's helpful to indicate to students that you don't expect an immediate answer. This legitimizes the silence and gives students an opportunity to formulate their responses. During Barbara's recitation lesson on *The Cay,* we saw her indicate to children that she wanted everyone to think for a while before responding:

> BARBARA: **What's one survival technique that CT used? [Children raise their hands.] Jim? [He had not raised his hand.]**
>
> JIM: **Using a carved twig for fire.**
>
> BARBARA: **Show us on the board how the twig was carved. While he's drawing, the rest of you think of another. [He draws a twig that has been carved. Barbara turns to the class.] Why would that burn more easily? [A few students raise their hands.] Everyone put your hands down and think for a minute. [There's a long pause. Then a few hands go back up; then some more. Finally Barbara nods to a student.]**
>
> GIRL: **Because there are more places to burn?**
>
> BARBARA: **Right.**

Allowing children to write an answer to your question is another way of providing them with time to think. Written responses also help to maintain students' engagement, because everyone has to construct a response. In addition, students who are uncomfortable speaking extemporaneously can read from their written papers. We observed an example of this strategy when Barbara's class began their study of *Sarah, Plain and Tall* (MacLachlan, 1985). Barbara gave them the following directions:

BARBARA: Read the first chapter silently. While you do that, I'm going to give each of you a piece of paper. Write down just a little bit about each of the characters you meet. [When students have finished reading and writing, Barbara regains their attention.] OK, you met Sarah. What did you learn about her?

Once you have selected someone to respond, it's also important to provide that student with an opportunity to think. This is another kind of wait time, and research has documented that here, too, teachers often jump in too soon (Rowe, 1974). Sometimes they provide the answer themselves or call on another child. This is particularly tempting if other students are frantically waving their hands. Watch the way Ken deals with this situation during a lesson on number sequences:

KEN: What is Sequence C? Robin? [Robin is silent. Other children in the class are waving their hands to answer and murmuring "ooh, ooh, Mr. K. . . ."] Let her take her time. This is tricky. Give her a chance. . . .

ROBIN: It's adding on every odd number, 1, 3, 5 . . .

KEN: Hmmm, I wonder if that continues . . .

Stimulating and Maintaining Interest

In previous chapters, we have discussed Jacob Kounin's classic study (1970) of the differences between orderly and disorderly classrooms. One finding of that study was that children are more involved in work and less disruptive when teachers attempt to involve nonreciting children in the recitation task, maintain their attention, and keep them "on their toes." Kounin called this behavior *group alerting*. Observations of our five teachers reveal that they frequently use group-alerting strategies to stimulate attention and to maintain the pace of the lesson. For example, watch how Courtney injects suspense into a phonics lesson on the short "a" sound:

COURTNEY: Everybody, close your eyes. I have something really special to share with you. [She takes out a picnic basket covered with a small quilt.] Okay, now open your eyes. What could be in here? [Her voice is filled with wonder.] Let's hear some predictions.

STUDENT: Snacks!

COURTNEY: Karen, what do you think?

STUDENT: Letters.

COURTNEY: What do you think, Lawrence?

STUDENT: Markers.

COURTNEY: Well, let me reach in here and take out one thing for us to see. Tomorrow we'll take out another thing. [She takes out a plastic apple.]

STUDENTS: It's an apple!

Challenges to students can also be a way of keeping them on their toes. During a math lesson, for example, Viviana told her students, "This next one is not baby stuff. This one you really have to think about and read the directions." The excitement in the room was almost palpable, and afterward we heard students murmuring, "This is easy, this is baby stuff, I can do this." Viviana's challenge is reminiscent of the behavior of "Teacher X," one of the subjects in Hermine Marshall's (1987) study of three teachers' motivational strategies. Marshall found that Teacher X frequently used statements designed to challenge students to think: "I'm going to trick you," "Get your brain started. . . . You're going to think," "Get your mind started," "Look bright-eyed and bushy-tailed" (stated, according to Marshall, "with enthusiasm and a touch of humor"). This frequent use of statements to stimulate and maintain student attention was in sharp contrast to the statements made by the other two teachers in the study. In fact, Teacher Y and Teacher Z *never* used the strategy of alerting students to pay attention, and they rarely challenged students to think. The vast majority of their directives were attempts to return students to the task *after* attention and interest had waned.

In the next vignette, we see Viviana teach about action verbs. Although this can be deadly dull, the room was alive with excitement because Viviana allowed her students to participate physically:

VIVIANA: **Let's stand up. Run in place. Run, run, run, run. Don't stop until I tell you to. [All the children run in place by their desks.] You are doing something. What are you doing?**

STUDENTS: **We're running.**

VIVIANA: **So run is an action. Something you are doing. OK, stop. Let's . . . hop. [Children begin to hop in place.] Are you doing something?**

STUDENTS: **Yes.**

VIVIANA: **What are you doing?**

STUDENTS: **We're hopping.**

VIVIANA: **So hop is an action, something you are doing. [The pattern repeats as children jump and then skip around the room back to their desks.]**

Providing Feedback

Research has demonstrated the importance of providing feedback to students (Fisher et al., 1980). But how can you provide appropriate feedback while maintaining the pace and momentum of your lesson? Barak Rosenshine (1986) reviewed the research on effective teaching and has developed a set of guidelines that may be helpful. According to Rosenshine, when students give correct, confident answers, you can simply ask another question or provide a brief verbal or nonverbal indication that they are correct. If students are correct but hesitant, however, a more deliberate affirmation is necessary. You might also explain *why* the answer is correct ("Yes, that's correct, because . . .") in order to reinforce the material.

When students provide an incorrect answer, the feedback process is trickier. If you think the child has made a careless error, you can make a simple correction and move on. If you decide that the student can arrive at the correct answer with a little help, you can provide hints or prompts. Sometimes it's useful to backtrack to a simpler question that you think the child can answer and then work up to your original question step by step.

There are times when students are simply unable to respond to your question. When that happens, there's little point in belaboring the issue by providing prompts or cues; this will only make the recitation sluggish. Ken allows students in this situation to "pass," and both he and Garnetta permit children to call on a friend to help. These practices not only help to maintain the pace but also allow students to "save face." Meanwhile, the teachers make a mental note that they need to reteach the material to the individuals having difficulty.

In the following vignette, we see Viviana recognize the need to reteach the concept of thirds to her whole class. Her students had been working on "halves" with Cuisenaire rods. After the students had seen that two yellow rods were equivalent to one orange rod, and that each yellow rod was one-half of the orange, Viviana asked the children to take the blue rod (the "nine" rod):

VIVIANA: Everyone have the blue rod? OK, divide it into equal parts.
ROBERT: [A student calls out] Three greens!
VIVIANA: Robert, by yelling out you are not being fair to the other children, because you don't give them a chance to figure out the answer. [She scans the room and sees that everyone has three greens lined up with one blue.] How many greens equal one blue?
STUDENTS: Three.
VIVIANA: If you give one green to your friend, how many are left?
STUDENTS: Two.
VIVIANA: Good. If you give one green to your friend, what *fraction* have you given away? [There is silence. Children look puzzled. A few children try a guess: 1/2? One? Two? Noting the extreme confusion, Viviana provides the answer.] You have given away *one-third*. And you kept *two-thirds*. We'll talk about this more tomorrow. Now we have to clean up and go to lunch.

Afterward, we spoke with Viviana about what had happened during the lesson. She told us why she had decided to "give up" on her question about thirds:

There was just too much confusion, and I didn't want the children to get frustrated. It was also too close to lunch time to start reteaching about thirds; when they're hungry it's hard to think. It was better to just tell them the answer. Tomorrow I can pick up from where we left off.

We also talked with Viviana about how to provide appropriate feedback when children's answers are clearly incorrect. She was very emphatic as she talked about the need to be honest and clear. We think her perspective is worth remembering:

I strongly believe that teachers should not sugarcoat their responses to children's answers for fear of hurting children's feelings. If the answer is wrong, the child needs to know it's wrong. You can reject an answer without rejecting a child. But you have to explain why the answer is wrong. I often ask other children to help out. When I get the right answer from another child, I go back to the first child and check to see if they now understand. It's important not to leave kids hanging.

Monitoring Comprehension

A simple way to assess comprehension is to have students respond overtly to your questions by answering chorally, putting thumbs up or down, or holding up cards. For example, you might give children cards reading "yes" or "no," colored red or green, or depicting a happy face or a sad face, which they then hold up in response to your yes or no questions. Another suggestion is to give each student a set of four cards labeled A, B, C, and D and ask questions in multiple-choice format (Leahy, Lyon, Thompson, & Wiliam, 2005). In mathematics, students can use number cards or operation sign cards to show you the correct answer. "Number fans" (Rief, 1993) are also useful for whole-group responses; they can be made by fastening together three small pieces of cardboard or index cards with the numerals 1, 2, and 3 written on separate cards to indicate "strongly agree" (1), "kind of agree" (2), or "disagree" (3). Students can also use small chalkboards or dry-erase boards to write one- or two-word responses (Narayan et al., 1990).

You can also have children manipulate some material at their seats and physically display their work. During one visit to Garnetta's class, she was reviewing division with her students. She had students work with colored blocks at their desks, while one student did the division problem at the chalkboard:

GARNETTA: OK, now count out 48. I see most of you have taken four ten blocks and eight ones blocks. Put the other ones away. We're going to divide the 48 by four. [There's a gasp, as if the children think that's too hard.] You're going to divide the 48 blocks into four groups. [One child murmurs, "Oh, that's easy!"] Rashad, you come to the board and do the problem while everyone else works with the blocks. OK, let's see how many you put in each group. [She scans the room to see how the students did on the problem.] I want only hands.

STUDENT: 12.

GARNETTA: Everyone, look up here at the problem on the board. Rashad, what did you get?

RASHAD: 12.

GARNETTA: OK, so we agree. Now let's do this problem. [She writes another problem on the chalkboard.]

You can also check on students' understanding by observing the performance of a "steering group"—a sample of students whose performance is used as an indicator that the class is "with you" and that it's all right to move on to a new topic. Be careful, however, about choosing students for the steering group. If you select only high achievers, their performance may lead you to overestimate the comprehension of the class as a whole.

During one discussion with Garnetta, she indicated that Joelle, a low-achieving student, was a key member of her mathematics steering group. She shared this example of how Joelle helps her to monitor the class's understanding:

> We were working on place value, and I wrote 382 on the board. I asked Joelle to tell us which number was in the ones column, which was in the tens column, and which was in the hundreds column and what that meant. He got it! That was a clue that the lesson was successful, and I confirmed it by sampling a couple of the other students.

Supporting the Participation of Diverse Learners

By understanding and appreciating the fact that students' home patterns of discourse may not match the discourse pattern used in recitation, you are better able to ensure that all students in your class—regardless of cultural background or gender—will have equitable opportunities to participate. Although there are no simple solutions, several guidelines may be useful. (These are summarized in the Practical Tips box on managing recitations on page 314.) First, teachers need to be conscious of their patterns of asking questions, using wait time, and providing praise (Arends, 2008). This means tracking which students you call on, how often you call on them, and how you respond to their answers. (Since it is difficult to monitor your own questioning patterns, it's helpful to have someone do this for you.) Second, it is essential to become familiar with the discourse patterns characteristic of your culturally diverse students (Arends, 2008). Before assuming that children are being disrespectful by calling out, for example, it's a good idea to ask whether this behavior could represent a culturally learned style of discourse that is appropriate and normal in settings outside of school.

Although accommodation to students' discourse patterns may be possible and appropriate at times, some educators (e.g., Delpit, 1995) argue that teachers need to be explicit about the discourse patterns that are expected (and usually implicit) in school. Indeed, the explicit teaching of this knowledge is considered a teacher's "moral responsibility," because it enables children to participate fully in the classroom community and the larger society (Gallego, Cole, & Laboratory of Comparative Human Cognition, 2001, p. 979). Thus our third guideline emphasizes the need to provide explicit instruction on the discourse pattern of recitations (I-R-E) and to allow children to practice these communication skills.

Finally, teachers can incorporate "alternative response formats" designed to engage all students rather than just one or two (Walsh & Sattes, 2005). Some we've already mentioned—such as choral responses, overt responses (e.g., "thumbs up" or "thumbs down"), and work samples (e.g., students individually solve a problem, perhaps on an individual chalkboard, and hold it up so the teacher can see). All of these require students to answer individually, but others allow children to work cooperatively before responding to the teacher's question.

✇ PAUSE AND REFLECT

Think about the strategies for managing recitations described in the previous section. What are the five most important things you will want to keep in mind as you plan a recitation?

These more active, participatory response formats may be more comfortable for children who find the traditional pattern of question-response-evaluation unfamiliar or intimidating.

DESIGNING AND IMPLEMENTING EFFECTIVE DISCUSSIONS

Thus far, the chapter has examined four major problems associated with recitations and has provided some suggestions for avoiding these problems. Now we turn to the second type of oral interaction, the discussion. As we said earlier, although the terms *recitation* and *discussion* are often used interchangeably, it is important to distinguish clearly between them. (Refer again to Table 11.1.)

Let's consider the following example of a discussion, which we witnessed in Garnetta's classroom. The class had just read a story entitled *Buford, the Little Bighorn* by Bill Peet (1993). Buford, "a scrawny little runt of a mountain sheep," has a huge pair of horns that cause him considerable difficulty throughout the story. At the very end, however, Buford discovers that his horns have some use after all. Using them as skis, he is able to escape from hunters and becomes a "star attraction" at a winter ski resort. The students are discussing whether Buford would ever consider returning his horns to the normal size.

GARNETTA: My ladies and gents, let's review how to behave in a discussion. If someone's talking, we don't cut them off, right? Raise your hand, and I'll recognize you. Remember, you can't just say "I agree" or "I disagree"—you have to be able to defend your answer. What does that mean? Sheneika?

SHENEIKA: You have to try to convince people you're right.

GARNETTA: OK, you have to give reasons why you think what you think. You have to explain. Luis, you want to start us off, tell us what you think, and give us some supporting arguments?

LUIS: Yes.

GARNETTA: Yes, he should get his horns trimmed? [Luis nods.] Why do you say yes?

LUIS: 'Cause they're too long, and if he fall down he can get hurt.

VICTOR: I disagree. In the story, when he fell, he ended up hanging on a tree. So the horns help him.

TANAYA: I disagree 'cause the horns made him fall in the first place. He should take off his horns so the hunters won't get to him.

GRANDON: I agree with Luis. If Buford don't get his horns cut, he'll trip and get hurt.

ALEESHA: Yeah, I agree with Luis too. He'll fall if he don't get them cut.

SHENEIKA: I disagree, because Buford, when he was walking, he fell, and his horns saved him.

VICTOR: Yeah, and if he get his horns cut off, then the folks from all over the world won't come and he won't be a big star.

GARNETTA: Do you want to say something, James?

JAMES: I don't want him to get his horns cut off because then he won't be able to ski.

Later that day, Garnetta talked with us about the discussion and the progress that students had made since the beginning of the year:

It used to be that two or three students dominated everything, and the others would not join the discussion. Victor used to jump on anybody who disagreed with him, and the other children actually seemed afraid to speak up. Now he's beginning to realize that other people are entitled to their opinions. Instead of just Victor and Lucia doing all the talking, just about everyone is willing to express an opinion. Sometimes I still have to intervene to make sure people get a chance to speak, but not as much. . . . They've made a lot of progress since the beginning of the year, but they still need the teacher to make sure they stick with the topic and listen to each other. If we want them to be problem solvers and to develop critical thinking skills, we've got to let them practice. And it takes practice on the part of the teacher too. We've got to learn to guide the discussion without taking over.

As Garnetta points out, it takes time to learn how to participate in a discussion, and it's not easy to break out of the teacher-dominated interaction pattern so characteristic of classrooms. But even kindergartners can begin to learn to talk and listen to one another. For example, Courtney frequently ends the day with a "sharing circle," another meeting component that is part of the Responsive Classroom approach. (Although the sharing circle would normally be part of morning meeting, Courtney has found that it works better at another time of day, because the morning meeting can become too long for her students to sit still.) Observing the children's interaction, it is clear that the children have been taught exactly how to participate in this event. Each child with something to share first states his or her information and then invites questions and comments from three children. Here's Michael's contribution:

MICHAEL: I went to Hershey Park. I am ready for comments and questions.
CHILD 1: Did you go in a pool?
MICHAEL: No, it was cold.
CHILD 2: Was there a pool of melted chocolate?
MICHAEL: No.
CHILD 3: Did you have fun?
MICHAEL: Yes.

When you're learning to lead a discussion, keep in mind three basic suggestions (Gall & Gillett, 1981). First, it may be wise to *limit the size of the group.* It's difficult to have a student-centered discussion with a large number of participants. One option is to use the "fishbowl" method, in which five or six students carry on the discussion in the middle of the room, while the rest of the class sit in a large circle around them and act as observers and recorders. Another solution is to divide the class into small discussion groups of five, with one student in each group acting as a discussion leader.

Second, *arrange students so they can make eye contact.* It's hard to speak directly to someone if all you can see is the back of a head. If at all possible, students should move their desks into an arrangement that allows them to be face to face. Finally, *prepare students for participating in a student-centered discussion by explicitly teaching the prerequisite skills:*

- Talk to each other, not just to the moderator.
- Give others a turn to speak.
- Ask others what they think.
- Allow others to have opinions without attacking them.
- Listen to others' ideas.
- Acknowledge others' ideas.
- Question irrelevant remarks.
- Ask for clarification.
- Ask for reasons for others' opinions.
- Give reasons for your opinions.

Because some students have difficulty taking turns, you can use a prop (e.g., a special pen, a wand, or a toy) to designate the speaker. The prop is passed from child to child. This encourages turn taking and helps children remember not to call out.

James Dillon (1994) also provides some extremely helpful guidelines for preparing and conducting discussions. (See the Practical Tips box.) Note that Dillon advises against asking questions during a student-centered discussion for fear of turning the discussion into a recitation. Although his concern is well-founded, other discussion experts believe that asking questions can be an appropriate and effective way to keep conversation going (McCrone, 2005). In fact, Stephen Brookfield and Stephen Preskill (1999) identify several kinds of questions that are especially helpful in maintaining momentum:

Questions that ask for more evidence

How do you know that?

What data is that claim based on?

What does the author say that supports your argument?

Where did you find that view expressed in the text?

What evidence would you give to someone who doubted your interpretation?

Questions that ask for clarification

Can you put that another way?

What do you mean by that?

What's an example of what you are talking about?

Can you explain the term you just used?

PRACTICAL TIPS FOR

DESIGNING AND IMPLEMENTING EFFECTIVE DISCUSSIONS

- *Carefully formulate the discussion question* (making sure that it is not in a form that invites a yes/no or either/or answer), along with subsidiary questions, embedded questions, follow-up questions, and related questions.

- *Create a question outline,* identifying at least three subquestions and at least four alternative answers to the main question.

- *Present the discussion question to the class,* writing it on the chalkboard, on an overhead transparency, or on paper distributed to the class. After reading the question aloud, go on to give the sense of the question, identifying terms, explaining the relevance of the question, connecting it to a previous discussion or class activity, and so on. End with an invitation to the class to begin addressing the question.

- Initially, *help the class focus on the question,* rather than giving answers to it. For example, invite the class to tell what they know about the question, what it means to them.

- *DO NOT COMMENT AFTER THE FIRST STUDENT'S CONTRIBUTION.* (If you do, the interaction will quickly become I-R-E.) In addition, do not ask, "What does someone else think about that?" (If you do, you invite statements of difference or opposition to the first position, and your discussion turns into a debate.)

- In general, *do not ask questions beyond the first question.* Use instead nonquestion alternatives: statements (the thoughts that occurred to you in relation to what the speaker has just said; reflective statements that basically restate the speaker's contribution; statements indicating interest in hearing more about what the speaker has just said; statements indicating the relationship between what the speaker has just said and what a previous speaker has said); signals (sounds or words indicating interest in what the speaker has said); even silence. (Dillon acknowledges that deliberate silence is the hardest of all for teachers to do. To help teachers remain quiet, he recommends silently singing "Baa, baa, black sheep" after each student's contribution.)

- *Facilitate the discussion by*
    Locating: "Where are we now? What are we saying?"
    Summarizing: "What have we accomplished? agreed on?"
    Opening: "What shall we do next?"
    Tracking: "We seem a little off track here. How can we all get back on the same line of thought?"
    Pacing: "Just a minute, I wonder whether we're not moving a little too fast here. Let's take a closer look at this idea . . ."

- When it is time to end the discussion, *help students to summarize the discussion and identify the remaining questions.*

Linking or extension questions

Is there any connection between what you've just said and what Rajiv was saying a moment ago?

How does your comment fit in with Neng's earlier comment?

How does your observation relate to what the group decided last week?

Does your idea challenge or support what we seem to be saying?

Hypothetical questions

What might have happened if Joey hadn't missed the school bus?

In the video we just saw, how might the story have turned out if Arnold had caught the ball?

If the author had wanted the teacher to be a more sympathetic figure, how might he have changed this conversation?

Cause-and-effect questions

What is likely to be the effect of the name calling?

How might the rumor affect the school play?

Summary and synthesis questions

What are the one or two most important ideas that emerged from this discussion?

What remains unresolved or contentious about this topic?

What do you understand better as a result of today's discussion?

Based on our discussion today, what do we need to talk about next time if we're to understand this issue better?

What key word or concept best captures our discussion today?

CONCLUDING COMMENTS

This chapter has focused on two different patterns of verbal interaction: recitations and discussions. It's important not to get them confused—to think that you're leading a discussion when you're actually conducting a recitation. Also keep in mind the criticisms that have been leveled against recitations, and reflect on how frequently you dominate (or wish to dominate) the verbal interaction in your classroom. Ask yourself whether you also provide opportunities for student-centered discussion, during which you serve as a facilitator (rather than a questioner) and encourage direct student–student interaction. Reflect on the level of thinking that you require from students. The classroom recitation can serve a number of useful functions, but *overuse* suggests that your curriculum consists largely of names, dates, facts, and algorithms (Cazden, 1988).

SUMMARY

This chapter began by examining some of the major criticisms of recitation, as well as the useful functions it can serve. It then distinguished recitations from discussions. Next, the chapter considered the hazards that recitations present to teachers and suggested a number of strategies for avoiding these problems. Finally, we looked at an example of a discussion, reflected on reasons for the infrequent use of discussion, and briefly considered a number of guidelines for managing this type of verbal interaction.

Characteristic Pattern of a Recitation

- I-R-E (teacher initiation, student response, teacher evaluation) or I-R-F (teacher initiation, student response, teacher follow-up).
- Quick pace.
- To review material, to elaborate on a text.

Criticisms of Recitation

- Gives the teacher a dominant role, the student a passive one.
- Lacks interaction among students.
- Emphasizes recall over higher-level thinking skills.
- Promotes public evaluation, which can lead to negative interdependence.

Five Functions of Recitation

- Provides opportunity to check on students' comprehension.
- Involves students in presentation of material.
- Allows for contact with individuals in a group setting.
- Helps to maintain attention level.
- Offers an opportunity to push students to construct more complete responses.

Characteristics of a Discussion

- I-R-R-R.
- Student-initiated questions.
- Student comments on contributions of peers.
- Slower pace.
- Intended to stimulate thinking, foster problem solving, and examine implications.

The Pitfalls of Recitations

- Unequal participation.
- Losing the pace, focus, and student involvement.
- Difficulty in monitoring comprehension.
- Incompatibility with communication patterns that children bring to school.

Designing and Implementing Effective Recitations

- Distribute chances for participation by
  Using patterned turn taking.
  Using names in a jar.
  Using a checklist.
  Gently encouraging silent students to participate.
  Ensuring that males and females have equal opportunity to participate.
- Provide time to think about answers before responding.
- Stimulate and maintain interest by
  Using group-alerting strategies.
  Using humor and novelty.
  Including challenges to students.
  Incorporating physical activity.
- Provide feedback without losing the pace.
- Monitor comprehension by
  Requiring overt responses.
  Observing a steering group.

- Support the participation of diverse learners.
    Be conscious of patterns of asking and responding to questions.
    Become familiar with discourse patterns of different cultures.
    Accommodate students' discourse styles where possible.
    Provide explicit instruction on discourse patterns of recitations.
    Use alternative response formats.

Designing and Implementing Effective Discussions

- Limit group size.
- Arrange students so they have eye contact.
- Teach discussion skills.
- Act as facilitator rather than questioner.
- Plan discussion questions (and subsidiary questions) and outline.
- At the beginning of the discussion, focus on the question, not on answers.
- After the initial question, use nonquestion alternatives to keep discussion going (or use questions very judiciously).
- Manage the discussion by locating, summarizing, opening, tracking, and pacing.

When planning your lessons, think about the extent to which you use recitations and discussions in your classroom. Think about the level of the questions that you ask: Are all of your questions low-level, factual questions that can be answered with a word or two, or are your questions designed to stimulate thinking and problem solving? Ask yourself whether you consistently dominate the interaction or also provide opportunities for real discussion among students.

Activities for Skill Building and Reflection

In Class

1. Your colleague has asked you to help him figure out why his students are not paying attention in class. He would like you to observe him and offer feedback. What follows is the transcript of a session you observed. Using what you know about distributing participation, stimulating and maintaining interest, and monitoring comprehension, identify the trouble spots in your colleague's lesson and provide three specific suggestions for improvement. When you enter the class, Mr. B. is perched on a stool in front of the room with the science book in his hand.

    Mr. B.   Who remembers what photosynthesis is? [No response.] Do you remember yesterday when we looked at green plants and we discussed how a plant makes its own food? [Mr. B. notices that Thea is nodding.] Thea, do you remember about photosynthesis?

    Thea: Yeah.

    Mr. B.   Well, can you tell the class about it?

    Thea: It has something to do with light and chlorophyll.

    Mr. B.   Good. Tom, can you add to this? [Tom was drawing in his notebook.]

    Tom: No.

Mr. B. Tom, Thea told us that photosynthesis had to do with light and chlorophyll. Do you recall our discussion from yesterday when we defined photosynthesis?

Tom: Sort of.

Mr. B. What do you mean? Didn't you write down the definition with the rest of the class? Look in your notebook and tell me the definition. [Tom starts to page through his notebook. Many of the students have begun to whisper and snicker. Some are looking in their notebooks.] How many of you have found the page where we defined photosynthesis? [Seven students raise their hands.] Good. Would somebody read to me that definition? Thea.

Thea: Photosynthesis is the process of forming sugars and starches in plants from water and carbon dioxide when sunlight acts upon chlorophyll.

Mr. B. Excellent. Does everyone understand? [A few students nod.] Good. Tomorrow we will be having a quiz about plants and photosynthesis. Tom, will you be ready for the quiz?

Tom: Sure, Mr. B.

Mr. B. OK, now let's all turn to page 135 in our science texts and read about the uses of plants.

2. Monitoring students' comprehension is sometimes problematic. Choose one of the following topics and suggest two different ways in which a teacher could elicit overt participation in order to assess student understanding.

   a. Main characters and their traits.
   b. Fractional parts.
   c. "Greater than" and "less than" symbols.
   d. Syllabication.
   e. Spanish vocabulary words.
   f. State capitals.
   g. Types of clouds.

On Your Own

1. Visit a classroom and observe a recitation. On a seating chart, map the verbal interaction by placing a check mark or an X in the "seat" of each child who participates. (See Figure 11.2 for an example.) Analyze your results, and draw conclusions about how widely and fairly participation is distributed in the class you visit.

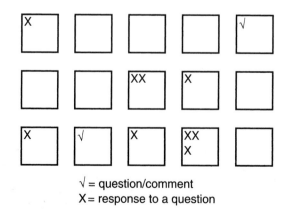

√ = question/comment
X = response to a question

Figure 11.2 On Your Own Exercise

2. We know that recitation and discussion are often confused. Observe and record 10 minutes of a class "discussion." Then, using the following checklist, which shows some of the properties of discussions, determine whether the verbal interaction actually meets the criteria for a discussion or is more like a recitation.
   - Students are the predominant speakers.
   - The verbal interaction pattern is not I-R-E but a mix of statements and questions by a mix of teacher and students.
   - The pace is longer and slower.
   - The primary purpose is to stimulate a variety of responses, to encourage students to consider different points of view, to foster problem solving, and the like.
   - Evaluation consists of agree/disagree, rather than right/wrong.

For Your Portfolio

Create two lesson plans, one that includes a recitation and one that includes a discussion. In sequence, list the questions that you will use for each. In a brief commentary, explain how these lessons differ from one another and why the chosen teaching strategy is appropriate for the content of the lesson.

FOR FURTHER READING

Brookfield, S. D., & Preskill, S. (2005). *Discussion as a way of teaching: Tools and techniques for democratic classrooms* (2nd ed.). San Francisco: Jossey-Bass.

This book offers a wealth of practical information on how to plan, conduct, and assess classroom discussions. The authors describe strategies for starting discussions and maintaining their momentum. A chapter on discussion in culturally diverse classrooms provides valuable information on eliciting diverse views and voices.

Gambrell, L. B., & Almasi, J. F. (Eds.). (1996). *Lively discussions! Fostering engaged reading.* Newark, DE: International Reading Association.

The first chapter of this book contrasts recitation and discussion and clearly explains the difference between the two in terms of the teacher's and students' roles. Other chapters offer practical strategies that teachers can use to foster discussions that promote literacy development. The book presents many examples of children collaboratively constructing meaning and considering alternative interpretations of a text in order to arrive at new understandings.

Henning, J. E. (2008). *The art of discussion-based teaching: Opening up conversation in the classroom.* New York: Routledge.

This is a valuable text for K–12 teachers who want to foster more student-centered discussion in their classrooms. The book provides practical advice for asking questions, guiding discussions, and keeping students involved. A particularly helpful section focuses on ways to support culturally and linguistically diverse students.

Walsh, J. A., & Sattes, B. D. (2005). *Quality questioning: Research-based practice to engage every learner.* Thousand Oaks, CA: Corwin Press.

Based on the authors' QUILT framework (Questioning and Understanding to Improve Learning and Thinking), this book discusses preparing questions, presenting questions, prompting student response, processing student responses, teaching students to generate questions, and reflecting on questioning practice. Walsh and Sattes suggest strategies to engage all students in the teacher's questions and prompt students to generate their own questions.

PART IV

PROTECTING AND RESTORING ORDER

Newspaper headlines about crime, violence, and vandalism convey a grim, frightening image of classrooms, but most of the misbehaviors that teachers encounter are far more mundane—inattention, talking to neighbors, not having homework done, calling out, and forgetting to bring supplies and books. Nevertheless, behaviors such as these can be aggravating and wearing, can take precious time away from teaching and learning, and can threaten a caring community. Clearly, teachers must have a way of thinking about such problems and a repertoire of disciplinary strategies for dealing with them effectively.

The two chapters in this section focus on strategies for responding effectively to instances of problem behavior. Chapter 12 begins with a set of principles to guide your thinking about how best to respond in a constructive fashion. We then consider a hierarchy of strategies for dealing with a variety of problem behaviors, starting with strategies that are minimally obtrusive and easy to implement and concluding with those that require considerable time and effort. In Chapter 13, we turn to the issue of school violence. First we look at the frequency and severity of school violence. Then we consider approaches for preventing and coping with hostile, aggressive, and dangerous behavior.

Both chapters echo themes heard in earlier chapters—namely, the importance of building community and fostering positive teacher-student relationships. When students are inattentive, resistant, or disruptive, it's easy to fall back on punitive, authoritarian reactions—"Stop that or else!" "Because I said so!" "Go to the principal's office!" "That's three days of detention!" But responses like this destroy relationships with students. Resentment builds, defiance escalates, and an atmosphere of "us against them" begins to take hold. Moreover, such responses are usually ineffective, leading teachers to conclude that "nothing can be done with these kids."

As we have stated in earlier chapters, research consistently indicates that students are more likely to engage in cooperative, responsible behavior and adhere to classroom norms when they perceive their teachers to be supportive and caring. Thus teachers who have positive relationships with students are better able to *prevent* inappropriate behavior. But we believe that *teacher-student relationships also play a key role in a teacher's ability to respond effectively to problem behaviors.* If your students perceive you as fair, trustworthy, and "on their side," they are likely to comply more readily with your disciplinary interventions.

RESPONDING EFFECTIVELY TO PROBLEM BEHAVIORS

Not too long ago, we spoke with Cheryl, a first-year teacher whose class was giving her a hard time. It was only October, but she was close to tears as she talked about the disrespectful and disruptive behavior of her fifth-graders. "I'm more like a cop than a teacher," she told us, and she was both surprised and dismayed by the antagonism she felt toward her students. She had always "loved children so much." What had gone wrong?

As we talked, it became clear that Cheryl's problem was not due to any lack of clear rules and routines or to boring, tedious instruction:

It's not like they don't understand what I want. On the first day of school, we talked a lot about the rules. You know, whisper quietly, don't interrupt, raise your hand to speak. . . . I thought we were off to such a great start. They were so well-behaved! But now they just don't seem to care. I'll remind them about a rule, like listening when the teacher is giving a lesson, and for a few minutes they're

OK, but then they start shouting out, getting up to sharpen pencils, throwing erasers back and forth. I get so frustrated, I just start yelling—something I said I'd never do. I don't know . . . I just don't understand how to get them to follow all those great rules I set up. Sometimes I tell them that we're not going to do any interesting things anymore, and I'm just going to give them worksheets to do every day. But that's not the kind of classroom I always dreamed of. I want my classroom to be exciting. I want my kids to love coming to school.

This first-year teacher had learned a sad fact of classroom life: Having clear, reasonable rules and routines doesn't automatically mean that everyone will follow them. At the beginning of the school year, students work hard at figuring out the teacher—determining teachers' expectations and requirements, the amount of socializing they will tolerate, and how far they can be pushed (see Figure 12.1). Most students will pursue their agendas within the limits the teacher sets, but they need to know those limits. This underscores the importance of communicating your behavioral expectations to students (the topic of Chapter 4)—and then *enforcing those expectations.* During our discussions on misbehavior, Garnetta, Ken, Barbara, Courtney, and Viviana repeatedly stressed the importance of following through on the rules and routines that you've planned and taught to your students. As Barbara put it, "If you tell kids to do something, then you have to make sure they do it. Otherwise, you're communicating that you don't really mean it."

In this chapter, we consider ways of responding to the problems you may encounter—from minor, nondisruptive infractions to chronic, more serious misbehaviors.

PRINCIPLES FOR DEALING WITH INAPPROPRIATE BEHAVIOR

There is little research on the relative effectiveness of disciplinary strategies (see Emmer & Aussiker, 1990), but six principles guide our discussion (see Table 12.1). First, *disciplinary strategies must be consistent with the goal of creating a safe, caring classroom environment.* You need to achieve order, but you also need to choose strategies that support your relationship with students, help them to become

Figure 12.1 *Source:* ADAM @ HOME © 1997 by UNIVERSAL UCLICK. Reprinted with permission. All rights reserved.

TABLE 12.1 Principles for Dealing with Inappropriate Behavior

1. Choose disciplinary strategies that are consistent with the goals of creating a safe, caring classroom environment and preserving the dignity of each student.
2. Keep the instructional program going with a minimum of disruption.
3. Consider the context when deciding whether or not a particular action constitutes misbehavior.
4. Be timely and accurate when responding to behavior problems.
5. Match the severity of the disciplinary strategy with the misbehavior you are trying to eliminate.
6. Be "culturally responsive," because differences in norms, values, and styles of communication can have a direct effect on students' behavior.

self-regulating, and allow them to save face in front of their peers. Richard Curwin and Allen Mendler (1988), authors of *Discipline with Dignity,* put it this way:

> Students will protect their dignity at all costs, even with their lives if pushed hard enough. In the game of chicken, with two cars racing at top speed toward a cliff, the loser is the one who steps on the brake. Nothing explains this bizarre reasoning better than the need for peer approval and dignity. (p. 27)

For more information about Curwin and Mendler's work, see Box 12.1.

In order to preserve your relationship with students and protect their dignity, it is important to avoid power struggles that may cause students to lose face with their peers. Our five teachers speak with misbehaving students calmly and quietly. They don't bring up past sins. They take care to separate the child's *character* from the specific *misbehavior;* instead of attacking the child as a person ("You're lazy"), they talk about what the child has done ("You have not handed in the last two homework assignments"). When more than a brief intervention is necessary, they try to meet with students privately.

On the second day of school, we witnessed a good example of disciplining with dignity in Garnetta's classroom. Even though it was so early in the school year, Tanya was already displaying the behaviors that had contributed to her notorious reputation:

 During the first hour of the morning, Tanya breaks down in tears, refuses to participate in a class activity, punches two children passing by her desk, and creates a fuss about her place in the bathroom line. She gets little work done without individual supervision, constantly asks Garnetta for assistance, and pouts if immediate help is not forthcoming. At 10:00, when Tanya is again in tears, Garnetta tells her class they have five minutes of free time. She goes over to Tanya and speaks quietly with her. The two of them go into the hallway. After a few minutes, Garnetta comes back alone; Tanya follows shortly. She sits down at her desk and begins to work on the assignment that Garnetta has just given. After about 10 minutes, Garnetta asks Tanya to go on an important errand to the office. We are astounded by the smile on Tanya's face as she leaves the room. She returns shortly, and there are no problems for the rest of the morning.

MEET THE EDUCATORS   BOX 12.1

MEET RICHARD CURWIN AND ALLEN MENDLER

Richard Curwin and Allen Mendler are widely known authors, speakers, consultants, and workshop leaders who focus on issues of classroom management, discipline, and motivation. Curwin has been a seventh-grade teacher, a teacher of children with emotional disturbance, and a college professor. Mendler is a school psychologist who has worked extensively with children of all ages in general and special education settings. Together they developed the *Discipline with Dignity* program, which was first published in 1988.

Some Major Ideas about Classroom Management

- Dealing with student behavior is part of the job.
- Management strategies must maintain the dignity of each student.
- Discipline plans should focus on teaching responsibility rather than obtaining compliance.
- In a typical classroom, 80 percent of the students rarely break rules and don't really need a discipline plan; 15 percent break rules on an occasional basis and need a clear set of expectations and consequences; 5 percent are chronic rule breakers. A good discipline plan controls the 15 percent without backing the 5 percent into a corner.
- Consequences for rule violations are not punishments. Punishment is a form of retribution; the goal is to make the violator pay for misconduct. Consequences are directly related to the rule; their purpose is instructional rather than punitive, because they are designed to teach students the effects of their behavior. Consequences work best when they are clear, specific, and logical.
- Teachers should have a range of alternative consequences so that they can use discretion in choosing the best consequence to match the particular situation.
- Teachers need to teach the concept that "fair is not always equal."

Publications

Curwin, R. L., & Mendler, A. N. *Discipline with Dignity* (2nd ed). 1999. Alexandria, VA: Association for Supervision and Curriculum Development.

Mendler, A. N., & Curwin, R. L. (1999). *Discipline with Dignity for Challenging Youth.* Bloomington, IN: National Educational Service.

Mendler, A. N. (2001). *Connecting with Students.* Alexandria, VA: Association for Supervision and Curriculum Development.

Curwin, R. L. (2003). *Making Good Choices: Developing Responsibility, Respect, and Self-Discipline in Grades 4–9.* Thousand Oaks, CA: Corwin Press.

Website: www.tlc-sems.com

Later, we ask Garnetta to reveal what happened in the hallway. She tells us that she began by asking Tanya what was bothering her. Tanya reported that the boy next to her had said her shoes were ugly. "Do you think they're ugly?" Garnetta asked. "No," Tanya replied. They spoke for a few minutes about her shoes and how it feels when somebody says something bad about the way you look. Although this clearly had not been the cause of Tanya's problems all morning, Garnetta let it go, assuring Tanya that she would talk to the boy about his comment. Garnetta then talked about how glad she was that Tanya was in her class, pointed out good things Tanya had done that morning as well as the things that had been problematic, and encouraged her to work hard for the rest of the morning. She told her to go to the bathroom, wash her face, get a drink, and then return to the room. "When I saw her working so well, I wanted to give her an immediate reward. Children like Tanya often don't get to go on errands, because teachers are sure they'll misbehave in the hallways. So I sent her on an errand to let her know that I trusted her and that I liked her and that I knew she had been working well."

In this vignette, we see how Garnetta tried to avoid embarrassing Tanya by speaking with her privately; how she demonstrated concern for Tanya's feelings about the boy's nasty comments; how she focused on the appropriate behavior Tanya had demonstrated that morning rather than on her misbehavior; and how she attempted to reinforce Tanya's on-task behavior and increase her feelings of self-importance by sending her on an errand. This encounter was not a magical cure. Although Garnetta was able to bring about definite improvements in Tanya's behavior, the child's problems were deep-rooted and persistent. Nonetheless, this vignette demonstrates the way Garnetta worked to communicate her expectations for appropriate behavior, while preserving Tanya's dignity and promoting a strong teacher–student relationship.

Second, when dealing with misbehavior, it is essential to *keep the instructional program going with a minimum of disruption.* Achieving this goal requires a delicate balancing act. On the one hand, you cannot allow inappropriate behavior to interrupt the teaching-learning process. On the other hand, you must realize that disciplinary strategies themselves can be disruptive. As Walter Doyle (1986) comments, interventions are "inherently risky" because they call attention to misbehavior and can actually pull students away from a lesson (p. 421). To avoid this situation, you must try to anticipate potential problems and head them off; if you decide that a disciplinary intervention *is* necessary, you need to be as unobtrusive as possible.

Watching our five teachers in action, it is clear that they recognize the importance of protecting the instructional program. In the following incident, Courtney doesn't even let an unexpected flying object derail her lesson:

 Students are seated on the rug in four straight rows for a mini-lesson on phonics. Courtney is giving directions for the upcoming activity. Suddenly, she is hit with a small wad of blue tape that someone has peeled off the rug. "Uh, oh, what is this?" She looks in the direction it came from, and the culprit squirms uncomfortably. "OK, we'll talk about this later." She continues with her lesson. Later, when students are working at their tables on the follow-up activity, Courtney approaches Natalie and kneels down next to her so they are on eye level. They talk very quietly.

Similarly, watch how Viviana sizes up a potentially disruptive situation and maintains the flow of her lesson:

 It is Halloween time, and Viviana's students have just returned from art class, where they made masks. They enter the room wearing the masks, obviously excited and proud of the way they look. Viviana stands at the chalkboard, about to begin a language arts lesson. She takes a long look at her students and waits for them to get settled. Then, she moves to her desk, takes out a mask, and puts it on. She moves back to the chalkboard and announces, "Since you have your masks on, I will wear one too. We will do language arts with our masks on." Later, she tells us: "I had only two choices. It was clear that if I made them take their masks off, I'd be fighting with them the whole period; my lesson would go down the drain. If I let them wear the masks, and even put one on myself, I could keep the lesson going and get them involved. I couldn't let my lesson fall apart.

The third principle of effective discipline is that *whether or not a particular action constitutes misbehavior depends on the context in which it occurs* (Doyle, 1986). There are obvious exceptions to this notion—punching another child and stealing property are obvious violations that always require a teacher response. But other behaviors are not so clear-cut. For example, in some classes, wearing a hat, sitting on your desk, chewing gum, and talking to neighbors are all misbehaviors, but in other classes these are perfectly acceptable. What constitutes misbehavior is often a function of a particular teacher's tolerance level or the standards set by a particular school. When determining a course of action, you need to ask yourself, "Is this behavior disrupting the ongoing instructional activity? Is it hurtful to other children? Does it violate established rules?" If the answer to these questions is no, disciplinary interventions may not be necessary.

 "I'm a fidgeter," Barbara tells us. "When I first went for an interview for a teaching position, my mother told me not to wear any jewelry, because she knew that I'd play with it while I talked. Because of this, I'm sympathetic to the fidgeters in my class. If a kid has trouble sitting still and crawls all over his or her chair, I don't do anything—unless it's bothering other people. Sometimes I hear a child singing softly while working. I'll check to see whether other people seem to be disturbed before doing anything. For me, that's the most important question: Is the behavior affecting others and denying them the right to instruction? If not, it's usually OK with me."

In addition to considering the classroom context, you need to be sensitive to conditions at home that make some children's lives a constant struggle. We recently learned about a second-grader who was frequently late to school because he had to get himself up, wake his younger brother (a kindergartner), prepare breakfast, and get them both to school. When he would appear at the door of his classroom 15 minutes late, his teacher would harshly berate him and send him to the office. It's true that the child was violating the school rule about not being tardy, but we think a more humane response would have been to welcome him to school with a warm hello, while working with the school social worker to see what could be done to improve the situation. After all, the fact that he got to school at all was quite an accomplishment.

On the other hand, teachers sometimes excuse the inappropriate behavior of certain students because "these kids can't help it"—when in fact they *can* help it, at least with support. We hear teachers say, "What can you expect, with a family situation like that?" or "These poor kids are going through so much at home, I hate to make their lives more difficult by enforcing rules." As well-intentioned as these teachers may be, not holding students accountable for inappropriate behavior that they could, in fact, regulate rarely helps. Children may protest limits, but they crave consistency, predictability, and structure—particularly when they live inconsistent, unpredictable, and unstructured lives out of school. Garnetta offers this touching profile:

 I have one girl in my class with serious behavior problems. Her mother is in and out of jail, and the child is shunted around to different relatives and friends. She's thin and frail, prone to tantrums, and very sensitive. She can't stand to be yelled at and needs a lot of TLC [tender, loving care]. I have to be more mellow with her than with the other kids. For example, when I tell her she has to do her work, she'll say, "OK, I'll be good, Mrs. Chain. Just give me a hug. Do you still love me?" I tell her, "I love you, and I'll hug you, but you still have to do your work."

The fourth principle is to *be timely and accurate when responding to behavior problems.* Jacob Kounin (1970) identified two common errors that teachers make when attempting to handle misbehavior in the classroom: timing mistakes and target mistakes. A timing mistake occurs when a teacher waits too long to correct a misbehavior. For example, a teacher might not realize (or has ignored the fact) that several students have called out responses without raising their hand and then sternly reprimands the next student who does so. Not only is this timing mistake unfair to that particular student, but calling out may have already become a habit for the students and thus will be much more difficult to curb than if it had been corrected immediately.

Target mistakes call attention to one particular student when in fact one or more others are at fault. A student may pull the hair of the girl in front of him—and the girl gets reprimanded for screaming in class. The student who threw the paper airplane that hit the teacher may go unnoticed while a student closer to the teacher is blamed for the incident. Mistakes like these are understandable, because instances of inappropriate behavior are often ambiguous and occur when the teacher is looking elsewhere. For this reason, care must be taken to respond accurately and in a timely manner.

The fifth principle emphasizes the importance of *making sure the severity of the disciplinary strategy matches the misbehavior you are trying to eliminate.* Research (e.g., Pittman, 1985) has indicated that some teachers think about misbehavior in terms of three categories: *minor misbehaviors* (noisiness, socializing, daydreaming); *more serious misbehaviors* (arguing, failing to respond to a group directive); and *never tolerated misbehaviors* (stealing, intentionally hurting someone, destroying property). They also consider whether the misbehavior is part of a pattern or an isolated event.

When deciding how to respond to a problem, it is useful to think in terms of these categories and to select a response that is congruent with the seriousness of the misbehavior. This is easier said than done, of course. When misbehavior occurs, teachers have little time to assess its seriousness, decide whether it's part of a pattern, and select an appropriate response. Nonetheless, you don't want to ignore or react mildly to misbehavior that warrants a more severe response, nor do you want to overreact to behavior that is relatively minor.

Finally, the sixth principle of effective discipline stresses *the need to be "culturally responsive," because differences in norms, values, and styles of communication can have a direct effect on students' behavior.* A good example of being culturally responsive comes from Cindy Ballenger's *Teaching Other People's Children* (1999). Ballenger, an experienced preschool teacher, expected to have little difficulty with her class of four-year-old Haitian children. To her surprise, however, her usual repertoire of management strategies failed to create a respectful, orderly environment. Her colleagues—all Haitian—were experiencing no difficulty with classroom management, so Ballenger had to conclude that the problem "did not reside in the children" (p. 32). She began to explore her own beliefs and practices with respect to children's behavior and to visit other teachers' classrooms to examine their "control statements." Eventually, Ballenger was able to identify several key differences between her own style of discourse and that of her Haitian colleagues. Whereas the Haitian teachers stressed the fact that they cared for the children and had their best interests at heart (e.g., "The adults here like you, they want you to be good children"), Ballenger frequently referred to children's internal states (e.g., "You must be angry"). Moreover, she tended to stress the logical consequences of children's behavior (e.g., "If you don't listen, you won't know what to do"), whereas the Haitian teachers articulated the values and responsibilities of group membership and stressed less immediate consequences, such as bringing shame to one's family. Once Ballenger had identified these differences in control statements, she made a deliberate effort to adopt some of the Haitian discourse style. Order in her classroom improved significantly.

As this vignette suggests, being culturally responsive means reflecting on the kinds of behaviors you judge to be problematic and considering how these might be related to race and ethnicity. For example, Gail Thompson (2004), an African American educator whose research focuses on the schooling experiences of students of color, notes that African American children are often socialized to talk loudly at home—a behavior that gets them into trouble at school. Listen to the mother of an eighth-grader who was starting to be labeled as a discipline problem at school for this reason:

> She's a loud person. My husband is a loud person, and when they get to explain themselves, they get loud. Their voices go up. Then, the teachers think she's being disrespectful. She's gotten a referral for that once. (p. 98)

Similarly, African American children tend to be more intense and confrontational than European American children; they are more likely to challenge school personnel, because they see leadership as a function of strength and forcefulness (rather than as a function of position and credentials); and they may jump into heated discussion instead of waiting for their "turn" (Irvine, 1990). Teachers familiar only with the dominant culture are likely to see these behavioral patterns as examples of rudeness and disruptiveness, to respond with anger, and to invoke punitive measures. In contrast, teachers who view the behaviors as reflections of cultural norms are better able to remain calm and nondefensive and to consider a variety of more constructive options (e.g., discussing classroom norms and the need for turn-taking in large groups). Indeed, they may actually come to see the benefits of allowing intensity and passion to be expressed in the classroom and broaden their definition of what is acceptable student behavior.

In addition, culturally responsive classroom managers are aware of the ways in which race and ethnicity influence the use of disciplinary consequences. Research conducted over 30 years repeatedly shows that African American and Latino students, particularly males, are disproportionately referred for behavior problems compared to their majority counterparts (Skiba et al., 2008). In fact, out-of-school suspension rates are between four and seven times greater for African American elementary school students than for European Americans (Raffaele-Mendez & Knoff, 2003).

What accounts for this disproportionality? One obvious explanation is that Black and Latino students violate class and school norms more often than their White peers. If this is the case, then disproportionate punishment is an appropriate response to inappropriate behavior, rather than an indicator of bias. Research on student behavior, race, and discipline, however, has yielded no evidence to support this explanation. In fact, studies suggest that African American students tend to receive harsher punishments for less severe behaviors (Skiba & Rausch, 2006). In addition, it appears that White students are more frequently referred to the office for "objective" offenses, such as vandalism, leaving without permission, and obscene language, whereas Black students are referred more often for "subjective" offenses—disrespect, excessive noise, and threat (Skiba, Michael, Nardo, & Peterson, 2002). In sum, it does not appear that racial disparities in school discipline are due to higher rates of misbehavior on the part of African American students. Instead, the evidence indicates that African American students are sent to the office and given punitive disciplinary consequences for less serious or more subjective reasons (Skiba & Rausch, 2006).

The implication is clear: To be culturally responsive classroom managers, teachers need to acknowledge their biases and values and think about how these affect their interactions with students. Some useful questions to ask yourself follow (Weinstein, Curran, & Tomlinson-Clarke, 2003).

- Am I more patient and encouraging with some students?
- Am I more likely to reprimand other students?
- Do I expect certain students to be disruptive based on their race or ethnicity?
- Do I use hairstyle and dress to form stereotypical judgments of my students?
- When students violate norms, do I recommend equal treatment of all students?

With these six principles in mind—preserving a safe and caring classroom environment, protecting the instructional program, considering the context, timely and accurately responding, selecting a disciplinary strategy that matches the misbehavior, and being culturally responsive—we turn now to specific ways of responding to inappropriate behavior.

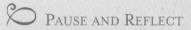

PAUSE AND REFLECT

Before reading about specific disciplinary interventions, think back to your own years as a student in elementary and high school. What disciplinary strategies did your most effective teachers use? What strategies did your least effective teachers use?

DEALING WITH MINOR MISBEHAVIOR

As we mentioned in Chapter 4, Jacob Kounin's (1970) classic study of orderly and disorderly classrooms gave research support to the belief that successful classroom managers have eyes in the back of their heads. Kounin found that effective managers knew what was going on all over the room; moreover, *their students knew they knew* because the teachers were able to spot minor problems and "nip them in the bud." Kounin called this ability *withitness,* a term that has since become widely used in discussions of classroom management.

How do "with it" teachers deal with minor misbehavior? How do they succeed in nipping problems in the bud? This section discusses both nonverbal and verbal interventions and then considers the times when it may be better to do nothing at all. (Suggestions are summarized in the accompanying Practical Tips box.)

Nonverbal Interventions

A while back, an 11-year-old we know announced that she could be a successful teacher. When we asked why she was so confident, she replied, "I know how to make *the look.*" She proceeded to demonstrate: her eyebrows slanted downward, her forehead creased, and her lips flattened into a straight line. She definitely had "the look" down pat.

The "teacher look" is a good example of an unobtrusive, nonverbal intervention. Making eye contact, using hand signals (e.g., thumbs down; pointing to what the individual should be doing), and moving closer to the misbehaving student are other nonverbal ways of communicating withitness. Nonverbal interventions all convey the message "I see what you're doing, and I don't like it," but because they are less directive than verbal commands, they encourage students to assume responsibility for getting back on task.

Nonverbal strategies are most appropriate for behaviors that are minor but persistent: frequent or sustained whispering, staring into space, calling out, walking around the room, playing with a toy, and passing notes. Nonverbal interventions not only allow you to deal with these misbehaviors, they enable you to protect and continue your lesson.

 It's a few days after Christmas vacation, and we are observing in Garnetta's classroom. During a creative writing activity, two boys seated across the room from each other begin a "shooting match," using their

PRACTICAL TIPS FOR

DEALING WITH MINOR MISBEHAVIOR

- *Use a nonverbal intervention:*

  Facial expressions.

  Eye contact.

  Hand signals.

  Proximity.

  Tokens or colored cards.

- *Use a nondirect verbal intervention:*

  State the student's name.

  Incorporate the name into the lesson.

  Call on the child to participate.

  Use gentle humor.

  Use an I-message.

- *Use a direct verbal intervention:*

  Give a succinct command.

  Remind students about a rule.

  Give a choice between behaving appropriately and receiving penalty.

- *Choose deliberate non-intervention* (but only if the misbehavior is minor and fleeting).

pencils as "guns." They make convincing gun noises. Garnetta is working with another child; she stops and looks hard and long at both boys. They look back, immediately stop what they're doing, and get back to work. Garnetta finishes her conversation and begins to circulate around the room. She stops at both boys' desks and checks their work.

As this anecdote illustrates, a nonverbal cue is sometimes all that's needed to stop a misbehavior and get a student back on task. In fact, a study of six middle school teachers (Lasley, Lasley, & Ward, 1989) found that *the most successful responses to misbehavior were nonverbal.* These strategies stopped misbehavior 79 percent of the time; among the three "more effective managers," the success rate was even higher—an amazing 95 percent.

The obvious advantage of using a nonverbal cue is that you don't distract other students while dealing with the misbehavior. As Barbara comments:

Whenever you're involved in a verbal confrontation with one child, the others are "free-timing it." They're listening to you instead of doing their work. If a child is playing with a car, it's much more effective to simply walk over and take it. That way it's gone, and you don't have to worry about it anymore.

Nonverbal interventions can also be tangible. For example, some teachers quietly put a small yellow or red card on a student's desk to communicate a first or second warning; a card with a sad face or a poker chip can also be used. Placing a hand on a student's shoulder or physically guiding a child to pick up a pencil and get to work are also unobtrusive, nonverbal interventions that teachers have found helpful. Remember the cautions expressed in Chapter 3, however, about physical contact with students. We know a student teacher who tried to get a student on task by taking the child's head in her hands and directing it away from the window toward the chalkboard. Later, the child complained about a stiff neck and accused the student teacher of "jerking" her head around. The student teacher immediately notified her cooperating teacher and principal about what had happened, and a phone call to the parents fortunately headed off further trouble. Incidents like these, however, underscore the importance of avoiding any physical interventions that could be interpreted as abusive.

Verbal Interventions

Sometimes you find yourself in situations where it's just not possible to use a non-verbal cue. Perhaps you can't catch the student's eye, or you're working with a small group and it would be too disruptive to get up and walk across the room to the misbehaving child. Other times, you're able to use a nonverbal cue, but it's unsuccessful in stopping the misbehavior.

In cases like this, you can use a *nondirective verbal intervention*. These allow you to prompt the appropriate behavior, while leaving the responsibility for figuring out what to do with the misbehaving student. For example, *simply saying the student's name* might be enough to get the student back on task. Sometimes it's possible to *incorporate the child's name* into the ongoing instruction. We witnessed Ken use this unobtrusive strategy during a small-group discussion:

 Brian is slouching down in his seat and appears inattentive. Ken is praising the comment of another student: "Did you see the way Joey made that into an analysis question? He didn't just say, 'Brian is slouching in his seat,' he said . . . ." Brian immediately sits up, with a small smile on his face and begins to participate in the discussion.

If the misbehavior occurs while you are giving a presentation or while a group discussion or recitation is going on, you can *call on the child to participate in some way or to answer a question.* Consider the following example:

 Viviana is conducting a whole-group reading lesson—"The Hen and the Bread." She asks the class, "What is make believe in this picture and what is real?" The children scrutinize the illustration, and one by one, hands go up into the air. She calls on a nonvolunteer who appears to be daydreaming. "Fernando, what is make believe in this picture?" He is brought back to the task, looks at the picture, and slowly responds.

Calling on a student enables you to communicate that you know what's going on and to capture the student's attention—without even citing the misbehavior. But keep in mind what we said earlier about preserving students' dignity. If you are obviously trying to "catch" students and to embarrass them, the strategy may well backfire by creating resentment (Good & Brophy, 2008). One way to avoid this problem is to alert the student that you will be calling on him or her to answer the *next question:* "Sharon, what's the answer to number 18? Taysha, the next one's yours."

The *use of humor* can provide another "gentle" way of reminding children to correct their behavior. Used well, humor can show students that you are able to understand the funny aspects of classroom life. But you must be careful that the humor is not tinged with sarcasm that can hurt students' feelings.

 Garnetta instructs her students to clean off their desks in anticipation of the next activity. One boy takes a paper, crumples it up into a ball, and sticks it in his desk. Garnetta makes big eyes and says, "I saw that paper go squish into your desk." The boy and the class laugh. He takes the paper ball and puts it in the wastebasket.

An "*I-message*" is another way of verbally prompting appropriate behavior without giving a direct command. I-messages generally contain three parts. First, the teacher *describes the unacceptable behavior in a nonblaming, nonjudgmental way.* This phrase often begins with "when": "When people talk while I'm giving directions . . . ." The second part describes the *tangible effect on the teacher:* "I have to repeat the directions and that wastes time. . . ." Finally, the third part of the message states the *teacher's feelings* about the tangible effect: "and I get frustrated." Barbara used a three-part I-message like this when her class failed to clean up after a particularly messy art activity: "When you leave the room a mess, I have to clean it up, and I may not want to do an activity like this again."

Here are some other examples of I-messages:

"When you come to class without your supplies, I can't start the lesson on time, and I get really irritated."

"When you leave your skateboard in the middle of the aisle, I can trip over it, and I'm afraid I'll break a leg."

Although I-messages ideally contain all three parts in the recommended sequence, I-messages in any order, or even with one part missing, can still be effective (Gordon, 2003). We've witnessed our teachers use "abbreviated" I-messages. For example, Viviana communicates the importance of not laughing at people's mistakes when she states: "If you laugh at me when I make a mistake then I'll feel bad." And Barbara honestly tells her class, "When you guys do that, it drives me up the wall."

There are several benefits to using this approach. In contrast to typical "you-messages" (e.g., "You are being rude," "You ought to know better," "You're acting like a baby"), I-messages minimize negative evaluations of the student. For this reason, they foster and preserve a positive relationship between people.

Because I-messages leave decisions about changing behavior up to students, this approach is also likely to promote a sense of responsibility and autonomy. In addition, I-messages show students that their behavior has consequences and that teachers are people with genuine feelings. Unlike you-messages, I-messages don't make students defensive and stubborn; thus students may be more willing to change their behavior.

Most of us are not used to speaking this way, so I-messages can seem awkward and artificial. With practice, however, using I-messages can become natural. We once heard a four-year-old girl (whose parents had consistently used I-messages at home) tell her nursery school peer: "When you poke me with that pencil, it really hurts, and I feel bad 'cause I think you don't want to be my friend."

In addition to these nondirective approaches, there are also *more directive strategies* you can try. Indeed, several African American educators (e.g., Delpit, 1995; Thompson, 2004) contend that these may be particularly well matched to the communication patterns of African American students. For example, Lisa Delpit, author of *Other People's Children: Cultural Conflict in the Classroom* (1995), observes that framing directives as questions (e.g., "Would you like to sit down now?") is a particularly mainstream, middle-class (and female) way of speaking, designed to foster a more egalitarian and nonauthoritarian climate. According to Delpit,

> Many kids will not respond to that structure because commands are not couched as questions in their home culture. Rather than asking questions, some teachers need to learn to say, "Put the scissors away" and "Sit down now" or "Please sit down now." (Valentine, 1998, p. 17)

As Delpit suggests, the most straightforward approach is to *direct students to the task at hand* ("Get to work on that math problem"; "Your group should be discussing the first three pages"). You can also *remind the student about the rule* or behavioral expectation that is being violated (e.g., "When someone is talking, everyone else is supposed to be listening"). Sometimes, if inappropriate behavior is fairly widespread, it's useful to review rules with the entire group. This is often true after a holiday, a weekend, or a vacation. Courtney found that a review of the rules and routines was needed in the second half of the year:

All of a sudden, all the signals I had been using to gain their attention stopped working. I think they got bored with them, and so I had to make up new ones. And I was amazed at the behavior problems that came up. From September to December, they were just so cooperative, and then in February, it suddenly happened. They were talking a lot more. It was chat, chat, chat. And I had never had hitting or punching in the beginning of the year, and all of a sudden, they started roughhousing. Even though I knew it was just a game, I was still surprised. I think they were more comfortable with each other and with me and with school. I'm glad about that, but we still had to do a review of how we behave in school.

Another strategy is to *give students a choice between behaving appropriately and receiving a penalty for continued inappropriate behavior* ("If you can't handle working in your group, you'll have to return to your seats"; "Either you choose to raise your hand instead of calling out, or you will be choosing not to participate in our discussion"). Statements like these not only warn students that a penalty will be invoked if the inappropriate behavior continues, they also emphasize that students have real choices about how to behave and that penalties are not imposed without reason. Ken often uses this strategy. For example, when a boy in his class repeatedly called out during a spelling test, despite nonverbal cues and nondirective reminders, Ken told him: "Barry, you either choose to be quiet, or you will lose the opportunity to play soccer with the rest of the class." Barry protested in a shocked tone: "What am I doing?" In response, Ken calmly described his behavior and its effects: "You're calling out and disturbing people in the room, including me."

Deliberate Non-Intervention

If misbehavior is extremely brief and unobtrusive, the best course of action may be *in*action. For example, during a discussion a student may be so eager to comment that she forgets to raise her hand; or someone becomes momentarily distracted and inattentive; or two boys quietly exchange a comment while you're giving directions. In cases like these, an intervention can be more disruptive than the students' behavior.

One risk of overlooking minor misbehavior is that students may conclude you're unaware of what's going on. Suspecting that you're not "with it," they may decide to see how much they can get away with, and then problems are sure to escalate. You need to monitor your class carefully to make sure this doesn't happen.

Another problem is that occasional ignoring can turn into full-fledged "blindness." This was vividly demonstrated in a study of a student teacher named Heleen (Créton, Wubbels, & Hooymayers, 1989). When Heleen was lecturing, her students frequently became noisy and inattentive. In response, Heleen talked more loudly and looked more at the chalkboard, turning her back on her students. She did not allow herself to see or hear the disorder—perhaps because it was too threatening and she didn't know how to handle it. Unfortunately, Heleen's students seemed to interpret her "blindness" as an indication that noise was allowed, and they became even more disorderly. Heleen eventually recognized the importance of "seeing" and responding to slight disturbances in order to prevent them from escalating.

DEALING WITH MORE SERIOUS MISBEHAVIOR

Sometimes nonverbal cues and verbal reminders are not enough to convince students that you're serious about the behavioral expectations that you've established. And sometimes misbehavior is just too serious to use these kinds of low-level responses. In cases like these, it may be necessary to use more substantial interventions to enforce your expectations for appropriate behavior.

The importance of enforcing expectations was clearly demonstrated in Emmer, Evertson, and Anderson's (1980) study of effective classroom management. When rule violations occurred in the classrooms of ineffective classroom managers, they often issued reminders and warned students of penalties, but they didn't act on their warnings. Inevitably, behavior problems increased in frequency and severity. In contrast, effective classroom managers dealt both quickly and predictably with rule violations. When they warned students that a penalty would result if the misbehavior didn't stop, the teachers made sure to follow through on the warning.

Emmer, Evertson, and their colleagues also found that effective classroom managers planned their penalties ahead of time. In some cases, teachers discussed penalties when they taught rules and procedures so that students would understand the consequences of violating a rule from the very beginning. We saw Garnetta do this with her students in Chapter 4. This practice prevents unpleasant "surprises" and may minimize protests of blissful ignorance: "But you didn't *tell* me that would happen!"

Selecting Penalties

It's often difficult for beginning teachers to decide on appropriate penalties. One frustrated student teacher told us:

> *I can't keep kids after school because they have to catch the school bus. I don't like keeping them in from recess or lunch because that's the only time I have for myself, and I've got to use it for preparation. My cooperating teacher says I'm not allowed to keep kids from going to "specials," because art, music, and physical education are legitimate, valuable parts of the curriculum. I was told by other teachers not to send kids to the office, because then the principal and my cooperating teacher will think I can't handle problems by myself. And my professors have told me never to use extra work as a penalty because kids will come to see schoolwork as punishment. So what's left?!*

We posed this question to our five teachers and learned about the types of penalties that they typically use. As a general rule of thumb, our teachers try to implement pentalties that are *logically related to the misbehavior* (e.g., Curwin & Mendler, 1988; Dreikurs, Grunwald, & Pepper, 1982). For example, if students make a mess at the science center, a logical penalty would be to make them clean it up. If a child forgets his book and can't do the assignment, he must borrow someone's book and do the assignment during free time or recess. A student who cannot work cooperatively in a group must leave the group until she decides she can cooperate. A student who hands in a carelessly done paper has to rewrite it.

Logical consequences differ from traditional punishments, which bear no relationship to the misbehavior involved. Examples are as follows: A child who continually whispers to her neighbor has to do an additional homework assignment (instead of being isolated). A child who forgets to get his spelling test signed by his parents has to stay in at recess (rather than writing a letter home to parents about the need to sign the spelling test). A child who continually calls out during a whole-class discussion has to stay after school and clean the hamster cage (rather than making a cue-card to post on his desk saying "I won't call out" or not being allowed to participate in the discussion).

The specific penalties used by our teachers are described below. As you read about each one, keep in mind that these five teachers have worked hard to build caring, trusting relationships with students. Undoubtedly, these relationships increase the likelihood that students will interpret the penalties not as punishments imposed by a hostile, dictatorial adversary, but as reasonable consequences enacted by a teacher who cares enough to insist that students behave the best they can (Bondy & Ross, 2008; Gregory & Ripski, 2008).

Expressions of Disappointment

We normally don't think of this as a penalty, but because students in these classes really like their teachers, they feel bad when their teachers are upset. In serious, almost sorrowful tones, our teachers express their disappointment and surprise at the inappropriate behavior and direct students to think about the consequences of their actions.

Loss of Privileges

In Barbara's, Garnetta's, and Ken's classes, students who consistently misbehave may lose the highly valued privilege of free time. If they have "forgotten" to do their homework, they need to do it during this time. Ken tells us that for his students, being eligible for the "student of the week" is extremely important; thus, losing eligibility for the week is also viewed as a serious penalty.

Time-Out

In all five classes, students who distract other students or fail to cooperate with their peers must move to another part of the room until they are ready to rejoin the group. Viviana tells her students, "You decide when you can come back." Courtney directs students who are disrupting a group lesson on the rug to go back to their tables and "stop and think." When Ken has a student who constantly talks too much, he and the student agree on a pleasant, quiet, and isolated place for the child to go if needed. They work out a signal that Ken uses to send the child to the agreed-upon spot if a verbal warning is ineffective.

Sometimes in-class time-out isn't possible or effective, and it's necessary to send a child out of the room. Barbara has worked out a system with another teacher so that she can send a child to his classroom if necessary. She simply writes the amount of time (e.g., "10 minutes") on a slip of paper that the child takes to the other teacher. In the other room, the child must sit quietly and do schoolwork, ignored by both teacher and students.

Time-out can be particularly effective with children who suffer from ADHD (Rief, 1993). These children have trouble dealing with the distraction and stimulation of the typical classroom environment; time-out can provide a much-needed opportunity to calm down and regain self-control. Try to direct the student to time-out in a calm, positive manner and to be specific about the behavior that is causing the problem (e.g., "Sean, I need you to keep your hands to yourself. Please go to the "think-about-it" chair until you are ready to sit without poking others" [Rief, 1993]).

A few cautions are in order (Walker & Shea, 1995). First, you need to consider the characteristics of the child receiving time-out. Time-out may work well for a disruptive, aggressive child who is socially oriented, but it may actually be rewarding for a withdrawn child who tends to daydream. Second, children need to understand the reason why they are being sent to time-out and what the rules are (e.g., sit quietly until a timer goes off; no participation in activities until time-out is over). Third, it's important to refrain from lecturing and chastising, because these can reinforce the inappropriate behavior. Fourth, the time-out area should be away from distraction and the possibility of interaction with others; however, it also needs to be a safe place that can be supervised. (For all these reasons, the hallway is *not* a good time-out area!) Fifth, time-out should be limited to approximately 2 to 5 minutes and should never exceed 10 minutes.

Written Reflections on the Problem

In Garnetta's classroom, students who consistently misbehave may have to write an essay about what they did, their thoughts about why it happened, and why it was inappropriate. In Ken's class, students who hurt other children write letters of apology to the individuals. Barbara sometimes has her students take out their journals and write about the problem that has occurred.

Visits to the Principal's Office

All five teachers believe that "kicking kids out" is a strategy that should be reserved for major disruption. Only rarely do any of them send a child to the principal. Nonetheless, they realize that in extreme cases (such as physical aggression), exclusion from the classroom and a meeting with the principal or disciplinarian may be necessary. Even so, Garnetta tells us, "I send along a note telling the principal to send the child back right away. I want my kids in here. They're not going to learn any of my curriculum in the principal's office."

Detention

Sometimes Garnetta, Ken, and Barbara require students to meet with them after school for a few minutes. This gives them an opportunity to speak privately with students about the inappropriate behavior and to explore possible causes. Usually it's even possible for a "bus student" to meet for a brief period of time. If it's necessary for students to stay longer, parents are notified ahead of time. Ken also keeps students in the room at lunch time (although, as the student teacher we quoted at the beginning of this section observed, this requires him to eat his lunch in the room also). During this time, students make up missing work, and Ken can talk with them in a more private, less rushed manner.

Contacting Parents

All the teachers contact parents promptly if a student shows a pattern of repeated misbehavior. For example, in Barbara's classroom, the first time children don't do homework, she reminds them about her expectations. If shortly afterward they "forget" again, she tells them, "It's my responsibility to let your parents know that you're not getting your work done and to ask them for help in seeing that you do it." She tries to say this not in anger, but with an expression of serious concern. She wants to convey the idea that "between the two of us, maybe we can help you get it together."

These seven types of penalties illustrate the ways in which Courtney, Viviana, Garnetta, Barbara, and Ken choose to deal with problems when they have a degree of flexibility. In addition, there are times when they are required to follow school policies mandating particular responses to specific misbehaviors. In Viviana's school, for example, the vice principal (who serves as the school disciplinarian) requires that teachers send students to his office in cases of continual defiance, use of profanity, and fighting. Be sure to find out what your school policies are with respect to serious problem behaviors.

It's also important to note that under *No Child Left Behind,* schools must have a plan for keeping schools safe and drug free. These plans must include discipline policies that prohibit disorderly conduct, the illegal possession of weapons, and the illegal use, possession, distribution, and sale of tobacco, alcohol, and other drugs. As a result, nearly all schools now have *zero tolerance* policies with pre-determined consequences for such offenses. Zero tolerance may also be applied to other problems, such as bullying and threatening. These policies usually result in automatic suspension or expulsion, although there may be wide variation in severity. Be sure to familiarize yourself with the zero tolerance policies in your school.

If you have students with disabilities in your classes, it's also essential that you consult with a special educator or a member of the child study team about appropriate intervention strategies. Serious behavior problems require a team effort, and parents, special education teachers, psychologists, social workers, and administrators can all provide valuable insights and suggestions. Also be aware that the Individuals with Disabilities Education Act (IDEA 2004) includes several stipulations about the rights of students with disabilities with respect to disciplinary procedures. For example, if the problematic behavior is "caused by" or has a "direct and substantial relationship" to the child's disability, removing the child for more than 10 school days may not be allowed.

> ✑ PAUSE AND REFLECT
>
> Review the various penalties that our five teachers generally use when dealing with inappropriate behavior. Which ones would you be most inclined to implement? Are there any with which you disagree?

Imposing Penalties and Preserving Relationships

It's frustrating when students misbehave, and sometimes we let our frustration affect the way we impose penalties. We've seen teachers scream at students from across the room, lecture students on their history of misbehavior, insinuate that they come from terrible homes, and attack their personalities. Clearly, behavior like this undermines children's dignity and ruins the possibility of a good relationship with them. How can you avoid creating a situation like this?

First, if you're feeling really angry at a student, it's a good idea to *delay the discussion.* You can simply say to a child, "Sit there and think about what happened. I'll talk to you in a few minutes." Barbara sometimes tells her students, "I'm really angry about what just happened. Everybody take out journals; we're all going to write about this situation." After a few minutes of writing, she's better able to discuss the misbehavior with students in a calm, dispassionate manner. Similarly, Ken may tell an individual student, "I do not like what I just saw. See me for a few minutes during free time so we can discuss this." Delaying discussion gives everyone a chance to cool off, and you'll be better able to separate the child's character from the child's behavior. Your message must be "*You're* OK, but your *behavior* is unacceptable."

Second, it's essential to *impose penalties privately, calmly, and quietly.* Despite the temptation to yell and scream, the softer your voice and the closer you stand, the more effective you tend to be (Bear, 1998). Remember, students are very concerned about saving face in front of their peers. Public sanction may have the advantage of "making an example" of one student's misbehavior, but it has the disadvantage of creating resentment and embarrassment. Numerous studies have found that students view public reprimand as the *least acceptable method* of dealing with problems (Woolfolk Hoy & Weinstein, 2006). Furthermore, the ability to be firm without using threats and public humiliation appears to be particularly important for students who are already disaffected or alienated from school. For example, interviews conducted with 31 "marginal" junior high school students who were judged to be at risk of school failure found that teachers were perceived as uncaring and unfair adversaries if they "engaged in public acts intended to convey an impression of authority: making examples of specific students, sending students from the room, and ordering compliance" (Schlosser, 1992, p. 135).

Our five teachers agree. When Garnetta reprimands a child, she moves over to the individual and speaks so softly that no one else can hear what is going on. Even when speaking to the whole class about misbehavior, her voice is amazingly soft and low—a striking contrast to her "instructional voice," which is loud and strong.

In the following example, Barbara tells how she dealt with Robert.

Robert was used to being the focus of the teacher's attention because of his annoying habits. I think he really enjoyed being yelled at, being the center of attention. His records indicated that he often seemed angry and unwilling to do what the rest of the class was doing. I knew I had to get him early on or he'd mess up my class. I vowed not to allow him to pull me off task. I decided to work with him individually, privately. In the beginning of the year he was chronically late to school and late to get started on everything. He'd have to sharpen his pencil, or rearrange his desk, or get a dictionary—he always procrastinated. So the first thing I did was take him aside and tell him what my expectations were. If he didn't get work done because he was late to school or late starting, then he had to miss free time. For three days after that he missed free time and was really angry with me. I refused to talk with him about his anger; I ignored it. Then he tried tears, and I ignored the tears. After the third day I reminded him about getting his work done. He got it done that day and had free

time. Robert needed to know that I meant what I said. In addition, of course, I made positive comments to him about other things, so he wouldn't think I was just picking on him.

Finally, after imposing a penalty, it's a good idea to get back to the student and *reestablish a positive relationship.* At the beginning of this chapter, we saw how Garnetta sent Tanya on an errand after meeting with her in the hall. Similarly, complimenting a student's work or patting a back communicates that there are no hard feelings.

Being Consistent

Beginning teachers are constantly told to "be consistent," and research certainly supports this advice (e.g., Emmer, Evertson, & Anderson, 1980). If teachers do not consistently enforce the rules, students become confused and begin to test the limits, which leads to an increase in problem behavior. On the other hand, teachers often feel trapped by the need for consistency. (See the discussion in Chapter 3 about being fair.) When a normally conscientious student forgets a homework assignment, it seems unreasonable to send the same note home to parents that you would send if a child repeatedly missed assignments. Furthermore, what is an effective consequence for one child may not be effective for another. Staying after school might be a negative experience for a child who was eager to go home to play; for a child who has nothing special waiting at home, staying after school could actually be a positive, rewarding experience.

In order to get out of this bind, it's desirable to develop a *hierarchy of generic consequences* that can be applied to all misbehaviors and that have enough flexibility that consequences can be tailored to the needs of particular individuals. Consider the following example:

First violation: Verbal warning
Second time: Private conference with teacher to decide on action plan
Third time: Call parents
Fourth time: Conference with child and parents to develop an action plan

It's also important to explain in advance to students that "fair is not always equal." It is impossible to have a single solution appropriate for everyone. Just as teachers design instruction to meet students' varying *academic* needs, they select consequences to meet students' varying *social* needs. Having a range of alternative consequences enables you to be *consistent* with respect to the behavior you expect from students, but *flexible* with respect to the selection of a consequence.

Penalizing the Group for Individual Misbehavior

Sometimes teachers impose a consequence on the whole class even when only one or two children have been misbehaving. The hope is that other students will be angry at receiving a penalty when they weren't misbehaving and will exert pressure on their peers to behave.

We decided to ask our five teachers what they think about this practice. Their responses were extremely consistent. All of them felt the practice was basically unfair and would undermine their efforts to create a caring community. They also believed the practice could backfire by teaching students that "it doesn't pay to be good since you'll be punished anyway." And Garnetta expressed concern about the animosity and physical fighting that might result from penalizing the group. She described instances of children vowing to "get back" at misbehaving students—"We'll take care of you after school."

When we asked our teachers whether there were any situations that would prompt them to impose group penalties for individual wrongdoing, there was also remarkable consistency. All four experienced teachers cited the problem of stealing and described times when they had kept children after school or denied them free time in order to address the problem. Listen to Garnetta:

 I said the whole class had to stay after school and explained that the girl's money was "missing." I told them we were going to help find it by spending a few minutes looking around the room. I said that if someone found the money they should put it on my desk. I helped to look too, and a few minutes later I went back to my desk. The money was there.

DEALING WITH CHRONIC MISBEHAVIOR

Some students with persistent behavior problems fail to respond to the routine strategies we have described so far: nonverbal cues, verbal reminders, and penalties. What additional strategies are available? In this section, we consider two basic approaches. First, we examine a *problem-solving strategy,* which views inappropriate behavior as a conflict that can be solved through discussion and negotiation. Next, we take a look at *four self-management approaches based on principles of behavioral learning*—namely, *self-monitoring, self-evaluation, self-instruction,* and *contingency contracting*—and then turn to *positive behavioral supports* (PBS), interventions designed to replace problem behaviors with new behaviors that serve the same purpose for the student.

Resolving Conflicts through Problem Solving

Most teachers think in terms of winning or losing when they think about classroom conflicts. According to Thomas Gordon, author of *T.E.T.—Teacher Effectiveness Training* (2003):

> This win-lose orientation seems to be at the core of the knotty issue of discipline in schools. Teachers feel that they have only two approaches to choose from: They can be strict or lenient, tough or soft, authoritarian or permissive. They see the teacher-student relationship as a power struggle, a contest, a fight. . . . When conflicts arise, as they always do, most teachers try to resolve them so that they win, or at least don't lose. This obviously means that students end up losing, or at least not winning. (p. 185)

A third alternative is a "no-lose" problem-solving method of conflict resolution (Gordon, 2003) consisting of six steps. In Step 1, the teacher and the student (or students) *define the problem.* In Step 2, everyone *brainstorms possible solutions.* As in all brainstorming activities, suggestions are not evaluated at this stage. In Step 3, the *solutions are evaluated:* "Now let's take a look at all the solutions that have been proposed and decide which we like and which we don't like. Do you have some preferences?" It is important that you state your own opinions and preferences. Do not permit a solution to stand if it is really not acceptable to you. In Step 4, you and the students involved *decide on the solution that you will try.* If more than one student is involved, it is tempting to vote on the solution, but that's probably not a good idea. Voting always produces winners and losers unless the vote is unanimous, so some people leave the discussion feeling dissatisfied. Instead, try to work for consensus.

Once you have decided which solution to try, you move to Step 5 and *determine how to implement the decision:* Who will do what by when? Finally, in Step 6, *the solution is evaluated.* Sometimes the teacher may want to call everybody together again and ask, "Are you still satisfied with our solution?" It is important for everyone to realize that decisions are not chiseled in granite and that they can be discarded in search of a better solution to the problem.

Gordon provides the following example of a teacher using the "no-lose" problem-solving method with her elementary class.

TEACHER: I have a problem that you can help me with. There's too much talking and I feel like I'm always having to quiet you down. I don't like that. There are times when I need to have quiet so I can teach, but when you're talking I have to repeat directions and go over material I've already talked about. Yet I know that you seem to have a need to talk. Let's think of all the things we can that might help meet my needs and your needs, too. I'll suggest some, and you suggest all you can think of. I'll list them on the board. Every suggestion will be listed without any comments. Later we'll discuss them and eliminate the ones you don't want and I don't want.

(The following alternative solutions are proposed and listed on the board:

1. Rearrange the seating.
2. Punishments.
3. Talk whenever you want to.
4. Have a certain time each day to talk.
5. Talk only when others are not talking.
6. No talking at all.
7. Teach one-half the class at a time (other half can talk).
8. Whisper.
9. Have only oral work.)

TEACHER: Now let's cross out the suggestions we really don't like. I'll cross out numbers two, three, and nine because I don't like them. [Note that it would have been good if the teacher had explained why she objects to these suggestions.]

(Various students suggest crossing out numbers six and seven.)

TEACHER: Now let's look at the remaining suggestions. How about number one, "Rearranging the seating"?

BETTY: You've tried that and it didn't work. (After a brief discussion, class agrees to cross that one out.)

TEACHER: "Have a certain time each day to talk"—what about that one?

(There are no objections to that solution.)

TEACHER: What about "Don't talk when others are talking," number five?

(There are no objections to that one.)

TEACHER: "Whisper." What do you think of that idea?

(There are no objections to that one.)

TEACHER: That leaves us with numbers four, five, and eight. Does anyone want to add anything? No? Okay, then, I'll copy this on paper and we'll all sign it. This is what we call a contract. It's an agreement the teacher and the class have signed. We both will try to live up to the contract. We'll try not to break the contract. (2003, pp. 236–237)

As Gordon points out, this problem-solving session did not go beyond Step 4. The teacher could have engaged the students in Step 5 by saying something like "All right now, how are we going to put this into action? What has to be done? Who is going to do it?" In addition, the teacher failed to move the class into Step 6, assessment. Nonetheless, the teacher did describe the problem in terms of an I-message, and she did share responsibility with the students for arriving at a solution to the problem.

Using a Behavioral Learning Approach

Behavioral learning principles emphasize external events (rather than thinking or knowledge) as the cause of changes in behavior (Woolfolk, 2007). Applied behavior analysis (also known as behavior modification) is the application of behavioral learning principles to change behavior; it involves the systematic use of reinforcement to strengthen desired behavior. Probably more research has focused on the effectiveness of applied behavior analysis than on any other classroom management approach, and dozens of books are available for teachers (e.g., Alberto & Troutman, 2006; Zirpoli, 2005).

In recent years, educators have stressed behavioral approaches that involve the student in *self-management:* self-monitoring, self-evaluation, self-instruction, and contingency contracting. The goal of these self-management strategies is to help students learn to regulate their own behavior. The perception of control is crucial in this process: When we feel in control, we are much more likely to accept responsibility for our actions.

In the next sections of the chapter, we describe these self-management approaches. Then we turn to a relatively new behavioral approach that focuses on teaching students appropriate behavior through *positive behavioral supports.*

Self-Monitoring

Some students may not realize how often they're out of their seats, how frequently they sit daydreaming, or how often they call out during class discussions.

Youngsters such as this may benefit from a self-monitoring program, in which students learn to observe and record their own behavior during a designated period of time. Interestingly, self-monitoring can have positive effects even when youngsters are inaccurate (Graziano & Mooney, 1984).

Before beginning a self-monitoring program, you need to make sure that students can identify the behaviors targeted for change. For example, some children may not know what "working independently" looks like. You may have to demonstrate, explicitly noting all the component parts: "When I work independently, I am sitting down, I am looking at the paper on my desk. I am holding my pencil in my hand." With young children, even demonstration may not be enough; pictures or photographs can help.

Students then learn how to observe and record their own behavior. This can be done in two ways. The first approach has individuals tally each time they engage in the targeted behavior. For example, students can learn to chart the number of math problems they complete during an in-class assignment, the number of times they blurt out irrelevant comments during a discussion, or the number of times they raise their hand to speak. For young children, the tally sheet might contain pictures of the appropriate and inappropriate behaviors. (See the "countoon" suggested by Jones and Jones, 2010, in Figure 12.2.) In the second approach, some sort of a timer is used to cue individuals to observe and record the targeted behavior at regular intervals. At the designated time, students mark a recording sheet to indicate whether they are engaged in the appropriate or inappropriate behavior. In one particular study (Cloward, 2003), using this approach increased time-on-task during independent seatwork for fourth-grade students with ADHD.

Both Barbara and Ken have used self-monitoring approaches with students who did not respond to the simpler, routine strategies we have discussed. In Ken's class, we watched as this masterful teacher was driven to distraction by Jason, a boy who continually talked to his neighbors, to Ken, and to himself. Nonverbal signals, verbal directives, and even penalties worked only momentarily. Eventually, teacher and student agreed that Jason would sit at a separate desk in an isolated corner of the room so that he would not disrupt other students. But even there he constantly muttered while working on assignments, blurted out comments during class discussions, and chattered with anyone passing by. When Ken spoke with him about this excessive talking, Jason denied that he was doing it. He seemed like an obvious candidate for a self-monitoring program. Ken describes the system that he and Jason developed:

 I decided to begin by focusing on only one of Jason's irritating behaviors—calling out during class discussions. I used the countoon form [see Figure 12.2] so Jason could record the times he raised his hand and the times he blurted out. In some ways, it wasn't entirely successful: I'd see Jason raise his hand even when he had nothing to say, just to collect marks on the positive side of the countoon. On the other hand, I frequently saw him start to blurt out a comment and then catch himself, so he wouldn't have to record a "call-out." And when he did call out, I could give him a look and he'd

Figure 12.2 Example of a "Countoon"
Source: Jones & Jones, *Comprehensive classroom management,* © 2001. Reproduced by permission of Pearson Education, Inc.

reluctantly realize that he had to make a check on that side of the countoon. That did make him more aware of his own behavior, and I did see some improvement.

In Barbara's case, self-monitoring proved useful with a child who continually left the room to go to the bathroom. As in Ken's situation, when Barbara spoke with Louis about how frequently he left, he adamantly rejected her claim. Finally, they decided that Louis would keep count. Barbara placed a tin of bingo markers next to the bathroom pass, which was kept on the chalkboard ledge near the door. Whenever Louis took the bathroom pass, he had to take a bingo marker and put it on his desk. Each day, Barbara and Louis counted the number of bingo markers on his desk. The chips served as indisputable, concrete evidence of his trips. Within days, the number of markers began to decrease.

Self-Evaluation

This self-management approach goes beyond simple self-monitoring by requiring children to judge the quality or acceptability of their behavior. Sometimes self-evaluation is linked with reinforcement—that is, an improvement in behavior brings points or rewards.

There is evidence that even young children can learn to do this. In one study (Sainato, Strain, Lefebre, & Rapp, 1990), four preschool children who displayed high rates of inappropriate behaviors (hitting, tantrums, continual talking, lack of social responsiveness) were taught to assess whether they had exhibited appropriate independent seatwork behaviors (listening to the teacher's directions, sitting appropriately, and working quietly). First, each child was photographed modeling the appropriate behaviors. These pictures were then mounted on construction paper, with a caption describing each behavior being modeled. Next to each picture were two faces: a happy face for "yes" and a frowning face for "no." The sheets of paper were covered with clear plastic and then placed in three-ring binders.

Each of the four children received his or her own personalized binder. At the end of each independent seatwork period (20 minutes), the children assessed whether they had exhibited the behaviors, marking the "yes" or "no" with an erasable grease pencil. The results demonstrated that even these very young children could learn to evaluate their behaviors accurately. Furthermore, the self-evaluations produced immediate, substantial improvements in the children's behavior.

Self-Instruction

The third self-management approach is self-instruction, in which children learn to give themselves silent directions about how to behave. Most self-instruction strategies are based on Donald Meichenbaum's (1977) five-step process of cognitive behavior modification: (1) An adult performs a task while talking aloud about it, carefully describing each part. (2) The child performs the task while the adult talks aloud (overt, external guidance). (3) The child performs the task while talking aloud to self (overt self-guidance). (4) The child performs the task while whispering (faded, overt self-guidance). (5) The child performs the task while thinking the directions (covert self-instruction). This approach has been used to teach impulsive students to approach tasks more deliberately, help social isolates initiate peer interaction, teach aggressive students to control their anger, and teach defeated students to try problem solving instead of giving up (Brophy, 1983).

Self-instruction has most often been used in special education classes or in one-to-one settings (e.g., between therapist and client), but a study by Brenda Manning (1988) suggests that it can be successful in general education classrooms as well. Manning worked with first- and third-grade students who had been identified by their teachers as exhibiting inappropriate behavior in class—shouting out, constantly being out of their seats, daydreaming, playing around with things in their desk, and disturbing others. Two times a week, for four consecutive weeks, Manning met with the children in a 50-minute session. First, she modeled appropriate behaviors (e.g., raising hands, staying seated, concentrating, keeping hands and feet to self). Then she had the students perform the behaviors while verbalizing aloud what to do: "If I scream out the answer, others will be disturbed. I will raise my hand and wait my turn. Good for me—see, I can wait!" Finally, students performed the behavior without speaking aloud, but they used "cue cards" as prompts ("I will raise my hand and wait my turn.") Observations of the students after the self-instruction training indicated significant increases in on-task behavior.

Although none of our five teachers has tried self-instruction with students, all have frequently used cue cards to prompt appropriate behavior. They tell us that Post-it notes are a useful "low-tech" tool for this purpose. Post-its can be stuck on desk tops to remind children not to call out, not to tattle, or not to whine. They can be stuck on lockers to help students remember to wear their glasses or to bring their books to class. And one student teacher with a tendency to dominate class discussions applied Post-its to her lesson plans to remind herself to "KEEP QUIET AND LET THE KIDS TALK."

Before we leave the discussion of self-monitoring, self-evaluation, and self-instruction, it is important to note that self-management strategies hold particular promise for students with disabilities in general education settings. Only a handful of studies have been conducted in inclusive classrooms (e.g., Rock, 2005), but they indicate that students with disabilities can be taught to use self-management to improve both their social and their academic performance. If you decide to try one of these self-management strategies, consult with your school's psychologist, a counselor, or a special education teacher.

Contingency Contracting

A contingency or behavior contract is an agreement between a teacher and an individual student that specifies what the student must do to earn a particular reward. Contingency contracts are negotiated with students; both parties must agree on the behaviors the student is to exhibit, the period of time involved, and the rewards that will result. To be most effective, contracts should be written and signed. And, of course, there should be an opportunity for review and renegotiation if the contract is not working.

Courtney developed a contingency contract with Ashley, a student in her class who was frequently off task. She wandered around, going to the restroom and disrupting other students. During morning meetings, she often called out and gave inappropriate responses to questions; when everyone else was sitting with "pretzel feet" in a circle, Ashley would be up on her knees just *outside* the circle, fidgeting with her name tag, her hair, or a toy (which she wasn't supposed to have brought to the meeting). According to Courtney, much of Ashley's behavior seemed to be an effort to get attention:

When I would talk to her about her behavior, she'd say, "You gonna call my mom and dad?"—almost as if she'd like that. And she's alienating the other children. She's bossy; she doesn't share; she hoards the markers; she annoys the kids whenever they have to work together; she doesn't follow directions; she doesn't stop and clean up when she's supposed to. When a new student came, Ashley's behavior got a lot worse. I think she didn't like it that someone else was getting a lot of attention. She stopped doing her work. This was a line she hadn't crossed before, and I decided I had to do something more systematic.

Courtney decided to develop a behavior contract with Ashley that would provide reinforcement for appropriate behavior (see Figure 12.3). She knew she had to choose reinforcers that Ashley really liked, such as spending time in the room with Courtney after school (instead of going to "after school care"). Second, she wanted the system to be manageable and simple. She decided to give Ashley a sticker after every instructional period in which she demonstrated on-task, cooperative behavior; they negotiated how many stickers she had to receive each day in order to earn 10 minutes after school with Courtney, and gradually the number increased. At first they assessed her behavior after every period, but eventually they did so only at snack (mid-morning), at lunch, after their "special," and at the end of the day. When the system had been in place for a month or so, we asked Courtney to tell us how it was working.

MY CONTRACT

I, Ashley, agree to:

    raise my hand when I have something to say

    stay in my own space at my carpet spot and at my table

I will earn a sticker for each part of the day that I am able to do these things.

7 stickers = 10 minutes after school with Miss Bell

_____

Ashley

_____

Miss Bell

Figure 12.3   Example of a Behavior Contract

 Her behavior has definitely improved, and she likes the system—almost too much, in fact! She was asking me every 10 minutes, "Can I count how many stickers I have?" It was too much for me to keep showing her, so we agreed that she would count only when we met to decide on whether she had earned a new sticker. I'm actually surprised by how honest she is. I'll ask her, "Do you think you earned your sticker?" and she'll say, "No, I should stop and think."

At first we decided that she'd have to get seven stickers (out of a possible 12) in order to spend time with me after school. Then we increased it to eight, then nine, etc. Things were working pretty well until we got to 12, when she seemed to backslide. I realized that if she messed up just once, she had no incentive to behave the whole rest of the day. So I decided we had to go back to saying she had to earn at least 10.

It's interesting how the other kids have gotten on board. After special, they'll come in and say, "Ashley was really good today at special. She should get a sticker." I was afraid that they would complain that she was getting stickers and they weren't, but that hasn't happened. Even at five, they seem to understand that she needs extra support. If they ask me why she has a sticker chart and they don't, I just say, "You make good choices, but Ashley needs a little help making good choices. This will help her." Also, I think the fact that she gets time with me after school works well; it's less obvious than if she got something during the day. And she's becoming the class computer expert because she spends the time playing computer games.

Overall, I'm pleased with the way it's working. Ashley really does like the system. She came up to me the other day and said, "What am I going to do next year, when you're not my teacher, and I don't have a sticker chart?" I told her, "Well, hopefully you're learning to make good choices and you won't need a sticker chart." She seemed satisfied with that answer.

Positive Behavioral Support and Functional Behavioral Assessment

Positive behavioral support (PBS) is based on the principle that behavior occurs for one of two reasons. Either it enables individuals to obtain something they desire (positive reinforcement) or it enables individuals to avoid something they find unpleasant (e.g., negative reinforcement). In other words, behavior happens for a reason, although the individual may not be conscious of this. Given this principle, PBS begins by investigating *why* a problem behavior occurs (i.e., what *function* or purpose it serves); teachers can then design an intervention to eliminate the challenging behavior and replace it with a socially acceptable behavior that serves the same purpose.

The process of investigating why the problem behavior occurs is known as *functional behavioral assessment* (FBA). FBA procedures have historically been used in cases of severe disabilities, and in fact, IDEA 2004 mandates that schools conduct FBAs of a student with disabilities if he or she is to be removed more than 10 consecutive school days or if the removal constitutes a change in placement. In recent years, however, FBA has also been widely recommended for use in general education classrooms with typically developing students and those with mild disabilities (Robinson & Ricord Griesemer, 2006).

FBA consists of several steps. First, it is necessary to *describe the problem behavior* in precise, measurable, observable terms so that two or more people could agree on the occurrence. This means that instead of saying, "Lauren is aggressive," you need to say, "Lauren pinches and shoves other children and takes their materials during center time." In the second step, *information is collected about the environmental events that occur before and after the student's behavior.* This is generally referred to as an A-B-C assessment, where A represents the antecedents of the behavior, B represents the behavior, and C represents the consequences. (Figure 12.4 shows a sample ABC recording sheet.) Because it generally isn't feasible to collect this information while you're teaching, you will probably have to arrange for someone else (e.g., a collaborating teacher, a teaching assistant, or a school counselor) to do the assessment while you provide instruction (or vice versa). It's also essential to conduct observations across several days and several time periods, so you can be confident that you are getting a representative sample of the student's behavior. Finally, make sure to observe at times when the target behavior typically occurs and at times when it typically does *not* occur. If you carry out this step carefully, you should then be able to answer the following questions (Kerr & Nelson, 2006):

In what settings does the behavior occur?

During what times of the day does the behavior occur?

Student **Ronald**   Date **10/11**

Observer **Mr. Green**   Time **9:15**

Setting/Activity   **Writing workshop**

Target Behavior(s) **Noncompliance/aggression**

Time	**Antecedents** (What happened before the behavior?)	**Behavior** (What did the student do?)	**Consequences** (What happened after the behavior?)
9:15	Teacher tells class to put writing materials away and get ready to go to gym.	Ronald keeps writing while other children begin cleaning up.	Teacher tells him to put writing folder and markers away and to help his table group clean up. Ronald keeps writing.
9:17	Teacher goes over to Ronald, crouches down to eye level, and says she needs him to clean up now.	Ronald crumples paper and throws it on the floor.	Teacher tells Ronald to sit in time-out chair until time for gym.
9:22	Teacher tells class to line up for gym class.	Ronald races over to door, shoves child who is 1st in line, and assumes position of line leader.	Teacher tells Ronald to go to back of line.

Figure 12.4   A Sample ABC Recording Sheet

Does the behavior occur in the presence of certain persons?

During what activities is the behavior more likely to occur?

During what activities is the behavior less likely to occur?

What happens to the student following the behavior?

How do others respond to the behavior?

Does the surrounding environment change in any way following the behavior?

In the third step of the FBA, *hypotheses are developed about the purpose of the behavior;* in other words, this is when you try to figure out what the child stands to gain. For example, let's assume that as a result of gathering information in Step 2, it has become clear that Justin is disruptive only during writing workshop (the antecedent), when he annoys the other children at his table cluster by taking their pencils, making silly noises, and falling out of his chair (the behavior). In response to this behavior, the teacher repeatedly tells him to "settle down and get to work" (one consequence). When this doesn't bring about a positive change, the teacher tells him to go to the time-out chair and think about how students are supposed to behave during writing workshop (another consequence). On the basis of this information, we can hypothesize that Justin's behavior enables him to avoid something he seems to find aversive—namely, writing workshop.

The fourth step is to *test the hypotheses you have developed* by creating a behavior intervention plan (BIP). This involves modifying some aspect of the environment and observing the effect. In Justin's case, because the writing task appears to be frustrating, the teacher might provide him with additional support (such as his own personal dictionary), allow him to seek assistance from a "writing buddy," and provide encouragement and further instructional guidance as needed. In addition, the teacher might stop responding to the inappropriate behavior and instead respond to appropriate behavior with smiles and praise. If *monitoring* (the fifth step) shows that the BIP is successful (i.e., the inappropriate behavior ceases), then the FBA is done. If the inappropriate behavior continues, you need to go back to the third step and develop some new hypotheses. Remember, however, that long-standing behavior does not change overnight; you may need to follow the plan for two or three weeks before deciding whether it is making a difference (Friend & Bursuck, 2002).

Although FBA is an extremely useful tool, it is not simple, and identifying the underlying function of a behavior may require the assistance of well-trained observers (Landrum & Kauffman, 2006). Therefore, we urge teachers to consult with special services personnel.

Positive behavioral support can also be a schoolwide effort designed to prevent problem behavior and promote social and academic goals (Lewis, Newcomer, Trussell, & Richter, 2006). This year, Courtney was a member of a schoolwide PBS team composed of the principal, the guidance counselor, a representative from each grade level and the related arts, members of the Child Study Team, and a parent. Together, the team worked to select and define three expectations for behavior: *Respectful, Responsible, Safe.* These behavioral expectations are now being taught to all students. A monitoring system will evaluate how well the program is working, and additional supports will be provided for children who continue to display problem behavior.

DEALING WITH THORNY PROBLEMS

Some problem behaviors seem to plague teachers regardless of where they are teaching. It's impossible to generate recipes for dealing with these problems, because every instance is unique in terms of key players, circumstances, and history. Nonetheless, it is helpful to reflect on ways to deal with them *before* they occur and to hear some of the thinking that guides the actions of our five teachers. In this section of the chapter, we will consider seven behaviors that keep teachers awake at night wondering what to do.

Tattling

Fortunately, tattling is generally confined to the lower grades; unfortunately, it can become an epidemic if allowed to go unchecked, creating a negative atmosphere and wasting instructional time. Furthermore, if tattling is encouraged or condoned, children receive the message that only "a higher authority" can settle disputes and resolve problems.

All five teachers stress the fact that children need to understand the difference between alerting the teacher to a dangerous or hurtful situation and reporting minor infractions or perceived injustices. This may require explicit lessons, during which the class discusses what tattling is, how it affects the atmosphere in the classroom, and why it is important to learn to settle one's own problems (Charles & Senter, 1995). Sometimes students need practice in distinguishing among situations that call for different responses: instances when a particular situation demands an immediate report to the teacher (e.g., you see a classmate about to jab someone with a pair of scissors); situations that they should try to resolve by themselves (e.g., your neighbor is mumbling to herself and it's annoying you); and situations that can be ignored (e.g., you see a classmate use the pencil sharpener when he shouldn't be doing so). Of course, if you encourage students to try resolving their own problems, then you need to equip them with some strategies. Courtney, for example, teaches her students to use I-messages if someone is being a bother:

First I modeled I-messages with my aide. We acted out a typical kinder-garten situation in which she pushes me, and I told her, "I don't like it when you push me because that hurts." I explained that when there is a problem in the classroom, we need to tell people how it makes us feel. I don't call it using an I-message; I call it "using your words." I had the kids do it with me, and then I had two kids at a time role-play. We practiced it a lot. It works well. The kids will come up to tell me about a problem, and I'll listen and then say, "Did you use your words?" If they say no, I tell them to go back and try that. It became clear that I wouldn't listen to them unless they had already tried it. If they use their words and that doesn't work, I'll go over and ask them what happened and coach them through it.

All the teachers try to convey the message that they are available for students when serious problems arise, but that they are not interested in hearing minor, petty complaints. When tattling does occur, they try to discourage it. Ken some-times asks, "Why are you telling me this?" When the student explains ("Well, he took my paper . . ."), Ken follows up with questions such as

What else could you do, besides telling me?
Is this serious?
Can you talk to him?
Do you want to write about it?

Garnetta also suggests that children write about the problem and promises to read what they have written later, when she has the time. This usually discourages any further discussion, unless the situation is really upsetting to the child. Then, of course, she acknowledges their feelings and tries to help them deal with the issues.

Very often, tattling occurs after lunch or recess, when students return to class with stories about problems that have occurred in the cafeteria or on the play-ground. Barbara deals with situations like these by telling students, "Unless you were hurt, I don't need to hear about it." If lunchtime or recess incidents begin to disrupt classroom life, however, it may be necessary to deal with the problem directly, either with the individual children involved or with the whole class. (See Barbara's problem-solving session described in Chapter 3.)

Cheating

As teachers increasingly emphasize collaboration, cooperative learning, and peer tutoring, both they and students are finding it harder to distinguish cheating from sharing. Furthermore, in classrooms where helping one another is the normal way of working, it can be difficult for students to shut off this mode of operation and move into individual, independent activities such as test taking. Desks arranged in clusters can also contribute to the difficulty. As we discussed in Chapter 2, clusters foster discussion and sharing—even during a test, when students are supposed to work independently.

It's obviously better to deal with cheating before it occurs, rather than afterward. This means finding ways to *reduce the temptation to cheat.* You can discuss cheating in a class meeting, during which you can explain the difference between helping and cheating, demonstrate the expected behavior for various activities, and have students distinguish between situations when it's appropriate to share ideas and situations when it's inappropriate. Given the advent of the Internet, it's also important (at least in the upper elementary grades) to explain what plagiarism is and to make it clear that you consider plagiarism a serious transgression. Many students don't consider copying and pasting from a website to be cheating (Ma, Lu, Turner, & Wan, 2007).

You can also explain the difference between *learning* and *performance* and make it clear that your job is to help students *learn.* One particular study (Anderman, Griesinger, & Westerfield, 1998) found that students are more likely to report that they have cheated when teachers are perceived as emphasizing performance over mastery (i.e., when it's more important to get an A on a test than to master the material). Similarly, students more often report that they have cheated when teachers rely on extrinsic incentives to stimulate motivation (e.g., giving homework passes to students who get As on a test) rather than trying to foster genuine interest in academic tasks.

In addition to reducing temptation, you can also take a number of simple precautions to *minimize opportunity.* When giving tests, for example, it's helpful to separate desks, circulate throughout the room, use new tests each year, and create different forms of the same test. In the case of standardized testing, it's a good idea to rearrange the desks several days in advance so that students can adjust to the new layout.

Obviously, despite all your precautions, incidents of cheating will occur. It then becomes necessary to confront the students involved. Some suggestions for handling those encounters are listed in the Practical Tips box.

You also need to think about your response to the child who *gives* help on a task. Often, the desire to follow the teacher's directions and to stay out of trouble clashes with a child's desire to assist friends who are having difficulty (Bloome & Theodorou, 1988). This may be a particular dilemma for children who come from

PRACTICAL TIPS FOR

DEALING WITH CHEATING

- *Talk privately.* Avoid creating a situation where the student may be publicly humiliated. This is likely to lead to a series of accusations and denials that get more and more heated.

- *Present your reasons for suspecting cheating.* Lay out your evidence calmly and firmly, even sorrowfully.

- *Express concern.* Make it clear that you do not expect this kind of behavior from this student. Try to find out why students cheated (e.g., Were they simply unprepared? Are they under a lot of pressure to excel?)

- *Explain consequences.* A common response to cheating is to give the student a low grade or a zero on the assignment or test. This seems like a sensible solution at first glance, but it confounds the act of cheating with the student's mastery of the content (Cangelosi, 1993). In other words, a person looking at the teacher's grade book would be unable to tell whether the low grade meant the student had violated the test-taking procedures or indicated a failure to learn the material. We prefer using a logical consequence—namely, having the student redo the assignment or test under more carefully controlled conditions. Some schools have predetermined consequences for cheating, such as detention and parental notification. If so, you need to follow your school's policy.

- *Discuss the consequences for subsequent cheating.* Alert the student to the consequences that will follow additional cheating incidents. If the student continues to cheat, investigate the reasons for this behavior. Students may cheat on a test because they watched television instead of studying, but they may also cheat because their parents are putting excessive pressure on them to achieve, because they have unrealistic goals for themselves, or because they do not have the skills or background necessary to succeed on the test (Grossman, 1995). Clearly, these different causes of the cheating call for different responses.

PAUSE AND REFLECT

How would you explain to a child whose culture stresses the importance of cooperation, friendship, and generosity that there are times when providing help on a task is *not* a good thing and may actually be considered cheating?

cultures that teach children to be generous; Hawaiian American and Hispanic students, for example, may feel that helping friends is a necessity even though the teacher views it as cheating (Grossman, 1995). A gentle reminder of the rules that apply in the school setting may be an effective first response to students who help others for this reason.

Stealing

Like tattling, most stealing incidents occur in the early grades when students have less control over their impulses and when they are still learning the difference between sharing and taking what doesn't belong to them. Again, it's important to help young children distinguish between these two situations. Usually, a simple reminder about rules related to personal property should help, but remember that a rule such as "respect other people's property" has to be clearly operationalized for children.

In addition to age, cultural differences also may play a role in the confusion between sharing and taking. Some cultures emphasize sharing and generosity, whereas others stress private ownership. For example, Herbert Grossman (1984) observes that when teachers try to explain that "what's mine is mine and what's yours is yours," Hispanic students may feel "bewildered, confused or even rejected and insulted" (p. 89).

If an incident of stealing does occur, and you know who the culprit is, you can have a quiet, private conversation about what has happened. If you are not sure that the child understands the difference between sharing and taking, it is best to avoid direct accusations: "I'm sure you forgot that his markers were in your backpack when you went home, but you need to bring them back tomorrow." When the child returns the markers, you can take a more instructional approach: "I'm glad you brought the markers back. You know, you shouldn't be putting other people's property in your backpack. Even though it was an accident, some people might call it stealing, and I know you wouldn't want to be accused of that."

Depending on the value of the property, the frequency of incidence, and the grade level you are teaching, it may be necessary to intervene more forcefully. As we mentioned earlier, all of our teachers have used whole-class pressure to have the stolen materials returned. Sometimes, you may even need to contact families or refer the problem to the principal.

Profanity

The use of profanity in school has risen as children have been increasingly exposed to inappropriate language at home and through the media. In deciding on a suitable response, it's useful to think about the reasons why students use profanity. Once again, age plays a role. Younger children may simply be echoing language they have heard used by friends, by family, or on television, with little or no understanding of the meaning. In this case, the appropriate response is instructional, not disciplinary. You need to explain that "we don't use words like that in school." You might ask the children whether they know what the words mean and suggest that they talk with their parents; it might also be helpful to contact parents and ask them to speak with their children.

Children may also use profanity because they hear it used frequently at home and it has become a regular part of their speaking vocabulary. In this case, you can make it clear that language like that is inappropriate and unacceptable in school. Barbara reminds students that *she* doesn't use that language at school, and she doesn't expect *them* to use it either.

Finally, there are times when students angrily direct profanity toward another student or the teacher. When this happens, you need to stress that using language to hurt other people will not be tolerated and that there are more acceptable ways of expressing anger. Sometimes children are so angry that they blurt out profanities without thinking about the context. In this case, it's wise to allow them time to calm down before trying to discuss what happened. It's also helpful to address the reasons for their anger before addressing the inappropriateness of their language.

Defiance

When we asked Courtney, Barbara, Garnetta, Ken, and Viviana to tell us about the ways they deal with defiance, our question was met with unusual silence. Finally, Ken ventured to explain that his students rarely acted in defiant ways, so it was hard for him to say what he'd do. The four other teachers murmured their agreement. We were initially skeptical, but as we talked, it became clear that the answer lay in the teachers' ability to prevent minor problems from escalating into major ones. Consider Garnetta's way of dealing with Laticia, a child who had "spent the entire second grade in the office":

Laticia was constantly picking fights, calling names, and talking back to her previous teacher. . . . Obviously, I couldn't wait to have her in my class. But when she came to me, one of the first things she said was "No one ever listens to me." I took that as my cue. I made sure to listen to her. And I'd always try to anticipate a problem. I'd see her beginning to act up—maybe going to poke someone—and I'd immediately go over and quietly tell her to come into the hall with me. I never got into an argument with her in front of everyone. I'd be real calm, and we'd go out, and I'd ask her what was happening. She'd tell me why she was mad, and I'd listen, and we'd talk about what she could do when she got that way. She hardly ever had to go to the office. But if I had let things go, the other child would have poked back. Then a fight would have erupted, and she'd have ended up in the principal's office again.

Defiant situations can usually be avoided if teachers follow Garnetta's model. Having said that, we still need to consider what to do if a student *does* become defiant. See the Practical Tips box for some suggestions.

One additional note: Children with oppositional defiant disorder (ODD) exhibit a pattern of defiant and hostile behavior, especially toward authority figures. If you have a child with ODD, he or she may need to be treated in specific ways outlined in his or her individualized education plan (IEP). In this case, it's important to discuss the child's behavior with a counselor.

Sexually Related Behavior

The need to consider children's developmental levels is particularly relevant here. In an early childhood classroom, it's not unusual to see children occasionally rubbing their genitals. Usually they will stop as soon as you divert their attention or get them more actively involved in the lesson. Viviana simply tells her first-graders that she wants to see everyone's hands on their desks. If the masturbation continues, however, she has a private conversation with the individual student:

I don't want to embarrass the child, but if I don't stop it, the other children will see and start to make fun. Maybe the child doesn't even know this is not proper to do in school. I'll say something like, "I don't want you to put your hands inside your pants. It's not bad, but it's not something people do at school."

PRACTICAL TIPS FOR

HANDLING DEFIANCE

- *Stay in control of yourself.* Even though your first inclination may be to shout back, don't. (It may help to take a few deep breaths and to use self-talk: "I can handle this calmly. I'm going to speak quietly.")

- *Direct the rest of the class to work on something* (e.g., "Everyone do the next three problems" or "Start reading the next section").

- *Move the student away from peers.* Talk to the student in an area where you can have more privacy. This eliminates the need for the student to worry about saving face.

- *Stand a few feet away from the student (i.e., don't get "in his face").* A student who is feeling angry and defiant may interpret closing in on him as an aggressive act (Wolfgang, 1999).

- *Acknowledge the student's feelings.* "I can see that you're really angry. . . ."

- *Avoid a power struggle.* "I'm the boss in here and I'm telling you to . . . ."

- *Offer a choice.* "I can see that you're really upset, and we'll have to talk later. But meanwhile, here are the choices. You can go to the office, or I'll have to send for someone to come and get you."

Depending on the situation, you might also contact parents, ask them to speak with their child, and suggest some simple ways of curbing the behavior—for example, having children wear pants that require a belt instead of pants with an elastic waist.

By the time students reach fourth grade, they generally know that masturbation is inappropriate in school. If you do see a youngster engaging in this behavior, however, you need to deal with the situation very discreetly—and before the other children notice and begin to taunt. Barbara uses this approach: "I've seen what you've been doing at your seat during quiet times, and it's not something you should be doing in school. Is everything OK?"

It's also necessary to consider developmental level when you see a child touching another child in a sexual way. Again, it's not unusual for kindergarten children to explore each other's bodies; a simple directive to stop and a reminder to "keep your hands to yourself" will usually take care of the matter. At intermediate grade levels (grades 4 through 6), students need to be aware of what constitutes sexual harassment and to know that it will not be tolerated in the school environment. They also need to know that they can report incidents of sexual harassment and that the adults in the school will take action.

At *any* elementary grade level, habitual masturbation and behaviors that are sexually precocious or explicit warrant investigation. Children who continue to masturbate even after you have spoken to them may have severe problems, and children who imitate adult sexual behavior may have witnessed such activity first-hand or experienced it themselves. In cases like these, you need to contact the appropriate child welfare agency. (See Chapter 5 for signs of abuse and reporting procedures.)

Failure to Do Homework

When students consistently fail to do homework assignments, it's important to consider just how valuable those assignments are and whether you have communicated that value to students. It's also important to reflect on how much homework you're assigning, whether it's too difficult for students to complete independently, and whether the time allotted is sufficient. Some additional strategies that can help increase the likelihood of students completing homework are listed in the Practical Tips box.

PRACTICAL TIPS FOR

INCREASING THE LIKELIHOOD THAT STUDENTS WILL DO THEIR HOMEWORK

- *Provide homework planners.* Not only do homework planners help students to remember their assignments, they also allow parents to see what homework their children have and send messages to the child's teacher using the planner. Homework planners have a particularly positive effect on students with learning disabilities and average-achieving students who have homework problems (Bryan & Sullivan-Burstein, 1998).

- *Provide choices.* For example, if children have to practice their vocabulary words, they might be allowed to use sentences including the words, do a word search, or make a flip book illustrating the words (D'Agostino, 2003).

- *In the beginning of the year, teach children how to do homework.* Talk about their experience with homework (What's been hard? easy? What have they liked? disliked?) Discuss how to manage time, how to find a quiet, appropriate space, and how to care for materials (Bates, 2003).

- *Review, collect, or grade assignments.* If you assign homework and then fail to check whether students have done it, you're conveying the message that the homework just wasn't that important. Not all homework has to be graded, or even collected, but it's wise to check that students have done it and to record that fact in your grade book.

- *Have children graph their homework completion.* Students can create their own graphs showing the homework assignments not turned in (red), those turned in complete and on time (green), and those turned in complete but late (yellow) (Bryan & Sullivan-Burstein, 1998).

- *Give "homework quizzes."* Some teachers give a daily quiz with one or two questions that are just like those assigned the night before for homework. In addition, they give a "homework quiz" every week or two. They select a few problems that were previously given for homework and allow students to refer to their homework papers, but not their books.

- *Require a "product" in addition to reading.* Students are far more likely to do reading if you also have them do something *with* it (e.g., use Post-it notes to mark your three favorite passages; list 10 words or phrases the author uses to give clues about the protagonist's character; generate three questions about the reading to ask your classmates).

- *Provide in-school support.* Sometimes students' home circumstances may interfere with doing homework. They may be in the midst of a family crisis. They may be living in an abusive situation. They may have after-school responsibilities (such as caring for younger siblings) that leave little time for schoolwork. In situations like this, you might work with the student to develop a plan for getting homework done in school.

Despite your best efforts, some students will still not turn in homework. In this case, you need to meet individually to discuss the problem, generate possible solutions, and decide on an action plan. This might include contacting parents and asking for their cooperation and assistance, writing a contingency contract, or assigning a "homework buddy" to help the student remember and complete homework.

WHEN DISCIPLINE VIOLATES STUDENTS' CONSTITUTIONAL RIGHTS

Before we leave the topic of disciplinary interventions, it's important to examine three situations in which well-meaning teachers may unknowingly violate students' constitutional rights. The first situation involves students' First Amendment rights. Consider the following scenario: A student comes to school wearing a t-shirt with a slogan and picture that you find offensive. Do you have the right to require him or her to remove the shirt or turn it inside out?

According to David Schimmel (2006), an expert on law and education, the answer is no—unless the student's expression causes substantial disruption or interferes with the rights of others. In 1969, the U.S. Supreme Court ruled that the First Amendment applies to public schools and that a student's right to freedom of expression "does not stop at the schoolhouse gate" (*Tinker v. Des Moines,* 1969, p. 506; cited by Schimmel, 2006). In that groundbreaking case, schools in Des Moines, Iowa, fearing disruption, had forbidden students to wear black armbands protesting the Vietnam War. The Court rejected the schools' argument, concluding that schools cannot prohibit expression just "to avoid the discomfort and unpleasantness that always accompany an unpopular viewpoint" (p. 509). Although subsequent Supreme Court decisions have narrowed *Tinker,* the basic principle remains intact—"that is, a student's nondisruptive personal expression that occurs in school is protected by the First Amendment even if the ideas are unpopular and controversial" (Schimmel, 2006, p. 1006). Given these judicial rulings, you need to be careful about disciplining students for controversial expression. Without question, you need to consult with a school administrator or the district's legal counsel before taking disciplinary action.

The second situation is when teachers unwittingly violate students' Fourth Amendment rights against unreasonable search and seizure. The case of *Watkins v. Millenium School* (2003) is illustrative (Schimmel, 2006). Ms. Apley, a third-grade teacher in Ohio, discovered that $10 was missing from her desk. She asked Shaneequa Watkins and two other students to open their book bags, empty their pockets, and turn down the waistband of their pants, but she didn't find anything. The teacher then took Shaneequa to a supply closet; there the girl was required to pull out her pants and underwear so Ms. Apley could look down them for the money.

In the subsequent lawsuit, the court ruled that the school's interest in maintaining order and instilling moral values did not outweigh Shaneequa Watkin's privacy interest. They wrote that "a reasonable teacher should have known that students have Fourth Amendment rights against unreasonable search and seizure" and that requiring a student to expose the private areas of her body without individualized suspicion is clearly unreasonable (p. 902; cited in Schimmel, 2006, p. 1009). Keep this judicial ruling in mind if you suspect that a student has stolen and hidden something. It's best to bring that person to the appropriate school official rather than undertake a search yourself.

Finally, another situation that involves students' Fourth Amendment rights is use of a form of time-out called "seclusion time-out," in which a student is removed from the classroom environment and placed alone in a room designated for this purpose. (Note that this is far more restrictive and controversial than the mild form of time-out used by our teachers.) In recent years, several lawsuits have been brought by parents contending that school districts had violated their children's rights by improperly using seclusion time-out. In the *Peters v. Rome City School District* (2002) decision, for example, a jury in New York awarded $75,000 to a family whose second-grade child had been placed in a time-out room for over an hour with the door held shut (Ryan, Peterson, & Rozalski, 2007). If current advocacy efforts are successful, this form of time-out may be entirely prohibited; meanwhile, seclusion time-out should be used only as a last resort, and only after checking carefully on school or district policies and procedures.

CONCLUDING COMMENTS

One afternoon after school, we talked with Garnetta about the problems her students bring with them to school. She displayed considerable empathy and insight into their home situations. Nonetheless, she emphasized that she had high expectations for their behavior and achievement:

It's up to us to teach students to be responsible, to have standards, and to demand that work gets done. We can't simply say, "They can't help it," or "They didn't do it, so it's a zero." You've got to discuss expectations and keep plugging away. I see so many kids kicked out of class, and I think to myself, "Did you talk with them? What did you try before you gave up and sent them out?" Some days I feel like I've had it too. But then I remind myself that I'm in charge of this classroom. I'm responsible for what goes on here.

Garnetta's comments illustrate two important characteristics of effective classroom managers. First, more effective managers are *willing to take responsibility* for managing their students' behavior, whereas *less effective managers tend to disclaim responsibility and refer problems to other school personnel,* such as the principal or the guidance counselor (Brophy & Rohrkemper, 1981). All five of our teachers take responsibility for the behavior of their students. They rarely refer students to the office. They recognize that they are "in charge" and that they are accountable for what happens in their classrooms.

Second, *effective managers (especially in high-poverty schools such as Garnetta's) can be characterized as "warm demanders"* (Bondy & Ross, 2008). This term aptly describes our teachers. As warm demanders, they genuinely care about their students and have deliberately built supportive, trusting relationships with them. At the same time, they insist that students meet high expectations. They accept the fact that problem behaviors will occur, but they believe in students' ability to improve. They make it clear that showing respect and behaving appropriately is non-negotiable. And, as Garnetta stressed, they keep "plugging away."

SUMMARY

This chapter discussed ways of responding to a variety of problems—from minor, nondisruptive infractions to chronic, more serious misbehaviors.

Guidelines for Dealing with Misbehavior

- Use disciplinary strategies that are consistent with the goal of creating and maintaining a safe, caring classroom environment.
    Separate the student's character from the specific misbehavior.
    Encourage students to take responsibility for regulating their own behavior.
- Keep the instructional program going with a minimum of disruption.
- Consider the context of students' actions. Behavior that is acceptable in one context may be unacceptable in another.
- Be timely and accurate when responding to behavior problems.
- Match your disciplinary strategy to the misbehavior.
- Be "culturally responsive," because differences in norms, values, and styles of communication can have a direct effect on students' behavior.

Strategies for Dealing with Minor Misbehavior

- Nonverbal interventions.
- Verbal interventions.
- Deliberate non-intervention for misbehavior that is fleeting.

Strategies for Dealing with More Serious Misbehavior

- Plan penalties ahead of time.
- Choose penalties that are logically related to the misbehavior.
- Impose penalties calmly and quietly.
- Reestablish a positive relationship with the student as quickly as possible.
- Be consistent.
- Develop a range of alternative consequences.

Strategies for Dealing with Chronic Misbehavior

- Problem-solving process
    Step 1: Define the problem.
    Step 2: Brainstorm possible solutions.
    Step 3: Evaluate solutions.
    Step 4: Decide on a solution to try.
    Step 5: Determine how to implement the decision.
    Step 6: Evaluate the solution.
- Behavioral learning approaches
    Self-monitoring.
    Self-evaluation.

Self-instruction.
Contingency contracting.
Positive behavioral supports and functional behavioral assessment.

Dealing with Thorny Problems

- Tattling.
- Cheating.
- Stealing.
- Profanity.
- Defiance.
- Sexually related behavior.
- Failure to do homework.

When Discipline Violates Students' Constitutional Rights

- A student's nondisruptive personal expression is protected by the First Amendment, even if the ideas are unpopular and controversial.
- The Fourth Amendment grants students freedom from unreasonable search and seizure, so consult with an administrator before searching students and their belongings.
- Be very cautious about using "seclusion time-out," because this very restrictive, controversial intervention may also violate students' Fourth Amendment rights.

Effective teachers are willing to take responsibility for managing students' behavior. They can also be characterized as "warm demanders" who build caring, supportive relationships with students, while also holding high expectations for behavior.

ACTIVITIES FOR SKILL BUILDING AND REFLECTION

In Class

1. When a misbehavior occurs, there usually isn't much time for careful consideration of logical consequences. We've listed a few typical misbehaviors for you to practice dealing with. In a small group, think of two logical consequences for each example.

    a. Your class monitor keeps forgetting to clean the gerbil cage, and it is beginning to smell.
    b. Tom always takes longer than the other children to get settled in after snack time, and most times he is still eating when it is time to get back to work.
    c. Rachel spends her computer time playing with the contents of her purse.
    d. As part of a laboratory group, Lou mishandles supplies, causing spills and complaints from his group members.
    e. Meagan draws all over Shelissa's face with a purple magic marker.
    f. Ross rubs glue all over his hands so that he can peel it off when it dries.
    g. Ariana returns her novel with many pages ripped and the cover missing.

2. In a small group, discuss what you would do in the following situation. You are reviewing homework from the night before. You call on James to do number 5. He slumps in his

seat and fidgets with the chain around his neck. You tell him the class is waiting for his answer to number 5. Finally he mutters, "I didn't do the f_____homework."

On Your Own

1. Beginning teachers sometimes overreact to misbehavior or take no action at all because they simply don't know what to do or say. First, read the examples given in the table. Then consider the situations that follow it, and for each, suggest a nonverbal intervention, a verbal cue, and an I-message.

Example	Nonverbal	Verbal	I-Message
A student writes on the desk	Hand the student an eraser.	"We use paper to write on."	"When you write on the desk, the custodian complains to me and I get embarrassed."
A student makes a big show of looking through her book bag for her homework, distracting other students and delaying the start of the lesson.	Give the "look."	"We're ready to begin."	"When you take so long to get your things out, I can't begin the lesson, and I get very frustrated about the lost time."

   a. A student is copying from another student's paper.
   b. A student takes another student's notebook.
   c. A student sharpens his pencil during your presentation.
   d. A student calls out instead of raising her hand.

2. One common misbehavior in many classrooms is students being off task (e.g., talking to other students while the teacher is presenting a lesson, or trying to distract other students).
   a. What might you conclude about the classroom norms or the classroom activities if this misbehavior is common?
   b. What might be some of the reasons for the students' off-task behavior?
   c. Given your responses to parts a. and b., what would be a reasonable teacher response?

For Your Portfolio

Develop a behavior modification plan (such as self-monitoring or a contingency contract) to deal with each of the following problems.
   a. Arthur is larger than the other children in your second-grade class. A day has not gone by that a child hasn't come to you complaining of Arthur's hitting, pushing, or teasing. You've talked to his parents, but they are at a loss about what to do.
   b. Cynthia, a fifth-grader, rarely completes her work. She daydreams, socializes with others, misunderstands directions, and gets upset when you speak to her about her incomplete work. The problem seems to be getting worse.

For Further Reading

Bear, G. G. (1998). School discipline in the United States: Prevention, correction, and long-term social development. *School Psychology Review, 27*(1), 724–742.

> This article reviews strategies used by highly effective classroom teachers to achieve the short-term goal of order and the long-term goal of self-discipline. Bear argues that effective teachers can be characterized by an authoritative style that combines strategies for preventing behavior problems, operant learning strategies for short-term management, and decision-making and social problem-solving strategies to achieve the long-term goal of self-discipline.

Gordon, T. (2003). *T.E.T.—Teacher Effectiveness Training.* New York: Three Rivers Press.

> In this updated edition of his 1974 classic, Gordon contends that both authoritarian and permissive approaches to dealing with young people in schools are destructive, "win–lose," power-based approaches. Instead, he advocates a "no-lose" approach to solving problems that protects the teacher–student relationship and promotes communciation and caring. He explains the concept of "problem-ownership" so that students can respond in appropriate ways.

Kottler, J. A., & Kottler, E. (2009). *Students who drive you crazy: Succeeding with resistant, unmotivated, and otherwise difficult young people* (2nd ed.). Thousand Oaks, CA: Corwin Press.

> This book gives teachers a model to assess, understand, and respond to challenging students. The authors cover a range of potential misbehaviors that are prevalent in teaching, and they provide advice and support from teachers, counselors, and administrators who have had previous experience in handling such issues in practice.

Obidah, J. E., & Teel, K. M. (2001). *Because of the kids: Facing racial and cultural differences in schools.* New York: Teachers College Press.

> Jennifer Obidah is Black; Karen Mannhein Teel is White. Together, they conducted a three-year study to explore the impact of racial and cultural differences on Karen's relationship with her primarily African American middle school students. In the process, the two teachers also had to learn to communicate with each other across racial and cultural boundaries. This book describes the challenges they faced as they tried to generate specific ways in which Karen could more effectively educate her African American students.

Thompson, G. L. (2004). *Through ebony eyes: What teachers need to know but are afraid to ask about African American students.* San Francisco: Jossey-Bass.

> Written in lively, conversational language, this book provides information and strategies to help teachers increase their effectiveness with African American students. Thompson talks about why some African American students misbehave in class and how teachers often unwittingly contribute to their misbehavior.

PREVENTING AND RESPONDING TO VIOLENCE

By the year 2000 all schools in America will be free of drugs and violence and the unauthorized presence of firearms and alcohol, and offer a disciplined environment that is conducive to learning. (HR 1804: Goals 2000: Educate America Act, 1994, Sec. 102)

In the late 1990s, a series of school shootings in Mississippi, Kentucky, Arkansas, Pennsylvania, Tennessee, and Oregon made it clear that this laudable national goal, adopted by Congress and signed by then President Clinton, was certainly out of reach. But nothing prepared the country for the events of April 20, 1999. On that day, two seniors at Columbine High School in Littleton, Colorado, shot and killed 12 students and a teacher before turning their guns on themselves. Overnight, the topic of school violence catapulted to the front page. Copycat shootings, bomb scares, and threats of violence created unprecedented terror and upheaval during the final weeks of the school year. Parents agonized about sending their children to school. Politicians, policy makers, and pundits talked about youth violence as a "national epidemic" and speculated on the causes (Drummond & Portner, 1999). Perceptions of an epidemic were heightened in 2000, when a six-year-old in Michigan took a gun to school and killed his first-grade classmate (Naughton & Thomas, 2000). Five years later the country was stunned again when a high school student went on a shooting rampage on the Red Lake Indian Reservation in northern Minnesota, killing his grandparents, five fellow students, a teacher, a security guard, and himself. Since then, additional school shootings by students have occurred in Wisconsin, Washington, Ohio, Tennessee, California, and Florida.

But just how widespread is school violence? Are Columbine, Red Lake, and these more recent shootings symptomatic of a growing epidemic, or are they horrible but isolated incidents? Let's look at some facts and figures.

HOW MUCH VIOLENCE IS THERE?

Information on the frequency and severity of school violence comes from the U.S. Departments of Education and Justice (Dinkes, Cataldi, & Lin-Kelly, 2007). The data show that from 1992 to 2005, crime in the nation's schools actually *decreased* from 50 violent incidents per 1,000 students to 24 violent incidents. From 1993 to 2005, the percentage of high school students who said they had been in a fight on school property declined from 16 percent to 14 percent. Similarly, the percentage of students who reported carrying a weapon such as a gun, knife, or club on school property within the previous 30 days also declined, from 12 percent to 6 percent.

Despite the decreasing percentages, violence remains a problem that must be confronted. In 2005, 129,000 students from ages 12 to 18 were victims of serious violent crimes at school, and an additional 74,000 students were victims of theft at school (Dinkes, Cataldi, & Lin-Kelly, 2007). Moreover, *perceptions* of violence are widespread and produce a great deal of anxiety (see Figure 13.1). After the Red Lake shootings, a Gallup/CNN poll reported that close to three-quarters of the American public believed such school shootings were likely to happen in their communities, and 60 percent did not think events like these could be prevented (Astor & Benbenishty, 2005). When asked to name the biggest problem that their school had to deal with, students from ages 13 to 17 mentioned violence, fighting, and school safety nearly twice as frequently as any other problem (Gallup Poll, 2005). Clearly, teachers and administrators must work to decrease students' fears and anxiety, as well as actual incidents of school violence.

Figure 13.1   *Source:* BALDO © 2001, Baldo Partnership. Dist. By UNIVERSAL UCLICK. Reprinted with permission. All rights reserved.

Many strategies that are effective for preventing violence have already been discussed in earlier chapters of this book. Getting to know your students, building respectful relationships, establishing orderly classrooms, curbing peer harassment and bullying, and working to meet students' learning needs all reduce the potential for violence. In this chapter we discuss additional strategies for preventing violence and then examine ways to react to violence if it occurs.

PAUSE AND REFLECT

With the issue of school violence so prevalent in the media, anxiety around this issue is normal for all teachers, but for novice teachers in particular. What are your fears associated with school violence? Talk to teachers in the school where you are observing or teaching about the school's procedures for dealing with issues of violence. Are there standard procedures in place? Knowing what to do in a crisis situation will not only ease anxieties but also may make a significant difference in the outcome.

STRATEGIES FOR PREVENTING VIOLENCE

Build Supportive School Communities

Although we focused on creating safer, more caring classrooms in Chapter 3, it's important to revisit this topic in relation to violence prevention. Numerous educators argue that violence prevention has to focus on the creation of more humane environments in which students are known and feel supported (Astor, Meyer, & Behre, 1999). The superintendent of Barbara's district echoes this sentiment:

> *A safe school is one that is responsive to students, where the staff knows the kids, where you can get help for troubled kids right away. . . . We don't talk much about metal detectors or security measures here. Our approach to violence prevention emphasizes connecting to kids and addressing their social–emotional needs. We try hard to make sure that one group isn't elevated over another . . . and to respect differences among kids.*

In line with the superintendent's beliefs about safe schools, Barbara's school has launched a major effort to create a schoolwide sense of community. A birthday board by the front door displays everyone's birthday on a giant calendar; in the hallways, grade-level bulletin boards allow every student to display a self-selected example of school work; and in addition to class rules, the school has adopted a set of "beliefs" that are posted in every classroom (see Figure 13.2).

Ken's school is also working to build a schoolwide community. Every teacher and every aide in the building has a "family" made up of two children from each grade level (1–5). The family has a name (Ken's family is the Golden Eagles), a color, and a special family signal. Every Tuesday morning at 11:00, families meet to do an activity together for about 20 minutes, such as a morning meeting. Families stay together through the years, enabling children to develop relationships across grade levels and to connect with another adult in the building.

Creating a supportive school community is more important than ever. Given the changing nature of families and economic conditions that require both parents

In this school . . .

- Everyone has a right to be respected and treated with kindness and courtesy. This means we will not treat anyone unfairly, laugh at them, ignore them, or hurt their feelings.
- Everyone has a right to feel safe. This means that we will not hurt anyone with our words or actions.
- Everyone has a right to hear and be heard. This means we will use Listening Position, Speaker Power, B.E.S.T., and Keep Calm.
- Everyone has a right to learn as an individual. This means we will support and appreciate the different ways that people learn by offering encouragement.

Figure 13.2   The Schoolwide Beliefs Adopted in Barbara's School

to work outside the home, many students spend more time in the company of peers than with adult family members. These peer relationships are not an adequate substitute for adult attention, so it is critical that teachers develop and nurture caring relationships with their students (Laursen, 2008).

Be Alert to Signs of Hate

According to a report from the Southern Poverty Law Center (2004), the number of hate crimes by youngsters has risen sharply since 9/11:

> [A] disproportionate number of assaults on Muslim-Americans were committed by teenagers. The same appears to be true for attacks against sexual and gender minorities, Hispanics and the homeless. And hate activity is no longer the province of white boys, though they are still the main offenders. Not only are more Hispanic and African-American kids getting involved in hate, but more girls as well. . . . [Furthermore,] in another demographic shift, the bulk of hate activity now bubbles up in the suburbs—among reasonably well-off youth. (p. 1)

As a teacher, you need to take note if book reports, essays, drawings, or journal entries convey messages of hate or violence, and you must report your concerns to the principal, a school counselor, or the district's affirmative action officer. Help students recognize hate symbols, such as swastikas, and derogatory labels for race, ethnicity, and sexual orientation. At Halloween time, discourage costumes that involve negative stereotyping (e.g., "gypsy" costumes or "homeless person" outfits); organizations that promote hate (e.g., Ku Klux Klan robes); and the display of weapons.

Know the Early Warning Signs of Potential for Violence

In 1998, the U.S. Department of Education and the Department of Justice published a guide to assist schools in developing comprehensive violence prevention plans (Dwyer, Osher, & Warger, 1998). The guide contains a list of "early warning signs" that can alert teachers and other school staff to students' potential for violence, as well as signs that violence is imminent. These appear in Tables 13.1 and 13.2.

TABLE 13.1 Early Warning Signs of Potential for Violence

Social withdrawal

Excessive feelings of isolation and being alone

Excessive feelings of rejection

Being a victim of violence

Feelings of being picked on and persecuted

Low school interest and poor academic performance

Expression of violence in writings and drawings

Uncontrolled anger

Patterns of impulsive and chronic hitting, intimidating, and bullying behaviors

History of discipline problems

Past history of violent and aggressive behavior

Intolerance for differences and prejudicial attitudes

Drug use and alcohol use

Affiliation with gangs

Inappropriate access to, possession of, and use of firearms

Serious threats of violence

Source: Adapted from Dwyer, Osher, & Warger, 1998.

TABLE 13.2 Imminent Signs of Violence

Serious physical fighting with peers or family members

Severe destruction of property

Severe rage for seemingly minor reasons

Detailed threats of lethal violence

Possession and/or use of firearms and other weapons

Other self-injurious behaviors or threats of suicide

Source: Adapted from Dwyer, Osher, & Warger, 1998.

It's important to remember that the early warning signs are not an infallible predictor that a child or youth will commit a violent act toward self or others (Dwyer, Osher, & Warger, 1998). Also, keep in mind that potentially violent students typically exhibit multiple warning signs. Thus, be careful about overreacting to single signs, words, or actions, and don't be biased by a student's race, socioeconomic status, academic ability, or physical appearance.

The difficulty of distinguishing between a real threat to safety and harmless student expression is underscored by a 2000 federal court ruling in Washington state (Walsh, 2000). In this case, a high school junior submitted a poem to his English teacher about a lonely student who roamed his high school with a pounding heart. The poem contained this passage:

> As I approached the classroom door,
> I drew my gun and threw open the door.
> Bang, Bang, Bang-Bang.

When it was all over, 28 were dead,
and all I remember was not felling [sic] any remorce [sic],
for I felt, I was, cleansing my soul . . .

The student's teacher alerted administrators, and the poem was reviewed by a psychologist, who determined that the student was unlikely to cause harm to himself or others. Nonetheless, the district decided to expel him on an emergency basis. After the student was examined by a psychiatrist, the district rescinded the expulsion, and the student completed his junior year. The boy's parents then sued the district, claiming that the school had violated his First Amendment right to free speech and asking that the expulsion be removed from their son's record. On February 24, 2000, a federal district judge ruled for the family, maintaining that the district had overreacted in expelling the student. She suggested that there were less restrictive ways in which the district could have ensured the safety of students and school personnel, such as imposing a temporary suspension pending psychiatric examination.

Stories like this can discourage teachers from reporting essays or artwork that contain threatening messages or behavior that suggests a potential for violence. But it's better to alert school officials about what you have learned than to ignore indicators and be sorry later. Find out what the reporting procedures are in your school: Do you report your concerns to the principal? to the school nurse? to a counselor? Do you notify parents? Remember that parental involvement and consent are required before personally identifiable information is shared with agencies outside the school (except in case of emergencies or suspicion of abuse). The Family Educational Rights and Privacy Act (FERPA), a federal law that addresses the privacy of educational records, must be observed in all referrals to community agencies (Dwyer, Osher, & Warger, 1998).

Be Observant in "Unowned" Spaces

In addition to knowing the early warning signs, teachers can help prevent violence by being observant in hallways, cafeterias, stairwells, and locker rooms—"unowned" spaces where violence is most likely to erupt. One study (Astor, Meyer, & Pitner, 2001) interviewed elementary and middle school students about the places in their schools that seemed unsafe and violence-prone. Areas that students perceived to be unsafe tended to lack adult supervision and monitoring and were overcrowded. As one elementary student put it,

[Fights are likely to occur] in the hallway . . . 'cause it's like the biggest space in the school. And like most teachers don't look in the hallway if they're going to get coffee.

Be Attentive to Whispers, Rumors, and Threats

The high-profile school shootings that we have witnessed in the last several years are what the Secret Service calls *targeted violence*—incidents in which the attacker selects a particular target prior to the violent attack. As part of the Safe School

Initiative of the U.S. Secret Service and the U.S. Department of Education, researchers studied 37 school shootings involving 41 attackers who were current or recent students at the school (Vossekuil et al., 2002). Here are some of their findings:

- Incidents of targeted violence at school are rarely sudden or impulsive. Typically, the attacker *planned* the attack in advance.

- In most of the cases, other people knew about the attack before it occurred. In over three-quarters of the cases, at least one person knew; in nearly two-thirds, more than one person knew. Some peers knew details of the attack, whereas others just knew that something "big" or "bad" was going to happen in school on a particular day.

- Most attackers engaged in some behavior prior to the incident that caused others concern or indicated a need for help.

These findings contradict the common perception that students who commit targeted acts of violence have simply "snapped." Nor are they loners who keep their plans to themselves. In a follow-up study, researchers interviewed 15 students who had known about potential threats of violence at their schools (Pollack, Modzeleski, & Rooney, 2008). They found that the school climate had an effect on whether or not these students reported the threats of violence. One student who knew of a weapon on school property was reluctant to come forward because he expected a negative reaction: "When you say something, you get in trouble or [get] interrogated by teachers" (p. 7). Additionally, many of the bystanders did not believe that the threats would be carried out, so they didn't tell anyone. This means that school staff must be attentive to whispers that something is afoot and must create a climate that encourages students to report rumors of potential violence. As Tonia Moore, the student assistance counselor (SAC) in Barbara's district, puts it, "You have to have your radar out all the time."

You also need to be aware of your district's policy regarding threats to harm another person, whether they are written or oral. For example, in Courtney's district, the superintendent of schools sent parents and guardians a letter explaining that the school district could "no longer disregard any threat as a hoax" and outlining the procedures to be followed in the event of a threat of violence. First, the building principal notifies the central office, calls the police, and contacts the parents of the accused student. Second, the student is disciplined and placed on home instruction until the school receives a written psychiatric report stating that the student does not pose a threat. Finally, the police, as part of their own investigation, take whatever action they deem appropriate.

De-escalate Potentially Explosive Situations

Explosive situations often begin benignly. You make a reasonable request ("Would you join the group over there?") or give an ordinary directive ("Get started on the questions at the end of this section"). But the student is feeling angry—maybe he has just been taunted and humiliated in the hallway; maybe her mother has just grounded her for a month; maybe the teacher in the previous class has ridiculed an answer. The anger may have nothing to do with you at all, but it finds its outlet in your class. In a hostile mood, the student fails to comply immediately and may even respond defiantly. Unfortunately, at this point, teachers often contribute to the escalation of a conflict by becoming angry and impatient. They issue an ultimatum: "Do what I say or else." And now teacher and student are combatants in a potentially explosive situation that neither of them wanted.

Let's consider an example (adapted from Walker, Colvin, & Ramsey, 1995) of a teacher–student interaction that begins innocuously enough but quickly escalates into an explosive situation:

> Students are working on a set of math problems the teacher has assigned. Michael sits slouched in his seat staring at the floor, an angry expression on his face. The teacher sees that Michael is not doing his math and calls over to him from the back of the room where she is working with other students.

TEACHER:	Michael, why aren't you working on the assignment?
MICHAEL:	I finished it.
TEACHER:	Well, let me see it then. [She walks over to Michael's desk and sees that he has four problems completed.] Good. You've done 4 but you need to do 10.
MICHAEL:	Nobody told me that!
TEACHER:	Michael, I went over the assignment very clearly and asked if there were any questions about what to do!
MICHAEL:	I don't remember that.
TEACHER:	Look at the board. I wrote it there. See, page 163, numbers 11–20.
MICHAEL:	I didn't see it. Anyway, I hate this boring stuff.
TEACHER:	OK, that's enough. No more arguments. Page 163, 11 through 20. Now.
MICHAEL:	It's dumb. I'm not going to do it.
TEACHER:	Yes you are, mister.
MICHAEL:	Yeah? Make me.
TEACHER:	If you don't do it now, you're going to the office.
MICHAEL:	F———— you!
TEACHER:	That's enough!
MICHAEL:	You want math? Here it is! [He throws the math book across the room.]

At first glance, it appears that the teacher is being remarkably patient and reasonable in the face of Michael's stubbornness, defiance, and abuse. On closer examination, however, we can detect a chain of successive escalating interactions, in which Michael's behavior moves from questioning and challenging the teacher to defiance and abuse, and for which the teacher is also responsible (Walker, Colvin, & Ramsey, 1995). Could the teacher have broken this chain earlier? The probable answer is yes.

First, the teacher should have been sensitive to Michael's angry facial expression and the fact that he was slouching down in his seat. Facial expression, flushing,

PRACTICAL TIPS FOR

MANAGING POTENTIALLY EXPLOSIVE SITUATIONS

- *Move slowly and deliberately toward the problem situation.*

- *Speak privately, quietly, and calmly.* Do not threaten. Be as matter-of-fact as possible.

- *Be as still as possible.* Avoid pointing or gesturing.

- *Keep a reasonable distance.* Do not crowd the student. Do not get "in the student's face."

- *Speak respectfully.* Use the student's name.

- *Establish eye-level position.*

- *Be brief.* Avoid long-winded statements or nagging.

- *Stay with the agenda.* Stay focused on the problem at hand. Do not get sidetracked. Deal with less severe problems later.

- *Avoid power struggles.* Do not get drawn into "I won't, yes you will" arguments.

- *Inform the student of the expected behavior and express the negative consequence of doing otherwise as a choice or decision for the student to make.* Then withdraw from the student and allow some time for the student to decide. ("Michael, you need to return to your desk, or I will have to send for the principal. You have a few seconds to decide." The teacher then moves away, perhaps attending to other students. If Michael does not choose the appropriate behavior, deliver the negative consequence. "You are choosing to have me call the principal.") Follow through with the consequence.

Source: Adapted from Walker, Colvin, & Ramsey, 1995.

squinty eyes, clenched fists, rigid body posture, pacing and stomping—these all suggest an impending eruption (Hyman, 1997). Second, teachers can usually avoid defiant situations if they do not corner a student, do not argue, do not engage in a power struggle ("I'm the boss in this classroom, and I'm telling you to . . .") and do not embarrass the student in front of peers. The accompanying Practical Tips box summarizes specific recommendations.

With this background, let's go back to Michael and see how the teacher might have dealt with the situation to prevent it from escalating.

Students are working on a set of math problems the teacher has assigned. Michael sits slouched in his seat staring at the floor, an angry expression on his face. The teacher notices Michael's posture and realizes that he is feeling upset about something. She goes over, bends down so that she is on eye-level with Michael, and speaks very quietly.

TEACHER: Are you doing OK, Michael? You look upset. [Teacher demonstrates empathy.]

MICHAEL: I'm OK.

TEACHER: Well, good, but if you'd like to talk later, let me know. [Teacher invites further communication.] Meanwhile, you need to get going on this assignment.

MICHAEL: I already did it.

TEACHER: Oh, good. Let me see how you did. [She checks the paper.] OK, you've done the first four, and they're fine. Now do the next four problems and let me see them when you're done. [She walks away, giving the student space.]

PAUSE AND REFLECT

Imagine an incident of aggressive behavior occurring in your classroom (e.g., a child explodes in anger and throws a book at another student). Think about the steps you would take to stop the aggression from escalating and to restore calm. What words would you use? Then continue reading and see, in the next section, how Garnetta handled an outburst that occurred in her classroom.

RESPONDING TO VIOLENCE

Coping with Aggressive Behavior

Despite your best efforts at prevention, there are times when students erupt in hostile, aggressive behavior. A girl screams profanities and knocks a pile of dictionaries to the floor. A boy explodes in anger and throws a chair across the room. Someone yells "I'll kill you" and hurls a notebook at another student. In situations like this—every teacher's nightmare—it's easy to lose self-control and lash out. That's the normal reaction. But teachers can't afford to react normally. That will only make things worse, and your responsibility is to make things better.

Let's consider an episode that occurred in Garnetta's classroom:

My class was working in small groups of three or four students on their "five senses" projects. Each group was collecting information on a different sense. I was circulating, helping groups that were having difficulty, directing others to additional resources. All of a sudden, I heard a commotion on the other side of the room. Larry had turned over the desk he was working at, and he was yelling to Jeffrey, "I'm going to get you after school." Jeffrey was on his feet, and he looked as though he was about to tackle Larry.

My first instinct was to shout, "Now stop that at once!" but I kept my cool and immediately started walking over to the two boys. The first thing I said was "Jeffrey, keep your hands down. Go over to the library corner. Larry, you come over to me." I kept repeating that. Finally, Larry looked at me and started coming toward me, mumbling under his breath about how Jeffrey's little brother had hit his [Larry's] younger sister for the last time. As we got closer, I put my arm around him (something that was natural since I had done that many times before) and quietly said, "Let's move over to the door so we can talk." I wanted to talk with him privately, but I also wanted to be able to keep an eye on the class. I told the rest of the students that I needed to speak with Larry but that I wanted them to continue working on their projects. I told them that if they acted responsibly, we would have lunch together in the classroom on Friday.

When we got to the doorway, a security guard was passing by. I asked him to go get the vice principal, Mr. Williams. Meanwhile, I tried to get Larry to calm down. It was clear he was still ready to burst. I said, "Obviously you're really angry about something. Tell me about it." He told me how Jeffrey's younger brother kept beating up his [Larry's] younger sister.

When Mr. Williams came, I explained what had happened. He took Larry to the office, along with Jeffrey (collecting the two younger siblings on the way), so that everyone could tell their version of the situation. I went back into the room, where my students all wanted to know what had happened, of course. I told them that the two boys were having a feud, but that they were going to talk about it with Mr. Williams and get everything settled. I complimented them on their behavior and got us back on track.

About 20 minutes later, Larry came back with a note from the vice principal saying that he needed to get his jacket and book bag because he was going home for the day. I gave him a hug and told him that I was glad to see he had calmed down. I told him that I could understand why he had been angry, but that we all needed to learn better ways to express our anger. I made sure he had the necessary materials so that he could work on his project at home. Once Larry left, Jeffrey came with the same note. I gave him a hug too and helped him pack up his things. I told him how glad I was that he had listened to me and not fought back.

After the boys left, Mr. Williams called on the intercom and asked me to stop by to see him at the end of the school day. I found out that it was the boys' mothers who were having the dispute, and they had dragged the kids in. Mr. Williams had met with them both, and they had agreed to see the school guidance counselor—with and without their children—to work out their problems. Given their agreement, he agreed not to suspend Larry.

My class handled itself really well during the whole thing—I was really proud of them. On Friday, I kept my promise: We had a pizza lunch together in the classroom.

Analysis of Garnetta's response to Larry's outburst reveals some important guidelines for dealing with aggression in the classroom. Let's examine her behavior more closely and consider the lessons to be learned.

1. Although Garnetta's first instinct was to shout, she remained outwardly calm and in control. By doing so, she was able to lower the level of emotion in the class and prevent the situation from escalating. She then directed Jeffrey to keep his hands down and to move to the library corner. This prevented Larry's aggressive actions from escalating into a full-scale physical fight. Next she issued quiet, firm, repetitive instructions for Larry to move away from Jeffrey and come over to her.

2. Garnetta's next action was to summon help by asking the passing security guard to get the vice principal. Never send angry, aggressive students to the office alone: You cannot be certain they will actually get there, nor do you

know what they will do on the way. If you do not have a telephone or intercom (and no security guard shows up at the right moment), quietly instruct a responsible student to go for assistance.

3. While Garnetta waited for the vice principal, she spoke privately and quietly with Larry in an attempt to defuse the aggression. She did not rebuke or threaten punishment. Instead, she acknowledged his anger and showed her willingness to listen.

Again, it's critical that you resist the temptation to "react normally" and lash out at the student. You need to speak slowly and softly and to minimize threat by not invading the student's space and keeping your hands by your sides. Allow the student to relate facts and feelings, even if it involves profanity, and use active listening ("So you were really furious when you found out what was happening . . ."). Do not disagree or argue.

If, despite your efforts to restore calm, the student's aggression escalates, it is best to move away unless you are trained in physical restraint techniques. Even then, don't use restraint unless you are strong enough and there are no other options. As Hyman (1997) emphasizes, "The last thing you ever want to do is to physically engage an enraged student who may be out of control" (p. 251).

4. Once Larry and Jeffrey were on their way to the office, Garnetta turned her attention to her class to determine how the other students were feeling and what to do next. She decided to briefly explain what was going on and to continue the lesson.

Sometimes your students may be so upset and frightened that it's impossible to continue working. The SAC in Barbara's district suggests that it's important to allow them to express their feelings:

> *If the students are upset, you have to give them the opportunity to talk about what happened and to acknowledge their fear. You don't want to pretend nothing happened and then send them on to the next class all churned up inside.*

5. When Larry came back to the room to get his belongings, he gave Garnetta the chance to reestablish a positive relationship. She gave him a hug, helped him to get his materials together, and acknowledged his anger. Her actions reassured him that he was still a member of the class and that he could learn from this.

Responding Effectively to Physical Fights

Physical fights are more likely to occur on the playground and in hallways and cafeterias than in classrooms. But what do you do if you're on the scene when a fight erupts? We asked the teachers that question one evening, as we talked about the problem of violence in schools. They were unanimous in their response; the steps they take are listed in the Practical Tips box. As we discussed the issue of fighting in school, the teachers repeatedly stressed the fact that *fights are fast.* They

> ### PRACTICAL TIPS FOR
>
> **RESPONDING EFFECTIVELY TO PHYSICAL FIGHTS**
>
> - *Quickly appraise the situation.* Is this a verbal altercation? Is there physical contact? Does anyone have a weapon?
>
> - *Send a responsible student for help.* Send for the nearest teacher and for the principal or vice principal. Once other people are there to help, it's easier—and safer—to get the situation under control.
>
> - *Tell students to stop.* Often, students don't want to continue the fight, and they'll respond to a short, clear, firm command. If you know the combatants' names, use them.
>
> - *Disperse other students.* There's no need for an audience, and you don't want onlookers to become part of the fray. If you're in the hallway, direct students to be on their way. If you're in the classroom, send your students to the library or to some other safe place.
>
> - *Do not intervene physically*—unless the age, size, and number of combatants indicates that it's safe to do so, or there are three or four people to help, or you have learned techniques of physical restraint.

can erupt quickly—so you don't have a lot of time to think through a response—and they're usually over in less than 30 seconds (although that can seem like a lifetime).

It's important to remember that you must report violent acts. Every school system needs to have a violent incident reporting system that requires you to report what happened, when and where it happened, who was involved, and what action was taken (Blauvelt, 1990).

CONCLUDING COMMENTS

In the wake of Columbine, school officials all across the country reexamined their safety and security measures. Schools mounted surveillance cameras, limited access during school hours by locking or monitoring doors, practiced "lock-downs" and safety drills, and either required clear plastic backpacks or banned them completely. Although enhanced security is a logical reaction to the threat of violent crime, some educators worry that security measures create a negative environment, turning schools into prisonlike, oppressive institutions (Astor, Meyer, & Behre, 1999; Berreth & Berman, 1997; Noguera, 1995).

It is clear that enhanced security systems alone will not solve the problem of school violence, nor will they allay students' fears and anxieties. Creating safer schools—and schools that *feel* safer—requires a collaborative effort to reach out to students and build a climate of tolerance and community. In the final analysis, it is the presence of caring administrators and teachers that holds the greatest promise for preventing violence.

SUMMARY

Although data on the frequency and severity of school violence indicate a decrease, students, teachers, and parents are fearful, and the perception that violence is increasing is widespread. This chapter presented a variety of strategies for preventing and responding to violence.

Strategies for Preventing Violence

- Build supportive school communities.
- Be alert to signs of hate.
- Know the early warning signs of potential for violence.
- Be observant in "unowned" spaces.
- Be attentive to whispers, rumors, and threats.
- De-escalate potentially explosive situations.

Responding to Violence

- Coping with aggressive behavior
    Prevent escalation.
    Summon help.
    Defuse the aggression.
    Reestablish a positive relationship with the aggressor.
    Determine how the other students are feeling.
- Responding effectively to physical fights
    Quickly appraise the situation.
    Send a responsible student for help.
    Tell the students to stop.
    Disperse onlookers.
    Do not intervene physically unless it is safe.

Metal detectors and security systems can only go so far. It's essential to build connections with students. In the final analysis, it is the presence of caring administrators and teachers that holds the greatest promise for preventing violence.

ACTIVITIES FOR SKILL BUILDING AND REFLECTION

In Class

Consider the following situations. In small groups, discuss what you would do in each case.

1. As students enter your classroom, you overhear a girl teasing Annamarie about being overweight. They go to their seats, but the taunts continue. Suddenly, Annamarie stands up, turns to the girl, and shouts, "You shut up! Just shut up, or I'll get you!"

2. Your students are taking a brief quiz on their homework. Those who have finished already are reading. As you circulate throughout the room, collecting the finished

papers, you notice that James is drawing gruesome pictures of people fighting with knives and guns. He has labeled one of the victims with the name of a classmate.

3. You catch Joe passing a note to Pete. It says, "Michael is a fag. Let's go after him at lunchtime."

4. You ask Carla where her homework is. She mutters something under her breath. When you tell her you didn't hear what she said, she shouts, "I didn't do it, you bitch!"

On Your Own

Interview an experienced teacher, the student assistance counselor, the school nurse, or a guidance counselor about the school's efforts to prevent violence. Find out answers to the following questions:

> If you think a student exhibits some of the early warning signs of potential for violence, to whom do you report your concern?
>
> Is there an official form to file?
>
> Do you contact parents?

For Your Portfolio

Document how you will establish a classroom climate in which students are comfortable telling you about threats of violence at school. Return to the artifacts you created when you completed the "For Your Portfolio" section of Chapter 3, and modify those artifacts to incorporate this chapter's material. Write a brief commentary explaining how you will help your students understand the importance of reporting threats.

FOR FURTHER READING

Colvin, G. (2004). *Managing the cycle of acting-out behavior in the classroom.* Eugene, OR: Behavior Associates.

> This book provides practical strategies for managing and preventing acting-out behavior such as defiance, tantrums, threats, resistance, avoidance, and classroom disruption at various levels. It presents a model of acting-out behavior that consists of seven phases. The characteristics of each phase are described via examples and case studies. Strategies are then presented for interventions that can be used for each phase.

Creating caring schools (2003). Theme issue of *Educational Leadership, 60*(6).

> This entire issue of *Educational Leadership* is devoted to the topic of creating caring schools. Topics include bullying, teasing, creating community, social-emotional learning programs, student-led class meetings, collaborative learning, and racial and ethnic tolerance.

Noguera, P. (1995). Preventing and producing violence: A critical analysis of responses to school violence. *Harvard Educational Review, 65,* 189–212.

> In this article, Pedro Noguera asks whether the strategies that schools adopt in response to "disciplinary problems," including violence, actually perpetuate violence. Noguera argues that "get-tough" disciplinary measures produce prisonlike schools, interrupt learning, and breed mistrust and resistance. He offers alternative strategies for humanizing school environments and encouraging a sense of community.

Teaching Tolerance is a magazine that is mailed twice a year at no charge to educators. It is published by the Southern Poverty Law Center, a nonprofit legal and educational foundation. (See listing below.) The magazine provides a wealth of information and resources on all aspects of promoting tolerance and respect and eliminating bias, oppression, and bullying (www.teachingtolerance.org).

ORGANIZATIONAL RESOURCES

The Anti-Defamation League (ADL), 823 United Nations Plaza, New York, NY 10017; 212-885-7970; www.adl.org. Dedicated to combating hate crime and promoting intergroup cooperation and understanding.

Committee for Children, 568 First Avenue South, Suite 600, Seattle, WA 98104-2804; 800-634-4449; www.cfchildren.org. Publishes *Second Step—A Violence Prevention Program* and *Steps to Respect—A Bullying Prevention Program.*

Drug Strategies, 1616 P Street, Suite 220, Washington, DC 20036, 202-289-9070, www.drugstrategies.com. Publishes a guide on conflict resolution and violence prevention curricula.

National School Safety Center, 141 Duesenberg Dr., Suite 11, Westlake Village, CA, 91362, 805-373-9977, www.nssc1.org. Resource for school safety information, training, and violence prevention.

The Safe and Drug Free Schools website for the U.S. Department of Education, 550 12th St. SW, 10th floor, Washington DC 20202-6450, 202-245-7896, www.ed.gov/offices/OESE/SDFS/news.html. Provides reports and articles on school safety and school violence.

The Southern Poverty Law Center, 400 Washington Avenue, Montgomery, AL 36104; 334-956-8200, www.teachingtolerance.org. The Teaching Tolerance project provides teachers at all levels with ideas and free resources for building community, fighting bias, and celebrating diversity.

Students Against Violence Everywhere (SAVE), 322 Chapanoke Rd., Suite 110, Raleigh NC, 27603, 866-343-SAFE, www.nationalsave.org. This student-driven organization helps students learn about alternatives to violence and encourages them to practice what they have learned through school and community projects.

References

The AAUW Report: How schools shortchange girls. (1992). Washington, DC: The AAUW Educational Foundation and National Education Association.

A field trip to the sea. (1999). Pleasantville, NY: Sunburst Communications.

Abd-Kadir, J., & Hardman, F. (2007). Whole class teaching in Kenyan and Nigerian primary schools. *Language and Education, 21*(1), 1-15.

Adams, R. S., & Biddle, B. J. (1970). *Realities of teaching: Explorations with video tape.* New York: Holt, Rinehart, & Winston.

Ainsworth, M.D.S. (1964). Patterns of attachment behavior shown by the infant in interaction with his mother. *Merrill-Palmer Quarterly, 10,* 51-58.

Ainsworth, M.D.S. (1967). *Infancy in Uganda: Infant care and the growth of love.* Baltimore, MD: Johns Hopkins University Press.

Akin-Little, K. A., Little, S. G., & Laniti, M. (2007). Teachers' use of classroom management procedures in the United States and Greece: A cross-cultural comparison. *School Psychology International, 28*(1), 53-62.

Alberto, P. A., & Troutman, A. C. (2006). *Applied behavior analysis for teachers* (7th ed.). Upper Saddle River, NJ: Pearson Prentice Hall.

Alfi, O., Assor, A., & Katz, I. (2004). Learning to allow temporary failure: Potential benefits, supportive practices and teacher concerns. *Journal of Education for Teaching, 30*(1), 27-41.

Allen, J. B. (2007). *Creating welcoming schools: A practical guide to home-school partnerships with diverse families.* New York: Teachers College Press.

Allen, J. B. (2008). Family partnerships that count. *Educational Leadership, 66*(1), 22-27.

Alvermann, D., O'Brien, D., & Dillon, D. (1990). What teachers do when they say they're having discussions of content area reading assignments. *Reading Research Quarterly, 25,* 296-322.

American Psychiatric Association. (2000). *Diagnostic and statistical manual of mental disorders* (4th ed., text rev.). Washington, DC: Author.

Anderman, E. M., Griesinger, T., & Westerfield, G. (1998). Motivation and cheating during early adolescence. *Journal of Educational Psychology, 90*(1), 84-93.

Anderson, K. J., & Minke, K. M. (2007). Parent involvement in education: Toward an understanding of parents' decision making. *Journal of Educational Research, 100*(5), 311-323.

Anderson, L. (1985). What are students doing when they do all that seatwork? In C. W. Fisher & D. C. Berliner (Eds.), *Perspectives on instructional time.* New York: Longman, 189-202.

Anderson, L. (1994). Assignment and supervision of seatwork. *International Encyclopedia of Education* (2nd ed.). Oxford: Pergamon Press, 5359-5363.

Anderson, L., Brubaker, N., Alleman-Brooks, J., & Duffy, G. (1985). A qualitative study of seatwork in first-grade classrooms. *Elementary School Journal, 86,* 123-140.

Anderson, R., Hiebert, E., Scott, J., & Wilkinson, I. (1985). *Becoming a nation of readers: The report of the Commission on Reading.* Washington, DC: National Institute of Education.

Antil, L. R., Jenkins, J. R., Wayne, S. K., & Vadasy, P. F. (1998). Cooperative learning: Prevalence, conceptualizations, and the relation between research and practice. *American Educational Research Journal, 35*(3), 419-454.

Arends, R. I. (2008). Learning to teach (8th ed). New York: McGraw-Hill.

Arlin, M. (1979). Teacher transitions can disrupt time flow in classrooms. *American Educational Research Journal, 16,* 42-56.

Aronson, E., Blaney, N., Stephan, C., Sikes, J., & Snapp, M. (1978). *The Jigsaw classroom.* Beverly Hills, CA: Sage.

Astor, R. A., & Benbenishty (July 27, 2005). Zero tolerance for zero knowledge. *Education Week.* Downloaded from www.edweek.org/ew/articles/2005.

Astor, R. A., Meyer, H. A., & Behre, W. J. (1999). Unowned places and times: Maps and interviews about violence in high schools. *American Educational Research Journal, 36,* 3-42.

Astor, R. A., Meyer, H. A., & Pitner, R. O. (2001). Elementary and middle school students' perceptions of violence-prone school subcontexts. *The Elementary School Journal, 101*(5), 511-528.

Atwater, R., & Atwater, F. (1966). *Mr. Popper's penguins.* New York: Scholastic.

Ayers, W. (1993). *To teach: The journey of a teacher.* New York: Teachers College Press.

Bailey, J. M., & Guskey, T. R. (2001). *Implementing student-led conferences.* Thousand Oaks, CA: Corwin Press.

Ballenger, C. (1999). *Teaching other people's children: Literacy and learning in a bilingual classroom.* New York: Teachers College Press.

Bates, A. (2003). Comments on homework. *Responsive Classroom Newsletter, 15*(4), 6.

Beane, A. L. (1999). *The bully free classroom: Over 100 tips and strategies for teachers K-8.* Minneapolis, MN: Free Spirit.

Bear, G. G. (1998). School discipline in the United States: Prevention, correction, and long-term social development. *School Psychology Review, 27*(1), 724-742.

Berk, L. E. (2009). *Child development* (8th ed.). Boston: Pearson/Allyn & Bacon.

Berreth, D., & Berman, S. (1997). The moral dimensions of schools. *Educational Leadership, 54*(8), 24-26.

Bickley-Green, C. (2007). Visual arts education: Teaching a peaceful response to bullying. *Art Education, 60*(2), 6-12.

Blauvelt, P. D. (1990). School security: "Who you gonna call?" *School Safety Newsjournal,* Fall, 4-8.

Bloome, D., & Theodorou, E. (1988). Analyzing teacher–student and student–student discourse. In J. E. Green & J. O. Harker (Eds.), *Multiple perspective analyses of classroom discourse.* Norwood, NJ: Ablex, 217-248.

Bodine, R. J., & Crawford, D. K. (1998). *The handbook of conflict resolution education: A guide to building quality programs in schools.* San Francisco: Jossey-Bass.

Bohn, C. M., Roehrig, A. D., & Pressley, M. (2004). The first days of school in the classrooms of two more effective and four less effective primary-grades teachers. *The Elementary School Journal, 104*(4), 269-287.

Bolick, C. M., & Cooper, J. M. (2006). Classroom management and technology. In C. M. Evertson & C. S. Weinstein (Eds.), *Handbook of classroom management: Research, practice, and contemporary issues.* Mahwah, NJ: Lawrence Erlbaum Associates, 541–558.

Bomer, R., Dworin, J. E., May, L., & Semingson, P. (2008). Miseducating teachers about the poor: A critical analysis of Ruby Payne's claims about poverty. *Teachers College Record, 110*(12), 2497–2531.

Bondy, E., & Ross, D. D. (2008). The teacher as warm demander. *Educational Leadership, 66*(1), 54–58.

Bonus, M., & Riordan, L. (1998). *Increasing student on-task behavior through the use of specific seating arrangements.* Chicago: Saint Xavier University & IRI/Skylight Field-Based Masters Program. ERIC Document Reproduction Service No. ED 422 129.

Bowlby, J. (1969). *Attachment and loss, Vol. 1: Attachment.* New York: Basic Books.

Bowlby, J. (1973). *Attachment and loss, Vol. 2: Separation.* New York: Basic Books.

Brady, K., Forton, M. B., Porter, D., & Wood, C. (2003). *Rules in school.* Greenfield, MA: Northeast Foundation for Children.

Brandt, R. (1989). On parents and schools: A conversation with Joyce Epstein. *Educational Leadership, 47*(2), 24–27.

Brendgen, M. B., Wanner, B., Vitaro, F., Bukowski, W. M., & Tremblay, R. E. (2007). Verbal abuse by the teacher during childhood and academic, behavioral, and emotional adjustment in young adulthood. *Journal of Educational Psychology, 99*(1), 26–38.

Brookfield, S. D., & Preskill, S. (1999). *Discussion as a way of teaching: Tools and techniques for democratic classrooms.* San Francisco: Jossey-Bass.

Brophy, J. (2004). *Motivating students to learn.* Mahwah, NJ: Lawrence Erlbaum Associates.

Brophy, J., & Rohrkemper, M. (1981). The influence of problem ownership on teachers' perceptions of and strategies for coping with problem students. *Journal of Educational Psychology, 73,* 295–311.

Brophy, J. E. (1983). Classroom organization and management. *The Elementary School Journal, 83*(4), 265–285.

Brophy, J. E., & Evertson, C. (1976). *Learning from teaching: A developmental perspective.* Boston: Allyn & Bacon.

Brown, D. F. (2004). Urban teachers' professed classroom management strategies: Reflections of culturally responsive teaching. *Urban Education, 39*(3), 266–289.

Brown, L. H., & Beckett, K. S. (2007). Parent involvement in an alternative school for students at risk of educational failure. *Education and Urban Society, 39*(4), 498–523.

Brown, M. W. (1949). *The important book.* New York: Harper & Row.

Bryan, T., & Sullivan-Burstein, K. (1998). Teacher-selected strategies for improving homework completion. *Remedial and Special Education, 19*(5), 263–275.

Campbell, L., Campbell, B., & Dickinson, D. (1996). *Teaching and learning through multiple intelligences.* Needham Heights, MA: Allyn & Bacon.

Cameron, C. E., Connor, C. M., & Morrison, F. J. (2005). Effects of variation in teacher organization on classroom functioning. *Journal of School Psychology, 43*(1), 61–85.

Cameron, C., Tate, B., MacNaughton, D., & Politano, C. (1997). *Recognition without rewards: Building connections.* Winnipeg, Manitoba: Peguis Publishers.

Cameron, J. (2001). Negative effects of reward on intrinsic motivation—A limited phenomenon: Comment on Deci, Koestner, and Ryan (2001). *Review of Educational Research, 71*(1), 29–42.

Cameron, J., Banko, K. M., & Pierce, W. D. (2001). Pervasive negative effects of rewards on intrinsic motivation: The myth continues. *The Behavior Analyst, 24*(1), 1–44.

Cameron, J., & Pierce, W. D. (1994). Reinforcement, reward, and intrinsic motivation: A meta-analysis. *Review of Educational Research, 64,* 363–423.

Cangelosi, J. S. (1993). *Classroom management strategies: Gaining and maintaining students' cooperation* (2nd ed.). New York: Longman.

Canter, L., & Canter, M. (2001) *Assertive discipline: Positive behavior management for today's classroom* (3rd ed.). Santa Monica, CA: Lee Canter & Associates.

Carbone, E. (2001). Arranging the classroom with an eye (and ear) to students with ADHD. *Teaching Exceptional Children, 34*(2), 72–81.

Carson, L., & Hoyle, S. (1989/90). Teaching social skills: A view from the classroom. *Educational Leadership, 47*(4), 31.

Carter, K., & Doyle, W. (2006). Classroom management in early childhood and elementary classrooms. In C. M. Evertson & C. S. Weinstein (Eds.), *Handbook of classroom management: Research, practice, and contemporary issues.* Mahwah, NJ: Lawrence Erlbaum Associates.

Cartledge, G., & Lo, Y. (2006). *Teaching urban learners: Culturally responsive strategies for developing academic and behavioral competence.* Champaign, IL: Research Press.

Cartledge, G., with Milburn, J. F. (1996). *Cultural diversity and social skills instruction: Understanding ethnic and gender differences.* Champaign, IL: Research Press.

Cary, S. (2007). *Working with second language learners: Answers to teachers' top ten questions.* Portsmouth, NH: Heinemann.

Catalano, R. F., Haggerty, K. P., Oesterle, S., Fleming, C. B., & Hawkins, J. D. (2004). The importance of bonding to school for healthy development: Findings from the social development research group. *Journal of School Health, 74*(7), 252–261.

Cazden, C. B. (1988). *Classroom discourse: The language of teaching and learning.* Portsmouth, NH: Heinemann.

Centers for Disease Control and Prevention. (2007). Surveillance summaries. MMWR 2007; 56(SS-1).

CHADD. (1993). *Attention deficit disorders: An educator's guide (CH.A.D.D. Facts #5).* Plantation, FL: Children and Adults with Attention Deficit Disorders.

Charles, C. M., & Senter, G. W. (1995). *Elementary classroom management* (2nd ed.). New York: Longman.

Charney, R. S. (2002). *Teaching children to care: Classroom management for ethical and academic growth, K–8.* Greenfield, MA: Northeast Foundation for Children.

Chilcoat, G. W. (1990). How to make seatwork more meaningful. *Middle School Journal, 21*(4), 26–28.

Child Welfare Information Gateway. (2008). Gay and lesbian adoptive parents. Available at www.enotalone.com/article/9874.html.

Children's Defense Fund. (2008). *State of America's children 2008.* Washington, DC: Children's Defense Fund.

Ching, C.L.P. (1991). Giving feedback on written work. *Guidelines, 13*(2), 68–80.

Chrispeels, J. H., & Rivero, E. (April 2000). *Engaging Latino families for student success: Understanding the process and impact of providing training to parents.* Paper presented at the Annual Meeting of the American Educational Research Association, New Orleans.

Christensen, L. (1994). Building community from chaos. In B. Bigelow, L. Christensen, S. Karp, B. Miner, & B. Peterson (Eds.), *Rethinking our classrooms: Teaching for equity and justice.* Milwaukee, WI: Rethinking Schools Limited, 50–55.

Clayton, M. K., with Forton, M. B. (2001). *Classroom spaces that work.* Greenfield, MA: Northeast Foundation for Children.

Cloward, R. D. (2003). Self-monitoring increases time-on-task of attention deficit hyperactivity disordered students in the regular classroom. *Dissertation Abstracts International Section A: Humanities & Social Sciences, 64*(5-A). US: University Microfilms International.

Cohen, E. G. (1972). Interracial interaction disability. *Human Relations, 25,* 9-24.

Cohen, E. G. (1984). Talking and working together: Status, interaction, and learning. In P. L. Peterson, L. C. Wilkinson, & M. Hallinan (Eds.), *The social context of instruction.* New York: Academic Press, 171-188.

Cohen, E. G. (1994a). *Designing groupwork: Strategies for the heterogeneous classroom* (2nd ed.). New York: Teachers College Press.

Cohen, E. G. (1994b). Restructuring the classroom: Conditions for productive small groups. *Review of Educational Research, 64*(1), 1-35.

Cohen, E. G. (1998). Making cooperative learning equitable. *Educational Leadership, 56*(1), 18-21.

Coles, A. D. (May 10, 2000). Educators welcome guidelines for diagnosing ADHD. *Education Week, 19*(35), 6.

Committee for Children. (2002). *Second step: A violence prevention program* (3rd ed.). Seattle, WA: Committee for Children.

Cook, L., & Friend, M. (1995). Co-teaching: Guidelines for creating effective practices. *Focus on Exceptional Children, 28*(3), 1-16.

Coontz, S. (May 13, 2007). Motherhood stalls when women can't work. *Hartford Courant.* Available at www.contemporaryfamilies.org.

Corbett, D., Wilson, B., & Williams, B. (2005). No choice but success. *Educational Leadership, 62*(6), 8-12.

Cornelius-White, J. (2007). Learner-centered teacher-student relationships are effective: A meta-analysis. *Review of Educational Research, 77*(1), 113-143.

Créton, H. A., Wubbels, T., & Hooymayers, H. P. (1989). Escalated disorderly situations in the classroom and the improvement of these situations. *Teaching & Teacher Education, 5*(3), 205-215.

Cronin, D. (2000). *Click clack moo—Cows that type.* New York: Simon & Schuster Books for Young Readers.

Crothers, L. M., & Kolbert, J. B. (2008). Tackling a problematic behavior management issue: Teachers' intervention in childhood bullying problems. *Intervention in School and Clinic, 43*(3), 132-139.

Cummins, J. (2000). *Language, power and pedagogy: Bilingual children in the crossfire.* Clevedon, UK: Multilingual Matters.

Curwin, R. L., & Mendler, A. N. (1988). *Discipline with dignity.* Alexandria, VA: Association for Supervision and Curriculum Development.

D'Agostino, T. (2003). Comments on homework. *Responsive Classroom Newsletter, 15*(4), 6.

Damon, W. (1977). *The social world of the child.* San Francisco: Jossey-Bass.

Davidson, A. L. (1999). Negotiating social differences: Youths' assessments of educators' strategies. *Urban Education, 34*(3), 338-369.

Davidson, C. (2007). Routine encounters during independent writing: Explicating taken-for-granted interaction. *Language and Education, 21*(6), 473-486.

Davis, B. (1995). *How to involve parents in a multicultural school.* Alexandria, VA: Association for Supervision and Curriculum Development.

Deci, E. L., Koestner, R., & Ryan, R. M. (1999). A meta-analytic review of experiments examining the effects of extrinsic rewards on intrinsic motivation. *Psychological Bulletin, 125*(6), 627-668.

Deci, E. L., Koestner, R., & Ryan, R. M. (2001). Extrinsic rewards and intrinsic motivation in education: Reconsidered once again. *Review of Educational Research, 71*(1), 1-27.

Delgado-Gaitan, C. (1992). School matters in the Mexican-American home: Socializing children to education. *American Educational Research Journal, 29*(3), 495-513.

Delpit, L. (1995). *Teaching other people's children: Cultural conflict in the classroom.* New York: The New Press.

Delpit, L. (2002). No kinda sense. In L. Delpit & J. K. Dowdy (Eds.), *The skin that we speak: Thoughts on language and culture in the classroom.* New York: The New Press, 31-38.

Denton, P., & Kriete, R. (2000). *The first six weeks of school.* Greenfield, MA: Northeast Foundation for Children.

deVoss, G. G. (1979). The structure of major lessons and collective student activity. *The Elementary School Journal, 80,* 8-18.

Diaz-Rico, L. T., & Weed, K. Z. (2009). *The crosscultural, language, and academic development handbook. A complete K-12 reference guide* (4th ed.). Boston: Allyn & Bacon.

Dillon, J. T. (1994). *Using discussion in classrooms.* Philadelphia: Open University Press.

Dinkes, R., Cataldi, E. F., & Lin-Kelly, W. (2007). *Indicators of school crime and safety: 2007.* (NCES 2008-021/NCJ 219553). National Center for Education Statistics, Institute of Education Sciences, U.S. Department of Education, and Bureau of Justice Statistics, Office of Justice Programs, U.S. Department of Justice. Washington, DC. (Can be downloaded at http://nces.ed.gov.)

DiPardo, A., & Freedman, S. W. (1988). Peer response groups in the writing classroom: Theoretical foundations and new directions. *Review of Educational Research, 58*(2), 119-149.

Dowd, J. (1997). Refusing to play the blame game. *Educational Leadership, 54*(8), 67-69.

Dowrick, N. (1993). Talking and learning in pairs: A comparison of two interactive modes for six- and seven-year-old pupils. *International Journal of Early Years Education, 1*(3), 49-60.

Doyle, W. (1983). Academic work. *Review of Educational Research, 53*(2), 159-200.

Doyle, W. (1985). Recent research on classroom management: Implications for teacher preparation. *Journal of Teacher Education, 36*(3), 31-35.

Doyle, W. (1986). Classroom organization and management. In M. C. Wittrock (Ed.), *The handbook of research on teaching* (3rd ed.). New York: Macmillan, 392-431.

Doyle, W. (2006). Ecological approaches to classroom management. In C. M. Evertson & C. S. Weinstein (Eds.), *Handbook of classroom management: Research, practice and contemporary issues.* Mahwah, NJ: Lawrence Erlbaum Associates, 97-126.

Dreikurs, R., Grunwald, B. B., & Pepper, F. C. (1982). *Maintaining sanity in the classroom: Classroom management techniques* (2nd ed.). New York: Harper & Row.

Drummond, K. V., & Stipek, D. (2004). Low-income parents' beliefs about their role in children's academic learning. *The Elementary School Journal, 104*(3), 197-213.

Drummond, S., & Portner, J. (May 26, 1999). Arrests top 350 in threats, bomb scares. *Education Week, 1,* 12-13.

Dwyer, K., Osher, D., & Warger, C. (1998). *Early warning, timely response: A guide to safe schools.* Washington, DC: U.S. Department of Education.

Eccles, J., & Wigfield, A. (1985). Teacher expectations and student motivation. In J. Dusek (Ed.), *Teacher expectancies.* Hillsdale, NJ: Lawrence Erlbaum Associates, 185-226.

Edwards, C., & Stout, J. (1989/90). Cooperative learning: The first year. *Educational Leadership, 47*(4), 38-41.

Elias, M. J., & Clabby, J. F. (1988). Teaching social decision making. *Educational Leadership, 45*(6), 52-55.

Elias, M. J., & Clabby, J. F. (1989). *SDM skills: A curriculum guide for the elementary grades.* Gaithersburg, MD: Aspen Publishers.

Emmer, E. T., & Aussiker, A. (1990). School and classroom discipline programs: How well do they work? In O. C. Moles (Ed.), *Student discipline strategies.* New York: SUNY Press, 129-165.

Emmer, E. T., Evertson, C. M., & Anderson, L. M. (1980). Effective classroom management at the beginning of the school year. *The Elementary School Journal, 80*(5), 219-231.

Emmer, E. T., & Gerwels, M. C. (April 1998). *Classroom management tasks in cooperative groups.* Paper presented at the annual meeting of the American Educational Research Association, San Diego, California.

Emmer, E. T., & Gerwels, M. C. (2002). Cooperative learning in elementary classrooms: Teaching practices and lesson characteristics. *The Elementary School Journal, 103*(1), 75-91.

Epstein, J. L. (2001). *School, family, and community partnerships: Preparing educators and improving schools.* Boulder, CO: Westview Press.

Epstein, J. L., & Becker, H. J. (1982). Teachers' reported practices of parent involvement: Problems and possibilities. *The Elementary School Journal, 83*(2), 103-113.

Epstein, J. L., Clark, K. C., & Jackson, V. E., with Language Arts, Science/Health, and Math Teachers. (1995). *Manual for teachers: Teachers involve parents in schoolwork (TIPS), language arts, science/health, and math interactive homework in the middle grades.* Baltimore, MD: Johns Hopkins University Press.

Epstein, J. L., Sanders, M. G., Simon, B. S., Salinas, K. C., Jansorn, N. R., & Van Voorhis, F. L. (2002). *School, family, and community partnerships: Your handbook for action* (2nd ed.). Thousand Oaks, CA: Corwin Press.

Erikson, E. H. (1963). *Childhood and society* (2nd ed.). New York: Norton.

Evertson, C. M., & Emmer, E. T. (2009). *Classroom management for elementary teachers* (8th ed.) Upper Saddler River, NJ: Pearson.

Evertson, C. M., & Weinstein, C. S. (2006). Classroom management as a field of inquiry. In C. M. Evertson & C. S. Weinstein (Eds.), *Handbook of classroom management: Research, practice, and contemporary issues.* Mahwah, NJ: Lawrence Erlbaum Associates, 3-16.

Farivar, S., & Webb, N. (1991). *Helping behavior activities handbook: Cooperative small group problem solving in middle school mathematics (Report to the National Science Foundation).* Los Angeles: University of California, Los Angeles.

Finders, M., & Lewis, C. (1994). Why some parents don't come to school. *Educational Leadership, 51*(8), 50-54.

Fischer, L., Schimmel, D., & Kelly, C. (1999). *Teachers and the law.* New York: Longman.

Fisher, C. W., Berliner, D. C., Filby, N. N., Marliave, R., Cahen, L. S., & Dishaw, M. M. (1980). Teaching behaviors, academic learning time, and student achievement: An overview. In C. Denham & A. Lieberman (Eds.), *Time to learn.* Washington, DC: U.S. Department of Education, 7-32.

Flowerday, T., & Schraw, G. (2000). Teacher beliefs about instructional choice: A phenomenological study. *Journal of Educational Psychology, 92*(4), 634-645.

Fordham, S., & Ogbu, J. U. (1986). Black students' school success: Coping with the "burden of 'acting white.'" *The Urban Review, 18*(3), 176-206.

Franek, M. (2005/6). Foiling cyberbullies in the new wild west. *Educational Leadership, 63*(4), 39–43.

Fraser, B. J., McRobbie, C. J., & Fisher, D. L. (April 1996). *Development, validation and use of personal and class forms of a new classroom environment instrument.* Paper presented at the annual meeting of the American Educational Research Association, New York.

Friend, M., & Bursuck, W. D. (2002). *Including students with special needs: A practical guide for classroom teachers.* Boston: Allyn & Bacon.

Froschl, M., & Gropper, N. (1999). Fostering friendships, curbing bullying. *Educational Leadership, 56*(8), 72–75.

Fryer, R. G. (2006). "Acting White." *Education Next, 6*(1), 53–59.

Fulk, C. L., & Smith, P. J. (1995). Students' perceptions of teachers' instructional and management adaptations for students with learning or behavior problems. *The Elementary School Journal, 95*(5), 409–419.

Fuller, M. L., & Olsen, G. (1998). *Home-school relations: Working successfully with parents and families.* Boston: Allyn & Bacon.

Gall, M. D., & Gillett, M. (1981). The discussion method in classroom teaching. *Theory into Practice, 19*(2), 98–103.

Gallego, M. A., Cole, M., & Laboratory of Comparative Human Cognition. (2001). Classroom cultures and cultures in the classroom. In V. Richardson (Ed.), *Handbook of research on teaching* (4th ed.). Washington, DC: American Educational Research Association.

Gallup Poll. (2005). Teens say safety issues top problem at school. Surveys conducted July 6–Sept. 24, 2005, ± 4% margin of error, sample size = 600. Accessed at http://www.gallup.com.

Gardner, H. (1995). Reflections on multiple intelligences: Myths and messages. *Phi Delta Kappan, 77*(3), 200–209.

Gardner, H. (1998). Reflections on multiple intelligences: Myths and messages. In A. Woolfolk Hoy (Ed.), *Readings in educational psychology* (2nd ed.). Boston: Allyn & Bacon.

Gay, G. (2000). *Culturally responsive teaching: Theory, research, and practice.* New York: Teachers College Press.

Gay, G. (2006). Connections between classroom management and culturally responsive Teaching. In C. M. Evertson & C. S. Weinstein (Eds.), *Handbook of classroom management: Research, practice and contemporary issues.* Mahwah, NJ: Lawrence Erlbaum Associates, 343–370.

Gearheart, B. R., Weishahn, M. W., & Gearheart, C. J. (1992). *The exceptional student in the regular classroom* (5th ed.). New York: Macmillan.

Giangreco, M. F., & Doyle, M. B. (2002). Students with disabilities and paraprofessional supports: Benefits, balance, and band-aids. *Focus on Exceptional Children, 34*(7), 1–12.

Gillies, R. M. (2002). The residual effects of cooperative-learning experiences: A two-year follow-up. *The Journal of Educational Research, 96*(1), 16–20.

Gillies, R. M., & Ashman, A. F. (1998). Behavior and interactions of children in cooperative groups in lower and middle elementary grades. *Journal of Educational Psychology, 90*(4), 746–757.

Ginsberg, M. B. (2007). Lessons at the kitchen table. *Educational Leadership, 64*(6), 56–61.

Good, T. L., & Brophy, J. E. (2008). *Looking in classrooms* (10th ed.). Boston: Pearson/Allyn & Bacon.

Goodlad, J. (1984). *A place called school.* New York: McGraw-Hill.

Gordon, J. A. (1998). Caring through control. *Journal for a Just and Caring Education, 4*(4), 418–440.

Gordon, T. (2003). *Teacher effectiveness training: The program proven to help teachers bring out the best in students of all ages.* New York: Three Rivers Press.

Gorney, C. (June 13, 1999). Teaching Johnny the appropriate way to flirt. *The New York Times Magazine,* 43-47, 67, 73, 80-83.

Governor's Task Force on Child Abuse and Neglect. (October 1988). *Child abuse and neglect: A professional's guide to identification, reporting, investigation, and treatment.* Trenton, NJ: Author.

Grandin, T. (2007). Autism from the inside. *Educational Leadership, 64*(5), 29-32.

Graves, T., & Graves, N. (1990). Things we like: A team-building/language development lesson for preschool–grade 2. *Cooperative Learning, The Magazine for Cooperation in Education, 10*(3), 45.

Graziano, A. M., & Mooney, K. C. (1984). *Children and behavior therapy.* New York: Aldine.

Greenwood, G. E., & Hickman, C. W. (1991). Research and practice in parent involvement: Implications for teacher education. *The Elementary School Journal, 91*(3), 279-288.

Gregory, A., & Ripski, M. (2008). Adolescent trust in teachers: Implications for behavior in the high school classroom. *School Psychology Review, 37*(3), 337-353.

Griffith, J. (1998). The relation of school structure and social environment to parent involvement in elementary schools. *The Elementary School Journal, 99*(1), 53-80.

Grossman, H. (2004). *Classroom behavior management for diverse and inclusive schools* (3rd ed.). Lanham, MD: Rowman & Littlefield.

Grossman, H. (1984). *Educating Hispanic students: Cultural implications for instruction, classroom management, counseling, and assessment.* Springfield, IL: Thomas.

Grossman, H. (1995). *Classroom behavior management in a diverse society.* Mountain View, CA: Mayfield.

Grossman, H., & Grossman, S. H. (1994). *Gender issues in education.* Boston: Allyn & Bacon.

Grossman, D. C., Neckerman, H. J., Koepsell, T. D., Liu, P. Y., Asher, K. N., Beland, K., Frey, K., & Rivara, F. P. (1997). The effectiveness of a violence prevention curriculum among children in elementary school. *Journal of the American Medical Association, 277*(2), 1605-1611.

Gruber, B. (1983). *Managing your classroom! An instant idea book.* Palos Verdes Estates, CA: Frank Schaffer.

Gruber, B. (1985). *Classroom management for elementary teachers. An instant idea book.* Palos Verdes Estates, CA: Frank Schaffer.

Gump, P. V. (1982). School settings and their keeping. In D. L. Duke (Ed.), *Helping teachers manage classrooms.* Alexandria, VA: Association for Supervision and Curriculum Development, 98-114.

Gump, P. V. (1987). School and classroom environments. In D. Stokols & I. Altman (Eds.), *Handbook of environmental psychology.* New York: John Wiley & Sons, 691-732.

Gumperz, J. J. (1981). Conversational inference and classroom learning. In J. Green & C. Wallat (Eds.), *Ethnography and language in educational settings.* Norwood, NJ: Ablex.

Gutman, L. M., & McLoyd, V. C. (2000). Parents' management of their children's education within the home, at school and in the community: An examination of African-American families living in poverty. *The Urban Review, 32*(1), 1-24.

Hagin, R. A. (2004). Autism and other severe pervasive developmental disorders. In F. M. Kline & L. B. Silver (Eds.), *The educator's guide to mental health issues in the classroom.* Baltimore, MD: Paul H. Brookes, 55-73.

Hansen, P., & Mulholland, J. A. (2005). Caring and elementary teaching: The concerns of male beginning teachers. *Journal of Teacher Education, 56*(2), 119-131.

Harmon, A. (August 26, 2004). Internet gives teenage bullies weapons to wound from afar. *New York Times,* pp. A1, A23.

Harrison, M. M. (Fall 2005). Bully on the bus. *Teaching Tolerance, 28,* 39–43.

Hastings, N., & Schwieso, J. (1995). Tasks and tables: The effects of seating arrangements on task engagement in primary classrooms. *Educational Research, 37*(3), 279–291.

Hatch, J. A. (March 1986). *Alone in a crowd: Analysis of covert interactions in a kindergarten.* Presented at the annual meeting of the American Educational Research Association, San Francisco. ERIC Document Reproduction Service No. ED 272 278.

Heilman, E. (2008). Hegemonies and "transgressions" of family: Tales of pride and prejudice. In T. Turner-Vorbeck & M. Miller Marsh (Eds.), *Other kinds of families: Embracing diversity in schools.* New York: Teachers College Press, 7–27.

Helmke, A., & Schrader, F. W. (1988). Successful student practice during seatwork: Efficient management and active supervision not enough. *Journal of Educational Research, 82*(2), 70–75.

Henderson, A. T., Mapp, K. L., Johnson, V. R., & Davies, D. (2007). *Beyond the bake sale: The essential guide to family-school partnerships.* New York: The New Press.

Henley, M., Ramsey, R. S., & Algozzine, R. F. (2002). *Characteristics of and strategies for teaching students with mild disabilities* (4th ed.). Boston: Allyn & Bacon.

Henning, J. E. (2008). *The art of discussion-based teaching.* New York: Routledge.

Heuveline, P. (2005). *Estimating the proportion of marriages that end in divorce.* A research brief prepared for the Council on Contemporary Families. Available at www.contemporaryfamilies.org.

Hidi, S., & Harackiewicz, J. M. (2000). Motivating the academically unmotivated: A critical issue for the 21st century. *Review of Educational Research, 70*(2), 151–179.

Hodgkinson, H. (1985). *All one system: Demographics of education, kindergarten through graduate school.* Washington, DC: Institute for Educational Leadership.

Hoover, J., & Oliver, R. (2008). *The bullying prevention handbook: A guide for teachers, principals and counselors* (2nd ed.). Bloomington, IN: Solution Tree.

Hoover-Dempsey, K. V., Bassler, O. T., & Brissie, J. S. (1987). Parent involvement: Contributions of teacher efficacy, school socioeconomic status, and other school characteristics. *American Educational Research Journal, 24*(3), 417–435.

Hoover-Dempsey, K. V., Bassler, O. T., & Burow, R. (1995). Parents' reported involvement in students' homework: Strategies and practices. *The Elementary School Journal, 95*(5), 435–449.

Hoover-Dempsey, K. V., & Sandler, H. M. (1997). Why do parents become involved in their children's education? *Review of Educational Research, 67*(1), 3–42.

HR 1804: Goals 2000: Educate America Act, 103rd Congress, 2nd session. 1994.

Hyman, I., Kay, B., Tabori, A., Weber, M., Mahon, M., & Cohen, I. (2006). Bullying: Theory, research, and interventions. In C. M. Evertson & C. S. Weinstein (Eds.), *Handbook of classroom management: Research, practice, and contemporary issues.* Mahwah, NJ: Lawrence Erlbaum Associates, 855–884.

Hyman, I. A. (1997). *School discipline and school violence: The teacher variance approach.* Boston: Allyn & Bacon.

Irvine, J. J. (1990). *Black students and school failure: Policies, practices, and prescriptions.* New York: Greenwood.

Irvine, J. J. (2002). *In search of wholeness: African American teachers and their culturally specific classroom practices.* New York: Palgrave.

Irvine, J. J., & Fraser, J. (May 13, 1998). Warm demanders: Do national certification standards leave room for the culturally responsive pedagogy of African-American teachers? *Education Week, 17*(35), 56.

Jackson, P. W. (1990). *Life in classrooms.* New York: Teachers College Press.

Johnson, D. W., & Johnson, R. T. (1980). Integrating handicapped students into the mainstream. *Exceptional Children, 47*(2), 90-98.

Johnson, D. W., & Johnson, R. T. (1989/90). Social skills for successful groupwork. *Educational Leadership, 47*(4), 29-33.

Johnson, D. W., & Johnson, R. T. (1995). *Reducing school violence through conflict resolution.* Alexandria: VA: ASCD.

Johnson, D. W., & Johnson, R. T. (1999). The three Cs of school and classroom management. In H. J. Freiberg (Ed.), *Beyond behaviorism: Changing the classroom management paradigm.* Boston: Allyn & Bacon, 119-144.

Johnson, D. W., Johnson, R. T., Holubec, E. J., & Roy, P. (1984). *Circles of learning: Cooperation in the classroom.* Alexandria, VA: Association for Supervision and Curriculum Development.

Jolivette, K., Stichter, J. P., & McCormick, K. M. (2002). Making choices—improving behavior—engaging in learning. *Teaching Exceptional Children, 34*(3), 24-30.

Jolivette, K., Wehby, J. H., Canale, J., & Massey, N. G. (2001). Effects of choice-making opportunities on the behavior of students with emotional and behavioral disorders. *Behavioral Disorders, 26*(2), 131-145.

Jones, E., & Prescott, E. (1978). *Dimensions of teaching-learning environments. II: Focus on day care.* Pasadena, CA: Pacific Oaks College.

Jones, F. H., Jones, P., Lynn, J., Jones, F., & Jones, B. T. (2007). *Tools for teaching: Discipline, instruction, motivation.* Santa Cruz, CA: Fredric H. Jones & Associates.

Jones, M. G., & Gerig, T. M. (1994). Silent sixth-grade students: Characteristics, achievement, and teacher expectations. *The Elementary School Journal, 95*(2), 169-182.

Jones, V. F., & Jones, L. S. (1986). *Comprehensive classroom management: Creating positive learning environments.* Boston: Allyn & Bacon.

Jones, V. F., & Jones, L. S. (2010). *Comprehensive classroom management: Creating communities of support and solving problems* (9th ed.). Upper Saddle River, NJ: Pearson.

Kagan, S. (1989/90). The structural approach to cooperative learning. *Educational Leadership, 47*(4), 12-15.

Karweit, N. (1989). Time and learning: A review. In R. E. Slavin (Ed.), *School and classroom organization.* Hillsdale, NJ: Lawrence Erlbaum Associates.

Kashti, Y., Arieli, M., & Harel, Y. (1984). Classroom seating as a definition of situation: Observations in an elementary school in one development town. *Urban Education, 19*(2), 161-181.

Katz, M. S. (1999). Teaching about caring and fairness: May Sarton's *The Small Room.* In M. S. Katz, N. Noddings, & K. A. Strike (Eds.), *Justice and caring: The search for common ground in education.* New York: Teachers College Press, 59-73.

Katz, S. R. (1999). Teaching in tensions: Latino immigrant youth, their teachers, and the structures of schooling. *Teachers College Record, 100*(4), 809-840.

Keith, S., & Martin, M. E. (2005). Cyber-bullying: Creating a culture of respect in a cyber world. *Reclaiming Children and Youth, 13*(4), 224-228.

Kerr, M. M., & Nelson, C. M. (2006). *Strategies for addressing behavior problems in the classroom* (5th ed.). Upper Saddle River, NJ: Pearson Prentice Hall.

Kershner, R., & Pointon, P. (2000). Children's views of the primary classroom as an environment for working and learning. *Research in Education, 64,* 64–78.

Kidder, T. (1989). *Among schoolchildren.* Boston: Houghton Mifflin.

Kim, D., Solomon, D., & Roberts, W. (April 1995). *Classroom practices that enhance students' sense of community.* Paper presented at the annual convention of the American Educational Research Association, San Francisco, California.

King, J. R. (1998). *Uncommon caring: Learning from men who teach young children.* New York: Teachers College Press.

King, L., Luberda, H., Barry, K., & Zehnder, S. (1998). *A case study of the perceptions of students in a small-group cooperative learning situation.* Paper presented at the Annual Conference of the American Educational Research Association. San Diego, California.

Kline, F. M., & Silver, L. B. (2004). *The educator's guide to mental health issues in the classroom.* Baltimore, MD: Paul H. Brookes.

Kohn, A. (1993). *Punished by rewards: The trouble with gold stars, incentive plans, A's, praise, and other bribes.* Boston: Houghton Mifflin.

Kohn, A. (1996). *Beyond discipline: From compliance to community.* Alexandria, VA: Association for Supervision and Curriculum Development.

Kottler, E. (1994). *Children with limited English: Teaching strategies for the regular classroom.* Thousand Oaks, CA: Corwin Press.

Kottler, J. A., & Kottler, E. (1993). *Teacher as counselor: Developing the helping skills you need.* Newbury Park, CA: Corwin Press.

Kottler, J. A., & Kottler, E. (2009). *Students who drive you crazy: Succeeding with resistant, unmotivated, and otherwise difficult young people* (2nd ed.). Thousand Oaks, CA: Corwin Press.

Kounin, J. S. (1970). *Discipline and group management in classrooms.* New York: Holt, Rinehart & Winston.

Kralovec, E., & Buell, J. (2000). *The end of homework: How homework disrupts families, overburdens children, and limits learning.* Boston: Beacon Press.

Krantz, P. J., & Risley, T. R. (September 1972). *The organization of group care environments: Behavioral ecology in the classroom.* Paper presented at the Annual Convention of the American Psychological Association, Honolulu. ERIC #ED 078 915.

Kriete, R. (2002). *The morning meeting book.* Greenfield, MA: Northeast Foundation for Children.

Kriete, R. (2003). Start the day with community. *Educational Leadership, 61*(1), 68–71.

Kutnick, P., Blatchford, P., Clark, H., McIntyre, H., & Baines, E. (2005). Teachers' understandings of the relationship between within-class (pupil) grouping and learning in secondary schools. *Educational Research, 47*(1), 1–24.

Kutnick, P., Ota, C., & Berdondini, L. (2008). Improving the effects of group working in classrooms with young school-aged children: Facilitating attainment, interaction and classroom activity. *Learning and Instruction, 18,* 83–95.

Kyle, D., & McIntyre, E. (2000). *Family visits benefit teachers and families—and students most of all.* CREDE Practitioner Brief #1. Santa Cruz, CA: Center for Research on Education, Diversity & Excellence.

Ladson-Billings, G. (1994). *The dreamkeepers: Successful teachers of African American children.* San Francisco: Jossey-Bass.

Ladson-Billings, G. (2001). *Crossing over to Canaan: The journey of new teachers in diverse classrooms.* San Francisco: Jossey-Bass.

Landrum, T. J., & Kauffman, J. M. (2006). Behavioral approaches to classroom management. In C. M. Evertson & C. S. Weinstein (Eds.), *Handbook of classroom management: Research, practice, and contemporary issues*. Mahwah, NJ: Lawrence Erlbaum Associates, 47–72.

Landsman, J. (2006). Bearers of hope. *Educational Leadership, 63*(5), 26–32.

Lasley, T. J., Lasley, J. O., & Ward, S. H. (1989). *Activities and desists used by more and less effective classroom managers*. Paper presented at the annual meeting of the American Educational Research Association, San Francisco.

Latham, A. S. (1997). Learning through feedback. *Educational Leadership, 54*(8), 86–87.

Laursen, E. K. (2008). Respectful alliances, *Reclaiming children and youth, 17*(1), 4–9.

Lawrence-Lightfoot, S. (2003). *The essential conversation: What parents and teachers can learn from each other*. New York: Ballantine Books.

Leahy, S., Lyon, C., Thompson, M., & Wiliam, D. (2005). Classroom assessment: Minute by minute, day by day. *Educational Leadership, 63*(3), 18–24.

Lee, J., & Bowen, N. K. (2006). Parent involvement, cultural capital, and the achievement gap among elementary school children, *American Educational Research Journal, 43*(2), 193–215.

Leinhardt, G., Weidman, C., & Hammond, K. M. (1987). Introduction and integration of classroom routines by expert teachers. *Curriculum Inquiry, 17*(2), 135–175.

Leishman, J. (2002). Cyberbullying: The Internet is the latest weapon in a bully's arsenal. Toronto: CBC News. Available at http://cbc/ca/news/national/news/cyberbullying/index.html.

Lepper, M., Greene, D., & Nisbett, R. E. (1973). Undermining children's intrinsic interest with extrinsic rewards: A test of the "overjustification" hypothesis. *Journal of Personality and Social Psychology, 28,* 129–137.

Levin, J., & Nolan, J. F. (2003). *What every teacher should know about classroom management*. Boston: Allyn & Bacon.

Lewis, T. J., Newcomer, L. L., Trussell, R., & Richter, M. (2006). Schoolwide positive behavior support: Building systems to develop and maintain appropriate social behavior. In C. M. Evertson & C. S. Weinstein (Eds.), *Handbook of classroom management: Research, practice, and contemporary issues*. Mahwah, NJ: Lawrence Erlbaum Associates.

Lindeman, B. (2001). Reaching out to immigrant parents. *Educational Leadership, 58*(6), 62–66.

Lindle, J. C. (1989). What do parents want from principals and teachers? *Educational Leadership, 47*(2), 12–14.

Lisante, J. E. (June 6, 2005). Cyber bullying: No muscles needed. Published on Connect for Kids (http://www.connectforkids.org).

Lopez, G. R. (2001). The value of hard work: Lessons on parent involvement from an (im)migrant household. *Harvard Educational Review, 71*(3), 416–437.

Lord, B. B. (1984). *In the year of the boar and Jackie Robinson*. New York: Harper & Row.

Lortie, D. (1975). *Schoolteacher*. Chicago: University of Chicago Press.

Lotan, R. (2006). Managing groupwork in the heterogeneous classroom. In C. M. Evertson & C. S. Weinstein (Eds.), *Handbook of classroom management: Research, practice, and contemporary issues*. Mahwah, NJ: Lawrence Erlbaum Associates.

Ma, H., Lu, E. Y., Turner, S., & Wan, G. (2007). An empirical investigation of cheating and digital plagiarism among middle school students. *American Secondary Education, 35*(2), 69–82.

MacLachlan, P. (1985). *Sarah, plain and tall*. New York: Harper & Row Junior Books.

Madden, N. A., & Slavin, R. E. (1983). Cooperative learning and social acceptance of mainstreamed academically handicapped students. *Journal of Special Education, 17,* 171–182.

Mamlin, N., & Dodd-Murphy, J. (2002). Minimizing minimal hearing loss in the schools: What every classroom teacher should know. *Preventing School Failure, 46*(2), 86–93.

Manning, B. H. (1988). Application of cognitive behavior modification: First and third graders' self-management of classroom behaviors. *American Educational Research Journal, 25*(2), 193–212.

Marshall, H. H. (1987). Motivational strategies of three fifth-grade teachers. *The Elementary School Journal, 88*(2), 135–150.

Martin, S. H. (2002). The classroom environment and its effects on the practice of teachers. *Journal of Educational Psychology, 22,* 139–156.

Marzano, R. J., Gaddy, R. J., Foseid, M. C., Foseid, M. P., & Marzano, J. S. (2005). *A handbook for classroom management that works.* Alexandria, VA: Association for Supervision and Curriculum Development.

Maslow, A. H., & Mintz, N. L. (1956). The effects of esthetic surroundings: Initial effects of three esthetic conditions upon perceiving 'energy' and 'well-being' in faces. *Journal of Psychology, 41,* 247–254.

McCaslin, M., & Good, T. L. (1998). Moving beyond management as sheer compliance: Helping students to develop goal coordination strategies. *Educational Horizons,* Summer, 169–176.

McCrone, S. S. (2005). The development of mathematical discussions: An investigation in a fifth-grade classroom. *Mathematical Thinking and Learning, 7*(2), 111–133.

McIntosh, K., Herman, K., Sanford, A., McGraw, K., & Florence, K. (2004). Teaching transitions: Techniques for promoting success between lessons. *Teaching Exceptional Children, 37*(1), 32–38.

McKinley, J. (March 25, 2009). Cities deal with a surge in shantytowns. *New York Times,* p. A1.

Meadan, H., & Monda-Amaya, L. (2008). Collaboration to promote social competence for students with mild disabilities in the general classroom: A structure for providing social support. *Intervention in School and Clinic, 43*(3), 158–167.

Mehan, H. (1979). *Learning lessons: Social organization in a classroom.* Cambridge, MA: Harvard University Press.

Meichenbaum, D. (1977). *Cognitive behavior modification.* New York: Plenum.

Miller, E. (1994). Peer mediation catches on, but some adults don't. *Harvard Education Letter, 10*(3), 8.

Milner, H. R. (2006). Classroom management in urban classrooms. In C. M. Evertson & C. S. Weinstein (Eds.), *Handbook of classroom management: Research, practice, and contemporary issues.* Mahwah, NJ: Lawrence Erlbaum Associates, 491–522.

Minke, K. M., & Anderson, K. J. (2003). Restructuring routine parent-teacher conferences: The family school conference model. *The Elementary School Journal, 104*(1), 49–69.

Montemayor, R., & Eisen, M. (1977). The development of self-conceptions from childhood to adolescence. *Developmental Psychology, 13*(4), 314–319.

Morine-Dershimer, G., & Beyerbach, B. (1987). Moving right along. . . . In V. Richardson-Koehler (Ed.), *Educators' handbook, a research perspective.* New York: Longman, 207–232.

Morrow, L. M. (2005). *Literacy development in the early years: Helping children read and write* (5th ed.). Needham Heights, MA: Allyn & Bacon.

Morrow, L. M., Reutzel, D. R., & Casey, H. (2006). Organization and management of language arts teaching: Classroom environments, grouping practices, exemplary instruction. In C. M. Evertson & C. S. Weinstein (Eds.), *Handbook of classroom management: Research, practice, and contemporary issues.* Mahwah, NJ: Lawrence Erlbaum Associates, 559–581.

Morrow, L. M., & Weinstein, C. S. (1982). Increasing children's literature use through program and physical design changes. *Elementary School Journal, 83*(2), 131-137.

Morrow, L. M., & Weinstein, C. S. (1986). Encouraging voluntary reading: The impact of a literature program on children's use of library centers. *Reading Research Quarterly, 21*(3), 330-346.

Morse, L. W., & Handley, H. M. (1985). Listening to adolescents: Gender differences in science classroom interaction. In L. C. Wilkinson & C. B. Marrett (Eds.), *Gender influences in classroom interaction*. Orlando, FL: Academic Press, 37-56.

Mulryan, C. M. (1992). Student passivity during cooperative small groups in mathematics. *Journal of Educational Research, 85*(5), 261-273.

Murawski, W. W. (2005). Addressing diverse needs through co-teaching. *Kappa Delta Pi Record, 41*(2), 77-82.

Myles, B. S., Gagnon, E., Moyer, S. A., & Trautman, M. L. (2004). Asperger syndrome. In F. M. Kline & L. B. Silver (Eds.), *The educator's guide to mental health issues in the classroom*. Baltimore, MD: Paul H. Brookes, 75-100.

Narayn, J. S., Heward, W. L., Gardner, R., III, Courson, F. H., & Omness, C. K. (1990). Using response cards to increase student participation in an elementary classroom. *Journal of Applied Behavior Analysis, 23*(4), 483-490.

National Coalition of Homeless Children and Youth. (2008). *Fact sheet #10, June 2008.*

National Commission on Excellence in Education. (1983). *A nation at risk: The imperative for educational reform*. Washington, DC: U.S. Government Printing Office.

National Crime Prevention Council (2003). Cyberbullying. Downloaded from www.mcgruff.org.

National Dissemination Center for Children with Disabilities. (2003). Pervasive developmental disorders. Fact sheet 20. (Downloaded from www.nichcy.org/pubs/factshe/fs20txt.htm)

National Dissemination Center for Children with Disabilities (2004). Learning disabilities. Fact sheet 7. (Downloaded from www.nichcy.org/pub/factshe/fs7txt.htm).

National Education Commission on Time and Learning. (1994). Prisoners of time. Available at http://www.emich.edu/public/emu_programs/tlc/toc.html.

National Institute on Alcohol Abuse and Alcoholism. (2004/2005). Alcohol and development in youth: A multidisciplinary overview. *Alcohol Research and Health, 28*(3). Available at http://pubs.niaaa.nih.gov/publications/arh283/toc28-3.htm.

National Law Center on Homelessness and Poverty. (2008). *Homelessness and poverty in America: Overview*. Washington, DC: National Law Center on Homelessness and Poverty.

Naughton, K., & Thomas, E. (March 13, 2000). Did Kayla have to die? *Newsweek,* 24-29.

NCELA. (2007). The growing numbers of LEP students, 2005-2006 Poster. Washington, DC: U.S. Department of Education. Retrieved 02/24/2009 from http://www.ncela.gwu.edu/stats/2_nation.htm.

Nelsen, J. L., Lott, L., & Glenn, H. S. (2000). *Positive discipline in the classroom* (3rd ed.). Roseville, CA: Prima.

Nelson-Barber, S., & Meier, T. (Spring 1990). Multicultural context a key factor in teaching. *Academic Connections,* Office of Academic Affairs, The College Board, 1-5, 9-11.

Nevin, A. (1993). Curricula and instructional adaptations for including students with disabilities in cooperative groups. In J. W. Putnam, *Cooperative learning and strategies for inclusion: Celebrating diversity in the classroom*. Baltimore, MD: Paul H. Brookes, 41-56.

New Jersey v. T.L.O., 105 S. Ct. 733 (1985).

Newby, T. (1991). Classroom motivation: Strategies of first-year teachers. *Journal of Educational Psychology, 83,* 195-200.

Newman, R. S., & Schwager, M. T. (1993). Students' perceptions of the teacher and classmates in relation to reported help seeking in math class. *The Elementary School Journal, 94*(1), 3-17.

Nieto, S., & Bode, P. (2008). *Affirming diversity: The sociopolitical context of multicultural education* (5th ed.). Boston: Allyn & Bacon.

Noguera, P. A. (1995). Preventing and producing violence: A critical analysis of responses to school violence. *Harvard Educational Review, 65*(2), 189-212.

Nucci, L. (2006). Classroom management for moral and social development. In C. M. Evertson & C. S. Weinstein (Eds.), *Handbook of classroom management: Research, practice, and contemporary issues*. Mahwah, NJ: Lawrence Erlbaum Associates, 711-731.

Oakes, J., & Lipton, M. (1999). *Teaching to change the world*. Boston: McGraw-Hill.

Obidah, J. E., & Teel, K. M. (2001). *Because of the kids: Facing racial and cultural differences in schools*. New York: Teachers College Press.

O'Connor, R. E., & Jenkins, J. R. (1996). Cooperative learning as an inclusion strategy: A closer look. *Exceptionality, 6*(1), 9-51.

O'Donnell, A., & O'Kelly, J. (1994). Learning from peers: Beyond the rhetoric of positive results. *Educational Psychology Review, 6*(4), 321-349.

Olds, A. R. (1987). Designing settings for infants and toddlers. In C. S. Weinstein & T. G. David (Eds.), *Spaces for children: The built environment and child development*. New York: Plenum, 117-138.

Olmsted, P. P. (1991). Parent involvement in elementary education: Findings and suggestions from the Follow Through program. *The Elementary School Journal, 91*(3), 221-231.

Olweus, D. (2003). A profile of bullying at school. *Educational Leadership, 60*(6), 12-17.

Oortwijn, M. B., Boekaerts, M., Vedder, P., & Fortuin, J. (2008). The impact of a cooperative learning experience on pupils' popularity, non-cooperativeness, and interethnic bias in multiethnic elementary schools. *Educational Psychology, 28*(2), 211-221.

Osterman, K. F. (2000). Students' need for belonging in the school community. *Review of Educational Research, 70*(3), 323-367.

Ostrander, R. (2004). Oppositional defiant disorder and conduct disorder. In F. M. Kline & L. B. Silver (Eds.), *The educator's guide to mental health issues in the classroom*. Baltimore, MD: Paul H. Brookes, 267-286.

Paley, V. G. (1992). *You can't say you can't play*. Cambridge, MA: Harvard University Press.

Patrick, H., Anderman, L. H., Ryan, A. M., Edelin, K. C., & Midgley, C. (2001). Teachers' communication of goal orientations in four fifth-grade classrooms. *The Elementary School Journal, 102*(1), 35-58.

Patall, E. A., Cooper, H., & Robinson, J. C. (2008). Parent involvement in homework: A research synthesis. *Review of Educational Research, 78*(4), 1039-1101.

Patton, J. E., Snell, J., Knight, W. J., & Gerken, K. (April 17-21, 2001). *A survey study of elementary classroom seating designs*. Paper presented at the Annual Meeting of the National Association of School Psychologists.

Payne, R. K. (2005). *A framework for understanding poverty* (4th rev. ed.). Highlands, TX: aha! Process.

Peet, B. (1993). Buford, the little bighorn. In R. C. Farr & D. S. Strickland (senior authors), *A most unusual sight. HBJ treasury of literature*. Orlando, FL: Harcourt Brace Jovanovich.

Pell, T., Galton, M., Steward, S., Page, C., & Hargreaves, L. (2007). Promoting group work at key stage 3: Solving an attitudinal crisis among young adolescents? *Research Papers in Education, 22*(3), 309-322.

Pietrangelo, R., & Giuliani, G. (2008). *Frequently asked questions about Response to Intervention: A step-by-step guide for educators.* Thousand Oaks, CA: Corwin Press.

Pittman, S. I. (1985). Cognitive ethnography and quantification of a first-grade teacher's selection routines for classroom management. *The Elementary School Journal, 85*(4), 541–558.

Pointon, P., & Kershner, R. (2000). Making decisions about organising the primary classroom environment as a context for learning: The views of three experienced teachers and their pupils. *Teaching and Teacher Education, 16*(1), 117–127.

Pollack, W. S., Modzeleski, W., & Rooney, G. (2008). *Prior knowledge of potential school-based violence: Information students learn may prevent a targeted attack.* U.S. Secret Service and Department of Education. Washington, DC: U. S. Government Printing Office. (Downloaded from http://www.ed.gov.)

Powell, R. R., Zehm, S. J., & Kottler, J. A. (1995). *Classrooms under the influence: Addicted families/addicted students.* Newbury Park, CA: Corwin Press.

Power, B., & Chandler, K. (January/February 1998). Six steps to better report card comments. *Instructor, 107*(5), 76–78.

Proshansky, E., & Wolfe, M. (1974). The physical setting and open education. *School Review, 82,* 557–574.

Raffaele-Mendez, L. M., & Knoff, H. M. (2003). Who gets suspended from school and why: A demographic analysis of schools and disciplinary infractions in a large school district. *Education and Treatment of Children, 26,* 30–51.

Reeve, J. (2006a). Extrinsic rewards and inner motivation. In C. M. Evertson & C. S. Weinstein (Eds.), *Handbook of classroom management: Research, practice, and contemporary issues.* Mahwah, NJ: Lawrence Erlbaum Associates, 645–664.

Reeve, J. (2006b). Teachers as facilitators: What autonomy-supportive teachers do and why their students benefit. *Elementary School Journal, 106*(3), 225–236.

Renewing Our Schools, Securing Our Future: A National Task Force on Public Education. (2005). Getting smarter, becoming fairer. Available at http://www.ourfuture.org/docUploads/gsbf_popup.html.

Richards, C., Pavri, S., Golez, F., & Murphy, J. (2007). Response to intervention: Building the capacity of teachers to serve students with learning difficulties. *Issues in Teacher Education, 16*(2), 55–64.

Rief, S. F. (1993). *How to reach and teach ADD/ADHD children.* West Nyack, NY: The Center for Applied Research in Education.

Robinson, S., & Ricord Griesemer, S. M. (2006). Helping individual students with problem behavior. In C. M. Evertson & C. S. Weinstein (Eds.), *Handbook of classroom management: Research, practice, and contemporary issues.* Mahwah, NJ: Lawrence Erlbaum Associates, 787–802.

Roby, T. W. (1988). Models of discussion. In J. T. Dillon (Ed.), *Questioning and discussion— A multidisciplinary study.* Norwood, NJ: Ablex, 163–191.

Rock, M. L. (2005). Use of strategic self-monitoring to enhance academic engagement, productivity, and accuracy of students with and without exceptionalities. *Journal of Positive Behavior Interventions, 7*(1), 3–17.

Roeser, R. W., Eccles, J. S., & Sameroff, A. J. (2000). School as a context of early adolescents' academic and social-emotional development: A summary of research findings. *The Elementary School Journal, 100*(5), 443–471.

Romero, M., Mercado, C., & Vazquez-Faria, J. A. (1987). Students of limited English proficiency. In V. Richardson-Koehler (Ed.), *Educators' handbook: A research perspective.* New York: Longman.

Rosenholtz, S. J., & Cohen, E. G. (1985). Status in the eye of the beholder. In J. Berger & M. Zelditch Jr. (Eds.), *Status, rewards, and influence*. San Francisco: Jossey-Bass, 430–444.

Rosenshine, B. (1980). How time is spent in elementary classrooms. In C. Denham & A. Lieberman (Eds.), *Time to learn*. Washington, DC: U.S. Department of Education, 107–126.

Rosenshine, B. V. (1986). Synthesis of research on explicit teaching. *Educational Leadership, 43*(7), 60–69.

Ross, R. P. (1985). Elementary school activity segments and the transitions between them: Responsibilities of teachers and student teachers. Unpublished doctoral dissertation, University of Kansas.

Rowe, M. B. (1974). Wait-time and rewards as instructional variables: Their influence on language, logic, and fate control. Part 1: Wait time. *Journal of Research in Science Teaching, 11,* 291–308.

Ryan, R. B., Peterson, R. L., & Rozalski, M. (2007). State policies concerning the use of seclusion timeout in schools. *Education and Treatment of Children, 30*(4), 215–239.

Ryan, R. M., & Connell, J. P. (1989). Perceived locus of causality and internalization. *Journal of Personality and Social Psychology, 57,* 749–761.

Ryan, R. M., & Deci. E. L. (2000a). Intrinsic and extrinsic motivations: Classic definitions and new directions. *Contemporary Educational Psychology, 25,* 54–67.

Ryan, R. M., & Deci, E. L. (2000b). Self-determination theory and the facilitation of intrinsic motivation, social development, and well-being. *American Psychologist, 55*(1), 68–78.

Sadker, D., & Sadker, M. (1985). Is the OK Classroom OK? *Phi Delta Kappan, 55,* 358–367.

Sadker, D., Sadker, M., & Thomas, D. (1981). Sex equity and special education. *The Pointer, 26,* 33–38.

Sadker, D., Sadker, M., & Zittleman, K. (2009). *Still failing at fairness: How gender bias cheats girls and boys in school and what we can do about it.* New York: Simon & Schuster.

Sainato, D. M., Strain, P. S., Lefebvre, D., & Rapp, N. (1990). Effects of self-evaluation on the independent work skills of preschool children with disabilities. *Exceptional Children, 56*(6), 540–549.

Sanoff, H. (1979). *Design games.* Los Altos, CA: William Kaufmann.

Sapon-Shevin, M. (1995). Building a safe community for learning. In W. Ayers (Ed.), *To become a teacher: Making a difference in children's lives.* New York: Teachers College Press.

Sapon-Shevin, M. (1999). *Because we can change the world: A practical guide to building cooperative, inclusive classroom communities.* Boston: Allyn & Bacon.

Sapon-Shevin, M. (2003). Inclusion: A matter of social justice. *Educational Leadership, 61*(2), 25–28.

Scarcella, R. (1990). *Teaching language minority students in the multicultural classroom.* Upper Saddle River, NJ: Prentice Hall Regents.

Schaps, E. (2003). Creating a school community. *Educational Leadership, 60*(60), 31–33.

Schimmel, D. (2006). Classroom management, discipline, and the law: Clarifying confusion about students' rights and teachers' authority. In C. M. Evertson & C. S. Weinstein (Eds.), *Handbook of classroom management: Research, practice, and contemporary issues.* Mahwah, NJ: Lawrence Erlbaum Associates, 1005–1020.

Schlosser, L. K. (1992). Teacher distance and student disengagement: School lives on the margin. *Journal of Teacher Education, 43*(2), 128–140.

Schlozman, S. C. (2001). Too sad to learn? *Educational Leadership, 59*(1), 80–81.

Schmoker, M. (October 24, 2001). The Crayola curriculum. *Education Week, 21*(8), 42.

Schmollinger, C. S., Opaleski, K. A., Chapman, M. L., Jocius, R., & Bell, S. (2002). How do you make your classroom an inviting place for students to come back to each year? *English Journal, 91*(6), 20-22.

Schniedewind, N., & Davidson, E. (2000). Differentiating cooperative learning. *Educational Leadership, 58*(1), 24-27.

Shalaway, L. (1989). *Learning to teach . . . not just for beginners.* Cleveland, OH: Instructor Books, Edgell Communications.

Shariff, S. (2004). Keeping schools out of court: Legally defensible models of leadership. *The Educational Forum, 68,* 222-232.

Shaw, C. (1947). *It looked like spilt milk.* New York: HarperCollins.

Sheets, R. H. (1996). Urban classroom conflict: Student-teacher perception: Ethnic integrity, solidarity, and resistance. *Urban Review, 28*(2), 165-183.

Shin, H. B., with Bruno, R. (2003). Language use and English-speaking ability: 2000. Washington, DC: U.S. Census Bureau. (Downloaded from www.census.gov.)

Shuy, R. (1988). Identifying dimensions of classroom language. In J. L. Green & J. O. Harker (Eds.), *Multiple perspective analyses of classroom discourse.* Norwood, NJ: Ablex.

Sileo, T. W., & Prater, M. A. (1998). Creating classroom environments that address the linguistic and cultural backgrounds of students with disabilities: An Asian Pacific American perspective. *Remedial and Special Education, 19*(6), 323-337.

Skiba, R., Horner, R., Gung, C. G., Rausch, M. K., May, S. L., & Tobin, T. (2008). *Race is not neutral: A national investigation of African American and Latino disproportionality in school discipline.* Paper presented at the Annual Meeting of the American Educational Research Association, New York, New York.

Skiba, R. J., Michael, R. S., Nardo, A. C., & Peterson. R. (2002). The color of discipline: Sources of racial and gender disproportionality in school punishment. *Urban Review, 34,* 317-342.

Skiba, R. J., & Rausch, M. K. (2006). Zero tolerance, suspension, and expulsion: Questions of equity and effectiveness. In C. M. Evertson & C. S. Weinstein (Eds.), *Handbook of classroom management: Research, practice, and contemporary issues.* Mahwah, NJ: Lawrence Erlbaum Associates.

Skinner, E. A., & Belmont, M. J. (1993). Motivation in the classroom: Reciprocal effects of teacher behavior and student engagement across the school year. *Journal of Educational Psychology, 85*(4), 571-581.

Slavin, R. E. (1995). *Cooperative learning: Theory, research, and practice* (2nd ed.). Boston: Allyn & Bacon.

Smith, B. (1998). *It's about time: Opportunities to learn in Chicago's elementary schools.* Chicago: Consortium on Chicago School Research. Available at www.ncrel.org/sdrs/areas/issues/envrnmnt/go/go6lk10.htm.

Smith, B. (2000). Quantity matters: Annual instructional time in an urban school system. *Educational Administration Quarterly, 36*(5), 652-682.

Smith, E. (2002). Ebonics: A case history. In L. Delpit & J. K. Dowdy (Eds.), *The skin that we speak: Thoughts on language and culture in the classroom.* New York: The New Press, 15-30.

Sobel, A., & Kugler, E. G. (2007). Building partnerships with immigrant parents. *Educational Leadership, 64*(6), 62-66.

Soodak, L. C., & McCarthy, M. R. (2006). Classroom management in inclusive settings. In C. M. Evertson & C. S. Weinstein (Eds.), *Handbook of classroom management: Research, practice, and contemporary issues*. Mahwah, NJ: Lawrence Erlbaum Associates, 461–490.

Southern Poverty Law Center. (September 2004). Hate among youth becomes widespread. *SPLC Report, 34*(3), 1.

Souvignier, E., & Kronenberger, J. (2007). Cooperative learning in third graders' jigsaw groups for mathematics and science with and without questioning training. *British Journal of Educational Psychology, 77,* 755–771.

Steele, F. I. (1973). *Physical settings and organization development.* Reading, MA: Addison-Wesley.

Stefkovich, J. A., & Miller, J. A. (April 13, 1998). *Law enforcement officers in public schools: Student citizens in safe havens?* Paper presented at the annual meeting of the American Educational Research Association.

Stigler, J. W., Lee, S., & Stevenson, H. W. (1987). Mathematics classrooms in Japan, Taiwan, and the United States. *Child Development, 58,* 1272–1285.

Stipek, D. J. (1993). *Motivation to learn: From theory to practice* (2nd ed.). Boston: Allyn & Bacon.

Stodolsky, S. S. (1984). Frameworks for studying instructional processes in peer work groups. In P. L. Peterson, L. C. Wilkinson, & M. Hallinan (Eds.), *The social context of instruction*. New York: Academic Press, 107–124.

Stodolsky, S. S. (1988). *The subject matters: Classroom activity in math and social studies.* Chicago: University of Chicago Press.

Strauss, S., with Espeland, P. (1992). *Sexual harassment and teens: A program for positive change.* Minneapolis, MN: Free Spirit.

Strong-Wilson, T., & Ellis, J. (2007). Children and place: Reggio Emilia's environment as third teacher. *Theory into Practice, 46*(1), 40–47.

Substance Abuse and Mental Health Services Administration (SAMHSA). (2003). *Results from the 2002 National Survey on Drug Use and Health: National Findings.* NHSDA Series H-22, DHHS Pub. No. SMA 03-3836. Rockville, MD: SAMHSA, Office of Applied Studies. Available at http://www.oas.samhsa.gov/nhsda/2k2nsduh/Results/2k2Results.htm.

Swap, S. M. (1993). *Developing home–school partnerships: From concepts to practice.* New York: Teachers College Press.

Tannen, D. (1995). The power of talk: Who gets heard and why. *Harvard Business Review, 73*(5), 138–148.

Tarr, P. (2004). Consider the walls. *Young Children, 59*(3), 88–92.

Taylor, T. (1969). *The cay.* New York: Doubleday.

Thompson, B. (2008). Characteristics of parent-teacher e-mail communication. *Communication Education, 57*(2), 201–223.

Thompson, G. L. (2004). *Through ebony eyes: What teachers need to know but are afraid to ask about African American students.* San Francisco: Jossey-Bass.

Tomlinson, C. A. (1999). *The differentiated classroom: Responding to the needs of all learners.* Alexandria, VA: Association for Supervision and Curriculum Development.

Towers, R. L. (1989). *Children of alcoholics/addicts.* Washington, DC: National Education Association.

Trueba, H. T., Cheng, L.R.L., & Ima, K. (1993). *Myth or reality: Adaptive strategies of Asian Americans in California.* Washington, DC: Falmer Press.

Trumbull, E., Rothstein-Fisch, C., Greenfield, P. M., & Quiroz, B. (2001). *Bridging cultures between home and school: A guide for teachers.* Mahwah, NJ: Lawrence Erlbaum Associates.

U.S. Census Bureau. (2008). Language spoken at home. American Community Survey. Washington, DC: U.S. Census Bureau. Retrieved 02/24/2009 from http://factfinder.census .gov/home/saff/main.html?_lang=en.

U. S. Department of Education, National Center for Education Statistics (NCES). (March 13, 1998). *Third international math and science study* (TIMSS). Available at http://nces .ed.gov/timss/video/finding3.htm.

U.S. Department of Health and Human Services, Administration of Children, Youth, and Families. (2008). *Child maltreatment 2006.* Washington, DC: U.S. Government Printing Office. Available at http://www.acf.hhs.gov/programs/cb/stats_research/index.htm#can.

Urdan, T., & Schoenfelder, E. (2006). Classroom effects on student motivation: Goal structures, social relationships, and competence beliefs. *Journal of School Psychology, 44*(5), 331–349.

Valentine, G. (Fall 1998). Lessons from home (an interview with Lisa Delpit). *Teaching Tolerance, 7*(2), 15–19.

Valenzuela, A. (1999). *Subtractive schooling: U.S.-Mexican youth and the politics of caring.* Albany: State University of New York Press.

Valli, L., Croninger, R. G., & Walters, K. (2007). Who (else) is the teacher? Cautionary notes on teacher accountability systems. *American Journal of Education, 113*(4), 635–662.

Vaughn, S., Bos, C. S., & Schumm, J. S. (2003). *Teaching exceptional, diverse, and at-risk students in the general education classroom.* Boston: Allyn & Bacon.

Vaughn, S., Gersten, R., & Chard, D. J. (2000). The underlying message in LD intervention research: Findings from research syntheses. *Exceptional Children, 67*(1), 99–114.

Vaughn, S., Levy, S., Coleman, M., & Bos, C. S. (2002). Reading instruction for students with LD and EBD: A synthesis of observation studies. *Journal of Special Education, 36*(1), 2–13.

Villa, R. A., Thousand, J. S., & Nevin, A. I. (2008) *A guide to co-teaching: Practical tips for facilitating student learning* (2nd ed.). Thousand Oaks, CA: Corwin Press.

Villegas, A. M., & Lucas. T. (2007). The culturally responsive teacher. *Educational Leadership, 64*(6), 28–33.

Vossekuil, B., Fein, R., Reddy, M., Borum, R., & Modzeleski, W. (2002). *The final report and findings of the Safe School Initiative: Implications for the prevention of school attacks in the United States.* Washington, DC: U.S. Secret Service and the U.S. Department of Education. Available at www.secretservice.gov/ntac/ssi_final_reprot.pdf.

Vygotsky, L. (1978). *Mind in society: The development of higher psychological processes.* (Eds. M. Cole, V. John-Steiner, S. Scribner, & E. Souberman). Cambridge, MA: Harvard University Press.

Walberg, H. J. (1988). Synthesis of research on time and learning. *Educational Leadership, 45*(6), 76–85.

Walde, A. C., & Baker, K. (1990). How teachers view the parents' role in education. *Phi Delta Kappan, 72*(4), 319–320, 322.

Walker, H. M., Colvin, G., & Ramsey, E. (1995). *Antisocial behavior in school: Strategies and best practices.* Pacific Grove, CA: Brooks/Cole.

Walker, J. E., & Shea, T. M. (1995). *Behavior management: A practical approach for educators.* Englewood Cliffs, NJ: Merrill/Prentice Hall.

Walker, J.M.T. (Ed.). (2009). A person-centered approach to classroom management. *Theory into Practice, 48*(2), 95–159.

Wallace, M. A., Cox, E. A., & Skinner, C. H. (2003). Increasing independent seatwork: Breaking large assignments into smaller assignments and teaching a student with retardation to recruit reinforcement. *School Psychology Review, 32*(1), 132–142.

Walsh, J. A., & Sattes, B. D. (2005). *Quality questioning: Research-based practice to engage every learner.* Thousand Oaks, CA: Corwin Press.

Walsh, M. (June 2, 1999). Harassment ruling poses challenges. *Education Week, 18*(38), 1-22.

Walsh, M. (March 8, 2000). Law update: A fine line between dangerous and harmless student expression. *Education Week,* 14.

Walters, L. S. (2000). Putting cooperative learning to the test. *Harvard Education Letter, 16*(3), 1-6.

Watson, M., & Battistich, V. (2006). Building and sustaining caring communities. In C. M. Evertson & C. S. Weinstein (Eds.), *Handbook of classroom management: Research, practice, and contemporary issues.* Mahwah, NJ: Lawrence Erlbaum Associates, 253-280.

Watson, M., in collaboration with Ecken, L. (2003). *Learning to trust: Transforming difficult elementary classrooms through developmental discipline.* San Francisco: Jossey-Bass.

Webb, N. M. (1984). Sex differences in interaction and achievement in cooperative small groups. *Journal of Educational Psychology, 76,* 33-44.

Webb, N. M. (1985). Student interaction and learning in small groups: A research summary. In R. E. Slavin, S. Sharan, S. Kagan, R. Hertz-Lazarowitz, C. Webb, & R. Schmuck (Eds.), *Learning to cooperate, cooperating to learn.* New York: Plenum.

Webb, N. M., Baxter, G. P., & Thompson, L. (1997). Teachers' grouping practices in fifth-grade science classrooms. *The Elementary School Journal, 98*(2), 91-113.

Webb, N. M., & Farivar, S. (1994). Promoting helping behavior in cooperative small groups in middle school mathematics. *American Educational Research Journal, 31,* 369-395.

Webb, N. M., & Mastergeorge, A. M. (2003). The development of students' helping behavior and learning in peer-directed small groups. *Cognition and Instruction, 21*(4), 361-428.

Webb, N. M., Nemer, K. M., & Ing, M. (2006). Small group reflections: Parallels between teacher discourse and student behavior in peer-directed groups. *The Journal of the Learning Sciences, 15*(1), 63-119.

Webb, N. M., & Palincsar, A. S. (1996). Group processes in the classroom. In D. Berliner & R. C. Calfee (Eds.), *Handbook of educational psychology.* New York: Macmillan, 841-876.

Weiner, L. (1999). *Urban teaching: The essentials.* New York: Teachers College Press.

Weinstein, C. S. (1982). Privacy-seeking behavior in an elementary classroom. *Journal of Environmental Psychology, 2,* 23-35.

Weinstein, C. S., Curran, M., & Tomlinson-Clarke, S. (2003). Culturally responsive classroom management: Awareness into action. *Theory into Practice, 42*(4), 269-276.

Weinstein, C. S., Tomlinson-Clarke, S., & Curran, M. (2004). Toward a conception of culturally responsive classroom management. *Journal of Teacher Education, 55*(1), 25-38.

Wengel, M. (1992). *Seating arrangements: Changing with the times.* Research/Technical Report. Eric Document Reproduction Service No. ED 348 153.

Wentzel, K. R. (1997). Student motivation in middle school: The role of perceived pedagogical caring. *Journal of Educational Psychology, 89*(3), 411-419.

Wentzel, K. R. (1998). Social relationships and motivation in middle school: The role of parents, teachers, and peers. *Journal of Educational Psychology, 90*(2), 202-209.

Wentzel, K. R. (2006). A social motivation perspective for classroom management. In C. M. Evertson & C. S. Weinstein (Eds.), *Handbook of classroom management: Research, practice, and contemporary issues.* Mahwah, NJ: Lawrence Erlbaum Associates, 619-644.

Wertsch, J. V. (1985). *Vygotsky and the Social Formation of Mind.* Cambridge, MA: Harvard University Press.

Wesley, D. (1976). *Heritage.* Lakeside, CA: Interact.

Wessler, S. (2008). Civility speaks up. *Educational Leadership, 66*(1), 44-48.

Wheldall, K., & Lam, Y. Y. (1987). Rows versus tables. II. The effects of two classroom seating arrangements on classroom disruption rate, on-task behaviour, and teacher behaviour in three special school classes. *Educational Psychology, 7*(4), 303-312.

Wigfield, A. & Eccles, J. S. (2000). Expectancy-value theory of achievement motivation. *Contemporary Educational Psychology, 25*(1), 68-81.

Wilkinson, L. C., & Calculator, S. (1982). Effective speakers: Students' use of language to request and obtain information and action in the classroom. In L. C. Wilkinson (Ed.), *Communicating in the classroom*. New York: Academic Press, 85-100.

Williams, M. (1993). Actions speak louder than words: What students think. *Educational Leadership, 51*(3), 22-23.

Williams, R. L., & Stockdale, S. L. (2004). Classroom motivation strategies for prospective teachers. *The Teacher Educator, 39*(3), 212-230.

Wodrich, D. L. (2000). *Attention-deficit/hyperactivity disorder: What every parent wants to know* (2nd ed.). Baltimore, MD: Paul H. Brookes.

Wolfgang, C. H. (1999). *Solving discipline problems: Methods and models for today's teachers.* Boston: Allyn & Bacon.

Wood, C. (1999). *Time to teach, time to learn: Changing the pace of school.* Greenfield, MA: Northeast Foundation for Children.

Woodruff, E. (1991). *George Washington's socks.* New York: Apple Paperback, Scholastic.

Woolfolk Hoy, A. (2007). *Educational psychology* (10th ed.). Boston: Pearson Education/Allyn & Bacon.

Woolfolk Hoy, A. W., & Weinstein, C. S. (2006). Student and teacher perspectives about classroom management. In C. M. Evertson & C. S. Weinstein (Eds.), *Handbook of classroom management: Research, practice, and contemporary issues*. Mahwah, NJ: Lawrence Erlbaum Associates, 181-219.

Xu, J., & Corno, L. (2003). Family help and homework management reported by middle school students. *The Elementary School Journal, 103*(5), 503-517.

Zhang, S. (1995). Reexamining the effective advantage of peer feedback in ESL writing class. *Journal of Second Language Writing, 4*(3), 209-222.

Zirpoli, T. J. (2005). *Behavior management: Applications for teachers* (4th ed.). Upper Saddle River, NJ: Pearson Education.

NAME INDEX

Abd-Kadir, J., 303
Adams, R. S., 35
Ainsworth, M. D. S., 120, 154–155
Akin-Little, K. A., 95
Alberto, P. A., 357
Alfi, O., 229
Algozzine, R. F., 125
Alleman-Brooks, J., 255, 256–257, 258
Allen, J. B., 54, 196
Alvermann, D., 308
AAUW Educational Foundation, 313
American Psychiatric Association, 127, 130, 133
Anderman, E. M., 367
Anderson, K. J., 161, 166, 187, 193
Anderson, L. M., 93, 109, 254, 255, 256–257, 258, 263, 348–349, 354
Anderson, R., 254, 256
Antil, L. R., 289, 292
Arends, R. I., 312, 322
Arieli, M., 35
Arlin, M., 206, 207, 210
Aronson, E., 290
Ashman, A. F., 293–294
Assor, A., 229
Astor, R. A., 380, 381, 384, 391
Atwater, F., 237
Atwater, R., 237
Aussiker, A., 335
Ayers, W., 224

Bailey, J. M., 186, 187, 196
Baker, K., 163
Ballenger, C., 341
Banko, K. M., 244
Barry, K., 278

Bassler, O. T., 163, 191, 192
Bates, A., 372
Battistich, V., 22, 88
Baxter, G. P., 277
Beane, A. L., 72
Bear, G. G., 353, 378
Becker, H. J., 163
Beckett, K. S., 167
Behre, W. J., 381, 391
Belmont, M. J., 92, 224
Benbenishty, R., 380
Berdondini, L., 274, 275
Berk, L. E., 117–118
Berman, S., 391
Berreth, D., 391
Beyerbach, B., 310
Bickley-Green, C., 84
Biddle, B. J., 35
Blauvelt, P. D., 391
Bloome, D., 259, 367
Bode, P., 7, 53, 62
Bodine, R. J., 80
Boekaerts, M., 274, 287
Bohn, C. M., 94, 114
Bolick, C. M., 39
Bomer, R., 151
Bondy, E., 350, 374
Bonus, M., 32, 46
Bos, C. S., 125, 127, 128, 129, 131, 254
Bowen, N. K., 166
Bowlby, J., 120, 154–155
Brady, K., 114
Brandt, R., 190
Brendgen, M. B., 56
Brissie, J. S., 163

Brookfield, S. D., 325, 331
Brophy, J., 76, 204, 224, 225, 226, 233–234, 245, 248, 250, 307, 310, 315, 346, 360, 374
Brown, D. F., 56
Brown, L. H., 167
Brown, M. W., 73
Brubaker, N., 255, 256–257, 258
Bruno, R., 121
Bryan, T., 372
Buell, J., 192
Bukowski, W. M., 56
Burow, R., 191, 192
Bursuck, W. D., 365

Calculator, S., 260, 279
Campbell, B., 230
Campbell, L., 230
Cameron, C., 246, 250
Cameron, C. E., 102
Cameron, J., 224
Canale, J., 237
Cangelosi, J. S., 368
Canter, L., 104
Canter, M., 104
Carbone, E., 32
Carson, L., 295
Carter, K., 96, 118
Cartledge, G., 54, 259
Cary, S., 124, 158
Casey, H., 42
Catalano, R. F., 56
Cataldi, E. F., 380
Cazden, C. B., 258, 303, 327
Centers for Disease Control and Prevention, 129

SUBJECT INDEX